HUMAN WELFARE

Human Welfare and Moral Worth

Kantian Perspectives

THOMAS E. HILL, JR.

CLARENDON PRESS · OXFORD

This book has been printed digitally and produced in a standard specification in order to ensure its continuing availability

OXFORD
UNIVERSITY PRESS

Great Clarendon Street, Oxford OX2 6DP

Oxford University Press is a department of the University of Oxford.
It furthers the University's objective of excellence in research, scholarship,
and education by publishing worldwide in

Oxford New York

Auckland Cape Town Dar es Salaam Hong Kong Karachi
Kuala Lumpur Madrid Melbourne Mexico City Nairobi
New Delhi Shanghai Taipei Toronto

With offices in

Argentina Austria Brazil Chile Czech Republic France Greece
Guatemala Hungary Italy Japan South Korea Poland Portugal
Singapore Switzerland Thailand Turkey Ukraine Vietnam

Oxford is a registered trade mark of Oxford University Press
in the UK and in certain other countries

Published in the United States
by Oxford University Press Inc., New York

© In this collection Thomas E. Hill Jr., 2002

The moral rights of the author have been asserted

Database right Oxford University Press (maker)

Reprinted 2008

All rights reserved. No part of this publication may be reproduced,
stored in a retrieval system, or transmitted, in any form or by any means,
without the prior permission in writing of Oxford University Press,
or as expressly permitted by law, or under terms agreed with the appropriate
reprographics rights organization. Enquiries concerning reproduction
outside the scope of the above should be sent to the Rights Department,
Oxford University Press, at the address above

You must not circulate this book in any other binding or cover
And you must impose this same condition on any acquirer

ISBN 978-0-19-925263-3

SOURCES AND ACKNOWLEDGEMENTS

I thank the following for permission to reprint the essays in this collection.

'Kantian Analysis: From Duty to Autonomy' was originally published as 'Kantianism' in Hugh LaFollette (ed.), *Blackwell Guide to Ethical Theory*, 227–476, © 2000, by Blackwell Publishers. Reprinted by permission of Blackwell Publishers.

'Is a Good Will Overrated?' originally appeared in *Midwest Studies in Philosophy: Moral Concepts*, xx (1996), 299–317. Reprinted by permission of Blackwell Publishers.

'Hypothetical Consent in Kantian Constructivism' originally appeared in *Social Philosophy and Policy*, 18(2) (2001), 300–29. Reprinted with the permission of Cambridge University Press.

'Beneficence and Self-Love' originally appeared as 'Beneficence and Self-Love: A Kantian Perspective' in *Social Philosophy and Policy*, 9(1) (1992), 1–23. Reprinted with the permission of Cambridge University Press.

'Reasonable Self-Interest' originally appeared in *Social Philosophy and Policy*, 14(1) (1997), 52–85. Reprinted with the permission of Cambridge University Press.

'Happiness and Human Flourishing' was originally published as 'Happiness and Human Flourishing in Kant's Ethics' in *Social Philosophy and Policy* (1998), 143–75. Reprinted with the permission of Cambridge University Press.

'Four Conceptions of Conscience' originally appeared in *Nomos*, XL (1998), 13–52. Reprinted by permission of New York University Press.

'Wrongdoing, Desert, and Punishment' was originally published as 'Kant on Wrongdoing, Desert, and Punishment' in *Law and Philosophy*, 18(1) (1999), 407–41. Reprinted with kind permission from Kluwer Academic Publishers.

'Punishment, Conscience, and Moral Worth' was originally published as 'Kant on Punishment, Conscience, and Moral Worth' in *The Southern Journal of Philosophy*, xxxvi, Supplement (1998), 21–71. Reprinted by permission of *The Southern Journal of Philosophy*, published by the Department of Philosophy, the University of Memphis.

'Moral Dilemmas, Gaps, and Residues' was originally published in H. E. Mason (ed.), *Moral Dilemmas and Moral Theory*, © 1996 by Oxford University Press, Inc. Used by permission of Oxford University Press, Inc.

Although I have no one but myself to blame for the deficiencies of these essays, I acknowledge gratefully the help that many others have given me. Some of these are mentioned in the notes within the essays, but my debt is wider than the notes indicate. The University of North Carolina at Chapel Hill provided more than basic institutional support, and The Social Philosophy and Policy Center at Bowling Green, Ohio, provided four stimulating conferences and a summer fellowship that contributed to four of the essays. A fellowship from the Institute for the Arts and Humanities at the University of North Carolina gave me time to work on ideas for other essays. My colleagues at the University of North Carolina have been generally encouraging and philosophically stimulating, and in a number of cases offered instructive criticism. For this I especially want to thank Bernard Boxill, Geoffrey Sayre-McCord, and Gerald Postema. Graduate students have often been helpful, and I have been especially fortunate to have a group of former students whose work and correspondence continue to stimulate my thinking about Kantian ethics and related matters. These include especially Lori Alward, Samuel Bruton, Richard Dean, Sarah Holtman, Andrew Johnson, Sean McKeever, Cynthia Stark, and Valerie Tiberius. I have learned from the work of many other Kantians and critics of Kant. There are too many to acknowledge properly, but a fuller acknowledgment would highlight Henry Allison, Marcia Baron, Sharon Byrd, David Cummiskey, Stephen Engstrom, Paul Guyer, Barbara Herman, Christine Korsgaard, Jeffrie Murphy, Onora O'Neill, John Rawls, Andrews Reath, J. B. Schneewind, Allen Wood, and no doubt others.

Several people have helped specifically in the process of preparing this volume for publication. As research assistants, Wendy Nankas, Vicki Behrens, Clea Rees, Shelby Weitzel at first and Adrienne Martin did editorial work that saved me from many errors. Their philosophical judgment, meticulous care, and sound advice were very helpful and much appreciated. Gucki Obler provided quick, reliable office support, with cheerful encouragement.

As before, family members have been very supportive. My father, whose dedication to reading and writing philosophy remains undiminished at age 93, continues to be an inspiration. Most of all, I am deeply grateful to Robin for her unfailing support and encouragement. Among other things, her practical help and good spirit enable me to write about theoretical matters and her empathetic understanding of real human problems helps me to remember the practical matters that, in the end, moral philosophy is about.

CONTENTS

Abbreviations for Kant's Works	x
Introduction	1
PART I. Some Basic Kantian Themes	11
1. Kantian Analysis: From Duty to Autonomy	13
2. Is a Good Will Overrated?	37
3. Hypothetical Consent in Kantian Constructivism	61
PART II. Human Welfare: Self-Interest and Regard for Others	97
4. Beneficence and Self-Love	99
5. Reasonable Self-Interest	125
6. Happiness and Human Flourishing	164
7. Meeting Needs and Doing Favors	201
8. Personal Values and Setting Oneself Ends	244
PART III. Moral Worth: Self-Assessment and Desert	275
9. Four Conceptions of Conscience	277
10. Wrongdoing, Desert, and Punishment	310
11. Punishment, Conscience, and Moral Worth	340
12. Moral Dilemmas, Gaps, and Residues	362
Bibliography	403
Index	413

ABBREVIATIONS FOR KANT'S WORKS

A   *Anthropology from a Pragmatic Point of View*, tr. Mary Gregor (The Hague: Martinus Nijhoff, 1974). Translated from *Anthropologie in pragmatischer Hinsicht abgefasst* (1798), in *Kants gesammelte Schriften*, ed. under the auspices of the Königliche Preussische Akademie der Wissenschaften (Berlin: Walter de Gruyter, 1908–13), [7: 117–333].

C1   *Critique of Pure Reason*, tr. Norman Kemp Smith (New York: St. Martin's Press, 1965). Translated from *Kritik der reinen Vernunft* (1781, 1787) in *Kants gesammelte Schriften* [first edition, 4: 1–252; second edition, 3: 1–594]. References to the first and second editions are indicated by the standard A/B abbreviation.

C2   *Critique of Practical Reason*, tr. Mary Gregor (Cambridge: Cambridge University Press, 1997). Translated from *Kritik der praktischen Vernunft* (1788), in *Kants gesammelte Schriften*, [5: 1–163].

C3   *Critique of Judgment*, tr. Werner S. Pluhar (Indianapolis: Hackett Publishing Co., 1987).

G   *Groundwork of the Metaphysic of Morals*, tr. H. J. Paton (New York: Harper and Row, 1964). Translated from *Grundlegung zur Metaphysik der Sitten* (1795), in *Kants gesammelte Schriften*, [4: 387–463].

Gg   *Groundwork of the Metaphysics of Morals*, tr. Mary Gregor (Cambridge: Cambridge University Press, 1997). Translated from *Grundlegung zur Metaphysik der Sitten* (1795), in *Kants gesammelte Schriften* [4: 387–463].

LE   *Lectures on Ethics*, tr. Louis Infield (New York: Harper and Row, 1963). Translated from *Eine Vorlesung Kants über Ethik*, ed.

Abbreviations for Kant's Works xi

Paul Menzer (Berlin: *im Auftrage der Kantgesellschaft*, 1924). A more recent and thorough translation is *Lectures on Ethics*, tr. Peter Heath and J. B. Schneewind (Cambridge: Cambridge University Press, 1997), [27: 3–732]. LE refers to the Infield edition; references to the Heath and Schneewind edition will be indicated in the notes.

MM   *The Metaphysics of Morals*, tr. Mary Gregor (Cambridge: Cambridge University Press, 1996). Translated from *Die Metaphysik der Sitten* (1797–8), in *Kants gesammelte Schriften*, [6: 203–491].

PP   *Perpetual Peace*, tr. H. B. Nesbit, in *Kant: Political Writings*, ed. Hans Reiss (Cambridge: Cambridge University Press, 1991). Translated from *Zum ewigen Frieden: Ein philosophischer Entwurf* (1795), [8: 341–86].

R   *Religion within the Boundaries of Mere Reason*, tr. Allen Wood and George di Giovanni (Cambridge: Cambridge University Press, 1998). Translated from *Die Religion innerhalb der Grenzen der blossen Vernunft* (1793–4), in *Kants gesammelte Schriften*, [6: 1–202].

RL   'On a Supposed Right to Lie because of Philanthropic Concerns', in Immanuel Kant, *Grounding of the Metaphysic of Morals*, tr. James Ellington, 3rd edn. (Indianapolis: Hackett Publishing Co., 1993), translated from *Über ein vermeintes Recht aus Menschenliebe zu lügen* (1797), [8: 425–30].

Numbers in square brackets refer to the relevant volume and page number of *Kants gesammelte Schriften*. This edition of Kant's works is commonly called the Akademie (or Academy) edition. When works of Kant other than those abbreviated above are cited, a full reference will be given in a footnote. Passages in other translations of Kant's works can be located by the marginal numbers, which indicate the Academy edition pages and are now included in virtually all translations.

Introduction

In a recent collection of essays, *Respect, Pluralism, and Justice: Kantian Perspectives*, I explored the implications of basic Kantian ideas for several practical issues, including cultural conflicts, political violence, and responsibility for the consequences of wrongdoing. The essays in the present volume continue the same sort of investigation with regard to other topics. Broadly speaking, the main topics here are, *first*, self-interest and regard for others (or 'human welfare') and, *second*, moral assessment of ourselves and others (or 'moral worth'). The first three essays provide background on certain central themes in Kant's ethics: a priori method, categorical imperatives, autonomy, the special value of a good will, and appeals to possible and hypothetical consent in moral arguments. Then the next essays raise particular questions regarding human welfare, for example: Are our obligations to help others prescribed and limited by our sentiments toward them? What reasons do we have to promote the welfare of others as well as our own? Is it our obligation to promote others' happiness as they conceive it or their 'human flourishing' as ancient philosophers define it? How demanding is the duty to promote others' happiness? Are some instances of helping supererogatory? Finally, the last four essays focus on the nature and grounds of moral assessments of persons as deserving esteem or blame for their choices. For example: How should we conceive of conscience? In what sense, if any, is it appropriate that we suffer for our wrongdoing? Is punishment justified because wrongdoers inherently deserve to suffer for their misdeeds? Is there anything morally worthy in our striving to avoid pangs of conscience and just punishment by our peers? In what sense, if any, should we feel *guilty* if we cause serious harm in tragic situations where we could find no better option?

The essays discuss Kant's explicit views on these topics, but they also consider how a reasonable contemporary Kantian theory might best address the problems. Scholars disagree, of course, about what is best and most central in Kant's work, and they also disagree about how to interpret particular passages. I do not pretend to offer a complete or definitive account of Kant's position, nor do I insist that my proposals for developing Kantian ethics point to the only reasonable paths to explore. As in previous essays, my aim is to respect the letter of Kant's texts as far as possible but also to identify, trace, and develop themes worthy of contemporary attention. At times these aims conflict, and then the best one can do is to suggest reconstructions that are to some extent compromises. Readers will have to assess these for themselves.

In selecting topics I was influenced by several factors. The guiding aim was to explore the resources and limits of a Kantian perspective by reviewing critically what Kant wrote on various issues that remain of interest today. For this purpose the essays in the present volume supplement not only those recently collected in *Respect, Pluralism, and Justice: Kantian Perspectives* but also some of my essays published earlier in *Autonomy and Self-Respect* and *Dignity and Practical Reason in Kant's Moral Theory*. The selection of topics in several cases was also influenced by invitations to conferences devoted to particular issues. This was the case with Chapters 3, 4, 5, 6, 9, and 12. I am grateful to the conference organizers for encouraging me to think more about the issues in question. Chapter 7 was prompted as a response to quite reasonable worries raised by David Cummiskey and Marcia Baron about my earlier (1971) characterization of Kant's principle of beneficence. In addition, I was drawn to many of the topics discussed in this volume, and previous ones, by my strong sense that some familiar questions about Kant's ethics have already been overworked and others too long neglected. In some other cases, the questions that I consider are not new but I have wanted to challenge familiar answers and call attention to different, and perhaps better, ways of looking at the issue.

The essays presented here and those in the previous volume are based on the conviction that Kant's works can be reasonably faulted on many counts but they remain a rich, and not yet fully tapped, resource for contemporary moral philosophy. This is not a new theme. In fact it now seems to be readily affirmed by most critics of Kantian ethics as well as by Kant scholars. What I hope readers will find interesting in these essays are the particular ways in which it is developed.

The essays, at least by default, accept many of the familiar objections to Kant's ethics. For example, as before, readers will find me impatient with Kant's endorsement of strict, inflexible moral rules and his radical ideas about noumenal wills. To some extent the latter can be interpreted as practical, normative points. I do not defend the idea that Kant's formulas of the Categorical Imperative can serve as simple decision procedures for solving moral problems. Nor do I address doubts about whether Kant has shown that it is always rational to be moral. I set aside, because I share, familiar doubts about the adequacy of Kant's ideas about nonhuman animals and certain human virtues. Kant's treatment of our moral responsibility to the needy may be inadequate to conditions in the world today. His conceptions of punishment and conscience, I agree, have a dark side that needs to be tempered with more hopeful and humane sentiments.

My main focus, however, is on what I find appealing in Kant's ethics, or at least on matters that promise to repay our efforts to rethink constructively what Kant has said. For example, I present in a favorable light Kant's ideas about the need for a priori method, duties understood as categorical imperatives, autonomy, and the special value of a good will. My account of Kant's views on reasons for acting, the possibility of altruism, and the duty of beneficence interprets them as quite close to common thought about these matters though in conflict with various popular philosophical theories. In my last four essays, I argue that, when separated from misunderstandings and inessential features, Kant's conceptions of conscience, judicial punishment, and moral dilemmas are more attractive than the alternatives to which they are often compared. A common theme in many of the essays is Kant's emphasis on individual freedom and responsibility. More than many moral theories, Kant's theory leaves it to individuals to choose how to live so long as they meet their moral responsibilities. To meet those responsibilities, however, requires moral vigilance, firm commitment, and good judgment as well as right action.

The essays are meant to be self-standing, and so reading them in a particular order is not necessary. I did not intend to presuppose a prior knowledge of Kant's writings on ethics, but readers with some familiarity with Kant's work will probably find the essays more helpful and challenging than others will. In order to make the connection between the essays more evident and to enable readers to select topics that most interest them, I provide below a brief summary or abstract of each essay.

I. *Some Basic Kantian Themes*. The aim of the two opening essays is to distinguish certain core ideas in Kantian ethics from more extreme associated ideas. Some of the associated ideas, I argue, have been mistakenly attributed to Kant. Others are indeed aspects of Kant's more radical and controversial thought, but, arguably, the core ideas are independent of these. For the most part, I suggest, the core ideas represent familiar assumptions of common moral discourse and practice. At least, on a proper understanding, they approximate these more closely than most have supposed. The third essay of this set surveys Kant's 'constructivist' procedures for justifying moral principles.

1. 'Kantian Analysis: From Duty to Autonomy' distinguishes radical from core interpretations of three important Kantian themes: that fundamental questions of moral philosophy require an a priori methodology; that duties are conceived as categorical imperatives; and that moral agents have autonomy of the will. A core idea is that an *a priori* method is required to analyze moral concepts and to reflect on whether morality and prudence are grounded in necessary requirements of practical reason. This relatively uncontroversial point, however, is often associated with the implausible idea that substantive moral issues can be settled in complete independence of empirical evidence. Similarly, the core idea that duties are conceived as categorical imperatives marks the familiar assumption that, unlike prudential and pragmatic principles, moral principles do not bind us simply because they promote our happiness or serve our personal ends. This common thought, however, is often conflated with Kant's unfortunate claim that various simple, substantive moral principles (e.g., about lying, revolution, and 'unnatural' sex) hold in all conditions, without exception. Again, Kant's idea of autonomy has been interpreted in a bewildering variety of ways, but arguably the core idea simply refers to certain capacities and dispositions that we must attribute to any agent who is subject to duties understood as categorical imperatives.

2. 'Is a Good Will Overrated?' offers an interpretation of the special value of a good will, which for Kant is the moral disposition expressed in morally worthy acts and the indispensable condition of being a good person. Kant's famous declaration that only a good will can be conceived as good without qualification has often been interpreted as a radical and distinctively Kantian thesis, but I argue that the core idea is a common-sense one. In brief, it is not that our decisions should be dominated by a self-righteous concern for our own moral purity but rather that we should not pursue any goods by means that we recognize to be morally wrong. The thesis, I suggest, is best understood, not as a guide to praise and blame, but as an indeterminate practical principle that becomes action-guiding only when supplemented by a standard of right and wrong (e.g. the Categorical Imperative). If Kant's writings at times encourage readers to stand on rigid principles in foolish disregard of disastrous consequences, the fault lies with his unwarranted belief that this rigidity is required by the Categorical Imperative, not with his initial affirmation that only a good will is unconditionally good.

3. 'Hypothetical Consent in Kantian Constructivism' is about the

justificatory force of arguments that appeal to actual, possible, and hypothetical consent. Despite certain popular views of Kantian ethics, Kant treats actual consent as having only a derivative and limited relevance to how we may be treated. A more fundamental standard for Kant is that practices are justified only if, as rational agents, we can consent to them as universal practices. Application of this standard, however, requires important assumptions about the context of choice and further standards of rationality that determine what universal practices it is possible, in the relevant sense, to will. When these are made explicit, the possible consent standard is essentially equivalent to a hypothetical consent standard that requires that practices conform to principles that any rational agent *would* will *in specified conditions*. The essay reviews the role of possible and hypothetical consent in Kant's use of the idea of an original contract as well as the Categorical Imperative. Finally, the essay discusses whether several familiar objections to the use of hypothetical consent arguments are applicable to Kant's ethics.

II. *Human Welfare: Self-Interest and Regard for Others*. The five essays in this section address questions related to our moral responsibility to promote human happiness or well-being. Although they are a selective rather than a comprehensive treatment of these issues, the essays take up a Kantian perspective on a wide range of issues: the possibility of altruism, the nature of happiness, the stringency of our duty of beneficence, and the relation between reasons to promote our own good and reasons to promote the good of others.

4. 'Beneficence and Self-Love' is primarily directed to the question: (1) Given the limits of our natural altruistic *sentiments*, is it possible for us to *act* as altruistically as duty seems to require? A Kantian answer requires attention to two further questions: (2) What are we morally required to do on behalf of others besides respecting their rights? (3) Why is this a reasonable requirement? The plausibility of Kant's position on the first issue, I suggest, depends on (a) a distinction between a deliberative point of view and a purely empirical point of view, (b) a moderate (not maximizing) interpretation of the imperfect duty of beneficence, and (c) adequate justifying grounds for accepting that duty. The reconstruction of Kant's position here makes use of a practical, not metaphysical, interpretation of Kant's controversial 'two perspectives' on the world.

5. 'Reasonable Self-Interest' contrasts common-sense ideas of what is reasonable with current philosophical ideas of rational choice: (1) maximizing self-interest, (2) efficiency and coherence in pursuit of one's

ends, (3) maximizing intrinsic value, and (4) efficiency and coherence constrained by a Kantian ideal of co-legislation. Contrary to usual assumptions, the last, I suggest, corresponds more closely to the common-sense ideas than any of the other models. This is not a proof of the Kantian ideal, or of common sense, but calls for rethinking assumptions.

6. 'Happiness and Human Flourishing' reviews the role of happiness in Kant's ethics and contrasts his ideas of happiness with the idea of human flourishing prominent in ancient philosophy. It considers possible reasons why Kant avoided the traditional ideas of human flourishing and instead worked with more subjective ideas of happiness. This was due, I conjecture, not merely to historical influences or misunderstanding of ancient philosophy but also to Kant's respect for individual freedom to choose, within moral limits, the way of life one prefers. The essay also replies to Michael Slote's charge that Kant requires us to devalue our own happiness relative to others'.

7. 'Meeting Needs and Doing Favors' addresses the controversial questions, (1) How demanding, in Kant's view, is the imperfect duty to promote the happiness of others? and (2) Is there any place or analogue in Kant's ethics for supererogatory acts—or acts that are, in some sense, morally good to do but more than is required? Here I suggest that the general duty to promote others' happiness, especially as presented in *The Metaphysics of Morals*, is an important but rather minimal requirement. Contrary to recent commentators, however, the fact that the general principle articulates only a rather minimal requirement does not mean that helping others in serious need is morally optional. Judgment in particular cases is not completely determined by the intermediate principles of *The Metaphysics of Morals*. Reflection from the moral framework expressed in the formulas of the Categorical Imperative can show why helping in many particular cases is morally demanded. Although Kant admittedly does not include a category of 'supererogatory' acts in his moral system, I argue that his position, reasonably construed, supports the common opinion that some acts are, in a sense, morally good to do but are not required. This discussion is a partial response to recent work of David Cummiskey and Marcia Baron.

8. 'Personal Values and Setting Oneself Ends' focuses on what individuals value and pursue when considered apart from moral considerations. These matters are ultimately relevant to our moral decisions under various Kantian principles, such as beneficence, but my concern here is with personal values as such. The essay begins by reviewing the various kinds of moral evaluation in Kant's theory in order to contrast

these with the sort of personal value judgments and decisions to be discussed. Then the two main issues are raised. First, in Kant's view, what value judgments, if any, are implicit when we set ourselves ends and adopt maxims? Are we necessarily committed to the judgments that the end is good and that it is good to act on the maxim? If so, 'good' in what sense? In particular, do these individual choices of ends and maxims implicitly commit us to the idea that the ends and maxims are worthy of endorsement from an impartial (and ultimately moral) point of view? Commentators often suggest that Kant held this view, and passages in the *Critique of Practical Reason* might seem to confirm it. If we assume it as a premiss, it becomes all too easy to deduce Kant's controversial thesis that all rational agents are implicitly committed to the moral law. The assumption, however, is implausible and examination of relevant texts raises doubts that Kant relied on it.

The second troublesome issue is whether Kant's idea of 'setting an end' as an 'act of freedom' implies a radical kind of voluntarism that is implausible from a present-day perspective. The suspicion is not entirely unwarranted, but I suggest that underlying the idea of freely setting ends are significant normative points that are separable from implausible kinds of voluntarism.

III. *Moral Worth: Self-Assessment and Desert.* The final four essays turn from questions of moral deliberation (for example, what should we do?) to questions of moral assessment (for example, how well have we been doing?) These are related, but assessment is more concerned with the moral worth of past acts and motives, whether we deserve esteem or blame for what we have done, and when it is appropriate to feel guilty. Kant emphasizes moral assessment of ourselves, and for this the idea of conscience discussed in Chapters 9 and 11 is crucial. The moral assessment of others is involved in judicial punishment, which is discussed in Chapters 10 and 11. I argue that moral judgments about a criminal's moral deserts have a more limited role in Kant's theory of punishment than is commonly thought. The third essay of this set, Chapter 11, inquires whether avoiding wrongdoing has any moral worth when it is motivated by pangs of conscience or fear of punishment. The final essay, Chapter 12, presents a Kantian position on the possibility of 'moral dilemmas' and 'gaps' in moral theory. I include it here because the final two sections consider whether it is appropriate to feel guilty for causing harm in a dilemma-like situation.

9. 'Four Conceptions of Conscience' contrasts Kant's view of conscience, and its merits, with alternative views. The alternatives include

Joseph Butler's theory of conscience, as well as two conceptions briefly reviewed in *Respect, Pluralism, and Justice*. Kant's view avoids the epistemological problems of the popular religious conception, but Kant's view shares the latter's assumption that conscience is experienced as an intuitive voice rather than a deliberative judgment. Kant's view denies the metaethical skepticism in the cultural relativists' conception, but it agrees with their claim that conscience expresses a dissonance between our acts and our moral beliefs rather than a perception of what is truly right or wrong. Finally, although Kant agrees with Butler that reason, in due reflection, is our only source of justified beliefs about what we ought to do, Kant distinguishes the roles of *reasonable deliberation* about what is right from *conscience* as inner judge of innocence or guilt by the standards of our own moral beliefs.

10. 'Wrongdoing, Desert, and Punishment' is about relations between wrongdoing and suffering because of our wrongdoing. Kant maintains that, although wrongdoers are intrinsically liable to suffer self-reproach and disapproval of others, wrongdoing does not entail 'deserving to suffer' in a sense providing intrinsic practical reasons to inflict suffering. Arguably, even Kant's most infamous remarks on punishment fail to show otherwise. Contrary to common impressions, Kant is best understood as holding a mixed theory in which retributive policies lack deep retributive justification. Although other factors are relevant, the need to preserve justice by credible legal threats plays a crucial role in justifying the practice of punishment. At the end I explore implications of this interpretation for a contemporary Kantian perspective on punishment.

11. 'Punishment, Conscience, and Moral Worth' concerns the moral worth of acting from certain motives that may seem morally suspect from a Kantian point of view. The controversial motives of sympathy and love have been the object of endless discussion, but my focus is on two relatively neglected motives associated with anticipating punishment and a troubled conscience. Like the anticipation of grief, I suggest, these can give rise to two importantly different sorts of motive, one of which is morally worthy from a Kantian perspective and the other is not. Even 'fear' of just punishment can express respect for other citizens as sources of moral law.

12. 'Moral Dilemmas, Gaps, and Residues' offers an explanation of Kant's denial that there can be any genuine moral dilemmas. It also criticizes Alan Donagan's claim that we can put ourselves in a moral dilemma *through our own prior wrongdoing* even though we cannot innocently fall into one. True moral dilemmas, in which one would be

wrong no matter what one did, are distinguished from tragic cases in which 'gaps' in moral theory leave us no resolution. Kant's moral theory, I suggest, has such 'gaps,' and arguably this is not altogether a bad thing. Questions then arise about 'residues' of feeling and attitude after we have been forced to make a choice in such a situation. Are feelings of guilt and special regard for those we have injured appropriate? How can Kantians grant that we 'should feel' anything at all? I explore how plausible answers to these questions can be given from a Kantian perspective without appealing to consequentialist reasons for training people to feel guilty when they are not.

PART I

Some Basic Kantian Themes

I

Kantian Analysis: From Duty to Autonomy

Among the most basic ideas in Kant's moral philosophy are these: that moral philosophers must use an a priori method, that moral duties are categorical imperatives, and that moral agency presupposes autonomy of the will. In the second section of his *Groundwork of the Metaphysics of Morals* Kant develops each of these ideas in an argument for his central thesis that the idea that we have moral duties presupposes that we are rational agents with autonomy. The conclusion and each step of the argument remain controversial. Kant's admirers usually see here a great advance in moral theory, but critics often find Kant's contentions obscure and implausible.

When a philosopher inspires such extremes of admiration and disdain as Kant does in his ethical writings, we may well ask ourselves whether Kant's friends and his critics are focusing their attention on the same ideas. Elementary misunderstandings of Kant's ethics are common, and serious Kant scholars often disagree about interpretations. Insightful core ideas may be dismissed or ignored because they are conflated with more radical, controversial ideas. My aim, then, is to do some much needed sorting among the doctrines attributed to Kant. What is central, and what is peripheral? What is commonplace, and what is radical? Which assertions are preliminary starting points, and which are the more remote conclusions? Considering these questions is necessary for a balanced assessment of the strengths and weaknesses of Kant's ethics.

In my remarks below I comment in turn on each of the major themes mentioned above, trying to separate the more widely appealing core points from the more controversial. The modest version of each basic theme, I suggest, leads naturally to the next. The three themes are the outline of an argument that the idea that we have moral duties presupposes the idea that we are rational agents with autonomy. To preview, my main suggestions will be these:

(1) Kant's insistence on an a priori method, in its modest version, stems in large part from his belief that moral theory should begin with an analysis of the idea of a moral requirement (duty). Despite his strong

rhetoric about setting aside everything empirical, Kant's main point was that empirical methods are unsuitable for analysis of moral concepts and defense of basic principles of rational choice. The reason that Kant insisted on an a priori method was not that he believed in rational intuition of moral truths, opposed naturalistic explanations, assumed that duties are imposed by noumenal will, or thought that empirical facts are irrelevant to moral decisions.

(2) Kant thought that analysis of the ordinary idea of duty showed that we regard duties as categorical imperatives. That is, when we suppose that we have a duty we are thereby supposing that we have sufficient (overriding) reason to act accordingly and not just because doing so furthers our (desire based) personal ends. The modest point here is not that duties must always be experienced as unwelcome demands that must be fulfilled from a sense of constraint. Kant's point is also independent of his dubious view that substantive principles regarding lying, obedience to law, sexual purity, etc., are exceptionless and applicable in the same way across all times and places.

(3) The analysis of duty is for Kant merely a step on the way to the conclusion that in thinking of ourselves as having moral duties we must think of ourselves as rational agents with autonomy of the will. The basic point is that in order to be a moral agent, with duties, one must be able to understand and be moved by the sort of reasons that categorical imperatives claim we have. Categorical imperatives are addressed to deliberating rational agents presumed able to follow reasons independent of their concern for happiness and personal ends. To think that we can guide our decisions by such non-instrumental reasons, we must conceive ourselves as agents that implicitly acknowledge and respect the noninstrumental rational standards presupposed by categorical imperatives. As moral agents we might not always live up to the standards that we acknowledge, but our capacity to follow them presupposes that we accept them as rational grounds for our decisions and judgments. More controversially, in regarding our duties as categorical imperatives we presuppose that our disposition to judge our conduct by these basic standards is a constitutive feature of being moral agents, and not something we have because of a prior commitment to following external authorities, tradition, or common sentiments. In a sense, then, particular duties can be understood as requirements that rational agents impose on themselves, and following them is a way of being self-governing.

I. THE A PRIORI METHOD IN MORAL PHILOSOPHY

Kant repeatedly emphasizes in the *Groundwork*, and elsewhere, that we cannot find answers to the fundamental questions of moral philosophy by empirical methods.[1] To gain a theoretical understanding of nature we must rely on experience. We must use empirical concepts as well as some basic categories of thought. Ordinary, common-sense knowledge of what there is, how things work, and what is needed to achieve our goals must also rely on experience. But moral philosophy, Kant insists, is not an empirical science, and its conclusions are not simply inferences from observations of human behavior, emotional responses, and social practices. Rather, to address the basic questions of moral philosophy, according to Kant, we must use an a priori method that does not base its conclusions on what we learn from experience. Kant rejects many of the prominent moral theories of his day (e.g., British 'moral sense' theories) because they treat moral questions as if they were empirical questions. He rejects, for example, Frances Hutcheson's view that moral goodness is a natural property of actions that causes human beings to feel approbation.[2] On this view, the answer to 'Which acts are morally good?' would be discoverable by observing what sorts of acts human beings tend to approve. Kant criticizes other theories for mixing empirical and a priori arguments in discussions of basic issues that, he thinks, should be approached in a purely a priori manner. For example, Kant strongly disapproves of moral philosophies that argue that helping those in need is right and reasonable *because* experience shows that charitable people tend to be happier than uncharitable people.

Why begin moral philosophy by an a priori investigation instead of empirical studies? The explanation, I think, concerns Kant's understanding of what the basic questions of ethics are. In the *Groundwork*, he describes his task as seeking out and establishing the supreme principle of morality.[3] Judging by how Kant then proceeds to argue, it seems that 'seeking out' the supreme principle is a matter of articulating an abstract, basic, and comprehensive principle that can be shown to be a deep presupposition in ordinary moral thinking. 'Establishing' the

---
[1] G, 74–80 [4: 406–12], and 92–4 [4: 425–7].
[2] J. B. Schneewind, *Moral Philosophy from Montaigne to Kant*, ii (Oxford: Oxford University Press, 1990), 503–24.
[3] G, 60 [4: 392].

principle, I take it, is the further task of showing that the principle is rational to accept and follow. In addressing the first task Kant begins, provisionally, by assuming some very general moral ideas that he takes to be widely accepted, in fact, part of ordinary rational knowledge of morality. These assumptions include the special value of a good will and the idea of duty as more than prudence and efficiency in pursuing one's ends. That these are only assumed provisionally is shown by the fact that, even at the end of the second section, Kant forcefully reminds us that his 'analytic' mode of argument has not proved we really have moral duties.[4] Instead, it only serves to reveal presuppositions of the common moral idea that we have duties. For all we know at this point, morality might be an illusion. Despite this disclaimer, the results that Kant claims to reach by the analytic method are significant: common moral belief presupposes that the several formulas of the Categorical Imperative are morally fundamental, that rationality is not exclusively instrumental, and that moral agents are to be seen as legislators of moral laws as well as subject to them. These particular conclusions, however, are supposed *results* of the a priori method of analysis, not assumptions used to justify the method. Other philosophers might radically disagree with Kant's results but still see the value of his analytic approach.

Kant's main idea is simple and familiar in philosophy. We make use of moral concepts, some of which seem pervasive and essential features of our moral thinking and discourse, even when we disagree in our particular judgments. By reflecting on the meaning, implications, and presuppositions of these concepts, we may be able to understand them, and ourselves, better. To say that the process of reflection is a priori is not to imply that it could be done by hypothetical persons with no empirical concepts or experience of life. It is just to say that we are examining our ideas in a rational reflective way, looking for their structure and presuppositions. The aim here is not to explain the causes or effects of behavior that seems to be guided by moral ideas but only to gain a clearer grasp of the content and implications of those ideas themselves. Experiments, surveys, and comparative studies of different cultures can be valuable for many purposes, but they do not serve the philosophical purpose that Kant's analytical method was meant to address.

There was another important reason why Kant wanted moral philosophy to begin with an a priori method. This stems from his conviction that believing that we are under moral obligation entails believing

[4] G, 112 [4: 444–5], 107–8 [4: 440–1], and 114–15 [4: 446–7].

that we are subject to a rational requirement of a special sort (a 'command of reason'). This conviction was embedded in a long tradition, and Kant thought that it was part of ordinary understanding of morality. The problem is that we can question whether the *apparent* rationality of moral demands is an illusion. In fact, reading the British moralists Hutcheson, Hume, and others would naturally raise doubts in those (like Kant) who were deeply influenced by the natural law tradition. Such doubts, Kant thought, call for a response, an effort to vindicate the apparent (and commonly believed) assumption that moral principles express requirements that we would be irrational to disregard.[5] A positive response to the doubts would be to supplement (and build on) the analytical argument mentioned above with further argument that we really have reason-based duties, or at least that it is necessary to presuppose this for practical purposes. To do so would be to show that morality is not a mere illusion. Like the task of analysis, this task, which Kant undertakes in the notoriously difficult third section of the *Groundwork*, is again not one that could be accomplished by empirical investigations. The problem is to establish that guiding one's life by certain principles is *rationally necessary*, that one always has *sufficient reason* to do so.

Even if (contrary to Kant) there are only prudential reasons for following moral principles, to show that following them is always rational is not *simply* a matter of collecting empirical data on the effects of various behavior patterns. One would also need to argue that we always have *sufficient reason* to do what most effectively promotes the effects deemed 'prudent,' and this is a contested philosophical thesis that is not itself subject to empirical proof (as even most non-Kantians would agree). But the inadequacy of using an empirical method alone becomes even more evident for those who grant Kant's thesis that morality imposes categorical imperatives.[6] According to this, moral principles are rationally necessary to follow, but their rational necessity is not merely prudential or based on hypothetical imperatives. This means (at least) that the reason for following moral principles cannot be simply that doing so serves to promote one's happiness or individual ends. Thus, the rationality of following moral principles could not be established by showing empirically that they are good guides to happiness or means that serve well our particular purposes. For not only is the idea of rationality a normative one (the previous point), but also the sort of sufficient reason that needs to be defended is

---

[5] G, 114–31 [4: 446–63].   [6] G, 82–8 [4: 414–20].

more than the (empirically discernible) efficacy of our actions in achieving our ends.

This is not the place to review and assess Kant's actual argument in defense of his idea that moral requirements are *rationally necessary* to follow and even *categorically* so. And this assessment, fortunately, is not necessary for present purposes. The need that Kant saw for an a priori method, at least in parts of ethics, can be seen in the *problems* he posed, independently of his particular solutions. The essential point is that *if* we understand moral demands as saying to us that it is *unreasonable* not to do what is demanded, then we want some explanation and defense, especially once the seeds of philosophical doubt have been raised. All the more, if we understand moral demands as purporting to tell us what is *categorically* rational to do, then we may question whether morality's claim to be categorically rational is defensible. If, like most contemporary philosophers, we understand that claims about what is *reasonable*, *rational*, supported by *reasons*, etc., are irreducibly evaluative, practical, claims, then it becomes clear that the problems cannot be resolved by empirical investigation alone. The problems may prove to be irresolvable, or perhaps even pseudo-problems (as Humeans think), but at least we can understand why Kant and others believe that any search for resolutions must start with rational, a priori reflection.

Now that we have uncovered Kant's rationale for thinking that we must employ an a priori method, we can respond to some common objections and clarify certain misconceptions about the method.

(1) One misunderstanding that might lead readers to be skeptical of Kant's methodology stems from the thought that the alternative to empirical methods in moral theory is appeal to rational intuition or rationalistic theological arguments. Hume's famous objections to deriving 'moral distinctions' from 'reason' seem primarily aimed at views of this type. If turned against Kant, however, objections to rational intuition and theological ethics would miss their mark, for Kant agrees with Hume in rejecting rational intuitionism and theology as the basis of ethics. Like Hume, Kant holds that the traditional a priori arguments for the existence of God are inadequate, that morality cannot be based in theology, and that reason is not an intuitive power that 'sees' independent moral facts. (Kant does not deny that there is 'knowledge' of moral principles and that there are 'objective' moral values, but moral validity is determined by, and so not independent of, what rational agents with autonomy could or would accept.)

(2) Some moral theorists, past and present, see their main task as explaining moral phenomena as a part of the natural world. It seems

obvious that we raise moral questions, praise and blame in moral terms, experience moral feelings (e.g., guilt, indignation), and are sometimes moved by our moral beliefs. Many philosophers committed to understanding the world, so far as possible, in naturalistic terms accept the challenge of trying to explain moral phenomena (behavior, feelings, etc.) without appeal to occult, theological, or other 'nonnatural' entities. The methodology needed for this project, it seems widely agreed, is empirical, at least in a broad sense. When we turn to Kant's moral philosophy we find that not only does he use terminology (e.g., the will, autonomy, intelligible world) that is outside what most naturalists consider their domain, he even insists that these moral terms cannot be understood entirely in naturalistic terms. Clearly his moral theory is not a successful fulfillment of the naturalists' project, and may even seem to reflect contempt for such a project. Thus an objection to Kant's a priori method might be grounded in the thought that it is a method that cannot successfully carry out the project that naturalists consider most important and may even show contempt for it.

It is true, of course, that Kant's moral philosophy is not an attempt to contribute to the naturalists' project, but this does not mean that he would regard it as an unfruitful or unimportant task for empirically oriented scientists and philosophers to undertake. Although Kant insists that the a priori tasks in moral theory must be undertaken first, he often refers to 'practical anthropology' as empirical work that should follow and supplement basic moral theory.[7] What he had in mind (and attempted rather casually and unsystematically) was not the full naturalists' project, but his theory of knowledge is friendly to that project, at least if no more is claimed for its results than can be validly inferred from experience. Kant is committed to the position (which in fact he believed that he had proved) that all phenomena are in principle explicable by empirical, natural laws. So, although he thought that for practical purposes we must employ normative ideas that are not reducible to empirical propositions, anything that can count as observable phenomena associated with moral practices must (in principle) be amenable to empirical study and understanding. And, although he denied that empirical science can establish moral truths or vindicate their rational claim on us, his theory of knowledge allows (indeed insists) that all the *observable facts* associated with moral and immoral acts can be studied and (in principle) comprehended from an empirical perspective. This is

---

[7] G, 55–6 [4: 387–8], and Kant's *Anthropology from a Pragmatic Point of View*, tr. Mary Gregor (The Hague: Martinus Nijhoff, 1997).

distinct from the practical perspective we must take up when we deliberate and evaluate acts.⁸ Each perspective has its legitimate and necessary use, and limits. So, although Kant thinks the basic questions of moral philosophy cannot be answered by empirical methods, he should happily encourage naturalists' ambition to understand the phenomena associated with moral activity *so far as possible* in naturalistic terms through empirical investigations.

(3) Again, some critics familiar with Kant's philosophy as a whole may suppose that Kant's insistence on an a priori method is based on his controversial idea that we must think of moral agents not only in empirical terms but also under the idea of free rational agency. This involves thinking of them as belonging to an 'intelligible world' that cannot be understood in the terms of empirical science.⁹ Hence one might suspect that Kant thought an a priori method of investigation in ethics is necessary because moral agents, as such, are not beings that we can comprehend empirically. But I think that this is a mistake, and in fact it gets the order of Kant's thought backwards. As we have seen, there are simpler and less controversial explanations for Kant's insistence on the a priori method. In fact he introduces the perspective of an intelligible world into ethics not as an initial assumption but rather as a point to which he believes his analysis of common moral knowledge finally drives him. Analysis of the idea of duty shows that it presupposes the idea of rational agents with autonomy, and this idea, he argues, can be squared with his earlier conclusions about empirical knowledge only if we think of these agents as 'intelligible' or noumenal beings.¹⁰ Many philosophers who find Kant convincing at the earlier stages dissent from this last stage of the argument. There is no doubt that Kant thought it an important part of his systematic moral theory, but it is not a beginning assumption used to justify his methodology. Rather, it is a final theoretical point to which (Kant thought) his particular a priori argument (not the method itself) drives us. In short, his controversial views about the ultimate 'Idea' of moral agents to which philosophical reflection forces us is not presupposed in the modest methodological procedures with which he begins.

(4) Finally, there is a persistent objection that, I suspect, rests partly on misunderstanding but partly on Kant's tendency to overstate his

---

⁸ See Henry Allison, *Kant's Theory of Freedom* (Cambridge: Cambridge University Press, 1990).   ⁹ G, 118–21 [4: 450–3].

¹⁰ Note, for example, that although Kant is committed to the possibility of noumenal 'causation' in the *Critique of Pure Reason*, his argument for beginning ethics with an a priori investigation precedes his conclusion that our conception of morality requires us to think of moral agents from a nonempirical standpoint. See G, 74–81 [4: 406–14] and 118–23 [4: 450–5].

insights. The objection proceeds as follows. First we note that the reasons we give for thinking that acts are right or wrong are typically empirical facts, e.g., 'That will kill him,' 'You intentionally deceived him,' 'She saved your life and needs help now,' 'No society could survive if it tolerated that.' Then we also note that most morally sensitive persons realize that the acts picked out by simple descriptions (e.g., 'killing', 'deceiving') may be wrong in one situation but right in another, depending on the empirical facts of the case. So a method that excluded empirical information, it seems, will not even consider facts that are crucial to determining what is right and what is wrong. Moral decisions must be made in a complex and richly diverse world, and so it seems foolish to suppose that we can discern what is right without knowing accurately and in detail (and so empirically) what this world is like and where we stand in it at the moment.

The objection would be appropriate and (I think) devastating if directed against a moral theorist who claimed that pure reason alone can discern what we ought to do in each situation. But few, if any, today make such a claim, and certainly Kant did not. Those who agree with Kant that some fundamental moral principles can be vindicated through the use of reason are well aware that we need empirical knowledge to apply these principles to our current circumstances. We need to judge whether and how moral principles are relevant, and this requires understanding based on experience. For example, that we should treat all persons with respect, Kant thought, is an ideal norm, not something empirical science or ordinary experience can establish; but, of course, respect and disrespect are expressed in a wide variety of ways that we learn only with experience in different cultural contexts.[11] Kant does not deny that we (rightly) cite facts in explaining the reasons why some particular act is morally required or forbidden; he merely agrees with Hume that empirical facts *alone* do not establish any 'ought' claim. Kant was indeed extremely rigoristic by not allowing that familiar moral principles (e.g., about lying) need to be qualified, but his rigidity on these matters cannot be blamed on his rejection of empirical methods for the basic issues in moral theory. Notoriously, Kant endorses some principles in an absolute, unqualified form, and most of us will agree that inflexible adherence to such rules is an over-simple response to complex moral problems. His extreme stand on lying, revolution, and sexual practices, however, does not follow from his thesis that moral philosophy should *begin* with a priori methods, e.g., of analysis.[12] The problem,

---

[11] MM, 209-13 [6: 462-8].

[12] MM, 176-7 [6: 422-3], 96-7 [6: 320], 178-9 [6: 424-5], and 'On a Supposed Right to Lie because of Philanthropic Concerns', in Immanuel Kant, *Grounding of the*

rather, lies in his thinking that rigid opposition to lying (etc.) is required by the Categorical Imperative.

There remains serious controversy, however, on two related points. *First*, many philosophers would deny that an a priori use of reason can establish even one basic moral principle. This objection comes not only from those who think that empirical methods can establish moral principles, but also from those who think that moral principles cannot be established by any method because they have no objective standing. This is a perennial controversy, but it is about the *results* that can be established by an a priori method rather than about the value of the method in general. *Second*, even those who side with Kant on the first point may reasonably worry that Kant himself tries to make *too much* of ethics independent of empirical knowledge. It is one thing, they may say, to suppose that some quite abstract, formal principles can be discovered and defended by an a priori method, but quite another (and more dubious) thing to exclude empirical facts when taking up other tasks of moral philosophy. For example, if moral philosophers, following Kant and Alan Donagan, want to try to work out a system of universally valid moral principles about substantive matters (such as lying, obedience to law, punishment, charity), then it seems only reasonable to expect that the construction must take into account our (limited) empirical knowledge about the human condition in general and about the diversity of contexts to which putative universal principles must be applied. It is still a matter of dispute how much empirical information Kant intended to exclude when he took up this project in *The Metaphysics of Morals*. His arguments often presuppose facts that could only be known empirically, but they also often raise the suspicion that his determination not to rely on empirical evidence has led to unwarranted rigidity and over-generalization. These worries and controversies cannot be lightly dismissed, but they do not call into question Kant's main reasons for adopting an a priori method for the basic issues in moral philosophy.

II. CATEGORICAL AND HYPOTHETICAL IMPERATIVES

The vocabulary and tone of Kant's writing about morality is disturbing to many readers, especially when they contrast this with the ethical

Metaphysics of Morals, tr. James Ellington, 3rd edn. (Indianapolis: Hackett Publishing Co., 1993), 63–7.

works of Hume and Aristotle. A good example is Kant's contention that there are *categorical imperatives* of morality. Kant focuses attention on what we morally *must* do, what is *necessary*, a *command* of reason, a *constraint* rather than an aid in the pursuit of happiness.[13] We are easily reminded of angry parents who tell us, in stern imperative tones, 'Do it at once, whether you want to or not.' So viewed, morality can seem to be dictatorial, not intrinsically appealing or personally fulfilling. Moreover, since Kant tells us that categorical imperatives are unconditional, absolute, apodictic as opposed to mere prudential 'counsels,' it is natural to assume that this means that moral rules are inflexible and admit of no exceptions. This assumption may seem confirmed when we read Kant's vigorous denial that we may tell a lie to save a friend from murder and his insistence that we must obey the law even if it is imposed by a tyrant.[14] Categorical imperatives then seem like demands that we must obey with the attitude of a dutiful soldier following orders, respecting the authority of law without regard to anything else.

Kant's moral theory no doubt contains features with which many ordinary readers, as well as opposing moral theorists, will disagree, but making some distinctions helps us to identify some possible misunderstandings and to sort the more controversial from the less controversial Kantian themes. There may remain disputes both about interpretation and plausibility, but I think that some core ideas that are manifestly at least part of Kant's thought are also quite widely accepted. Three questions, in particular, need to be considered: (1) Are categorical imperatives to be seen as disagreeable orders from an alien power with whom we cannot identify, mere pressures that we see no good reason to follow apart from possible rewards and punishments? (2) Are moral principles, as categorical imperatives, necessarily inflexible and exceptionless? (3) Is a motivating respect for principles that are categorical imperatives necessarily a sense of constraint rather than concern for the good of others?

Despite what one might initially suppose, Kant's basic position on each of these questions, I think, is quite compatible with common opinion (among philosophers and non-philosophers alike). This is not to deny, however, that Kant accepts some further related ideas that remain more controversial. Let us begin with what I take to be the core idea that moral duties are categorical imperatives, and then we can return to the three questions just mentioned.

---

[13] G, 82–8 [4: 414–21].
[14] 'On a Supposed Right to Lie because of Philanthropic Concerns', and MM, 127–33 [6: 316–23], and 176 [6: 371].

Kant's remarks about categorical imperatives can be confusing because although he explicitly says that there can only be one categorical imperative he repeatedly writes as though there are many. Kant lists several 'formulas' of the Categorical Imperative, which he says are 'at bottom the same,' but he also refers to more specific principles, such as 'Don't lie' and 'Punish all and only the guilty' as categorical imperatives.[15] No doubt he had in mind a primary (or strict) sense of the term when he was writing as if there is only one categorical imperative, but he then helped himself to a secondary (or less strict) sense of the term when writing about further principles that (he believed) were warranted by 'the Categorical Imperative' (in the strict sense). On this hypothesis, the discrepancy (from singular to plural) becomes harmless, even though there remain questions in various contexts about which sense he had in mind.

Categorical imperatives (in both senses) are *imperatives*, which Kant calls 'commands of reason.' All imperatives express the idea that something ought to be done, either because it is good in itself or because it is good as a means to an end that is in some way valuable. Through the idea of 'ought' they express a relation ('necessitation') between what is rational to do (an 'objective principle') and the not so perfectly rational choosers ('imperfect wills') that can do what is rational but might not.[16] So, in other words, imperatives say (truly) that we have good reason to do something even while acknowledging (implicitly) that we might in fact not do it. This applies to 'hypothetical imperatives,' e.g., 'one ought to exercise if one aims to be strong,' as well as to 'categorical imperatives,' e.g., 'one ought to treat human beings with respect.'

What, then, makes an imperative *categorical*? For both the primary and secondary senses, the core idea is that the reasons for following a 'categorical imperative' are not merely that doing so will promote the ends that one happens to have, such as becoming rich or (more generally) being happy. Following categorical imperatives may often promote our personal ends, but it may not always do so. Making us happy and helping us get what we want is not what makes moral principles *categorical* imperatives; they are rational to follow, even if doing so does not make us happy or promote our personal ends. They express the idea that it is good and rational to act as they prescribe, but, unlike hypothetical imperatives, they do not simply say what is good to do as a means to getting or achieving what we want.

---

[15] G, 88–104 [4: 420–37], MM, 14 [6: 221], and MM, 105 [6: 331].
[16] G, 81–4 [4: 412–17], 69n [4: 401].

Furthermore, as Kant uses the term, categorical imperatives do not merely say that we have *some* reason to do what they prescribe. They assert that we have sufficient reason, *overriding* other considerations.[17] We always ought to follow categorical imperatives, even if they conflict with what we otherwise would have reason to do based on self-interest and our personal projects. So categorical imperatives do not simply give us 'some' reason to act; they give us sufficient reasons, all things considered, reasons that override other considerations. This point, however, should not be confused with the idea that moral rules are always specific, simple, and inflexible, allowing no exceptions or variation for extraordinary circumstances. Kant himself did insist on *some* moral principles (e.g., against lying) in this rigid form, but nothing in the core idea of categorical imperatives prevents them from being vastly complex and justifiably filled with qualifications ('unless,' 'so long as,' 'but only if'). Moreover, as Kant says, some ethical principles only say that we ought to adopt certain indeterminate ends (e.g., the happiness of others), without specifying exactly what, or how much, one must do to promote the ends.[18] These too are supposed to be categorical imperatives, for they say we must, for overriding reasons, adopt the prescribed ends, whether or not doing so promotes our happiness and personal projects. So categorical imperatives do not have to be inflexible, rigoristic rules of conduct. In labeling an 'ought' judgment as a 'categorical imperative' we express the belief that it is an all-things-considered, overriding moral requirement, backed by reasons not entirely dependent on what serves to promote the ends we happen to have. The requirement could be simple and sweepingly general (as Kant regarded 'Never lie'), but it could be vastly complex and qualified. We should not confuse issues about the scope and complexity of moral principles with issues about the sort of reason we have to follow them. Kant's claim that we are under categorical imperatives is addressed to the latter.

---

[17] For example, if it is a categorical imperative not to give false witness, then the (moral) reasons not to give false witness override or defeat the consideration that you might make some money by doing so. In other words, all things considered, you should not bear false witness. The question naturally arises, 'What should one do if two different categorical imperatives conflict?' Kant's response was that this is a conceptual impossibility. There cannot be genuine conflicts of duty, only competing grounds or considerations relevant to determining what one's duty is. Thus, if two alleged categorical imperatives give contradictory directions, then we must regard one of them as mistaken, or only valid in a more qualified form. I discuss this problem in more detail in Ch. 12 of this volume. For a somewhat different view, see Alan Donagan, 'Moral Dilemmas, Genuine and Spurious: A Comparative Anatomy', *Ethics*, 104 (1993), 7-21.

[18] MM, 147-56 [6: 382-94].

Beyond these core ideas, Kant held that the one 'Categorical Imperative' (in the strict sense) that he formulated (in several ways) is an unconditional and unqualified requirement of reason, applicable in all human conditions and implicitly acknowledged in common moral judgments. Unlike the principle behind instrumental reasons, which we call 'the Hypothetical Imperative,' it does not simply prescribe taking the necessary means to desired ends. It can be established as rationally necessary, Kant thought, without reliance on empirical studies of human nature, and we can and should be motivated by respect for it apart from any other interests that might be served. It expresses what our own reason, independently of inclination, requires of us, and so we cannot help but acknowledge its authority (even when we fail to meet its requirements). Kant seems at times also to believe that more specific principles (e.g., about lying, obeying the law, and sexual practices) are derivative categorical imperatives, shown by the basic Categorical Imperative to be unconditionally required in *all human conditions*, without exception.[19] These ideas are understandably more controversial than the basic points we have been discussing.

The core idea, however, remains just that moral duties impose categorical imperatives in the sense that we have sufficient, overriding reason to fulfill our moral duties, independently of whether doing so will promote our own happiness or serve our individual ends. Even this core idea is rejected by those philosophers who insist that practical rationality is always nothing but taking efficient means to desired ends, but Kant's view, I suspect, is closer than theirs to ordinary moral opinion and most of Western tradition in moral theory.[20] We think, for example, that Hitler was wrong and *unreasonable* to kill millions of European Jews and this was not just because it was a poor means for him to get what he most wanted. The moral prohibition on murdering people, it is commonly thought, should override personal ambitions; so Hitler had sufficient reason not to do the killing, even though he wanted to.

Now let us return to our earlier questions. (1) It should be clear that

---

[19] I use capital letters to indicate the basic principle, the Categorical Imperative, and small-case letters for the derivative principles, categorical imperatives.

[20] Aristotle and most other ancient moral philosophers, I think, do not accept that we have reason to be moral only as a means to some desired end independent of it. The Aristotelian view, for example, is apparently that virtue is a constituent part of 'happiness,' not a mere means to it. We cannot say, either, that he sees moral requirements as 'independent' of what promotes our happiness, but it is important that 'happiness' for Aristotle is not merely a subjective state or merely an end that we inevitably desire. See Julia Annas, *The Morality of Happiness* (Oxford: Oxford University Press, 1993). See also Ch. 6 of this volume.

categorical imperatives are not to be viewed as orders from an alleged alien authority. Unlike commands from parents, military superiors, and legal authorities, they are conceived as expressing 'objective principles,' that is, principles that anyone in the context would follow if sufficiently guided by reason. They are supposed to tell us what is good in itself to do, not what someone demands that we do.[21] As discussed more fully in the next section of this essay, a key Kantian doctrine is that basic moral requirements are laws we legislate to ourselves as rational persons with autonomy. We are not morally bound by any alleged requirement unless it is backed by principles that we can recognize as what we ourselves, as rational, self-governing persons, will for ourselves and others. There are various ways of understanding this, but all clearly rule out the idea that categorical imperatives are imposed by alien authorities and give us reasons only by threats of punishment or promise of rewards. The authority of moral principles is, as it were, the authority of our own reason, our best judgments, all things considered, as to what we ought to do. Moral reasons are *our* reasons; they guide us, rather than goad us.[22] What they require need not be unpleasant or disagreeable at all; but even when it is, we cannot pursue other projects in disregard of them without going against our own best judgment, suffering conflict of will, and inviting self-contempt. These implications of Kant's idea of moral autonomy may be doubted, but at least they make clear that Kantian categorical imperatives would be grossly misunderstood if they were seen as commands of some alleged 'authority' independent of our own reason.

(2) It should also be clear that substantive categorical imperatives need not be simple, exceptionless rules, like 'Never lie.' As noted above, Kant himself believed that there are such absolute rules, but this dubious belief does not follow from the concept of a categorical imperative. What follows is that, no matter how richly complex and filled with 'unless' and 'so long as' clauses, a categorical imperative should always be respected, not subordinated to other considerations. To call a specified requirement a 'categorical imperative' is to make a summary

---

[21] In later writings, trying to reconcile his moral philosophy with some minimal religious beliefs, Kant says that, once we determine through reason what our duties are, we can and should think of them as if they are commands of God (exemplifying pure practical reason). But this does not alter the main point. Duties are not derived from personal orders, should not be followed from fear of punishment or hope of reward, and are binding only because rationality requires them.

[22] For an illuminating discussion of this distinction, see David Falk, 'Guiding and Goading', in his *Ought, Reasons, and Morality* (Ithaca: Cornell University Press, 1986), 42–66.

judgment, saying that, all things considered, reason requires a certain course of action. If we believe that a principle states merely a morally relevant consideration, then it should not be called a categorical imperative; for that label is appropriate only when all relevant factors have been taken into account and an all-things-considered conclusion on a particular act or act type has been reached. We can say, trivially, 'categorical imperatives must be obeyed, no matter what' because the claim is implicit in what is meant by a categorical imperative. Again, however, nothing follows about the complexity and scope of the principles that summarize our reasonable all-things-considered moral judgments about lying, revolution, sex, promises, etc., i.e. the principles we might take to be categorical imperatives. In short, we should not confuse two distinct questions: (a) How much (if at all) should moral principles about lying, killing, obeying the law, etc., be qualified by explicit or implicit exceptions? and (b) Are moral principles *categorical imperatives*? The core issue for the second question is whether moral principles, no matter how many or few qualifications they contain, are overridingly rational to follow and not simply because doing so promotes the personal ends of the agent.

(3) Finally, a categorical imperative is not something we must follow from a sense of constraint. We do not need to grit our teeth and focus on the requirement as a 'command,' to which we are 'bound' and 'subject.' We can often, and should, fulfill our moral responsibilities with our mind focused on the good we can do, rather than our own goodness or need to submit to authoritative commands. This requires some explanation.

To be sure, Kant does imply that in general we are not only authors of moral laws but *subject* to them.[23] As *imperatives* they express a relation of *necessitation* between our imperfect wills and objective principles, i.e. the principles that we would follow invariably if we acted in a fully rational way.[24] Moreover, Kant says that conforming to duty has 'moral worth' only if done 'from duty'.[25] But none of this, I think, implies that we are *always or typically* averse to doing what we should or that we need to feel 'constrained' in order to do it. If we are in fact reluctant to do what we should, then the thought that doing so is an *imperative* to which we are *subject* may serve to move us (or not); but the thought is not essential, I think, to the idea of governing ourselves by principles that are categorical imperatives. Kant did tend to suppose that self-interest is such a strong motive that recognition of the moral

---

[23] G, 98–102 [4: 431–4].   [24] G, 80–1 [4: 413].   [25] G, 65–7 [4: 397–9].

law inevitably causes in us feelings of 'respect,' and he describes this respect as a partly painful feeling, akin to fear, a sense of our 'self-conceit' being humbled by recognition that what is morally required is not always what we most want to do.[26] This dark, and perhaps overly pessimistic, view of human psychology, however, is not an implication of the core idea that moral requirements are categorical imperatives. That idea is about the sort of reasons that favor acting as we morally should, leaving open whether on particular occasions acting for those reasons will be experienced as being constrained or obedient to authority. An important point to note here is that all 'imperatives' have two sides, as it were. They express 'objective principles,' or rational principles that even a 'holy will' would follow, and yet they do so in a form ('ought') that also conveys the idea that imperfect wills, i.e. those who do not automatically follow them with God-like regularity, are *bound* to obey them, *must* do so, and feel *constrained* when tempted to do otherwise.[27] When we consider our thoughts and feelings in fulfilling our various duties, then, there are several possibilities.

First, we might desire to do something incompatible with what we ought to do but nevertheless understand and respect the reasons behind the moral principle. Here it seems natural to suppose that we are moved both by the moral reasons and by a sense of being under appropriate constraints. Suppose, for example, you are asked to testify in a legal case and telling the truth will prove embarrassing to you and your friend, but you recognize and respect the moral reasons for obeying the law and testifying truthfully and you conclude that, all things considered, this is your duty. If you tell the truth, you do so because you respect the good reasons for doing so but also with a sense of being constrained to do so contrary to your wishes. Or, better, you have had to *constrain yourself* to act on principle rather than inclination. This is the sort of case, I think, that Kant most often highlights.

Second, we might desire to do something incompatible with what we accept as duty but without understanding or even considering the good reasons for accepting it as duty. We might have just relied on common

---

[26] C2, 62–75 [5: 71–89].
[27] 'Holy will' is Kant's term for the will of any being conceived (as God often is) as necessarily willing what is rational, without temptations or the possibility of willing in an irrational way; G, 81 [4: 414]. Such a will is perfectly guided by rational principles (regarding what is good) but these principles do not impose imperatives or duties on a holy will. Such a will would be a member of the 'kingdom of ends' as a 'completely independent being,' one whose will (along with the rational will of all members) legislates the moral laws but without being 'subject' to the laws as authoritative constraints; G, 100–1 [4: 433–4].

opinion or the authority of another person. Here we would fulfill the duty with a sense of constraint but not from respect for the reasons behind it. Insofar as we have really accepted the opinion that we have the moral duty, then by Kant's analysis we must suppose that *there are* sufficient, overriding reasons but we are not aware of them and so cannot be moved by them. An example might be a person who restrains sexual impulses according to commonly accepted opinions about what is permissible, but who never considers why those restraints are required.

Third, now that we see that the elements of Kant's paradigm case (i.e., the first case above) are separable, we can consider another possibility. That is, we might recognize and respect the reasons for a particular moral requirement but have no inclination or reason to act otherwise. The suggestion is not that we *never* think of duty, but just that in the case at hand there is no need for constraint because nothing even prompts the thought of not doing the right thing. Suppose, for example, your child is badly cut from a fall and needs hospital treatment immediately. In fact, as you would agree if asked, it is your duty to take the child to the hospital, but the constraints and imperatives of moral duty are not at all what is on your mind. Nor are you thinking 'The child is *mine* and so I must help.' Your love draws your attention to the need of Ken or Leah, the individual person in front of you perceived concretely.[28] The life and interests of *this* child are so clear and vivid that abstract thoughts about all human beings' reasons for helping other human beings are not what is on your mind. But, still, what primarily moves you in the particular context are features of it that would give anyone reason to act similarly in relevantly similar cases. It is not that the child is named 'Ken' or 'Leah,' or anything else in particular. It is not primarily, certainly not only, that the child shares your genes or has lived with you for several years. You are moved by a direct concern for the life and vital interests of the real person, and these are the very sort of reasons about which moral principles speak in more general terms.

---

[28] Kant thought that acts that express a moral attitude (e.g., a commendable regard for persons as ends) are not acts 'from inclinations,' such as 'pathological love' (i.e., a feeling distinct from commitments of will made for good reasons). So in the case imagined here I am supposing that the love is not so blind and detached from your general commitments and moral attitudes. It is also not a driving force, as conceived on a mechanical model, although it alerts you to concrete needs and you may act *with* love (lovingly). My claim now is not that Kant's statements about acts 'from duty' are compatible with his acknowledging that our imagined case is a 'morally worthy' act, but only that it is a case of acting for the reasons behind recognizing the aid as a 'duty,' and so should have been counted as morally worthy.

Your reasons, I would say, are moral reasons insofar as they manifest in the particular case the sort of attitude that the more abstract principles of humanity and beneficence call for. The motivation does not fail to show respect for moral reasons just because it was not the result of a deduction from abstract moral generalizations to particular cases. It seems, then, that we can be moved by the relevant moral reasons without experiencing them as constraints and without even thinking of them in the form of abstract generalizations. If so, even imperfect moral agents, like us, who often experience moral requirements as constraints, need not always do so. In at least some circumstances we can act as categorical imperatives prescribe, responding directly to the reasons behind them, without experiencing them as constraints or even thinking of them abstractly as duties.

Would Kant count these acts as 'from duty' and so 'morally worthy'? The answer is not entirely clear because the idea of duty includes the two elements (moral reasons and constraint) that can work separately in ways that Kant did not discuss. Even if Kant assumed that the sense of being (self-) constrained is an essential part of acting 'from duty,' a reasonable extension of Kant's view would, I think, grant that the crucial feature of morally worthy acts is that they manifest responsiveness to the sort of basic reasons that underlie moral principles.

III. AUTONOMY OF MORAL AGENTS

Kant argued, still by an analytical method, that there can be only one Categorical Imperative, which he expressed initially in his famous formula of universal law.[29] In a complex and controversial course of argument, he contended that this formula expresses essentially the same basic moral idea as his later formulas, including the formula of autonomy.[30] According to this formula, we must act under the idea that moral agents legislate or will for themselves universal laws, as rational beings, independently of their particular desires as sensuous human beings. Thinking of ourselves as under the Categorical Imperative, then, requires thinking of ourselves as rational agents with what Kant calls autonomy of the will. Thus, assuming Kant's analysis of the idea of moral duty as the idea of being subject to categorical imperatives and so bound by the Categorical Imperative, then believing that we have

---

[29] G, 88 [4: 420–1].
[30] G, 88–100 [4: 420–33] and 104–8 [4: 437–40].

duties commits us to a conception of ourselves as rational agents with autonomy. Now there is much in this whole argument that for present purposes we can bypass. The core point is Kant's thought that we must attribute at least a modest sort of autonomy to moral agents because we think of them as having the capacities and dispositions to guide their decisions by categorical imperatives. Kant also affirms a more robust, and controversial, conception of autonomy, in line with his stronger claims about the Categorical Imperative, but let us begin with the more modest idea.

What sort of agents could be subject to categorical imperatives? All imperatives are rational requirements addressed to those who can fulfill them but might not, and so the agents must be able to follow the rational requirements, recognized as such. That is, they must be disposed to acknowledge and follow them because they are requirements that express good reasons or are based on good reasons. Since being under an imperative implies the possibility of acting against reason, agents subject to categorical imperatives may in fact fail to follow them, and may even act against them; but insofar as we suppose the agents *ought* to follow the imperatives, we must assume that they *can*. Already it is clear, then, that agents subject to categorical imperatives cannot be complete slaves to the impulses and desires of the moment, for that implies inability to regulate conduct by rational reflection, even about future consequences to oneself. At a minimum the agents must be able to act for reasons, reflecting on facts and interests over time. This much is implicit even in the idea that they can follow hypothetical imperatives. Since, however, categorical imperatives are defined as principles rational to follow independently of how well they serve our happiness and particular personal ends, agents subject to them must also be able and disposed to recognize reasons to act beyond those of instrumental rationality. Their deliberations are not restricted to considering what will satisfy their immediate desires, what will make them most happy in the long run, and what will achieve their desires for others. Apart from these considerations, they also acknowledge reasons of another kind, considerations that also other agents, so far as they are rational, accept as reasons and not just because their desires as individuals would be served. Agents subject to categorical imperatives, then, cannot take the fact that they can satisfy a particular desire or interest as sufficient, by itself, to give them a reason to act; for they realize that further reflection, on rational considerations not so tied to their personal concerns, may give them reason to disregard, suppress, or even try to eliminate that desire or interest. Furthermore, if they judge that, all things considered, these reasons are sufficient to constitute duty, understood as a categorical imperative, they regard them as overriding reasons—determining what they ought to do, despite any inclination not to.

Agents conceived in this way have the main elements of a modest Kantian idea of autonomy.[31]

In thinking of agents as having desires but able to reflect to determine whether those desires, all things considered, provide good reasons, we are already attributing to them a necessary condition of autonomy. To follow categorical imperatives, however, agents must also be able to acknowledge and act on reasons that are more than requirements to take the means to satisfy their desire-based ends. This is a further feature of Kant's idea of autonomy. When we add that, to follow categorical imperatives, they must respect these special reasons as overriding their desire-based reasons, we have a fuller, but still modest, idea of Kantian autonomy. Some philosophers deny that moral agents must have autonomy even in this limited sense, but the ideas regarding autonomy that draw the most controversy go beyond the basic points mentioned so far.

First, Kant held that moral agents, in a sense, impose moral requirements on themselves. They are *authors* of moral laws as well as *subject* to them. They can be compared to autonomous states, bound to no higher authority, with a power to govern themselves in accord with their own constitution, without needing the approval of any further authority. These metaphorical descriptions may be understood in several ways, but some basic points seem clear. Rational agents with autonomy identify with the perspective from which moral judgments are made so that that they see moral requirements not as externally imposed, for example, by cultural norms or divine commands. They cannot, then, knowingly act contrary to their moral beliefs without inner conflict and self-disapproval. When they act from moral principle, they are governing themselves by their own standards; and when they act immorally, they are in conflict with deep commitments essential to them as moral agents. Also, in conceiving of moral agents as 'authors' of moral laws, Kant implicitly contrasts his idea of rational autonomy with rational intuitionism. That is, reason does not simply 'perceive' moral facts as things that exist independently of the use of reason by moral agents; rather moral agents determine particular moral requirements through reasoning from a basic moral perspective (as if legislating according to values inherent in their constitution).

Second, Kant apparently thought that virtually all sane, competent

---

[31] For more detail, see 'The Kantian Conception of Autonomy', in my *Dignity and Practical Reason*.

adult human beings have the characteristics of autonomy that his analysis revealed as essential to moral agency. This, however, is a point of faith beyond what his analytical argument aims to establish. That argument, at best, shows that the idea of a moral agent who acknowledges duties presupposes that such an agent is rational and has autonomy. But whether all, or even most, functional adult human beings are moral agents in this sense cannot be settled by conceptual analysis, and Kant, of course, did not undertake any empirical investigations to give evidence for his assumption. In our times, after the Holocaust, it is harder to share Kant's faith that a moral point of view is universally acknowledged as authoritative. Kant tries to make sense of moral life by offering an abstract model of moral agents with certain essential features; but whether that model fits this or that person, i.e. whether they are moral agents in his sense, depends on what we find when we try to employ it. Merely finding examples of sociopaths who fail to be moral agents in Kant's sense, however, does not show that Kant's argument was incorrect or his model valueless. Instead, it would confirm doubts about the common eighteenth-century faith, which Kant shared, that all minimally rational human beings implicitly acknowledge moral standards. Some Kantians will defend Kant on the point; and some critics may argue that Kant's model does not even fit ordinary moral agents. Controversy here is not easily resolved.

Third, Kant held that rational agents with autonomy can act from pure practical reason alone. When they act from respect for overriding moral reasons, then, they are not to be understood simply as acting on good (morally approved) *sentiments* as opposed to other desires and inclinations. It is a familiar Kantian theme that they act on principle, where the governing maxim is not of the form 'I will do X because, as it happens, X promotes Y, which I want' but, rather, 'I will do X, regardless of its effect on what I desire.' The claim that we can act from pure practical reason, however, goes beyond these familiar Kantian themes. A sophisticated Humean, for example, might accept those themes but insist that the agent's underlying motive for adopting the maxim of duty is a strong, but 'calm,' sentiment in favour of so acting. The feelings that move us are not always reflected in the maxims we use to guide and explain our conduct. Even Kant conceded this when he repeatedly insisted that we do not know for sure what moves us to act even when we take ourselves to be acting for the best moral reasons. It is clear, however, that Kant meant to deny the Humean thesis that all motivation must stem from sentiments. Insofar as we take ourselves to be moral agents, Kant argues, we must conceive ourselves as *capable* of being moved by practical reason alone. Sometimes we may be moved by mere sentiment when we think we are guided by reason alone, but we must suppose that we can do what reason requires even if we lack any feeling prompting us to do so. Here Kant goes beyond claims we have explicitly discussed previously, and Kant's view is widely disputed.

There is, however, a way of understanding Kant's point that is less radical than what is usually attributed to him. Kant denies that all action must be motivated by sentiment, feeling, inclination, or sensuous desire, but these terms can be interpreted broadly or narrowly. Similarly, when Kant insists that we can act from reason alone, we can think of 'reason' in more or less radical metaphysical ways. If we interpret desires and sentiments narrowly as felt internal pushes and pulls, then Kant's denial that these must be present as motivating causes of all action is more plausible. If, however, we interpret 'desire' broadly as just a given disposition to act, then Kant does not deny that we 'desire' to follow moral principles. In fact he insists that all moral agents have, inescapably, a predisposition to morality, even though he attributes it to our rational nature rather than our sensuous nature. Again, if 'reason' is given a narrow Humean interpretation, it cannot motivate any act because it is merely an 'inert' power to discover natural facts and relations of ideas. But Kant agrees with Hume that reason, so construed (as 'theoretical reason'), is not by itself a source of motivation. To have practical reason, according to Kant, is (among other things) to be disposed to acknowledge certain procedural norms for choice, and so in the broad sense it is a kind of 'desire' that can figure in practical explanations of why agents choose to act as they do. Humeans question whether these normative commitments are special in ways that warrant attributing them to our nature as *rational*, as opposed to sensuous, beings. Kant, and followers, think that there are good reasons for the attribution. This is a dispute that needs more work on both sides; but it is rarely discussed in a fruitful way. This, I think, is largely because Kant's normative position tends to be conflated with his widely rejected appeal to the distinction between noumena and phenomena, to which I turn next.

Fourth, the core ideas of autonomy suggested here also fall short of the most controversial ideas that Kant introduces when he tries to reconcile his ethics with the conclusions he reached in his *Critique of Pure Reason*. In the third section of the *Groundwork*, and other writings, Kant argues that to attribute to moral agents the sort of freedom of will that morality requires we must think of them as belonging to an 'intelligible world' as well as the 'sensible world.' The idea of responsible choice employed in practical discussions cannot be reduced to or fully explained by empirical phenomena: a fact that is marked by saying that wills are *noumenal*, in contrast with what is known through experience (the *phenomenal*). Autonomous wills cannot be known as substances in space and time, subject to empirical causal laws. We can 'think' but not 'comprehend' their existence as 'causes' of a nonempirical kind. These are features of Kant's thought that have led many to reject his ethical theory altogether. It is significant, however, that Kant does not start with them as the elements from which to build his ethical theory, even though the views were largely reflected in his earlier *Critique of Pure Reason*. Rather Kant argues first from (supposedly) common moral thought to general normative principles, and only then develops the extreme metaphysical picture (or nonpicture) to square his ethics with the rest of his philosophy. Less radical contemporary interpretations of this aspect of Kant's thought regard it as only an attempt to distinguish two perspectives on human action, the *theoretical/empirical perspective* appropriate to natural science and the *practical/evaluative perspective* when we think about reasons for acting, obligation, and responsibility. This interpretative strategy is to admit that the practical perspective is committed to irreducibly normative ideas, but deny that it is inseparably committed to a faith in mysterious entities outside of space and time. It is not supposed to be a denial of the conclusions of science but another way of thinking and talking about the same human conduct that psychologists study from the empirical perspective. Even this two perspectives approach is, of course, unconvincing to many critics, and obviously much depends on how in particular the less radical account of the practical conception is spelled out.

2

Is a Good Will Overrated?

In the history of ethics there are few, if any, lines more widely known and quoted than Kant's declaration at the beginning of his *Groundwork of the Metaphysics of Morals*, section I.

It is not possible to conceive anything at all in the world, or even out of it, which can be taken as good without qualification, except a *good will*.[1]

Readers sympathetic to Kant's perspective commonly take this claim about the special value of a good will to be a cornerstone of his ethics, a distinctively Kantian doctrine that is intuitively appealing as well as deeply grounded. Though usually agreeing that Kant's thesis is bold and distinctive, those unsympathetic to Kant's views often reject it as contrary to common sense and unsupported by argument. Most critics accept that to have a good will is a good thing, but they frequently suspect that Kant exaggerates the value of a good will relative to other values. The consequence, it is often thought, is that Kant's ideal moral agents would be moralistic rather than humane in dealing with others and obsessed with their own moral purity instead of properly concerned with the important, real world issues, such as violence, unjust institutions, and debilitating poverty.

My aim here is to encourage and to begin rethinking about the alleged special value of a good will. Looking at the context of Kant's thesis, i.e., its place in the course of argument in the *Groundwork*, should help us to find an interpretation that both makes sense of the texts and reveals Kant's thesis to be more sensible than it commonly appears to critics. When interpreted sympathetically and in context, Kant's thesis, I shall suggest, is perhaps less distinctive and controversial than both critics and sympathizers have assumed. On my reading the thesis has a practical, choice-guiding function, but can be employed only in conjunction with Kant's fuller account of the fundamental features of a moral attitude. In effect it is just one of Kant's many ways of affirming that in deliberation moral considerations should be overriding. If properly

[1] G, 61 [4: 393].

understood, I suggest, this does not endorse excessive moralistic attitudes towards others or undue preoccupation with one's own moral purity, though it is at odds with certain deflationary views about the place of morality in a good life.[2]

To further discussion, I will sketch a sympathetic reconstruction of Kant's thesis about the special value of a good will and compare this reading on some points with alternatives. My main concern, however, is to explain the proposal and some of its implications, so that we can begin to reflect about whether it is plausible, first, as a moral thesis and, second, as the core of what Kant was saying. In a brief essay of this sort I cannot undertake the detailed review of texts and comparison with other scholarly accounts that a more thorough treatment of the subject would require. However, I think that my general characterization of Kant's conception of 'a good will' is not particularly controversial among Kant scholars. My practical (or choice-guiding) reading of 'good without qualification' is no doubt more controversial; but here again, though my reading differs sharply from some earlier commentators, I expect that a number of contemporary scholars will find it congenial with their views.[3] In any case, my aim here is not to establish the novelty of the account or to engage in fine textual disputes about it, but rather to put it forward as an interpretative hypothesis and moral thesis worthy of further consideration.

I. THE CONTEXT OF THE THESIS

Although my primary aim is not textual exegesis, noting some points about Kant's aims and strategy of argument in the first chapter of the *Groundwork* may help to guide our understanding of Kant's thesis about the special value of a good will.

---

[2] Nietzsche, Michael Slote, Susan Wolf, and Bernard Williams apparently hold such 'deflationary' views. See Friedrich Nietzsche, *Beyond Good and Evil: Prelude to a Philosophy of the Future*, tr. Marion Faber (Oxford: Oxford University Press, 1998), and *On the Genealogy of Morality*, tr. Maudemarie Clark and Alan Swensen (Indianapolis: Hackett Publishing Co., 1998), Michael Slote, *From Morality to Virtue* (Oxford: Oxford University Press, 1992), Susan Wolf, 'Moral Saints', *Journal of Philosophy*, 79 (1982), 419–39, and Bernard Williams, *Ethics and the Limits of Philosophy* (Cambridge, MA: Harvard University Press, 1985), and *Moral Luck: Philosophical Papers, 1973–1980* (New York: Cambridge University Press, 1981).

[3] Two important essays should be mentioned here but will not be discussed: Christine M. Korsgaard, 'Two Distinctions in Goodness', *Philosophical Review*, 92 (1983), 169–95, and 'Kant's Analysis of Obligation: The Argument of Foundations I', *Monist*, 73 (1989), 311–40.

First, a point that is obvious but often not fully appreciated is that Kant's thesis about the special value of a good will belongs to *ethics*, which is a branch of *practical* philosophy. That is, the context is an inquiry about what practical reason tells us in response to the question, 'What ought I *to do*?' This contrasts with theoretical philosophy which deals with what exists in the world and how we can understand it. Unlike Hume, Kant is not primarily concerned to explain empirically, from a third-person perspective, the phenomena of moral feelings and the development of moral language and institutions.[4] Nor does he focus, like Hume, on how we *assess* the characters of the people we observe, *commending* them for their virtues and *disapproving* of them for their vices. Instead, Kant's major concern is to determine reasonable prescriptions for conscientiously deliberating moral agents, who are assumed to be facing real options for choice, and, further, to give a philosophical account of the conception of moral agency that must be presupposed in accepting such prescriptions.

This general aim should be kept in mind when we try to *interpret* Kant's thesis about a good will's special value. That thesis is not intended to describe the world, natural or supernatural, but to guide deliberative choice or at least provide the first step towards finding a choice-guiding principle.[5]

Second, it is important not to forget that Kant's thesis about a good will is the opening step in a chapter entitled 'Passage from Ordinary Rational Knowledge of Morality to Philosophical.'[6] Thus we begin by provisionally assuming, and then analyzing and developing, the 'knowledge' that ordinary people have of morality insofar as they are rational. Thus the declaration that nothing but a good will is good without qualification is not meant to be surprising. Because the thesis is so abstract and general, some clarification and illustration may be needed; but, if

---

[4] Kant does not deny, however, that empirical explanations of such phenomena are possible, for he is committed by his 'two perspectives' doctrine to the view that all observable phenomena are in principle explicable in terms of empirical causal laws.

[5] By 'choice-guiding principle' here I mean a principle that primarily serves (perhaps in conjunction with other such principles) to prescribe how one ought to choose to act or, as Kant might say, 'to determine one's will.' The contrasts I have in mind are principles of *moral assessment*, indicating when someone is worthy of praise or blame whether we can know this or not, and *impractical speculative evaluations*, such as a claim that one kind of universe would be 'better' than another though it is utterly beyond human capacities to influence which, if either, is realized.

[6] G, 61 [4: 393]. Each of the next chapters carries the discussion into deeper philosophical territory, as indicated by the titles: chapter II, 'Passage from Popular Moral Philosophy to a Metaphysics of Morals', and chapter III, 'Passage from a Metaphysics of Morals to a Critique of Pure Practical Reason'. See G, 74 [4: 406] and 114 [4: 446].

Kant is right that he has articulated what is common knowledge, then, for all practical purposes, a proof should not be necessary. This is not to say that Kant expects that everyone will find that the thesis expresses the evaluative priorities by which they themselves actually live, but only that he expects that, on reasonable reflection, they can see that the thesis expresses the priorities that they believe morality requires, that is, it expresses the attitude they have when fully conscientious.

This second point is relevant to the *interpretation* of Kant's thesis in that it casts doubt on any reading that renders that thesis radically counterintuitive. Kant *could* have been mistaken about what ordinary conscientious people think, but we should not assume so without good reason.

Third, we need to keep in mind that the explicitly stated aim of the *Groundwork* is 'to seek out and establish the supreme principle of morality.'[7] The supreme moral principle is what is expressed in the various forms of the Categorical Imperative, which together characterize the fundamental commitments inherent in the attitude of a moral deliberator and are supposed to be useful in guiding deliberation about what one ought to do.[8] Judging by what Kant actually tries to do in the first two chapters of the *Groundwork*, 'seeking out' the principle means not merely articulating it but giving a step-by-step course of argument to show that the principle that is finally articulated as 'the supreme moral principle' *really is* such, that is, really is the most comprehensive and basic principle presupposed in common moral thought. This task ('seeking out') is distinct from '*establishing* the supreme principle,' which from the third chapter of the *Groundwork* we can infer is the task of defending the common presumption that the principle is *rationally* binding.[9]

The relevance of this general point about Kant's aim is that it reminds us that Kant's thesis about the good will is just the first step in the argument of chapter 1, the purpose of which is to show that the choice-

---

[7] G, 60 [4: 392].

[8] Kant, like others at the time, sometimes used 'principle' for an action-guiding prescription but also at times used it more broadly to refer to deep dispositions supposed to motivate conduct. Thus, in a sense, the supreme principle of morality could be said to be 'autonomy,' meaning not something formulated as a prescription 'One ought' but the complex moral disposition presupposed in all who acknowledge the moral law. But this is a complication I shall set aside, treating the 'supreme principle' here as the principle of rational willing that is supposed to be expressed in the forms of the Categorical Imperative.

[9] My interpretation of these tasks, several of Kant's formulations of the Categorical Imperative, and several other matters pertinent to my discussion in this essay are developed in my *Dignity and Practical Reason*.

guiding principle that Kant identifies as the supreme principle of morality is simply a development of familiar ideas taken for granted in common moral thought. More specifically, it suggests that the supreme principle (in at least one 'formal' version) has more or less the same practical import as the common-sense idea with which the chapter begins, namely, that a good will, and nothing else, is conceivable as good without qualification.[10] If so, that initial thesis is best understood as itself choice-guiding, even if by itself only formally and incompletely so. The main purpose of introducing the thesis, then, is concern with 'What ought *I* to do?' not 'When should people be morally praised?' or 'What states of the universe are most desirable, from an agent-neutral perspective?'

Fourth, Kant's strategy in 'seeking out' the supreme principle is, in effect, to characterize a good will more fully in a series of steps, each specifying further what (Kant supposed) is implicit in the common idea of a good will. To summarize briefly, first Kant considers a good will as we suppose it to be when actually motivating someone in morally problematic human conditions. Here we take it to be what underlies acts 'from duty,' as most apparent when one does what is morally required despite having no discernable nonmoral interest or inclination to do so.[11] Next, further characterizing the good will as (apparently) expressed in those cases, Kant notes that it cannot be *identified* as 'the will to promote *E*,' where *E* stands for any of the various particular ends that philosophers have proposed as the goal of an ethical life (e.g., 'perfection,' pleasing God, 'flourishing' as a human being, or the general happiness).[12] Nor, he adds, can the will be *identified* as 'a will that produces desirable results.' Rather, the identifying mark of a good will would be its 'maxim' or 'principle of volition,' i.e., maxim to act as one ought (whether or not one thereby achieves objectives that one desires). In a third step the same motive, 'duty' (i.e., good will in action), is further described as 'respect for the law,' where *laws* are explained as principles of choice that all would follow if fully rational.[13] Finally, in two

---

[10] Any version of the supreme principle that plausibly expresses essentially the same idea as that a good will and nothing else is good without qualification would have to be understood as quite *formal*, in the sense that it is not sufficient by itself, without further specification and supplement, to prescribe in particular what one ought to do. Consider, for example, the injunction 'Conform to universal law' that precedes the more familiar 'universal law formula' at G, 70 [14: 402] and G, 88 [4: 420] and Kant's interpretation of that universal law formula when not yet 'typified' in C2 58–62 [5: 67–71].

[11] See G, 64–7 [4: 397–9].

[12] Kant makes this point and those mentioned in the next two sentences at G, 67–8 [4: 399–400].

[13] G, 68 [4: 400–1].

quick steps, these descriptions are said to show that a good will's principle could only be 'conformity of actions to universal law as such' and then this idea (perhaps mistakenly) is treated as equivalent to the basic formula, 'I ought never to act except in such a way that I can also will that my maxim should become a universal law.'[14]

The relevance of Kant's step-by-step argument, as sketched above, to the controversy about whether a good will is overrated is that the argument is the place where Kant's conception of a good will is gradually unfolded and developed. Though paraphrased in different ways, the content of this idea, as revealed in the argument, is a full commitment to act as rationally/morally required, whether or not this is in accord with one's interests and inclinations. Further, it suggests that, for practical purposes, maintaining one's good will and giving it unqualified priority simply amounts to choosing always to 'conform to universal law as such,' i.e., to do what one understands to be always rationally/morally required for everyone and never to do what one understands to be always rationally/morally forbidden for everyone, regardless of what nonmoral interests and inclinations need to be sacrificed for this.[15] This suggests that the way one abandons one's good will or momentarily fails to honor its priority is by choosing, for the sake of satisfying some nonrequired interest or inclination, to do what one understands to be (rationally/morally) wrong. If so, to say 'Maintain your good will, giving it priority above everything else' would express basically the same prescriptive idea as 'Conform to universal law as such,' which was the penultimate choice-guiding principle to which Kant's whole argument in chapter one was leading. The argument pattern gives us reason to expect such an equivalence, and so we have some reason to understand Kant's thesis about the special value of the good will as, in effect, a preview of the familiar choice-guiding theme: do what is right, regardless of your inclinations or personal ends. So construed, the thesis would not prescribe preoccupation with one's

---

[14] G, 69–70 [4: 401–2]. Since 'universal laws' are principles of conduct that, necessarily, every fully rational person would follow, the first step implies that the principle to which a good will, as such, is committed is something like 'I'll do what is required, and nothing that is forbidden, by the principles rationally binding on everyone.' This characterizes the commitments of a good will in quite formal terms, inadequate (until supplemented) to guide particular choices. The final step, equating this idea with the familiar universal law formula of the Categorical Imperative, is puzzling because it equates the previous formal commitments with what is apparently a more substantive one, capable of guiding deliberation without further moral premisses. Much more needs to be said about this puzzle, but resolving it, I hope, is not essential for the issues about a good will that are my main concern here.

[15] I say 'rationally/morally' here because at this stage Kant is provisionally taking for granted as the common view of morality that duty is a requirement of full rationality.

own moral purity, nor would it invite moralistic efforts to make others morally good. Not being a guide to moral praise and blame, it would not imply that only a good will is relevant to the moral assessment of character. Also, since it does not itself specify what duty requires, it would not imply that a morally good agent would let the world suffer in misery rather than deviate from a particular moral precept, construed narrowly and inflexibly.

Fifth, the immediate context of Kant's declaration that a good will, and nothing else, is good without qualification is a review of other good things that, without due reflection, one might take to be unqualifiedly good.[16] In a passage reminiscent of the opening of Aristotle's *Nicomachean Ethics*, Kant first introduces the idea of a very special value. For Aristotle this was the *final good for human beings*, and for Kant this is the *uniquely good without qualification*. Then, like Aristotle, Kant 'argues' that one and only one thing could have such value; this was 'happiness' for Aristotle, but it is 'a good will' for Kant. The 'arguments' in both cases are essentially clarifications and illustrations of the value judgments in question, implicitly relying on the reflective good sense of a morally knowledgeable audience to recognize the correctness of the priorities expressed in those judgments. Then, it seems, both Aristotle and Kant go on through the rest of their books to specify more fully, as well as to supplement and defend, their initial claims: that happiness is the final end for Aristotle, that a good will is uniquely good without qualification for Kant. Setting aside questions about actual historical influence, there seems to be another striking similarity in the approaches of Aristotle and Kant. Kant, in a manner similar to Aristotle, seems to be addressing an audience presumed to be initially asking, 'How should I live?' and more specifically, 'Among the various kinds of good things that human beings can have, are there any *worth seeking, cherishing, and hoping for in a special way*, for example, unconditionally, in all contexts, as never worth sacrificing or subordinating for other goods?' Aristotle proposes 'happiness,' which encompasses many elements in a wisely ordered package (e.g., virtue, use of reason, good fortune, pleasure). Kant proposes 'a good will,' though he grants that a more *completely* good life would include not only good will and virtue but also well-deserved happiness.[17]

The significance of Kant's taking this perspective to begin his discussion of ethics is that it strongly suggests that his thesis about the special value of a good will is *not* about how to mete out praise and blame and

[16] G, 61–2 [4: 393–4].
[17] This complete good is the Summum Bonum described in the 'Dialectic' for *Critique of Practical Reason*, 116 ff.

not about how to produce (impartially) the greatest amount of some agent-neutral value. The goods Kant explicitly reviews are intelligence, wit, judgment, courage, resolution, constancy of purpose, power, wealth, honor, health, and happiness.[18] These are traits and possessions that are often thought to contribute to a 'good life,' but, with a few exceptions, they are not even candidates for being the criteria for ordinary assessments of persons as morally good or bad. Kant did not suppose his audience so confused as to need reminding that people are not *morally* better by virtue of being smarter, richer, and happier. Rather, he supposes them to be wondering, 'What good things in life, if any, are *worth my* pursuing, cherishing, holding on to, developing, hoping for, etc., in any and all contexts, no matter what might have to be sacrificed for them?'

Kant assumes his audience has 'ordinary rational knowledge of morality,' and this limits their answers to what they can *reasonably and conscientiously* count as worth pursuing and cherishing in all contexts. For example, because they (supposedly) find morally distasteful the 'coolness' and 'uninterrupted prosperity' of thoroughly corrupt people, they are expected to see that they do not, on reflection, count self-control and contentment as worth having in all contexts. Thus moral disapproval and distaste in contemplating others are among the clues Kant invokes to show that we do not regard certain goods worth pursuing and hoping for in all contexts, but this does not mean that he is primarily concerned with criteria for moral assessment here. The point of proclaiming that the only unqualified good is a good will, accordingly, is not to give, in a few sentences, a complete theory of moral praiseworthiness; the point is rather to call attention to the value priorities of reasonable, conscientious agents, when they deliberate about what sort of life to pursue. In such deliberation, Kant implies, moral considerations constrain one from choosing the life of a cool, prosperous scoundrel. The suggestion, however, is just that a good will must be an ingredient in any life worth pursuing, not that the only factor relevant in assessing a person's moral character is whether the person has a good will. Again, though one should not sacrifice one's good will by deliberately doing wrong to obtain other goods, such as wealth, this common-sense idea should not be confused with the moralistic thought that the dominant aim of a good person is to produce as many 'good wills' as possible. From the perspective of those with 'ordinary rational knowledge of morality,' having a good will is a *necessary* feature of any

---

[18] G, 61 [4: 393–4]. See also G, 64 [4: 396].

II. THE IDEA OF A GOOD WILL

good life, but it is not the only good or the complete good for oneself, nor is it our responsibility to produce it in others.

Kant discusses a good will, and other moral concepts, on different levels. In the first section of the *Groundwork* Kant clearly means to discuss an idea of 'good will' that he assumes is familiar to virtually all moral agents, for his generalizations about a good will are offered as familiar aspects of ordinary rational knowledge of morality. In subsequent chapters and later works, however, Kant interprets the idea in the special terminology of his larger framework of philosophical thought, but the technical account is supposed to be consistent and coherent with the ordinary understanding. Here I focus mainly on what Kant says in his earlier, less technical discussion.

We need to distinguish the questions, 'What is a good will?' and 'What *special* value does it have?' In his famous opening remarks in section one of the *Groundwork* Kant presupposes for a while that we understand well enough what a good will is, i.e., what are the features of a person's will that make it a 'good' rather than 'bad' one.[19] His

[19] One might suppose, with common sense, that wills can be not only good and bad, but also 'so-so,' neither good nor bad but in between. But in his later work on religion Kant seems to reject this possibility, arguing that fundamentally one's will, if not good, is bad. See *Religion within the Boundaries of Mere Reason*. This, I take it, is because its goodness depends on whether one is deeply committed to the basic life-maxim 'to do my duty, whatever the circumstances' and either one is committed to this or one is not, there being no middle ground. If one professed as one's basic life-maxim 'to follow duty, except when the costs are very great,' this would reveal a bad will even though virtually all one's acts were in accord with duty. Actually, in Kant's terminology, strictly speaking, this qualified 'maxim' expresses an inherently self-defeating, irrational attitude, a deep determination to live with unresolved conflict of will. This is because a commitment to 'duty' is a commitment to do what is categorically required, whatever the costs, and so the qualified maxim both expresses that commitment and yet partially takes it back. It says, in effect, 'I will do what I acknowledge rationally required (and so demanded by my own rational will) regardless of costs, and yet I will not do it when the costs are very high.' Alternatively, perhaps, the qualified maxim might be read as using 'duties' in quotation marks (what Hare has labeled the 'inverted commas' use). Then it would express the attitude, 'I will do the sort of acts that others call "duty" but only if the costs are not very great.' Unless one had reason, beyond the costs, to suppose that what others call 'duty' is mistakenly so called, then the maxim would still express an attitude that Kant would regard as immoral.

The case of the qualified maxim (with an explicit 'escape clause'), we should note, can be distinguished from familiar cases of human frailty and *weakness* of will where one wills without qualification to do duty but fails from lack of effort, weakness of will, confusion, self-deception, etc. Note too that the point here does not imply that all acts are

concentration is on a thesis that he wants to identify, drawing from common knowledge of morality, about the special way a 'good will' should be valued. We should not treat it as the same, in kind or rank, as ordinary goods we might pursue or wish for in planning or reflecting about the course of our lives; it alone is 'good without qualification,' 'above all else,' the 'condition' of other goods. Before turning to what this means, let us consider briefly what a good will is, i.e., what are the features of a will that qualify a will for the special evaluation, 'good without qualification.'

A good will is not just a will that *is* good; it is a will to *do* good. That is, it is a 'will' to act well; and the relevant standards of 'acting well' are those of 'reason.' Reason sets nonmoral as well as moral standards, prescribing efficiency and prudence as well as duty; but its moral demands, which override all others, are clearly Kant's primary concern in his discussion of the special goodness of a good will.[20]

A good will is a 'will' to act as reason prescribes, not merely a 'wish' or a 'good feeling' about doing so. It is not merely a tentative intention, held as revisable if costs and benefits change; the paradigm of a good

---

either requirements of duty or wrong, there being no room for the 'indifferent' or for 'supererogation.' The point is that, in its basic deepest commitment on a life-maxim, one's 'will' is good or bad, not something in between. Persons of both good and bad will do many things, I assume, that are morally indifferent, in cases where moral duty is not at issue. Kant's point in *Religion*, which I have described above, is of course controversial, and it is not clear that it coheres with everything Kant says about a 'good will' in other works. My subsequent comments will not rely on accepting it.

[20] I set aside here difficult and controversial questions about whether merely contravening reason's nonmoral advice, if one unfailingly wills to do one's moral duty, means that one partially lacks 'a good will' in the sense of the first section of the *Groundwork*. Kant's *focus* is clearly on the value of maintaining a morally good will, relative to other (nonmoral) goods for which one might be tempted to sacrifice it. For simplicity, I will interpret and assess Kant's remarks about the value of a good will as if restricted to such morally significant choices. In a fuller account, complications might need to be added.

Some would question whether, strictly, it is even possible to 'will' against nonmoral rational 'rules of skill' and 'counsels of prudence,' but on my interpretation this must be possible if there are hypothetical *imperatives* as Kant defines these. I should note, too, that, on my reading, hypothetical imperatives never unequivocally prescribe anything contrary to moral duty, for they always leave one a rational option to abandon one's end and even, if need be, to suspend temporarily one's pursuit of happiness. Thus one can always avoid violating either hypothetical or categorical imperatives. My interpretation of these matters is spelled out in more detail in *Dignity and Practical Reason*, chs. 1 and 7 especially. Given my reading, it is a mistake to think that sacrificing personal goods (even happiness) for duty would be a failure of nonmoral reason and so make one's 'will' overall less good, for a perfectly good will could satisfy the (conditional) demands of rational efficiency and prudence as well as rational moral demands. The controversial case, which I have set aside, is whether failing to follow nonmoral reason in the absence of contrary moral demands makes one's will 'less good' in the relevant sense.

will, in any case, includes a readiness (if necessary) to 'strain every means' to do what one wills.[21] To have a will to do something implies being disposed to do it, but a good will is not a blind, instinctual, or habitual disposition, operating independently of thought. We might call it a 'firm commitment' or 'resolve,' if we remember that there need not be any particular time when the agent made an explicit resolve or 'act' of commitment. Unlike many other good things, whether one has a good will or not is supposed to be 'up to oneself.' That is, assuming one has the capacities necessary for being a moral agent at all, then neither circumstances nor other people can, strictly speaking, 'make' one have, or lose, a good will. At least this is what Kant insists that we must presuppose, for all purposes of 'practical' deliberation.

A person shows a good will on a particular occasion when the person 'wills' to act well on that occasion, but this, we assume, is the expression of a 'will' that is more than a passing, momentary state of mind. We have, or lack, 'a good will' as a feature of our character, a more or less stable readiness to respond to reason when the occasion requires. From the perspective of ordinary moral thought, we acknowledge that good persons might allow themselves to become corrupt, thereby losing or giving up their good wills. Also people with bad wills can reform, developing a good will.[22] But a person who is not displaying or 'acting from' a good will at the moment may nevertheless have a good will as a character trait. For example, you may be a person who is ever ready to do whatever rational morality demands, but for the moment, in the absence of such demands, you are just playing cards for fun.

For Kant, I believe, there is an equivalence between what it is *rational* to will to do and what it is *good* to will to do; but we cannot determine the latter first independently of the former. Goodness, in this context, is not something discovered in the natural world; but neither is it a Platonic Form or Moore's nonnatural 'intrinsic value.' Working out what is rational to will is basically the same thing as working out what is good to will. Thus, a thoroughly 'good will' *wills* both *what is most rational* and *what is best to do*. Kant interprets 'ought' as the characteristic form of an imperative, which states what is rational and good to do in a way that expresses how it constrains, binds, or 'necessitates' those who have 'imperfect wills,' i.e., who can will what is rational but

---

[21] G, 62 [4: 394].
[22] When we try to interpret these matters in terms of Kant's 'two perspectives,' viewing the will as 'noumenal' and so in some sense atemporal, we run into conceptual difficulties; and so I set these aside, instead keeping closer to the common-sense level of understanding of the phenomena of moral reform.

might fail. Given this, we can also say that, if imperfect (as all human beings are), persons with good wills *will to do what they ought to do.* Since in moral contexts the relevant 'oughts' are categorical imperatives, or 'duties,' we can add further that, in (imperfect) human beings, a good will *wills to do whatever duty requires, regardless of whether this serves one's personal ends.*[23]

We cannot delve very deeply here into how Kant understands or interprets 'will' when he leaves the level of common-sense discussion and tries to express his points in the framework and vocabulary of his critical philosophy. However, a few main points drawn from that discussion may be expressed rather simply. For example, persons' 'wills' are their capacity to make things happen in the world (e.g., move their bodies and other objects) while being guided by their ideas of 'principles' and 'laws.' Basically, this means they act for reasons, which can in principle be reconstructed by citing not only their wants but also the policies, plans, and ideals to which they are committed.[24] For practical purposes, we see ourselves as acting on maxims or policies, not unavoidably fixed by our factual beliefs together with our antecedent desires, but freely chosen in view of both our desires and the ideals we find ourselves committed to as rational deliberating agents. Kant held that among these ideals, which we do not 'choose' but cannot help but recognize as rationally authoritative, are those expressed in the various formulations of the Categorical Imperative. Thus every human being, with enough rationality to count as a moral agent, has inevitably a basic respect for the moral law as the authoritative voice of reason, no matter how badly in fact they may choose to act. The voice, moreover, is not heard as that of an alien commander but as, in a sense, the voice of one's own best rational judgment. This is, in effect, Kant's version of the idea of universal conscience. It provides a necessary part of the background for the claim that each moral agent, no matter how bad, can still acquire a good will; for the rudimentary disposition to it, a proto-goodwill, is always present in a moral agent, waiting only to be affirmed by the free commitment to follow it, above all else.[25] To make that commitment is to adopt, as a deep, life-structuring principle, the maxim 'I will do my duty, no matter what.' Often, of course, the maxim will be irrelevant to the

---

[23] Many of these points are expressed at G, 80–8 [4: 412–20]. My interpretation is developed in *Dignity and Practical Reason*, especially ch. 1, pp. 17–37.

[24] These ideas are expanded in *Dignity and Practical Reason*, chs. 5 and 7, pp. 76–96 and 123–46.

[25] Kant develops these ideas most fully in *Religion within the Boundaries of Mere Reason* and *The Metaphysics of Morals*.

particular choices at hand and then, as it were, the good will is inoperative; that is, a person can *have* a good will, even though not at the moment *manifesting or expressing* it.

Kant assumed, no doubt too readily, that most duties are simple, straightforward, easy to discern, and known well enough by virtually all civilized adults for whom he wrote. Thus he said relatively little about the problem of erring conscience, beyond noting that its source is commonly in our self-serving wish to justify exceptions to moral rules for ourselves. Good people would know and fight this tendency, and so for the most part, Kant assumed, those with good wills would know what is right and do it. He did not anticipate, apparently, that someone might have a genuine and firm commitment to duty but be so deeply misguided about the requirements of duty that, in the name of duty, he could do what most reasonable people would call atrocities. This raises the question, how deeply wrong about duty could a person be and yet still have a good will? Clearly, there must be limits. Kant would never have declared a good will to be good without qualification if he had imagined one could have a good will just by being committed to 'duty' construed as Himmler apparently saw his duty.[26] As the natural law tradition acknowledged, persons with the best will can sometimes make factual errors that lead them to do *wrong* in the sense *contrary to what reason, when used without error, prescribes*; but one whose alleged commitment to 'duty' was accompanied by complete ignorance or grossly distorted understanding of the fundamentals of a moral attitude could not fairly be said to have a 'good will,' as I believe Kant understood this. A person of Kantian good will is not unerringly right in the details of her judgments; but her commitment is to *moral duty* as understood (in fundamental points) more or less the way Kant presents it, not to 'duty' no matter how this is conceived. One does not have a good will in Kant's sense, for example, because one places military duty or other conventional duties above all else.

There are many other subtle and difficult questions one can raise about Kant's view of the nature of a good will—for example, questions about whether there can be degrees of good will and whether (and, if so, how) a good will can be weak. But enough has been said, I hope, to allow us to turn our attention now to Kant's normative claims about the special value of having a good will.

---

[26] I doubt that it should count as a good will in the Kantian system either if duty is conceived as Bentham or J. J. C. Smart conceived duty. One need not suppose that every person with a good will knew and agreed with every point in Kant's moral philosophy,

III. WHAT IS THE SPECIAL VALUE OF A GOOD WILL?

Kant opens his discussion in the *Groundwork* by declaring that *only* a good will is good without qualification, but he soon implies more: that is, something is good without qualification *if* (as well as *only if*) it is a good will. Kant adds later that a good will is good 'above all else' and is the 'condition' of the goodness of other things, but on my understanding of the claim that a good will and nothing else has this sort of value, these later claims are simply implications of the primary claim, to which I now turn.

It may help to explicate Kant's idea of unqualified goodness by contrasting it in several ways with G. E. Moore's idea of *intrinsic value*.[27] The first contrast is that Moore conceives of intrinsic value as a *metaphysical property* that *exists in* the various things that are good. It is a simple, nonnatural property that supervenes on natural properties of experiences, objects, and even whole states of the universe. It is a nonrelational property, not defined or identified by its being what is rational for persons to choose. Moore held that there are no 'criteria' for determining what has intrinsic value, but supposedly there is a fact of the matter about which things have it and to what degree. Such facts, however, are conceptually independent of whether anyone desires, cares about, or has any reason to pursue intrinsically good objects, and so, notoriously, on Moore's theory it is difficult to say *why* everyone *ought* to try to bring about the greatest possible amount of intrinsic value.

This metaphysical idea of intrinsic value is significantly different from Kant's practical idea of unqualified goodness, for the latter is an idea, not about a metaphysical property 'in' things, but about what is rational to choose in the face of certain options. What is unqualifiedly good, as I understand this, is what it is reasonable to choose to pursue, preserve, and cherish without regard to special conditions. To affirm it is to affirm a relation between rational agents and possible objects of choice, not to postulate a 'simple' property. Such affirmations are normative prescriptions, not speculative claims about a nonnatural world. Even if there are disagreements about what *is* unqualifiedly good, there

but a person of good will presumably has some commitment to ethics with the general shape and spirit of Kant's (which is like much traditional ethics).

[27] Moore presents his ideas about intrinsic value in several works, most prominently in *Principia Ethica* (Cambridge: Cambridge University Press, 1903) and *Ethics* (Oxford: Oxford University Press, 1912).

should be no deep mystery about why we *care about* (and think we *ought to preserve*) what we *judge to be* unqualifiedly good.

Further, unqualified goodness is not a pervasive dimension of value in terms of which all things can be compared and ranked. It is a kind of value, in fact, that Kant thinks only one thing (a good will) has. Moreover, Kant does not regard 'good willing' as a kind of quantifiable, agent-neutral value that we should try to promote throughout the world, for he repeatedly insists that each person's responsibility to others is to respect their moral and legal rights and, beyond that, to promote their happiness, not their moral goodness ('perfection').[28] No one can 'make' another have a good will, Kant thought; threats and inducements can influence another's *behavior*, but not 'cause' them to have, or lose, *a good will*. To pander to others' moral weaknesses and to tempt them to abandon their good wills is no doubt objectionable, but to act as if it is our responsibility to make others morally good is a failure to respect their moral autonomy.

Moore sometimes described the things having intrinsic value as 'good as ends,' as opposed to merely 'good as a means' to other things. But this idea does not capture Kant's idea of unqualified goodness either, for Kant held that personal goals that individuals set themselves are 'good as ends' so long as they are not contrary to moral law. These are 'relative' goods, of value *to* the individuals who adopted the goals in view of their desires and interests. But Kant also maintains that, once chosen, these personal ends must be regarded as valuable (to some degree) by everyone; for everyone has an imperfect duty to 'make the ends of others his own.'[29] That is, everyone has some moral reason to facilitate, or at least not interfere with, others' realization of their (permissible) goals. Clearly, then, Kant did not think that only a good will is 'good as an end,' and so goodness as an end is not the same as unqualified goodness.

Again, Moore (and others) sometimes conceive of what is intrinsically valuable as what we judge good when we consider it in isolation from all effects and accompaniments.[30] The pleasure of a heroin 'high,' for example, might be regarded intrinsically good in this sense even by those who believe the overall consequences of taking heroin so bad that no one should ever do it. The point is that, in isolation from its effects, 'that pleasure itself' would be something valuable. Even sadistic pleasures, some might argue, are intrinsically valuable, assuming the

[28] See MM, 150–2 [6: 385–8].
[29] See G, 95–8 [4: 428–30], especially 98 [4: 430].
[30] G. E. Moore, *Ethics*, 27.

pleasure can be imagined separate from the motive, because 'the pleasure itself' would be judged worth having when considered apart from the 'accompanying' malice and intentional harm. But this idea of what would be judged valuable *when isolated from features of its context* is importantly different from Kant's idea of 'good without qualification,' as I understand this, for the latter implies 'good *in any context* whatsoever.' The drug addict's 'high' and the sadist's pleasure at torturing an innocent person are obviously not good within all contexts, especially if one understands this, practically, to mean 'worthy of choice.' Similarly, many things Kant assumes we will recognize at once as not 'good without qualification' may be considered good in isolation from the negative effects and distasteful associations they may have in some contexts: for example, happiness, good health, a keen intelligence, and self-control. Some critics, noticing this fact, use it to criticize Kant's 'argument' that only a good will is good without qualification;[31] but, to the contrary, the proper lesson to draw, I suggest, is that Kant's 'good without qualification' did not mean 'good in isolation.'

To summarize my proposals more positively, to say that a good will is good without qualification is to say that it is worthy of choice in all contexts, that is, something reasonable to maintain, pursue, cherish, and the like, in any and all contexts where we face a choice that brings into question how we value a good will relative to other goods. To add that all *other things* are only good *with qualification* means, in effect, that when one must choose between a good will and any other good, the latter must be abandoned. This seems clearly to be what Kant had in mind, even if it is not *formally implied* merely by saying that a good will and nothing else is good without qualification; for Kant explicitly indicates that a good will is above all other goods and that the relevant qualification or 'condition' of the goodness of other things is their compatibility with a good will.[32] The general point seems clear: when circumstances force a choice between a good will and goods of other kinds (or, indeed, anything else), then the fully reasonable, conscientious agent always opts for the former and is willing to sacrifice the latter.

IV. TO WHAT CHOICES DOES THE THESIS APPLY?

The question then arises, what are the contexts of choice that are pertinent here? That is, when might one have to choose between a good

---

[31] For example, W. D. Ross in his commentary, *Kant's Ethical Theory* (Oxford: Clarendon Press, 1954), 9–12.
[32] See, for example, G, 61 [4: 393] and 64–5 [4: 396–7].

will and some other good? Before trying to assess the plausibility of Kant's claim that a good will always should take precedence, we need to address this issue about the range of cases to which the claim is to be applied.[33] To respond briefly, there are three main contexts to explore: choices to protect the good wills of others; choices about whom to praise; and choices that preserve one's own good will.

Protecting the Good Will of Others

We have already noted that Kant rejects the idea that we have a responsibility to maximize good willing in the world or to even *make* those close to us maintain a good will. But one might speculate that, by placing the value of a good will above other goods, Kant demands that we must never, at any cost, try to corrupt others or tempt them away from doing their duty. The choice context, one might imagine, could be something like this. Suppose a guard at a German concentration camp in World War II has a good will but has been duped by Nazi propaganda into believing that his prisoners were justly sentenced and are about to be sent to work camps where they will be well treated. Unaware that they are in fact innocent people about to be shipped off to further misery and death, he firmly believes it is his moral duty to guard them securely. Resistance workers, plotting the prisoners' escape, despair of convincing the guard of the truth, but they are convinced that they can lure him from his post by offering a bribe that he, being weak, will not refuse. To do so, they suppose, would save many innocent people from misery and death; and the only cost they foresee is the corruption of the guard, his loss of a good will. We can imagine them wondering, does the special value of a good will imply that they must let the prisoners die in misery rather than play on the guard's weakness? Here the common suspicion that Kant has overrated a good will naturally arises, for the humane choice seems to be to offer the bribe.

If one thought Kant's doctrine applicable to such cases, one might still perhaps make a case for offering the bribe by arguing that this does not, strictly speaking, *make* the guard act contrary to his duty and so lose or tarnish his good will. If he is to some extent corrupt already, saving lives may warrant taking advantage of his corruption. But this response

---

[33] Context of application may also be important when we consider the relation between Kant's claim that only a good will is unqualifiedly good and his claim, which might seem to contradict this, that 'humanity' or 'rational nature' in persons has unconditional value as an 'end in itself.' Though I shall not pursue the matter, I think that these claims can be reconciled because the relevant contexts of choice are not the same and their prescriptions, in principle, cannot conflict. Presumably both can be honored in all contexts.

strikes me as quite artificial and unnecessary. It too readily concedes the underlying consequentialist picture that good willing is an agent-neutral value to be promoted, preserved, and protected *whenever possible*, and merely tries to avoid the counterintuitive results by insisting (with Kant) on our limited power over others' wills. A more plausible reading, I suggest, would reject that picture altogether. Instead we would understand Kant's thesis, as the context suggest, as an affirmation that *one* should never sacrifice *one's* good will for other things, where, for practical purposes, this simply means *do not* do what you understand to be *wrong* in order to gain other goods, for yourself or anyone. So construed, the thesis contains no imperative concerning the production or protection of good wills in others; it simply tells each person not to violate (perceived) moral requirements in the pursuit of nonmoral goods or even conditional moral goods. There are no doubt moral reasons for generally trying to avoid tempting others, playing on their moral weaknesses, and the like; but this was not the point Kant was making when he affirmed that a good will is unqualifiedly good, contrasting it in this respect to other personal goods (wealth, health, happiness, etc.) that we want. There, at that initial stage, his point was more basic and familiar: in effect, 'there are many other goods to pursue, but none for which it is worth selling your (moral) soul.'

Praising and Blaming

Commending and criticizing, in various forms, are activities we engage in voluntarily. One might suppose, then, that Kant's thesis about the special value of a good will can guide our choices about when and how to direct our moral praise and blame. Kant's point, one might imagine, is that we should morally praise people for their good wills and for nothing else, and, conversely perhaps, we should morally blame people for their lack of good will and nothing else. An extreme example of the sort of choice to which Kant's thesis would be relevant, on this suggestion, is something like the following.

Suppose one person, Finefellow, lacks a good will but has every other fine character trait compatible with this one failing. For example, one might (initially) imagine that Finefellow has a natural sympathy, an aversion to harming others, and a developed firm disposition to conform to social rules that are useful and just (though not because they are so). We might add self-control, prudence, courage, as well as energy, efficiency, and a natural delight in promoting peace and alleviating poverty. Suppose, in contrast, another person, Goodheart, has a good will but lacks every other good trait except those inseparable from a good will. For example, though Goodheart will do his duty once he sees it, he lacks sympathy and so often fails to see how he hurts others. He finds it pleasant to see others in misery, though (because of his good will) he takes care not to be the wrongful cause of their suffering. He is inept, a natural coward, prone to be impulsive and weak, often in violation of useful social rules, though of course he does not mean to be. Here is a context, one might think, in which Kant's thesis about the special value of a good will applies, telling us unequivocally to condemn Finefellow and give Goodheart full marks as a morally good person. If so, again it may seem that Kant has overrated the value of a good will, for many will see Goodheart as less praiseworthy than Finefellow.

Now many Kantians, I suspect, will defend the controversial claim that Finefellow, lacking a good will, is morally worthless and Goodheart, having a good will, has all it takes to be fully commendable on moral grounds, despite his other displeasing and even harmful traits. In support, they might call attention to the fact that Goodheart and Finefellow, if described consistently, must be quite unlike ordinary people in important respects. Normally, if one really has a good will, one will notice and try to alter traits that prove displeasing and destructive to oneself and others, for example, Goodheart's 'natural' cowardice, lack of sympathy, impulsiveness, ineptitude, and finding pleasure in others' misery. A person with a good will, then, could not persist in having such traits unless, unlike most human beings, he was utterly incapable of recognizing and improving his character. Similarly, if one really lacks a good will, then one is highly unlikely to have developed the pleasing and useful traits that Finefellow was said to have. Self-control, courage, sympathy, and respect for socially useful rules are traits that people normally need to work conscientiously (with a good will) to develop and maintain. Having these good traits is usually a sign that a person has a good will, just as having Goodheart's bad traits is commonly a sign that a person lacks a good will. Thus 'intuitions,' or first reactions, in favor of Finefellow are likely to be skewed by false assimilation of their special cases to familiar ones. Once the contrast is fairly described and fully understood, one might argue, our reflective judgments will assess Goodheart as morally superior to Finefellow.

Actually Kant did not focus much on issues of moral praise and blame, and what he does say about the assessment of character is more complex and qualified than the view generally attributed to him. To be sure, he thought that having a good will is a necessary condition of being a morally good and virtuous person; but he did not think it sufficient for being virtuous or morally ideal. In *The Metaphysics of Morals* Kant implies that virtue goes beyond good willing; it is a developed inner strength and fortitude that enables one to do what is right despite obstacles.[34] A virtuous person does not do duty grudgingly, and virtue brings its own reward, a kind of moral pleasure in fulfilling duties of virtue.[35] We should cultivate sympathetic feelings, and so they too are part of the morally ideal person's character. Even in the *Groundwork*, Kant implies that there are other traits besides a good will that are worthy of praise, provided they are traits of someone who also has good will.[36]

Although Kant does express these and other controversial views about the assessment of character, his skepticism about our knowledge of motives severely limits the practical importance such assessments have in his ethics. He does say that we should conscientiously scrutinize ourselves to avoid bad motivational attitudes,[37] but he repeatedly insists that we cannot know with any confidence whether we have a good will.[38] Nor do we know when others have a good will, for people can behave decently from many other motives. Even in dealing with vicious criminals, Kant implies, the state must punish, not because it has a basic responsibility to make the wicked suffer, but rather because its basic responsibility is to maintain a just system of law and order, by means of uniformly applied rules that define certain 'external' acts as crimes and lay down penalties 'equal' to the offense.[39] There is surprisingly little room in his ethics for moralistic praising and blaming.[40]

In sum, both the limited role of praise and blame in Kant's theory and Kant's aims and argument in chapter 1 of the *Groundwork* (as reviewed earlier) suggest that Kant's initial declaration of a good will's special value should not be construed as a thesis about how to mete out moral praise and blame.

---

[34] See MM, 145–6 [6: 380] and 156 [6: 394]. Anne Margaret Baxley gives a thorough and subtle treatment of the relation between a good will and virtue in 'Kant's Theory of Virtue: The Importance of Autocracy', PhD dissertation, University of California, San Diego, 2000.

[35] MM, 154 [6: 391].   [36] G, 61–2 [4: 393–4].

[37] MM, 188–91 [6: 438–42] and 196–7 [6: 446–7].

[38] For example, G, 74–5 [4: 406–7].

[39] See *Dignity and Practical Reason*, ch. 9, pp. 176–95, and B. Sharon Byrd, 'Kant's Theory of Punishment: Deterrence in its Threat, Retribution in its Execution', *Law and Philosophy*, 8 (1980) 151–200.

[40] *Dignity and Practical Reason*, 176–95.

Preserving One's Own Good Will

My conclusion, then, is that Kant's thesis is concerned, at least primarily, with contexts in which one could gain certain nonmoral (or conditional) goods that one wants only by abandoning *one's own good will*. Moreover, the relevant way in which one could abandon one's good will is simply to choose, deliberately, to do what one understands to be morally wrong.

Without this last stipulation, we would invite critics to construct moral dilemmas where one cannot preserve one's current good will without sacrificing one's future good will. They might, for example, ask us to imagine the following paradoxical situation. Terrorists give you a choice of killing some innocent people or being subjected to drug-aided 'brain-washing' that will corrupt your character and cause you to lose your good will. If you think it is wrong for you to do the killings, then it seems you must sacrifice either your current good will or your future good will. Both choices, the critics might argue, fail to treat a good will as good without qualification.

Some Kantian purists might want to take on this challenge, thereby admitting that Kant's thesis is applicable here. They might argue, for example, that, given Kant's conception of freedom, no drug or mind-control techniques could *cause a person to abandon* his or her good will. Physical and mental abuse could, of course, bring it about that I no longer remain a person with a good will, for the abuse might destroy my life or reduce me to a babbling, amoral animal. But, from a Kantian perspective, to do such things to me is not to make me *abandon* or willfully destroy, disregard, or disrespect my good will; for so long as I remain a competent moral agent, I can continue to *try* to resist the terrorists' mind-bending techniques, and once I cease to be a competent moral agent, nothing I do can count as *my* abandoning my good will. Thus, it might be argued, the case is not really a moral dilemma; for it is clear that what I should do is to refuse to kill the innocent people and then try my best to resist the 'brainwashing.' If resistance proves futile and I am reduced by the terrorists to an amoral animal, that would be a personal tragedy but not a case of my deliberately sacrificing my good will for something else. So long as I am willing to resist others' efforts to corrupt me, I am not devaluing either my current good will or my potential for a good will in the future.

This reply may be appropriate Kantian casuistry, but to many (including myself) it may seem unrealistic. On my interpretation of Kant's thesis, it is also *unnecessary*; for the practical import of Kant's thesis, as I see it, concerns only contexts where the imagined conflict is between what one must do to maintain one's current good will and what one would have to do to gain nonmoral goods, such as wealth, power, and happiness, or conditional moral goods, such as courage and self-control.[41]

Even when Kant's thesis is applied only to these special contexts of choice, there is a final objection that may arise. That is, Kant's thesis may strike some critics as encouraging us to be preoccupied, to an unreasonable degree, with our own purity and inner worth when in fact we should direct our attention ('outward') to the larger issues of war, poverty, and social injustice. In an extreme form, the objection is that Kant's thesis implies that no amount of any other good for any number of people could warrant the slightest deviation from rigid, exceptionless moral prohibitions on lying, promise-breaking, disobeying the law, and so on, because any such deviation would sacrifice or tarnish one's own precious 'good will.' Unless these objections rest on misunderstanding, it seems clear that Kant has overrated a good will.

Given my reading of Kant's thesis, however, these objections miss their mark. Kant did in fact endorse certain moral precepts in an absolute, exceptionless form, which is unacceptable to both his critics and to most of those sympathetic to his basic moral theory. The most notorious example is lying, which Kant said was wrong even to save the life of a friend.[42] There are also other cases, for example, pertaining to sexual activity, that seem now to be the result of uncritical acceptance of a particular cultural heritage rather than the conclusion of serious moral thinking.[43] Insofar as the objections above are motivated by dissatisfaction with these aspects of Kant's 'applied ethics,' I think that they are appropriate and should readily be conceded. They are not, however, objections to Kant's thesis about the special value of a good will, on my

---

[41] The way in which one might have to choose between one's good will and self-control, courage, and intelligence is harder to imagine, but we can imagine an agent, like Faust, offered a 'deal' by the legendary Satan—'I will give you all these traits, and more, just for giving up your integrity and good will.' Some contemporary critics of 'morality' might say, 'Why not, what's the catch?' They are the relatively few people, I believe, who are really in disagreement with Kant's thesis regarding the special value of a good will, on my interpretation. These critics raise a deep challenge that I have not addressed here, a challenge (unlike some I have considered) which cannot be dismissed as due merely to misunderstanding.

[42] See Kant's 'On a Supposed Right to Lie because of Philanthropic Concerns', in Immanuel Kant, *Grounding of the Metaphysics of Morals*, tr. James Ellington, 3rd edn. (Indianapolis: Hackett Publishing Co., 1993), 63–7.

[43] See for example, MM, 178–80 [6: 424–6].

reading; for that thesis says nothing about how much time, relatively, one should spend thinking about whether one's will is good and, more importantly, the thesis itself says nothing specific about how to decide what one's duty is. To determine what to do in a hard case, where sticking to normal moral practices would have disastrous consequences for world peace and the like, we need to appeal to the ideals and procedures expressed in the several forms of the Categorical Imperative. When we do, then despite what Kant himself thought, it is far from obvious that clear, informed thinking from that perspective warrants the inflexible precepts about lying, etc., that Kant himself endorsed.[44] In any case, the inflexibility of particular moral precepts is not a consequence of Kant's common-sense claim about the value of a good will. That thesis, as we have seen, is that *once you have determined in independent reflection what your duty is*, then do your duty rather than pursuing some good that in the context can be achieved only by violating your duty. *If* telling a lie, breaking a promise, or disobeying the law is strictly necessary to prevent a horrible war or some other disaster and *if*, further, your best moral judgment is that the exceptional circumstances override the normal presumptions against lying, promise-breaking, and disobeying the law, then in fact the only way to honor and preserve your good will is to follow your best judgment and deviate from the normal rules. As a conscientious moral deliberator, you must choose to do what you understand to be right, regardless of what other goods are lost and no matter what familiar presumptive moral rules you must deviate from. Basically, that is what it means to treat a good will as good without qualification, as I have been interpreting Kant's claim.

Readers may object that I have reduced Kant's thesis to something obvious and trivial. The proper response, in my opinion, is that it was meant to be obvious, and it is not trivial. It is a formal point, which is choice-guiding only in conjunction with a more specific understanding of what moral duty is. In Kant's thought it is not trivial, for he believed that by successive paraphrases and supplements he could arrive at a version of the supreme moral principle which illuminates our conception of duty and is just a short step away from a more substantive action-guiding formula. In contemporary philosophy it is also not trivial, for it affirms as a part of ordinary rational thought something that a number of philosophers now deny, namely, that an unqualified commitment to moral requirements is a reasonable constraint on the

---

[44] See *Dignity and Practical Reason*, ch. 9, pp. 196–225.

pursuit of the other good things that life may offer. In other words, things that may be desirable in other contexts are not worth pursuing if the cost is to do, quite deliberately, what in your own best judgment is morally wrong.

3

Hypothetical Consent in Kantian Constructivism

I. PROLOGUE: KANTIAN CONSTRUCTIVISM AND MORAL EPISTEMOLOGY

Epistemology, as I understand it, is a branch of philosophy especially concerned with general questions about how we can know various things or at least justify our beliefs about them. It questions what counts as evidence and what are reasonable sources of doubt. Traditionally, epistemology focuses on pervasive and apparently basic assumptions covering a wide range of claims to knowledge or justified belief rather than very specific, practical puzzles. For example, traditional epistemologists ask 'How do we know there are material objects?' and not 'How do you know which are the female beetles?' Similarly, *moral* epistemology, as I understand it, is concerned with general questions about how we can know or justify our beliefs about moral matters. Its focus, again, is on quite general, pervasive, and apparently basic assumptions about what counts as evidence, what are reasonable sources of doubt, and what are the appropriate procedures for justifying particular moral claims.

If we were to assume that moral beliefs are substantially like beliefs about the empirical features of the world, then moral epistemology would face the task of explaining the apparent disanalogies between the procedures of giving evidence for empirical propositions and providing reasons for moral claims. If, instead, we supposed that fundamental moral propositions are about nonempirical objects in the same way that fundamental propositions of mathematics are (on some interpretations), then moral epistemology would face a different set of problems. The special problems raised by moral *realism* of both kinds, and by skeptical doubts about the underlying assumptions of each kind, are

---

I am grateful to Andrews Reath, Shelly Kagan, Philip Pettit, Thomas Pogge, David Copp, Geoffrey Sayre-McCord, and David Brink for helpful comments on earlier drafts of this essay.

so frequently discussed that they may seem to exhaust the field of moral epistemology. However, there are other questions about justification that should count as belonging to moral epistemology. For example, although Kantian constructivists typically try to avoid realist/antirealist epistemological disputes, they still need to face general questions regarding moral knowledge or justified belief as understood in their constructivist theories. What do they count, most generally, as grounds for substantive moral claims? If moral principles are 'constructed,' what are the building materials and what is the procedure of construction?

'Kantian constructivism,' unfortunately, is a broad label that has been used to characterize significantly different views.[1] A common theme in these views is that moral principles are to be seen as the outcome ('constructions') of certain procedures of thought (or will) rather than as facts about the world (empirical or nonempirical). Ideas about what these procedures are vary, but Kantian varieties of constructivism require us to consider what universal principles all persons 'could' or 'would' endorse if they were thinking rationally and in a position specified as appropriate.[2] Some Kantian constructivists hold that the moral truth or justification of substantive moral claims *consists* in their being the

---

[1] Ideas of Kantian constructivism can be found in the work of Immanuel Kant (on some interpretations), John Rawls, Onora O'Neill, and others who comment on their work. See, for example, Immanuel Kant, *Groundwork of the Metaphysics of Morals*, ed. and trans. Mary Gregor (Cambridge: Cambridge University Press, 1998); John Rawls, 'Kantian Constructivism in Moral Theory', *Journal of Philosophy* 77(9) (1980): 515–72; reprinted in Samuel Freeman, ed., *John Rawls Collected Papers*, (Cambridge, MA: Harvard University Press, 1999), 305–58; John Rawls, *A Theory of Justice* (Cambridge: MA: Harvard University Press, 1999); John Rawls, *Political Liberalism* (New York: Columbia University Press, 1993); Onora O'Neill, *Constructions of Reason* (Cambridge: Cambridge University Press, 1989), esp. ch. 11; Onora O'Neill, *Towards Justice and Virtue: A Constructive Account of Practical Reasoning* (New York: Cambridge University Press, 1996); Brian Barry, *Theories of Justice* (Berkeley: University of California Press, 1989), vol. 1 of *A Treatise on Social Justice*; David O. Brink, *Moral Realism and the Foundations of Ethics* (Cambridge: Cambridge University Press, 1989); Thomas E. Hill, Jr., *Dignity and Practical Reason in Kant's Moral Theory* (Ithaca, NY: Cornell University Press, 1992), ch. 11; and Thomas E. Hill, Jr., *Respect, Pluralism, and Justice: Kantian Perspectives* (Oxford: Oxford University Press, 2000), chs. 2, 4, 8.

[2] Onora O'Neill's views might seem to be an exception here because she criticizes Rawls for arguing from a hypothetical idealized choice situation (see O'Neill, *Constructions of Reason*, 207–13; and O'Neill, *Towards Justice and Virtue*, 44–8), but her arguments from the thought that everyone 'cannot share' certain principles presuppose at least some modest rationality conditions (as well as other background conditions) in her procedure of construction. Thus, my broad characterization of Kantian constructivism includes O'Neill's position, but nothing substantive in my discussion depends on fine points about how we use this broad term of classification.

product of the appropriate procedure of construction; others affirm only that the procedure and outcomes are valid or useful for 'practical' or 'political' purposes. Some take an agnostic position on the metaphysical and epistemological issues in debates about moral realism, while others take a negative (antirealist) stance; generally, however, constructivists have been disinclined to engage in these debates. One theme that is quite common among these diverse Kantian constructivist positions is that moral philosophy is itself 'practical,' a claim usually understood as implying that moral philosophy's results are not derived from (or refutable by) science and metaphysics.

To simplify, I will restrict my discussion, for the most part, to one version of Kantian constructivism: namely, Kant's moral theory as I interpret and partially reconstruct it.[3] Kant holds that knowledge and justified belief about moral matters are based not on theoretical (or 'speculative') reason but on practical reason. Both are forms of rational reflection, but theoretical reason is concerned with what exists whereas practical reason is concerned with what ought to exist. The distinction, as Kant interprets it, is important, for it is incompatible with the realist idea that moral values and imperatives are objects in the world to be discovered empirically, by intuition, or through speculative metaphysical thinking. For Kant, morality is, in a sense, the *product* of practical reason, not merely some independent thing that reason discovers.

This controversial feature of Kantian constructivism, however, is not essential to my main concerns in this essay. The important feature for present purposes is that Kant offers, in several forms, practical constructivist procedures for determining what moral principles to accept. That is, he proposes, at least as workable heuristic devices, several kinds of reflection that draw conclusions about what we ought to do from premises about what rational, free, and appropriately situated persons could or would willingly accept. In this way, like John Rawls's theory of justice, Kant's moral theory is constructivist even if certain ultimate premises (about rationality and the appropriate deliberative perspective) are not themselves 'constructed.' The Kantian procedures, in contrast to Rawls's, are to be found in the various formulas of the Categorical Imperative (Kant's supreme moral principle) and in Kant's idea of an original contract.

---

[3] In this essay, I will only describe aspects of Kant's moral theory when they are immediately relevant to my questions about the justificatory roles of actual, possible, and hypothetical consent. Fuller discussions of Kant's moral theory are contained in Hill, *Dignity and Practical Reason in Kant's Moral Theory*, esp. ch. 11, and Hill, *Respect, Pluralism, and Justice*, esp. chs. 1, 2, 4, 8.

My main question, then, is this: *within Kantian constructivist procedures*, what are the roles of actual consent, possible consent, and hypothetical consent in guiding and justifying particular moral beliefs? This is one question of moral epistemology about the commitments of Kantian constructivism. There are other such questions, of course, that moral epistemologists may want to raise. For example, they may reasonably question whether Kantian constructivists are warranted in the stance they take on the moral realism debates. If the constructivists' position (like Kant's, in my view) is not realist, what justifies this? If their position (like Rawls's) is agnostic, what justifies its claim to be independent of the realist/antirealist issues? Another legitimate epistemological question would be to ask how the basic procedures of construction endorsed by Kantian constructivism can themselves be justified. These further questions, however, will not be my concern here.

II. OUTLINE AND PREVIEW OF CONCLUSIONS

In everyday life we often argue that acts or practices are wrong because appropriately placed persons *do* not, *could* not, or *would* not consent to having them take place. Moral philosophers commonly use all of these forms of argument, but they often privilege one or another form as basic, treating the others as derivative and constrained. Kant and contemporary Kantians are no exceptions. Any moral theory that is Kantian in spirit will specify ways that we must not treat others without their actual consent, but regarding basic principles Kantians generally acknowledge that the crucial question is either 'Is the principle *possible* for all to accept and follow?' or 'What principles *would be* agreed on by ideally free and rational agents?' The first question is primary for Onora O'Neill, for example, while the second is primary for Rawls. It is a matter of controversy which question *should* be primary in our efforts to interpret and extend Kant's ethics.

Within Kantian theory, then, how are we to understand attempts to justify moral claims by appeals to actual consent, possible consent, or agreement under hypothetical conditions?[4] What are the relations

---

[4] Although for some purposes it might be important to distinguish 'consent,' 'agreement,' and 'will,' I use them more or less interchangeably here. It may be more natural to speak of the 'consent' of actual persons to particular proposals and the 'agreement' of ideal rational agents on general principles, but using the terms more flexibly helps to highlight the comparisons I want to make.

among these types of claims? Are the differences between them fundamentally important? Are familiar objections decisive against the idea that whether moral and political principles are justified is determined by what ideal rational agents would agree to in specified hypothetical conditions?

I begin with some remarks about the role of different forms of consent and agreement in the *Groundwork of the Metaphysics of Morals* (hereinafter *Groundwork*), and then I turn to Kant's political philosophy, especially his use of the idea of an original contract.[5] In both contexts, what Kant treats as fundamental is not what people *actually* consent to, but what is *possible* for them to will. Though important, appeals to actual consent presuppose a background of practices and principles that must be justified by asking what (rational) agents could or would agree to as standards for everyone. In the *Groundwork*, which I focus on in Section III, Kant's basic standard usually refers to possible willing rather than hypothetical agreement. For example, Kant's *universal law formula* of the Categorical Imperative says: Act only on maxims that you *can will* as universal law.[6] What it is possible to will, in the relevant sense, is that which can be willed in a presupposed context of choice without contravening certain presupposed standards of rationality. These standards can be interpreted as minimum standards (e.g., logical consistency) or as more robust standards (e.g., treating humanity as an end in itself). In the *kingdom of ends formula* of the Categorical Imperative, the formula on which my essays often rely, Kant suggests that the basic moral test is to ask what rational agents *would* agree to, rather than what they *could* agree to. I suggest, however, that this formal difference is not in itself deeply significant.[7] The rational standards on which the 'could will' test relies can (though they need not) be expressed in terms of what rational agents necessarily 'would will if rational.' Moreover, under the kingdom of ends formula, the prohibitions that hypothetical

---

[5] For Kant's references to an original contract, see Hans Reiss (ed.), *Kant: Political Writings*, 2nd edn. (Cambridge: Cambridge University Press, 1991), 77, 79, 80–3, 85, 91 (from Immanuel Kant, 'On the Common Saying: "This May Be True in Theory, but It Does Not Apply in Practice"' [hereinafter 'Theory and Practice']), 94, 99–100 (from Immanuel Kant, 'Perpetual Peace'), 140, 158, 162–4 (from Immanuel Kant, *The Metaphysics of Morals* as edited by Reiss [8: 295], [8: 297], [8: 299–302], [8: 305], [8: 311] ... [8: 314], [8: 351] ... [6: 315], [6: 375], [6: 640-2]).

[6] The universal law formula is one of several ways that Kant expresses the Categorical Imperative. Kant, Gg, 15 [4: 402], 31 [4: 421]. A fuller discussion of the universal law formula follows in Section III.

[7] Kant sets forth the kingdom of ends formula at Kant, Gg, 41–4 [4: 433–7]. A fuller discussion of this formula follows in Section III.

rational agents would will are just those that are rationally necessary for them to will, given their situation.[8] Both formulas, then, presuppose as background some general standards of rational willing. Furthermore, whatever substantive permissions and prohibitions, if any, would be legislated for our condition by perfectly rational legislators must constrain what we can (rationally) will as universal law. Thus, what we *could* will under Kant's universal law formula may depend on what we *would* will under his kingdom of ends formula. Treating Kant's ethics as primarily concerned with *possible* willing, then, is not in itself a way of avoiding the apparent problems in reconstructions that express his basic ethical test in terms of what it is to which rational agents *would* agree.[9] The merits of either approach for further developments of Kantian ethics depend, in the end, on the details of how the standards of rationality and other features of the imagined choice problem are spelled out.

Review of Kant's use of the idea of an original contract as a test for constitutions seems to confirm these general points; I will engage in such a review in Section IV. The basic standard of assessment is not whether all or most citizens actually consent to the constitution, or did so in a historical contract. The test is whether it is logically possible for citizens to have a united will on a proposed constitution if they are rational and in an appropriate position to choose. Again, the relevant standards of rationality may be interpreted thinly or thickly, and the merits of the test for different purposes will vary accordingly. Whether the test is expressed in terms of hypothetical agreement or possible agreement does not seem deeply significant.

In Section V, I conclude the essay by suggesting that several common objections to arguments that appeal to hypothetical agreement for justificatory purposes do not undermine the force of such arguments, at least as used in Kant's ethics as I reconstruct it. For example, hypothetical consent is not merely a weak practical substitute for actual consent in particular cases where actual consent should be the standard. Also, Kantian theory does not attempt to reduce values to empirical facts about what everyone with certain descriptive characteristics would

---

[8] The kingdom of ends formula invites us to ask what laws rational agents would will. As I reconstruct the idea, it is assumed that the hypothetical agents are fully rational, and the question is what they would necessarily will *qua rational* (and properly informed) agents regarding all the possible general permissions and prohibitions that we might want to assess. Thus, they would (necessarily) will a prohibitive law if and only if it is rationally necessary for them to will it in the context in question. See Hill, *Dignity and Practical Reason*, chs. 3, 11.

[9] For an example of this sort of reconstruction, see O'Neill, *Constructions of Reason*, 206–18.

agree to. The theory makes explicit use of idealizations, but I argue that these idealizations are not of a kind that should alienate us from conclusions drawn from the theory. Next, I respond to an apparent dilemma that confronts any theory that purports to draw moral principles from the thought that everyone would agree to those principles under certain (ideal) conditions. The objection is that either the theory presupposes independent standards of rationality or it does not; in the first case, reference to hypothetical agreement may be unnecessary, and in the second case, hypothetical agreement would be arbitrary and so its results would have no moral force. The best Kantian response, I suggest, is to embrace the first horn of the dilemma, admitting that Kantian hypothetical agreement presupposes independent rational standards, but argue that this does not necessarily undermine the value of using the Kantian constructivist model. Finally, I note that, although Kantian hypothetical-agreement arguments will not necessarily convince extreme rational egoists, they were not designed for that purpose.

III. ACTUAL CONSENT, POSSIBLE WILLING, AND HYPOTHETICAL RATIONAL AGREEMENT IN THE *GROUNDWORK*

A. *Possible Consent, not Actual Consent, is Basic under Kant's Formulas*

In various ways the *Groundwork* affirms the importance of obtaining the actual consent of those affected by our actions; this is a moral consideration prominent in appeals to 'autonomy' in contemporary applied ethics. We expect Kantian ethics, more perhaps than any other, to place severe limits on what we can do to others without their consent. Yet although actual consent is important, Kant's fundamental ethical principle is not a requirement to respect the actual consent of those affected by our actions. The sphere of actions that are 'up to the individual,' such that others may not interfere with them without the individual's consent, is determined by principles and practices that lie in the background of our everyday encounters. Normally we take for granted that we may not use others' property or touch them intimately without explicit or implicit consent. Usually we do not stop to think deeply about general principles regarding property and bodily integrity, but when questions arise about what requires consent and why, we need to address the more general issues.

Consider an example of Kant's in which disregard of the right of another to consent or dissent seems especially prominent. In taking money from another through a false promise to repay the loan, a person tries to escape difficulties in a way that leaves his victim no choice of whether or not to consent to giving up his property with no prospect of repayment.[10] Moral assessment of this case does not start from the absurdly impractical assumption that we may do something that affects another person if and only if the other person actually consents. Kant condemns the lying promisor's disregard for another's consent in the context of a particular set of practices—namely, promises and property. These practices include shared understandings relevant to the case. For example, it is part of the practice of promising that saying 'I promise to do X' alleges an intention to do X. One should not say 'I promise to do X' if one lacks the intention, although for good reasons, saying this in the appropriate context creates a binding promise even when (secretly) one has no intention to do what one says. Practices governing property authorize the man who needs money to take funds if they are given or loaned, but not if the gift or loan is obtained on false pretenses, especially deception regarding the parties' understanding of the nature of the transaction. Under these practices, consent has justificatory force only under certain complex conditions. For example, the mere fact that the deceived party *accepted* the promise as genuine and *consented* to the loan does not justify by itself the lying promisor's taking money from him.

Kant's arguments against the lying promisor, if sound, would show that given our practices, what he does is wrong.[11] Thus, the arguments presuppose practices that define when actual consent is necessary, but

---

[10] Kant, Gg, 32 [4: 423].

[11] My remarks here are not meant as a literal interpretation of Kant's arguments. To provide such an interpretation, much more preparatory work would be needed, including identifying the relevant maxim. (A maxim is a subjective principle, or personal policy statement, that summarizes, in a way relevant for moral assessment, one's understanding of what one intends to do, one's purpose, and one's underlying reasons.) My suggestion is that, Kant aside, practices of various kinds typically determine when consent is (and is not) needed, and so justifications of the form 'He consented and so it is permissible' require moral evaluation of the practice to which one is implicitly appealing. When the issue is what practices are justifiable in the way they demand consent (or not), Kant's formulas of the Categorical Imperative move us to another level. The universal law formula, for example, asks whether we can will our maxim as universal law, but 'the maxim' needs to be described in a way that appropriately reflects our practice-laden understandings.

they are not arguments that appeal to actual consent. Kant condemns the lying promisor on the grounds that (a) the agent's maxim of profiting from lying promises *cannot* be willed as universal law, and (b) the victim *cannot* share the agent's end.[12] The first argument, if sound, would show that the lying promisor in Kant's example is wrong because one cannot rationally will as a universal law maxims that reflect disregard for certain requirements inherent in our practices of promising and property—namely, the requirement not to say 'I promise' with apparent sincerity unless one has the requisite intention, and the requirement not to seek a loan under false pretenses. Respect for the (appropriately informed) lender's consent is required by these practices. These practices themselves, however, may ultimately need to be tested by asking whether the agent who uses them *could (rationally) consent* to a maxim to support and conform to them as universal practices. How, more specifically, the test posed by the universal law formula should be interpreted and whether it is ultimately tenable are, of course, disputed questions that I set aside for present purposes.

Kant's second argument, which derives from his *humanity formula* of the Categorical Imperative, focuses not on whether the lender actually consented to the loan but on whether he *could* agree with the borrower's end in making the false promise.[13] It is assumed that the lender consented to make the loan but did not consent to lending money that the recipient had no intent to repay. The problem, Kant implies, is that the lying promisor took what the lender had an antecedent right to (as a result of the background practices), and did so for ends that the lender 'could not share.' The point, surely, is not that it would be *impossible* for the lender to want the borrower to use the money for the borrower's own purposes, for the lender might be so generous that he would have given the borrower the money had he asked. The problem, it seems, stems from the fact that the borrower had an aim that is crucially relevant, under our practices, to the transfer of property—namely, the aim to bring about a transfer of the lender's property to the borrower without the borrower giving anything (now or later) in return. This is

---

[12] Kant, Gg, 32 [4: 422], 38 [4: 429–30].

[13] Kant expresses the humanity formula of the Categorical Imperative at ibid. 38 [4: 429]: '*So act that you use humanity, whether in your own person or in the person of any other, always at the same time as an end [in itself], never merely as a means.*' He then, almost immediately, applies this principle to the example of someone who tries to borrow money without intending to repay. Arguably there is more to the argument from the humanity formula, at least implicitly, than is captured in the idea that we must treat persons as those who can share (or 'contain in themselves') the end of the action, but the further ideas are not important for present purposes.

an end that the deceived lender cannot share *when he makes the loan* because, necessarily, lending is transferring one's property to another with the understanding that the other party means to return it or repay the lender.[14] Under the practice of loaning, it is logically impossible for both parties to share the crucial intention of the borrower while engaging in the mutual act that constitutes the making (and receiving) of a loan. Whether or not we think that this argument is morally decisive, its implication, as before, is that one's treatment of another is justified only if the other party *could* consent in appropriate conditions (e.g., if not deceived about the first party's intention). The treatment does not become legitimate just because the person *actually* consents to the act as he or she (mistakenly) understands it.[15]

B. Appeals to Possible Consent Presuppose Further Normative Standards

Though I have only presented one so far, Kant actually develops two universal law formulas of the Categorical Imperative; each of these invokes a standard that refers to what an agent *can* will. As noted above, Kant's universal law formula says that we must act only on 'that maxim' which we can 'at the same time' will as a universal law; that this formula involves possible willing is relatively straightforward. The *universal law of nature formula*, which Kant puts forth soon after he states the universal law formula, says that we must act as if our maxims were to become, through our will, universal laws of nature.[16] Examples Kant

---

[14] A complication I ignore here: Suppose the would-be borrower pretends that he intends to repay and the would-be lender does not believe him but pretends that he does. Has a loan been made? I suppose so, for the lender could complain afterward when the borrower does not repay, and the borrower could not defend his not paying, when he learns that the lender did not believe him, by saying, 'I do not owe you anything because you never believed that I would give the money back.' Therefore, the 'understanding' the lender needs, perhaps, for a loan to exist is not strictly that the borrower intends to return the money, but just that the borrower intends (in borrowing) to cause the lender to believe that he intends to return the money. The lender in Kant's example, we may suppose, has this understanding. In fact, it is natural to suppose that the lender will transfer the funds only because he thinks that the borrower intends to give them back, and with this understanding the lender, in making what he understands is a *loan*, cannot share the borrower's end, that is, that the borrower get money cost-free (i.e., without repaying it).

[15] There are other ways to interpret Kant's humanity formula, but under any plausible interpretation, it places limits on what actual consent can justify and helps to explain why actual consent, though important, is not always decisive.

[16] The universal law of nature formula is expressed at Kant, *Groundwork*, 31 [4: 421]. Scholars differ on whether the difference between the universal law formula and the universal law of nature formula is significant, but for my present purposes it is not. Because of their structural similarity, the two formulas are often referred to collectively as 'the universal law formulas.'

provides make clear that this test is really about whether we can, or could if we had the power, will our maxim as such. Hence, this formula seems to involve possible willing, not ideal willing in hypothetical conditions.

Both textual considerations and charity, however, give us reasons to understand that the tests proposed under the universal law formulas ask whether an agent can *reasonably* will her maxim as universal law (i.e., *reasonably* will her maxim and at the same time will that all may, or do, adopt and follow it). Kant's concern is with what we can will *as rational beings*, even if the full idea of pure practical reason has not yet been invoked.[17] What someone who is crazy, inconsistent, or even very stupid can will is not what matters. Likewise, one's inability to will that everyone adopt a particular maxim is not morally relevant if the reason one cannot will this is that one suffers from some psychological quirk (e.g., 'I could not will for anyone to eat *that*') or some rationally indefensible individual bias (e.g., 'I would be revolted if those people were allowed to eat with us'). Furthermore, maxims that one cannot will for everyone to act on merely because contingent circumstances make it in fact impossible for everyone to act on them are surely not to be condemned just for that reason.[18] Each of these points underscores that for Kant, the test of one's being able to 'possibly consent' to maxims becoming universal law is really a matter of the *absence of any relevant*

---

[17] That is, the universal law formulas do not themselves specify the underlying standards that determine what we can will reasonably and what we cannot. There are many different ideas about what these specific standards count as irrational willing: for example, willing what proves to be logically impossible, having an incoherent set of intentions, willing that everyone adopt one's maxim even though this would defeat one's initial purpose in adopting it, willing contrary to the rationally necessary value of humanity in a person, and so on.

[18] Consider a policy under which individuals drink a certain kind of wine on their birthdays. One can imagine a case in which, because of scarcity, it would be impossible for everyone to follow this policy. If in fact only a few people want to act on the policy, however, the scarcity of the wine should not be taken as any reason to condemn the policy for those few who want to adopt and act on it. The general point here has been noted often. For example, Kurt Baier presents a 'universalizability' requirement analogous to Kant's (though different), and he qualifies his principle 'doing X should be forbidden by the morality of the group if it would be harmful for everyone to do X' by adding, along with other stipulations, 'provided doing X is an indulgence and not a sacrifice' (Kurt Baier, *The Moral Point of View* (Ithaca, NY: Cornell University Press, 1958), 211). If we interpret the universal law formula to say that maxims are wrong to act on unless we can will them as *permissible* for everyone to act on, then, in cases where only a few want to act on a maxim, the maxim could turn out to meet the formula's test even though it is not possible in fact for everyone on Earth to act on it. See Thomas Pogge, 'The Categorical Imperative', in Paul Guyer (ed.), *Kant's Groundwork of the Metaphysics of Morals: Critical Essays* (Lanham, MD: Rowman and Littlefield, 1998), 189–213. Whether or not maxims can be as specific as the policy in my example above remains a controversy.

rational bar to consent. This raises a question: what are the further relevant standards of rational willing beyond what has already been formally given (namely, that rational wills act only on maxims that they can, as rational, will as universal laws)?

Defenders of Kant's universal law formulas suggest different answers to this question, and none, I suspect, are entirely satisfactory. A few points seem clear. For example, when we try to decide what we can will as universal law, we can assume that the set of principles that we will must meet rational standards of logical consistency and coherence. No doubt we would also take for granted what I call *the Hypothetical Imperative*, a general principle stating that we must take the necessary means to our ends or else revise or abandon those ends. We might assume that other formal principles of rational choice are applicable as well.[19] Since the other forms of the Categorical Imperative (i.e., the kingdom of ends formula and the humanity formula) are supposed to involve tests of rational necessity, they should impose some constraints on what we can rationally will as universal law.[20] For example, the humanity formula suggests that we cannot rationally will any maxim as universal law if it treats humanity in any person as a mere means and not at the same time as an end in itself. However, to introduce further substantive moral principles as intuitive rational standards for what can be willed as universal law seems at odds with Kant's aims in presenting and illustrating the universal law formulas, even if introducing such principles would provide some practical advantages.[21] For example, we may think that it is intuitively irrational to prefer superficial popularity to deep personal relationships, but Kant apparently aims to provide a rational test for moral decisions that does not rely on particular intuitive beliefs of this sort.

If we accept that general standards of rational willing are presupposed in assessing what we can and cannot will as universal law, then asking

---

[19] For more on the Hypothetical Imperative, see Hill, *Dignity and Practical Reason*, chs. 1, 7. Other principles of rational choice that might well be taken for granted are, for example, those that Rawls calls 'counting principles'; see Rawls, *A Theory of Justice*, 361–5.

[20] Some may argue that these later formulas cannot add significantly to the universal law formulas on the ground that the later formulas are derivative, but this is debatable. In any case, a reconstructed Kantian moral perspective can make use of ideas of autonomy and humanity as an end in itself in attempts to apply the universal law formulas. Doing so may help to deflect some familiar arguments against the universal law formulas, though problems with those formulas will remain.

[21] If, as it seems, in using Kant's decision-guiding procedures we are supposed not to rely on further, substantial intuitive assumptions about what we have 'reasons' to do and prefer, then this is a way in which Kant's procedures for justifying our decisions to others

what we *could* rationally will no longer appears to be deeply different from asking what we *would* rationally will. Of course, 'could' and 'would' are not identical in meaning, but the relevant Kantian tests, it seems, are inseparable. We could will a maxim (rationally) as a universal law if doing so is consistent with all principles that we would necessarily will *qua* rational. Furthermore, as rational legislators in a kingdom of ends, we would necessarily will prohibitions of acts the maxims of which could not be (rationally) willed as universal law.[22] Rational standards do not have to be expressed by reference to what rational agents would necessarily will; one can use the apparently simpler form, 'It is rationally necessary to X.' Yet expressing the standards by reference to what rational agents would necessarily will may make us less tempted to picture the standards as self-standing objects of intuition rather than as procedures inherent in practical reasoning.[23]

C. The Role of Actual, Possible, and Hypothetical Rational Agreement under the Kingdom of Ends Formula

Kant's idea of a kingdom of ends has been a source of inspiration to many, but its interpretation remains controversial. Here I can only

differ significantly from the procedures proposed by T. M. Scanlon in his recent book, *What We Owe to Each Other* (Cambridge, MA: Harvard University Press, 1998).

[22] In general, it does not follow from 'We could not rationally will X' that 'We would rationally will not-X,' for in some contexts it is possible that we neither rationally will X nor rationally will not-X. My point, however, does not depend on this false inference. Kant's universal law formula and kingdom of ends formula provide the context here. The kingdom of ends is a highly idealized model. We assume that its legislators are perfectly rational, appropriately informed, and have a will in favor of or against all the possible permissions and prohibitions that we might put to them. The analogy with a divine will is obvious. In calling the formula of universal law a Categorical Imperative, Kant claims that fully rational persons, as such, will that they not act according to a maxim if it is impossible to will that maxim as a universal law. Therefore, if acting as described in a given maxim cannot be (rationally) willed as universal law, then rational legislators in the kingdom of ends must will that they, and anyone relevantly like them, not act in that way. This is just what 'legislating' in this context amounts to, for the ideal kingdom of ends is not a legal system in which public offenses are defined and sanctions are imposed. Without any sanctions, necessary rational willing of the Kantian 'legislators' against an act is supposed to make not acting that way imperative for us as imperfectly rational beings.

[23] Such 'objects of intuition' would be, for example, nonnatural intrinsic values as conceived of by G. E. Moore, or Platonic Forms as they are often interpreted. See G. E. Moore, *Principia Ethica* (Cambridge: Cambridge University Press, 1903), ch. 1. Julia Annas's paper, 'Moral Knowledge as Practical Knowledge', *Social Philosophy and Policy*, Vol. 18, No. 2 (2001), 236–59 criticizes the common view that Platonic Forms are intuited independent objects or properties like Moore's intrinsic values.

comment on a few points. The first few remarks are needed, for the sake of historical accuracy, to supplement my previous discussions of the kingdom of ends. Those earlier discussions deliberately emphasized certain features of Kant's idea of a kingdom of ends in order to highlight its similarities to Rawls's constructivism and its differences from Kant's universal law formulas. In the process, however, I may have suggested a somewhat exaggerated picture of the centrality of the idea of a kingdom of ends in Kant's ethics, its similarities with Rawls's idea of hypothetical agreement, its advantages over the universal law formulas, and the closeness of the analogy between the kingdom of ends and political communities. So I begin with some brief cautions on these points.

In the past I have proposed possible reconstructions of the kingdom of ends formula that make it look like a moral analogue to Rawls's appeal to an original position (with important differences).[24] As I have noted, there are problems with trying to square this kind of reconstruction with all that Kant actually says, and with trying to make the kingdom of ends formula the centerpiece of Kantian ethics.[25] For example, Kant himself does not think of the formula as a better practical guide to moral decisions than are the universal law formulas. In the *Groundwork* he says that the universal law formula is a better practical guide, and in *The Metaphysics of Morals* he writes as if the humanity formula is also more useful for practical purposes.[26] In discussing the kingdom of ends, Kant seems less concerned to offer yet another guide to practical decision-making than to highlight his ideal of moral motivation independent of contingent interests.

In an earlier paper I suggested that the kingdom of ends formula avoids the problem of maxim description that plagues the universal law formulas.[27] The problem of maxim description is this: there is no definitive way to decide what the relevant maxim of our proposed act is, and yet whether or not we can will our 'maxim' as universal, and hence whether or not the act is right or wrong, depends on how the maxim

---

[24] Hill, *Dignity and Practical Reason*, 58–66, 243–50; Hill, *Respect, Pluralism, and Justice*, 33–56, 220–30.
[25] Hill, *Dignity and Practical Reason*, 65–66; Hill, *Respect, Pluralism, and Justice*, 36, 51–5.
[26] Kant, Gg, 44 [4: 437]. It is the humanity formula that Kant appeals to most frequently in later moral arguments, especially in the second part of *The Metaphysics of Morals*. See Immanuel Kant, *The Metaphysics of Morals*, tr. Mary Gregor (Cambridge: Cambridge University Press, 1996), 173–218 [6: 418–74].
[27] Thomas E. Hill, Jr., 'The Kingdom of Ends', in Hill, *Dignity and Practical Reason*, 58–66.

is described. The kingdom of ends formula avoids this problem, I suggested, because unlike the universal law formulas, it does not make essential use of the idea of a maxim. This suggestion, however, goes beyond, and probably against, Kant's own view because (a) he did not seem to acknowledge the problems regarding maxim descriptions, and (b) there is some evidence that he thought that the way we 'legislate' in the kingdom of ends is by acting only on maxims that we can will as universal laws.

Although Kant describes the kingdom of ends in political metaphors that suggest an ideal community in which members jointly make the laws of the community (as authors) and obey them (as subjects), he also explicitly draws an analogy between the kingdom of ends and a harmonious order or realm of nature.[28] The 'laws' that we conceive of agents giving to themselves in the kingdom of ends differ from the laws of states (even a possible world state) because they are moral requirements that, as such, do not impose coercive external sanctions (e.g., legal punishment) and are not limited to our 'external acts.'[29] Kant alludes to the 'sovereign' of the kingdom of ends, but this is just a 'holy will' that wills essentially the same as all the members do.[30] The only difference between the sovereign and the kingdom's members is that, because it lacks a liability to temptation, the sovereign is not properly said to be 'subject' to the laws, which are willed by everyone in the kingdom. This picture is very different from that of a secular head of state, whose authority depends on his power and who can make and enforce corrupt laws.

These cautions are important for purposes of historical accuracy, but they are compatible with the basic point that the kingdom of ends formula puts before us an ideal that treats moral requirements as the normative 'laws' that agents, as lawgivers, *would* give themselves (as subjects) if they were rational and autonomous. The kingdom of ends is not actual, but possible and ideal; it is conceived abstractly as how things would be if everyone did his or her duty and if God were cooperative in making nature allow the ends of the virtuous to be satisfied. We are supposed to act by the laws of a possible kingdom

[28] Kant, Gg, 44 [4: 436], 45-6 [4: 438-9].
[29] See Kant, *The Metaphysics of Morals*, 20-2 [6: 218-21].
[30] Kant refers to a possible 'sovereign' of a kingdom of ends that is also head of the realm of nature, implying a power to harmonize the two, presumably in a way that allows the natural end (happiness) of the virtuous to be realized. Kant, Gg, 41 [4: 433], 46 [4: 439]. This power, so used, would give us an additional motive to follow the laws of the kingdom, but is not necessary for its authority (or even for adequate motivation).

of ends even if others do not.³¹ The members are not merely abstractly conceived, but idealized, for they make laws rationally in a way that makes possible a harmonious system of ends and their lawgiving is not improperly influenced by particular interests. The political metaphors of 'lawgiving,' being 'subject' to laws, a 'sovereign,' 'the union of different rational beings under common laws,' 'validity' of laws, and the like invoke the model of (idealized) secular legislation.

Some passages in Kant's work, however, suggest that we give ourselves laws in the kingdom of ends by following the principle 'never to perform an action except on a maxim such as can also be a universal law.'³² The idea suggested here is that we must find the normative rules of the kingdom by generalizing from our reflections on whether various particular maxims can be willed as universal laws. This would mean that the universal law formula is the primary working decision-making guide (as Kant suggests after his review of the formulas).³³ Kant's texts, I think, are ambiguous about this. Nevertheless, the suggestion here is about just *how* the members of the kingdom legislate. It does not deny that, with the kingdom of ends formula, Kant endorses a model of morality in which justified moral principles are those principles to which idealized agents would rationally agree. What remains to be seen, however, is whether or not the suggestion that members of the kingdom legislate by using the universal law formula is useful for extensions of Kantian moral theory. This depends on whether the universal law formula's possible-will standard can fulfill the hopes that Kant, and some contemporary Kantians, have for it without falling back on implicit appeals to things that would or would not be agreed to by idealized rational agents. I doubt that the standard can do this, but I will not pursue the issue here.

Although there are different views about the interpretation and importance of the kingdom of ends formula, the views seem compatible with the following main points that I have wanted to emphasize. Under this formula, the fundamental Kantian standard judges principles and practices by considering what, as rational, persons necessarily would agree to from a certain perspective; this process, however, is inseparable from the consideration of what we could and could not rationally will. When and why actual consent is required must be judged by considering what we could and would will if we were rational in a presupposed sense.

---

³¹ Kant, Gg, 45 [4: 438].   ³² Ibid. 42 [4: 434], 45 [4: 434].
³³ Ibid. 43–4 [4: 436].

IV. KANT'S IDEA OF AN ORIGINAL CONTRACT: CONDITIONS, PURPOSE, CONTENT

Kant uses arguments that call for thought experiments about what agents could or would consent to (or rationally agree upon) in many places besides the *Groundwork*. In the political works, Kant sometimes refers to a possible 'general will' behind laws or policies. For example, the test that the supreme authority should use to determine the rightness or justice of legislation, he says, is to ask whether the laws *could* have been produced by the united will of the people.[34] Now, however, let us focus not on this test for particular legislation but on the idea of an original contract that lies behind the authority of a legislator to make laws. Kant mentions the idea, but all too briefly, in many works, primarily 'On the Common Saying: "This May Be True in Theory, but It Does Not Apply in Practice"' (hereinafter 'Theory and Practice'), 'Perpetual Peace,' and *The Metaphysics of Morals*.[35]

Kant uses the idea of an original contract for purposes quite different from those of other philosophers who invoke the idea. In contrast to Locke, Kant does not use the idea of an original contract to argue that we ought to obey just governments because we, or our ancestors, actually promised or contracted to obey. Nor is his purpose to argue, with Hobbes, that obedience is rational because submission to a particular kind of constitution would be the only possible point of agreement among rational self-interested persons in a very dangerous state of nature.[36] Kant's idea of an original contract is incompatible with some putative constitutions, but does not yield a particular one as the only rational alternative to a state of nature. Kant argues that only a republican form of government captures fully the spirit of an original contract, but he allows that, given limited options, rational persons in a state of nature could endorse a less-than-ideal constitution. Finally, Kant does not use the idea of an original contract, as Rousseau initially

---

[34] See Reiss (ed.), *Kant: Political Writings*, 79 [8: 297] (from Kant, 'Theory and Practice').

[35] See, for example, ibid. 77, 79, 80, 83, 91 [8: 295], [8: 297], [8: 299], [8: 301–2], [8: 311] (from Kant, 'Theory and Practice'), 99–100 [8: 351] (from Kant, 'Perpetual Peace'), 143, 158, 162, 163, 164 [6: 318–19], [6: 335], [6: 340–2] (from Kant, *The Metaphysics of Morals* as ed. by Reiss).

[36] A Hobbesian state would not have separation of powers of the sort that Kant's ideal constitution would have, and there would be no grounds of justice on which enlightened critics could criticize the legislation of the sovereign. States that meet Hobbes's stipulations could differ in various other ways (e.g., they need not be a hereditary monarchy), and so my reference to 'a particular kind of constitution' is relative.

did, to argue that existing governments have no moral claim on our obedience because their supposed authority rests on a grossly unfair, and hence void, social contract.[37]

Instead, Kant invokes the idea of an original contract to test whether constitutions are compatible with the idea of right (*Recht*) and whether they conform fully to the requirements of practical reason.[38] Any provision in a constitution, real or imagined, is supposed to be rationally indefensible if that provision could not be endorsed in an original contract expressing the united will of the people. Unfortunately, Kant suggests narrower and broader ways of understanding the necessary conditions for an original contract.[39] On the narrower understanding, all that is required for the possibility of an original contract on a constitution is that the constitution must outline a genuine system of law. In asking whether there could be an original contract on a constitution of some kind, then, we are checking whether the constitution provides for what is essential to a *juridical condition*. To determine this, we would not need to rely on special Kantian moral assumptions, but only on the idea of rule of law. For example, in Kant's view, some alleged constitutional systems (e.g., those with gaps in sovereignty) are objectionable because they fail to meet fully the logically necessary conditions for a legal order. These flawed constitutions, in effect, do not completely remove us from a state of nature.

On a broader understanding, Kant aims to determine higher stan-

---

[37] See Jean-Jacques Rousseau, *Discourse on the Origin of Inequality*, in Rousseau, *The First and Second Discourses together with Replies to Critics*, ed. and tr. Victor Gourevitch (New York: Harper and Row, 1986).

[38] Note that I include here two aims that I distinguish later. I leave aside whether there are other uses, though it seems that there are. In particular, Kant seems to appeal to the idea of an original contract, along with argument that it would be a duty in a state of nature to enter a civil order, to support a claim that we are *morally*, as well as legally, bound to obey the ruler of our state. What I have in mind here is the claim that under any legal constitution, no matter how badly designed and executed, we must see the ruler as the representative of the united will of the people, for the alternatives are a state of nature or a lack of final legal authority. The language of 'united will' in both Rousseau and Kant strongly suggests an attempt at moral justification. This raises many problems, and so for present purposes I am limiting my discussion to the use of the idea of a possible original contract for arguments that purport to say what cannot (for conceptual or moral reasons) be in a constitution.

[39] The evidence for this is complex and ambiguous, involving a significant controversy about the interpretation of the *Rechtslehre* that Thomas Pogge describes in his paper, 'Is Kant's *Rechtslehre* Comprehensive?', *Southern Journal of Philosophy*, 36, supplement (1997), 161–87. Here I will only attempt to characterize some possible alternative readings in a general way, to show their relevance to the discussion of types of consent, without undertaking the detailed review of passages needed for a definitive account. Among the problems here is that Kant uses the idea of an original contract in several different works, and it is doubtful that we should assume that remarks in one context automatically carry over to the other contexts.

dards for constitutions, namely, standards for judging whether they are fully compatible with what is right and just. The question to ask now is not 'What is necessary and sufficient for a system of enforced rules to constitute a civil order with a *legal* right to my obedience?'[40] Rather, it is 'What is *morally* defensible, given some basic *moral* assumptions, as the sort of constitution that we should hope and work for through whatever means are appropriate to our station?'[41] The latter question places the emphasis not so much on what is essential to law, but on what is essential to legal orders that meet certain basic moral principles applicable to coercive systems that satisfy those conditions established by the first question. Kant apparently aims to answer each of these questions. Sometimes the narrower understanding makes the most sense of his arguments, but at other times the broader reading is needed. I shall return to this distinction shortly.

Kant uses the idea of an original contract in arguments for a variety of conclusions. These include the following:

(1) There can be no original contract endorsing a constitution that allows the state to be bought, inherited, or given away (as, it seems, some monarchs in eighteenth-century Europe wanted to allow).[42]
(2) There cannot be united will on a constitution that incorporates a right of revolution[43] or a right of the people to abrogate the original constitution.[44]

---

[40] Note that even though this is not a moral question, it has a proper (though limited) place in Kant's overall project to lay out the basic moral limits and requirements on political and legal institutions and conduct. This is so at least insofar as Kant has moral arguments that legal systems ought to be maintained and respected. Thus, even if, as some suggest, the doctrine of law in *The Metaphysics of Morals* is a module setting out the necessary conditions of a juridical condition independent of the moral principles in Kant's moral theory, it still has an appropriate place in *The Metaphysics of Morals* when this is viewed as a work the primary purpose of which is to lay out moral conditions on law, political institutions, and personal choices.

[41] The qualification regarding appropriate means is needed because Kant believes that the means by which different people may work for constitutional reform are strictly limited. Philosophers can use public reason to criticize a constitution, but active resistance and revolution are forbidden. (We employ 'public reason' when, as citizens, we participate in reasonable critical assessment of governmental laws and policies through newspapers, books, public speeches, etc., as opposed to what we may say privately or as representatives of special nonpublic institutions, such as a church or a club.) Rulers under nonrepublican constitutions may (and should) gradually work for reform, but even they are restricted in what they may do. The reason for the reference to 'hoping' is that Kant's ideal constitution serves not only as a practical action guide, but also as a point of reference when we look hopefully (as we should) for progress in history.

[42] Reiss (ed.), *Kant: Political Writings*, 94 (from Kant, 'Perpetual Peace') [8: 344].

[43] See ibid. 80–3 (from Kant, 'Theory and Practice'), 127 (from Kant, 'Perpetual Peace'), 162 (from Kant, *The Metaphysics of Morals*) [8: 299–302], [8: 382–3], [6: 340].

[44] Ibid. 83 (from Kant, 'Theory and Practice') [8: 302].

(3) There can be no united will on a constitution that allows permanent hereditary political privilege.[45]
(4) There can be no united will on a religious constitution that permanently prohibits questioning the officially sanctioned religious beliefs.[46]
(5) Any original contract, whatever the 'letter' of its provisions regarding the mode of government, must be presumed to be made in the 'spirit' that nonrepublican forms of government should gradually and continually be reformed, in legal ways, until they in effect conform to the ideal of a republic.[47]
(6) An original contract must be presupposed to account for the authority needed to make definite and secure property rights, which would be only 'provisional' in a state of nature.[48]
(7) Generally, the idea of an original contract obliges the head of state to avoid acts of tyranny, to make only laws that could come from the united will of the people, and to respect the people's innate rights to equal freedom of external action under universal laws.[49]

Kant also argues, contrary to Cesare Beccaria, that an original contract does *not* rule out capital punishment, for the parties to the contract, as such, have a will only regarding what is permissible in general, as opposed to a will regarding particular outcomes for their individual situations.[50] At another point, echoing Rousseau's language, Kant says that an original contract involves giving up natural (lawless) freedom for civil liberty backed by one's own lawgiving.[51] An original contract is not a historical event, but an a priori standard. It is the foundation of all actual public contracts, and in fact all public rights.[52] It cannot do anyone an injustice, presumably because it is supposed to represent each person's will.[53]

---

[45] See Reiss (ed.), 79 (from Kant, 'Theory and Practice'), 99 (from Kant, 'Perpetual Peace'), 153 (from Kant, *The Metaphysics of Morals* as ed. by Reiss) [8: 297], [8: 351], [6: 329].

[46] Ibid. 58 (from Immanuel Kant, 'An Answer to the Question: "What is Enlightenment?"') [8: 39–40].

[47] Ibid. 163 (from Kant, *The Metaphysics of Morals* as ed. by Reiss) [6: 340–1].

[48] Kant, *The Metaphysics of Morals*, 53 [6: 265–6].

[49] Reiss (ed.), *Kant: Political Writings*, 73, 79–81 [8: 289, 297–9] (from Kant, [8: 350–1] 'Theory and Practice'), 99 (from Kant, 'Perpetual Peace').

[50] Kant, *The Metaphysics of Morals*, 108 [6: 335]. Kant refers to Beccaria's influential work, Cesare Bonesana, Marchese di Beccaria, *On Crimes and Punishments* (New York: Bobbs-Merrill, 1963).

[51] Kant, *The Metaphysics of Morals*, 92–3 [6: 315].

[52] Reiss (ed.), *Kant: Political Writings*, 164 [6: 341], [8: 297] (from Kant, *The Metaphysics of Morals* as ed. by Reiss); see also ibid. 79 (from Kant, 'Theory and Practice').

[53] Ibid. 79 [8: 297] (from Kant, 'Theory and Practice').

Who are the supposed parties to the original contract? Kant's implicit answer is that these are all the people, across time, who are in a state under common laws.⁵⁴ However, since the arguments from the idea of an original contract are not supposed to rely on variable contingent circumstances, the differences among individuals and even cultures should not affect whether a united will on a certain constitution is possible in the relevant sense. If we like, we can think of the parties as a mix of malicious and kindhearted folk, the naturally greedy and the naturally generous, but the acceptability of constitutional provisions should not turn on the parties' individual temperaments and preferences.⁵⁵

This brings us to a crucial question: what sorts of factors does Kant envision as rendering an original contract impossible? It seems clear that Kant is not thinking of contingent obstacles. The empirical fact that some people, for subjective psychological reasons, would refuse to consent to a given contract does not mean that such a contract is 'impossible' in the relevant sense. For example, an original contract on a republican form of government does not count as impossible, for Kant's theoretical purposes, just because some individuals' superstitions, pathological distrust of authority, or ideological dogmas would block any effort actually to achieve unanimous agreement on it. What is relevant, Kant implies, is logical impossibility (assuming, no doubt, certain general background conditions). The idea of an original contract, Kant says, provides an 'infallible a priori standard.'⁵⁶ To apply the standard to proposed laws, checking whether they are compatible with the idea of an original contract, we are supposed to ask whether or not it is 'self-contradictory' to suppose that the people unanimously agree. 'For so long as it is not self-contradictory to say that an entire people could

---

⁵⁴ It can be questioned whether Kant means to include women in this category, because he assumes women are merely 'passive citizens' without sufficient independence to be allowed the vote. If, as it should be, women were meant to be included as parties to the hypothetical original contract, then women could be treated as 'passive citizens' only if enlightened women and men alike would accept a constitution with this provision when they take up an appropriate genderless point of view. Assigning women second-class citizenship would surely fail this test, despite what Kant himself apparently thinks.

⁵⁵ Presumably, at least for some uses of the idea of an original contract, this does not mean that tests of the acceptability of provisions completely abstract from empirical facts about human nature and the human condition in general; rather, it suggests that such tests only abstract from the specific preferences and temperaments that vary from person to person, culture to culture. Some more strictly a priori arguments about the acceptability of provisions may proceed just through analysis of the idea of law, but there is no way that Kant could reasonably suppose that he could spin out all the conclusions listed above—that is, (1)–(7)—without presupposing general facts about human nature.

⁵⁶ Reiss (ed.), *Kant: Political Writings*, 80–1 (from Kant, 'Theory and Practice') [8: 297–9].

agree to such a law, however painful it might seem, then the law is in harmony with right.'[57] Presumably, Kant has at least two reasons for discounting disagreements based on various subjective psychological factors. On the one hand, if a constitution were rendered objectionable just because these factors would prevent unanimous agreement on it, then probably no constitution would be justified. On the other hand, even if there were a *de facto* agreement on a constitution despite these obstacles, this by itself would not, in Kant's view, justify the constitution. What matters is whether the agreement or disagreement is appropriately grounded in rational considerations. Regarding law and politics, as with morality in general, actual consent cannot justify basic principles but, to have force, must presuppose them.

The factors anticipated as the sort that might render an original contract on a proposed constitution impossible, I suggest, depend on whether in the context Kant's aim is narrower or broader in the ways previously mentioned. Suppose first that the aim is simply to determine a priori the essential conditions for establishing a legal system that maintains a juridical condition as opposed to a state of nature. In this case, the only barrier to an original contract on a proposed constitution would be that it is incompatible with the very idea of a legal order. Rational parties seeking to establish a legal order could not agree to such an arrangement because, unlike many options, it would fail to serve their end. The minimum standards of rationality presupposed here as what all rational persons *would* agree to need be nothing more than the Hypothetical Imperative and the ability to understand the idea of a juridical condition and its implications. It is this standard that might show that a constitution cannot contain a (legal) right to revolution.

Now suppose that the aim of invoking the idea of an original contract is to argue that certain constitutions fall short of broader standards of justice. That is, suppose the aim in invoking the idea of an original contract is to show that only constitutions that meet certain more demanding standards count as morally defensible and fully 'just' (as we might use the term).[58] The aim here is not to distinguish constitutions that require loyalty from those that do not, but rather to identify the basic features constitutions must have to be (morally) worth working and hoping for. Given this aim, what would be the factors that

---

[57] Reiss (ed.), *Kant: Political Writings*, 81 (from Kant, 'Theory and Practice') [8: 299].

[58] I add the qualification because our common practice is to use 'just' as a more general term of moral assessment than Kant did. Many traditional moral philosophers did use our broader sense; Hobbes and others narrowed the term's use such that its application was limited to those realms of activity that can be enforced by secular authorities.

might, in a relevant way, prevent an unqualified agreement on a constitution?[59] Any reasonable reconstruction of Kant's answer will need to bring in at least Kant's basic ideas of the innate rights to freedom and equality, which he affirms throughout his political writings. Constitutions fall short of the ideal if they could not be the result of an original contract among rational agents who affirm these fundamental rights, their own as well as those of others. Hence, the rational standards presupposed in arguments that an original contract on a given constitution is impossible are moral standards, broadly conceived. To say more exactly what Kant presupposes in his all-too-brief arguments from the original contract is difficult, but it seems clear that he does not mean to presuppose his whole moral theory, nor even all its basic principles. For example, if we were to invoke all the implications of treating humanity as an end in itself when we evaluate constitutions, we would strike out far more provisions than those that are ruled out by the seven conclusions listed above. However, to show that those provisions incompatible with the listed conclusions could not themselves be part of an unqualified contract, it seems clear that at least Kant's moral assumptions about the basic freedom and equality of persons are needed. For example, these assumptions are needed to rule out hereditary political privilege and permanent religious requirements. Similarly, without those assumptions it is hard to make sense of Kant's claim that only a republican form of government satisfies fully the spirit of the original contract. All the more, the assumptions must be at work when, in 'Theory and Practice,' Kant tells us that the idea of an original contract obliges every legislator to frame his laws such that they could have been produced by the united will of the whole nation.[60]

On both the narrower and broader understandings of the appeal to an original contract, the basic pattern of argument seems the same. That is, on both understandings, constitutions are condemned if it is *impossible* for those taking an appropriate perspective to have a rational agreement on them, and determination of what is impossible in the

[59] I add 'unqualified' because Kant holds that there could be, and we must assume that there is, a united will on an original contract on any constitution that establishes the existing juridical order, no matter how far from ideal that constitution might be. What the higher standards prevent is rational agreement on such a constitution as a permanent arrangement. With no other viable options in certain periods of history, we can and should endorse whatever *de facto* government gives us rule of law, but we can form a united will on imperfect constitutions only with the understanding that these will be gradually, continually, and legally reformed to resemble a republican constitution. This, I take it, is the spirit of the original contract. See Reiss (ed.), *Kant: Political Writings*, 163 (from Kant, *The Metaphysics of Morals* as edited by Reiss) [6: 340–1].
[60] Ibid. 79 (from Kant, 'Theory and Practice') [8: 297].

relevant sense presupposes standards on which all rational persons *would* (*qua* rational) agree.

V. SOME OBJECTIONS CONSIDERED: IS KANT'S APPEAL TO HYPOTHETICAL AGREEMENT MISGUIDED?

Many objections have been raised against philosophers' use of the idea of agreement under hypothetical conditions. Kant uses this idea, I have suggested, in several different contexts—for example, in his discussions of both the kingdom of ends formula and the idea of an original contract. Let us consider briefly some of these objections.

A. Is Hypothetical Agreement merely a Proxy for Actual Agreement?

One reason for initial skepticism about arguments that turn on claims about hypothetical agreement is that they can be used to make highly dubious moral claims in particular contexts. For example, a distant cousin of a homeowner might try to justify his trespass onto the owner's property by saying 'They would not mind my using their house while they are away and cannot be reached.' When someone dies without a specific will, family members sometimes just help themselves to favorite items in the estate, appealing to the thought 'I am sure she would want me to have this.' People who, for personal reasons, refuse to consent to life-prolonging medical treatments may be forced to undergo them because, it is said, 'they would consent if they were thinking rationally.' In the background of these cases are practices regarding property, wills, and medicine that, for good reasons, insist on actual consent as the norm for using another's property, establishing an inheritance claim, and authorizing invasive treatment of another's body. These practices typically allow that sometimes we can appeal to evidence of what a person would have consented to as a substitute for the person's actual consent. Such appeals, however, are in a shady area relevant only when it is clear that it is impossible to get the actual informed and competent consent of the person whose presumptive rights are being set aside. Actual consent is taken to be the norm; hypothetical consent is a poor substitute, worth considering only because, unfortunately, we do not have the express and competent consent of those affected by a decision. The worry about relying on hypothetical consent in this context is that the more crucial factor in justifying our treatment of others—that is, their actual consent—will be ignored or bypassed just because someone can argue, abstractly, that the relevant parties *would* consent if properly informed. The worry about using hypothetical consent to justify moral and political principles, then, would be the suspicion that such arguments will be used illegitimately to bypass or override the actual consent of the people who must live under the principles.

How seriously must we take this worry as an objection to Kant's use of the idea of hypothetical agreement in his abstract discussions of the kingdom of ends and the original contract? Are his appeals to hypothetical agreement simply a dangerous substitute for what primarily justifies institutions, namely, actual consent? I think not. Regarding particular questions such as 'When is one entitled to enter another's house?' the normal standard is 'When the owner actually consents.' We allow hypothetical consent to serve as the second-best alternative in special circumstances where there is no opportunity to ask for actual consent, as when a genuine friend justifies entering my house without actual consent (e.g., to police patrolling the neighborhood) by saying, 'He would have consented, had he been available, for I am sure he would want me to check on the cat.' The background here is an ongoing set of complex conventions regarding trespassing on personal property that, for good reasons, make actual consent the norm but allow exceptions for cases in which the purposes of the conventions are not well served by rigid insistence on actual consent. This, however, is not the context when our question concerns standards for the basic social institutions themselves. When we ask whether these conventions themselves are justified, we cannot take for granted that the norms that are familiar and intuitive for particular cases are the relevant ones. Simply to apply those familiar norms in the assessment of basic institutions would be to suppose that, except in rare cases where actual consent cannot be consulted, moral practices (such as promising) and political institutions (such as constitutions) are justified when and only when people actually consent to them. As Kant recognized, however, even universal agreement does not make something right, nor is universal agreement required. Far from being necessary and sufficient for justification, actual readiness to consent to background institutions in fact often depends on ignorance, prejudices, and uncritical acceptance of whatever norms are familiar.

Kant invokes the idea of hypothetical agreement for very general abstract purposes. The kingdom of ends formula is supposed to express a combination of the basic normative ideas present in other formulas of the Categorical Imperative, and the idea of an original contract is supposed to express basic standards of practical reason for any constitution. Given that his aim is to articulate and apply these ideas as standards for our actual moral practices and political institutions, Kant cannot presuppose the requirements for actual consent that are defined by those practices and institutions. When we are trying to determine some general features of any justifiable practice, many of the specific, historically conditioned reasons for and against consenting to actual particular practices are irrelevant. Kant's ideas of a kingdom of ends and an original contract, then, are not merely a second-best proxy for a universal actual consent that would better serve his purposes if only it were possible to achieve.[61]

B. Does the Appeal to Hypothetical Rational Agreement Reduce Values to Facts?

A second source of worry about Kant's use of the idea of hypothetical agreement might be the suspicion that such a use commits the same sort of error—the *naturalistic fallacy*—as do certain contemporary reductive theories of value. These theories equate value judgments with judgments about what we would prefer or choose in specified hypothetical situations. Such theories commit the naturalistic fallacy because they treat normative claims as if they were empirical or metaphysical claims. An example would be a theory stating that what is *good* for a person to choose is what that person *would in fact choose* if fully informed, reflective, and put through a course of 'cognitive psychotherapy.'[62] The arguments against such reductive analyses are familiar, and it is not necessary to review them here. I mention them only to note that they reflect a concern about some hypothetical-agreement arguments that does not apply to Kant. Kant's basic commitments are incompatible with any

---

[61] It must be admitted that any pattern of argument used to justify political institutions, whether it appeals to hypothetical agreement or not, can be abused; one must also concede that the conditions stipulated as appropriate idealizations that must be realized for a hypothetical agreement to count can always be challenged. Furthermore, I am not claiming that Kant's own use of possible and hypothetical agreement, for example, in appeals to the idea of an original contract, are altogether satisfactory. My more modest aim is to argue that the appeal to hypothetical agreement in itself is not to be dismissed on the several grounds reviewed in this section. The devil, and maybe the angels, are in the details.

[62] See Richard Brandt, *A Theory of the Good and the Right* (Oxford: Clarendon Press, 1979), 113–29. Cognitive psychotherapy is a 'process for confronting desires with relevant information, by repeatedly representing it, in an ideally vivid way, and at an appropriate time' (ibid. 113).

attempted reduction of claims about duty and justice to empirical or even metaphysical facts. A Kantian claim that rational contractors would agree regarding a constitution cannot be tested by rounding up and questioning people who meet purely descriptive criteria of rationality. Moral ideals of freedom and equality are presupposed on the broader interpretation of the conditions necessary for an original contract, and even the narrower interpretation of these conditions presupposes norms of coherence in willing. It should be obvious, too, that Kant's ideal of a kingdom of ends invokes normative ideas of rationality, autonomy, humanity as an end in itself, and abstraction from morally irrelevant differences. We cannot determine simply by empirical investigation or metaphysical argument what such members of the kingdom of ends would agree upon.

Even if it seems at times that Kant wants to project his normative claims about what practical reason can and cannot will as if they can be thought of as metaphysical facts about a nonempirical (*noumenal*) world, this still would not be the disturbing reduction of value to fact that most philosophers have worried about. Their concern is primarily about identifying values with natural or metaphysical properties that can be specified independently of the values in question.[63] Thus, on their view, goodness cannot be reduced to promoting the survival of the species or to obeying orders of a powerful Creator because these concepts are definable without any reference to evaluative notions. When Kant tries to square his ethical thought with his earlier work in epistemology and metaphysics, he suggests that we should think of the source of moral commands, a pure rational will, as something *noumenal* or, in other words, beyond what can be located in space and time and comprehended empirically. Kant grants, however, that our moral consciousness is our only ground for supposing that we are subject to the demands of a pure rational will, and moral reflection is our only basis

---

[63] G. E. Moore famously objected to identifying normative concepts with descriptive ones. Such identification is prominent among the errors he called 'the naturalistic fallacy.' See Moore, *Principia Ethica*, ch. 1. Moore held that 'intrinsic value' is a nonnatural, nonrelational, unanalyzable property that we can know by intuition. This identifies intrinsic value as a real metaphysical property that certain states of affairs have, and so it might seem at first to reduce values to descriptive facts. However, unlike typical metaphysical accounts of goodness, Moore's theory leaves no way to discover or even make sense of the property in question except by using the terms 'good,' 'valuable for its own sake,' and so on. What he calls 'intuition' is, for all practical purposes, just evaluation without appeal to argument. Hence, despite initial appearances, his seemingly 'metaphysical' account of intrinsic value does not reduce it to descriptive (nonevaluative) facts. In this one respect, I suggest, Moore's view is like Kant's, though Kant and Moore differ very substantially in other ways.

for saying what a pure rational will would endorse. Since everything we can say about such a will derives from ethics, not from intuition or value-neutral metaphysical theory, it is no reduction of value to fact to claim that moral principles are those that pure rational wills would agree upon. The claim asserts a connection between certain related value concepts, not a derivation of value concepts from merely descriptive ones.

C. Are the Parties to Hypothetical Agreement so Idealized that Their Conclusions are Irrelevant to Us?

A third source of problems with Kant's use of hypothetical agreement might be that hypothetical points of view could be so alien to us that we have no reason to care about principles that would be agreed upon from those perspectives. More specifically, a perspective may 'idealize' the parties to a hypothetical agreement in ways that render their vastly simplified choices irrelevant to ours.[64] For example, although it may be entertaining to read utopian fantasies about altruists in a world of unlimited abundance, these provide no grounds for us to adopt the moral and legal codes that would be workable in such situations. Even Rawls's more realistic 'original position' is idealized in ways that have raised doubts about whether *we* have any reason to respect the principles that *they*, the hypothetical persons in that position, would adopt. In general, even if it is established that ideal legislators would agree that everyone should act on a certain principle, it does not follow, without further argument, that we ought to follow that principle when it conflicts with actual practices. Sticking with the less optimal actual practices may be justified, all things considered, especially if the actual practices are quite good, underlie existing legitimate expectations, and would be very costly to change. Determining the ideal solution for idealized conditions may be helpful as a background for reflection on what should be done under real conditions. Theorists use idealizations in an objectionable way, however, if they draw conclusions about what should be done in imperfect conditions directly from what they judge appropriate for ideal conditions.

These are concerns that must be taken seriously, but whether they amount to a decisive objection to the use of hypothetical agreement must be assessed in the context of each particular theory. The fact that a theory uses idealizations is not in itself a problem. In science as well

---

[64] See, for example, O'Neill, *Towards Justice and Virtue*, 44–8.

as in moral philosophy, when our theories assume conditions unlike (and perhaps better or neater) than the situation to which they are to be applied, we must be sensitive to the differences between the theoretical assumptions and the actual conditions at hand. The question is whether the idealizations adequately serve a good purpose. They can be helpful in different ways. Idealizing theories may simplify problems in a harmless way if the ideal conditions are a fairly close approximation of actual conditions. Another way idealizations can be helpful is that in applying a theory, we can often find satisfactory ways to adjust our judgments about actual situations by taking into account the differences between the idealized conditions and the actual conditions. Practical scientists, for example, modify the equations appropriate for objects falling in a hypothetical perfect vacuum in order to take into account the air resistance encountered by actual falling objects.

A third way that idealizations can serve a good purpose is by deliberately forcing us to consider a worthwhile perspective. Some moral theories, for example, articulate a conception of the best possible perspective to try to adopt when evaluating imperfect real-world conditions. It is appropriate, given their aim, that such theories characterize ideal moral deliberators as better in some ways than we actually are in practice. To simplify with an imaginary example, suppose moral theorists specify that ideal deliberators about the real problem of racial conflict should be intelligent, well informed about the problem, and free from racial prejudice; these theorists may then argue that from this perspective certain affirmative action programs would be adopted. Many questions and doubts could be raised about such an argument, but it would be bizarre to object that the theorists have unduly idealized the deliberative perspective.[65] This would suggest that, in thinking about the problem, it is better to be more stupid, ignorant, and prejudiced.

Whether Kantian ethics employs troublesome idealizations is a large and important issue. Kant attributes to the legislating members of a kingdom of ends autonomy, a kind of rationality, and the ability to see things in abstraction from personal differences. These idealizations,

[65] Practically minded critics would naturally focus on the specific reasons offered to show that such ideal deliberators would adopt the programs in question, but philosophers would probably also question whether it serves any useful purpose to characterize ideal deliberators first rather than turning immediately to moral arguments for the programs. This latter concern seems a natural one to raise about the simple argument in my example because its account of ideal deliberators is so thin, but whether it is an important worry about more subtle and complex arguments of the same structure is less obvious. My discussion of the fourth objection to hypothetical-agreement theories returns to this issue briefly.

or some modified version of them, can be seen as useful and harmless extensions of widely shared ideals for deliberation about general moral principles. When seen this way—as I have argued elsewhere that they should be[66]—their use need not be alienating. However, this issue is obviously too complex and controversial to pursue here.

Instead, let us briefly consider Kant's use of the idea of an original contract. Does this employ a reasonable and helpful idealization? Whether it does depends, of course, on the purpose for which the idea is used. Kant's purpose, I take it, is to set out at least minimal conditions for the rational and moral justification for thinking that no state constitution should contain certain provisions (e.g., those establishing permanent hereditary political privileges). Recall that Kant apparently has at least two different sets of working assumptions about what is necessary for there to be a united will on a constitution. His first, narrower view is that what is necessary is merely that the constitution structure a logically possible system of law. Here there is no worrisome idealization unless one has crept in under the idea of 'law.' We may question Kant's ideas about what is essential to a legal order and his assumption that such a system is the only alternative to lawlessness, but objections on these points alone are not charges that Kant is engaging in the troublesome kind of idealization that I have described. Kant does not assume, for example, that everything in the real world that is called a legal order actually satisfies his conditions; for example, he does not claim that all real-world legal orders lack gaps in authority. Articulating a certain conception of a legal order by laying out its necessary conditions can be of use for theoretical purposes, for the conception can provide a model relevant to deliberations about real-world conditions without decisively determining what should be done. In merely doing this, a theorist is not guilty of the alienating kind of idealization. Whether a theorist is in fact guilty of this charge depends on whether, *without adequate further argument*, the theorist draws from his idealization conclusions about how actual social systems *should* be structured. Since Kant does not hesitate to make prescriptions for real-world conditions, whether we conclude that he is guilty of the troublesome kind of idealization will depend in the end on how we understand and assess the strength of his reasons for applying his model.

Consider briefly Kant's broader view of the necessary conditions for a united will on an original contract. This view employed idealizations, but arguably not the troublesome kind that render the possibility of

---

[66] See Hill, *Respect, Pluralism, and Justice*, ch. 2.

ideal agreement irrelevant to our concerns. Unless we reject the rights of freedom and equality presupposed by Kant's broader view, we should not be indifferent to arguments that hypothetical constitution-makers who, among other things, accept these as basic rights could not endorse, in an original contract, any constitution with certain provisions.[67] Such arguments do not purport to ground these basic rights in the idea of an original contract, for the rights at this stage are presupposed, not 'constructed.' Whether such arguments are rationally compelling depends, of course, on whether the presupposed rights are independently well grounded. The arguments, we may say, take for granted certain ideals, but again, this is not to concede that they indulge in the troublesome sort of idealization we have been considering. They do not assume falsely that in the real world everyone accepts the basic rights; rather, they only assume that as a normative matter, persons *should* be guaranteed those rights. The conclusions of such arguments (e.g., that permanent hereditary political privileges are unjust) are not based on a failure to understand the differences between our imperfect world and a more ideal one. Some aristocrats, Nietzscheans, and postmodernists may reject the presupposed rights, but that would call for a separate debate. For most of us, it would be quite bizarre to complain that what the hypothetical parties to an original contract could agree on is irrelevant to us because they, given their commitment to basic rights of freedom and equality, are more ideal than we are.

D. Is Hypothetical Agreement a Standard that is Either Arbitrary or Useless?

My reply to the previous objection invites another objection commonly raised to theories that try to justify principles by arguing that they are, or would be, prescribed by ideal legislators. The objection can be put in the form of a dilemma: either the ideal legislators are guided by substantial reasons, or else their prescriptions are arbitrary. Both options have objectionable implications.[68] On the one hand, if there are substantial reasons why the ideal legislators prescribe the principles in question, then those reasons—not the fact that ideal legislators prescribed the principles—are what give the principles force. Reference to legislators'

---

[67] Kantian arguments of this sort are analogous to arguments at what Rawls calls 'the constitutional stage' of applying the Rawlsian basic principles of justice. See Rawls, *A Theory of Justice*, 172–4.
[68] Andrews Reath, Shelly Kagan, and Philip Pettit convinced me of the need to respond to this apparent dilemma.

'legislative' choices seems irrelevant if the same principles could be justified directly by appeal to the substantial reasons that supposedly guide the legislators' choices. On the other hand, if the ideal legislators make arbitrary choices that are not based on good reasons, then the fact that they prescribe a principle seems to give us no reason to respect it.[69]

Kantian ethics, as I understand it, is clear about which horn of this dilemma it must avoid at all costs, and so the important question is whether there is any devastating force in the other horn. What seems obvious is that Kant does not think that what members of a kingdom of ends would legislate and what would be rationally excluded from an original contract are arbitrary choices. If we can find no adequate reasons why the hypothetical legislators or original contractors would accept or reject proposals, then Kantian theory has no grounds for attributing choices to these legislators or contractors. As noted already, however, Kant's thought experiments about what would or would not be agreed to in a kingdom of ends and in an original contract *presuppose* standards of rational choice that are not themselves products of choice or construction in the hypothetical-choice situations. Thus, Kantian constructivism is not subject to the complaint that it renders moral principles arbitrary.

How damaging, then, is the other horn of the dilemma? Kantian theory, I think, should concede that principles justified by reference to the hypothetical choices of members of the kingdom of ends might in principle be justified by more direct appeal to the rational standards presupposed by their alleged legislative choices. For similar reasons, it should not be denied that reference to the idea of an original contract could in principle be replaced by direct invocations of the rational standards presupposed in arguments that there could be no original contract on constitutions with certain provisions. In principle we might, for example, argue against such constitutions directly from the presupposed innate rights to freedom and equality. Whether these concessions pose a serious problem, however, depends on at least two questions. First, need Kantian constructivism claim to offer hypothetical-agreement arguments that are free from all presuppositions about rational and moral choice beyond what these arguments themselves can establish?

---

[69] The dilemma posed here is analogous to the 'Euthyphro problem,' which is a dilemma that Socrates poses in Plato's dialogue, *Euthyphro*. Either what is pious (or righteous) is so because it pleases the gods or else what is pious (or righteous) pleases the gods because it is pious (or righteous). If the former is true, piety (or righteousness) seems to be arbitrary; if the latter is true, then the gods do not determine what is pious (or righteous), but merely respond to an independent truth about piety (or righteousness).

The proper response, in my opinion, is that so long as the aims and limits of the constructivism are clear, there is nothing in itself objectionable about starting with assumptions that are not themselves the products of construction.[70] Kantians should not hesitate to admit that their thought experiments presuppose certain standards, nor should they hesitate to try to clarify what those standards are. Kantians need not contend that their constructivist procedures can justify substantive moral principles without making any initial assumptions about rationality and morality. The assumptions they do make, like those in any theory, may be questioned and debated, but unless constructivists claim to derive moral principles without any potentially disputable assumptions, there is no problem in principle with the constructivists' procedure. Constructivist arguments are not undermined by the mere fact that they are built with some equipment and tools that constructivists cannot claim to have constructed.

The second question is this: even if direct appeals to rational presuppositions of hypothetical-agreement arguments could in principle achieve the same results that the arguments themselves yield, is there any theoretical or heuristic value in arguing by reference to hypothetical agreement? To answer this question, we need to work out more of the details of the Kantian appeals to hypothetical agreement. The constructivist question 'What would be agreed upon in such-and-such a hypothetical ideal situation?' may bring together several evaluative assumptions, explicit and presupposed, to bear on a particular topic in a way that is more convenient and fruitful than treating those assumptions as so many separate premises in a direct argument. In addition, expressing standards as rational guides and constraints on hypothetical choices may discourage attempts to reify those standards as self-standing natural or supernatural facts. In any case, it is not a fatal objection to a proposal that the same job could be done another way.

E. Will Arguments from Hypothetical Agreement Convince Egoistic Amoralists?

Finally, another source of suspicion about Kantian appeals to hypothetical agreement might be the thought that such agreement does not

---

[70] Onora O'Neill's constructivism is more ambitious in this regard than is the general account of constructivism that I am discussing here (which is closer to Rawls's position), for she aims to build her arguments from only thin, formal assumptions. See Onora O'Neill, 'Constructivism in Kant and Rawls', in Samuel Freeman (ed.), *The Cambridge Companion to Rawls* (Cambridge: Cambridge University Press, forthcoming).

provide arguments adequate to convince a 'rational egoist' who has little regard for others. The short-term response to this claim must be that the point of hypothetical-agreement arguments in Kantian constructivism is to work out and defend certain principles as being morally justified, not to convince egoists lacking any moral commitment that they have purely self-interested reasons for accepting these principles. What we can say to such persons, if they exist, is another matter. Despite his insistence on the rationality of moral conduct, Kant in fact does not develop an answer that one could give to the utterly uncommitted egoist. He assumes that all moral agents have legislative reason (*Wille*), which forces on us, as it were, recognition of the authority of the moral law even when we violate it. He is even committed to the idea that, in a sense, we *actually will* for ourselves (at least as a standard) conformity to whatever rational agents with the most basic Kantian moral commitments *would agree* upon. Yet this presupposition of a deep 'actual consent' to moral law is far from the everyday idea of actual consent with which I began this essay. The sort of 'actual consent' presupposed by Kant, reflected in his discussion of the inescapable 'fact of reason,' is clearly not an actual readiness, or even public commitment, always to be fully governed by moral standards. It is an acceptance of the authority of the moral law, but, as we know, this is not always accompanied by a wholehearted resolve or commitment to obey.

VI. CONCLUSION

The primary question in this essay has been how to understand the justificatory role of actual, possible, and hypothetical consent within Kant's ethics. Kant's theory has been treated as one among several possible versions of Kantian constructivism. A brief review of the Categorical Imperative's various formulations and of Kant's idea of an original contract provides the basis for several conclusions. Contrary to what discussions of applied ethics often assume, Kant regards *actual* consent as having only a derivative and qualified relevance to how we may be treated. For Kant, a more basic standard is that practices are justified only if we *can*, as rational agents, consent to them being universal practices. To apply this standard, however, we must make assumptions about the context of choice and the rational principles that determine what it is possible, in the relevant sense, for us to will. When the assumptions necessary to make the standard plausible are made explicit, it turns out that, in effect, the possible-consent standard can be expressed as a hypothetical-consent standard. Hypothetical-consent standards condemn practices that are contrary to principles that any rational agent *would* will *under specified conditions*. The apparent simplicity, then, of the possible-consent test that asks 'What can we will as universal law?' is deceptive. This test is not a way of avoiding the hard, controversial questions raised by hypothetical-consent standards. What are the principles and conditions of rational choice that are being presupposed when one applies these standards? Are these presuppositions defensible? Furthermore, when these presuppositions are made explicit, do the presupposed standards support intuitively plausible moral judgments? Particular versions of hypothetical-consent standards (such as that presented by Rawls's original position) raise special problems, but arguably the several objections to hypothetical consent that I consider in this essay are not decisive objections to the Kantian version of such a standard.

PART II

Human Welfare: Self-Interest and Regard for Others

4

Beneficence and Self-Love

I. QUESTIONS, ASSUMPTIONS, AND PREVIEW

What, if anything, are we morally required to do on behalf of others besides respecting their rights? And why is such regard for others a reasonable moral requirement? These two questions have long been major concerns of ethical theory, but the answers that philosophers give tend to vary with their beliefs about human nature. More specifically, their answers typically depend on the position they take on a third question: To what extent, if any, is it *possible* for us to act altruistically?[1]

I want to thank all those who made helpful comments on an earlier version of this essay, especially Jean Hampton, Christine Korsgaard, Geoffrey Sayre-McCord, Ellen Frankel Paul, Andrews Reath, and Michael Zimmerman.

[1] The familiar idea of *altruism* is notoriously hard to pin down, and philosophical definitions can vary as widely as those of the contrasting term, *egoism*. I do not want to limit my general discussion by insisting on a specific definition, but roughly I mean by 'altruistic acts' those done to benefit others and not motivated by self-interest. They are done 'for the sake of others' from motives such as sympathy, respect, group loyalty, or moral duty. The idea of 'self-interest,' unfortunately, is almost as slippery as the ideas of 'egoism' and 'altruism,' but when more than a common-sense understanding is needed, I favor the characterization suggested by Gregory S. Kavka in his account of 'Narrow Egoism.' That is, acts motivated by self-interest have as their ultimate end 'personal benefits,' as best identified by a list of examples. Kavka's list includes 'pleasure, [avoidance of] pain, wealth, security, liberty, glory, possession of particular objects, fame, health, longevity, status, self-respect, self-development, self-assertion, reputation, honor, and affection' (Gregory S. Kavka, *Hobbesian Moral and Political Theory* (Princeton: Princeton University Press, 1986), 42).

Here I set aside, as nonaltruistic, acts done *both* for others and for oneself, even though for some purposes these might be called 'altruistic' in another sense. Also, importantly, I do not assume, as some do, that acts done for the sake of others are done out of compassionate or sympathetic *feelings* towards others, for I want to count among altruistic acts those done to benefit others because one believes that helping others on such occasions is what one morally should do. In such cases, on the Kantian view, the aim or *end* one seeks is others' welfare and nothing further, but the motivating *principle* is to act as one believes morally right, and the accompanying *feeling* may be respect for moral principle rather than compassion. It should be noted further that altruistic acts, as understood here, need not be motivated by *general benevolence* (i.e., a concern for the welfare of human or sentient beings in general) rather than concern to help particular individuals.

Theories that provide related answers to these three questions can differ radically. At one extreme, for example, is an egoist position often attributed to Hobbes.[2] This denies the possibility of genuine altruism and argues that reason and morality can only require us to look out for others to the extent that doing so will serve our own long-term self-interest. Others, like Hume, suppose that sympathy for others is a basic feature of human nature; and, on this assumption, some even argue (beyond Hume) that our moral duty is to count each other person's happiness as having the same weight in our decision making as our own. Theories at both extremes tend to draw conclusions about how we should treat others from initial beliefs about how we are naturally inclined to feel about them. There are, of course, many intermediate positions, with subtle variations, between these extremes.

In my discussion I describe some main features of one of these less extreme positions—what I call 'a Kantian perspective'—on my initial three questions though, I focus primarily on the third issue (the *possibility* of altruistic conduct). In labeling the position 'Kantian' I mean only to acknowledge respectfully that the position in question has roots in Kant's ethical theory, not to raise historical and interpretative questions about Kant's texts. My main purpose is to put the ideas in question on the table for consideration, not to do textual exegesis.

My project is limited in another way as well. I want to consider our questions about altruism as they might arise for us when we take up a practical, deliberative, and conscientious point of view.[3] We want

---

[2] The view in question is a combination of psychological egoism and ethical egoism, as these terms are generally understood. Whether Thomas Hobbes actually was an unqualified egoist in these senses is a matter of controversy, which turns partly on the exact definitions of relevant senses of 'egoism' and partly on the interpretation of familiar passages. It is clear that Hobbes acknowledged that we sometimes act from *apparently* altruistic motives, for example, 'pity' and 'compassion,' but his definitions can be read as efforts to reinterpret such terms in a way compatible with psychological egoism and its denial of *genuine*, i.e., actual, altruism. For finer distinctions and varying views on Hobbes, see, for example, the following: C. D. Broad, *Five Types of Ethical Theory* (London: Routledge & Kegan Paul, 1930), 54; Richard B. Brandt, *Ethical Theory* (Englewood Cliffs, NJ: Prentice-Hall, 1959), ch. 14, especially 370–1; William K. Frankena, *Ethics*, 2nd edn. (Englewood Cliffs, NJ: Prentice-Hall, 1973), ch. 2, especially p. 15; James Rachels, *The Elements of Moral Philosophy* (New York: Random House, 1986), chs. 5 and 6; Jean Hampton, *Hobbes and the Social Contract Tradition* (Cambridge: Cambridge University Press, 1986), ch. 1, especially 19–24; and Kavka, *Hobbesian Moral and Political Theory*, ch. 2, especially 44–51.

[3] As I intend these terms, we take a 'practical, deliberative' point of view when we think seriously about reasons for and against policies or courses of action, and this perspective is also 'conscientious' when our background assumption, and indeed our point, in deliberating is that we intend to do what is morally right. Conscientious people, of

answers appropriate for sincere deliberation about what we can do, what we should do, and why. From this perspective our questions are not idle speculative ones, for we want not merely to understand the world but to change it in some ways—or at least to act responsibly in it. In addition, I want to assume that the practical task before us is not primarily how to persuade and motivate others to do what we believe they should. Rather, the task is first and foremost to determine how we ourselves should act.

Given these assumptions, as deliberators we ask what we should do because we mean to do what we should. We seek good reasons for acting, not merely for predicting or explaining how people do behave. Nevertheless, what we learn from psychology is potentially important, for in trying to decide what *to do*, we must set aside any alleged 'oughts' that we *know* we *cannot* fulfill. When deliberating as conscientious persons, we are not entertaining or responding to the doubts of moral skeptics who ask, 'Are moral judgments *objective*?'—'Are obligations *real*?' Nor are we trying to answer amoralists who pose the challenge, 'Show me why I should *care* about morality at all.'

Thus, for present purposes I am supposing that, like most people who bother to discuss ethical issues, we accept some minimal moral limits to how we may treat others. We are not doubting, for example, that there are some reasonable moral principles against theft, fraud, promise-breaking, murder, rape, and torture. But, realizing that many are inclined to accept such minimal constraints as morally sufficient, we raise further questions. For example, 'Isn't it optional whether we give to charity, do favors, and generally give regard to the concerns of others, provided that we fulfill our strict obligations of honesty, promise-keeping, noncoercion, and the like?' Even if we enjoy helping others and know that others like us better when we do, we may still wonder, 'Isn't this beyond duty, a matter of preference, "nice" to do but not wrong to omit? If not, why not?' And, seeing rampant greed and selfishness, we ask, 'Is it possible for human beings to be altruistic as, some say, duty requires?'

In sum, we pose our questions about altruism as conscientious agents who accept certain core moral constraints but have questions and disagreements about the nature, grounds, and limits of their moral

course, may have different views about what is morally right, but they have in common a commitment to act on their best judgment about this. Here I assume only that *in taking up the conscientious perspective* we seek what is right with the intent to do it, not that we are all moral saints, *always* perfectly free from weakness of will, negligence, and perversity.

obligations to act beneficently towards others.⁴ This means that our concerns are more specific than those of moral skeptics; but they should not be confused with even more particular questions that individuals may raise in special contexts. For example, suppose a volunteer has worked long and hard for strangers (or even competent adult family members) whose basic needs are provided for, who refuse to avail themselves of ample opportunities, and who show her neither gratitude nor reciprocity. Then to ask, in these circumstances, 'Do I have any obligation to help them further?' is not to ask our more general question about the duty of beneficence but rather to doubt its application to a quite specific, though perhaps all too common, situation. To take another example, suppose that a woman comes to see that she has diminished herself by constantly submitting to male demands that women devote themselves to others, and she wonders, 'Is it wrong for me to concentrate my energies on myself now?' Her concern is more specific and contextually focused than my opening questions, which were about our general obligation to help others, rather than about how such an obligation directs us to act in troublesome special contexts.

Kant addresses these questions, more or less from the point of view described above, in several works, but his most sustained discussion of the duty of beneficence is in the second part of *The Metaphysics of Morals.*⁵ There Kant takes for granted that his audience has followed him through (or is not now doubting) his earlier attempts to characterize the fundamentals of a moral attitude, to confront doubts about its rational authority, and to establish the principles of justice and respect prior to beneficence. The problem is not to judge how the general duty of beneficence applies to particular cases, but to say in general what it requires and why, while granting that human beings have a limited natural disposition to help others and cannot call up sympathetic feel-

---

⁴ The point of specifying that we are to address the questions in this essay as conscientious deliberating agents is methodological, not rhetorical. What one can take for granted, what is in doubt, and even what one is looking for can vary with the context of discussion of normative matters. Purposes and working assumptions tend to shift as one moves within contemporary philosophical literature from abstract philosophical arguments about 'moral realism,' to practical debates on specific moral issues, to general explanatory accounts of moral belief and behavior from a third-person perspective. Ideally, we expect that reasonable conclusions in these different contexts will eventually cohere, but in the meantime it is only good procedure to keep in focus the background aims and assumptions of each particular discussion.

⁵ Kant's position on the possibility of altruism is inseparable from his ideas of autonomy and practical freedom, discussed in many of his major works. For commentary and detailed references, see Henry E. Allison, *Kant's Theory of Freedom* (Cambridge: Cambridge University Press, 1990).

ings at will. The questions are about our duty to others, not about how to get others to do their duty. Kant never doubted that his audience could hear the voice of duty, once clearly expressed, even if he was not an optimist about how regularly they would heed it.

The Kantian position, as I understand it, offers practical alternatives to opposing extremes with regard to the three questions that I posed at the beginning of this essay.

First, what beneficence towards others is morally required? An answer at one extreme is the minimalist idea that helping others (beyond the requirements of justice and contractual obligations) is optional, and at the opposing extreme is the maximalist idea that one must always help others, provided doing so does not diminish the general welfare impartially viewed. The Kantian position is that beneficence is a moral duty, but a wide, imperfect duty of virtue, unenforceable and constrained by prior requirements of justice and respect.

Second, why is beneficence a duty? Some would attempt to answer by reference to the demands of God, social convention, or our compassionate natures; others would appeal to a metaphysical belief in the reality of intrinsic values, perceived by us but not constituted by their relation to human or divine thoughts and feelings. The Kantian alternative attempts to ground a duty of beneficence in our acknowledgment that, as rational agents, we each value ourselves in a special way and, as conscientious agents, we are committed to evaluative consistency and a constraint to act only in ways that we believe we could defend before others in morally appropriate joint deliberations.[6]

Third, can we act altruistically? Here the extremes are the belief that

---

[6] Here I paraphrase what Kant expresses in his more specialized terminology and what I explain more fully in the last section of this essay. What I call 'conscientious agents' are roughly, in Kant's terms, (*imperfectly*) *rational agents* that acknowledge that they are subject to *duties*, conceived as *categorical imperatives*. This implies a 'will,' though not an invariably effective disposition, to conform to what one judges (or 'knows') to be morally obligatory. Kant held that all (even imperfectly) rational human beings have such a will; and so, though he implied that there are rational requirements that are not duties, he believed that 'rational agents' are also 'conscientious' (as I use the term here). In saying that (for Kant) conscientious agents are 'committed to evaluative consistency,' I allude (rather imprecisely) to the standards expressed in the universal law formula of the Categorical Imperative, which is discussed briefly in the last section of this essay. The constraint of defensibility 'before others in morally appropriate deliberations' is drawn from the 'kingdom of ends' formula, not discussed in this essay. I present a more thorough view of some of these matters in my collection of essays *Dignity and Practical Reason*, especially chs. 1, 3, 7, 10, and 11, and in ch. 2 of my recent anthology *Respect, Pluralism, and Justice*. See also H. J. Paton, *The Categorical Imperative* (London: Hutchison, 1947); and Onora O'Neill, *Constructions of Reason* (Cambridge: Cambridge University Press, 1989).

natural self-regard makes genuine altruistic conduct impossible and the belief that natural sympathy makes it possible and even common. The Kantian position, by contrast, is that, once we see the reasons for doing so, we can guide our conduct by a limited principle of beneficence, no matter how warm or cold our feelings towards others may run. That we can do so, at least in normal circumstances, is not refuted by empirical evidence and is presupposed in our conception of ourselves as moral agents.

My primary focus will be on the Kantian position with regard to the third question, whether or not we are capable of acting altruistically. But since Kant's response on this issue is not complete without reference to his answers to the first two questions, these will be considered (more briefly) in Sections IV and V.

II. DIVERSE OPINIONS ON THE PREVALENCE OF BENEVOLENT FEELINGS AND THEIR RELEVANCE FOR ETHICS

Beliefs vary about what we *can* do for others, and these beliefs tend to influence in various ways views about what we *should* do for others. Let us review some variations.

1. Some believe that altruistic conduct is impossible, and thus conclude that there is no moral obligation to be altruistic. Moral arguments for accepting other-regarding principles, on this view, must appeal at some point to self-interest. Hobbes is often thought to be a prime example. By nature, he held, we always act for the sake of some good for ourselves. What is called 'compassion,' he tells us, is really one's 'grief for the calamity of another ... [that] ariseth from the imagination that a like calamity may befall [oneself],'[7] and the laws of nature that prescribe accommodation and forbid hatred are derivative from the primary law directing one to further one's own interests.[8]

2. Others hold, less radically, that though concern for others for their own sake is occasionally possible, due to human nature such other-regarding concerns can only be rare, unstable, and restricted in scope

---

[7] Thomas Hobbes, *Leviathan*, ed. C. B. MacPherson (Baltimore: Penguin Books, 1951), part I, ch. 6, p. 126. This passage, as Jean Hampton has reminded me, can be interpreted in several ways. A reading that assimilated Hobbes's point to Hume's account of sympathy would allow that acts moved by compassion (as Hobbes defines it) could count as altruistic. See the references in n. 2 above.

[8] Ibid., part I, chs. 14 and 15.

(e.g., to family, friends, and associates). If one assumes that altruistic acts must be motivated by altruistic feelings, then the belief that altruistic feelings are severely limited tends to undermine belief in a general obligation to act for the sake of others. It seems pointless, and even dangerous, to expect people to act from selfless regard for others if, because of human nature, such motives are uncommon, unreliable, and narrowly focused. Even if one imagined oneself to be the rare exception, having frequent, strong, and wide-ranging compassion, one could only try to make *oneself* act from this motive and could not fairly or reasonably prescribe the same to all. 'Ought' in this context implies 'can', and to regard a principle as a basic moral principle is to understand it as a standard for everyone. If an individual lacks and cannot acquire a kind or degree of benevolent feeling, then that person cannot be under obligation, all things considered, to have such a feeling or to take action that requires this feeling as a motive. And if *most* people are similarly lacking, then it seems doubtful that having and acting on the motive can be a *basic* moral obligation even for the few who have the capacity for it.

3. Many who agree that altruistic feelings are in fact rare in our world may nevertheless believe that this is an ideal motive, within human capacities, and that we are obligated to cultivate it. What our observations show, they may argue, is that people *do not* (often) act from altruistic feelings, but not that they *cannot*. Various explanations may be given for the fact that most do not develop and act from their capacity for this ideal motive. The failure may be attributed, for example, to pervasive problems that, according to some theological and social theories, can eventually be overcome or transcended: for example, original sin, capitalism, or the use of inadequate techniques of socialization.

If pressed with the objection that it is foolish and dangerous to expect people to act on motives that are in fact quite uncommon, idealists may reply in different ways. Some Christians may say that love for all, even though rare, has a supreme value and that one should have faith that God will prevent or compensate for the disasters that seem predictable when one trusts that people can be more loving than evidence shows them capable of being. Some revolutionary idealists, confronted with the same objection, may reply that indeed we should not count on most people, as currently conditioned, to act from anything less than selfish motives, but after the revolution, they may argue, radically altered social conditions will mold new personalities in which other-regarding motives dominate.

4. Another common view is that compassion and general benevolence

are not only possible in rare circumstances but are powerful and pervasive features of human nature. This belief about human psychology can also influence moral views. For example, the belief makes it easier to affirm utilitarianism as a theory of moral obligation, for it sets aside the alleged problem that human beings cannot consciously strive for the greatest happiness for all without ulterior motives. Believing that general benevolence is a powerful natural motive would also make it more reasonable for utilitarians (and others) to believe that we need not and so (given costs) should not resort to state coercion, manipulation, and indoctrination to maintain a decent social order. More radically, the belief that benevolence is natural may be regarded as the *basis* for an altruistic ethics. For example, some philosophers seem to hold that an ethics that prescribes acting for the good of others *follows* from their empirical beliefs that benevolence is a powerful natural motive, and that people tend, when disinterested, to look favorably on acts motivated by benevolence.[9]

III. THEORETICAL AND PRACTICAL PURPOSES, AND THE PROBLEM OF THE POSSIBILITY OF ALTRUISM FOR KANTIANS

Kant's view on the possibility of altruism is an important alternative to the views sketched above, but it is not so much an intermediate position on the same scale as it is the introduction of another way of thinking. Kant does not try to settle the issue by determining the extent to which we naturally have, or can acquire, benevolent or sympathetic feelings. Instead, he invites us to see ourselves as agents, trying to decide what to do, in a setting where human motives are mixed and difficult to discern in most cases. As a deliberating agent, one looks at empirical evidence about one's own inclinations and the motives of others as potentially relevant background information, but not as data sufficient

---

[9] This view is at least suggested by various philosophers who interpret moral judgments as expressing sentiments of impartial spectators, but my unqualified summary of the position no doubt oversimplifies their views. See, for example, David Hume, *Moral and Political Philosophy*, ed. Henry D. Aiken (New York: Hafner, 1948), especially 175–84 and 249–61. See also selections from Adam Smith and Joseph Butler in L. A. Selby-Bigge (ed.), *British Moralists* (Indianapolis: Bobbs-Merrill, 1964), 255–336 and 181–254; and Roderick Firth, 'Ethics and the Ideal Observer', *Philosophy and Phenomenological Research*, 12 (1952), 317–45. For a contemporary defense of natural altruism as, in some sense, the basis for morality, see Lawrence Thomas, *Living Morally: A Psychology of Moral Character* (Philadelphia: Temple University Press, 1989).

by themselves to determine which option one should choose. What one can introspect and infer from one's past behavior about one's own current inclinations is not seen as a glimpse at an inner mechanism of wheels and levers from which one can predict what one will do or calculate what one should do. Rather, all this merely sets the factual scene within which one must undertake the deliberative task of deciding reasonably what to do.

To move beyond these metaphors, a distinction needs to be made between two importantly different purposes one can have in thinking about the world, human motives, one's particular situation, and what one can and cannot do. One purpose is to gain theoretical understanding of the phenomena we observe. With this aim we seek to describe, comprehend, explain, and predict human behavior by empirical generalizations conceived as causal laws.[10] The other purpose is to decide reasonably, in practical deliberation, what to do in the factual situation in which one finds oneself. The two sorts of purposes necessarily require somewhat different presuppositions and methodologies. When we deliberate, for example, we presume that we have genuine options, that our reasoning can (and should) direct our decisions, that our decisions typically manifest themselves in our behavior, and that our behavior has some effects on the rest of the world. We presuppose that we can and will act for reasons that we can assess, with some objectivity, as better or worse. We are looking for reasons for choosing to act this way or that, intending to act as reason directs, and this is not the same as seeking to discover the physical or psychological events, conditions, and laws by reference to which an observer might predict and explain the resulting behavior.[11]

A. *The Theoretical Task of Empirical Explanation*

Now, when guided by the first (theoretical) purpose, what are the basic features of human motivation that we can infer from our observations?

---

[10] Kant maintained that the idea of agent-initiated causation (e.g., I intentionally moved the lever with my hand) is importantly different from the idea of event causation (e.g., the explosion knocked my hand against the lever and/or my hand's movement caused the lever to move). All events, Kant argued, have prior causes sufficient to produce them with necessity, but from a practical point of view, we can and must think of agents as initiating causal sequences without being determined to do so by prior causes. See C1, 464–79 [A: 532–58, B: 560–86], G, 114–31 [4: 446–63], and C2, 62–75 [5: 72–89].

[11] Both the agent's (normative) reasons for choosing and explanatory causes may be referred to as 'the reasons why' the agent acted, and this ambiguity can cause confusion. See Stephen Darwall, *Impartial Reason* (Ithaca: Cornell University Press, 1983), 28–9.

The details of Kant's view are subject to scholarly controversy, but the main picture is clear enough for present purposes. Human beings have variable impulses and inclinations, as well as steady interests, that stem from their 'sensuous nature.' They *find* themselves feeling drawn and repulsed by various things, including other people. They do not acquire these feelings by choice, and they cannot simply choose to be rid of them. Though individuals vary in their particular desires, most have some mixture of self-regarding and other-regarding concerns. The latter, however, tend to be weaker and less reliable. Self-love may in fact underlie all or most of what appears to be altruistic feeling.[12] Everyone, by nature, wants to be happy.[13] Though Kant held that no one has a very definite and coherent idea of what his or her happiness would consist in, he clearly did not suppose that for most of us happiness (in this world) consists in sacrificing our own pleasures, material comfort, and security to satisfy intrinsic desires for others' welfare.[14]

On the Kantian view, then, preference for oneself over others is a strongly felt, pervasive human tendency, perhaps even the ultimate source of our other-regarding affections. Moreover, it seems quite foreign to a Kantian perspective to suppose that human nature is so malleable that we can be molded by social conditions into predominantly other-regarding creatures. Through something analogous to religious conversion, Kant thought, individuals may reorder their principles of action, but this may leave their selfish feelings and tendencies unaltered.[15] General benevolence and sympathy are far too weak and unreliable to maintain a decent social order; for that purpose punishment, even 'an eye for an eye,' is needed.[16] In fact, Kant suggests, in designing a system of public justice, we should assume no altruistic or even conscientious motivation, but instead should provide incentives sufficient to govern even a group of (prudentially rational) fiends.[17]

Empirically, then, we find some limited (and perhaps mixed) benevolent feelings, but these are too unreliable to encourage hope for widespread altruistic conduct. This is not the whole empirical story, however. We also find feelings that are *called* 'respect,' 'guilt,' 'sense of obligation,' and so on, accompanied by talk of 'principles,' 'reasons,' and 'duties'; and, oddly enough, we observe that people show tendencies to act correspondingly, even when they show no signs of sympathetic feelings. We find, I suppose, that people do act in ways that benefit others,

---

[12] See C2, 19–20 [5: 22].   [13] G, 83 [4: 415].   [14] G, 85–6 [4: 418–19].
[15] R, 65–73 [6: 44–53].   [16] MM, 104–8 [6: 331–5].
[17] See Kant, *Perpetual Peace*, tr. H. B. Nisbet, in *Kant's Political Writings*, ed. Hans Reiss (Cambridge: Cambridge University Press, 1970), 112 [8: 366].

despite apparent costs to themselves, more often than we would have predicted from our estimate of the prevalence of benevolent feelings. Sometimes we hear people *saying* that feelings of 'obligation' and 'respect for duty' moved them, but for all we know empirically, such reported feelings may simply be masks for deeply self-interested motives or conditioned responses to early training. Whatever their deep motives, we observe that sometimes people do *behave* in ways that benefit others, responding to the thought that another is in need, even at considerable cost to their apparent interests. Since they do, we infer that they can.

These observations, Kant granted, do not contradict the working assumption, found in most sciences, that there must be a causal explanation for all phenomena, whether we can identify it or not. In fact, he believed that he had proved that the principle 'every event has a cause' is necessary to human understanding of the world.[18] Thus, the fact that apparently altruistic behavior is not found to be always preceded by identifiably egoistic feelings, such as desire for personal benefit, does not mean that such behavior has no causes. The practical terms we typically use in making sense of human action (intending, willing, choosing, adopting policies, assessing reasons, accepting responsibility, etc.) are not precisely definable variables that could fit into any exact science, but this fact, again, is supposedly compatible with there being causes of all human behavior.[19] In sum, we must suppose for theoretical purposes that altruistic acts, if any, have causes, but empirically we find that, whatever the causes, human beings do at times benefit others even contrary to perceived personal benefit, with the typical feelings and verbal signs we associate with intentional and principled action.

B. *The Practical Purposes of Deliberation*

Let us turn now to the second reflective standpoint, which is distinguished by Kant from the theoretical stance just considered. This second standpoint is that of practical deliberation, and its purpose is to answer the normative question 'What ought I to do?' From this practical perspective, how does a Kantian view the possibility of altruism?

First it should be noted, and if necessary emphasized, that reasonable practical deliberators must take empirical facts very seriously. They must try to understand the feelings of others and their own dispositions in

---

[18] C1, 218–33 [A: 189–211, B: 232–56], 409–15 [A: 445–52, B: 473–80], and 443–9 [A: 497–507, B: 525–35].
[19] G, 118–29 [4: 451–61].

order to give due weight to each, when appropriate, in assessing what they should do. But as practical deliberators we seek these facts as background information, characterizing the scene within which we must make a choice. For example, finding, by introspection or self-observation over time, that I enjoy playing tennis more than helping out at the homeless shelter (or the reverse) may be a relevant fact to consider as I weigh the reasons for and against scheduling my time in a certain way; but I cannot assume that such facts alone determine the answer to my practical question, because the basic principles of reason and morality do not make what I *ought* to do simply a function of how I feel. Nor is what I ought to do determined simply by how my act will affect the feelings of others, or by whether it maximizes good feeling 'for everyone, all considered.'

Further, if empirical facts establish that human beings never do and indeed *cannot* act in certain ways, then, knowing this, in deliberation I cannot reasonably treat acting in these ways as an option. Imagine, for example, that I am aware that scientists have discovered, in a series of horrible experiments, that no one can persist in a plan to protect others if tortured to a certain measurable degree. Then, if confronted with the prospect of such torture, I can be sure that I will 'crack' just as others have; and knowing that I cannot withstand the torture, I cannot sincerely deliberate about whether to do so, treating this as one of my options.[20] I could, of course, deliberate about whether to *try as long as possible*, and to do so might be a heroic gesture; but if I were *fully* convinced that I could succeed in achieving an end (e.g., not giving any information under torture), it would be conceptually impossible for me to deliberate about whether to achieve that end.[21] Similarly, if empirical psychology gives decisive evidence that people do not and cannot always maintain benevolent feelings towards those who grossly abuse

---

[20] This is a conceptual point. That is, if a person really knows and is immediately and fully aware that it is impossible for him to do something, then it does not make sense to describe the person as 'deliberating.' I might stand before a thousand-pound weight mouthing the words 'Shall I—or shall I not—lift it?'—but anyone who knows that I know that I cannot lift it will also know that I am joking.

[21] In most actual cases, perhaps, those who face torture do not know for certain that they cannot withstand the degree of torture that they will receive. Even a glimmer of hope that one might succeed, despite weighty but not decisive evidence, might be enough to enable one to 'decide' to succeed. One can also self-deceptively 'half-believe,' contrary to solid evidence and one's own 'best judgment,' and sometimes, no doubt, doing so has good results. But the main point remains that deliberating about what to do presupposes seeing oneself as having options, and empirical evidence can sometimes show quite decisively that ways we might wish to act are not in fact options.

them and their children, then, knowing this, I could not deliberately make it a policy to have nothing but love in my heart for everyone, no matter what.

These are merely special instances of the obvious point that, in deliberating about what one ought to do, one *cannot sincerely* consider as an option something one *knows* that one cannot do. Moreover, except in special circumstances, one *cannot reasonably* treat something as an option when available empirical evidence *most strongly indicates* that one cannot do it.[22] For example, since there is ample evidence that human beings cannot run a three-minute mile or hold their breath for an hour, one cannot, unless ignorant, deliberate about whether to do these things; and 'trying' is unreasonable. All this seems only common sense.

Unfortunately, Kant at times seems to suggest a contrary view, that is, that we must first determine our duty independently of empirical evidence and then simply infer (from 'ought' implies 'can') that we can do it. To proceed this way in general would be foolish, for certain limits to our capacities can be empirically determined and (by 'ought' implies 'can') these limits are also constraints on what we can reasonably judge that we ought to do. If empirical investigation is inconclusive regarding what we can do, leaving room for hope, sometimes there may be special considerations for first thinking, 'What should we do if we can?' and then proceeding to make resolutions and plans in the faith that we can act accordingly, despite some counter-evidence. But to proceed from 'duty' to 'can' in this way makes sense only in special conditions. Even William James, who carried pragmatic faith to an extreme, called for a 'will to believe' in possibilities only when empirical evidence did not weigh against them.[23] (Similarly, in the *Critique of Pure Reason* Kant is careful to speculate about agent-initiated causation only after trying to establish that there could be no empirical evidence against believing in it.)[24] Kant's main ideas about practical deliberation, I think, are not incompatible with the common-sense position on these matters. In any case, the 'Kantian' perspective I am sketching here will take for granted that common-sense position.

---

[22] The special circumstance that might make it reasonable to try to do what seems almost certainly impossible (thereby *treating* it as an option) might be, for example, the fact that nothing else can save one's life or one's friends.

[23] William James, *The Will to Believe and Other Essays* (New York: Dover, 1956).

[24] See especially 'The Third Antinomy', C1, 409–17 [A: 445–55, B: 473–84], 422–30 [A: 462–76, B: 490–504], and 439–59 [A: 491–523, B: 519–51]. Regarding Kant's views on causation, see n. 10 above.

C. The Case for Doubting that Altruism is Possible

The relevant question, then, is neither whether our behavior is uncaused nor whether our options for choice are unlimited. Obviously, there is much that we cannot do even if we choose to, and also much that we cannot even choose to do. The question at hand is whether we can, by choice, be altruistic in the ways necessary for there to be a genuine and meaningful duty to be altruistic. Can I reasonably consider it 'up to me' in the senses presupposed if I am to make the practical judgment 'I ought'? The possible obstacles to believing in my freedom to be altruistic are not special individual circumstances, such as my being penniless, paralyzed, or isolated from others. Nor are the obstacles the (already conceded) general thesis that all behavior has causes, or the (empirically unsupported) particular belief that human beings never behave in ways beneficial to others without perceived personal benefit. The main challenge to the idea that it is 'up to us' whether to be altruistic comes from three claims: that what motivates us to act are the feelings we have at the time; that we cannot simply choose what to feel; and that genuine benevolent feelings towards others, if not impossible, are rare, unstable, and directed to our close associates. Thus, allegedly, we will act for the sake of others only if we feel warm towards them; but our warm feelings are severely limited, and whether we feel warm, cool, or hotly antagonistic towards others is not something we control by will.

Simply noting that we can to some extent cultivate dispositions to feel kind towards others does not solve the problem for Kantians. Admittedly, by doing things now we can sometimes affect our feelings in the future, but this process is indirect, difficult, and often ineffective. More importantly, acknowledging an ability to influence one's later feelings indirectly would give one no reason to believe that one can be altruistic now, when (let us suppose) one is feeling rather cool towards others. But it seems odd to suppose that the duty of beneficence, if there is one, would bind us only when we are 'in the mood.' It seems almost as bizarre to think that, to those feeling cool to others, the duty says merely, 'Do what will indirectly *result* in your being in an altruistic mood, so that then your feelings will *cause* you to give proper help to others.'

IV. CONDITIONAL KANTIAN ANSWER: THE POSSIBILITY OF REASONABLE BENEFICENCE

Kant, of course, held that we have a duty of beneficence and that we can act as it requires. How then does he respond to the challenge sketched above, that we are moved by our feelings, which are not 'up to us' and tend to be nonaltruistic? The reply, I think, has several parts worth considering separately.

1. Since the challenge suggests that we cannot simply choose to be altruistic, the first step is to clarify the relevant idea of 'being altruistic.' More specifically, in order to consider whether we can be altruistic, as many think duty requires, we need first to define the sort of altruism that we suppose morality demands. For Kant this is the duty of beneficence.[25] This is not a duty to feel warm towards others, but to take action to promote the happiness of others. Strictly, it is a duty to make it one's 'maxim' to promote the (morally permissible) ends of others. But the duty is 'nonjuridical'; it is not the correlative of *rights* of those we may help, and one cannot be legitimately coerced to comply with the duty.[26] Moreover, the duty is an 'imperfect duty' of the 'widest' obligation. As such, it leaves 'playroom' for free action, and does not specify how much, to whom, or when one should be beneficent. What is strictly *wrong* is to reject the principle of beneficence, that is, to refuse to count the ends of others as important in one's deliberations.

On Kant's view, it is only reasonable (as well as an 'indirect duty') to pursue one's own happiness, and, contrary to Bentham, what one morally ought to do is not determined by what will maximize happiness overall, counting each person's pleasures and pains (of equal intensity, duration, etc.) as equal on a quantitative scale to each other person's.[27] Promoting the happiness of others is also not the prima facie duty of beneficence as W. D. Ross influentially defined it. There are two important differences.[28] First, Kant held that, though the duty

---

[25] MM, 151–7 [6: 388–95], 161–2 [6: 401–2], and 198–208 [6: 448–61]. Kant claims that we do have a duty of beneficence of the sort he describes, but at this point in the essay we should consider it merely a *supposed* duty, because we have not yet considered any reasons for it and are still considering the question whether it is possible for us to do what it prescribes. If we assume now that beneficence is really a duty, then we could *simply infer* that we can conform to it because, in the relevant senses, 'ought' implies 'can.' But obviously that would be too facile a reply to those egoists who (relying on the idea that 'cannot' implies 'not ought') would argue the reverse, i.e., that we have no duty of beneficence because acting altruistically (they say) is impossible.

[26] These distinctions are discussed at length in Mary Gregor, *Laws of Freedom* (Oxford: Blackwell, 1963); and also in my *Dignity and Practical Reason*, ch. 8.

[27] See Jeremy Bentham, *An Introduction to the Principles of Morals and Legislation*, especially chs. 1 and 4. The work is available in many editions, including *A Fragment on Government and An Introduction to the Principles of Morals and Legislation*, ed. Wilfrid Harrison (Oxford: Blackwell Publishers, 1960).

[28] See W. D. Ross, *The Right and the Good* (Oxford: Clarendon Press, 1930), 16–47. A prima facie duty, according to Ross, is a feature of an act that would make the act an actual duty (i.e., a duty, all things considered) if there were no conflicting moral

of beneficence allows much room for individual choice about when and how much to help others, one is strictly required to make it one's principle (maxim) to promote the happiness of others.[29] Second, despite this, Kant's imperfect duty of beneficence is more lenient in practice than Ross's prima facie duty of beneficence, for unlike Ross's, Kant's principle does not imply that it is one's actual duty to promote others' happiness on every occasion when one can and other duties are absent.

The importance of these points for the issue at hand is this: by circumscribing *what* altruism requires, Kant makes it more plausible that we can be altruistic as required. What is obligatory is adopting a modest maxim of beneficence and choosing over time to act accordingly. The demands on action are flexible and limited, and there are no demands for warm sentiments. This by itself does not resolve all doubts about the possibility of altruism, however, for some will say that no one *can* act as the duty of beneficence requires unless driven by other-regarding sentiments.

2. Another background claim important to the Kantian answer is that the empirical evidence, as reviewed above, does not establish that we cannot behave in the ways that the duty of beneficence directs.[30] Observation raises doubts about the depth and frequency of purely altruistic feelings, but it reveals that people do sometimes, and so can, contribute to the good of others, even at some cost to themselves. Whatever their deep motives, which we may never know fully, some apparently adopt the policy of beneficence and act accordingly.

This alone is not sufficient to dismiss relevant doubts about the

---

considerations. Examples of such features include: that an act fulfills a promise, that it returns a favor, that it promotes someone's happiness, or that it makes reparation for past wrongs.

[29] Kant's view, as I understand it, is that everyone is strictly required to maintain as an effective guiding principle (or maxim): 'Promote the happiness of others, counting their (permissible) ends as among your own ends.' Like Ross's prima facie duty of beneficence, this principle does not specify exactly how, when, or how much one must do for others. (For qualification, see Ch. 7 of this volume.) Unlike Ross, however, Kant held that the duty of beneficence cannot be fully satisfied by helping others unless one makes it a principle to do so. (Kant also implies, even beyond this, that one must maintain the principle for moral reasons, not merely for self-interested reasons; but this introduces complications best left aside here.) On Ross's view, *adopting the maxim* as one's personal action-guiding standard is neither a prima facie duty nor an actual duty. For Ross the principle 'It is a prima facie duty to promote the happiness of others' is supposed to be a self-evident truth that once recognized tends to motivate, but one can satisfy this principle by doing what makes others happy even if one never makes it a principle to do so.

[30] See Section III (A) above.

possibility of altruism, however; for observation merely shows that beneficence is within human capacities, not that you and I, at the time of deliberation and action, can act beneficently. There are many things that are within human capacities in the sense that people can do them when they are in the mood (cry, fall asleep, make love, be creative), but one cannot always simply choose to be in the mood. Experience, one might argue, leaves it unsettled whether at particular moments of choice I can or cannot maintain and follow a maxim to benefit others.

3. There are certain general presuppositions that anyone who is sincerely deliberating must make. Without these we can only predict or 'wait and see' what we do, rather than trying to decide reasonably what *to do*. Most obviously we presuppose that we have some *options* before us that we can take and we can refrain from taking. Moreover, when we deliberate we consider *reasons* for choosing to do one thing rather than the other. These can be expressed as propositions that we believe to be true and that upon reflection we count in favor of or against an option: e.g., that eating more now will make me sick, that telling the truth about Jill will anger Harry, or that giving to Oxfam will lessen a child's misery.

Even the feelings we have at the moment, so far as we can recognize them, enter deliberation as possible considerations for or against options.[31] The fact that we have them is potentially relevant information, to be reviewed along with information about how we expect to feel later, how others are affected, and much besides. Of course, we also 'experience' our sentiments of the moment as yearnings, leanings, aversions, inclining us for or against options; but, if sincerely deliberating, we do not see the sentiments as pushes and pulls, like vector forces, determining what we will do.[32] When, for example, I feel an urge to abandon a writing project, have a snack or write an insulting letter, then in reasonable deliberation *the fact that* I have such an urge is a proposition to review in my project to find which option is supported by the

---

[31] Unrecognized feelings, of course, cannot enter the deliberation. That is, though sometimes they may unfortunately distort our judgment in ways we are helpless to prevent, the fact that they may be present is irrelevant to the question under deliberation, 'What ought I to do?' Learning empirically that unrecognized feelings can skew our judgments gives us reason to be wary and to seek greater self-awareness; and in extreme cases, e.g., where afterthought reveals a pattern, suspecting that my judgment is likely to be skewed may be a reason not to try to deliberate at all. But once an issue is up for deliberation, I must treat facts about how I feel, like all other facts, as data for reasonable decision making, not as controlling forces.

[32] This Kantian (and, I believe, common-sense) view of deliberation contrasts significantly with that of Hobbes. See *Leviathan*, part I, ch. 6, pp. 127–8.

best reasons. Only when that is settled can I treat the urge as an aid, or obstacle, in carrying out my plans.

4. A crucial further presupposition of deliberation, on the Kantian view, is that one can act on what one judges to be the best reasons. If one deliberates reasonably one has already excluded from the list of options any action that one has strong reason to believe one cannot do; so addictions and any susceptibility to 'irresistible impulses,' if empirically substantiated as special incapacities, have already been accounted for. Absent these, deliberative reflection must proceed on the assumption that after reviewing the possible pros and cons, one can act as directed by what one judged to be the best reasons. To do so, after all, is the point of the project of deliberating. The idea is to determine what *to do*, not merely to consider what would be desirable if one were to do it. So only what we believe to be options are on the agenda.

5. Now we can imagine the following objection arising. Suppose you have assessed the background of your problem, estimated the consequences, and identified as well as you can the inclinations you have for and against. Suppose, further, that you have weighed these considerations appropriately, giving due regard (or disregard) to each. Now having made a reasonable deliberate decision as to what you ought to do, you must act. Let us grant that in your deliberations it was reasonable to assume that you could act a certain way, e.g., beneficently, but you could not be aware of the very state of mind/desire/preference that you would be in at the moment you set yourself to act. This state consists of impulses and sentiments that may be different from those you identified in deliberation, and this state, rather than your deliberative judgment, may be what finally moves you. If the unidentified feelings actually present at the moment of action are not predominantly warm towards others, then, for all your fine deliberations, you may not act on your reasoned decision to act beneficently. Call this 'weakness of will' or whatever, the presumption in deliberation that you can and will follow your final judgment as to what you ought to do may prove false.

To this objection, the Kantian reply might go as follows. First, admittedly we do often observe that people act contrary to their professed judgments as to what they ought to do. Knowing this, even when deliberating I should perhaps acknowledge that it is possible that I will not in fact act on my best judgment. But since the point of deliberation is to find the best reasons in order to act on them, when deliberating I must *intend* to do so and thus anticipate that I will. For purposes of my deliberative task (e.g., trying to decide whether to act beneficently), the *possibility* that I will deviate from my best judgment in the end is simply irrelevant.

Now if I had overwhelming *antecedent* evidence that I *could* not act in a certain way (e.g., beneficently) even if I tried, then *that* would be relevant to my deliberative task (making it reasonable for me to rule out acting beneficently as an option). But, by hypothesis, this is not the situation in question. The objection under consideration hypothesized that momentary inclinations might prevent me from following even my best deliberations, which must have already taken into account the available antecedent evidence as to what I can and cannot do. In sum, lacking powerful empirical evidence that I cannot act beneficently if I judge this best, it still makes sense to continue to deliberate about this. And the mere possibility that unknown conditions will somehow prevent me from behaving as I judge best is irrelevant to my task, for it is not a reason for or against deciding that I ought to do the beneficent thing.

Behind the objection above there seems to lie a picture of human acts and motives that does not fit well with either science or how we conceive of ourselves. The model seems to be this: inner impulses mechanically cause the behavior that immediately follows. Terms from our practical vocabulary (desiring, liking, feeling inclined, etc.) are transported into quasi-scientific explanations, even though what they refer to is not measurable and often is not even identifiable before the behavior it is said to cause. Also, the model does not fit our normative conception of ourselves as agents in typical cases. Except in extraordinary cases, for example, we do not count momentary contrary sentiments as excusing us from acting as we judge we ought. Imagine: 'I knew that I should meet you at noon as I promised, but I couldn't because I felt an urge for a pizza.' Or: 'I thought I should donate but, just as I was about to, a sudden feeling of greed made me refuse.'

Thinking practically, we suppose that in most cases our feelings incline but do not coerce, that they are potentially relevant data for decision making and not forces that bypass deliberative processes, and that weakness of will is often just *willing weakly* rather than *lacking willpower*.[33] These ideas, in any case, are the presuppositions of the Kantian perspective that I am trying to characterize.

---

[33] This distinction, admittedly controversial, is discussed at length in 'Weakness of Will and Character', in my collection of essays *Autonomy and Self-Respect*, 9. Roughly, the idea is that what we call 'weakness of will' is often not a disability beyond the agent's control (*lack of willpower*) but rather the agent's pattern, for which he or she may be responsible, of making half-hearted efforts, breaking and fudging resolutions, and not following through on projects and commitments (*willing weakly*).

6. Another assumption of the Kantian perspective is that our inclinations in deliberation are not necessarily good reasons to act. What reason prescribes is not simply a function of how one feels at the time of decision (or even of anticipated satisfactions over time). That we desire or feel a preference for doing something is not *necessarily* any reason to do it; though, of course, we naturally count it as a reason in the absence of countervailing considerations. What facts are good reasons in favor of a project is something that must be determined by reflecting under rational procedural constraints, not something fixed in advance by nature or anyone's authority.[34]

Since we presuppose that we can act on the best reasons and that our feelings at the moment do not always correspond to what we judge good reasons, we are committed to the idea that we can do what we consider reasonable, whether or not this conflicts with what we feel inclined to do. The upshot is this: we can now see that Kantian deliberation presupposes that we *can* act beneficently, independently of how we are feeling towards others, *if we acknowledge good reasons for doing so.* We can act on our best reasons, and these are not a function of how warm or cold we feel toward others but are rather something to be worked out in an appropriate sort of reflection. Thus, the historical debate about how common, pure, and stable altruistic feelings are becomes irrelevant from the Kantian perspective, for on this view the practical issue about the possibility of altruism does not turn on what *sentiments* we have but rather on whether we can find adequate *reasons*, on reflection, for adopting at least the modest maxim of beneficence. We must now turn, at least briefly, to this final issue.

V. IS BENEFICENCE A REASONABLE REQUIREMENT?

From a deliberative perspective, then, we must suppose that we can act beneficently if there is adequate reason to do so. For Kantians addressing doubts about the possibility of altruism, therefore, the remaining question is whether the alleged duty of beneficence is really a require-

---

[34] The ideas expressed here, as well as some in the preceding three sections, are part of what Kant seems to have meant in claiming that it is necessary in conceiving ourselves as moral agents to take ourselves to have *autonomy* of the will. For further discussion, see my *Dignity and Practical Reason*, ch. 5; my *Autonomy and Self-Respect*, ch. 12; and Allison, *Kant's Theory of Freedom*, ch. 5.

ment of reason. This is a large topic, but for now a few comments must suffice.

First, we have already noted a number of points that tell us something about what the Kantian argument for beneficence must be like. For example, since having an inclination or sentiment does not necessarily give one a reason to act, we could not simply infer a duty of beneficence from sentiments of benevolence, even if these were universal and felt by all impartial spectators. Because the duty is supposed to stand regardless of variations in the warmth of our feelings towards others, the reason for acknowledging the duty must not vary with such feelings. An enlightened concern for one's own interest would meet this criterion, supposing (with Joseph Butler and others) that beneficence coincides with self-interest. But Kantians cannot rely on an argument from enlightened self-interest, for the duty of beneficence is supposed to be a categorical imperative, binding us independently of our interests. Appeals to the authority of tradition, community values, and God's commands will not serve the purpose, for the reasons the Kantian seeks are ones that any reasonable, conscientious agent will acknowledge, if thinking deeply and clearly. Thus, many of the traditional arguments for helping others are ruled out at the start.

Kant addresses the problem in several places. In the *Groundwork*, the final example to illustrate two formulations of the Categorical Imperative is a case where a person who is well-off considers refusing to help others who are 'struggling under great hardships.'[35] Here the problem whether to help is narrower, and perhaps easier to handle, than some other cases that could fall under the imperfect duty to promote the happiness of others. A principle of 'mutual aid' might suffice: that is, a principle prescribing that one help those in need if the cost to oneself is little. (Compare the more general characterization of the duty of beneficence: make it one's principle to promote the permissible ends of others.) Even in *The Metaphysics of Morals* Kant's arguments are focused on cases where one can help someone in need (as opposed, say, to 'doing favors' for the well-off). To simplify, then, let us also concentrate, for now, on the imperfect duty of beneficence only as it applies to cases of needy recipients and comfortable givers.

Kant argues for a duty of beneficence not only from the universal-law formula of the Categorical Imperative, but also from the formula of humanity as an end in itself.[36] An even more persuasive case might be

---

[35] G, 90 [4: 423] and 98 [4: 430].   [36] Ibid.

made, I suspect, from a reconstructed formula of the kingdom of ends.[37] But here I will discuss only arguments that appeal to the universal-law formula. There are variations even in these arguments, but some main points remain the same. Here is one version.[38]

The reason that it is a duty to be beneficent is this: since our self-love cannot be separated from our need to be loved (helped in case of need) by others as well, we therefore make ourselves an end for others; and the only way this maxim can be binding is through its qualification as a universal law, hence through our will to make others our end as well. The happiness of others is therefore an end that is also a duty.[39]

The argument here appeals to certain ideas that appear in virtually all versions: (i) the fact that we have a special self-regard (self-love, concern for our happiness, valuing our humanity as an 'end in itself'); (ii) the fact that, as human beings, we have needs that only others can meet (their assistance, their love); and (iii) a general moral assumption that we should consider what we are proposing to do from a broader perspective, looking beyond the immediate case and our own projects toward what would be reasonable 'universal laws.' This moral assumption, of course, is what Kant tried to express in several formulations of the Categorical Imperative.

There are different ways to reconstruct the Kantian rationale for beneficence, depending on how one construes the famous universal-law formula of the Categorical Imperative.[40] The details are controversial, but some points seem clear enough.

---

[37] Kant presents this formula in G, 100–2 [4: 433–4] and 105–7 [4: 438–9]. And my efforts to reconstruct it are cited in n. 6 above.

[38] Some other versions are the following: '... every morally practical relation to human beings is a relation among them represented by pure reason, that is, a relation of free actions in accordance with maxims that qualify for a giving of universal law and so cannot be selfish.... I want everyone else to be benevolent toward me ... ; hence I ought also to be benevolent toward everyone else' (MM, 200 [6: 451]). 'To be beneficent, that is, to promote according to one's means the happiness of others in need, without hoping for something in return, is everyone's duty.

'For everyone who finds himself in need wishes to be helped by others. But if he lets his maxim of being unwilling to assist others in turn when they are in need become public, that is, makes this a universal permissive law, then everyone would likewise deny him assistance when he himself is in need, or at least would be authorized to deny it. Hence the maxim of self-interest would conflict with itself if it were made a universal law, that is, contrary to duty. Consequently the maxim of common interest, of beneficence toward those in need, is a universal duty of human beings, just because they are to be considered fellow men, that is, rational beings with needs, united by nature in one dwelling place so that they can help one another' (MM, 202 [6: 453]).

[39] MM, 155–6 [6: 393].

[40] For some of the many interpretations, see the following: Christine Korsgaard,

For example, though the rationale begins with the fact that we love ourselves and need the love and help of others, the point is not that it actually pays to be beneficent. The point is not simply that if you scratch others' backs, then they *will* in fact scratch yours. That, of course, is not always true: sometimes no one helps the helpers. More importantly, what is to be justified is a moral duty, i.e., a categorical imperative, and this prescribes what one ought to do, whether it serves one's interests or not. Even if helping others is not the best strategy to obtain help when we need it, Kant holds that we cannot reasonably refuse all help to others.

It is also clear that the initial assumptions are not special claims about individual circumstances but rather quite general features of the human condition, namely, that we are the sort of creatures who have self-love and need the love and help of others. The degree to which individuals have self-love and need help varies, but that may not matter since the principle to be justified does not specify any particular amount that one is required to help others. Self-love, having happiness as an end, and wanting things that may require the assistance of others are features of us as human beings with feelings, but the concerns in question are not rare and unstable, as (in Kant's opinion) altruistic feelings are. Moreover, self-love obviously gives us steady reasons for acting, even though our particular moods may vary. Indeed, our concern for happiness, at least when not in conflict with moral demands, gives us reasons that typically override the reasons provided by particular desires and aims.

One common way of reconstructing the Kantian argument, drawing particularly from the *Groundwork*, runs as follows.[41] It is wrong to act on maxims that one cannot will as universal law. A person who repeatedly refused to help others in need, failing to adopt even an indefinite policy of promoting the ends of others, would be acting on the maxim: 'I'll never help others, even when their need is great and the cost to me is little.' As 'universal law,' this would be: 'Everyone will [or may] never help others, even when their need is great and the cost of helping is

---

'Kant's Formula of Universal Law', *Pacific Philosophical Quarterly*, 66 (1985), 24–47; Onora O'Neill, *Constructions of Reason* (Cambridge: Cambridge University Press, 1989), 81–104; Onora [O'Neill] Nell, *Acting on Principle* (New York: Columbia University Press, 1975); Nelson T. Potter and Mark Timmons (eds.), *Morality and Universality: Essays on Ethical Universalizability* (Dordrecht: Reidel, 1985); M. G. Singer, *Generalization in Ethics* (New York: Alfred A. Knopf, 1961), 217–99; and Barbara Herman, 'Mutual Aid and Respect for Persons', *Ethics*, 94 (1984), 577–602.

[41] G, 90–1 [4: 423].

little.' As a reasonably prudent person, aware that everyone is liable to fall into need, you 'could not will' such a law. To do so would conflict with your 'will' to pursue happiness prudently. Hence it is wrong for you to act on your maxim to refuse to help others. The only way to avoid this is to make it a policy to help others sometimes. If something is the only way to avoid doing wrong, then it is a duty. Hence it is your duty to adopt the policy to help others sometimes.

Now, there seems to be something right about this; but when we try to construe it as a rigorous argument, all sorts of problems arise. Most obviously, we need criteria for how to specify a maxim, more information about what enables one to will or not will a universal law, and some account of why the universal-law formula of the Categorical Imperative is a morally necessary assumption. Kant's critics and sympathizers have played with these problems for many years, but I remain doubtful that they can ever be resolved sufficiently to justify using the universal-law formula as a rigorous moral decision procedure—or even as a loose and partial action-guide *operating independently of other moral judgments*. But there are some other ways of thinking of the Kantian rationale for beneficence. These are obviously not rigorous proofs that helping others is rational. Rather, to twist a phrase of Daniel Dennett's they are 'conscience pumps.'[42]

In one version of the argument for beneficence, Kant says that we 'make ourselves an end for others.' This suggests a consideration that is true for virtually everyone. Though we no doubt have a current desire that we be helped in the future if we should become needy, this is not all. We also have accepted and asked for help in the past; we are willingly dependent on others' help now; and, if honest, we should admit that we intend to ask for and count on help from others later. That is, we in fact *will* the help of others in past activities, current dependencies, and future plans. In effect, we ask others to give some consideration to our ends when they set their own plans and goals.

The moral question, then, is this: Can we conscientiously ask and expect others to limit their own pursuit of self-interest to help us if we are unwilling to reciprocate? The minimal moral assumption here is that we cannot demand sacrifices from others when we are unwilling to sacrifice for anyone, unless we could cite special facts that might justify this. Sometimes, of course, there will be morally relevant differences between my situation and theirs, but one could not honestly and real-

---

[42] Dennett's phrase is 'intuition pumps.' See Daniel Dennett, *Elbow Room* (Cambridge: MIT Press, 1984), 12.

istically claim that such differences justify my not helping as a rule. It is logically possible, but practically absurd, to judge that there are relevant differences in every case between others' helping and my helping.

This familiar line of thought does not pretend to be a rigorous deduction, and it frankly calls for morally informed judgment as well as honest thinking and realistic assessment of the facts. Nonetheless, it uses the main ideas that Kant appeals to in his arguments, and for those who take our initial perspective of reasonable, minimally conscientious agents, it may be enough for practical purposes.

A few may object on the grounds that they sincerely try to avoid accepting help from anyone. They declare a policy of 'rugged individualism,' swim or sink, every dog for himself, show no pity and ask for none. Let us imagine that their record gives evidence of their sincerity: for example, they have often risked ruin and death by refusing to accept aid from others. Now to appeal to them to acknowledge that they have in fact 'made themselves an end for others' seems insufficient.

This suggests a possible way of extending the Kantian rationale. The idea that we *will* the help of others, making ourselves an end for them, need not be construed as our making actual demands for others' help (though most of us do). What we 'will,' in Kantian theory, is not identical with what we wish, or even ask for. Often it refers to our deep commitments based on what we count as good reasons, considerations that survive critical rational reflection. So we might construe the idea that we will the help of others, not as saying that we actually demand it, but rather as claiming that, if we reflect deeply, we will realize that it only makes sense for others to help us when we are in dire need. In effect, the question is: 'Given the facts, don't you really think that there are good and sufficient reasons for you to ask for help when you need it and to expect others to give it sometimes?'

The point of the question would not be to prove that one should be beneficent. The aim would be simply to focus attention on the case closest to our hearts, so we can see more clearly that we are committed to a judgment that presupposes a duty of beneficence. Thinking first of your desperately needing help may serve to pump the conscientious judgment 'They should help me.' But to say they 'should,' that it is only reasonable for them to help, calls for a general principle to support it. In saying, as reasonable and minimally conscientious persons, 'They should help,' we are not just saying that it serves my self-interest—or theirs. We have implicitly moved to a level of reflection where we critically review policies of helping and refusing to help in general, or as 'universal laws.' Here, presumably, most will find that they cannot conscientiously approve of the 'no help' policy. The 'argument' cannot force them or prove that they must, but it turns moral reflection in the right direction.

These brief and loose remarks are not meant to endorse the idea that we strictly perceive or 'intuit' what is right, even though I used the metaphor of 'seeing.' In Kantian ethics, what is right specifically is the product of rational reflection of an appropriate kind. At times we can 'see' without lengthy discussion what is implied by our deepest rational commitments, but this calls for confirmation in thorough discussion. Compare an employer's 'intuition' that his employee is a thief: it may be useful, even reliable, but it is no substitute for evidence. Thus, when I claim that we 'see' that the principle of beneficence is reasonable when we deliberate from a minimally conscientious Kantian perspective, I must acknowledge the need for a deeper, more thorough account of the moral point of view and of why, from this standpoint, beneficence is reasonable. To do this more thorough job in a Kantian theory, we need to give more weight to the later versions of the Categorical Imperative, give up thinking of these formulas as direct action-guides for specific cases, and be willing to trim, refurbish, and repair the grand old edifice that Kant himself constructed. And, unless we can find ways to illuminate them, we may need to abandon some of the darker rooms.

5

Reasonable Self-Interest

I. INTRODUCTION

Philosophers have debated for millennia about whether moral requirements are always rational to follow. The background for these debates is often what I shall call 'the self-interest model.' The guiding assumption here is that the basic demand of reason, to each person, is that one must, above all, advance one's self-interest. Alternatively, debate may be framed by a related, but significantly different, assumption: the idea that the basic rational requirement is to develop and pursue a set of personal ends in an informed, efficient, and coherent way, whether one's choice of ends is based on self-interested desires or not. For brevity I refer to this as 'the coherence-and-efficiency model.' Advocates of both models tend to think that, while it is sufficiently clear in principle what the rational thing to do is, what remains in doubt is whether it is always rational to be moral. They typically assume that morality is concerned, entirely or primarily, with our relations to others, especially with obligations that appear to require some sacrifice or compromise with the pursuit of self-interest. If there are any self-regarding moral duties, on this view, they must be derivative from duties to others—they must be understood, for example, as what we must do to remain fit to fulfill our responsibilities as parents, friends, citizens, etc.[1] Moral philosophers who share these assumptions have naturally supposed that their primary task is to answer the question 'Why be moral?' or, in other words, 'How can we show that fulfilling one's moral obligations to others will also

I would like to thank David Brink, Stephen Darwall, Chris Morris, Michael Slote, and Ellen Frankel Paul, for their helpful comments on an earlier draft of this essay.

[1] By 'self-interest' I mean to include, roughly, one's welfare, what is good for one, what is beneficial to one insofar as one is concerned with one's own well-being. 'Self-regard' has broader uses. For example, a self-regarding duty may be simply to treat oneself in a certain way (e.g., protecting one's health) even if the justification has nothing to do with one's personal interest in one's own welfare but stems instead, say, from one's promise to a spouse. To act out of 'self-regard,' however, seems properly understood as the same as acting out of self-interest. My understanding here, I hope, simply follows ordinary usage.

satisfy reason's nonmoral demand that one always advance one's self-interest or pursue one's personal ends in an informed, efficient, and coherent manner?' Any attempted answer, obviously, must appeal to contingent facts, such as the (supposed) inner rewards of virtue and the personal benefits of having a secure reputation for honesty and fair dealing.[2] Despite heroic efforts of philosophers to 'defend' morality along these lines, there seems to be an emerging consensus that, although such contingent arguments may be adequate to convince most of us under normal conditions, they fail to show that it is *always* rational to be moral.

A radically different picture of the relations between reason, self-interest, and morality draws both (moral) other-regarding requirements and (nonmoral or moral) self-regarding requirements from a common source, our judgments of intrinsic value. According to this picture, which I label 'the consequentialist model,' we judge many things to be good as means (e.g., money, possessions, reputation, and power), but their value ultimately depends on their usefulness in promoting what we judge to be good as an end and 'intrinsically valuable' (e.g., pleasure, happiness, friendship, and/or intellectual activity). Having a good reason to do something, on this model, amounts to being able to promote an intrinsic value (e.g., pleasure) or hinder an intrinsic disvalue (e.g., pain). The most rational thing to do would be whatever, on balance, one has the most good reason to do, that is, whatever contributes most to the greatest possible sum of intrinsic value. From this basic requirement of reason, we can derive both self-regarding and other-regarding requirements. Some hesitate to use the label 'moral' for the rational requirement to promote intrinsic values, such as pleasure, *in oneself*, but such self-regarding imperatives have the same *source* as other-regarding imperatives and the same *strictness*, assuming comparability in other respects. To show that it is reasonable to fulfill our other-regarding obligations, on this account, one must use the same method needed to show that limited pursuit of self-interest is reasonable. In both cases, that is, one needs to argue that the conduct in question maximizes (positive) intrinsic value. This general picture underlies utilitarianism of many kinds and, more broadly, most consequentialist theories. Like the first approach, the consequentialist model has a long history but remains open to serious doubts: for example, doubts about whether *objective* intrinsic value judgments are possible, about whether

---

[2] According to the coherence-and-efficiency model, one can also appeal to empirical facts about our other-regarding desires, because this model does not assume that the ends one wants to fulfill are all benefits for oneself.

(even if so) rationality requires each person to maximize such 'agent-neutral' goods, and about whether the prescriptions justified by such a method would closely resemble what we recognize as 'morality.'

Regarding the relations among reason, self-interest, and morality, various forms of the self-interest model, the coherence-and-efficiency model, and the consequentialist model have largely dominated contemporary discussions; but there is an alternative worth considering. I label this alternative 'the Kantian model' because its main elements are drawn from Kant's work, but I do not intend to explicate, or even to endorse, all aspects of Kant's views about practical reason. My aim, instead, is, first, to *describe* this Kantian idea of the connections between reason, self-interest, and morality; then, to *contrast* it with the three classic models sketched above; and, finally, to draw attention to how well the Kantian model fits with (what I take to be) views widely shared among ordinary people without prior commitments to philosophical theories. That the Kantian view has striking affinities with the assumptions of 'common sense,' I concede, is no proof of the correctness of either the Kantian view or the common assumptions; but it is a fact, I suggest, that warrants giving the Kantian view on these matters more serious consideration than it usually receives in contemporary discussions.

For ease of exposition I will begin with *what I take to be* a 'common-sense' view, relatively unencumbered with the technical terminology of philosophical theories. Although I will try to present this in a way that reveals it as a familiar and sensible perspective, I do not plan to defend it against skeptics or even to *argue* that it is a widely held view.[3] Instead, my aim is merely to call attention to ways in which the view I attribute to common sense is at odds with the three philosophical models sketched above, but not with the Kantian model that I shall sketch. In fact, I suggest, the common-sense view is just the practical result that the Kantian model, reasonably construed, supports and explains.

[3] These tasks are obviously too much to take on here. Defending what I call 'the common-sense view' would by itself be a major philosophical project, and establishing its credentials as very widely held among many otherwise diverse peoples would be a very challenging sociological/historical task. Neither is necessary for my purposes, though admittedly my conclusions will be of less interest to those who deny the plausibility or the breadth of appeal of the view I attribute to common sense. The main point is that this view, sketched here in familiar, nontechnical language, seems to have more affinity with the Kantian model, despite the austere Kantian terminology, than with the self-interest model, the coherence-and-efficiency model, or the consequentialist model. Readers, I expect, will find this claim more striking and important the more they agree with my conjecture that what I call 'the common-sense view' is plausible and widely held; but the extent to which they agree on this is a matter for each to judge.

Although this conclusion is modest, it is not insignificant; for, if I am right, the Kantian model, which is often dismissed because of its alien terminology or its (supposed) dubious metaphysical commitments, turns out to represent something closer to our ordinary, pretheoretical views than it is usually thought. This may help us to 'make sense' of the Kantian view, even if we choose in the end to reject it; and, since widely shared views are at stake, it may lead us to question more seriously the background assumptions of the alternative, currently dominant models of practical rationality.

One brief caveat is needed before I proceed. Since my aim is to compare certain general 'models,' 'perspectives,' or background assumptions that characterize various debates about reason, self-interest, and morality, I will need to paint with a broad brush, leaving many matters of detail for later. Obviously, contemporary choice theorists give subtly different accounts of how efficiency, coherence, and information figure in instrumental reasoning; consequentialism comes in many varieties; and Kantians differ among themselves regarding which are the most 'essential' features of Kant's philosophy. There are many 'in house' debates over fine points among advocates of the same general 'model,' and these are not to be disparaged. My hope, however, is that we may gain some further understanding by taking, in addition, a broader 'overview' of some major differences in approach. Too often, I suspect, those deeply committed to very different approaches fail to understand one another because they raise questions and look for answers in terms that make sense only within their background framework of thought. Objections that seem decisive to some, then, strike others as utterly without force, and larger issues about the merits and disadvantages of the alternative frameworks are too often ignored.

II. A COMMON-SENSE VIEW OF REASON, SELF-INTEREST, AND MORALITY

If we try to suspend our commitments to philosophical theories, I suspect, we will not find ourselves talking so much of 'principles of rational choice,' 'practical reason,' and the like, but rather about what we have 'good reasons' to do, what is 'reasonable,' 'makes sense,' and so on.[4] Technical distinctions between empirical reason and pure reason,

[4] In my discussion I will deliberately deviate from the philosophical practice of distinguishing 'rational' from 'reasonable,' e.g., as explicitly done in John Rawls, *Political*

instrumental and noninstrumental reason, etc., will not appear, but of course we will make use of such common expressions as 'a selfish reason,' 'a moral reason,' 'good as a means,' 'desirable as an end,' 'morally good,' 'good *for* me,' etc., as well as metaphors such as 'reason demands...,' 'passion overcoming reason,' 'listening to reason,' 'reason surrendering to impulse,' etc. What we are after is what a 'reasonable' person would do, what we 'have the best reasons' to do, what 'makes most sense' to do; what we want to avoid is what is 'unreasonable,' 'crazy,' 'makes no sense,' 'is unwise,' 'inadvisable,' 'against all good reason.'

There are distinctions here to be noticed, even in the metaphors. For example, sometimes reason *demands*, but often it *permits* many choices, and sometimes it *advises without demanding*. In other words, there are some things it is utterly unreasonable to do; but there are many things such that one could as reasonably do them or something else, because there is no better reason to do the one than the other; and, finally, there are other things such that one has, on balance, some good reason to do them, but one would not be properly criticizable as 'unreasonable' for not doing them.[5] This last point, incidentally, contrasts with an assumption often shared by philosophers, especially those who work within the first three 'classic' models, namely, that it is always irrational not to act on the very best reasons. On this view, it seems, reason *demands* when there is the slightest balance of reasons for an act; it *permits* an act only when there is an even balance of reasons for and against; and it never merely *advises without demanding*, that is, never asserts that there is, all things considered, some reason to do something even though not doing it would not be unreasonable.

Liberalism (New York: Columbia University Press, 1993), 48–54. Ordinary language does not honor a sharp distinction here, though there are subtle differences in the various 'reason' expressions we use. The Kantian view of reason, I shall suggest, is closer to a common-sense idea of the reasonable than the thinner and more technical idea of the rational in contemporary philosophy, but I continue to use 'rational' in a broader sense (including the reasonable) as a reminder that (as I believe) philosophers have kidnapped that ordinary term for their own purposes. This was a well-meaning offense, no doubt, but it is a constant source of confusion at the intersection of technical and nontechnical discourse.

[5] This idea fits well with Rudiger Bittner's suggestion that prudential reason does not 'demand' but merely 'advises.' See his *What Reason Demands*, tr. Theodore Talbot (New York: Cambridge University Press, 1989), esp. chs. 6 and 7. The idea is, I believe, congenial with the position developed by Michael Slote in *Beyond Optimizing: A Study of Rational Choice* (Cambridge, MA: Harvard University Press, 1989).

A. Reasonable Self-Regard

To begin, let us try to set aside other-regarding reasons and to focus instead on the nonderivative reasons we have for taking an interest in ourselves, securing our own good, and so forth. One aspect of the common-sense view, I think, is that reasonable persons will place a very high priority on securing those conditions that are necessary for them to continue living as reasonable agents with adequate (or, ideally, full) possession of basic human capacities of body and mind. For example, to sacrifice one's sight or hearing, or an arm or leg, to satisfy a particular self-regarding desire unrelated to such a basic capacity would typically be regarded as utterly foolish and unreasonable. To preserve one's life, at least so long as one retains a certain minimum level of human capability, has long been regarded a paradigm of the concern for oneself that reason demands, at least when the interests of others are not at issue.[6] Quite often, I find, people regard it as morally objectionable, as well as foolish, to ignore these more stringent demands of reasonable self-interest, but the considerations most uncontroversially considered moral seem to be other-regarding ones.

If we can free ourselves from the influence of the various theoretical models, we will also recognize, I think, that the common-sense view is that reason does not dictate all or even most self-regarding choices. That is, for each person there is a wide range of options, most of the time, among which the person is 'free' to choose, without being irrational or unreasonable. Often there will be no antecedent reason to choose one option over the other; neither choice would be more or less reasonable. What color clothes to wear on a given day, whether to have strawberry or chocolate ice-cream, and whether to vacation in the mountains or at

---

[6] I pass over several matters of detail here, partly because I suspect that they may not be settled features of the overlapping views I call 'common sense.' For example, is it ever reasonable to sacrifice one's sight, or life, to complete some personal project that one has come to treasure above all, assuming (artificially) that others' interests are not involved? For our purposes, it is enough to say that common sense holds that reasonable people place *a very high priority* on life and basic human capacities. Questions can also arise, of course, about what the basic capacities are and what degree of maintenance is rationally required. That one should try to preserve one's sight and limbs is uncontroversial, but does reason demand that we train our bodies to the peaks of athletic fitness? It is generally conceded that to 'fry one's brains' on drugs is foolish, regardless of the pleasures one might gain; but to what extent does reason demand that we develop our intellectual acuity, memory, etc.? More theoretical issues that I pass over here concern how the 'unreasonableness' of self-destructive behavior is to be explained. Some hold that it is inherently irrational; but one might argue that it merely reflects means–ends incoherence or cognitive confusion, given that the human desire to survive and thrive as human is in fact deep and virtually universal in us.

the beach are familiar examples. A reasonable person may, and typically will, choose 'whichever he or she prefers,' we say. However, there is no *demand* to uncover some fact (the 'preference') and then follow that, on pain of irrationality.[7] When we deliberate, a felt inclination to do something is not necessarily a good reason for doing it, and similarly the fact that one feels inclined to favor one option over another does not necessarily make that choice more reasonable.[8] Our inclinations may be destructive to ourselves as well as to others (e.g., jealous rage); but they may also simply be pointless, utterly unrewarding when indulged (e.g., an urge to hear or see something disgusting). In neither case do we *need* to conclude that they give us 'some reason' to satisfy the inclination.[9] Of course, in the absence of any contrary reasons, we typically *will* choose to do what we feel more inclined to do; and so after acting we often cite such de facto 'preferences' to explain what moved us to act as we did. If we understand 'preferences' in this way, as *given* 'leanings' or 'feeling inclined,' then our preferences are among the things we reasonably deliberate about and among the factors that move us to act, but they are not things we are rationally constrained to follow or maximally fulfill.

There is another sense of 'preference,' I think, but this again is not a sense that supports the idea that reason restricts our permissible self-regarding choices by demanding that we follow (or maximally fulfill)

---

[7] Here I am also supposing that common sense differs from the position of Richard Brandt and others who maintain, roughly, that the rational thing to do is to efficiently pursue maximum satisfaction of the desires one *would* have if fully informed, subjected to 'cognitive psychotherapy,' etc. See Richard B. Brandt, *A Theory of the Good and the Right* (Oxford: Clarendon Press, 1979), esp. 110–29; and Brandt, 'The Concept of Rational Action', *Social Theory and Practice*, 9 (1983), 143–64. For criticism of theories of this type, see, for example, Allan Gibbard, 'A Noncognitivist Analysis of Rationality in Action', *Social Theory and Practice*, 9 (1983), 199–221; Don Loeb, 'Full Information Theories of the Good', *Social Theory and Practice*, 21 (1995), 1–30; and Connie S. Rosati, 'Persons, Perspectives, and Full Information Accounts of the Good', *Ethics*, 105(2) (1995), 296–325. Some desires and preferences that common sense recognizes as quite foolish or crazy may be revealed as such by exposure to more information in cognitive psychotherapy, but it seems doubtful that common sense is committed to the *general* thesis that choices based on desires that would be extinguished under such a process are thereby irrational. (Brandt, I should note, introduces his definitions as stipulative and makes no claims that they conform to common sense.)

[8] I explain and try, informally, to make this view persuasive in my *Autonomy and Self-Respect*, ch. 12.

[9] The same point, I believe, applies to the hypothetical inclinations that we would have with full information and cognitive psychotherapy, but this is more controversial. In any case, this more sophisticated controversy—whether members of a special class of hypothetical filtered, informed desires always give us reasons—involves technical complications about which we should not expect 'common sense' to have an opinion.

our preferences. When we seem to be citing 'preferences' as *good reasons* for acting, I think, the preference is usually not a discovered fact of being inclined but rather a choice, a verdict, or an endorsement. In the absence of compelling reasons, in deliberation we review our options and their anticipated outcomes, etc., often feeling inclined one way and then another in the course of our reflections. The conclusion—what, for various reasons, we choose or endorse as our ranking of options—we commonly speak of as our 'preference.' Once one has deliberately formed a preference, this gives one 'good reason' to make certain other appropriate choices; but, as a mere preference, it is seen as revisable. That is, again in the absence of compelling counter-reasons, one can typically reconsider and, if one likes, endorse a different ranking of options, thus deliberately reversing the order of previous preferences. In short, although reasonable people 'do what they prefer,' absent contrary other-regarding or self-regarding reasons, it is not a demand of reason that we make our self-regarding choices so that they fulfill some *given* set of inclinations or preferences. Mere inclinations are not in themselves good reasons to act, and we may reasonably alter our preferences.

So far I have suggested that, in common opinion, reason demands concern for preserving one's life and human capacities but permits a wide range of options for each person. Among the things permitted, however, there is a distinction between what is rationally indifferent and what is rationally advisable but not mandatory. Like 'supererogatory' acts in the moral sphere, we think of some self-regarding acts as, from a rational deliberative point of view, good to do but not required. That is, there is some reason to do the act in question, but not a reason of the kind and strength to warrant thinking an agent 'irrational' or 'unreasonable' for not doing it. There is an ideal of being fully governed by relevant 'good reasons,' and one who fails to do what one judges to be supported by 'the best reasons' falls short of this ideal; but I suspect this ideal is more honored in theory than in practice. An example of what reason 'advises,' in the sense I have in mind, might be choosing to exercise slightly harder and eat even less fat when one already maintains an above-average but not quite ideal dietary and exercise program.[10]

---

[10] Another possible example is the choice of a less expensive brand of food, judged equally as tasty and nourishing as another brand which has a more attractive package. If the cost difference 'means' relatively little to one, it seems not unreasonable to choose the slightly more expensive brand even though one realizes that, on reflection, the pretty package 'means' even less and thus one has slightly better reason to choose the less

In each of the cases discussed above, I am supposing that common sense regards the conclusions as independent of other-regarding reasons. I mean not only that the conclusions about what reason demands, permits, and advises are *applicable* to situations where only self-regarding considerations are relevant, but also that the grounds for the claims do not stem indirectly from duties or rational requirements regarding others. It is unreasonable not to take steps to preserve oneself and one's human capacities, for example, and not just because we must be alive and fit to fulfill our other-regarding duties.

A final note here may help to avoid misunderstanding. My main concern has been to identify a common-sense view of the sorts of self-interested *ends* that any reasonable person is expected to have.[11] The central points were that, by common opinion, it would be unreasonable not to take an interest in one's survival and in maintenance of one's basic human capacities; but, beyond this (and perhaps a few other special concerns), we may reasonably choose among a variety of possible ends; and we are not rationally constrained to make particular choices of ends according to whether and how strongly we happen to feel inclined toward them. There are, of course, many further common-sense ideas about the *procedures* of rational deliberation and planning, once the ends have been fixed, that I have not discussed. One may have reasonable ends but plan and carry out their pursuit in quite irrational ways (e.g., relying on superstitions, failing to review options, wasting resources, ignoring conflicts with other ends, etc.). Common sense also recognizes another paradigm of irrationality, I think, namely, the weakness or incoherence of will shown by failing to take available means,

---

expensive brand. This point that it is not always unreasonable not to act on the best reasons has been more thoroughly discussed by others and is not a major thesis on which I want to insist. I note, however, that common sense's apparent adoption of this idea may be subject to several different explanations. One may be that, in the case in question, the agent, on reflection, endorses the end of having the pretty package now, thus making it his or her 'preference,' despite realizing that he or she would not endorse this ranking as a general policy. That current preference, as a reflective endorsement, is itself a good reason for acting, absent compelling counter-reasons, and thus tips the scale of reasons in favor of now buying the more expensive and attractive package. We can say that the opposite choice also would not have been unreasonable, for, had the agent made it, he or she would no doubt have endorsed the end of saving a little money now over having the pretty package, and thus again would have been acting on the stronger reasons.

[11] I am referring here to the *content* of the ends that a person may reasonably be expected to have, as opposed to (further) constraints on the adoption of ends, which I count as *procedural*, having to do, for example, with ascertaining that they are attainable, compatible with one's other ends, internally consistent, etc.

which one knows are necessary, while nonetheless stubbornly refusing to 'give up' the end.[12]

B. *Reasonable Concern for Others*

Let us now consider common opinion about what reason demands, permits, and advises with regard to the interests and concerns of others, insofar as our focus is exclusively on these (rather than, for example, on self-interest). Again, in real life, acts and policies that affect others almost always have an impact on the agents themselves, but we can still ask what reasons others' interests and concerns give us in themselves, i.e., considered apart from their impact on self-interest. The question is not about *how to rank* reasons of self-interest versus other-regarding reasons, but rather about what reasons an agent has, if any, that have their source in the interests of others without being grounded in the agent's self-interest.

The main point here, I believe, is quite obvious, though details may be controversial. That is, common sense holds that any reasonable person counts certain basic interests of others as providing him or her with reasons to do, or refrain from doing, various things, provided that various exception-making circumstances are not present. If, for example, I encounter someone severely injured and it costs me nothing very significant, on balance, to prevent his loss of life, intense suffering, etc., then I have some reason to do so, unless certain special circumstances obtain. Various exceptions have often been allowed, but are increasingly challenged in modern times: for example, the basic interests of persons have been discounted because they are enemies, defectives, racial inferiors, outlaws, immoral, despised by gods, etc. Even in these cases, it is not clear whether those who disregarded the interests of these persons did so because their interests do not 'count' at all or rather because other interests (e.g., social order, one's own survival, pleasing the gods, etc.) were overriding. It is not easy to get our neighbors to acknowledge, *practically*, that the suffering in war-torn or famine-struck foreign countries gives us reason to contribute to relief, but almost all will grant that in principle we should help, provided we could do so effectively and at little cost.[13] All the more, most people in

---

[12] These controversial cases are treated more fully in my discussions of hypothetical imperatives, in *Dignity and Practical Reason*, chs. 1 and 7.
[13] Most people, no doubt, think that it matters how many others are as well-situated to help, whether the victims are 'remote' in distance and affiliation, etc. I am not supposing, then, that most people accept Peter Singer's demanding standards for sharing

the contemporary world, I believe, acknowledge that, *absent any reason to the contrary*, one should refrain from killing, maiming, and severely harming other human beings. And, though urgent self-interest and 'justice' are common excuses for overriding the basic interests of others, virtually no one would publicly affirm that whim, personal dislike, or minor financial gain are adequate 'reasons' to override these interests. Putting out a small effort to save the lives of other nonthreatening, innocent human beings is just something reasonable people must do, whether they happen to feel like doing so or not.

The common-sense view, then, seems to be that reason demands that we treat the basic interests of others, in most cases at least, as potential reasons for us. What about their personal preferences—the innocent ends and activities they endorse for themselves? Here, I suggest, common sense is more permissive, but still gives some weight to the personal preferences of others, again provided certain conditions are met. Prominent among these conditions would be that their preferred ends and activities are not immoral, destructive of others, and the like. Assuming this condition is met, however, most would grant, I think, that one should refrain from interfering with another's preferred projects, and should perhaps even aid them, at least if there was virtually no cost to oneself to do so. That I have a preference for doing something (which is not in itself immoral or irrational) is a (revisable) reason for me to do it; but the fact that someone else prefers that I not do it is also some reason, at least worth considering, that I not do it. Since there are thousands, even millions, of people with whom one may come into contact, the reason we must acknowledge as arising from any random individual's personal preferences will be relatively small, compared to all other possible considerations (including the preferences of others). Thus, common sense takes the rather indefinite view that each permissible preference is 'some (small) reason' in favor of acting to promote it, but there are so many other ways to act with as much reason that, in effect, reason permits a wide range of choice as to when and how one promotes the personal preferences of others. A practice of squelching or ignoring them for no reason at all, however, would be unreasonable.[14]

---

resources, but only that most would grant that, other things being equal, one has 'some reason' to help if one *can* help effectively and at very little cost. (See Peter Singer, *Practical Ethics*, 2nd edn. (Cambridge: Cambridge University Press, 1993), ch. 8, esp. 229–46).

[14] We should note, however, that one's own preference, or reflectively endorsed inclination, not to do a particular favor for someone is also a reason that one may often take

Finally, to draw out the parallel with self-regarding reasons, I suppose that common sense acknowledges that, from its regard for others, sometimes reason *advises* us to act in a certain way without demanding that we do so. The sort of case I have in mind is, say, where an option would apparently promote the personal preferences of quite a few people as opposed to an alternative that would promote the equally strong preferences of somewhat fewer, and contrary reasons of other kinds (e.g., self-interest, justice) are inapplicable. Here, I imagine, we might say that it is usually 'better' to do the former, and even that there seems to be 'somewhat more reason' to do so; but nonetheless, unless one has special responsibility for the larger group, one would not be criticizable as irrational or unreasonable if one did the latter. Common sense does not, I think, treat 'reasons' in such cases in the quasi-mathematical way we sometimes think of 'evidence' *weighing* in favor of a hypothesis. Others' (permissible) preferences are various factors for a reasonable person to consider favorably, but they are not measurable factors that can be added up to yield a rational requirement.[15]

This brief review of reasons acknowledged by 'common sense' is not meant to be exhaustive. For simplicity I have concentrated on just two types of self-regarding and other-regarding reasons—basic human interests and personal preferences—but for other purposes a fuller list and more subtle distinctions might be introduced.[16]

C. Weighing Self-Interest and Concern for Others

Clearly there are many differences of opinion about how a reasonable person weighs the various factors when self-interested and other-

into account. When I really prefer not to do a favor, then, I am not ignoring the preferences of others 'for no reason.' This is not to say that my preference not to do favors is always, or even generally, a *sufficient* reason to make it reasonable to refuse the favor; but it is a reason, often relevant.

[15] I should note that I am thinking of cases where we only consider that *someone* has a personal preference, setting aside special relationships. For example, if I am legally appointed to be impartial executor of funds for underage heirs, then I might be explicitly obliged to satisfy more of their permissible preferences, other things being equal, rather than fewer, in fulfilling my task; but that is a very special context. I might also note that the common-sense permissibility of not acting on the 'best' other-regarding reasons stemming from others' preferences might be explained in terms of an overriding self-regarding permission to choose for oneself, without counting the numbers, where to invest one's 'charity' efforts (in promoting the preferred ends and activities of others). But these matters go beyond my main concerns here.

[16] I leave aside, for example, the familiar view that the fact that an act would cause an animal extreme pain is a reason for anyone to refrain from it, whether they 'prefer' to or not. See n. 55.

regarding concerns conflict. In very broad outline, however, I think there is considerable agreement. For example, most would agree, I think, that certain basic human interests (in life, limb, sight, etc.) are so important to each person that it is unreasonable, barring special explanation, to make someone sacrifice a basic interest so that another person can satisfy some nonbasic, minor preference. Thus, other things being equal, it is unreasonable to expect elderly persons to terminate their lives early just to provide a few extra dollars for greedy heirs who prefer for them to die at once. Similarly, it would be unreasonable, other things being equal, for me to let someone else die, when I could save the person at virtually no cost to me, just because his death would save me a few dollars or because I wish the person dead. To act in these ways would be not just immoral but quite unreasonable, for there are compellingly better reasons for preserving the life in each case than for the alternative. People may disagree to some extent on exactly which goods are basic and of high priority, relative to others; but that there are such differences that require placing strong other-regarding considerations above weak self-regarding ones is surely a widely shared belief.

When we ask where a reasonable person draws the line between self-regard and other-regard, there is, I suspect, no determinate common-sense answer. Most people, as Michael Slote notes, are not so 'neutral' as to accept the basic utilitarian position—each person's welfare should count the same in our deliberations, *ceteris paribus*, as each other person's. Other quantitative alternatives, such as 'Give about 50 percent regard for self and 50 percent regard for *all others*,' seem odd to me, not because I am sure that common sense demands more—or less—but because they presuppose that ordinary opinion converges on some determinate quantitative division.[17]

The explanation of this, I suspect, lies in a second main point about the ranking of self-interest and concern for others: to a great extent,

---

[17] See Michael Slote, *From Morality to Virtue* (New York: Oxford University Press, 1992). Slote gives an extensive description of 'common-sense morality' as he sees it, noting where it diverges from utilitarianism (pp. 31–84). He argues that common-sense *morality* is incoherent in various ways, but that common-sense views on *virtue* are more plausible. Regarding virtue, he suggests, common sense seems to give *roughly* equal regard to self and to all others: 'I am saying that our ordinary thinking about the virtues treats the category of trait-possessor and the category of "other people" (i.e. people other than the trait possessor) as of roughly equal importance, and this latter suggests (perhaps it does more than suggest, but I don't at this point want to claim any more than it suggests) an ideal of character and action that, for any given choice of agent/possessor, exemplifies roughly equal concern for the agent/possessor and for others treated as a class or category to which everyone other than the agent/possessor belongs' (p. 98).

conflicts between the interests of different people already fall under moral and social rules, developed over time, and endorsed as reasonable by one's community and tradition. Thus, one does not need to confront all such conflicts with only a simple formula, like '50 percent for me, 50 percent for others,' to guide one's decisions. We have many presumptions already in place: murder is wrong; self-defense is permissible if necessary, proportionate, etc.; one should aid others in need if it costs one little, but great risk and self-sacrifice are supererogatory; the fact that a person owns something is a reason to respect his consent as to its use; and so on.[18] Common sense treats most of these rules as open to exception and possibly revision, but as quite unreasonable to ignore, barring very special circumstances. Such rules, assumed to be mutually advantageous in a broad sense, determine for us in many types of cases when self-interest must yield and when it may take precedence. The rules, in effect, define for each agent an area of permissible choice and an area of responsibility, without imposing a need to think in terms of percentages of weight one must give to self-regarding and other-regarding considerations. Perhaps, for example, even though I am far from destitute, the $100 in your pocket would bring me more pleasure, or satisfy more intense preferences of mine, than it would for you; nonetheless, you may reasonably keep the money and even refuse to engage in such speculative cross-person comparisons because the money is *yours* and, on the common view, our property rules (regarding such cases, at least) are reasonable.

What makes these accepted rules reasonable, when they are—and by what criteria are they reasonably criticized and revised? Here we move from the heart of pretheoretical common sense to the borders of *theory* of moral and practical reason. Insofar as there is an answer that can be attributed to most people, it will be complex, I suspect, acknowledging that many factors need to be taken into account to find the *most reasonable rules*, just as (most often) many factors were probably causally contributory in the development of the *actual rules* we find in our culture. Considerations of consequences in terms of pleasures and pains (a philosophical favorite) are relevant; but so too are considerations of distributive justice, of desert, of the value of special relationships, of needs for respect, peace, and room for autonomous choice.

---

[18] It is common now for philosophers to insist that the 'shoulds' and 'reasons' requiring concern for others be labeled 'moral' in contrast to the 'nonmoral' or 'rational' 'shoulds' and 'reasons' pertaining to self-interest and efficient pursuit of one's ends; but common sense, I think, does not draw such a sharp line, and to insist on it here would beg questions that are at issue (e.g., what makes reasons 'moral'?).

Virtually any theory that reduced the reasons for moral rules to one type of substantive value would inevitably, I think, leave out considerations commonly thought relevant. The rules are seen as constraints that reasonable people would agree on, if viewing the matter properly; but they serve to affirm and secure many different values.

III. COMMON SENSE AND SOME NON-KANTIAN IDEAS OF PRACTICAL REASON

Let us review, in broad outline, some familiar philosophical accounts of practical reason in order to compare and contrast these with the several ideas I have attributed to 'common sense.' The point, I should repeat, is not to refute or confirm these theories, as coincidence with ordinary thought is admittedly no proof of correctness. Rather, the point for now is simply to understand better some major ways in which distinct perspectives on reason, self-interest, and morality differ.

A. The Self-Interest Model: Deliberative Rationality as the Intelligent Pursuit of Self-Interest

Sometimes philosophers suggest that to deliberate well, using reason most appropriately, is to make full and good use of one's cognitive powers to determine what courses of action will best promote one's self-interest. One acts reasonably, then, by following the conclusion of such deliberation or, when time is limited, by following one's best estimate, in the circumstances, as to what the conclusion would be if one could deliberate more thoroughly, etc.[19] Views of self-interest vary of course, and so do the procedures of deliberation believed most effective in finding the means to promote it. Some try to reduce self-interest to a

---

[19] The view I sketch here is akin to what is often called 'ethical egoism,' i.e., the view that what one *morally ought* to choose is just what maximizes one's self-interest. (Another version says that it is always *morally permissible* to do what maximizes one's self-interest.) By contrast, the view I sketch is about what it is *reasonable* to choose. The latter view, I suspect, is more common, but some philosophers apparently hold both the view I sketch and some form of ethical egoism. Uncontroversial historical examples are hard to find, but surely among the best candidates to illustrate the self-interest model of reasonable choice would include Epicurus, Thomas Hobbes, and Henry Sidgwick. See A. A. Long and D. N. Sedley, *The Hellenistic Philosophers* (Cambridge: Cambridge University Press, 1987), 102–57; Thomas Hobbes, *Leviathan*, ed. C. B. Macpherson (Baltimore: Penguin Books, 1968), part I, esp. pp. 110–222; Henry Sidgwick, *The Methods of Ethics*, 7th edn. (Chicago: University of Chicago Press, 1962), 119–95. See also Derek Parfit, *Reasons and Persons* (Oxford: Clarendon Press, 1984), esp. chs. 1 and 6.

common denominator of pleasure, or pleasure/pain balance; others interpret it in terms of satisfaction of desires, or of filtered 'informed' desires and aversions; some (G. E. Moore?) may treat it as obtaining the most 'intrinsically valuable experiences' for oneself; others, more pluralistic, treat one's self-interest in terms of expected 'personal benefits,' identified by enumeration.[20] There are different ways of coping with different probabilities of costs and benefits, with better and worse 'qualities' of experience, and with tensions between how one conceives one's future good now and how one may conceive it later.[21] These differences, fortunately, do not matter for purposes of the broad-stroke comparisons that concern me here.

What is important in order to avoid confusion, however, is to understand that, according to the self-interest standard I have in mind here, 'self-interest' is conceptually distinct from the interests of others. Many have argued, of course, that *in fact* pursuit of self-interest and promoting the interests of others coincide, yielding the same recommendations for action.[22] But even to make this traditional argument is to suppose that the ideas of self-interest and other-interest can be distinguished. In fact, your happiness and welfare may be so dependent on the happiness and welfare of certain other people that what makes them unhappy will make you unhappy, but presumably you can at least entertain the idea that this might change and that you might thrive while they suffer. Or, if this is too hard to imagine in your own case, you can no doubt conceive that others, less loving, find themselves in that situation where they can distinguish their self-interest from that of others.

Although my primary aim is not to evaluate the various perspectives under review, I cannot resist saying in passing that, despite its notable history, the self-interest model of rationality seems to me incredibly implausible. The theory, we must note, is not merely the theorist's affirmation of a personal policy to pursue self-interest above all, together with the claim that, for her or him, this is a rational policy. The theory

---

[20] The latter is proposed in Gregory S. Kavka, *Hobbesian Moral and Political Theory* (Princeton: Princeton University Press, 1986), 42.

[21] Another variation worth noting is a view that while the 'objectively rational thing to do' is what best promotes self-interest, because self-interest is best served by not pursuing it directly it is not rational for us, most of the time, actually to engage in deliberation about what will best promote self-interest. The view is a response to the 'paradox of egoism,' the alleged fact that it is not most in one's self-interest deliberately to pursue what is most in one's self-interest.

[22] See, for example, Joseph Butler, *Five Sermons*, ed. Stephen Darwall (Indianapolis: Hackett Publishing Co., 1983). For a rather different strategy of argument, see Robert G. Olson, *The Morality of Self-Interest* (New York and Chicago: Harcourt, Brace, and World, Inc., 1965).

is more general than that, implying that anyone who deliberately pursues the good of another without regard to whether it proves best for himself or herself is irrational in doing so.[23] Moreover, the theory implies that people are also irrational if they pursue other ends, say, intellectual or artistic goals, for their own sake, without explicit regard for (and not because of) any benefits that success might bring them. To declare irrational so much of what we apparently do would seem to require strong justification. But what reason can one give for the self-interest theory? Surely it is not a conceptual or 'analytic' claim, because there are no grounds for supposing that the many theorists as well as nonphilosophers who deny the claim are thereby saying something self-contradictory. Nor would the claim that it is 'intuitive' or 'self-evident' be convincing, given how controversial it is. Historically, the case for it seems to turn on assertion of psychological egoism as an empirical generalization about human nature.[24] However, as Joseph Butler, David Hume, and others have argued, once psychological egoism is separated from certain tautologies with which it has been confused, it is easily seen to be empirically false.[25] In any case, even if true, the fact that people always do pursue their own advantage would not show that it is somehow a requirement *of reason* to do so. If psychological egoism were true, then admittedly it would be futile to *preach* that we should take into account reasons other than self-interested ones. Again, however, that point is no support for the self-interest theory as a

---

[23] Even the indirect self-interest theory mentioned above (in n. 21) has implausible consequences, though less blatant ones. On that view, anyone who deliberately pursued the greater good of others at a slight sacrifice of his or her own good would be doing something 'objectively irrational'; and any pursuit of the good of others as an end at all would be irrational unless *grounded somehow* (e.g., by prior policy decisions) in one's aim for one's own best self-interest. Although the theory is consistent, it involves the bizarre claim that people who deliberate and act well are in most cases doing so in order to pursue ends quite different from the egoistic end that, according to the theory, really justifies their acting as they do. See Michael Stocker, 'The Schizophrenia of Modern Moral Theories', *Journal of Philosophy*, 73 (1976), 453–66.

[24] Psychological egoism comes in many forms, but for now it may suffice to characterize it as the view that it is an unalterable law of human nature that every human being always aims ultimately for what he or she believes is in his/her best self-interest, and for nothing else. A somewhat weaker version, i.e., 'each person is so constituted that he will look out only for his own interests,' is well discussed in James Rachels, *The Elements of Moral Philosophy* (New York: Random House, 1986), 53–64.

[25] See Butler, *Five Sermons*; David Hume, *Enquiries Concerning Human Understanding and Concerning the Principles of Morals*, 3rd edn., ed. L. A. Selby-Bigge and P. H. Nidditch (Oxford: Clarendon Press, 1978), 212–32; Joel Feinberg, 'Psychological Egoism', in Feinberg, *Reason and Responsibility*, 4th edn. (Encino, CA: Dickenson Publishing Co., 1978), reprinted in George Sher (ed.), *Moral Philosophy* (San Diego, New York, and Chicago: Harcourt Brace Jovanovich, 1987), 1–15.

normative theory of rationality. In fact, it highlights the implausibility of the psychological egoism on which it was supposed to depend, for it seems obvious that preaching norms of rationality other than the self-interest theory has not been utterly futile, as a matter of fact.

That the self-interest theory conflicts with our common-sense assumptions should be obvious now. Although both agree that individuals, generally, have good reason to preserve themselves and maintain their basic human capacities, the self-interest theory makes rationally mandatory many acts and policies that common sense sees as optional. First consider cases not involving others. If I choose to forgo a number of virtually cost-free pleasures or choose to indulge a minor short-term whim at the acknowledged cost of more (minor) future benefits, then the self-interest theory regards this as quite irrational.[26] Common sense, however, takes a more permissive view, so long as the benefits sacrificed were not vital human interests. An expression of that view, as I imagine it, would be this: 'The future benefits, perhaps, give you some reason to resist the whim, but you would not be unreasonable to go for the alternative, if you like; as long as you realize what you are doing, do as you please.' It is tempting to add, on behalf of common sense: 'The choice to sacrifice virtually cost-free pleasures, though within the bounds of reason, is nonetheless quite unusual, not at all what one would expect.' On reflection, however, it is not clear to me that this is true. Philosophical theories lead us to expect that no one knowingly turns down virtually cost-free pleasures, but in fact the phenomenon seems all too common.

Next consider cases involving the interests of others. Here the conflict with common sense is even more evident. The self-interest theory implies that to choose to give any benefit to another when one does not expect any benefit to oneself, not even the 'pleasure of giving,' would be contrary to reason. Any sacrifice of one's own perceived long-term self-interest, however slight, for the sake of the enormous benefit of many others, would be irrational, according to the theory. Many

---

[26] When I refer to 'virtually cost-free pleasures,' I do not mean to deny that there may always be some costs in opportunities, time, effort, etc. What I have in mind (more strictly) are significant pleasures (not very minor or barely discernable ones) that can be obtained at very small, insignificant costs so that, on balance, the costs are negligible for practical purposes. It is regrettable, I think, but not contrary to demands of practical reason that people often let the quality of their lives be somewhat diminished by minor but persistent habits of self-denial of pleasures of this sort. Perhaps fuller understanding of why they do this would help to free them from such habits, but the appropriate response, I suggest, is not a charge of irrationality of choice but sympathetic encouragement to 'lighten up.'

philosophers argue, of course, that in the long run a policy of immediate self-sacrifice in such cases tends to benefit the agent and thus is a good strategy for maximizing benefits for oneself. However, whether true or not, this thought will seem quite unnecessary to most commonsense deliberators; for the latter, I think, are quite ready to grant that they already have 'good reason,' even 'sufficient reason,' to make the minor self-sacrifice, and this is not because they expect to get a compensating personal 'kick' from helping others. Again, when the choice falls under certain legal, social, or moral rules that are seen to be (for the most part) mutually advantageous, the self-interest theory would demand, on pain of irrationality, that we break such rules whenever we can achieve a long-term, on balance, personal benefit from doing so, no matter how slight this benefit might be or how great the losses others may suffer as a result of our violating the rule. But common sense, as I have said, seems to grant in such cases that the rules give us a good, and usually sufficient, reason to conform, even when this is (to some degree) contrary to our long-term maximum self-interest.

B. *The Coherence-and-Efficiency Model: Deliberative Rationality as Seeking Means–Ends Coherence and Efficiency*[27]

Currently a more common perspective on rational choice is the idea that rational deliberation is simply a process of working toward an appropriate fit between the ends one adopts and the means one uses to achieve them. The view accepts Hume's idea that our ends are not *in themselves*

---

[27] A principle of efficiency, as I understand this, would direct us, given fixed goals, to take means that are least costly in terms of resources, or, given fixed resources, would direct us toward a higher degree of satisfaction of our ends. If all our values are commensurable and expressible in terms of some common denominator, then it might be possible (and many would say desirable) to dispense with 'coherence' and reduce rational choice to efficiency, seen as choosing so as to bring about the greatest possible amount of that value (which might be, for example, 'preference-satisfaction'). The model I call 'coherence and efficiency' does not assume that all values are commensurable and thus introduces standards of informed reflection and coherence among means and ends, distinct from and beyond efficiency. For example, if certain means are necessary to an end, one must choose the means or else give up the end; to hold on to an end while refusing to take the necessary steps to achieve it is a form of practical incoherence. (We might be incapable of such incoherence if we were immune to self-deception.) Similarly, it is generally a mark of incoherent (though possible) practical thinking to pursue goals that undermine one's other goals or to employ means that violate the values that were the basis for choosing one's goals. Finding himself in such a situation, a reasonable person will make some adjustment in his set of goals to make them more 'coherent,' even if there is no quantitative measure of value to indicate *which* ends among his incoherent set of ends should be revised or abandoned.

either rational or irrational, though they might be *called* 'irrational' in a *derivative* sense if adopted because of irrationally formed beliefs about the factual background situation. What is practically irrational, in a straightforward sense, is to select inappropriate means, *given* the set of ends that the agent has in fact adopted.[28] Examples include violations of what John Rawls calls 'the counting principles': using more resources than needed to achieve a set of ends; choosing means that achieve a less inclusive set of ends than one might with the same resources; choosing the means less likely than others to achieve the ends, where other things are equal; and so on.[29] These are 'counting principles' because they enable us to determine what is unreasonable in some cases simply by 'counting' up resources spent and ends achieved, without evaluating or ranking the ends themselves.

Another familiar principle that remains neutral regarding the nature of the ends, and thus naturally suits the coherence-and-efficiency model, is the Hypothetical Imperative. In a version reconstructed from Kant, this says: If there are means available and necessary to achieve your end, then you (rationally) must take those means—*or give up the end*.[30] This last qualification is important, for there is nothing irrational about deliberately changing your ends. What is irrational, even incoherent, is to refuse to take known necessary means without at the same time revising the set of ends one professes and sees oneself as having. When we first will an end, we necessarily intend ('will') that at some time we will take some means to achieve the end. Typically, however, neither the end nor the 'taking some means' is willed unrevisably. If we find out later that the only available means are too costly, in terms of other things we care about, then it is reasonable to drop the end, which takes away the reason to adopt the costly means. Rawls's counting principles presumably must be understood as similarly qualified. They tell us what to do if, but only so long as, we continue to affirm the initial set of ends; but under various conditions, revising one's ends is quite reasonable. The upshot of all these principles is that they demand that the deliberator

---

[28] This point, incidentally, goes beyond Hume, as I understand him. For Hume, acts, choices, and preferences cannot be 'contrary to reason,' except in the derivative sense mentioned. If they involve wasting resources, taking unnecessary risks of failure, etc., they are foolish and imprudent but not, strictly speaking, irrational. But the coherence-and-efficiency model treats such inappropriate selection of means to fixed ends as a paradigm of practical irrationality.

[29] John Rawls, *A Theory of Justice* (Cambridge, MA: Harvard University Press, 1999), 361–5.

[30] I discuss this principle at some length in *Dignity and Practical Reason*, chs. 1 and 7.

seek efficiency and coherence in selecting means to his or her ends, a process which involves both apt selection of means and thoughtful adjustment of one's ends.

Virtually any sensible account of practical reason will *include* principles of efficiency and coherence between means and ends. What is distinctive about what I call 'the coherence-and-efficiency model' is that it assumes that principles of this sort are *sufficient* for practical rationality. In particular, the model denies (with Hume) that reason tells us what specific ends we must adopt or what rules we must follow.

Now, how does this second model square with the common-sense view? Consider, first, self-regarding considerations. The coherence-and-efficiency standard is permissive in many ways that common sense would approve; for, by abstaining from evaluation of ends, the standard allows that reasonable people may adopt quite different ends, even ends that involve self-sacrifice and seem quite bizarre to others. Thus, while reason demands means–end coherence and efficiency, it permits, in principle, virtually any act one chooses, provided one can knowingly endorse a means–ends package that recommends the act. Only human nature, and one's individual character, limit the content of what one may reasonably do.

The permissiveness of the coherence-and-efficiency model, however, is too unlimited to accord with common-sense views. For example, unlike the common-sense view, it does not require that a person place a high priority on his or her own life and limb. Most people, most of the time, may in fact adopt these as high-priority ends; but if one chooses not to, then, by the coherence-and-efficiency standard, there is nothing irrational in that, provided one makes the appropriate adjustments in one's set of ends and means.[31]

The conflict with ordinary opinion is even sharper in cases involving the vital interests of others. The coherence-and-efficiency standard, for example, agrees with Hume's dictum, which Hume no doubt knew would outrage 'common sense,' that it is not unreasonable to prefer the destruction of the whole world to the scratching of one's finger.[32] Even if by doing something easy, and of little or no cost to myself, I would prevent the imminent misery of many others, the coherence-and-efficiency model does not count that as 'a good reason' *in itself* for me to

---

[31] According to the coherence-and-efficiency standard, it is not in itself irrational, for instance, to risk one's life for trifles, but if one has that attitude, it is unwise to invest much in long-term projects.

[32] David Hume, *A Treatise on Human Nature*, ed. L. A. Selby-Bigge (Oxford: Clarendon Press, 1995), 416.

do it. The model's advocates will quickly add that, *if* I care about others or about the rewards of their good opinion (as most people do), *then* I have good reason to take the preventive action. But this is not enough to square with common opinion, as I see it; for the latter holds that I would be unreasonable not to prevent the harm to others, *whether or not I happen to care for them or for my reputation*. Similarly, the coherence-and-efficiency model must recommend that a person break any conventional legal or moral rule if, all things considered, doing so is the best means to the ends he or she reflectively endorses (or 'prefers' most). But with regard to murder, rape, torture, betrayal of friends, etc., common opinion seems firm in its view that it is unreasonable to do these things as means to one's ends, even if they are effective and coherent with one's other ends.

C. *The Consequentialist Model: Deliberative Rationality as Seeking to Maximize Intrinsic Value*

Another way of looking at the aims of reasonable deliberation is an analogue of the moral principle of utilitarianism. Typically, utilitarianism is regarded as a basic normative principle that distinguishes between what is morally right and what is morally wrong to do. The root idea, which is subject to many refinements, is that acts are morally right or wrong depending solely on their consequences, and that consequences are better or worse depending upon whether they promote happiness or the reverse.[33] The starting point is the idea that happiness, or some alternative, is objectively an intrinsic value, regardless of whose happiness it is, and unhappiness, or perhaps something else, is intrinsically bad, no matter who has it. Then a course of action is recommended or proscribed according to whether or not it, or the general acceptance of a related moral code, promotes the most intrinsic value possible in the circumstances. Often this sort of theory is presented as a standard of 'objective right' rather than as a deliberative guide; and it is usually treated as a *moral* standard, which leaves open the question of whether

[33] There are many important distinctions that have emerged from the vast literature on utilitarianism and consequentialism, but I hope no harm is done by my oversimplifying here. For other purposes, for example, one might note that 'consequences,' as usually understood, are not all that counts in many versions, e.g., G. E. Moore's; for acts themselves, as distinct from their consequences, could have intrinsic value. See G. E. Moore, *Principia Ethica* (Cambridge: Cambridge University Press, 1903), 1–21. The many subtle variations on 'rule-utilitarianism,' as well as 'motive-utilitarianism,' are also highly significant in many discussions, but not, I think, here.

it is always *rational* to be moral.[34] But the analogue that I want to consider is an idea about what should guide reasonable deliberation in general, rather than a criterion of ('objective') moral rightness. Essentially, the idea is that the fact that doing something would promote an intrinsic value is a good reason for doing it, just as the fact that something would have an intrinsically bad effect (or hinder an intrinsic value) is a reason not to do it. The most reasonable course to take in deliberation, then, would in general be to seek sensibly and effectively to promote, on balance, the most intrinsic value possible.[35]

If we were dissatisfied with the other perspectives on deliberative rationality that we have considered because of their apparent conflicts with 'common sense,' then we might find some features of the current (consequentialist) perspective attractive. Notably, the latter derives both self-regarding reasons and other-regarding reasons from a common source, and thus it is not committed to the view that the good of others gives us reasons to act only indirectly when and because promoting the good of others also promotes our own good (or aids in the coherent-and-efficient satisfaction of our personal ends). Although empirical assumptions are needed, it seems one could argue plausibly from the consequentialist standard that virtually everyone has strong *presumptive* reasons to place a high priority on preservation of his or her own life and the maintenance of his or her basic human capacities; for these seem to be prerequisites for realizing intrinsic value in one's own life, if anything is.[36] If so, everyone would also have strong presumptive reasons to preserve the lives and basic capacities of others; for these are, to the same extent, prerequisites for realizing intrinsic value in the lives of others. This requirement to count the basic good of others as weighing heavily in our deliberations may also make the consequentialist standard closer than the self-interest and coherence-and-efficiency models to common-sense views about how reasonable people rank self-interest

---

[34] Some argue that encouraging people to use the utilitarian principle as a deliberative guide would result in less than the most possible intrinsic value; and for this reason they recommend that, for the most part, we (or common folk) rely on familiar specific moral rules as our deliberative guides. See R. M. Hare, *Moral Thinking* (Oxford: Clarendon Press, 1981), 44–64.

[35] Here I am thinking that 'the most intrinsic value, on balance' is the result when negative intrinsic values are 'subtracted' from positive ones. (That we can really perform such calculations is, of course, a fiction.)

[36] We need, in addition to empirical premises, also some account of intrinsic value, such as Mill's, which allows us to identify such value as happiness, or high-quality happiness, or Aristotelian thriving, or something similar. See J. S. Mill, *Utilitarianism* (Indianapolis: Hackett Publishing Co., 1988), 7–11.

and other-regard. At least it seems quite plausible to suppose that most consequentialist theories will uphold the common-sense idea that to be reasonable a person must be ready to sacrifice some minor interest of his or her own if necessary and sufficient to avert a major disaster to many other people. Moreover, consequentialists should also readily endorse the idea that, other things being equal, it is unreasonable for a person to sacrifice his or her most intense and stable interests merely to satisfy the whims of others. Sophisticated consequentialism, such as Richard Brandt's rule-utilitarianism, can argue that reasonable legal, social, and moral rules will not dictate our every move but rather will leave each of us a considerable area of freedom within which we may do as we please.[37] Since, by definition, consequentialist theories justify rights-conferring rules only by reference to their expected long-term results, they cannot *start* from an antecedent right to liberty, and they will need to appeal to strong empirical premises, claiming the overall benefits of leaving people free within certain limits to do as they please.

In other ways, however, the consequentialist model seems far removed from common-sense views. It has often been argued, for example, that in various real and hypothetical cases *consequentialism as a moral theory* conflicts with common-sense opinion about what it is morally right to do;[38] and, since common sense supposes it is only reasonable to do the morally right thing, these conflicts translate into conflicts between common sense and our analogous *consequentialism as a theory of reasonable deliberation*. In my opinion, these conflicts are deep and serious, not to be dismissed *ad hoc* by conjuring up new consequences each time troublesome counterexamples appear or by inventing new epicyles in the definition of consequentialism. My view here, however,

---

[37] See, for example, Richard B. Brandt, 'Toward a Credible Form of Utilitarianism', in Hector-Neri Castaneda and George Nakhnikian (eds.), *Morality and the Language of Conduct* (Detroit: Wayne State University Press, 1965), 107–43; and Brandt, *A Theory of the Good and the Right* (*supra* n. 7), 163–99. For the distinction between 'act' and 'rule' varieties of utilitarianism and consequentialism, see n. 41 below.

[38] Many introductory texts and anthologies on ethics, as well as professional books and articles, offer such 'counterexamples' to utilitarianism together with discussions of rule-utilitarian, or other consequentialist, devices to circumvent these problems. See, for example, Sir David Ross, *The Right and the Good* (Oxford: Clarendon Press, 1930), 16–47; James Rachels, *The Elements of Moral Philosophy* (New York: Random House, 1986), 90–113; William K. Frankena, *Ethics* (Englewood Cliffs, NJ: Prentice Hall, 1973), 34–43; Alan Donagan, *The Theory of Morality* (Chicago: University of Chicago Press, 1977), 172–99; Donagan, 'Is There a Credible Form of Utilitarianism?', in Michael D. Bayles (ed.), *Contemporary Utilitarianism* (New York: Doubleday Anchor Books, 1968); J. J. C. Smart and Bernard Williams, *Utilitarianism: For and Against* (Cambridge: Cambridge University Press, 1973); and David Lyons, *Forms and Limits of Utilitarianism* (Oxford: Clarendon Press, 1965).

is admittedly controversial, and I shall not press it. Instead, I just want to point out something that should be less controversial, namely, that at least when considered *as a theory of reasonable deliberation*, consequentialism is at odds with how people actually think about choices in ordinary life. According to direct- or act-consequentialism, for example, in deliberation my concern should be entirely forward-looking, aimed at promoting the most (or best balance of) intrinsic value (e.g., happiness) that I possibly can. But common sense counts many backward-looking considerations as also relevant, and not just derivatively so: promises, past injustices, debts of gratitude, a history of friendship, etc. Moreover, people do not ordinarily think of it *as their responsibility* to consider and weigh impartially every (intrinsic) good and bad to every person, however remote. Consequentialists sometimes concede this point, claiming that we are justified, in most ordinary contexts, in restricting consideration of costs and benefits more locally because wider-ranging deliberations in those ordinary contexts prove counter-productive. Nonetheless, there is still a conflict, for the common-sense view is that no such justification is needed. That is, there is no reason to *presume* in the first place that my deliberations are reasonable only if I weigh every interest (or 'intrinsic good') for every person equally with the comparable interest (or 'intrinsic good') of every other, including myself, my family, and my friends. Since there is no such presumption, there is no need to try to 'justify' all of our more narrowly focused deliberations from a remote, impartial God's-eye point of view.[39]

This is not to deny that impartial weighing of interests has its place: for example, in courts of law, in government policy making, in arbitration of family disputes, and the like. Even here, though, the range of interests to be impartially considered is limited by the decision maker's jurisdiction as well as various rules of relevance. Beyond this, common-sense morality also acknowledges a fundamental equal moral status for all human beings, and this means that in discussing the formulation and implications of basic moral principles, we must keep in mind that these are not designed to serve the special interests of any particular group as opposed to another, and therefore in applying the principles we must try not to be influenced *inappropriately* by our own special attachments and circumstances.[40] But even this general feature of common-sense

---

[39] On this point, the self-interest standard and the coherence-and-efficiency standard seem quite correct; the Kantian disagreement with them lies elsewhere, as should become evident later.

[40] The need for the qualification 'inappropriately' here should be evident; for *some*

morality does not amount to the sort of *impersonal* weighing of interests (or 'intrinsic values') that consequentialists have prescribed for moral debates; and, even more obviously, it is not a plausible standard, or even a presumptive standard, that ordinary opinion endorses for all reasonable deliberation.

Since many other problems in direct- or act-consequentialism are ameliorated by a move to rule-consequentialism, one might initially expect that an analogous move might help square our *consequentialism as a standard of reasonable deliberation* with common sense.[41] Moving in this way to a dual standard for deliberation helps resolve the immediate problem, but it seems only a superficial improvement. That is, the rule-consequentialist can agree with common sense that in most everyday deliberations, agents can quite reasonably restrict the range of interests (or 'intrinsic values') they consider, because doing so is a part of a policy that, in the long run, has the best consequences, when all interests (or 'intrinsic values') are considered impartially. (Another part of that useful policy, presumably, is that ordinary deliberations be constrained by various substantive moral rules.)[42] But then the problem seems only removed a step. Assuming they could understand the philosophical move to rule-consequentialism, the representatives of common sense might respond as follows: 'Why do you presume that our ordinary deliberations are reasonable only if they would be recommended from the alien perspective of consequentialist rule-makers, who (unlike us) debate and decide rules with intrinsic concern for *nothing but*

---

attention to our actual circumstances, including our particular loves and hates, is often relevant to the reasonable application of general moral principles. What is needed now is more constructive effort to work out standards of appropriateness of particular concerns in various contexts and less rhetoric about the evils of impartialism (or the opposite).

[41] 'Act-consequentialism' generally refers to any theory of normative ethics that affirms, perhaps with minor modifications, that one acts in the right (or best) way if and only if one does what will (or probably will) have the best results, compared to one's options, in the long run, considering all persons (or all sentient beings). 'Rule-consequentialism' generally refers to any version of normative ethics that affirms, perhaps with minor modifications, that one does what is right (or best), among one's options, if one acts as directed by an ideal (or actual) moral code, or set of rules, such that general acceptance of that code (which is not the same as perfect conformity to it) by most people in the relevant community would have the best results in the long run, considering all persons (or sentient beings). Consequentialists differ among themselves as to what makes results 'good' and whether there need always be a quantifiable 'best.' 'Utilitarians' are often considered consequentialists who reduce 'good results' to pleasure and pain, or at least benefits and setbacks to the welfare of individuals (but this usage does not fit G. E. Moore's ideal utilitarianism). See the citations in n. 38.

[42] Endorsing this idea, a colleague of mine says that we should *be* utilitarians but *think like* Kantians.

maximizing (or at least impartially promoting) what they consider good *consequences*? Do we really suppose that reason requires us to submit to their principles and policies simply because these seem well-calculated (or estimated) to raise the relevant population's average or total level of "good results," no matter how the benefits and burdens are distributed? Their vantage point, however lofty, is not ours, nor are we committed to regarding it as authoritative. Even if such rule-makers were wonderfully well-informed and purely impartial, why should I suppose that, to be reasonable, *I* must submit all my life-projects, interests, and even my promptings of conscience to these legislators for approval or disapproval?' There are various responses that consequentialists can offer, and, though I remain skeptical, I acknowledge that they should eventually be examined respectfully and in detail.[43] For present purposes, it should suffice to note that common sense does not initially acknowledge that reason demands submission of its deliberative practices to the rule-consequentialist standard; thus, even if a good argument for this is forthcoming, it would speak in favor of a *revision* of common sense, rather than a *reconciliation* between common sense and rule-consequentialism.

IV. A KANTIAN MODEL: DELIBERATIVE RATIONALITY AS COHERENT AND EFFICIENT PURSUIT OF ONE'S ENDS CONSTRAINED BY RESPECT FOR IDEAL CO-LEGISLATION

In this final section, I want to sketch an alternative idea of deliberative rationality that I draw from Kant. The sketch will admittedly have to leave many details open, and I will not be concerned to defend its

---

[43] Strategies for showing the rationality of adopting rule-utilitarianism are discussed in Hare, *Moral Thinking*, ch. 12, and Brandt, *A Theory of the Good and the Right*, chs. XI and XVII. Advocates of either of our first two models of rational deliberation would need to argue from empirical evidence that it is, derivatively, rational to adopt rule-consequentialism as a moral philosophy. Also, I suspect confusion about 'intrinsic value' sometimes gives a false appearance of supporting the thesis that trying to maximize intrinsic value, directly or by rules, is rationally necessary. If one defines 'intrinsically valuable' as 'having properties that provide good reasons for anyone to favor the thing,' or something like this, then the move to justify maximizing intrinsic value could at least get started. But traditionally, from classic utilitarians to Moore and his successors, this has not been what is meant. Bentham, for example, identified intrinsic value with certain sensations, and Moore treated it as a metaphysical, simple, nonnatural, supervenient quality. In both cases, intrinsic value is conceptually independent of what we have reason to choose.

credentials as Kantian.[44] My hope, however, is that the sketch is sufficient to suggest some interesting points of comparison with common sense and some contrasts with the three philosophical models reviewed above.

The Kantian model assumes that human beings have both self-interested and other-regarding desires, even if the self-regarding ones have a tendency to dominate in conflict situations. Viewed from a practical standpoint, however, human choices are not simply the result of whatever competing desires and aversions we have at the moment. We have a capacity to review options, consider consequences and precedents, develop norms, strategies, and personal values, and then to choose, in the light of all these, what ends we will adopt and what policies we will follow in pursuing them. We act according to *rationales*, or complexes of beliefs, policies, and deep normative commitments. Even when our motive is inclination, the explanation is not that the inclination caused the behavior (as if it were some inner force moving a machine). Rather, though we might have done otherwise, we endorsed the end of satisfying that inclination (perhaps having seen no reason not to) and chose some means to satisfy it, according to the general norm of the Hypothetical Imperative.[45] Merely having an inclination is not in itself a reason for doing anything, though naturally in the absence of any reason to the contrary, we commonly endorse satisfying our inclinations; i.e., we adopt doing so as an end. Having adopted an end gives us some reason to take necessary means to it, but not a *compelling* reason. This is because freely adopted ends are also revisable, and they (rationally) must be revised if the only means available to satisfy them conflict with some unconditional rational norm.

As human beings who are adult and not severely defective, we are *rational* beings in at least the *minimal sense* that we find ourselves inescapably committed to certain norms for deliberation and thought that have certain features which have led Western tradition to identify them with our 'rational nature.' Exactly what these features are is not easy to say, but, very roughly, the dispositions of thought and

---

[44] My aim here is merely to reconstruct and summarize a Kantian position rather than to show how it is drawn from Kant's texts; but for purposes of comparing my sketch with Kant's writings, the main texts to consider are the following: Immanuel Kant, *Groundwork of the Metaphysics of Morals*, *Critique of Practical Reason*; *Religion within the Boundaries of Mere Reason*; and *The Metaphysics of Morals*.

[45] This is not to suggest the silly view that we actually go through all these steps consciously every time we make significant choices. The elements are meant to reflect aspects of what is involved, often as background beliefs and commitments, when, as we ordinarily say, 'his reason for doing that was . . . ,' and the like.

deliberation that we identify with our 'rational nature' are those that especially reflect, for example, our concerns for consistency, coherence, conceivability, wider and wider explicability, discovery by methods of reflection, intersubjective justifiability, and having beliefs that are (in senses appropriate to the context) universal and necessary. Perhaps, too, our 'rational' dispositions are seen as dispositions to submit to the standards, among those we find in our own practices of thought and deliberation, that, even on persistent reflection, we cannot help but see as authoritative, whether we like it or not.

What are these rational norms which we are disposed to regard as authoritative? Some are, of course, norms of logic and general principles of empirical understanding, but our concern is with norms of practical reason. Clearly the Hypothetical Imperative is part of the Kantian view, and other principles of instrumental reasoning might well be added.[46] Insofar as both the Hypothetical Imperative and other instrumental principles are understood so as to allow for the revision of ends, it is always rational to respect those principles.[47] They cannot, by themselves, dictate action against unconditional rational moral norms, if there are any.

What other practical standards of reasonable deliberation are there? Let us consider the negative side of the Kantian position. First, the Hypothetical Imperative and other instrumental principles alone are insufficient to account for everything that, as human beings, we count as rationally mandatory. These principles, taken by themselves, allow that all sorts of murderous conduct would be rational, for example, for persons who adopt extremely inhumane ends; but on the Kantian view there are compelling reasons not to destroy human lives for cruel and sadistic purposes.

Second, Hume was right to criticize the previous rationalistic tradition that too readily pronounced all its favorite substantive values 'self-evidently rational.' Reason is not an intuitive access to a Platonic realm of values; and mere analysis of the concept of 'rational beings' can establish neither that they are peace-loving, generous, and law-abiding nor that they are relentlessly power-hungry, exclusively self-interested, or, for that matter, committed to any other familiar set of substantive values. Such values are too variable and controversial to have a plausible claim to be overridingly authoritative and intersubjectively

---

[46] Other instrumental principles might be, for example, those that Rawls (in *A Theory of Justice*, 364) calls 'counting principles.'

[47] I develop this view of the Hypothetical Imperative in *Dignity and Practical Reason*, chs. 2 and 7.

justifiable for all who share the dispositions we associate with our 'rational' nature. Thus, the most *basic* universal norms of practical reason, if there are any, will not be expressible in terms of *substantive* ends that any rational person must pursue.[48] The basic norms will not include, for example, 'Promote peace,' 'Increase pleasure and diminish pain,' 'Obey God's commands,' 'Maximize your power to survive,' or even 'Seek to flourish according to your *telos* as a human being.' Instead, they will have more to do with a general *orientation* or *attitude*, and with *procedures* necessary for rational deliberation.[49]

Third, various attempts to identify a common denominator in all the different things that people have considered valuable as ends misconstrue the nature of value judgments. For example, theories that are 'naturalistic,' in the sense introduced by G. E. Moore and refined by others, commonly confuse descriptive claims about what people in fact take interest in and evaluative claims about what is worthy of interest.[50] This complaint would apply not only to simple theories, such as R. B. Perry's 'value = any object of interest,' but also to complex, sophisticated theories, such as Richard Brandt's, that identify value as the objects of desires that are informed, stable, and capable of surviving a special cognitive scrutiny.[51] Kant's complaint is not that such views commit a 'naturalistic fallacy,' but that they confuse (1) that which it is conditionally and contingently reasonable to choose with (2) that which it is necessarily reasonable to choose. What is fundamentally valuable is that which it is necessarily rational to choose, and none of the natural properties that 'naturalists' identify with value (being desired, pleasure, an object of interest, fitness for survival, etc.) have this characteristic. Nothing becomes valuable, for example, *simply* by virtue of being an object of interest, not even if the interest is informed, stable, and capable

---

[48] The distinction between 'substantive' and 'nonsubstantive' is perhaps relative to context, just as the line between 'specific' and 'nonspecific' is. Thus, I am not claiming that the Kantian basic norms of rational deliberation are so 'formal' as to have no action-guiding or deliberation-constraining content at all, but am only trying to contrast them with more specific and controversial substantive principles such as 'Maximize your wealth and power,' 'Follow God's commands,' 'Choose the most pleasant life,' and 'Promote the greatest happiness of the greatest number.'

[49] For example, the moral attitude is one that values humanity in each person and constrains an agent's choices by principles determined by trying to deliberate according to the procedural standards of the Kantian legislative perspective, to be sketched below.

[50] See, for example, Moore, *Principia Ethica*, 1–21; William K. Frankena, 'The Naturalistic Fallacy', *Mind*, 48 (1939), 464–77; and R. M. Hare, *The Language of Morals* (Oxford: Clarendon Press, 1952), 79–93.

[51] See Ralph Barton Perry, *Realms of Value* (Cambridge: Harvard University Press, 1954), 3, 107, 109; and Brandt, *A Theory of the Good and the Right* (*supra* n. 7), ch. 6.

of surviving cognitive psychotherapy.[52] A similar point would apply to the idea of objective 'intrinsic values,' as conceived by Moore and others. Since these are allegedly real, simple, nonrelational 'properties' of things in the natural world (especially 'experiences'), the claim that doing something would produce intrinsic value does not in any way imply that we *have a reason* to do the act. It is logically possible to be perfectly rational and yet indifferent to intrinsic value, in Moore's metaphysical sense, just as one can be indifferent to various natural properties.

More constructively, Kant's positive account of norms of reason (beyond instrumental principles) is implicit in the progressive development of his idea of the Categorical Imperative. Although the idea has implications that can be expressed as positive prescriptions, the tone and guiding thought is perhaps better expressed in terms of reasonable *constraints* on our pursuit of personal projects. The first formula, roughly, tells us *not* to act on maxims that we could not *reasonably* choose for everyone;[53] but, for the most part, the criteria of reasonable choice (as well as identification of maxims) are left for later formulas. The humanity formula says that 'rational nature' *in each person* is to be treated as an objective 'end in itself,' a special unconditional value setting limits on how any person may be treated.[54] On a thin reading, the central point is that, in determining what is permissible, it is not simply *your reason* (as the first formula might have suggested) but *reason in each person* that must be consulted and satisfied. The 'practical reason' that we do and must regard as authoritative in our deliberations is a faculty that we *share*, and not merely in the weak sense in which we might 'share' a desire for self-preservation, money, or domination of others in competition.[55] As in logic and science, reason

---

[52] By 'fundamentally valuable' here I mean only moral and nonmoral values as defined or characterized in the most general terms, not the more specific values that we might draw from such general characterizations in the light of empirical facts.

That persons have dignity for Kant was morally fundamental; that adultery is wrong was derivative. Similarly, that each person's 'happiness' consistent with duty is good for that person would be a basic point about personal value, whereas that playing games is good for everyone, or any particular person, would be derivative (if true). The naturalists' error, from the Kantian perspective, was not in their (correct) recognition that empirical facts about what we want, find satisfying, etc., are crucially relevant to most of our value judgments; it was rather that they *identified* the value judgments with judgments about natural properties.

[53] G, 88–92 [4: 420–5].   [54] G, 95–8 [4: 427–30].

[55] I distinguish the 'thin' from the 'thick' interpretation of the humanity formula of the Categorical Imperative in 'Donagan's Kant', in my *Respect, Pluralism, and Justice*. Neither interpretation, I should note, makes explicit any grounds for the decent treatment of animals, although neither denies that there are such grounds or implies that the

is a capacity that enables all who use it properly to determine (or work more closely toward) conclusions justifiable to all, despite the fact that the world appears differently to individuals from their various perspectives, and despite the fact that their diverse desires often pull them toward conflicting policies and value judgments.[56] We treat persons as mere means when we blatantly ignore the need to obtain their consent in order to be able reasonably to do certain things to them.[57] More generally, we treat their rational nature as an end in itself only if we could justify our treatment *to them*, insofar as they are willing to consider the matter from the same shared perspective of common reason.

Later formulas of the Categorical Imperative begin to fill in some of the further conditions needed to make the Kantian idea of common practical reason workable. For example, each person with practical reason is to be seen as having 'autonomy of will' and thus as being ready to acknowledge as finally authoritative those basic principles, and only those, of which one can identify oneself, together with others, as the 'author' or 'legislator' in a sense implying that one is committed to them as a legitimate standard for oneself.[58] That we will such principles as legislators with 'autonomy' implies further that what moves us to accept them is not our attachment to the particular (rationally optional) personal goals and projects that our desires as individuals incline us toward, but rather some general concerns that all reasonable human beings have.[59] The model of legislation from the perspective of legislators in a

---

ground is merely Kant's unsatisfactory argument that cruelty to animals creates habits of cruelty to people. A theory that, in the end, cannot convincingly articulate good grounds for the decent treatment of animals is woefully incomplete, as Kant's critics have often pointed out.

[56] Kant's aim is similar in some respects to Hobbes's, when Hobbes, after noting that in a state of nature we each call the objects of our diverse desires 'good,' insists that we need a common authoritative standard to determine a 'good' that all will acknowledge. See Hobbes, *Leviathan*, 120–1. For Hobbes, the standard, of course, was the Sovereign's voice, once the state was established—whereas Kant's standard, the voice of 'practical reason' is a construct from ordinary reasonable deliberation, namely, an ideal of duly constrained joint deliberations of persons presumed to have certain general dispositions (traditionally associated with our 'rational nature').

[57] This is meant as an example, with obvious gaps, not a general criterion of treating someone as a mere means. Sometimes, of course, coercion is justified and a person's failure to consent is not a barrier; to sort cases, we need, among other things, to appeal to the idea of hypothetical consent or justifiability to the person under specified ideal conditions.

[58] G, 98–102 [4: 431–4].

[59] Note that among these concerns would be the general concern with one's own happiness: that is, wanting, within the bounds of reason, to realize some large set of jointly possible ends that one endorses upon reviewing the many diverse things one feels inclined toward. This concern, of course, will be important, though not the only factor, in applying the abstract idea of reasonable deliberation to actual conditions.

'kingdom of ends' brings together these, and some other, aspects of the Kantian ideal of reasonable deliberation. It is important, for example, that legislators take into account that each person has a set of 'private ends,' even though, as legislators they must 'abstract from the content' of those ends when they make laws.[60]

Moreover, for purposes of applying the Categorical Imperative, Kant introduces a thicker idea of 'humanity as an end in itself,' presumably an interim conclusion about what rational autonomous co-legislators would agree to. This is the idea that each person, qua rational agent and legislator, has dignity, an 'unconditional and incomparable worth,' without 'equivalent.'[61] Thus, there is, Kant thought, a rational presumption in favor not only of using one's rational powers, but of preserving them from harm (by avoiding drunkenness, gluttony, and suicide), developing them (by education and self-scrutiny), and honoring them (through self-respect and respect for others). The idea that dignity, unlike 'price,' admits no equivalents, amounts to an important constraint upon deliberation from the legislative perspective, namely, that legislators must not think of the value of *persons*, like that of *things*, as subject to rational trade-offs (for example, they must not reason, as they would about things, that two are worth twice as much as one).[62]

Pulling these ideas together, the main point is that reasonable deliberation, beyond instrumental reasoning, is deliberation *constrained by* this constructed ideal of joint legislation of rational agents with autonomy. An alleged consideration in favor of doing something is a 'good reason' for doing it only if the consideration is compatible with what lawmakers, as defined by the model, would accept. What makes a concern or requirement 'moral,' rather than 'nonmoral,' is not whether it is other-regarding or self-regarding but, rather, whether it would be deemed 'necessary' from the proper legislative perspective. Moral requirements are 'categorical' in that, from that common perspective of shared reason, one must respect them regardless of whether or not they serve one's interests or inclinations.[63]

---

[60] G, 100–2 [4: 433–5].

[61] G, 102–3 [4: 135–6]. See also my 'Donagan's Kant'.

[62] My efforts to work out this legislative model (and to identify the problems with it) so far include mainly chs. 2, 3, 4, 10, and 11, in my *Dignity and Practical Reason*; 'A Kantian Perspective on Moral Rules', and 'Donagan's Kant', in my *Respect, Pluralism, and Justice*. An application of the idea, independent of Kant, can be found in my *Autonomy and Self-Respect*, ch. 6.

[63] The supreme moral principle, what is supposedly expressed in the various forms of the Categorical Imperative, is 'categorical' (indeed supposedly the only 'categorical' imperative) in a further, stronger sense, implying that to show its rational necessity, unlike that of derivative principles, one does not need empirical premises. (Here I report the Kantian view without endorsing it.)

Kant himself seemed to have confidence, perhaps faith, that reasonable people with minimum effort could reach agreement on what rules would be approved and what policies would be ruled out by the proper use of our shared practical reason; but contemporary readers, I suspect, will find this incredible, or at least an exaggeration.[64] In the face of acknowledged disagreement, a natural extension of Kant's idea, I suggest, would be the following. Each person's responsibility, as a reasonable and moral agent, is to do his or her best, so far as the seriousness of the issue warrants the effort, to judge what should be approved from the legislative perspective. That is, one needs to try to work out what 'bills' the legislators have most reason to endorse. In doing so, one must rely on one's own honest, conscientious reflections guided by the conditions of the ideal perspective;[65] but since the outcome one seeks is justifiability to all who take up the perspective, one cannot reasonably avoid consulting others and taking their judgments into account when they differ from one's own. The regulative ideal, what we could call 'the objectively right,' is the point (if there is one) at which the best reflections of all reasonable deliberators would converge; but (despite what Kant himself thought) we can never be sure that there will be such convergence points on the various issues about which we deliberate. For practical purposes, then, when moral judgments of reasonable people differ, the best a conscientious agent can do is to *act on his or her own judgment*, after due consultation and weighing the judgments of others.[66] In doing so, without negligence, one would be blameless, but not necessarily objectively right. At best there is a workable

---

[64] The idea that reasonable Kantian legislators would reach agreement is more plausible, though perhaps still not guaranteed, when the principles are quite general and leave some room for possible exceptions—e.g., 'Everyone should make some efforts to contribute to the happiness of others.' Even specific, unqualified principles may be reasonably presumed to be agreeable to all who take up the legislative perspective (with its stipulated attitude and constraints)—e.g., 'One should not torture and kill human beings solely for the amusement of oneself or others.' Those who insist on the inevitability of disagreement are usually focusing on borderline 'hard cases,' are not heeding the Kantian constraints on moral deliberation, or both.

[65] It should be clear that this ideal construction of a legislative perspective makes no pretense at being describable, or defendable, entirely in 'neutral,' nonevaluative terms—although how various 'evaluative' terms are to be analyzed remains a matter of controversy.

[66] There is a trivial sense, of course, in which one always acts, if one acts intentionally, on one's own judgment; but what I have in mind is something else. There is a possibility of judging (even after consultation with others) that one thing is best, but then doing instead what 'most people' judge best *simply because they say so* (rather than because they have convincing reasons). It is this latter kind of 'acting against one's judgment' that goes against the conscience of a responsible agent.

standard for conscientious living, not for infallible conformity to moral 'truth.'

The details of this ideal perspective are underdetermined and controversial even among Kantians, but enough of a sketch has been given, I hope, to enable us to draw some general contrasts and comparisons with the views of reason, morals, and self-interest reviewed earlier.

First, the Kantian view, like the consequentialist one, does not give rational priority to self-interest or satisfaction of one's own preferences. There is, as it were, a common rational source for both self-regarding and other-regarding requirements. Thus, on the Kantian view, though the question arises why it is really rational to follow the (self-regarding and other-regarding) norms we call 'moral,' the task of answering this question is not equated with showing that what is *obviously rational* (self-interest or preference-satisfaction maximization), despite appearances, really supports what was *dubiously rational* (moral regard for others). Whether the issue concerns one's own life or the life of another, the question to ask is whether reasonable, autonomous legislators, under the various Kantian constraints, can justify to each other the treatment that is proposed.[67] In effect, the Kantian idea of reasonable deliberation (like common sense) has built into it concern for the 'voice' of every reasonable person.[68]

Second, Kant's conclusions about rational self-interest are, broadly speaking, coincident with two main points I attributed to common sense earlier. That is, one is rationally required to place a high priority in deliberation on self-preservation and the maintenance of one's human capacities; but otherwise, assuming compatibility with duties to others, what particular personal ends one adopts is rationally optional. When

---

[67] Alternatively, if they cannot agree on the specific treatment, can they justify to each other some general principles governing institutions that might acceptably arbitrate residual disagreements on specific issues?

[68] Skeptics about the necessary rationality of morality should not feel cheated by this stipulation, for the stipulations are aspects of an *analysis* of deliberation from a moral point of view and *not* covert attempts to allay or circumvent skeptical doubts. Skeptical worries can still be raised at a different point: why accept the results of *what Kantians call 'reasonable deliberation'* as authoritatively binding on ourselves? At this point, one might argue, Kant's *arguments* seem to run out and he must appeal to 'the fact of reason,' i.e., the supposedly inescapable sense of moral consciousness that we have some genuine moral duties. What Kant in the end defends is that, by analysis, we see that, if you accept the fact of reason, you must accept that rational deliberation goes beyond instrumental reason in the ways I have sketched. But if you really reject the 'fact of reason,' not just by saying that it is intellectually unproven but by freeing yourself (like a sociopath?) from the moral attitude and purging your dispositions to judge and act according to it, then probably neither Kant nor anyone else has an *argument* that will change you.

we are adequately fulfilling our moral duties to others and the basic self-regarding duties, reason does not *demand* further either that we pursue life-enriching, 'higher-quality' pleasures or that we try to *maximize* (informed) preference-satisfaction. Coherence and consistency in one's set of means and ends is enough. For example, if we respect others' rights, help others to some extent, avoid suicide, drunkenness, neglect of our talents, etc., we are rationally and morally free to pursue our various diverse ways of life.[69]

Third, Kant agrees with the common-sense view that reason demands that we constrain our pursuit of self-interest by a mandatory regard for others. For example, reasonable moral deliberation, he thinks, favors attitudes of gratitude, beneficence, and respect, as well as principles regarding contracts, property, and legal authority. The justification is not that in the long run such constraint will prove beneficial to oneself; on the contrary, these duties are binding even if opposed to self-interest. Here again, Kant's account is more like the consequentialist model of reason than the previous ones. Moreover, like the views of some consequentialists (but not all), Kant's conclusions accord with the common-sense view that, beyond our strict duties to others, there is much 'playroom for free choice' regarding when, how, and how much we undertake efforts on behalf of others. There is room for the morally indifferent; Kant ridicules one who would deny this as one who 'strews all his steps with duties, as with mantraps.'[70] Beneficence is a 'wide, imperfect duty of virtue': unenforceable, flexible, not a response to 'rights,' and leaving a wide latitude for choice in when and how to fulfill it.[71] As in the common-sense view, what one owes to others is not measured in terms of percentages of time and effort for others versus for oneself, but is rather spelled out roughly in legal systems and traditional ethical principles that, like common sense, typically give priority to life and integrity of body and mind.

Finally, unlike consequentialist models, the Kantian view maintains the primary importance of the moral agent in ways that, I believe,

---

[69] The 'etc.' here refers to the rest of the various perfect and imperfect duties that Kant argues for in the *Groundwork*, *The Metaphysics of Morals*, and various political writings. For the latter, see Hans Reiss (ed.), *Kant: Political Writings* (Cambridge: Cambridge University Press, 1991). The list includes more duties than I explicitly mentioned, but the main point is that both moral and nonmoral reason leave considerable leeway for individual choice of way of life.

[70] MM, 167 [6: 409].

[71] MM, 150–4 [6: 387–91] and 198–208 [6: 448–61]. Interpretation here is somewhat controversial. My interpretation and evidence can be found in *Dignity and Practical Reason*, ch. 8.

accord with common sense. Thus, despite the ultimate appeal to a shared faculty of human reason, the Kantian view is arguably not as objectionably 'impersonal' and 'impartialist.' Here, in conclusion, are a few reflections that may suggest what I have in mind.

The starting point of Kantian reflection on reason, self-interest, and morality is supposed to be the perspective of an ordinary reasonable and conscientious person, deliberating about what he or she ought to do (but prepared to follow the philosophical argument wherever it leads). It is by analyzing the ordinary consciousness of being under duties, supposedly, that one is able to articulate the ideal of co-legislation by reasonable, autonomous agents; and it is the fact that the latter is (supposedly) merely an extension of the former that explains why we regard the latter to be authoritative for us. Thus, the moral point of view is not a 'view from nowhere,' nor is it the alien idea of detached utility-maximizers. It is supposed to be the abstractly articulated presuppositions of ordinary conscientious agents.

Further, although the model of co-legislation requires us to consult and take seriously the moral opinions and arguments of others, in using it one is not expected to suspend or subordinate one's own conscientious judgments. Where there is disagreement among apparently reasonable conscientious agents, one must try, after due consultation and listening, to judge what ('bills') to propose as the most reasonable and thus most justifiable to all (under the constraints of the legislative perspective). Unlike in Brandt's theory of value, empirical facts about everyone's hypothetical preferences (even if known) would not by themselves fix determinate answers to value questions; and as with Rawls's initial 'original position,' stipulated features of the choosing parties fix determinate answers only at a certain very general level. As a would-be Kantian legislator, one is aiming at justif*ability* to all who try to take up the proper perspective. But the fact that most others firmly persist in disagreeing with me does not force me, on pain of irrationality, to grant that their majority judgment is better than mine. The Kantian model is not so tightly defined as to permit, regarding most issues, the simple deduction that all legislators would agree on certain results. And the differences between real people trying to adopt the perspective and the ideal of legislators who fully instantiate it are so great that one cannot simply infer from the fact that one differs from (or agrees with) most other people that one's own judgment is mistaken (or correct). In using the Kantian model as a guide, there will always remain a need to make one's own conscientious judgments.

In the face of real moral disagreement with others, in fact, the Kantian position (as I see it) is that each person has the responsibility *to act on his or her own best moral judgment*. Due consultation with others, weighing their arguments, etc., are necessary if one is to take seriously that one is looking for what can be justified to all; but to follow majority judgments just because more people share them would be to deny one's responsibility as an autonomous agent.

Another way in which the moral agent has priority in Kantian ethics is that most, if not all, duties are *agent-relative*, in a certain sense. They do not say, for example, 'Murders ought to be prevented,' but rather 'You ought not to commit murder.' Typically they direct each agent not to commit certain acts (murder, theft, lying, promise-breaking, adultery, etc.) and to perform others (debt-paying, aiding those in dire need, etc.), rather than putting forward a goal (such as general happiness) as worthy of pursuit, the more the better. Each agent is thus especially 'responsible' for his or her own conduct within a defined sphere, and whether others act likewise in comparable circumstances is typically 'not one's business.' Individual law-abiding agents are to be trusted, when possible, to carry out their specific and limited responsibilities; and beyond this they are largely free to do as they please. A conscientious person, then, can usually plan a course of life for him- or herself that is both morally sound and individually satisfying. At least, we do not face a general, ever-present, and all-encompassing responsibility to maximize good outcomes, or minimize wrongdoing, throughout the world.

Similarly, we have agent-relative rights. That is, each person, Kant thought, has a sphere of reasonably protected liberty to pursue his or her own ends without interference from others. Each has a permissible space, the boundaries of which may be legitimately crossed only with that agent's consent. Thus, just as I am not under an all-encompassing responsibility to promote good outcomes or prevent wrongdoing in the world, I am not *subject* to an all-encompassing moral authority of others to treat me in any manner that would minimize crime and immorality or otherwise promote the best states of the world. In this respect, in a Kantian world one's life is *more one's own* than in a consequentialist world, at least more so than in an act-consequentialist world.

Even if rule-consequentialists should argue for just the same boundary rules as Kant endorses, their mode of argument for them, I suspect, would involve both questionable empirical premises (that respecting the 'boundaries' always maximizes good results) and an impersonal, alien point of view. Most ordinary conscientious people, I believe, are deeply disposed and publicly committed to some limited form of *reciprocity* with others. Roughly, they are prepared to constrain their self-interested pursuits, within some limits, provided that others will do likewise. They are willing to treat the most vital interests of others as worthy of mutual protection insofar as they are assured similar protection for their own vital interests. They will even count nonvital personal preferences of others as worthy of *some* consideration for noninterference or aid, provided that others will do likewise and that sufficient liberty for one's own projects is ensured. Even those free-riders who refuse such minimal cooperation, I imagine, often tend to acknowledge as reasonable the complaints of those whose restraint they exploit. Though naturally and reasonably reluctant to give up their freedom, most people are prepared to listen to good reasons offered by others as to why, in limited ways, everyone's yielding such freedom makes sense from their common-sense perspective. Now, my thought is just that the Kantian legislative perspective is essentially an abstract expression and refinement of such basic commitments as these, and that these, in turn, are dispositions that we associate with being 'reasonable' in everyday life, not outbursts from a hidden noumenal realm. By contrast, the rule-utilitarian legislator is more than an extension of common reasonable commitments. It may be, as some suggest, an 'angelic' disposition, this willingness to devote oneself to rules, whatever they may be, that would best satisfy an overriding desire for maximum human welfare, impartially distributed.[72] But the Kantian, like anyone of common sense, cannot help but wonder, 'Why is it reasonable for *me*, or *you*, to count the rules so derived as authoritative for *us*?'

[72] See Hare, *Moral Thinking*, 44–64.

6

Happiness and Human Flourishing

I. INTRODUCTION

Ancient moral philosophers, especially Aristotle and his followers, typically shared the assumption that ethics is primarily concerned with how to achieve the final end for human beings, a life of 'happiness' or 'human flourishing.' This final end was not a subjective condition, such as contentment or the satisfaction of our preferences, but a life that could be objectively determined to be appropriate to our nature as human beings. Character traits were treated as moral virtues because they contributed well toward this ideal life, either as means to it or as constitutive aspects of it. Traits that tended to prevent a 'happy' life were considered vices, even if they contributed to a life that was pleasant and what a person most wanted. The idea of 'happiness' (or human flourishing) was central, then, in philosophical efforts to specify what we ought to do, what sort of persons we should try to become, and what sort of life a wise person would hope for.

In modern philosophy this ancient conception of 'happiness' has been largely replaced by more subjective conceptions. Not surprisingly, then, happiness plays a different, and usually diminished, role in modern moral theories. Immanuel Kant is a striking, and influential, example of this trend. Viewing happiness as personal contentment and success in achieving the ends we want, he argues that morality is a constraint on the pursuit of a happy life rather than a means to it or an element of it. Even the moral duty to contribute to the happiness of others is more limited in Kant's moral theory than in most other modern theories that (like Kant) abandon the common ancient conceptions of 'happiness.'

These are apparently major disagreements about the importance of happiness and human flourishing in a moral life, and it is natural to wonder what are the reasons for the disagreements and how deep they run. As a step toward understanding the contrasts better, I shall try to sort out and describe briefly several different aspects of Kant's moral theory, as I understand it, especially concerning how happiness and human flourishing are (or are not) relevant to ethics. My project here is not to defend Kant's position, but to clarify it and at times to explore Kant's reasons for holding it. Some of Kant's points, as we shall see, are widely accepted, but others are highly controversial. Some are basic to his ethical theory, but others prove not to be. All of the points are open to dispute, but in some cases, I suggest, the dispute rests on a misunderstanding of Kant's position.

My discussion here is part of a larger project, which is to distinguish Kant's basic moral theory from unwarranted particular conclusions, to show its appeal so far as possible, to call attention to its shortcomings as I see them, and to suggest modifications to make Kantian ethics more plausible at least on some issues.

Since 'happiness' (*eudaimonia*) in ancient ethics, understood as human flourishing, is generally distinct from what Kant calls happiness (*Glückseligkeit*), I need at first to explain what I take these ideas to be, at least sufficiently for purposes of subsequent discussion. Then my questions are: How did Kant restrict the role of happiness in his moral theory? And why did he endorse happiness, rather than human flourishing, as the primary nonmoral good for individuals?[1]

II. THE IDEAS OF KANTIAN HAPPINESS AND HUMAN FLOURISHING

What is happiness, and what is it to flourish? Much of the history of Western ethics is devoted to these questions, and the answers have varied in complex and subtle ways that defy brief summary. For present purposes, however, what we need are some stipulations sufficient to fix ideas for subsequent discussion. Here, then, I will merely propose a working understanding of *human flourishing* that I hope will be sufficient to pose the issues on which I want to focus, and then I will contrast this with *happiness* as Kant conceived this.

---

[1] By calling happiness a 'nonmoral' good in Kant's ethics, I have in mind several points. For example, in Kant's view, a happy person is not necessarily a morally good person and a vicious person is not necessarily unhappy. Happiness is a natural end that each person has, but the pursuit of (one's own) happiness is not a moral requirement—except indirectly, when its neglect would increase our temptations to neglect our duties. So far as it is compatible with morality, each person's happiness is a (conditional) good for that person, that is, something rational (but not a duty or virtue) for the person to pursue. We have a duty of beneficence to others, but this directs us to help them to achieve the (permissible) ends they choose, not to improve their characters or to fulfill a moral ideal. Having a good will (roughly, a will to do what is right) is, by contrast, a moral good, for maintaining a good will is necessary and sufficient for being a morally good person. It is an unconditional good, a fundamental requirement of morality.

Plants, animals, and human beings are said to flourish, or not, depending on how well they are doing by some presupposed conception of what is good for things of their kind. They flourish, or thrive, *as* plants, *as* animals, or *as* human beings. They may be said to flourish as a more specific kind of thing, natural or conventional. For example, a particular plant may be said to flourish as a bush (or as a decorative rose bush); a certain animal may be said to flourish as a bird (or as a wild bird of prey); and a particular person may be said to flourish as a hunter (or as a nomadic Buffalo hunter). The relevant criteria of flourishing (as an X) are sometimes part of the meaning of 'flourishing' and the term for the kind in question, but they may be merely commonly accepted evaluative standards. As the ancients emphasized, they are typically associated with natural tendencies: birds fly, fish swim, plants grow and draw nourishment through roots, etc. We think of things as not fully flourishing (as a certain kind) when they are impeded in these characteristic functions, when they are 'damaged,' 'injured,' 'deformed,' or 'degenerate.' In speaking of human beings, animals, and even (sometimes) plants, we invoke notions of striving and fulfillment: in general an X flourishes more fully as an X when the strivings it has as an X are fulfilled or at least partially successful. In human beings and higher-order animals, flourishing (as human or animal) is commonly thought to be marked by a sense of well-being and a significant degree of contentment about one's present condition or prospects. Being content, however, does not mean that one is flourishing, for contentment is merely a subjective sense of well-being that can persist despite serious disease, malfunctioning natural capacities, and imminent collapse. Notoriously, in human beings, narcotic drugs cause feelings of contentment in diseased, mentally damaged addicts who are far from flourishing as human beings.

These points seem obvious, I hope, because they reflect more or less how flourishing is usually understood today, even apart from philosophical theories. Together the points make the term 'flourishing' in some respects less misleading than 'happiness' for purposes of expressing ancient ideas of the final good for human beings. 'Happiness,' as often noted, now often stands for temporary euphoria, mindless contentment, a warm glow, or pleasure without worry. By common opinion now, one can be happy for a few moments, then unhappy, then happy again, and so on; but the same does not hold for *flourishing as a human being*. Admittedly, a person who is flourishing could be suddenly incapacitated or destroyed, but the description typically refers to a pattern of strivings and fulfillments, etc., over a significant period of time, not to something as variable as moods, sensations, and other passive states.

This current view of human flourishing reflects some of the basic ideas of 'happiness' in ancient philosophy, and no doubt owes much to that source.[2] Ancient moral philosophy includes variations as well as similarities, of course, but for present purposes we may treat Aristotle's account of 'happiness' (or human flourishing) as a paradigm.[3] The core of this idea, as I understand it, is as follows. 'Happiness,' properly conceived, describes an active, complete life that necessarily includes being virtuous and using practical reason in deliberation. Characteristic, natural, 'essential' human capacities are developed and fulfilled together in a 'happy' life. Community, moral exemplars, effort, and good fortune are supposed to be necessary, at least as causally enabling conditions. Whether acting in certain ways is conducive to a person's 'happiness' or not is an objective matter that the person can discern if wise and virtuous; but ordinary, imperfect people often misjudge what is required. The particulars of a 'happy' life vary from person to person, but not simply with their actual desires, considered preferences, or chosen ends. A 'happy' life is pleasant and all that a wise person could (realistically) want, but a pleasant and content life is not necessarily a 'happy' one. In a perfectly 'happy' (and so virtuous) life, natural desires have been shaped into a harmonious system appropriate to the circumstances, and thus, in a sense, our main desires would be satisfied, not frustrated or

---

[2] My brief sketch of a contemporary view of human flourishing is just a summary of how I interpret common understandings of the idea, but few philosophers seem to discuss it independently of the texts of Aristotle and other ancient philosophers. John Cooper uses the term 'human flourishing' to capture (roughly) Aristotle's idea of *eudaimonia* or 'happiness,' and he credits Elizabeth Anscombe for suggesting this translation. See John Cooper, *Reason and Human Good in Aristotle* (Cambridge: Harvard University Press, 1975), 89–143, esp. p. 90n.; and G. E. M. Anscombe, 'Modern Moral Philosophy', *Philosophy*, 33(124) (1958), 1–19. Other scholars prefer 'happiness' as the appropriate translation, while making clear that Aristotle's conception of 'happiness' differs from familiar contemporary conceptions. See, for example, Julia Annas, *The Morality of Happiness* (New York: Oxford University Press, 1993); Nancy Sherman, *The Fabric of Character* (Oxford: Oxford University Press, 1989); Anthony Kenny, *Aristotle on the Perfect Life* (Oxford: Oxford University Press, 1992); and Richard Kraut, *Aristotle and the Human Good* (Princeton: Princeton University Press, 1989).

[3] See Aristotle, *Nicomachean Ethics*, tr. Terence Irwin (Indianapolis: Hackett Publishing Co., 1985), esp. book I. Many similarities and variations are described in detail in Annas, *The Morality of Happiness*. Since my aim is to emphasize the contrasts between Aristotle's idea of 'happiness' (or human flourishing) and quite different Kantian ideas, in referring to Aristotle's *eudaimonia* I will either use the term 'human flourishing' or else use quotation marks ('happiness').

repressed, in such a life. Without this special shaping, however, the goal of 'satisfying all our desires' is far from the ideal of a 'happy' life.

Kant seems to shift between several ideas of happiness. In all cases, though, happiness is conceived as something more subjective, indeterminate, and variable from person to person than human flourishing is typically thought to be. Kant agrees with Aristotle and others that *virtue* (at least as Kant understands this) requires much more than satisfying our desires and feeling content. We must use practical reason to determine objectively what is morally right and virtuous to choose. But by sharply distinguishing virtue and happiness, Kant splits elements that are apparently *combined* in Aristotle's idea of human flourishing.[4] The moral element (virtue) Kant then treats as objective, common to all human beings, distinct from desires, and discerned by reason. But the other element (happiness) he treats as subjective, relative to individuals, desire-based, and not very well served by reason.

Sometimes Kant writes of happiness as something familiar and attainable (with luck): e.g., as 'preservation,' 'welfare,' and 'well-being.'[5] Most often, however, Kant characterizes happiness as an unattainable goal, something we can only approximate: e.g., as 'an absolute whole, a maximum of well-being in my present, and in every future, state.'[6] Sometimes the goal seems to be lasting *contentment*: e.g., 'satisfaction with one's state, so long as this is lasting,' and 'a rational being's consciousness of the agreeableness of life uninterruptedly accompanying his whole existence.'[7] At other times the central idea is *getting all that we desire*: e.g., 'total satisfaction' of our 'needs and inclinations' and 'all inclinations combined in a sum total.'[8] The differences here seem not to have concerned Kant. In fact, sometimes he brings the different ideas together: e.g., happiness is 'that everything should always go the way you would like it to—[that is,] continuous well-being, enjoyment of life, complete satisfaction with one's condition.'[9]

---

[4] Strictly speaking, Kant splits virtue (as he conceives it) from happiness (as he conceives it), but not Aristotelian 'virtue' from Aristotelian 'happiness.' 'Virtue,' according to Kant, is a 'capacity and considered resolve' and 'strength' to resist 'what opposes the moral disposition *within us*' (MM, 146 [6: 380], 153 [6: 390], and 156 [6: 394]). A virtuous person, then, must have not only a will to do what is right (a 'good will') but also a resolve to resist temptations and strength of will to do so. Virtue, according to Aristotle, requires reshaping or getting rid of desires that might compete with our doing the right thing; and thus Aristotle's fully virtuous person, being temperate rather than merely continent, has no need for the *strength of will to resist temptations* that Kant refers to.

[5] G, 93 [4: 395]. See also MM, 152 [6: 389]. [6] G, 67 [4: 399].
[7] MM, 152 [6: 389], and C2, 19–20 [5: 22].
[8] G, 73 [4: 405] and 67 [4: 399]. [9] MM, 223 [6: 480].

Kant realizes that all of our inclinations cannot be jointly satisfied and that we do not have any determinate idea of what this total satisfaction would be for us. Usually we have an even less determinate idea of the happiness of others. For practical purposes, then, the aim of promoting happiness, for oneself or another, must be understood more modestly: roughly, as trying to contribute to the satisfaction of some significant portion of the person's set of inclination-based ends.[10] Similarly, when happiness is interpreted as contentment, promoting happiness must be understood as increasing a person's contentment or subjective sense of well-being. The aim of promoting someone's happiness, understood as a practical aim, cannot be that the person will achieve total satisfaction of desire or uninterrupted contentment for a lifetime. That is obviously impossible to achieve, and, knowing this, we cannot seriously count it as a goal.

III. THE LIMITED ROLE OF HAPPINESS IN KANT'S ETHICS: OLD ISSUES

Kant reacted strongly against moral theories, ancient and modern, that, in his opinion, misunderstood and overrated the value of happiness or failed to acknowledge adequately the moral constraints on the pursuit of happiness. Much of his work in ethics in fact seems devoted to putting happiness in its place. There are several distinguishable ways that he attempted to limit the role of happiness in moral theory, and each has been disputed. The controversies on most of these points have been debated for many years, and thus I shall comment only briefly on them. But a recent objection raised by Michael Slote has not been so thoroughly aired.[11] Since I think that it rests on an important misunderstanding that should be corrected, I examine it critically in Section IV.

A. Happiness Is Not an Unconditional Good

In Kant's moral theory, happiness is not valuable in some of the ways, and to the degree, that it is in other moral theories. According to Kant,

[10] This characterization is quite vague, but inevitably so, for several reasons. Our ends tend to be indeterminate; our priorities for cases of conflict are often undecided; and it is unclear to what extent ignorance, irrationality, and misjudgment in a person's adoption of ends is supposed to modify or cancel the judgment that helping the person to realize those ends would be promoting the person's happiness.

[11] Michael Slote, *From Morality to Virtue* (New York: Oxford University Press, 1992), 39–57.

only a good will is 'good without qualification,' and thus happiness is only conditionally good.[12] Qualified or conditional goods, in Kant's sense, are not worthy of pursuit by rational agents in all possible contexts, but only when certain conditions obtain. Conditional goods, like happiness, might seem good when we try to consider them apart from particular contexts, but an unqualified good must be worthy of choice in all contexts.[13]

Kant grants, however, that happiness is an end that all human beings have. It is human nature to seek happiness for oneself. Moreover, we tend to pursue it for its own sake, not merely as something good as a means to other things. Thus, even though Kant denies that happiness is an unqualified good, he grants that we tend to treat happiness, at least from our individual perspectives, as 'good in itself' in a familiar, everyday sense.[14] We want happiness not for any further purpose it may serve, but just for what it is, and it is fully rational to act on this desire if doing so is compatible with duty and virtue.

Kant, however, does not treat happiness as something that has 'intrinsic value' in the ways that this term has been understood by G. E. Moore, W. D. Ross, R. B. Perry, C. I. Lewis, and others.[15] In Kant's

---

[12] G, 61–2 [4: 393–4]. I rely on a (possibly controversial) interpretation explained in Ch. 2 of this volume.

[13] G. E. Moore thought that the way to see what is 'good in itself' is to consider the item in question 'in isolation' from everything else, i.e., 'apart from all effects and accompaniments.' Here 'in itself' is taken quite literally: just look into the thing itself and you will see its goodness. (See G. E. Moore, *Principia Ethica* (1903; Cambridge: Cambridge University Press, 1959), and Moore, *Ethics* (1912; Oxford: Oxford University Press, 1965).) This is not the ordinary use of the term, I think, nor is it Kant's. Crucially, it is not what Kant means by 'unconditionally good.' See Christine Korsgaard, 'Two Distinctions in Goodness', *Philosophical Review*, 92, no. 2 (1983), 169–95; and Ch. 2 of this volume.

[14] There is some disagreement among Kant scholars, I think, about whether Kant admits that there are individual-agent-relative values, things that are merely *good to or for a person* in a sense that does not necessarily give others reasons to act (e.g., to help or refrain from interference). (I say 'individual-agent-relative' here to distinguish the values in question from those that might be described as 'rational-agents-relative.' In a sense, all value according to Kant stems from what persons rationally will and thus is not something that could exist independently of all (possible) valuing agents.) Of course, it is agreed that Kant's view is that insofar as attainment of happiness is consistent with morality, the happiness of every person is something that we have some moral reason to promote; and thus 'morally permissible happiness,' in Kant's view, is not *simply* valuable to the person who would attain it. The disagreement, I think, concerns whether Kant acknowledged the category of value judgments entirely relativized to individual agents. This is discussed further in Ch. 8 of this volume.

[15] See, for example, Moore, *Principia Ethica*; Moore, *Ethics*; R. B. Perry, *General Theory of Value: Its Meaning and Basic Principles Construed in Terms of Interest* (New York: Longmans, Green, 1926); C. I. Lewis, *An Analysis of Knowledge and Valuation* (La Salle, IL: Open Court, 1947); and W. D. Ross, *The Right and the Good* (Oxford:

theory there are no *intrinsic values* as Moore understood the term; that is, there are no intuited nonnatural properties that 'supervene' on natural properties (e.g., aspects of experiences of sentient beings). Kant's theory is also incompatible with the view that intrinsic values exist as natural properties, such as being 'objects of interest' (Perry), satisfying 'experiences' (Lewis), or being desired for themselves when we are fully informed (Brandt). Kant's view, as I understand it, is that things are good or valuable by virtue of being the objects of rational willing, and what it is rational to will is not a question that can be settled entirely by empirical means—or by intuition. In deliberating about right and wrong, then, we cannot assume that happiness has a natural or intuited 'intrinsic value' always tending in favor of the acts that promote it. Unlike many philosophers, Kant does not think that each potential increase in someone's happiness has a quantity of value on a scale of commensurable values so that we have good reason for doing what will bring about that increase unless that bit of value is 'outweighed' by more value that we can bring about by other options.[16]

Although Kant says that happiness is a natural end for human beings, he rejects the idea that happiness is a final, self-sufficient end for human beings in Aristotle's sense.[17] For Aristotle, as I understand him, a life of 'happiness' (in his special sense) contains within it all the valuable sorts of things that any human being could reasonably want, mixed in the proportions appropriate to the context as judged by a practically wise person. Moral virtue, in Aristotle's view, is an essential constituent of such a 'happy' life, and Aristotle apparently thought that no one would be wrong to live such a life, or to aim to do so, in any circumstances.[18] Kant conceives of happiness more narrowly (without virtue

---

Oxford University Press, 1930). These are classics of intrinsic value theory. In discussions of environmental ethics the term has reappeared in recent years, but without much attention to the controversies that earlier theories of intrinsic value raised. See, for example, D. S. Mannison, M. A. McRobbie, and R. Routley (eds.), *Environmental Philosophy* (Canberra: Australian National University Research School of Social Sciences, 1980). For a more contemporary use of the term, see Thomas Hurka, *Perfectionism* (New York: Oxford University Press, 1994).

[16] G, 102 [4: 434–5].
[17] G, 83 [4: 416]; Aristotle, *Nicomachean Ethics*, book 1, ch. 1.
[18] I distinguish living a 'happy' life from aiming to do so because it seems possible that fully virtuous persons could be living a 'happy' life (in Aristotle's sense) while for the most part not holding the ideal of this sort of life as a deliberative goal; for example, they could be concentrating instead on the particular choices at hand (in the manner of one with acquired virtues). The deliberate pursuit of a 'happy' life might be more appropriately the ideal for novices who are not yet fully virtuous or for certain special decisions that require consciously reviewing one's life as a whole.

as a necessary ingredient) and insists that a happy life (so conceived) would not be a good life, or a worthy end, unless it could be pursued and achieved without violating moral requirements (which are not derived from a prior assumption that happiness is always good as an end).

Kant's position here on the value of happiness is controversial, of course, but it is perhaps more widely shared than we might at first think. Aristotelians should have no *substantial* disagreement with Kant on these points about the limited value of happiness as Kant, more narrowly, conceives it; for Aristotelians do not affirm the unqualified goodness of happiness in that sense.[19] Even intuitionists, such as Moore and Ross, are not committed to the idea that happiness is something unqualifiedly good—that is, good to pursue in all contexts—and their intuitionism of value allows that there may be better ends to pursue than happiness, better even than the greatest happiness of the greatest number.[20]

When Kant's position is properly understood, then, objections stem mostly from two sources: (1) classic utilitarians who treat 'the greatest happiness' as an unconditionally good end to pursue, and (2) advocates of intuitionism and naturalism in value theory who rightly see Kant as denying their understanding of what constitutes value. These are old, much-debated issues, and among contemporary philosophers Kant has much good company on his side.[21]

---

[19] Kant would not fully accept Aristotle's view about the value of happiness even in Aristotle's sense, but their views are closer regarding that.

[20] Ross, like Moore, was an intuitionist regarding 'intrinsic value,' but, unlike Moore, he was not a consequentialist who thought that the right thing to do is always to maximize intrinsic value. See Ross, *The Right and the Good*.

[21] Although interpretation is controversial, Bentham and Mill, as usually understood, represent classic utilitarianism; see Jeremy Bentham, *A Fragment on Government and an Introduction to the Principles of Morals and Legislation*, ed. Wilfred Harrison (Oxford: Blackwell, 1960); and John Stuart Mill, *Utilitarianism*, ed. George Sher (1863; Indianapolis: Hackett Publishing Co., 1979). G. E. Moore and W. D. Ross are intuitionists with regard to intrinsic value; R. B. Perry and C. I. Lewis advocate the sort of naturalism that is intended here. Few, if any, contemporary philosophers defend the intuitionist position. Critics of classic utilitarianism are legion, but the most often cited is John Rawls, *A Theory of Justice* (Cambridge, MA: Harvard University Press, 1999). Naturalistic definitions of value are also widely rejected. See, for example, R. M. Hare, *Freedom and Reason* (Oxford: Oxford University Press, 1963); Allan Gibbard, *Wise Choices, Apt Feelings* (Cambridge, MA: Harvard University Press, 1990); Simon Blackburn, *Spreading the Word* (Oxford: Oxford University Press, 1984); and Christine Korsgaard, *The Sources of Normativity* (New York: Cambridge University Press, 1996).

B. Happiness Is Not the Ultimate Criterion of Right Action

Kant holds that it is not always morally right to do what you expect will maximize happiness. This is not merely because consequences are uncertain, for Kant is also committed to the stronger claim that there are many things that would be wrong to do even if we knew that they would actually maximize happiness. This goes beyond what I have already said, although perhaps not in an obvious way. Utilitarians often base their thesis that we always *ought* to do what promotes the greatest happiness on an assertion that happiness is *good* in itself, or intrinsically valuable; but they can affirm the former without the latter. That is, they can endorse a utilitarian theory of right without taking a stand in value theory. They can do this simply by asserting that the right thing to do is whatever maximizes happiness (or expected happiness) without arguing for this from the prior premiss that happiness is intrinsically valuable. They may be challenged to produce new 'grounds' for their utilitarian principle, but they would at least avoid dispute with Kantians (and others) about whether happiness is *unconditionally good*. Perhaps needless to say, their main dispute with Kantians (about what is right to do) would remain unsettled.

C. Happiness Is Not the Unqualified Goal of Moral Rules

Kant's theory not only affirms moral principles that constrain the pursuit of the general happiness, it is also incompatible with the rule-utilitarian idea that these principles themselves are justified because their general adoption as norms promotes the greatest happiness in the long run.[22] There is, I believe, a reasonable reconstruction of

---

[22] For often-cited statements of rule-utilitarianism, see J. O. Urmson, 'On the Interpretation of the Philosophy of J. S. Mill', *Philosophical Quarterly*, 3 (1953), 33–9; Richard Brandt, 'Toward a Credible Form of Utilitarianism', in Hector-Neri Castaneda and George Nakhnikian (eds.), *Morality and the Language of Conduct* (Detroit: Wayne State University Press, 1965); John Rawls, 'Two Concepts of Rules', *Philosophical Review*, 64 (1955), 3–32; and David Lyons, *Forms and Limits of Utilitarianism* (Oxford: Clarendon Press, 1965). Rule-utilitarianism developed in response to objections to 'act-utilitarianism,' which holds that in every case we ought to act in the way that would maximize utility even if this would contravene important rules (actual and ideal) that are generally useful. The standard objection was that act-utilitarianism would endorse acts of injustice (e.g., false witness, even murder) in cases where these acts would promote (even slightly) more utility. Rule-utilitarianism tries to block this objection by maintaining that we should follow the generally useful rules of justice, even in these cases. But there are subtle differences in different versions of rule-utilitarianism.

David Cummiskey argues that, despite Kant's own beliefs contrary to utilitarianism of

Kant's fundamental framework for moral deliberation that, like rule-utilitarianism, distinguishes deliberation about moral rules from deliberation guided by moral rules, but in Kant's theory, unlike in rule-utilitarianism, specific rules are not identified or 'legislated' because their adoption would maximize happiness.[23] Kantian deliberation about norms is constrained by the requirements implicit in the formulas of the Categorical Imperative, especially the idea of persons as ends in themselves.[24] Even at the highest level of deliberation about rules, then, we cannot endorse rules that express or encourage the idea that individuals are like exchangeable commodities, each having some value of a sort that is commensurable and permits calculated trade-offs.

D. Strict Moral Rules Forbid Exceptions That Might Prevent Unhappiness

Kant does not merely reject the extreme utilitarian stand regarding the morality of promoting happiness. That alone would disturb only relatively few contemporary moral philosophers. Notoriously, Kant also severely limited the role of happiness in his moral theory by endorsing substantive rules of conduct that make very strict demands and admit few, if any, exceptions. The most often cited example is probably Kant's stand on lying (even for 'benevolent purposes'), but his condemnation

---

all sorts, features of Kant's basic moral theory, when followed out consistently, lead to a kind of consequentialism that is akin to rule-utilitarianism. See David Cummiskey, *Kantian Consequentialism* (New York: Oxford University Press, 1996). I disagree, but cannot argue the point here.

[23] I sketch such a reconstruction in ch. 2 of *Respect, Pluralism, and Justice*. See also chs. 10 and 11 in my *Dignity and Practical Reason in Kant's Moral Theory*; and ch. 8 of *Respect, Pluralism, and Justice*.

[24] In Kant's moral theory, 'the Categorical Imperative' represents the most fundamental moral requirements, expressed in an imperative form—as a '*command* of reason' (G, 83 [4: 413] and 84 [4: 416]). It is supposed to be an unconditional requirement of reason that grounds particular moral duties, which are morally and rationally binding even if they do not serve our self-interest or further our chosen ends. Kant presents the Categorical Imperative in several formulas, which he suggests amount to the same basic idea (G, 103–4 [4: 436–7]). The interpretation of these formulas, whether they are equivalent, and even how many there are remain controversial. The first formula is: 'Act only on that maxim through which you can at the same time will that it should become a universal law' (G, 88 [4: 421]). A variation, used in Kant's examples, is: 'Act as if the maxim of your action were to become through your will a universal law of nature' (G, 89 [4: 421]). This is followed by the influential 'humanity formula': 'Act in such a way that you always treat humanity, whether in your own person or in the person of any other, never simply as a means, but always at the same time as an end' (G, 96 [4: 429]). Kant writes of both 'humanity' and 'persons' as 'ends in themselves,' which have an 'unconditional and incomparable worth' as opposed to mere 'price' (G, 102 [4: 434]).

of 'defiling oneself by lust,' adultery, 'unnatural crimes,' 'murdering oneself,' revolutionary activity, and other matters is also unconditional.[25] Even when Kant explicitly mentions a permissible exception to principles in his theory of justice, this often merely highlights how unusually strict and inflexible his principles are. For example, at one point Kant grants that we may (and must) disobey an official state order if it requires us to do something 'immoral in itself,' but this (rarely mentioned) concession calls attention, by way of contrast, to Kant's remarkably strong claim that in all other cases we must obey the law, even when the law is maliciously imposed by a tyrant.[26] To take another example, Kant concedes that the strict duty of state officials to execute those who commit murder excludes the case in which for the sake of 'honor' a mother kills her 'illegitimate' infant. Kant says that because the child 'is born outside of the law,' it has 'stolen into the commonwealth (like contraband)' and so 'the commonwealth can ignore its existence' and also 'its annihilation.'[27] Few of us, I imagine, will want to insist on execution of the mother in this case, but Kant's discussion of it (as only one of three exceptions) does little to improve, and may even worsen, Kant's image as an inflexible, insensitive, perhaps even callous, 'man of principle.'

By endorsing his strict principles, Kant goes far beyond others who agree with him on the weaker thesis that the pursuit of personal and general happiness is subject to moral constraints. Ross, for example, holds that the duty to promote happiness can be, and often is, overridden by other prima facie duties (fidelity, justice, reparation, noninjury, gratitude, and self-improvement), and other nonconsequentialists allow 'built in' exceptions to moral rules to accommodate certain special cases in which sticking to the rules without those exceptions would have a disastrous effect on the happiness of many people. Similarly, rights theorists now usually characterize particular rights as 'defeasible,' even

---

[25] In a late essay, Kant takes the extreme stance that a person would not have a right to tell a lie to an assassin to save a friend from murder. See Immanuel Kant, *Grounding for the Metaphysics of Morals*, with 'On a Supposed Right to Lie because of Philanthropic Concerns', tr. James W. Ellington (Indianapolis: Hackett Publishing Co., 1981), 63–7. Most contemporary admirers of Kant, I think, reject this position. See, for example, Alan Donagan, *The Theory of Morality* (Chicago: University of Chicago Press, 1977), 88–9. For Kant's controversial position on other matters, see MM, 178–9 [6: 424–5], 62–3 [6: 278–9], 130–5 [6: 363–9], 176–7 [6: 422–3], and 93–8 [6: 316–23].

[26] MM, 93–8 [6: 316–23], 136 [6: 371]; see also Hans Reiss, 'Postscript', in Hans Reiss (ed.), *Kant: Political Writings* (Cambridge: Cambridge University Press, 1991), 267–8. See also R, 153n [6: 154n].

[27] MM, 108–9 [6: 336].

if the potentially overriding considerations cannot be spelled out in advance. Quite unlike the disputes mentioned earlier, then, the dispute provoked by Kant's stand concerning inflexible principles pits Kant against most other moral theorists.

Once again, I do not want to pursue further the issue that I have identified, but my reason is not the same as in previous cases. Here the Kantian side of the dispute is so extreme and (in my view) implausible that discussions of it seem to me quite tiresome and 'academic' in the pejorative sense. Although Kant's rigoristic principles concerning lying, obedience to law, etc., were no doubt an important part of his own personality and moral thinking, there is little in his basic moral theory, I believe, to support his extreme stand on these substantive issues.[28] For example, as is often noted, a full and honest articulation of the maxim behind many conscientious lies would be more subtle and context-sensitive than those mentioned in Kant's examples. So to consider them 'as if universal laws of nature,' we should not be thinking of possible worlds in which everyone lies whenever they please, or for selfish reasons, or for many other reasons that we could not sensibly choose for everyone to act on.[29] Kant's polemical argument, given late in life, against the right to lie to someone who threatens to murder a friend is question-begging.[30] Kant argues that if one lied and unexpectedly the lie led the murderer to his victim, then the death of the victim would be imputable to the person who lied (as well as the killer); but this claim *presupposes* Kant's conclusion that telling the lie is wrong regardless of the circumstances. If we suppose, to the contrary, that lying is the right thing to do in the specified circumstances, then there is no reason to insist that the liar would be to blame for the death if, unforeseeably, the conscientious lie resulted in the murderer finding the victim.

Also, the idea that we should not treat persons 'merely as means,' which is often cited as the source of Kant's strictest principles, does not really support them, at least if that idea is interpreted in the way that makes most sense of Kant's arguments for it.[31] Those arguments, I think,

---

[28] My point is that Kant endorsed some particular principles as absolute that are indefensible even within his own basic theory, not that there are no defensible principles that hold without exception. Much depends on how the forbidden activity is described. When motives are included in the description, it becomes more plausible that we can describe acts that are always wrong, e.g., 'torturing someone merely for your amusement.' Some labels—e.g., 'murder' and 'rape'—seem implicitly to indicate an unacceptable motive.

[29] G, 89 [4: 421].

[30] Kant, 'On a Supposed Right to Lie because of Philanthropic Concerns' (*supra* n. 25).

[31] G, 95–6 [4: 427–9]. Kant's humanity formula has been interpreted in many differ-

support a relatively formal prescription, which I call the 'thin interpretation' of the humanity formula. The main idea is that, whereas Kant's universal-law formula explicitly calls for us to consider what we ourselves could will as universal laws, the humanity formula requires us to consider what the practical reason of those who are affected by our acts could approve. We must take up the perspective of those adversely affected by (or otherwise rationally opposed to) our treatment of them. Usually these are other people, but we can, in the relevant sense, mistreat ourselves. Thinking of the humanity (or 'rational nature') of potentially mistreated persons as an end in itself requires that our principles be justifiable to them, at least insofar as they too take up the moral perspective. It also prevents us from basing our decisions of principle on the idea that the value of persons is (in principle) quantifiable and relative to their social standing, usefulness, capacity for happiness, etc. But none of this implies that substantive moral rules (e.g., regarding lying, sex, revolution, and punishment) must be absolute or subject to only a few rare exceptions.

From the thin idea of 'humanity as an end,' together with some further assumptions, Kant moved to a more substantive working notion of what we must do to treat persons as ends, rather than merely as means. This thicker idea, with which Kant works in *The Metaphysics of Morals*, places high priority on acting in ways that protect, develop, and 'honor' rational nature in human beings, who are presumed to be free and equal (in certain Kantian senses). Respect for these 'rationally necessary' values would guide Kantian moral 'legislators' away from familiar consequentialist thinking and (arguably) would give them reason to adopt quite stringent principles regarding murder, coercion, deception, manipulation, treating people with contempt, and so on. These value priorities should also lead us, more than Kant himself acknowledged, to give positive support for institutions and practices that increase everyone's opportunities to live as rational, free persons. But the main point for present purposes is that merely by making our 'rational nature' a higher value priority than happiness, even Kant's thicker conception of 'humanity as an end' does not provide grounds for his absolute, and nearly absolute, practical principles.

A question more interesting, and potentially more rewarding, than whether Kant was right to hold such inflexible principles is how a moral theory that is Kantian in a broad sense (i.e., one that starts from

ent ways. My view is developed in my essay collection *Dignity and Practical Reason* (*supra* n. 23), 38–57, 197–225; and in chs. 5 and 8 of my *Respect, Pluralism and Justice*.

specified basic points in Kant's theory) can determine what exceptions to various moral principles should be acknowledged. To say that exceptions should be allowed whenever 'much,' or 'very much,' or 'very, very much' happiness would be lost otherwise seems un-Kantian in spirit and invites a familiar 'slippery slope' argument. (If it is all right to torture someone to save a million lives, why not a million minus one, a million minus two—and so on?) A reasonable response requires more thorough explanation and defense of the basic Kantian moral constraints on deliberation. These constraints are supposed to be expressed in the various formulations of the Categorical Imperative, but those fundamental prescriptions need to be combined and further refined before they can be used convincingly to answer the consequentialists' doubts.

E. The Purpose of Government is to Secure Justice, Not to Promote Happiness

Kant maintains that the proper aim of government is not to promote happiness but to secure justice. The fundamental principle of justice says, in effect, that it is not right to hinder the 'external freedom' of another person that would be allowed under a system of 'universal laws' that respects the equality and freedom of all.[32] John Rawls's first principle of justice is quite similar to this, and was perhaps inspired by it.[33] Kant offers little explicit interpretation of his own principle, but his main focus was apparently on 'negative' freedoms such as freedom from murder, slavery, and theft. Kant does, however, allow for government assistance to the needy, and it is arguable than Kant's basic theory of justice supports even stronger policies of assistance.[34] There are also

---

[32] MM, 24 [6: 230–1]. See also Reiss (ed.), *Kant: Political Writings*, 73–4, 80 [8: 289–90] (from 'Theory and Practice'). 'External freedom' is the ability to act as one chooses without hindrance from others. Kant holds that the exercise of external freedom is unjust when it is incompatible with the equal freedom of all under universal laws. We exercise our external freedom through intentional acts, but external freedom is contrasted with two kinds of internal freedom presupposed by moral agency: that is, the ability to act without being determined by natural causes (negative freedom) and 'being a law to oneself' (rational autonomy or positive freedom). See G, 114 [4: 446–7].

[33] Rawls's first principle says that 'each person is to have an equal right to the most extensive scheme of basic liberties compatible with a similar scheme of liberties for others.' John Rawls, *A Theory of Justice* (Cambridge, MA: Harvard University Press, 1999), 53. The interpretation of this principle is discussed in a later section (ibid. 201–51).

[34] See James Rosen, *Kant's Theory of Justice* (Ithaca: Cornell University Press, 1991), 173–208; and Paul Guyer, 'Kantian Foundations for Liberalism', *Jahrbuch für Strafrecht und Ethik/Annual Review of Law and Ethics*, 5 (1997), 121–40; reprinted in Guyer (ed.), *Kant on Freedom, Law, and Happiness* (Cambridge: Cambridge University Press, 2000).

reasons to believe that Kant's general moral theory, if applied with a fuller understanding of social realities than Kant apparently had, would justify us in taking a broader view than Kant did of what constitutes the 'freedom' that justice is meant to protect.[35] In any case, it seems clear that Kant is committed to the view that the primary function of government is the protection of the equal liberties of citizens as opposed to promoting their happiness.

Discussion of the issue between Kant and others here would echo many contemporary debates in political philosophy, but it would have some special features. Kant's arguments do not depend on the claims that ('external') freedom is intrinsically valuable, that only individuals know what best promotes their happiness, or that our freedom (or right) to act as we choose is morally unlimited until we make a contract to the contrary. Rather, Kant begins with the idea that practical reason permits 'external freedom' to act only in ways such that the exercise of this freedom could coexist with the similar freedom of others (the universal principle of justice).[36] The corollary, in Kant's view, is that coercion is justified to 'hinder hindrances to freedom.'[37] That is, violations of the principle of justice may be opposed by force, and, given the conditions of human life, we have reason to authorize a sovereign power to try to prevent such violations and reason to obey its commands. Kant holds that the sovereign power in a state ought to conform to the moral requirements of practical reason, but (notoriously) he insists that citizens ought to obey the *de facto* laws even if the sovereign power violates those moral requirements—except in the limiting case in which the sovereign demands that we do something 'wrong in itself.'[38] The upshot is that, whether his political theory is interpreted narrowly or broadly, Kant would have sided with contemporary political philosophers who deny that the aim of government is to make citizens happy and who say, instead, that its only legitimate aim is to respect rights and maintain the conditions for just relations among citizens.

Kant's grounds for his position go back to the basic idea that moral

---

[35] For example, freedom might be understood to include the more positive idea of having certain basic opportunities and resources to live a full life as a rational, autonomous person, and, if so, unjust 'hindrances to freedom' might include more than murder, slavery, theft, and the like. Sarah Holtman develops this idea in an excellent Ph.D. dissertation, 'Kant, Justice, and the Augmentation of Ideal Theory', University of North Carolina, Chapel Hill, 1996.

[36] MM, 24 [6: 230–1]. [37] MM, 25 [6: 231].

[38] MM, 23–6 [6: 230–3] and 95–8 [6: 318–23]. My interpretation of Kant's views on these matters differs somewhat from that presented in Rosen, *Kant's Theory of Justice*, 115–72.

principles, even regarding political matters, are just those principles that reasonable and autonomous persons would acknowledge, given adequate understanding and acceptance of the fundamentals of the moral point of view. The justifying framework is analogous to that of Rawls in some respects, but it is a mistake (as Rawls has acknowledged) to treat these as identical or even very closely similar. Kant's claim that 'freedom,' not happiness, is the primary value in political matters seems to depend on an implicit assumption that rational autonomous human beings would place a higher priority on state protection of their equal opportunities to live as rational end-pursuing agents than on state efforts to promote the various ends that they seek under the name of happiness. Kant may have thought that empirical evidence would confirm this assumption, but I suspect that Kant also took for granted that it is a necessary feature of our *rationality* that we have a strong preference for 'external' freedom over the merely desire-based values that we include under our conception of happiness.[39] The idea, perhaps, is that although being enslaved or imprisoned does not necessarily destroy our rationality and autonomy of will, we cannot develop and use our full powers to live as rational autonomous agents without external liberty.[40]

Although Kant's concern to preserve freedom under a just social order is not reducible to a concern to promote the happiness of citizens, it should be obvious that the former encompasses much that utilitarians would recommend as means, or necessary conditions, for maximizing happiness. Thus, it is not surprising to find that Mill agrees with Kant to a considerable extent on what justice requires, at least in ordinary cases.[41] Mill and Kant make their recommendations on different

---

[39] Kant divides human nature into rational nature and sensuous nature. We learn about our sensuous nature empirically—for example, by observing how we feel and act in various circumstances. We cannot help but think of ourselves also as persons with practical reason, and philosophical examination of the idea is supposed to show that this requires attribution to ourselves of some rational dispositions distinct from the desires, impulses, and inclinations attributed on the basis of experience. Kant seems to suppose that human beings have a preference for freedom to live as rational autonomous persons over satisfaction of other desires both because this is a common desire, hard to repress, and also because it is a rational disposition and we are rational (or so we must assume).

[40] The suggestion assumes that Kant thought we have a rational disposition, not only to avoid making irrational choices, but also to develop and exercise our practical rationality over time by pursuing morally necessary ends and pursuing happiness within the limits of our duties. Insofar as we think of the relevant 'external liberties' as those needed to fulfill this rational disposition (with due respect to others), then it makes sense to say that it is not just our desires but also our rational nature that places a high priority on these external liberties.

[41] See Mill, *Utilitarianism* (supra n. 21), 41–63; and J. S. Mill, *On Liberty*, ed. Elizabeth Rapaport (Indianapolis: Hackett Publishing Co., 1978).

Happiness and Human Flourishing

grounds, and they disagree about the permissibility of making exceptions for special cases; but Kant's rhetoric against making happiness the goal of government should not blind us from the fact that his ideal of justice, if realized, would provide much of what we need to be happy, but lack in an unjust world.

IV. CONCERN FOR HAPPINESS IN CHARACTER, MOTIVES, AND DELIBERATION

A. Old Issues About Happiness as a Moral Ideal, Motive, and Reason for Acting

In several related ways, Kant denies that the moral assessment of our character, motives, and deliberation depends on our efforts and success in pursuing our own happiness. Consider, for example, the idea that human happiness has *moral value*, not merely in the sense that it is morally right to promote the happiness of others (or happiness in general) but also in a sense implying that living a happy life is a *moral ideal*. The suggestion, in other words, is that living a happy life is a mark of a *morally good person*. In this respect being happy would be like being honest and being courageous, except that it is a more comprehensive characteristic. Those who seem to accept this idea probably have a conception of happiness that is radically different from Kant's; nevertheless, it is worth noting that Kant does not endorse this idea. Kant counts happiness (in his sense) as *morally valuable* only in the sense that it is something we have a limited duty (and right) to promote: more specifically, in Kant's view we have an imperfect duty to adopt a maxim to promote the happiness of others as one of our ends and a qualified permission (as well as an indirect duty) to pursue our own happiness.[42]

Furthermore, in Kant's view, acting to promote our own happiness, while often permissible, is normally not something 'of moral worth.' A maxim of the form 'I shall do X in order to increase my happiness,' according to Kant, 'has no moral content.'[43] We do not become worthy

---

[42] MM, 149–52 [6: 385–8] and 198–203 [6: 448–54]. An imperfect duty, according to Kant, is somewhat indefinite regarding what actions are required to fulfill it. Imperfect duties contrast with perfect duties, which have the form 'Always do X' or 'Never do X.' Typically, as with beneficence, an imperfect duty is a duty to make it a matter of principle (maxim) to pursue a broadly described end (such as 'the happiness of others') for moral reasons. This leaves open, as a matter of judgment (but not unlimited discretion), when, how much, and in what ways to promote the end. See Ch. 7 of this volume.   [43] G, 66 [4: 398].

of moral esteem by trying to be happy. Sometimes, Kant allows, we might act to increase our happiness out of respect for our 'indirect' duty to do so (to keep ourselves from temptations), but here the morally commendable motive is duty, not desire for happiness. Kant says that reason directs us to work toward the *summum bonum*, which is the union of virtue and the morally appropriate happiness that virtuous persons deserve.[44] Again, however, the point is not that concern for happiness itself is morally commendable. Even pursuit of the *summum bonum* is of moral worth only when it is 'from duty.'

Similarly, in Kant's view, when we deliberate about what to do, the fact that an act will enhance our happiness is not in general a reason for assessing that act as a moral duty. The consideration 'this will make me happy' is not something that usually weighs in favor of the conclusion 'this is what I morally ought to do.'[45] Kant concedes a minor exception; for, as noted earlier, he thinks that we should not ignore our own happiness to a degree that would make us so needy or depressed that we would be tempted to neglect our duties to others. The idea, I suppose, need not be just that if we are needy and depressed we will be inclined to steal, and the like. More generally, miserable people tend to dampen the spirits of others, and thus out of concern for the happiness of others we need to pay at least some attention to our own happiness. Kant's main points remain, however: for the most part, we are not morally good by virtue of our rational pursuit of happiness; and the ends that should guide our moral deliberations are our own perfection and the happiness of others, not our own happiness.

B. A New Issue: Does Kant Make Us Devalue Our Own Happiness Relative to That of Others?

Kant's views summarized above (in Section IVA) about the moral assessment of character, motives, and deliberation are widely shared, I believe, at least among those who conceive of happiness (more or less) as Kant did. But Michael Slote, in his recent book *From Morality to Virtue*, raises the possibility of a different way that effort and success in the pursuit of happiness might be relevant to the assessment of persons. Slote recommends that we should move beyond *morality* to nonmoral assessments of character as virtuous or vicious, admirable or despicable, from an ordinary, common-sense perspective. From this point of view, Slote argues, whether we are virtuous or not depends significantly on

[44] C2, 92–101 [5: 110–20].   [45] C2, 19–24 [5: 21–6].

our attitude and conduct with respect to our own happiness. For example, if we are virtuous, we will affirm the importance of our own happiness and will not sacrifice it too readily. In fact, Slote suggests at one point that if we are virtuous we will count our own happiness as (approximately) equal in importance to us as the happiness of all other persons combined.[46]

The issue now is not, as before, a controversy about how severely our pursuit of happiness is constrained by moral requirements. Slote's opposition to Kant, as I understand it, is not merely the usual complaint that Kant's inflexible principles leave us too little permission (or right) to do what we think will make us happy. Rather, the objection is that Kant requires us to 'devalue' our own happiness, relative to the happiness of others. He supposedly urges us *as moral agents* to value others' happiness but not our own—or at least to subordinate our own happiness to the happiness of others. Thus, it seems, there is an objectionable 'asymmetry' in Kant's ethics between a virtuous attitude toward our own happiness and a virtuous attitude toward the happiness of other people.

Slote's charge against Kant's ethics is similar in kind to a suspicion raised by Nietzsche and Ayn Rand, namely, that traditional moralists, such as Kant, advocate a self-effacing, debilitating, self-sacrificing 'altruism' that no clear-thinking, rational person could accept.[47] These writers prompt us to ask, Why is it a virtue to be more concerned for the happiness of others than our own? and, Why shouldn't we get as much credit for 'doing for ourselves' as we get for 'doing for others'? Taking these questions seriously makes virtue ethics seem more appealing than Kant's ethics because virtue ethics seem to place greater importance on the intelligent pursuit of our own happiness than on any duty to be concerned for the happiness of others.[48]

[46] Slote may intend a somewhat different point, namely, that character traits that are virtues are so because our having them tends to promote our own good and the good of all others combined more or less equally. This claim would not imply that a virtuous person actually has the policy or attitude of weighing others' good equally with his or her own. Slote does not explicitly identify a person's good with happiness, I think, and therefore the position that I describe is only 'suggested' by his remarks. See Slote, *From Morality to Virtue* (*supra* n. 11), 4–57, 98.

[47] See, for example, Ayn Rand, *The Virtue of Selfishness* (New York: New American Library, 1964); and Friedrich Nietzsche, *On the Genealogy of Morals*, tr. Walter Kaufmann and R. J. Hollingdale (New York: Vintage Press, 1968).

[48] 'Virtue ethics' refers to a cluster of moral theories that hold that the primary concern of moral theory should be to explain good and bad moral character traits (virtues and vices) rather than right and wrong action. How to define 'virtue ethics' more specifically is a matter of controversy. See, for example, Roger Crisp and Michael Slote, *Virtue Ethics* (Oxford: Oxford University Press, 1997). This includes a useful bibliography.

Why suspect Kant of requiring us to devalue our own happiness? One might think that Kant's denial that we have a direct duty to promote our own happiness reflects his belief that we should value our own happiness less than we should value that of others. In fact, Kant repeatedly implies that most people *care* much more about their own happiness than the happiness of others. This, in his view, is a natural fact, not subject to moral appraisal. In a sense, *valuing* is not merely caring but also implies a stable attitude that we adopt or reaffirm on reflection, a disposition that we have for reasons and that we intend to maintain.[49] But, even so, I think that Kant also believes that it is human nature for us to tend to *value* our own happiness more than the happiness of others and that there is nothing immoral or unreasonable about this.[50] At times, it seems, we may love another so much that the other person's happiness means more to us than our own, but this is not the attitude toward others that we normally have and maintain on reflection.[51]

In the ordinary sense intended here, *valuing* our own happiness more than others' happiness does not imply that we will choose to act to further our happiness whenever we can. Valuing is a positive attitude involving many dispositions to make certain choices in various circumstances, but it is not like a steady vector force that constantly pushes us in a certain direction no matter what the conditions. When our pursuit

[49] I draw (and oversimplify) here from an excellent philosophy Ph.D. dissertation by Valerie Tiberius, 'Deliberation about the Good: Justifying What We Value', University of North Carolina, 1997.

[50] I distinguish here *valuing* something from *judging that, all things considered, it is good to pursue or have in the relevant context*. I suppose that a person who is resolute in never immorally pursuing happiness might still *value* being happy in general—for example, might desire it, intend to satisfy the desire when doing so is morally permissible, feel disappointment at losing happiness even when this is morally necessary, and affirm these desires and attitudes on reflection. A fully *virtuous* person, perhaps, values happiness only insofar as it is not immoral to gain it or have it, for (in Kant's view) the correct moral *judgment* is that happiness is only a conditional good, and a fully virtuous person may have learned to *value* such goods only when the condition for their value is satisfied. The tendency to value our happiness over that of others, I think, Kant would ascribe to human nature as something that we cannot entirely overcome. Having the tendency is not our fault, in Kant's view, nor is it entirely regrettable (because it feeds competition on which progress depends). Our primary moral responsibility with respect to this tendency is not to try to transform or transcend it by training our sensibility, but rather not to let the tendency lead us to act in ways that violate or neglect our duties to others and to ourselves.

[51] In *Civilization and Its Discontents*, Freud stresses the rarity of such love and argues that the ideal of equal love of all persons is both contrary to human nature and not an admirable ideal. (See Sigmund Freud, *Civilization and Its Discontents*, tr. Joan Riviere (London: Hogarth Press, 1930).) Needless to say, many Christians profess a different belief.

Happiness and Human Flourishing 185

of happiness conflicts with that of others, we need to make a moral judgment about the case. Is it a matter of fair competition? Or is it a violation of others' rights for us to continue to pursue happiness in the way we initially wanted to? If we value our own happiness more than the happiness of the others, we may *prefer* to win the competition ourselves (in the first case), and we may *wish* that we could have permissibly done what we first wanted to do (in the second case)—we may even wish this more than we wish that the others could satisfy their initial desires. But none of this is incompatible with a Kantian good will. A good will, the unconditionally good moral disposition, does not require us to care about and value equally the happiness of all persons, for all purposes, in all contexts. What it requires is wholehearted commitment to constraining all our pursuits by the principles that can ultimately, at the highest level of moral deliberation, be justified to all persons who have equal moral standing and who are willing *for purposes of this deliberation* to abstract from the particular features of their special attachments and circumstances. Kant's moral theory, as I understand it, attributes an equal basic moral standing, dignity, or 'unconditional and incomparable worth' to all persons, but this is for purposes of determining our moral responsibilities and rights, not for governing our everyday preferences where these are not at issue.

One might think that Kant's ethics makes us devalue our own happiness in an objectionable way just because it requires us to recognize all persons as having equal basic moral worth. The objection might be that Kantian 'equal worth' inevitably leads to a utilitarian (or consequentialist) moral decision procedure, and therefore makes us devalue our happiness in just the ways that utilitarianism is often thought to do. The argument might run as follows: If each person has the same value, then the happiness of each should have the same value, other things being equal; and, since more value is better than less, the happiness of two persons must be more valuable than the happiness of one, other things being equal, and in general the more happiness, the more value; therefore, if we acknowledge the equal moral worth of all persons, we are committed to bringing about, directly or indirectly, the happiness of each random person as much as our own. The objection, as should now be clear, relies on the mistaken assumptions that all 'worth' or 'value' in Kant's theory, even dignity, is in principle commensurable and quantifiable and that right action consists in maximizing value. The basic equality that Kant attributes to all persons is not a matter of 'same size shares' of value understood in this way but, rather, a matter of having the same standing in a system of rights and duties and in the ideal deliberative processes that determine what these rights and duties are.

Slote's main reason for saying that Kant's ethics makes us devalue our own happiness, as compared to that of others, seems to be Kant's thesis that the 'ends which are duties' are the happiness of others and our own perfection, not our own happiness. Kant's corollary is that we have a quite extensive *direct duty* to promote the happiness of others but only a quite limited and *indirect duty* to promote our own happiness. If we assume (mistakenly, I think) that what we judge to be our duties must be a simple reflection of what we 'value,' then we might think that the asymmetry in Kant's claims about our duties regarding ourselves and others shows that Kant thinks that right-minded people will value the happiness of others more than their own. At least, it might seem that Kant thinks that we should act as if we valued others' happiness more than our own.

Slote's main objection, as I noted, is apparently not that Kant's ethics requires us to *do* more for others than for ourselves or even that it grants us no *right* to pursue our own happiness to a reasonable degree. The special feature of Slote's complaint is that it presses the charge that Kantian ethics makes us 'devalue' our own happiness even if it 'permits' us to pursue it to a reasonable degree. This, it seems, is because Kant makes it a *direct duty* (within limits) to promote other people's happiness but only an *indirect duty* and *permission* (within limits) to pursue our own. Slote's assumption seems to be that we must value more what we judge we have a duty to promote than what we have a right to pursue. This is a dubious assumption, but the best way to deflate the objection is to reconstruct Kant's reasons for his asymmetry thesis and its corollary. The most plausible reconstruction, I will argue, does not presuppose or entail that we should count our own happiness as less valuable than any other person's happiness. The reasons why promoting our own happiness is merely an indirect duty and a permission, while promoting that of others is a direct duty, do not reflect a difference in the 'value' of the two kinds of happiness, but rather a difference in the way respect for autonomy is displayed when we are dealing with the interests of others and when we are dealing only with our own interests.

Kant's explicit reason for denying that we have a direct moral duty to promote our own happiness is that we are already naturally inclined to promote our happiness. He did not mean, I take it, that we can never have a duty to do something that we have a natural inclination to do. The idea of duty includes the idea of being 'necessitated' or constrained by reason, but we can be constrained to act in a way that we are already inclined to act if, despite that inclination, we may still fail to act as we should. Otherwise, Kant would have to conclude that we can have no duty to promote the happiness of others if we have a natural inclination to do so, which seems absurd. So what is the point? Why does the natural inclination to promote our own happiness block a duty to do so, whereas a natural inclination to promote the happiness of others does not?

One might suppose that the answer is that Kant thought our desire for our own happiness is much stronger and more pervasive than our benevolent impulses. I have no doubt that Kant thought this, but the belief does not explain why Kant should think that there is *no* direct duty to promote one's own happiness. Perhaps, one might think, Kant's idea is that our self-love is so strong that it is not, on balance, worth the psychological costs to make 'a moral case' out of our occasional failures to take up harmless opportunities to further our own happiness. Most of the time we do not need a moral reminder, much less a call to 'duty,' to pay attention to our own happiness, and multiplying our duties needlessly may have a depressing effect. By contrast, one might think, our benevolent impulses are so weak that unless there is an acknowledged duty to promote the happiness of others, we will rarely do so, to the detriment of us all. These are reasonable rule-utilitarian thoughts, but there is, I think, a better Kantian reason for denying that we have a direct duty to promote our happiness.

To see this, let us first try to construct a Kantian argument *in favor of* a direct duty of beneficence. Consider the issue from the point of view of a Kantian moral legislator, a member of 'the kingdom of ends' who respects humanity as an end in itself. Suppose that prior duties of justice, respect, mutual aid, and self-perfection have already been agreed upon. A good case can be made for endorsing a further imperfect duty of beneficence, at least provided that the duty allows a reasonable 'playroom for free action.'[52] Such a duty, let us suppose, requires us to count the happiness of others as a good end to promote, but it is indeterminate regarding exactly when, how, and how much one must do to

---

[52] There is controversy among commentators about how to interpret the indeterminacy or 'playroom' in Kant's principles. This room for discretion is construed narrowly by David Cummiskey in his *Kantian Consequentialism* and by Marcia Baron in her *Kantian Ethics (Almost) without Apology* (Ithaca: Cornell University Press, 1995). Mary Gregor accepts a broader interpretation that allows more moral discretion regarding the balance between charity and our own projects. The main features of my understanding of Kant's principle, which is also broad, are indicated in *Dignity and Practical Reason* 147–75, and Ch. 7 of this volume.

promote the happiness of others, and thus allows space for the reasonable pursuit of one's own projects. The general adoption of such a principle can be expected to benefit everyone, so far as we can tell in advance of particular situations, and it seems to violate none of the basic Kantian value priorities and constraints. If this is the argument for beneficence to others, one might wonder, why shouldn't Kantian legislators prescribe a similar principle of *self-beneficence*, making it analogously an imperfect duty to promote one's own happiness? After all, one might think, this is just what we would do unless we fail to *value* our own happiness as much as others' happiness, or unless we imagine that each person's own happiness *should* be less important to him or her than others' happiness. On this line of thinking, then, Kant might at first seem to be committed to the idea that we should devalue our own happiness, relative to that of others, because he did not include in his moral system any direct duty to promote our own happiness analogous to his principle of beneficence.[53]

But we need to rethink the analogy. Let us consider more specifically what sorts of acts the duty of beneficence requires. Kant, like most of us, did not suppose that this is a duty to promote the ends of others *whether they want us to or not*.[54] We are supposed to help others in their projects but, barring special circumstances, not without regard to whether or not they consent. They need not always give express consent, of course, but the basic point is that we should not try to make people happy against their will. Coercion is justified in many circumstances to prevent people from violating others' rights, and giving crucial lifesaving aid to people who profess not to want it seems relatively unproblematic if those in danger are obviously unable at the time to think clearly. But doing unwanted 'favors,' working on others' projects for them without their consent, and so on, is meddlesome and disrespectful of the autonomy of those we mean to help, even if they would be happier if we were successful. Thus, we must understand the duty of beneficence to others as qualified: one should promote the permissible ends of others *only if this is what they choose*.[55] Our would-be benefi-

---

[53] As noted earlier, Kant says that we have an 'indirect' duty to promote our own happiness, but this does little to help meet Slote's objection because this duty is only an application of our more general duties, e.g., to respect the rights of others and to promote their happiness (along with our own 'perfection').

[54] 'I cannot do good to anyone in accordance with my concepts of happiness (except to young children and the insane), thinking to benefit him by forcing a gift upon him; rather, I can benefit him only in accordance with his concepts of happiness' (MM, 203 [6: 454]).

[55] There are, of course, many refinements that would need to be made if we were

ciaries normally have the right to block our altruistic efforts on their behalf. If they choose for us not to promote their ends, then doing so is no longer a way of fulfilling our imperfect duty of beneficence.

Now consider what sort of 'beneficent' acts an analogous duty of *beneficence to oneself* would require, if such a duty were possible. It would be an imperfect duty, limited by justice, respect, etc., to promote our own permissible ends (the ends belonging to our conception of a happy life for us), and it would be indefinite with respect to exactly what, in what way, and how much one must do toward this end. But now it must be qualified in the same way that the principle of beneficence to others is qualified. That is, it would have to be our 'duty' to promote our own permissible ends provided that we (at least implicitly) consent to do so, that is, provided that doing so is not against our will. In other words, the 'duty' would tell us that we 'must' contribute somehow, and to some extent, to our own happiness, by trying to fulfill the (permissible) ends that we already have, but that we are 'morally required' to do this only if we so choose. It is doubtful whether it is even coherent to suppose that I might adopt a general policy of not furthering my own happiness, that is, a policy of not taking the means to achieve the various (permissible) ends that I have. But, supposing for now that this is possible, the analogy with beneficence to others implies that if I, as the would-be beneficiary, withhold consent to the 'self-beneficent' acts (by choosing not to do them), then I, as the would-be benefactor, cannot fulfill a duty (not even an 'imperfect' duty) by performing such acts.

Now it becomes clear, however, that such a 'duty' of self-beneficence is conceptually impossible. We could cancel such an alleged duty at will, and a 'duty' that we could cancel at will is no duty at all. We are not bound by chains if they are so loose that we can throw them off whenever we choose. What comparing the duty of beneficence to others with a supposed duty of self-beneficence reveals is just that the latter is an incoherent idea. Kant's denial of such a 'duty,' then, does not show that he thinks that we should devalue our own happiness relative to others'.

The duty of beneficence to others (with its consent requirement) limits our moral freedom in dealing with others in several ways that seem quite reasonable: we must make it a principle to regard their happiness as an

---

trying to articulate the principle as subtly and completely as possible. For example, qualifications are needed regarding cases where the person who refuses help is incompetent, obviously 'not herself,' etc. But what I have said is enough, I hope, for present purposes.

end, and our contributions toward this end (typically) require at least the implicit consent of the intended beneficiary. Kant's position on beneficence, however, can be seen as respectful of freedom in another way. That is, it reaffirms our moral freedom to accept or decline anticipated efforts by others to promote our happiness. The duty of beneficence to others respects our freedom insofar as it permits us (as a rule) to reject the efforts that we do not want others to make to further our personal projects. Similarly, Kant's denial that there is a parallel duty of beneficence *to oneself* respects our freedom by permitting us (morally) to decline to make our own efforts to promote those projects when we do not want to. *Prudence* often counsels us, even when we are reluctant, both to make our own efforts and to accept the aid of others toward achieving the ends encompassed in our conception of happiness.[56] *Moral duty*, however, does not demand it.

It should be noted that the argument against a duty of beneficence to oneself does not amount to a general argument against Kant's 'duties to oneself,' even though that argument is similar to the argument M. G. Singer offers against all 'duties to oneself.'[57] The key to the argument is that we cannot be 'bound' by a 'duty' if we can release ourselves from that (alleged) duty at will, but the 'duties to oneself' that Kant affirms, unlike self-beneficence and keeping 'promises to oneself,' are not the sort of duties from which we have reason to suppose that we could release ourselves. If we had obligations to keep 'promises to ourselves' that were perfectly analogous to our obligations to keep promises to others, then it seems natural to suppose that we could (normally) 'release ourselves' at will because (normally) the recipient of a promise can release the promisor whenever he or she chooses. But a duty not to debase the humanity of other persons and treat them with utter contempt is not a duty from which they can release us, and so the analogous duty to avoid debasing our own humanity in a self-contemptuous way would not be a duty from which we could release ourselves.[58]

Let us return to Kant's explicit argument against a duty to promote our own happiness, which appeals to our natural inclination to pursue our own happiness. This is not the argument that I suggested above, but it is compatible with that argument. One way of understanding the

---

[56] Even prudence, however, normally allows options, for it is a conditional rational imperative to promote our own happiness, and our working conceptions of happiness are neither fixed nor completely determinate. Insofar as Kant conceives of happiness as satisfying freely chosen, desire-based ends, we can often avoid doing something that previously seemed necessary for happiness by modifying the ends we choose to pursue.

[57] M. G. Singer, *Generalization in Ethics* (New York: Alfred A. Knopf, 1961), 311–18.

[58] I discuss these issues more fully in 'Promises to Oneself', in my *Autonomy and Self-Respect* 138–54.

relevance of Kant's reference to natural inclination is as follows. Recall that the duty to promote others' happiness is indefinite; in its basic form, it is a duty to *make it one's maxim* to include the happiness of others among one's own ends. Basically, then, the analogous 'duty' of beneficence to oneself would have to be an indefinite 'duty' to include one's own happiness among one's ends. This is something that everyone is inclined to do, according to Kant. Adopting a maxim to pursue an end is supposed to be more than just being inclined toward that end; it presupposes some degree of reflection and the power to choose otherwise if there is a sufficient reason to do so. But all rational persons with that natural inclination, Kant assumes, will adopt at least a general, indefinite policy of pursuing a set of personal ends (their conception of happiness for them) at least when there is no sufficient reason not to. That is, Kant supposes not merely that we are inclined by nature to pursue our own happiness but also that we all 'freely' endorse our own happiness as an end—a higher-order end that encompasses many particular ends, though it is not necessarily our dominant end. Given Kant's idea of duties (categorical *imperatives*) as rational principles that we can but *might not* follow, we cannot say, strictly speaking, that it is a *duty* to make our own happiness an end, even though it is rational to do so.

Our own happiness is always an end we have, but we do not always attend to it as much as we need to in order to fulfill our duties to others. Thus, we might fail to promote our own happiness on particular occasions when we should. This makes it possible for Kant to speak of an 'indirect duty' to promote our own happiness, for this is not a duty to adopt happiness as a general (and indefinite) end but, rather, a duty to do particular things required by reason that we *might not* otherwise do. The upshot of this line of thought is that the analogy with a duty of beneficence to others is blocked, not because of our *inability to avoid* endorsing our own happiness as a general higher-order end, but because there is no reason to expect that any rational person would want to try. In any case, Kant's grounds for denying a duty of beneficence to oneself do not imply that we do or should count our own happiness as less valuable than the happiness of persons whom we dutifully try to help.

V. KANT'S FOCUS ON HAPPINESS RATHER THAN HUMAN FLOURISHING

We have seen many ways in which the concept of happiness (as Kant understands it) is of limited importance in his ethics. Many philosophers, ancient and contemporary, regard what they call 'happiness' as more important in ethics than Kant regards happiness in his sense. They may agree with Kant on many points about happiness in his sense; but when contemporary philosophers turn to Kant to see his position on 'happiness' in the ancient (human flourishing) sense, they are likely to be disappointed. This is partly because Kant has very little to say about flourishing as a human being, as distinct from happiness in his sense. Kant mentions ancient philosophers from time to time, but he seems to suppose for the most part that their conception of 'happiness' is more or less the same as his. The disappointment of many contemporary philosophers with Kant's position is also likely to be due to the fact that, although Kant does not discuss human flourishing explicitly, his theory commits him to placing more severe limits on the role of human flourishing in moral thinking than they can accept. In this section, I will simply summarize some of these limits, as I see them, and speculate briefly about why Kant might have insisted on them. The reason is not, I suggest, merely Kant's misunderstanding of ancient philosophers, his personal eccentricities, a preoccupation with other matters, or an insensitivity to the human desire to flourish. It has more to do with his awareness of the distinctness of individuals and his respect for freedom.

A. The Limited Role of Human Flourishing in Kant's Ethics

The first thing to consider is whether Kant's limits on happiness (in his sense) also carry over to human flourishing. Comparison is difficult if we suppose that having a 'good will' and having virtue (in Kant's sense) are necessary constituents of human flourishing—a possibility to be considered later. For now, let us suppose otherwise. That is, let us assume that, although fulfilling certain essential and good dispositions of human nature is necessary to flourishing as a human being, satisfying Kantian moral constraints, even the basic ones, is not included in the idea of human flourishing as a necessary part. We assume, then, that it remains an open question whether our having a Kantian good will is conducive to our flourishing as human beings. This is a common assumption and a reasonable one if we understand 'flourishing' in the usual ways (without presupposing Kant's theory).

Now it seems clear, given the assumption just mentioned, that Kant is committed to a limited role for human flourishing as well as for happiness in his sense. For example, human flourishing cannot be an unconditional good or an 'intrinsic value' as intuitionists and naturalists understand this. This is because one could flourish without having a good will, which for Kant is the only 'unconditional good,' and Kant does not acknowledge intuited or natural intrinsic values. Obviously Kant must deny that whatever maximizes human flourishing is morally right, for the price of bringing about the most flourishing could be treating humanity in some persons as a mere means. Similarly, since Kant holds that the sole or primary aim of government is to secure justice, he must disallow government efforts to promote human flourishing if they employ unjust means or fail to enforce justice among citizens. Also, the same grounds that support Kant's denial that we have a direct duty to promote our own happiness (in his sense) would also tend to undermine any alleged direct duty to further our own flourishing as human beings. Assuming that it is normally up to others whether or not we can dutifully contribute to their flourishing, acknowledging an imperfect duty to promote others' flourishing does not imply that we should acknowledge a parallel *duty* to promote our own.

In addition to these ways in which Kant limits the role of both happiness and human flourishing in ethics, there are at least two further ways in which Kant relies on judgments about happiness but not on judgments about human flourishing. The first concerns the principle of beneficence. This, in Kant's theory, is an imperfect duty to promote others' happiness (in Kant's sense), not a duty to contribute to others' flourishing as human beings.

Now, of course, if everyone wants to flourish as a human being, then regard for the (Kantian) happiness of others would often promote their flourishing. This is because, wanting to flourish, they would tend to include flourishing in their conception of their happiness, and, insofar as they do, our contributing to their flourishing would tend to promote their happiness. If, as many think, it is *wise* to make flourishing as a human being our dominant personal end (at least when this is compatible with moral requirements), then our respect for others as rational (and thus potentially wise) might lead us to encourage them to seek happiness in ways that promote their flourishing, and might lead us to prefer helping them when they do. Even so, however, Kant's idea of the duty of beneficence remains distinct from the idea of a duty to promote others' flourishing as human beings. Even if we, and they too, do not know what will contribute to their flourishing, the Kantian duty urges us to promote the (permissible) ends that they set for themselves. It is up to others to determine what will make them happy, and all such judgments, Kant thought, are uncertain. Within the 'room for choice' allowed by the principle of beneficence, we may select our beneficiaries as we choose; thus, we may to some extent choose to promote happiness where it will best contribute to flourishing, but the principle does not demand this.[59]

The second way that Kant relies on judgments about happiness rather than judgments about human flourishing has to do with prudence. Kant suggests that we are under a hypothetical imperative to take the necessary means to our happiness (in his sense). This is supposed to be a nonmoral requirement of reason, the application of which is limited by moral principles. Because of the indeterminacy, even partial incoherence, of our conceptions of our happiness, applying this general requirement only gives us inexact rules of thumb or 'counsels of prudence.' Like all hypothetical imperatives, these counsels are only conditionally rational to follow. The advice that they seem to give on particular occasions is overridden when it conflicts with our moral responsibilities, and also we may often set it aside without irrationality simply by altering the ends that we choose to include in our conception of happiness. In these ways, Kant views the imperative 'to do what we must to be happy' as quite restricted. It is striking, though, that he does not propose a general imperative of prudence concerning human flourishing. Even if it would be a good idea to adopt flourishing as a dominant end, Kant's theory of rational prudence seems to allow us, within moral limits, to choose our ends and set our priorities independently of any guiding aim to realize as well as we can the natural ('essential') human potentialities required for 'flourishing as a human being.'[60] We would be under a (nonmoral) hypothetical imperative to do what we must to flourish only if we chose to make that our end.

[59] It is important to keep in mind that the principle of beneficence, a quite indeterminate ('imperfect') duty to adopt the happiness of others as an end, is not the only moral consideration regarding how to treat others that we must take into account when deliberating about what to do in particular situations. We must also respect others' rights, treat them with respect, show proper gratitude, and so on. The principle of beneficence by itself does not tell us when, how, or how much to do for others. For this, we need good judgment guided by the Categorical Imperative. For example, the basic idea of humanity as an end in itself does not leave it as 'optional' whether to throw a life-preserver to someone about to drown or to wait to 'help' someone else later.

[60] Note, however, that Kant treats certain aspects of 'human flourishing' as matters that it is *morally impermissible* to ignore or neglect. For example, according to Kant, there is a 'perfect duty to oneself' to avoid suicide and an imperfect duty to oneself to 'develop and increase (one's) natural perfection' of body and mind (MM, 176-8 [6: 422-4] and 194-5 [6: 444-6]). Unlike Aristotle, Kant insists on a sharp distinction between rational prudence and morality. Then he does not place the ideal of human flourishing under rational prudence as a necessary end, but rather makes the pursuit of some aspects of it an imperfect *moral duty* to oneself. Thus, although he denies the right of prudential reason to demand that we pursue the ideal of human flourishing as an end, he makes room in his moral theory to affirm aspects of that ideal as requirements of reason.

As before, if we assume that human flourishing is something objective, discernible, and naturally desired, then following Kant's prescriptions regarding happiness should tend to promote it—but not always. By being prudent, in Kant's sense, we would generally contribute to our flourishing so long as our adoption of particular ends is guided intelligently by our natural desire to flourish. But Kantian prudence will not lead to flourishing if we have strong conflicting desires and adopt our ends more randomly. So the main point remains: Kantian prudence explicitly calls for intelligent pursuit of our (permissible) ends, whatever these may be, not for wise choices contributing to our thriving as human beings.

B. Possible Explanations

Why would Kant want to focus on happiness (in his sense) rather than on human flourishing? If we speculate about causal influences, there are many possibilities. For example, Kant was probably influenced by the modern rejection (by Hobbes and others) of the models of human nature that dominated the ancient and medieval worlds. Although Kant believed that for some purposes we should look at the world through teleological lenses, his view of human desires is closer to Hobbes's than to Aristotle's—that is, desires are seen as diverse, fluctuating, conflicting, unmalleable impulses that are, in themselves, not good or bad, rational or irrational. Kant thought that we tend to see happiness as the impossible ideal of satisfying all of our desires, but that with intelligence we can select a subset of compatible desires to try to satisfy (others need to be resisted or repressed). Like Hobbes, Kant denied that desires can be shaped by reason into a harmonious system of mutually cooperative motives in the way the classic ideas of human flourishing seem to presuppose.

Also, a partial explanation may be found by paying attention to Kant's project. He was not asking, in a general way, how a wise person would live. His primary questions, instead, were about the idea of moral duties and the necessary presuppositions of believing that we have such duties. His concern was to determine what, if anything, it is rationally *necessary* to think and to do. His method was to try to separate the elements of something familiar and then to focus attention on one aspect apart from the rest. The main elements of human nature, he thought, are reason, desire, and our ability to choose; accordingly, the main elements of a good life, he thought, must be governing one's choices by pure practical reason (a good will) and the satisfaction of our desires (happiness).⁶¹ The more complex idea of human flourishing does not readily fit into this picture. There is more to living well than doing our duty, but Kant's main questions were about the latter—and about the constraints it imposes on satisfying our desires. Many of the concerns that generate philosophical theories about human flourishing lie beyond the ethics of duty, as advocates of virtue ethics often remind us. To some extent, then, Kant's leaving aside questions about human flourishing is understandable in that these questions lie outside his central project. But this cannot be the whole story.

Another partial explanation might be Kant's recognition of our vast ignorance about what exactly it takes to enable different individuals to flourish as human beings.⁶² Even if we can say formally, or in very general terms, what it is to flourish as a human being, determining what in particular this or that individual needs in order to flourish in various contexts is extremely difficult. What will contribute to individuals' happiness (in Kant's sense) should be easier to discern because it is a matter of promoting whatever particular ends they set themselves, and typically those who want help will tell us what their ends are. Thus, although certainty here is impossible, we can often be effective in contributing to someone's happiness, as the duty of beneficence requires, even when neither they nor we know what it would take to make them flourish. For similar reasons, it seems that we can often enhance our own happiness (in Kant's sense), as prudence requires, even though we are ignorant of what would really contribute most to our flourishing. We may not know what is best for us, in that sense, but we know what our goals are. Again, however, our relative ignorance of the requirements of flourishing is hardly a sufficient reason for disregarding it in ethics.

Another possibility is that we are not merely ignorant of the facts about what makes individuals flourish; rather, it may be that there is

---

⁶¹ Kant treats 'practical reason' as reason concerned to determine what we *ought to do*. This contrasts with 'theoretical reason,' which is concerned with understanding the world as it actually is. Practical reason is called 'pure' when it serves to determine what we ought to do independently of our natural desire for happiness and our individual inclinations. This contrasts with 'empirically conditioned' practical reason, which tries to determine what we ought to do *in order to* satisfy our desire to be happy and to achieve our personal ends. Kant argues that pure practical reason is the source of the most fundamental moral principle, the Categorical Imperative. A person fully committed to following the fundamental moral principle has a 'good will' and is 'worthy to be happy.' The most complete good is a good will combined with deserved happiness, but having a good will alone is not enough to make one happy and being happy does not entail that one has a good will. See C2, 12–20 [5: 15–22] and 92–5 [5: 110–13].

⁶² See, for example, G, 85–6 [4: 418–19].

not 'a fact of the matter' to discern here. We can conjecture, then, that Kant, like many contemporary philosophers, was skeptical about the concept of human flourishing itself—that he doubted whether the concept was sufficiently determinate and psychologically defensible to serve a vital role in moral theory. If Kant had this skepticism, however, we would expect him to express it in criticism of classic theories that make human flourishing central; but, as far as I know, he did not. Perhaps he thought that this task of criticism had already been done; but more likely, I suspect, he just did not raise the issue.

Although no doubt many factors contributed, I suspect that a major reason why Kant made happiness, rather than human flourishing, the operative concept in the principle of beneficence and the imperative of prudence was his intense concern for individual freedom. At least this seems to be so if we focus on Kant's idea of happiness as fulfilling freely chosen ends rather than as feelings of contentment. Consider beneficence first. When would it matter whether our duty is to promote others' (permissible) happiness or to promote their flourishing as human beings? If we know more about the one than the other, that would make a difference; but let us suppose that we are equally knowledgeable (or ignorant) regarding both. Given this, how might concern for others' happiness and concern for their flourishing diverge?

A contribution to their flourishing will help them fulfill certain ends toward which human beings are *characteristically* prone to act, but these are not ends that all individuals want or endorse as their personal goals. To flourish means to develop and exercise common human potentials that are widely regarded to be natural, good, rewarding, and admirable to fulfill, but it is not necessarily compatible with doing what one loves to do, prefers on reflection to do, or sees as most expressive of 'who one is' as an individual. To promote others' flourishing when it diverges from their happiness (in Kant's sense) would be to place higher priority on their fulfilling their characteristic human dispositions than on their loves, considered preferences, and self-expression as individuals. Philosophers have often argued that these will not in fact diverge significantly for those who are thoughtful and well-informed (and perhaps well-trained), but our question presupposes that they can diverge. When moral responsibility and virtue are 'built in' to the concept of flourishing, then virtually all moral philosophers rank it as more important than individual loves, considered preferences, and self-expression *when these conflict with morality*. Again, however, our question concerns flourishing in a sense that is not so morally loaded. We assume, then, that happiness and human flourishing can diverge, and it is not yet obvious why beneficence should be more concerned with one rather than the other.[63]

My suggestion is just that, in addition to other factors, respect for individual freedom to choose one's own particular way of life, within moral limits, may have been a significant reason for Kant's giving priority to happiness over human flourishing in the ways that I have described. Even if there is a discernible fact that certain individual ends contribute better than others to fulfilling characteristic, natural human capacities, Kant says only that our responsibility in helping others is to respect *their* choices of the ends they want to pursue, provided the ends are not immoral. If they respect their basic duties to others and to themselves, then it is up to them to decide what to include in their pursuit of happiness, and we should respect that, rather than trying to make them flourish in another way. Admittedly, Kant says that we all have a duty to develop our mental and physical capacities, but he classifies this as a duty *to ourselves* that is not the business of others to enforce. Moreover, the requirement is an imperfect duty that leaves wide discretion as to how much, and in what ways, to develop these capacities. Undeniably Kant was moved by ideals of human perfection, for individuals and humanity in general, but his moral theory reflects a strong counterbalancing concern for allowing individuals to choose, and judge, for themselves, even if they choose less than what would best promote their flourishing.

Admittedly, if the duty of beneficence were a duty to promote others' flourishing rather than their happiness, then we would still be free (as potential beneficiaries) to refuse others' efforts to promote our flourishing when it promised to interfere with the preferred personal projects that we count as part of our happiness. The requirement of the consent of beneficiaries discussed earlier, we can assume, should apply here as well. Kantian beneficence, however, urges others to give us positive aid in our efforts to achieve the (permissible) ends we prefer, not merely to 'back off' when we do not want a certain kind of aid. In this it positively affirms and facilitates our attempts, within moral limits, to pursue the ends we choose for ourselves as individuals even if these are, at times, in conflict with the generic, supposedly objective, end of

---

[63] It must be remembered that we are concerned here with beneficence that does not violate justice, due respect for persons, or other obligations. Also, I assume that our duties to give lifesaving aid, to meet essential human needs, etc., are justifiable as high-priority duties in Kant's ethics on grounds that are not simply applications of the very general and indeterminate duty to promote others' happiness. That duty, as I understand it, concerns contributions to others' happiness beyond those more elementary duties (even though Kant does not separate these issues in *The Metaphysics of Morals*).

flourishing in characteristically human ways. If the normative appeal of the latter is as strong and pervasive as many think, then we can expect that wise individuals will freely choose to make it the core of their conceptions of happiness, and then promoting their flourishing would be a way of promoting their happiness. But this would not be because the idea of human flourishing necessarily has an overriding claim on us, but rather because we place a moral value on the ability of all human beings to choose and effectively pursue their happiness as they conceive it.

It seems a plausible conjecture that the same concern could lie behind Kant's limiting prudential requirements to the rational pursuit of happiness, rather than human flourishing. Prudence requires that we respect the Hypothetical Imperative regarding the ends that we actually choose, not that we do everything possible to promote our flourishing as human beings.[64] That is, the requirement of prudence is to adopt a set of desire-based ends and then, when one can, to take the necessary steps to achieve them or else revise the ends. Prudential reason does not condemn us as irrational if, instead of doing all we can to flourish in a characteristically human way, we choose a more eccentric individual course.[65] Thus, at least if we attend adequately to the imperfect duty to develop our minds and bodies, and if we fulfill our other duties, then, in Kant's view, the requirements of prudence as well as morality would leave us free to choose the ends that we prefer even when we anticipate that they will not maximally promote our flourishing as human beings.

My remarks in this section, as I mentioned, presuppose that flourishing as a human being is conceptually independent of being virtuous. But we might look at the whole matter differently. In Kant's view, our rational predisposition to morality, like our sensible nature as desiring beings, is an indispensable part of our nature—even if it is not, in the same sense, a 'natural' part.[66] So none of us, Kant thought, could live

---

[64] By 'the Hypothetical Imperative' I mean the most general principle behind our reasoning that we ought to do various particular things because they are necessary as a means to furthering our ends. The Hypothetical Imperative tells us to take the necessary means (when available) to the ends that we choose to pursue or else abandon these ends. A more complete explanation is given in my *Dignity and Practical Reason*, chs. 1 and 7.

[65] Critics of the Kantian perspective might object that it must be irrational to choose personal projects that we know are not 'the best' for us, but the objection presupposes the controversial claim that the course that does most to cause us to meet the descriptive criteria for 'flourishing as a human being' is also 'best' in a normative sense.

[66] The predisposition to acknowledge moral principles as authoritative in our decision making, according to Kant, is something that we must attribute to ourselves as rational

without inner conflict and self-disapproval if we pursued personal happiness by plainly immoral means. In a sense, then, he granted that we, human beings, cannot completely fulfill our most fundamental dispositions without virtue. Moreover, like many of his religious predecessors, he held that we should have faith that if we are truly virtuous we may, somehow (but not in this life), receive the happiness we deserve.[67] Thus, despite having separated virtue and happiness for practical purposes of choice, he acknowledged an ideal of human flourishing that unites them, after all, at least as something to hope for.

VI. CONCLUSION

My aim here has been to distinguish, summarize, and (at times) explain the place that the ideas of happiness and human flourishing have (or lack) in Kant's ethics. It is easy in reading Kant to get the impression that Kant is out to 'put happiness in its place,' which he sees as more restricted than many moral philosophers do. And readers of ancient philosophers will readily notice that Kant tends to ignore human flourishing, the favorite concept in virtue ethics. But it is also easy to confuse Kant's various claims on these matters and to exaggerate some of them. In any case, my hope has been that identifying and sorting out these different claims may facilitate discussion between Kantians and others, making further discussion more fruitful by focusing it on more specific issues. Some of Kant's claims about happiness, I have suggested, are rather uncontroversial; some of them, admittedly, are indefensible even within his basic framework; and some of them, though controversial, remain in dispute partly because of misunderstanding. The traditional and familiar ideas of human flourishing (as distinct from happiness in Kant's sense) do not have a prominent role in Kant's ethics, and I have speculated about several reasons why this might be so. This was due, I suggested, not merely to historical influences, misunderstanding of ancient philosophy, or preoccupation with other matters, but also to Kant's respect for individual freedom to choose, within moral limits, the way of life we prefer.

---

moral agents, but it is not an aspect of our nature that we discover and understand empirically as, for example, we come to know our desires and feelings.

[67] See C2, 102–10 [5: 122–32].

7

Meeting Needs and Doing Favors

Philosophers have long disagreed about the extent, as well as the grounds, of our obligations to help others. At one extreme is the radical libertarian view that our only obligations are to respect rights (of property, contract, and the like), and so charity is optional (or a matter of virtue, not duty). Another extreme is exemplified by Peter Singer's consequentialist claim that, absent special contingencies, we should give to the needy until doing more would reduce us to their level of need.[1] A sensible feature of Kant's ethics, I have always thought, is that it places our general obligation to help others between these two extremes and leaves further questions to judgment about particular cases. That is, Kant supplements his framework of rights with a general, but indefinite requirement of beneficence applicable to all, but he leaves to judgment questions about the particular times, ways, and extent that we must help. Kant also thought that judgment guided by the Categorical Imperative would leave substantial room, in nonemergency situations, for moral agents to pursue their own happiness. This latitude is not derivative, as it would be for utilitarians, from a duty to maximize aggregate happiness. Moreover, Kant's position accords with the common idea that some beneficent acts are morally praiseworthy but would not have been wrong not to do. Arguably, but more controversially, some praiseworthy acts are in significant respects like what others have called *supererogatory* acts.

This understanding, for the most part, fits with the interpretations of H. J. Paton and Mary Gregor.[2] Recently, however, this understanding

---

Parts of this essay stem from 'Author Meets Critics' sessions at the Pacific Division meetings of the American Philosophical Association on David Cummiskey's *Kantian Consequentialism* (1997) and Marcia Baron's *Kantian Ethics (Almost) without Apology* (1998). I am grateful for their responses as well as detailed comments by Jens Timmerman. Portions of this essay were presented at St Andrews University, the University of Minnesota, the University of Michigan, and Washington University (St Louis), and I appreciate the helpful comments from those audiences.

[1] Peter Singer, 'Famine, Affluence, and Morality', *Philosophy and Public Affairs*, 1 (1972), 229–43.
[2] H. J. Paton, *The Categorical Imperative: A Study in Kant's Moral Philosophy*

of Kant's position has been forcefully criticized.[3] Many of the objections, I believe, rest on misunderstandings, but, before turning to these, I shall restate positively what I take to be the best reconstruction of Kant's position.[4] This requires me at least to clarify and supplement what I have previously written on these matters. My primary aim is to explain Kant's position on our duties to help others as I now understand it, but I shall also indicate why I think certain objections from Cummiskey and Baron miss the mark.

A few preliminary remarks about my project here may help to prevent further misunderstanding. First, in the modern world, more than ever, there are many people in dire need who could be helped at relatively little cost to those of us who are well off. Private charity no doubt will always be needed, but effective remedies require greater efforts by governments and international organizations that can command and coordinate the necessary resources. Justice, and not merely beneficence, calls for this. Arguably, Kant's theory of justice, reasonably extended, would call for more stringent governmental responsibility for meeting basic needs than Kant himself acknowledged.[5] My concern in this essay, however, is limited to what Kant calls a 'duty of virtue,' namely, beneficence or the duty to make it our maxim to treat others' happiness as an end. It is important to remember that this is not the only source of our responsibility to combat poverty, famine, and preventable diseases.

Another caveat is that my main concern in this essay is primarily the interpretation of Kant's position on the general duty of beneficence, not its defense or application to particular circumstances. Although in my view Kant's position is more defensible than the more rigoristic alter-

(London: Hutchison, 1947, and Philadelphia: University of Pennsylvania Press, 1971), 148, 194; Mary J. Gregor, *Laws of Freedom* (Oxford: Blackwell, 1963), ch. 7, esp. pp. 103–8.

[3] See David Cummiskey, *Kantian Consequentialism* (New York: Oxford University Press, 1996) and Marcia Baron, *Kantian Ethics (Almost) without Apology* (Ithaca: Cornell University Press, 1995).

[4] Some of the points of controversy have to do with interpretation of passages in Kant's works, but some of the objections of Baron and Cummiskey, I think, are due to misunderstandings of an early (1971) article of mine that they discuss at length. Not all the controversy is a matter of miscommunication, however. Both Baron and Cummiskey cite evidence for their readings of Kant, and, all the more, they present forcefully the objectionable implications of certain extreme interpretations that they reject.

[5] See, for example, Paul Guyer, 'Kantian Foundations of Liberalism', *Kant on Freedom, Law, and Happiness* (Cambridge: Cambridge University Press, 2000), 235–61; Allen D. Rosen, *Kant's Theory of Justice* (Ithaca: Cornell University Press, 1993), 173–208; and Sarah Holtman, 'Kantian Justice and Poverty Relief', *Kant-Studien* (forthcoming).

natives that some propose, I will not argue that point here. Also it is not my current project, though it would be a worthy one, to work out what Kant's formulas of the Categorical Imperative, reasonably reconstructed, would prescribe for particular cases of helping others about which (in my view) the general duty of beneficence is indeterminate.

My remarks are divided as follows. In the first section I summarize my initial account of the imperfect duty of beneficence. Then, in the second section I supplement this by highlighting eight points that may help to prevent misunderstanding. In the third section I examine some controversial texts that David Cummiskey cites as evidence against my account. In the fourth section I comment briefly on further critical arguments by Cummiskey, and in the final section I respond to Marcia Baron's denial that there is a significant place in Kant's ethics for supererogatory acts.

I. THE LATITUDE IN IMPERFECT DUTIES: THE INITIAL ACCOUNT

In an earlier paper, 'Kant on Imperfect Duties and Supererogation', I reviewed the passages in which Kant distinguishes perfect and imperfect duties, commenting on various ways in which they might be interpreted.[6] My conclusion was that Kant's distinction, at least in *The Metaphysics of Morals*, is best understood as follows.

Strictly speaking,

what the moral law prescribes in addition to the actions demanded or prohibited by principles of perfect duty is that each person adopts certain maxims for guiding his other actions. What is required [by imperfect duties], at least directly, is that we take to heart certain principles, not that we act in certain ways. For example, what we can *directly* infer from the moral law is that we ought to adopt the maxim to promote the happiness of others, not that this or that beneficent act is obligatory.[7]

Perfect duties directly prescribe or prohibit *actions* rather than the sort of indefinite *maxims* (to promote ends) prescribed (directly) by imperfect duties. We never satisfy the requirements of imperfect duty simply by doing or refraining from 'external acts' from nonmoral motives, such as giving money to charity to impress people. A morally appropriate

---

[6] 'Kant on Imperfect Duty and Supererogation', *Kant-Studien*, 61 (1971), 55–77. This is reprinted in my collection of essays *Dignity and Practical Reason*, 145–75.
[7] *Dignity and Practical Reason*, 150. Italics added.

attitude is part of the requirement.[8] This is not a point of dispute among commentators.

Any command directing us to *adopt a maxim* to promote an end, such as others' happiness, also has implications for how we ought *to act*. 'For example, if a person with the usual abilities and opportunities did nothing to promote the happiness of others, he would thereby show that he did not really adopt a maxim of beneficence.'[9] These implications of imperfect duties *for action* can be expressed in the form 'Sometimes, to some extent, one ought . . .' as opposed to the more definite form of perfect duties, 'Always one ought . . .' or 'One must never . . .'. No one, I think, disputes that imperfect duties imply act principles of this form, as a minimum; the controversy is about what more they imply.[10] For example, do they imply that one must always act to promote the end prescribed by an imperfect duty, whenever one can, unless there is some other duty that one is trying to satisfy?

The paradigms of imperfect duties of 'widest' obligation, beneficence and development of our talents, allow a nontrivial kind of latitude that perfect duties do not.[11] This is because, by themselves, they imply only indefinite act principles of the form, 'Sometimes, to some extent, do things to promote the end . . .' Of course, all principles prescribing how we should act leave us some 'latitude' for *judgment* (whether the principle is applicable in a given case) and also for *choice* (how to carry out the requirement). For example, 'We ought to keep valid contracts' leaves some room for judgment as to whether certain putative contracts are valid, and even if it is a contract to pay a definite sum money at a

---

[8] Strictly speaking, what are required beyond the 'external act,' say, of giving money are two things: holding the happiness of others as an end to which one is committed and doing so from respect for moral law. This second 'requirement' is only 'wide and imperfect in terms of its degree, because of the frailty (*fragilitas*) of human nature' (MM, 196 [6: 446]).

[9] *Dignity and Practical Reason*, 151.

[10] Strictly speaking, the duty to adopt the maxim to count the happiness of others as our end *implies* that we ought to do things to promote the end only if we add the obvious assumption that we have the ability and opportunity actually to promote the end sometimes.

[11] Perfect duties, of the form 'Always X' or 'Never X,' can in fact leave us leeway in particular cases to decide when, how, and even to what extent to do something prescribed. Consider, for example, a promise to contribute to a friend's political campaign. Act principles of the form 'Sometimes, to some extent do X . . .', which are inferred from the wide imperfect duties, may in particular circumstances leave little or no important leeway, as when we face a last opportunity to do X even to a minimal extent. Kant's wide imperfect duties, such as beneficence and developing our talents, seem to allow more leeway of a significant kind than is allowed by the perfect duties that Kant discusses; but what in particular we are strictly required to do on various occasions depends on judgments that go beyond these principles.

particular time, we may be able to pay by check or cash, and, if by cash, in one, ten, or twenty dollar bills. Since the act principles derivative from imperfect duties have the form 'Sometimes, to some extent, one ought . . .', they leave room for choice of another kind.

Once we decide that a principle of perfect duty ['Always X' or 'Never X'] applies to our situation [i.e., doing X is now an option for us], then we have no choice but to do what it prescribes [X, or avoiding X] though there may be many ways of doing this. However, even if we know that one of the widest [act] principles of imperfect duty ['Sometimes do X'] applies [i.e., doing X is an option for us], we may still do something we would rather do [than X] which is not commended by a principle of duty, provided that we stand ready to do acts of the prescribed sort on some other occasions.[12]

I explicitly claimed this sort of latitude only for a subset of imperfect duties, not all, i.e., the paradigms of the 'widest' imperfect duties, beneficence and the development of talents.[13] Nevertheless, it is this claim that has proved to be most controversial.

Finally, as I noted, Kant's classification of duties contains some anomalies. For example, the so-called 'perfect duties to oneself,' such as a duty to avoid lying, drunkenness, and 'defiling oneself by lust,' are not easily construed as duties to adopt ends and so fit uneasily into Kant's

---

[12] *Dignity and Practical Reason*, 157. The bracketed words were added here for clarification. The explanation originally given in terms of a principle 'applying to' a situation is not as clear as it might be. Examples should make the point clear. Suppose the principle is 'Never lie,' which Kant regarded a principle of perfect duty. This 'applies' to any instance in which one is tempted to lie or seriously say what one believes to be false with the intent to deceive. It leaves no option with regard to the content indicated in the principle: there is no latitude with regard to whether to lie or not. Of course, the principle allows latitude regarding the means of satisfying the principle. Barring special considerations, one may, as one pleases, choose to avoid lying by telling the truth, by refusing to answer questions, or by carefully avoiding any situations in which one will be obliged to answer. Now consider the imperfect duty to develop one's talents or, more specifically, the act principle that it implies (assuming normal opportunities): Sometimes, to some extent, one ought to do things to develop one's talents. The form of the principle ('Sometimes, to some extent . . .') assures us that even if the principle 'applies,' in the sense that we are in a situation where we have an opportunity to do things to develop our talents, we may still (according to *this principle* at least) choose to do something we would rather do provided, over time, we do not neglect our talents. Even if we choose to take the opportunity now to develop our talents there is still, as with perfect duties, some latitude regarding the means. For example, if it is an educational opportunity, one might study logic or engineering; and if it is an opportunity for learning logic alone, one might take this course or that, use this study technique or that, and so on.

[13] *Dignity and Practical Reason*, 156. The point is worth noting because Marcia Baron expresses concern that if the duty of beneficence is a model for all imperfect duties, then on my interpretation the imperfect duty of moral self-perfection would also allow much latitude for choice, permitting us to be morally lax (Marcia Baron, *Kantian Ethics (Almost) without Apology*, 99–102).

general description of ethics as concerned with 'duties of virtue.'[14] Duties of respect are counted among the imperfect ethical duties but have a strictness characteristic of perfect duties.[15] Also, the duty of moral self-improvement is anomalous in ways I shall explain shortly.

II. IMPERFECT DUTIES: EXPLANATION AND QUALIFICATION

This initial account was evidently open to misunderstanding as well as controversy. Some of the earlier claims must be clarified, and some background assumptions need to be highlighted. My supplementary remarks are divided into eight distinguishable points.

First, the full import of Kant's principle of beneficence is not fully conveyed by saying that it implies an act principle of the *form* 'Sometimes, to some extent promote the happiness (or permissible ends) of others.' That at least such a principle is implied, assuming normal opportunities to help, is clear, and it is also clear that Kant does not mean to imply 'Always help when you can.' Already we have noted that the principle of beneficence also requires adopting the happiness of others as an end and doing so on moral grounds. To do less is to fall short of what it strictly requires.[16] But there is a further point. Kant obviously understood the principle as requiring us to make the happiness of others a serious, major, continually relevant, life-shaping end. It is not enough to include it along with minor, time-limited, minimally constraining goals, like keeping our campus free from litter, contributing to the local children's soccer team, and the like. The happiness of others is one of only two main ends that we have duties to promote, the other being our own perfection.[17] The general requirement to promote others' happiness, then, is meant to be a major, serious, always potentially relevant moral consideration, and nothing less than whole-hearted, unqualified willing this as an end will satisfy the requirement.

Although on my account the principle of beneficence requires serious commitment, still the only universal act principle, applicable to all cir-

---

[14] MM, 176–88 [6: 421–37].   [15] MM, 211 [6: 464].

[16] The principle of beneficence is labeled an 'imperfect duty,' but expresses a categorical imperative, a strict requirement to adopt the maxim to make the permissible ends of others one's own end.

[17] MM, 153–6 [6: 390–4]. Also, the *Summum Bonum* toward which our duties are to be seen as directed is the ideal combination of virtue and happiness for all: C2, 92–100 [5: 110–19].

cumstances, that we can infer from this has the basic form of a wide duty: 'Sometimes, to some *significant* extent, promote the permissible ends of others.'[18] We cannot infer the stronger principle with the form of perfect duties: '*Always*, whenever given a permissible opportunity, promote the end of the happiness of others.' Nor does it follow that we must always promote the happiness of others when able *and not fulfilling other duties*. Despite occasional suggestions to the contrary, Kant did not intend these strong claims. He says, for example, 'This duty [of beneficence] is only a wide one: the duty has in it a latitude for doing more or less, and no determinate limits can be assigned to what should be done. The law holds only for maxims not determinate actions.'[19]

Second, the labels 'perfect duty' and 'imperfect duty' primarily categorize *principles* of *The Metaphysics of Morals* that are quite general though more specific than the Categorical Imperative. Unlike the Categorical Imperative, which is supposed to be a comprehensive guide, they are restricted in their focus (to property, contracts, punishment, lying, beneficence, gratitude, respect, etc.), but they are supposed to articulate universal requirements for all foreseeable human conditions. When we try to apply the terms 'perfect duty' and 'imperfect duty' to particular acts or very specifically described act types, confusion is likely to result.[20]

---

[18] By 'the general principle of beneficence' I mean the general duty to promote the happiness of others, or (more strictly) to make the happiness of others an end of ours by adopting the maxim to promote that end. Kant's illustrations and arguments, however, are often focused more specifically on cases of helping those *in need* rather than 'doing favors' to those who are not 'needy' (see Gg, 33 [4: 423], MM, 201–2 [6: 452–3]). What counts as a need, Kant acknowledges, may vary with individual sensibilities. How far we ought to sacrifice part of our welfare to others without hope of return 'depends, in large part, on what each person's true needs are in view of his sensibilities, and it must be left to each to decide this for himself' (MM, 156 [6: 393]).

[19] MM, 156 [393].

[20] David Cummiskey, rightly noting that in certain specific circumstances, there may be no permissible alternative to helping someone in need, writes of helping in those circumstances as a perfect duty (in the sense of obligatory strength) even though it is derived (he thinks) from the alleged imperfect duty of beneficence. Similarly, he argues we may have 'wide duties' regarding various ways of fulfilling more general duties alleged to be 'perfect' (*Kantian Consequentialism*, 119, 120–1). Cummiskey's project here is to show that the perfect/imperfect duty distinction is unclear and, on any of several familiar interpretations, does not, by itself, provide an argument for thinking our duty to promote happiness is constrained in a way incompatible with consequentialism. Some of the unclarity can be resolved, I think, if we restrict the use of the terms to the purpose for which Kant primarily employed them in his mature work, namely, the classification of the general principles in his systematic metaphysics of morals. I agree with Cummiskey that merely labeling principles as 'perfect' or 'imperfect' provides no *argument* against consequentialism. Kantian reasons are needed why one principle (for example, not to lie) and not another (for example, beneficence) should be labeled 'perfect duty.'

For example, Kant's general prohibition on participation in revolution is aptly called a 'perfect duty' because of its 'Never do this' form, but we should not conclude from this that the ways of fulfilling this duty are all strictly mandatory. In some circumstances, the general prohibition might be satisfied in any of several ways, among which we may choose as we please: by refusing to sign the revolutionary declaration and giving aid to the cause, by joining the loyalist army, or by silently leaving the country altogether. Other circumstances may leave no significant options. The general duty to promote our talents is aptly classified as a wide imperfect duty because, as Kant says, it 'determines nothing about the kind and extent of the actions themselves but leaves a latitude for free choice.'[21] Nevertheless, it would be misleading to infer that all the particular acts that count towards fulfilling it should be called 'imperfect duties,' for extreme circumstances may leave us no significant latitude for choice. For example, in dire straits an unfortunate person might have only one (permissible) chance to escape a debilitating, brain-numbing life of physical labor. Given background conditions, taking the chance might be strictly required because nothing else would count as having seriously made developing her talents an end. It would be misleading to call the strict specific requirement (to take the chance to escape) an 'imperfect duty,' even though the principle behind this particular strict requirement is still aptly labeled a wide imperfect duty to develop our talents. A similar point applies to beneficence.[22]

Third, calling a duty 'perfect' implies that it trumps the general considerations to which 'imperfect' duty principles direct our attention. That is, the terms are meant to imply that we should never violate a duty labeled 'perfect' merely to promote an end that 'imperfect' duty principles require us to adopt and pursue. Strictly, principles correctly classified as perfect and imperfect duty cannot conflict simply because the labels indicate their relative priority. This is just a matter of what the labels imply, not a substantive claim that, by itself, can be used in

---

[21] MM, 195 [6: 446].

[22] Restricting the terms 'perfect duty' and 'imperfect duty' to the general principles is important because it blocks the following mistaken inference: (1) the general principle of beneficence is an imperfect duty (Kant); (2) therefore, in particular cases helping people in need is always an imperfect duty (a dubious inference); (3) imperfect duties always allow latitude and never strictly demand a particular type of action (Hill's interpretation); (4) therefore, on Hill's interpretation it is never strictly mandatory to help persons in need (a repugnant conclusion). This inference may partly explain Cummiskey's rejection of my minimalist ('anemic') interpretation of the general principle of beneficence (3). My proposal, however, blocks the inference from (1) to (2) because it reserves the term 'imperfect duty' for the general principle. It also clarifies (3) by making it explicitly restricted to the use of 'imperfect duty' regarding general principles.

an argument for or against consequentialism. Given these labels, it remains a substantive, and controversial issue, which duties are 'perfect,' which 'imperfect,' and how exactly they should be stated. Principles of perfect duty, as I construe them, can have built-in exception clauses, as in 'Never resist lawful authorities except when ordered to violate others' rights.'[23] If, as many think, our obligation to help people (for example, to save lives) on a particular occasion leaves us no permissible option to telling a lie, breaking a promise, or rebelling against an oppressive government, then the proper conclusion for them to draw is not that sometimes imperfect duties trump perfect duties but rather that it is a mistake to think that the prohibitions of lying, promise-breaking, and revolution are perfect duties in the unqualified form that Kant suggests.

Fourth, because of its content, the supposedly 'imperfect' duty to promote our own moral self-perfection as an end is an anomalous special case that does not serve as a model for beneficence.[24] The minimal act principles derived from duties to promote ends such as happiness and development of talents have the form 'Sometimes, to some extent, do what promotes X,' but if the obligatory end is explicitly described as an optimal condition or 'the most possible' of some good, as in the case of a duty of moral *perfection*, then we can infer more than the minimal act principles. For example, if we take seriously moral *perfection* as an end, then we must accept '*Never* do what you believe to be wrong' and '*Always* exercise due care to check your moral judgments.' More radically, given Kant's ideas of moral perfection, we can infer 'Keep striving, within human limitations, to do what's right for the right reasons.'[25] These are significantly different types of

---

[23] Kant acknowledges this exception at R, 153n [6: 154n]. In *Perpetual Peace* Kant indicates that the ideal is that perfect duties should not incorporate necessary qualifications as a list of seemingly *ad hoc* 'exceptions' but instead that they should express the point in a more unified way in the content of the principle (PP, 97–8n [8: 348]). For example, 'Never kill a person, except when the person is wrongfully threatening your life or has committed a capital crime' might be more acceptably replaced by 'Never kill innocent persons.' If such transformations conveyed exactly the same ideas, the change in form would be merely cosmetic; but presumably Kant intends that the simpler form should identify the common feature in the exceptional cases. In my example the simpler principle apparently goes beyond, but includes, the exceptional cases mentioned in the first.

[24] Kant says that the duty is 'narrow and perfect in terms of its quality but it is wide and imperfect in terms of its degree, because of the frailty (*fragilitas*) of human nature.' He adds that the duty is 'narrow and perfect *with regard to* its object (the idea that one should make it one's end to realize),' but '*with regard to* the subject it is only a wide and imperfect duty to oneself' (MM, 196 [446]).

[25] Marcia Baron notes, quite rightly, that Kant's duty of moral self-perfection is more

requirement from those derivative from 'Adopt the happiness of others as an end.' What is needed is not attention to a special range of moral requirements regarding what we should do (for example, about helping others and developing talents), but rather attention to our deliberative processes in all cases of potential moral importance and to our reasons for complying with moral requirements. Kant implies that this 'imperfect' duty has a strictness that other imperfect duties may lack, but this is not well translated by saying it implies act principles of the sort 'Always, whenever possible, do more things of a certain kind (those that contribute towards moral perfection).' That would suggest a Stoic novice's program of moral exercises, like foregoing a drink of cool water when thirsty, holding one's hand in the fire to develop fortitude later useful for fulfilling duty, etc. This, however, is not Kant's point. Rather, the point is that we should, to the extent possible, strive to do what is morally required and for the right reasons, though absolute perfection in this is beyond the reach of human beings.[26] To say this is not to add

stringent than the duties of beneficence and development of natural talents, and she argues that this duty 'stiffens' the duty of beneficence so that it is at least misleading to express the latitude that it allows in some of the ways I did. When supplemented with the duty of moral self-perfection, she maintains, one may not allow one's endeavors to help others 'to be circumscribed by the limitations of one's personality' (*Kantian Ethics (Almost) without Apology*, 100). For example, we should not let our 'insensitivity and lack of compassion' or anger at unhappy people determine our choice as to whether, how, and how much, to help others. For this reason, she thinks, it is misleading to say that the wide imperfect duties allow the 'freedom to choose to do x or not on a given occasion, *as one pleases*, even though one knows that x is the sort of act that falls under the principle, provided that one is ready to perform acts of this kind on some other occasions.' On p. 101 Baron quotes this phrase from *Dignity and Practical Reason*, 155, adding the italics. The proper response, in my view, is that it is not simply the general principle of beneficence that imposes the restriction but instead the duty of moral self-perfection. The latitude allowed by the general principle of beneficence is often restricted in particular cases by other relevant moral principles. The basic principle of beneficence by itself, as I see it, typically lets a generally beneficent person pass up some opportunities to promote others' happiness without specifying the range of permissible motives for doing so. Consideration of our own happiness, and so even 'that it pleases us' to do so, are acceptable motives so far as the principle itself tells us, as long as we have sincerely and wholeheartedly adopted the happiness of others as an end. Of course, other moral principles must guide and constrain our judgment in particular circumstances: sometimes not helping is ungrateful, disrespectful, unjust, or, more generally, not properly responsive to humanity in a person. The duty of moral self-perfection together with other duties will oppose doing anything with certain vicious motives, such as avarice, malice, servility, contempt for others, and so it follows that we must not choose not to help others from such motives. These constraints, however, are not written into the principle of beneficence; they stem from further grounds of obligation that we must consult when judging on particular occasions whether we must help or may pass up the opportunity.

[26] MM, 154–5 [6: 391–3], 196 [6: 446–7].

to the list of 'things to do' in the usual sense, but to urge due care in our moral deliberation and morally appropriate motivation in fulfilling our duties. Because the special requirements in this duty to perfect ourselves morally stem from the nature of the end in question (maximum striving towards the end), it is not a model for the duty of beneficence (which does not specify the end as 'the most possible' contribution to the happiness of others).[27]

Fifth, and most importantly, the principle of beneficence, as I understand it, is a minimal moral requirement, regarding helping others, that expresses what everyone, everywhere, must do, leaving open the question whether in specific circumstances morality requires more. *The Metaphysics of Morals* states Kant's view of the most general requirements of morality valid for all human beings at all times, or at least for those human conditions that he anticipated competent moral agents in foreseeable conditions would face. The *Rechtslehre* proposes principles of practical reason governing the shape of justifiable social institutions, at least conditions they must meet to be fully justifiable. The *Tugendlehre* states principles that all persons, regardless of their many differences in institutions and culture, should follow in their relations to one another and their own capacities. The principles are supposed to be derivable from (or at least constrained by) the Categorical Imperative, in its various forms,[28] and they do not preclude the possibility that

---

[27] This point is significant with respect to the criticisms of Baron and Cummiskey because, given my interpretation of the latitude in the duty of beneficence, equating the latitude in the duties of beneficence and moral self-improvement would have the consequence, contrary to Kant, that the latter requires only a minimal level of moral decency and effort. As Baron puts it, 'virtue would be optional and the duty to improve oneself would be incumbent only on those who, morally speaking, are especially derelict' (*Kantian Ethics (Almost) without Apology*, 42). Cummiskey offers the same objection: 'According to the anemic interpretation of imperfect duties, we should find Kant saying that one must "sometimes, to some extent" strive to be more virtuous, but if on a particular occasion one is inclined to satisfy an inclination instead, that is fine' (*Kantian Consequentialism*, 111). The explanation given here about why the duty of moral self-perfection is special should suffice to meet the objection. Also it should be noted that my initial account granted that some duties that Kant officially counts as imperfect, such as the duties of respect for others, do not allow the sort of latitude that the 'paradigms of imperfect duty, the duties of beneficence and the development of talents' do. That wider latitude was not attributed to the duty of moral self-improvement. *Dignity and Practical Reason*, 156–7.

[28] There are textual issues here. In the introduction to *The Metaphysics of Morals*, as well as the *Groundwork*, there is evidence that the Categorical Imperative guides and constrains all other principles in a system of principles that is called a metaphysics of morals. But Kant also suggests that the basic principle of *Rechtslehre*, the universal principle of justice (*Recht*) is a postulate, not derivative from anything else. Some scholars think that the doctrine of law, or some elements of it, was thought to be an independent module, developed from more minimal commitments than Kant's basic moral theory. See

the Categorical Imperative may be needed to guide our judgment regarding specific cases that fall under them.

The general imperfect duty of beneficence in *The Metaphysics of Morals*, taken by itself, does not determine when in particular circumstances helping is strictly required. Moral deliberation, guided by the various forms of the Categorical Imperative, presumably has more to say about helping others than is strictly implied by the rather minimal principle concerned with what everyone, everywhere, must do, regardless of particular circumstances.[29] Judgment from the Categorical Imperative and other (derived) principles regarding more specifically described circumstances should determine that often we have more stringent duties of aid than the minimal universal principle requires—and sometimes the general presumption that aiding is good may even be cancelled for a particular case. We should not assume that every issue about helping is determined *through* the intermediate, minimal universal principle of beneficence. Particular occasions when we can help others are complex and diverse, and there is no reason to suppose that the only relevant moral consideration guiding our judgments about whether, how, and to what extent we are required to help would be the indefinite imperfect duty of beneficence that expresses the minimal requirement for all persons regardless of circumstances. Considerations of justice, gratitude, respect, and friendship can be highly relevant.[30] They can be grounds for judging that on a particular occasion, helping is not at all optional.

Sixth, there are important distinctions to be made among the cases that fall under the very general principle of beneficence. Meeting basic needs for life and functioning as a rational autonomous agent are clearly more important than doing pleasing favors for someone well off. It is

---

Thomas Pogge, 'Is Kant's *Rechtslehre* Comprehensive?' *Southern Journal of Philosophy*, 36, supplement (1997), 161–87.

[29] This point was expressed briefly in a footnote in my initial account: *Dignity and Practical Reason*, 153, n. 5. It is obviously important because otherwise my interpretation of the latitude allowed by the general principle of beneficence would entail the absurd result that helping those in need is always optional. Cummiskey notes this absurd consequence, apparently thinking that it follows from my account: *Kantian Consequentialism*, 116, 119. Baron notes the qualification in my footnote but still argues for a 'stiffened' interpretation of the general principle of beneficence: *Kantian Ethics (Almost) without Apology*, 101.

[30] Even the principle of moral self-perfection might be relevant, in ways that Marcia Baron indicates, making a requirement to help in certain circumstances more stringent than it might otherwise be. For example, if not helping would be indulging some attitude that we have moral reason to alter. See her *Kantian Ethics (Almost) without Apology*, 99–101.

reasonable to suppose that judgments about the stringency of the requirement to help in particular cases would vary depending on whether it is a case of sacrificing minor personal pleasures to meet others' basic needs, a case of foregoing some personal pleasure to give a similar sort of pleasure to another, a case of sacrificing some of our basic necessities to meet others' basic needs, or a case of sacrificing our basic needs merely for the personal pleasures of others. (There are, of course, other possible cases, and the degrees of need, and other factors, may matter.) Kant is clearly committed to the priority of basic needs. A proper regard for the humanity of each person as an end would leave us the least latitude in cases where sacrifices of our minor pleasures can satisfy others' basic needs.[31] We can expect to have the widest latitude to forego opportunities to promote others' happiness when the beneficent act would be doing unsolicited favors irrelevant to anyone's basic needs.[32] For example, to further a nonmoral personal project very important to our happiness, we may forego chances to volunteer to contribute to others' minor personal projects. These common-sense points are not reflected in the general principle to promote others' happiness, I suggest, because that principle was supposed to state a basic requirement relevant regarding all opportunities to help others, not a comprehensive guide for deciding when one must help and when one has permissible options.

Seventh, although Kant states the principle of beneficence more generally, in examples and arguments he in fact focuses mostly on what are now known as cases of 'mutual aid' where we can help someone in great need at relatively little cost to ourselves. For example, regarding the sample case in the *Groundwork* Kant argues from the Categorical Imperative that the agent's failure to help a person in distress when he

---

[31] The incomparable worth of our 'humanity,' or 'rational nature,' would obviously give us reason to favor meeting needs essential to living as a rational agent over giving pleasant luxuries. Kant's discussion of duties to oneself also reflects this priority: avoiding suicide and taking care of our health, for example, are said to be quite strict duties whereas giving ourselves innocent pleasures is not: MM, 176–8 [6: 421–4], 180–1 [6: 427–8].

[32] This is relevant to the objections of Cummiskey and Baron because the most obvious cases where helping others is strictly required are cases in which we can meet someone's basic need at little cost to ourselves and no one else can help. Cummiskey's cases of saving people from drowning are of this sort: *Kantian Consequentialism*, 116, 119. Clearly any interpretation of Kant's position would be objectionable if it took the latitude in the general principle of beneficence to mean that such rescues are optional, all things considered, or that an acceptable alternative would be to skip the rescues and to choose instead to take flowers to a home for the elderly. In my view, the general principle of beneficence does not by itself determine the proper priority in such cases, but good judgment guided by the Categorical Imperative is supposed to.

easily could was quite strictly wrong. The judgment on the particular case turns not only on a description of the external circumstances but also on the agent's attitude.[33] To judge the man in Kant's example strictly wrong not to help is compatible with Kant's suggestion, in a footnote, that the *general* duties to aid and further the ends of others are 'imperfect duties' that allow some 'exception in the interest of inclination.'[34] Here it seems that 'imperfect duty' characterizes the general principle of beneficence (to promote the happiness of others), not particular cases of mutual aid such as the case described in the *Groundwork* example. The former articulates the most general minimum standard for all cases of helping, and the latter is reached not simply by 'applying' that standard but by arguing directly from the Categorical Imperative for a stricter obligation in special circumstances. Applications of the Categorical Imperative to particular cases evidently do not have to go *through* the general principle of beneficence as an intermediate step.

Note that Kant's examples are just that—particular sample cases in which an agent's circumstances and maxim are explicitly described and further background conditions are assumed. The use of the Categorical

---

[33] Gg, 33 [4: 424]. This point is relevant to my disagreement with Cummiskey because, if we ignored it, Cummiskey's 'robust' interpretation of the duty of beneficence would seem to gain support from the fact that Kant evidently thought that the person who refuses to give aid in his *Groundwork* example is quite strictly wrong. My point is that we cannot generalize to a stringent interpretation of the general principle of beneficence from a particular example in which Kant uses the Categorical Imperative to show that a person refusing aid with a certain attitude and in specified circumstances was strictly wrong.

[34] Kant does not actually say that imperfect duties allow exceptions in favor of inclination, but only that perfect duties do not. This suggests by contrast that imperfect duties do, but it is not strictly entailed. Kant may have been alluding to others' use of 'imperfect duty' without meaning to endorse it. In any case the expression is potentially misleading. Whenever we have a duty, all things considered, it is morally necessary to conform, i.e., to do just what is prescribed whether it is a specific action, adopting an end, or doing *some* acts towards an end. Being inclined to do otherwise would never be an adequate reason not to fulfill the duty. If making 'exceptions in favor of inclination' meant not doing our duty because we did not want to, Kant obviously would never allow it. The phrase may, however, refer to the latitude within the principles that describe our duties or, as we say, to 'exceptions built into the principle.' Suppose the content of a principle tells us to adopt and contribute to a certain end but leaves it optional when and how much. Then if we contribute on many occasions but choose—even from inclination—to pass up another particular opportunity to do so, we have not illegitimately 'made an exception' to what this principle requires but invoked a permission implicit in the principle. Other principles, of course, may close the options for particular cases that the general principle allowed. I thank Jens Timmerman for his comments on the controversial phrase discussed here though he probably still disagrees with my position.

Imperative as a guide to moral judgment is illustrated by arguments to show that the agent, with that maxim and in those specified circumstances, would be strictly wrong to act as initially proposed (briefly, to commit suicide to end pain, to make a lying promise to improve his financial lot, to neglect his talents to indulge pleasures, and to refuse to relieve distress when he easily could). The conclusion is that the agents in the illustrative stories would be wrong to act on their specified maxim. This does not generalize beyond 'No one should act on *that maxim* (reflecting *that* attitude in *those* circumstances).' Most important, we should resist the common temptation to suppose that we can generalize from these cases to either (a) how the universal duty regarding others' happiness should be stated or (b) how to sum up the full range of moral considerations relevant to cases in which we have an opportunity to promote others' (permissible) ends. The *Groundwork* examples were not intended to do these jobs: the first (a) was left to *The Metaphysics of Morals* and the second (b) was not attempted by Kant and is probably impossible. Misguided attempts to over-generalize from Kant's *Groundwork* examples naturally lead to thinking that Kant's principle of beneficence is more determinate and stringent than it is.

Eighth, in my initial account I suggested that, although Kant did not put the point this way, in effect he held that many beneficent acts are '*good* to do but not required.'[35] This is not an altogether inappropriate description, but it can be misleading. It is appropriate if it is understood to mean just that many beneficent acts are 'meritorious' and 'more in the way of duty than he can be constrained by law to do,' as Kant uses these terms.[36] It is also sometimes appropriate, in my view, if it means 'not required but morally worthy.'[37] The phrase 'good to do but not required' would be misleading, however, if understood as saying that the acts fall into a category of acts that we can identify in advance as always morally optional but to the credit of those who do them. Judgment will always be required in particular cases to determine whether helping someone is necessary or not. Meritorious acts do more than law can compel us to do and more than others can demand as their right.[38]

---

[35] *Dignity and Practical Reason*, 172–3.
[36] See, for example, MM, 19–20 [6: 227–8], 153–4 [6: 390–1].
[37] Gg, 10–3 [4: 397–400]. A particular act that is not required may be one among many ways that we pursue an end that it is a duty for us to have. In my view if we adopt and continue to affirm the end from duty and we pursue it because of this respect for moral reasons, then this should suffice for counting as 'morally worthy' any of the many particular acts we might choose to advance the end even though those particular acts were not required.
[38] MM, 19–20 [6: 390–1]. Kant appears to be concerned in this context with what

Since the imperfect duty of beneficence does not specify when, how, or to what extent we must promote the obligatory end, there will presumably be many possible ways and times of contributing to others' happiness that we may permissibly choose to pass up, even if we are not doing so to fulfill another duty. If, however, respect for moral law motivated the adoption of the end, then doing such an act should count as 'morally worthy' even though the agent is aware that neither law nor ethical duty strictly demands that particular act. The mere fact that an act is 'good to do but not required' in this sense does not, by itself, qualify it as 'supererogatory' in an ordinary sense.[39] Certainly it does not mean that the act is on a list of 'extra credit' activities that we can take, independently of context, as optional.

The phrase 'good to do but not required' would also be misleading as an expression of Kant's view of beneficent acts if it were taken to imply that morality recommends that we do such acts, *the more of them the better*. So understood, 'good to do but not required' would suggest that the moral ideal is to do as many beneficent acts as possible, at least when not responding to other duties, and that doing fewer than this taints one as morally inferior, adequate perhaps but falling short of what morality recommends to us. This understanding would invite the sort

---

can be legally demanded and enforced rather than, as I earlier thought, with moral law. If so, by saying that someone's meritorious act is 'more in the way of duty than he can by law be constrained to do' Kant does not affirm or deny that extraordinary efforts to make others happy can be 'more in the way of duty than *moral* law demands.' Such efforts, however, are a kind of thing that having an obligatory end requires of us (namely, working towards others' happiness), and some of these efforts in particular contexts are *more* of that kind of thing than the imperfect duty of beneficence requires because one could have been sincerely committed to the end without doing quite so much.

[39] As Henry Allison pointed out in a discussion, my initial account seems to imply that *every* beneficent act done because a person dutifully adopts the happiness of others as an end is 'good to do but not required.' That is, every act of this kind is 'morally worthy' (because of the moral motive) but not required as a *particular* way of promoting the obligatory end. If we were to identify the 'supererogatory' simply as what is 'good to do but not required,' as my earlier account may at times have suggested, then all morally motivated benevolent acts would count as supererogatory. This would be quite counter-intuitive, even though 'good to do but not required' is a common way of characterizing the supererogatory. What I called 'the best candidate' for a supererogatory act in Kant's system, however, was not merely 'good to do but not required' in the above sense but had further special features. Most importantly, no alternative was required by more stringent duty (or other imperfect duties), the agent had adopted the moral end, and he or she 'had often and continually acted on it.' The example was a case in which a person 'who had conscientiously helped others and given to charities all his life' gave a minor 'treat' to a neighbor child who was not needy: *Dignity and Practical Reason*, 168–9.

of objection that Susan Wolf famously expressed in her 'Moral Saints' paper: that is, Kantian morality presses us not only to be dutiful and virtuous (just, beneficent, etc.) but also, as we say, 'to do as much good' as possible, and this (she argues) is incompatible with our being interesting, diverse, creative, wonderful people.[40]

Kant, however, does not imply that beneficent acts are 'good to do' in the sense that leads down this path. Acts of 'moral worth' deserve our esteem as manifestations of an agent's commitment to moral standards, but there is no mandate to 'do as many as possible' acts of moral worth. The moral goodness (or esteem-worthiness) of a person depends on whether or not the person has a good will, but it is not measured by the *number* of acts in which the person is moved by a good will.[41] Similarly, in calling a particular act 'meritorious' and 'more in the way of duty than [we] can be constrained by *law* to do' Kant evidently means that it would violate no one's rights to omit the act because the act is not *owed* to the individuals who benefit from them. The phrase does not imply that the act is of a kind such that we will be morally better persons the more of them we do.

To illustrate this last point, consider a nonmoral case. John cherishes Mary's bringing him flowers as an act manifesting her having made it an end to please him, which reflects her commitment to their friendship. This is so even though her bringing flowers was not required by their friendship and, besides, she has done many such things already. His cherishing her doing this carries no judgment that it was a kind of act, the ideal for which is literally 'the more the better.'[42] By analogy, from a moral point of view, we may regard as 'morally worthy' Susan's giving flowers to a stranger insofar as it manifests her having made the happiness of others an end, which in turn reflects her commitment to humanity as an end in itself. This is so even though her giving flowers to the stranger was not morally required and, besides, she has done many such things already. Our moral esteem for what Susan did does

---

[40] Susan Wolf, 'Moral Saints', *Journal of Philosophy*, 79 (1982), 419–39.

[41] The assumption that we must do as many acts of moral worth as possible lies behind the objection that by Kant's theory we should deliberately strew our path with temptations so that we may more often act from duty rather than from inclination.

[42] This eighth point is relevant not only to Susan Wolf's objections that Kantian ethics demands too much, but it is also important in assessing the insistence of Baron and Cummiskey that Kant has no place for 'supererogatory acts.' Acknowledging that some beneficent acts are 'good but not required' in the sense I have endorsed does not imply that we could specify a minimum of moral requirement beyond which helping others is always 'extra credit' and so we may shut off our moral attention, relax, and do entirely as we please. As I explain in the last section of this essay, Marcia Baron argues forcefully against trying to specify such a minimum requirement.

not imply a judgment that it was a kind of act, the ideal for which is 'the more the better.'

Some particular acts (but not all) that are not morally demanded in the circumstances promote a morally necessary end *to a greater extent* than either the indefinite principle of beneficence or judgment from Categorical Imperative strictly requires. If the agents adopted and continued to affirm the end from duty and did these beneficent acts because of this, then these acts should count as 'morally worthy' even though the agents were not strictly required to do those particular acts *or even as much of this sort of thing as they have already done*. These special acts are not only 'good but not required' but also, in a sense, *more* 'in the way of duty' than the *moral* law requires. This last feature comes closest to familiar ideas of supererogatory acts, but, as before, there are no grounds for inferring that in advance of particular cases we could specify an area of life 'fenced off' from duty within which we can suspend our moral attention or treat others' welfare as of no concern to us.[43]

These remarks are not meant to endorse a lax, indulgent attitude about our moral duties to help others. My point is a conceptual one about ways we may classify morally significant acts, not a substantive thesis about which cases belong in each category. The best candidates for being acts that are 'good to do but not required,' do more toward a moral end than necessary, and yet are not necessarily commendable as 'the more the better,' would no doubt be doing minor unsolicited favors rather than meeting basic needs.

III. DAVID CUMMISKEY ON CONTROVERSIAL TEXTS

The eight supplementary points sketched above should suffice to answer many of the concerns that Baron and especially Cummiskey expressed about my relatively minimalist interpretation of Kant's general principle of beneficence. Given those points, for example, this interpretation does not imply that helping others is always morally optional, that we need only to avoid being morally derelict, that we may choose to do favors for friends rather than save the lives of strangers, or that we could specify a minimum of required beneficence beyond

---

[43] See Marcia Baron, *Kantian Ethics (Almost) without Apology*, 41.

which helping is always optional but the more the better.⁴⁴ This is only to say, however, that the interpretation does not have certain implausible implications, as some thought. Cummiskey and Baron, however, do not rest their case against the interpretation on the claim that it has morally unacceptable implications. They appeal directly for evidence to some controversial texts. In reviewing these, I will concentrate on Cummiskey's interpretations because they are most at odds with my account.

David Cummiskey sharply disagrees with my initial account of imperfect duties as he understands it. He complains that, 'perhaps under the influence of an article by Thomas Hill, it has become somewhat of a dogma that Kantian beneficence, since it is only an imperfect duty, only requires that one help others "sometimes, to some extent".' He calls this 'the anemic interpretation' in contrast to his 'robust' one, which holds that the general principle of beneficence demands that 'one ought to do a beneficent act *whenever one can*, unless one chooses to follow instead some other principle of imperfect duty.'⁴⁵ Later, to bring the robust interpretation more in line with his consequentialism, Cummiskey suggests that Kant must not have meant what he said when said that there is no (direct) duty to promote our own happiness.⁴⁶ Accordingly, he modifies the robust interpretation to say that 'the principle of beneficence is a duty to promote the happiness of all, not just others, in accordance with the principle of equality.' He understands 'the principle of equality' here in a qualified consequentialist way. That is, with three qualifications, his robust beneficence principle requires us to maximize aggregate happiness. The qualifications are (1) that we do not violate perfect duties (a condition later set aside), (2) that we give priority to values associated with our rational nature, and (3) that we may sometimes attend

---

⁴⁴ In order not to disrupt the exposition, I addressed objections from Cummiskey and Baron in nn. 11, 18, 20, 21, 24, 26, 31, 32, and 37. Some similar concerns are expressed by Daniel Statman in 'Who Needs Imperfect Duties?' *American Philosophical Quarterly*, 33(2) (1996), 221–4.
⁴⁵ *Kantian Consequentialism*, 110; my italics. Cummiskey claims (p. 110) that 'the robust interpretation is compatible with a derivative, more moderate, and nuanced set of secondary principles that guide one's actions and decisions in the concrete context of day-to-day life.' Thus, like many consequentialists, he grants that a robust consequentialist basic principle may justify a limited freedom to choose to favor one's friends and oneself in certain ways, as a derivative policy. He insists, however, that the latitude these policies allow must be 'derived from the more basic general principles, which will include the robust principle of beneficence' (p. 110).
⁴⁶ Ibid. 112. I discuss Cummiskey's interpretation of the relevant passage shortly under the text (3), quoted on p. 224.

instead to other imperfect duties. Except for the qualifications, this is a requirement so stringent that it should please even Peter Singer.[47]

Cummiskey appeals to several key texts to support his robust interpretation, and he challenges defenders of the weaker interpretation, saying provocatively that 'the textual support, not to mention the philosophical basis, for this *anemic interpretation* is inversely proportional to the conviction of those who defend it.'[48] I remain unconvinced. What accounts for the sharpness and fervor of Cummiskey's attack on the 'anemic' position may be his thought that it has the implausible implications that I mentioned. What he offers in support, however, are questionable interpretations of several key passages. Among these are the following.

(1) Kant asserts that 'ethics', which requires us to make the happiness of others an end, does not 'give laws for actions' but 'only for the maxims of actions.' It follows, he says, that 'ethical duties are only of wide obligation.' He explains as follows:

if the law can prescribe only the maxim of actions, not actions themselves, this is a sign that it leaves a play room (*latitudo*) for following (complying with) the law, that is, the law cannot specify precisely in what way one is to act and how much one is to do by the action for the end that is a duty.[49]

But Kant adds the following caution: 'But a wide duty is not to be taken as permission to make exception to the maxims of actions but only as permission to limit one maxim of duty by another (e.g., love of one's neighbor in general by love of one's parents), by which in fact the field for virtue is widened.'[50]

Earlier, following Mary Gregor, I explained the passage this way: 'what Kant seems to be saying is that, whereas we may (and indeed must) restrict the number of times we are prepared to act on one maxim (e.g., to develop our talents) by adopting another maxim (e.g., to promote the happiness of others), we may not let our concern for one maxim keep us from adopting another.'[51]

But Cummiskey vigorously objects as follows:

Now this conclusion seems true, indeed obvious, and it is also entailed by the passage—but it is simply not what the passage in question says. The passage

---

[47] Singer, 'Famine, Affluence, and Morality'.   [48] *Kantian Consequentialism*, 110.
[49] MM, 153 [390]. Cummiskey's discussion is on pp. 111 and 116 of his book.
[50] MM, 153 [390].
[51] *Dignity and Practical Reason*, 152. Cummiskey quotes this at p. 110 of his book. See Gregor, *Laws of Freedom*, 195–6.

says that the wideness of imperfect duties is 'only a permission to limit one maxim of duty by another'; that is, we may not take the wideness of imperfect duties as a permission to make non-duty-based exceptions to the demands of imperfect duty; in more Kantian jargon, we cannot make inclination-based exceptions to the maxim of actions that would promote the obligatory end. We can, however, let inclination determine which imperfect duty we will act on and to what extent.[52]

Cummiskey's argument, and also my earlier explanation, overlook a distinction that Kant makes here between general 'maxims of actions' (*Maxime der Handlungen*) and more specific 'maxims of duty' (*Pflichtmaxime*). Ethics, Kant says, gives laws only for the maxims of actions, not for actions. It tells us not merely that we must not act on certain maxims, but, positively, that we must make it our maxim to pursue the ends that are duties. The 'maxims of actions' in this context, then, are apparently general maxims that we are required to adopt, most basically, to make the happiness of others and our own perfection our ends. The 'maxims of duty' that Kant mentions here are 'love of one's parents' and 'love of one's neighbor in general.' These may also count as 'maxims of action' that everyone is required to adopt, but they refer to maxims indicating more specific ways to act on the general, indeterminate 'maxim of action' to promote the happiness of others somehow. The maxim of love of parents must be something like 'promote my parents' happiness,' and the maxim of 'love of neighbor in general' is presumably 'promote the happiness of all persons that I may affect.' The first is clearly a more specific, derivative maxim than the general, indeterminate maxim to promote others' happiness, and arguably this is true of the second as well. What was the point, then, of Kant's phrase 'only a permission to limit one maxim of duty by another'? A possibility consistent with my account of imperfect duties is that we are permitted to limit our efforts to promote others' happiness under one of these more specific 'maxims of duty' for the sake of promoting it under a different one. For example, some may devote more effort to caring for an ailing parent than to doing public charity work, but others may do the opposite. Presumably there are other specific 'maxims of duty,' such as 'love of children,' that describe other specific ways of fulfilling the general duty of beneficence; and how much we should devote to each of these maxims is not determined by rules. Since there are similar options under the other general maxims of action, such as to develop our talents, the 'field' for virtuous activity is 'widened.'

[52] *Kantian Consequentialism*, 110–11.

On this interpretation, 'a wide duty not to be taken as a permission to make an exception to the maxim of actions' implies that we may never exempt ourselves from any of the obligatory 'maxims of action,' such as developing talents, beneficence, or even, more specifically, love of parents. In other words, we have some choice among various ways of furthering the end of happiness in others, just as we have some choice about what talents to develop; but it is still a strict duty sincerely and wholeheartedly to adopt the happiness of others (and developing our talents) as ends. Kant warns us, in the passage, that by calling these general duties 'wide' and 'imperfect' he did not mean to suggest otherwise.

This reading seems natural and squares well with my less rigoristic account of the wide imperfect duties. It does not deny that we may also wholeheartedly adopt and permissibly pursue our own happiness as an end. Also nothing here implies that, assuming perfect duties are satisfied, I must promote others' happiness unless I am promoting other required ends. All the more, there is no implication that we may pursue our own personal ends only when it would be allowed by an impartial judge of what maximizes the general happiness.[53]

Cummiskey interprets Kant's phrase 'not as a permission to make exception to the maxim of actions' as *saying* 'not . . . as a permission to make non-duty-based exceptions to the demands of imperfect duty,' but this is unwarranted, perhaps even question-begging. The issue is how stringently to understand 'the maxim of action' regarding others' happiness that the moral law prescribes. In my view, it is an indefinite maxim to make the happiness of others an important end, but it does not specify when or how much to do toward that end. On Cummiskey's interpretation, the maxim of action specifies that we must do everything possible to further others' happiness unless we are engaged in fulfilling some other duty. By itself Kant's statement that we must 'not make exception to the maxim of actions' is neutral between these interpretations. It tells us to be guided unfailingly by the relevant obligatory maxim of action, never doing less than it demands; but this does not tell us specifically what it demands, which is what is at issue. On my view, it is often not making 'exception to the demands of imperfect duty' to do something non-obligatory for our own happiness.

(2) Following the passage quoted above, Kant continues: 'The wider the duty, therefore, the more imperfect is a man's obligation to action;

---

[53] Cummiskey, as I noted, is not a hedonistic utilitarian but has a two-tiered value system, giving priority to promoting the good of persons as rational agents.

as he, nevertheless, brings closer to *narrow* duty (duties of right) the maxim of complying with wide duty (in his disposition), so much the more perfect is his virtuous action.'[54]

Kant's point, I think, is that the more resolutely and without qualifications we are determined to comply with wide duties (from respect for morality) the more virtuous we are when we act on this resolution. This does not tell us, one way or the other, exactly what or how much is demanded by a wide duty such as beneficence. The passage has to do with the spirit and strength of will with which we determine that others' happiness will be for us an important end.[55] It is not a specification of the content of the wide duties, and so not, as Cummiskey says, a requirement 'to develop the strength of character that would result in *all one's actions being self-governed by the ends that are duties.*'[56] Later, as Cummiskey notes, Kant remarks that one 'should strive with all one's might that the thought of duty for its own sake is the sufficient incentive *of every action conforming to duty.*'[57] Here Kant does not say, as Cummiskey seems to think, that *every action* should be, as far as possible, motivated by the thought of duty. His point is that in complying with duty we should do so from respect for the moral reasons behind the requirements, rather than ulterior motives, at least so far as we can control our motivations in this way. This is not a specification of the content of duty but a point about the spirit in which we should fulfill our duties. Thus it lends no support to the rigoristic interpretation of the general principle of beneficence.

In commenting on this same passage regarding the motive of duty, Cummiskey charges that the 'anemic interpretation' would imply that

---

[54] MM, 153 [390].

[55] Narrow duties of right have the form 'Always do . . .' or 'Never do . . .'. 'The maxim of complying with wide duty' seems most plausibly to refer to the maxim expressing an individual's stand with regard to complying with her wide duties. This might be 'From duty I will always comply, never failing to count others' happiness as an important end' or 'From duty (and self-love) I will comply sometimes, giving some weight to others' happiness when I am not too busy with my own major projects.' To bring our maxim of complying with wide duty in our disposition closer to narrow duties of right, then, would be to make our maxim approximate more closely the first resolute maxim rather than the second half-hearted one. Neither, however, specifies what or exactly how much we will do for others. The first expresses resolution always to do what is required, not always to promote others' happiness maximally unless engaged with other duties. Actions expressive of this firm resolution are, by Kant's account of virtue, more virtuous: MM, 46 [6: 381], 153 [6: 390].

[56] *Kantian Consequentialism*, 111; my italics.

[57] MM, 155 [6: 393] (emphasis added). 'Conforming to duty' (*pflichtmässigen Handlungen*) here, I assume, means not merely morally permissible but doing what we have a duty to do.

we should strive to be virtuous only 'sometimes, to some extent,' but the response to this should be clear from what has already been said.[58] My initial account did not attribute to moral self-perfection the 'Sometimes, to some extent...' form applicable to beneficence and developing talents. Moreover, this is not an arbitrary exclusion, for, as explained in the previous section (point 4), the special content of the end of moral self-perfection accounts for the difference.

(3) Another contested passage from *The Metaphysics of Morals* is so important it is best to quote it at length:

> I want everyone else to be benevolent toward me...; hence I ought also to be benevolent toward everyone else. But since all *others* with the exception of myself would not be *all*, so that the maxim would not have within it the universality of a law, which is still necessary for imposing obligation, the law making benevolence a duty will include myself, as an object of benevolence, in the command of practical reason. This does not mean that I am thereby under an obligation to love myself (for this happens unavoidably, apart from any command, so there is no obligation to it); it means instead that lawgiving reason, which includes the whole species (and so myself as well) in its idea of humanity as such, includes me as giving universal law along with all others in the duty of mutual benevolence, in accordance with the principle of equality, and *permits* you to be benevolent to yourself on the condition of your being benevolent to every other as well; for it is only in this way that your maxim (of beneficence) qualifies for a giving of universal law, the principle on which every law of duty is based.[59]

This passage tells us that we are all 'lawgivers' regarding beneficence and that we may be 'benevolent' to ourselves if we are to others. As lawgivers with a dignity equal to any other we must not discount our own interests when we make a universal principle (or 'law') regarding benevolence. One way that our universal law principle can acknowledge the importance of our own happiness is to prescribe, as it does, that we should be *objects of others' benevolence*. Kant goes further, however. Our lawgiving reason includes each of us (as lawgivers of equal dignity) in the principle of benevolence as persons *permitted to be 'benevolent' to themselves* and so allowed to place value on their own happiness. The 'principle of equality' here may refer to the dignity of every person because this, as an 'unconditional and incomparable worth,' is an equal standing we all have under the moral law.[60] Alternatively, the 'principle of equality' may refer to 'the innate right of equal-

---

[58] *Kantian Consequentialism*, 111.
[59] MM, 200 [6: 451].   [60] Gg, 42–3 [4: 434–6].

ity,' which is 'independence from being bound to others more than one can in turn bind them.'⁶¹ In either case it is clearly not the consequentialist idea that each pleasure, interest, or aim of a person should be assigned a prima facie equal weight when we deliberate what to do. Nor is there reason to suppose that the principle asserts the prima facie equality, for all deliberative purposes, of each individual's having what is valuable, taking into account Cummiskey's two-tiered value system. Kantian equality is equal moral recognition and respect for persons, not a requirement to weigh every personal value equally in a consequentialist calculus.

Kant is explicit that the way we acknowledge the equality of persons as moral lawgivers is to include in our maxim of beneficence a *permission* (not obligation) to attend to our own happiness. Kant has already given compelling reasons why he counts this as a *permission*, not a duty, to promote our own happiness, and, contrary to Michael Slote, it is clear that this 'asymmetry' does not imply that we are to 'devalue our own happiness.'⁶²

Cummiskey's misappropriation of the passage in question for his purposes lends a false appearance of support for his robust interpretation. He claims that, even if we read the passage literally as meaning 'permission,' then it lends no support to the 'anemic interpretation' because 'the conclusion I may now draw is that I may promote my own happiness, rather than the happiness of others, provided that doing so is compatible with a mutual and equal regard for the happiness of all others.'⁶³ The mistake here, in my view, is to suppose that by referring to 'the principle of equality' in the passage quoted Kant meant to endorse 'mutual and equal regard for the happiness of all others' as utilitarians understand this, that is, as calling for maximizing the average or aggregate happiness. Kant's point is that the duty of beneficence, whatever its content, must bind each person in the same way and yield the same permissions to each person.

Kant distinguishes 'benevolence in *wishes*' from 'beneficence,' which is 'active, practical benevolence' that makes 'the well-being and happiness of others my *end*.'⁶⁴ Since our passage concerns what we prescribe as 'lawgivers,' it cannot be about benevolence in wishes. Although our benevolent wishes tend strongly to favor ourselves, we can wish for the

---

⁶¹ MM, 30 [4: 237–8].
⁶² MM, 151–2 [6: 387–8]. I discuss Slote's position in some detail in 'Happiness and Human Flourishing', Ch. 6 in this volume.
⁶³ *Kantian Consequentialism*, 113.
⁶⁴ MM, 200–1 [6: 451–2]. See also 155–6 [6: 393].

happiness of everyone without limit 'since [in contrast with beneficence] nothing need be done with it.'[65] In this sense, we can 'love our neighbor as ourselves.'[66] Active beneficence, however, is more difficult, especially 'if it is to be done from duty.'[67] This duty varies with the 'closeness,' in some sense, of persons to me. Kant says, 'For in wishing I can be equally benevolent to everyone, whereas in acting I can, without violating the universality of the maxim, vary greatly the degree in accordance with the different objects of my love (one of whom concerns me more deeply than another).'[68] This does not rest well with the interpretation of 'the principle of equality' from which Cummiskey draws his 'robust' principle of beneficence.

(4) From the *Groundwork*, Cummiskey tries to draw support from several passages. First, to illustrate the moral worth of acting from duty, but not from sympathy, Kant begins with a general remark: 'To be beneficent where one can is a duty.'[69]

This acknowledges that there are limits to what we can do for the happiness of others but repeats the theme that, in the range of cases where we can do something, we must be beneficent. This does not yet tell us, however, exactly what the duty of beneficence requires and what latitude it allows. The context of the remark is not (as in *The Metaphysics of Morals*) a discussion devoted to the general principle of beneficence. Instead, it is Kant's effort to highlight the moral worth of

[65] MM, 155 [6: 393].   [66] MM, 200–1 [6: 451–2].   [67] MM, 155 [6: 393].
[68] MM, 201 [6: 452]. Perhaps surprisingly, Kant says that 'in benevolence I am closest to myself' and implies that '[I] am closest to myself (even in accordance with duty).' 'Benevolence' here, he explains, refers not to wishes but to practical, active beneficence. Varying the *degree* of our active beneficence according to the closeness of persons to us, he says, is not a violation of the requirement to make our maxim of promoting happiness universal (in the appropriate sense). Thus my pursuing the happiness of myself and my special loved ones to some greater degree than I pursue the happiness of a comparable group of strangers is not by itself inconsistent with the kind of regard for persons as moral equals that Kant's ethics demands. In the same passage Kant even suggests that our *obligation* of beneficence to those closer to us is greater than it is to those more removed. For reasons explained earlier, however, in the special case of beneficence to ourselves this reasonable concern for our own happiness becomes a *permission* rather than an *obligation*. This permission to favor our own happiness to some degree, it should be noted, is not a secondary principle derived (as under utilitarianism) from a more basic duty to promote the general happiness, impartially determined by weighing each comparable bit of happiness of each person equally.
[69] Gg, 11 [4: 398]: 'Wohltätig sein, wo man kann, ist Pflicht.' The translation Cummiskey uses says 'to help when you can' but Gregor's more literal translation is 'to be beneficent where one can.' The latter more clearly leaves it open what is required to 'be beneficent,' that is, the passage does not specify the requirements involved and latitude allowed. What mattered for Kant's purpose in the context was just to have a particular example in which helping someone in distress is a duty.

doing duty from duty. He thus focuses attention on the grieving philanthropist who helps people 'in distress' from duty, not sympathy. Kant does not offer a general account of the conditions and limits on what it takes to 'be beneficent' but only a particular context where helping is required. My interpretation, as I have noted, is compatible with the common-sense idea that there are many such contexts.

When Kant returns to a case of required helping to illustrate how the universal law formula could be a guideline, the discussion does not substantially help Cummiskey's case. Again, the context is not a general characterization of the requirements of beneficence, but rather Kant's attempt to illustrate how the Categorical Imperative can guide moral judgment in particular cases. He selects a case in which an unsympathetic person is confronted with someone in distress 'whom he could very well help.'[70] Kant argues that he would be wrong to act on his maxim of never volunteering to give aid but only doing what justice demands. We cannot, however, generalize from this argument to the rigoristic principle of beneficence. In fact Kant's argument does not even purport to show that it is *always* wrong not to help someone in distress when we very well could, for the argument turns on Kant's ascription of a certain maxim to the agent which reflects the agent's attitude and reasons for refusing. The absence of relevant conflicting duties is also assumed in the particular case.

Significantly, in a footnote Kant explicitly postpones offering his explanation of the perfect/imperfect duty distinction as a task for *The Metaphysics of Morals*. So we should not rest much on his classification of the duty of beneficence as 'imperfect' in this context. Even if we were to take it seriously, however, it would lend no support to Cummiskey's 'robust' interpretation because what little Kant does say suggests that, unlike perfect duties, imperfect duties 'admit of exception in favor of inclination.'[71]

(5) Although again the *Groundwork* should not be a major source for interpreting Kant's idea of imperfect duties, another passage is worth considering. Concerning the same example as before, Kant says that there is 'a positive agreement' with the idea of humanity as an end in itself only when 'everyone also tries, *so far as he can* ['*soviel an ihm ist*'], to further the ends of others. For the ends of a subject who is an end in himself must, if this conception is to have its *full* effect on me, be also, *as far as possible*, my ends.'[72]

---

[70] Gg, 33 [4: 423]. Kant's phrase is 'denen er auch wohl helfen könnte.'
[71] Gg, 31n [4: 422].   [72] Gg, 39 [4: 430]; my italics.

One might question whether Kant intended that everything that would result from 'positive agreement' with the idea of humanity and its having a '*full* effect on me' is a strict requirement of duty, but let us grant that. Is there compelling evidence for Cummiskey's rigoristic interpretation in the phrase '*so far as he can*' (or 'so far as in him lies,' as Paton translates it)?[73] Cummiskey assumes that this phrase means that, unless in the service of other duties, we always must do as much as possible towards others' happiness, but there is another, more plausible interpretation.[74] The phrase, like 'as far as possible' in the last sentence of the quotation, acknowledges that there can be limits to our ability to do what the passage prescribes, namely, *try to further others' ends* and *to make their ends our ends*. There are not really two separate prescriptions here, for we would not be making others' ends our own if we never tried to further them. Our natural dispositions as primarily self-serving creatures are formidable obstacles to our completely achieving the ideal, but we must *try* 'as far as possible' to do so. On this reading, what we must do 'as far as in us lies' is to adopt and so make sincere efforts to further the happiness of others as an end. This itself is a difficult assignment, but it is not an exact and rigoristic specification of when, how, or to what extent our activities must be devoted to this end. It does not imply, for example, that, whenever other duties are absent, we must do *as many as possible* beneficent acts or do whatever will *maximize* others' happiness.

(6) Another controversial passage from *The Metaphysics of Morals* is the following:

That human being can be called fantastically virtuous who allows *nothing to be morally indifferent* (*adiaphora*) and strews all his steps with duties, as with mantraps; it is not indifferent to him whether I eat meat or fish, drink beer or

---

[73] Gg, 39 and G, 98 [4: 430]. Note that we get different interpretations depending on what we take the phrase 'so far as he can' to modify. Cummiskey evidently assumes that it modifies 'further the ends of others,' but on this reading the passage would require us (implausibly) to devote all our time and resources to furthering others' ends. He himself adds the qualifications that we must not violate perfect duties and may instead devote time to other imperfect duties, but, as those qualifications are not in the text, Cummiskey's reading seems quite implausible. If, instead, we take the phrase 'so far as he can' to modify 'try,' then the point could be that we should, so far as we can, fight our natural selfishness and try to do things that help others successfully realize their ends.

[74] It should be noted that in Cummiskey's view our own happiness is to be counted as much as any other person's in determining what our duties are. Thus, in his view, sometimes promoting our own happiness will count as acting 'in the service of duty.' His view is not simply Kant's thesis that there is an 'indirect' duty to promote one's own happiness in order to avoid falling into a condition that would lead to our failing in our duties to others.

wine, supposing that both agree with me. Fantastic virtue is a concern with petty details which, were it admitted into the doctrine of virtue, would turn the government of virtue into a tyranny.[75]

In my initial account I suggested that this passage speaks in favor of understanding the general duty of beneficence as less demanding than it would be on Cummiskey's rigoristic interpretation. The latter, as I understand it, would count acts as morally indifferent relative to alternatives only when all of these options happen to make an equal contribution to obligatory ends, and it would condemn any act that made less than the greatest possible contribution. Although admittedly this is not what Kant had in mind as 'fantastic virtue,' arguably it still threatens to 'strew our steps with duties as with mantraps.' To be sure, Cummiskey's rigoristic interpretation allows us to argue that, for contingent reasons, making a maximal contribution to obligatory ends will permit (and even require) us sometimes to relax and tend our own gardens. For the sake of others, we need to refresh ourselves for another day's good works. Besides this, Cummiskey's interpretation requires us to regard promoting happiness in general as an obligatory end.[76] It treats each person's happiness, including our own, as having a (prima facie) equal claim in determining our duties in particular cases. Thus, Cummiskey's interpretation (contrary to what Kant actually says) makes attending to our own happiness to some extent a direct duty, not merely (as Kant allows) a permission and an indirect duty derivative from our other duties. Even with these qualifications, however, Cummiskey's account still makes the permission to accommodate self-interest quite limited and derivative. It is granted only because at a more basic level we have the determinate duty always to promote the most possible human good. This requires us, at least in principle, to see all our steps as encumbered with a single duty always maximally to promote an all-encompassing end.

As Cummiskey rightly notes, the context of the passage in question is not a discussion of the latitude in imperfect duties but a discussion of virtue and a pseudo-virtue ('fantastic virtue').[77] Cummiskey infers that all the passage suggests is that the doctrine of virtue is not concerned with petty details. He adds, pointedly, that this would support

---

[75] MM, 167 [6: 409].
[76] As noted before, Cummiskey would have us promote happiness in a way that respects the priorities in his two-tiered value system, with values associated with rationality above others. In subsequent discussion I will take this point for granted without mentioning it explicitly.
[77] *Kantian Consequentialism*, 111.

my 'anemic interpretation' only if we suppose that the 'pains and projects of others are petty details.'[78] My explanations in the previous section should make clear that my less rigoristic interpretation does not treat 'the pains and projects of others' (in general) as 'petty details' that we may ignore. Cummiskey is right, however, that Kant's rejection of 'fantastic virtue' is not by itself significant evidence for my interpretation of Kant's general principle of beneficence. Because 'fantastic virtue' is moral obsession with petty details, its rejection would be compatible with treating the duty to promote happiness as maximally demanding in principle but as recommending, for contingent reasons, that we focus our energies on the most important issues and not waste them on relatively insignificant details. Despite that, it still seems to me that aspects of the passage do not sit comfortably with the rigoristic interpretation. This is because that interpretation, in theory, makes every small difference in the effects of our acts on happiness a potential shift in our duties. Even if for practical purposes they matter little, the smallest details may in principle be decisive in determining what one should do. Without special countervailing considerations, the rigoristic reading leaves relatively little room for the morally indifferent, multiplies our duties beyond what Kant's other remarks suggest, and makes the smallest effects relevant in principle to all moral decisions even if from a common-sense perspective they are 'petty details.'

IV. CUMMISKEY'S FURTHER ARGUMENTS

Cummiskey wants to show that there are no adequate textual grounds for not developing Kantian moral theory as a two-tiered consequentialist theory. He grants that Kant himself was no consequentialist, but he maintains that Kant has no adequate argument against consequentialism and that in fact basic aspects of Kant's theory (especially the humanity formula) commit him to consequentialism. As one part of this project, Cummiskey asserts that the perfect/imperfect duty distinction is irrelevant to the issue, for it provides no reasonable argument for thinking that the duty of beneficence should be constrained by nonconsequentialist concerns.[79] The distinction does not, he argues, support agent-centered prerogatives to favor our own happiness more than consequentialism would allow, and, further, it does not even provide reasons for thinking that so-called perfect duties have priority over the general

[78] *Kantian Consequentialism*, 112.   [79] Ibid. 114–22.

duty of beneficence. He distinguishes three ways of interpreting the perfect/imperfect duty distinction and argues that none of these gives us reason to resist his Kantian consequentialism. The three basic ideas are: (1) imperfect (or 'wide' duties) are less binding than perfect (or 'narrow') ones, (2) imperfect duties *only* prescribe ends whereas perfect duties prescribe actions, and (3) wide duties have no correlative rights whereas perfect duties do.

Before turning to details, I should say that it seems to me that Cummiskey's main point is quite right. That is, on any of these interpretations, the distinction between perfect and imperfect duties by itself is no obstacle to consequentialism or any other theory. As I have said, the labels carry implications but it is a substantive issue whether there are any perfect duties and, if so, what they are. To claim that, for example, 'Never lie' is a perfect duty is to *claim* a severe restriction on consequentialism, but the issue between Kant and the consequentialist on this is entirely about the reasons for and against thinking that 'Never lie' is a perfect duty. What is puzzling is why Cummiskey supposes that nonconsequentialist Kantians think otherwise. Kant's classification of certain duties (such as prohibitions of suicide, lying, servility, and injustice) as 'perfect' and others (such as beneficence and developing our talents) as 'imperfect' *expresses* a priority that Kant thought to be justified; but why would anyone, even Kant, suppose that merely labeling the duties this way justifies the alleged priority?

Regarding the first distinction, Cummiskey supposes that his opponents mistakenly infer from (a) the correct idea that the duty of beneficence is 'wide' in the sense of normally leaving many choices about how to fulfill it to (b) the mistaken idea that beneficence is less obligatory than narrow duties.[80] His argument presupposes his earlier dubious textual arguments for his 'robust' interpretation of beneficence. He also implies without warrant that his opponents believe that the imperfect duty *to adopt the happiness of others as an end* is not as binding as perfect duties, say, not to lie; but even my 'anemic' interpretation has no such implication. Again implying that his opponents would deny it, Cummiskey fervently argues that if we cannot save all when many are drowning, we are strictly 'obliged to help all we reasonably can.' As we have noted, however, this judgment about the particular circumstances is not ruled out by my account of the general duty of beneficence.

Regarding the second interpretation (Alan Donagan's), Cummiskey

[80] Ibid. 155–20.

cites the following argument from Shelly Kagan.[81] Conceivably, all of the ways for someone to promote others' happiness might be violations of what Kant calls 'perfect duties.' Thus the fact that beneficence is a wide (imperfect) duty 'cannot entail that [it] can be fulfilled without violating a perfect duty.' In such a case where the implications of a wide duty conflict with perfect duties, 'there is no reason for concluding that perfect duties provide a stronger ground of obligation.'[82] This is a clever but misplaced argument. Of course, in the fantastic circumstances described (where literally all means of helping others are violations of what Kant regards as perfect duties), there would be an *apparent* 'conflict of duties.' If such cases occurred, as Donagan rightly argues, a Kantian moral theory must grant that, unless there is an error in the reasoning to one or the other horn of the apparent dilemma, the description of the duties must be revised.[83] Despite Kant's rigorism regarding what he alleges to be perfect duties, the best move would be simply to qualify those principles. For example, 'Never lie' needs to be qualified to allow lies to terrorists for the sake of helping their victims. The main point remains: the perfect/imperfect duty distinction itself was never supposed to refute consequentialism. Kagan's objection invites us to rethink the grounds for supposing that there are perfect duties incompatible with consequentialism, but this is an old and substantive issue. It is not a special problem in Kant's terms for classifying duties or in Kantians' (alleged) misguided attempts to draw substantive conclusions from them.

Regarding the third way of distinguishing perfect and imperfect duties (Jeffrie Murphy's), Cummiskey argues that whether duties are imperfect (wide) or perfect (narrow) does not correspond with whether they yield positive or negative requirements or whether or not they are associated with assignable rights.[84] The main problem again is that Cummiskey assumes that Kantians mean for the distinction itself to refute consequentionalism, but what separates Kantians from consequentialists are substantive, not terminological, differences about the scope and grounds of our obligations.

Cummiskey offers other arguments for his more robust (and ulti-

---

[81] *Kantian Consequentialism*, 118; Alan Donagan, *The Theory of Morality* (Chicago: University of Chicago Press, 1977), 63. Cummiskey cites correspondence with Shelly Kagan.
[82] Cummiskey, *Kantian Consequentialism*, p. 118.
[83] See Alan Donagan, 'Moral Dilemmas, Genuine and Spurious: A Comparative Anatomy', *Ethics*, 104 (1993), 7–21.
[84] *Kantian Consequentialism*, 120–2; Jeffrie Murphy, *Kant: The Philosophy of Right* (London: Macmillan, 1970), 51.

mately consequentialist) treatment of beneficence. The most important is a complex argument that Kant's most basic moral principle, as expressed in the formula of humanity, entails consequentialism. What is especially Kantian, he argues, is its two-tiered value system in which consequences associated with human *dignity* take precedence over those of mere *price*. Both dignity and price, in his view, are commensurable scales of value, though value of the first sort takes precedence over value of the second. The key is his interpretation of the Formula of Humanity as an End in Itself. According to this, features of human lives associated with living as rational agents have special value ('dignity') that is intrinsic and has priority over mere 'price,' but this special value is commensurable within the category of the things that have it. The value attaches not to individual ('token') persons but aspects of the lives they may lead. That humanity is an end in itself is not an inflexible constraint on consequentialist thinking. It only puts a priority on our thriving as rational beings over our flourishing as sensuous beings. Since this special value attaches to features of human lives that we can promote more or less, Cummiskey argues that we ought to promote as much as we can.

Cummiskey's argument deserves a detailed examination that I will not attempt here, but I should make at least a brief comment. Parts of Christine Korsgaard's early papers and (alas) my own may suggest this kind of reading, and Cummiskey does a service by drawing out the unKantian implication of this reading.[85] A better understanding of dignity, in my view, would not treat it as a high-priority but commensurable kind of value but as a status, analogous to equal standing under the law, or as a 'value' always to be honored and respected but not the sort of thing which we could even try to maximize. As ends in themselves persons have a status 'against which we should never act,' not a kind of value that we need to produce more of. To be sure, Kant says that when the conception has full effect on us we will try to further their (permissible) ends, but this is because we value them as rational agents with their own ends. It is not because their dignity is a value attached to features of human lives that inherently should be maximally brought about. It is primarily the status of a co-legislator of moral law, a position to be respected by never treating the person by principles that could not be justified to the person himself (when willing to take up the moral perspective). This is too long a story to develop here, but I mention it

---

[85] See Korsgaard, *Creating the Kingdom of Ends* (Cambridge: Cambridge University Press, 1996), especially 106–32, and my *Dignity and Practical Reason*, especially 38–57.

only to indicate where further discussion of Cummiskey's position must focus.

V. MARCIA BARON ON DUTY AND SUPEREROGATION

My initial account of Kant's moral categories proposed that, although Kant does not acknowledge a category of supererogation, his scheme for classifying actions leaves room for meritorious acts that have the main features of what some philosophers at the time were calling 'supererogatory.'[86] Since then much has been written about supererogation, and the concepts and author's aims have not always been the same. Marcia Baron has written an admirably detailed and thoughtful defense of Kant's moral theory as a theory that wisely (in her opinion) excludes ideas of supererogation.[87] Her view is compatible with mine on many, if not most, major points. Remaining points of disagreement, however, deserve some comment.

Different Conceptions of Duty

One aspect of Baron's defense of Kant is to argue that Kant has been misunderstood in ways that make his moral theory seem implausible, even repugnant. In support Baron argues that contemporary readers are misled by differences between Kant's idea of *Pflicht* and current ideas of 'duty.' Contemporary philosophers, she notes, often follow Mill in thinking 'It is part of the notion of duty in every one of its forms that a person may rightfully be compelled to fulfill it.'[88] 'Duty,' Mill says, 'is

---

[86] *Dignity and Practical Reason*, 170–1.
[87] See, for example, Marcia Baron, 'Imperfect Duties and Supererogatory Acts,' *Jahrbuch für Recht und Ethik/Annual Review of Law and Ethics*, 6 (1998), 57–71, and 'Kantian Ethics and Supererogation,' *Journal of Philosophy*, 84 (1987), 237–62; Susan [Jake] Hale, 'Against Supererogation', *American Philosophical Quarterly*, 28 (1991), 273–84; David Heyd, *Supererogation: Its Status in Ethical Theory* (Cambridge: Cambridge University Press, 1982); Patricia McGoldrick, 'Saints and Heroes: A Plea for the Supererogatory', *Philosophy*, 59 (1984), 523–8; Gregory Mellema, *Beyond the Call of Duty: Supererogation, Obligation, and Offense* (Albany: State University of New York Press, 1991); Philip Montague, 'Acts, Agents, and Supererogation', *American Philosophical Quarterly*, 26 (1989), 100–11; Onora [O'Neill] Nell, *Acting on Principle: An Essay on Kantian Ethics* (New York: Columbia University Press, 1975); Elizabeth M. Pybus, 'A Plea for the Supererogatory: A Reply', *Philosophy*, 61 (1986), 526–31; Gregory Trianosky, 'Supererogation, Wrongdoing, and Vice: The Autonomy of an Ethics of Virtue', *Journal of Philosophy*, 83 (1986), 26–40; Susan Wolf, 'Above and Below the Line of Duty', *Philosophical Topics*, 14 (1986), 131–48.
[88] *Kantian Ethics (Almost) without Apology*, 15.

a thing that may be exacted from a person, as one exacts a debt.'[89] The colloquial use of 'duty,' in her view, is even farther from Kant's use, for 'the word "duties" suggests jejune tasks that one performs perfunctorily, many of which are duties in virtue of institutional arrangements and the expectations of one's profession.'[90] 'To some', she notes, 'a paradigmatic usage of "duty" is "military duty".' Duties in our colloquial sense, she suggests, can be 'imposed from without', 'frequently outweighed', and even 'immoral' to fulfill.[91] By contrast, Baron rightly points out, 'duty' for Kant 'does not stand for something that is imposed from without.' Rather, she says, 'duty' and its plural 'duties' refer to *'whatever one morally ought to do.'*[92]

It is essential, surely, not to confuse Kant's idea of (moral) duty with mere institutional requirements, military duty, and cultural norms that happen to be enforced by social pressures. I suspect, however, that Baron's expression—'whatever one morally ought to do'—does not fully capture Kant's idea of duty either.[93] 'Morally ought' is broader than Kant's *Pflicht*.

First—perhaps a minor point—it is common to distinguish moral ideals from moral requirements, even if Baron disapproves of this practice. The distinction might naturally be expressed, in a moral discussion, by saying 'In this situation I realize that it is not necessary to X, but I think that I ought to.' Here the moral 'ought' may be meant to express an ideal beyond duty, even in Kant's sense. Baron thinks that the proper distinction to make, which is adequate for all that we should want to say, is Kant's distinction between perfect and imperfect duties. But this is not quite the same distinction that is often made between (particular) acts that are morally ideal and those that are morally necessary. Since the term 'ought' (intended morally) is often used to express ideals distinct from perfect and imperfect duties, it probably is not the best expression to convey Kant's idea of duty.

Second, I think that Kant's conception of *Pflicht*, like our familiar idea of *moral duty*, is meant to convey the idea of *constraint*, being *bound*, *subject* to the law, under *commands* (of reason), *conscripts* (not volunteers) in the moral field. Critics are not altogether wrong about the tone of Kant's moral vocabulary. It is not just about what is 'good' and 'virtuous' to do. Even 'virtue' for Kant seems to be a kind of

---

[89] John Stuart Mill, *Utilitarianism* (Indianapolis: Hackett Publishing Co., 1979), 47.
[90] *Kantian Ethics (Almost) without Apology*, 15–16.
[91] Ibid.   [92] Ibid. 16, 17. The italics are mine.
[93] Philosophers often use 'morally ought' as a rough synonym of *Pflicht*, and generally there is no harm in doing so. But when we explicitly try to spell out the Kantian idea of duty in contrast to contemporary usage, more caution is called for.

strength of will resulting from lifelong moral struggles. The expression 'morally ought' doesn't quite capture all this.

To be sure, Baron is quite right to emphasize that Kant thinks that only perfect juridical duties can be 'exacted like a debt' by society. His general idea of duty, however, is different from Mill's. Perhaps surprisingly, Kant did not encourage the enforcement of morals by informal social sanctions, and he held that legal sanctions were supposed to be for 'external acts' contrary to law, not for the neglect of 'ethical' duties.[94] Kant emphasizes that, apart from injustices enforceable by law, individuals are to be responsible for their own moral conduct. For the most part, we are not to try to force others to be good through social pressures and informal sanctions. In this way, Kant's idea of nonjuridical duty no doubt differs from some common ideas of duty today.

For better or worse, however, Kant retains the idea of sanctions commonly associated with duty, even imperfect duty. Granted, his 'duties of virtue' often leave much discretion in the ways we fulfill them, they leave open questions of casuistry, and they leave some room within limits for each of us to pursue happiness in our own way. But it is *categorically imperative* to fulfill imperfect duties as well as perfect ones. The latitude (*Spielraum*) they allow is in *how*, not *whether*, we fulfill them. To fail is to be subject to trial and punishment in the inner court of *conscience*, in which an inner judge passes sentence and makes us suffer for failing to live by our best moral judgments. The suffering, Kant reminds us, can be torment.[95] Kant did not think that we should oppress others with our moral judgments on their character, but he thought that an inevitable (perhaps conceptually necessary) feature of understanding that we have moral duties, even imperfect duties, is being liable to suffer the pangs of self-disapproval if we fail. Those who want to construct compromise positions between Kant's view and virtue ethics may want to abandon this aspect of Kant's position, but to do so requires more 'apology' for Kant's ethics than Baron suggests is necessary.

Supererogation: Basic Points of Agreement

In *The Metaphysics of Morals* Kant divides duties into several types: juridical and ethical duties, perfect and imperfect duties, and (among imperfect duties) duties of wider and narrower obligation. He does not

---

[94] MM, 145 20-2 [6: 218-21], [6: 379-80]. Also see 'Kant's Anti-Moralistic Strain' in *Dignity and Practical Reason*, ch. 9.
[95] MM, 156 [6: 393-4], 189-90 [6: 438-40].

describe an additional category of supererogatory acts, and critics of Kant whom Baron labels 'supererogationists' have criticized Kant for not acknowledging and providing a proper space for supererogatory acts.[96] In my initial account I proposed an interpretation of Kant's divisions among the types of duties and how these divisions affect judgments about the moral worth of our acts. Reviewing several conceptions of supererogatory acts then current and relevant texts apparently for and against my claim, I concluded, 'There seems, then, good reason to grant that Kant has a place in his moral scheme for supererogatory actions, even though his conception differs somewhat from those conceptions.'[97] In Kant's scheme the closest analogue to the acts that others label 'supererogatory,' I suggested, would be morally worthy acts of a kind that fulfill the widest imperfect duties (for example, beneficence) in situations where the particular act could have been permissibly omitted, even for the sake of pursuing a nonmoral project of our own. In addition, as in the example of giving a child a treat cited earlier, the agents have more than amply demonstrated their commitment to the obligatory end by sincere and continual efforts on other occasions. Omitting to take the opportunity to do someone a favor on a particular occasion, I thought, is sometimes permissible in a situation where the agent has already been expending great effort to help this person and others, where the favor is not urgently needed, and so on. It was assumed that judgment and awareness of other potentially relevant considerations is called for here. Assuming appropriate motivation, such acts, I suggested, are morally worthy. They are 'good,' at least in that sense, and they do more toward an obligatory end than required. Paradoxically, since Kant says that only acts from duty have moral worth, in order to be 'good (morally worthy) but not required' it seems that acts would always have to be done in the false belief that they are required by duty. In response to the problem but going beyond Kant, I suggested that a 'not unreasonable extension' of Kant's position would be to grant that there can also be moral worth in acting 'upon one's disposition to live by whatever demands *and ideals* are implicit in a

---

[96] The first influential critic of Kant on supererogation was J. O. Urmson in his often reprinted 'Saints and Heroes', in Joel Feinberg (ed.), *Moral Concepts* (London: Oxford University Press, 1969), 60–73.

[97] *Dignity and Practical Reason*, 171. The accounts of supererogation under discussion were those of Chisholm and Feinberg: Roderick Chisholm, 'Supererogation and Offense: A Conceptual Scheme for Ethics', *Ratio*, 5 (1963), 1–14, and Joel Feinberg, 'Supererogation and Rules', *Ethics*, 71 (1961), 276–88. Paul Eisenberg argued that Kant has no place for supererogation in 'Basic Ethical Categories in Kant's *Tugendlehre*', *American Philosophical Quarterly*, 3 (1966), 255–69.

rational, moral life.'[98] The suggestion was that duties of virtue, which are broadly characterized as duties to adopt maxims to promote certain ends, not only make substantial *demands* on our conduct but also *encourage* further efforts beyond what can reasonably be judged (in context) as strictly required.[99]

Baron agrees, apparently, with my basic interpretation of Kant's position, even that Kant can, 'without inconsistency, recognize that there are particular acts that, in certain circumstances, it is good to do but not morally required to do.'[100] The key difference between supererogatory acts in this 'weak sense' and supererogatory acts in the strong sense that Baron opposes is that the latter are *types of act* identifiable as optional *without reference to the particular agent's context, principles, and past performance*. What she especially opposes is the idea that we could specify a simple and complete list of moral duties and supererogatory act-types in the way a teacher might lay out homework requirements and 'extra credit' opportunities. In this, she is surely right, both about Kant and about good moral theory.

It looks at first as if Baron wants to do more than reject this 'simple and complete list' picture because she insists that we can only judge particular acts, not act-types, to be supererogatory.[101] This suggests that we cannot describe in advance of actual historical situations any sort of act that would be supererogatory if it were to be performed, but I doubt that this is what she means. Descriptions of 'act-types' can be extremely rich with detailed specifications of the situation, the agent's state of mind, aims and hopes, past history, character, relationships, cultural setting, and so on. If (as Baron concedes) we can judge actual historical acts to be supererogatory in their contexts, then surely they must be so judged because of some set of these features of the acts and, if so, at least very specifically described *types* of acts can be characterized in advance as supererogatory. At least this must be possible *in principle*, and only an implausible form of particularism would hold that

---

[98] *Dignity and Practical Reason*, 172.

[99] This will seem implausible, of course, if we *equate* the imperfect duty to adopt a maxim to promote a moral end (the primary form of imperfect duties) with what in the initial account I called 'WIP principles,' i.e., principles of the form 'Sometimes, when C one ought to X' (*Dignity and Practical Reason*, 162). The implausibility stems from the fact that logically the latter are fully satisfied when one or two acts of type X in C have been done. As I noted, however, Kant's principles of imperfect duty are always, strictly speaking, in the form of duties to adopt maxims (typically to further an end) and so they are not fully captured by the WIP principles associated with them (ibid. 149–50). Beneficence, for example, requires a moral commitment to others' happiness as an end, not merely (as in the corresponding WIP principle) acting sometimes to help others.

[100] *Kantian Ethics (Almost) without Apology*, 32.   [101] Ibid. 32–3.

the judgments in advance are impossible *in fact* even though actual acts can be judged to be supererogatory in their contexts. So, probably what Baron means is not literally that act-types cannot be judged to be supererogatory but only that act-types cannot be judged to be supererogatory unless the types are specified in *very substantial detail* with reference to a *type of agent-in-a-context* (indicating, among other things, the agent's motives, principles, and performance record). If the specific features needed to judge an act supererogatory are so complex as to defy easy summary, then this would sufficiently serve Baron's desire to combat the moral complacency that is encouraged by lists of easily identifiable minimal duties and extra credit acts 'beyond duty.' For that purpose, there is no need to deny that act-types can be judged supererogatory.

Supererogation: Baron's Critique

Despite our substantial agreement, Baron argues that my proposed extension of Kant's official position would be rejected by Kant and for good reasons. Although admittedly the term 'supererogation' may now be too ambiguous to be helpful in characterizing Kant's position, Baron's objections still puzzle me. Kant does not use the terminology with which I characterized 'supererogatory' acts: 'ideals,' principles that 'encourage' beyond what they command, and acts 'good to do though not obligatory.' Baron does not complain about this deviant (or not Kantian) terminology, however, and (as noted above) she even allows that Kant can, without inconsistency, hold that some particular acts are 'good but not morally required.' Instead she offers objections of two sorts. The first line of objection is that admitting a 'category' of supererogatory acts would have certain morally undesirable consequences.[102] For example, it might encourage people to see everyday moral requirements as trivial, lead them to try to substitute supererogatory acts for fulfilling their duties, and cause them to think of morality as for special saints and heroes rather than as something 'within everyone's reach and incumbent on all.'[103] In support she cites familiar passages in which Kant criticizes sentimental moralists for emphasizing examples of 'so-called noble (super-meritorious)' deeds and exhorting us to do 'sublime and magnanimous' things, not because of duty but because of our own special merit or nobility.[104]

[102] Ibid. 36–40.   [103] Ibid. 38.
[104] Ibid. 36, 38. C2, 72 [5: 84–5], 127–9 [5: 157], R, 69 [5: 48–9].

These objections are not compelling, in my view, for several reasons. Most obviously, the objections do not even purport to show that it is *false* to say that there are supererogatory acts. They are at best reasons not to *say* this, even if it is true, or at least not to spread the word in public. The passages cited from Kant would at most show that he wanted moralists not to emphasize the supererogatory, not that he denied it. In fact, however, these passages are not even about the general category of supererogation, as I understand it. What Kant opposes is moralists' use of emotion-pumping examples of extraordinary heroism and appeal to elitist motives rather than a common sense of duty. This does not imply that Kant rejects the general idea that, in some contexts, acts can be morally good but more than strictly required. Also, what would bring about the untoward effects that Baron anticipates is not simply acceptance that there are some acts in a 'category' of supererogation but rather *beliefs about what sorts of acts are in that category*. If the rich in our world think that giving to alleviate poverty is always merely supererogatory, then this is a moral belief with terrible consequences. But it is not simply the belief that some (properly specified) types of act are morally good but more than required. Baron and Kant want not to encourage the thoughts that ordinary duties are trivial and that we can ignore justice if we are heroic and magnanimous, but these thoughts stem from bad judgment about the *content* of the class of acts 'good to do but more than required' and its role in a moral life, not from recognition that some acts may be appropriately so described.

Baron offers a second line of objection. The first and more general objection is that 'dividing what Kant means by "duty" into what one really must do and what, as Hill puts it, would be good to do' would 'make much of morality optional.'[105] It would 'fragment' morality by introducing 'a fence' separating duty from 'what I may do, if I please.'[106] Assuming that we stay within the bounds of our perfect duties, it allows us to say regarding imperfect duties, 'I have done my duty and now my time and choices are all mine' and 'Any other attention to morality is, for me, strictly optional.'[107]

Several points here should be clarified. First, my proposal was not to divide what Kant means by 'duty' into duty in a narrower sense and what is merely good to do. The basic imperfect duties, for Kant, are duties to adopt certain moral maxims, and to do this is not merely 'good' but a duty, strictly required. These basic duties have implications for how we should act, not merely for our inner thoughts. So they

---

[105] *Kantian Ethics (Almost) without Apology*, 41–2. [106] Ibid. 41. [107] Ibid.

support derivative act principles of the form 'Sometimes do X' (where X here stands for acts promoting a moral end, such as the happiness of others). These are also principles of duty that are not optional: we are required to fulfill them. What is 'good but not required' is not a new category in Kant's general system of moral principles, and my proposal was not that Kant treats some of his principles of duty as principles of supererogation. So the proposal is not to 'divide' his system of duties into narrow duty and supererogation. The suggestion that particular acts might be 'good but not required' concerns a kind of conclusion we might reach when *applying* the system of principles, guided by the Categorical Imperative, with good judgment in light of the facts in certain particular (or specific) situations. The idea is that the conclusions we may reach, after full consideration of the situation (including motive, agent history, etc.), are not simply that an act (actual or hypothetical) is 'morally mandatory,' 'wrong,' or 'morally indifferent.' To the contrary, sometimes we may reasonably judge that doing an act, in the context from the presumed motive, would be 'good but not required' and in fact even 'more than required.' No doubt this is a judgment that many of us make too often, for self-serving reasons, and without adequate grounds; but this is no reason to suppose that it is never the correct or most reasonable conclusion. Acknowledging the possibility of such judgments does not 'fragment' morality in any objectionable way. We employ a rich and subtly diverse set of moral concepts in everyday life, and we should not construe Kant as trying to erase some of these unless we have very good grounds.

Again, it is no doubt morally suspect to try to draw a 'fence' around favorite self-indulgent activities that meet 'minimal' moral standards with the thought that no further 'moral attention' is ever needed about the choices within the protected sphere. We can never abandon our responsibility to notice and respond to the morally relevant dimensions of our choices, but merely granting that some acts are 'good to do but not required' does not deny this elementary point. Also, it is somewhat misleading to say that characterizing acts as 'morally good to do but not required' is the same as saying simply that they are 'optional.' The former implies that the acts in context are not morally mandatory, and so we may choose (or 'opt') to do something else (even for nonmoral reasons) without being guilty of violating or neglecting our moral duties; but simply calling them 'optional' suggests, beyond this, that our moral commitments give us no reason at all to consider doing them.[108]

---

[108] Possibly Baron's worry about describing beneficent acts as 'good to do' stems from the thought that saying 'It is a *duty* to adopt as an end the happiness of others and actively promote this end to some (unspecified) extent' does not formally entail any

Baron expands her objection by calling attention to Kant's idea that we have a duty to strive to be morally better.[109] As she rightly notes, this is incompatible with an attitude of complacency about our characters.[110] She takes this to be opposed, or 'in tension,' with my account, but, for reasons stated earlier in this essay, I do not think that my account encourages moral complacency.[111]

The main worry expressed by both Baron and Cummiskey is that my account encourages moral laxity by making helping others optional in cases where Baron and Cummiskey believe it should be required. Although we may still disagree about some cases in the end, my earlier discussion, I hope, shows that their concern was to a large extent misdirected. The problem, if there is one, is not with a too minimal interpretation of the general principle of beneficence but with the current lack of fully satisfactory arguments from the formulas of the Categorical Imperative to show in which particular cases promoting others' ends is morally mandatory and in which cases it is not. The most important reason why the problem is not with the general principle of beneficence was stated earlier, but I conclude with a brief summary, as follows.

From the widest, imperfect duty to adopt a moral end we can derive derivative act principles of the form 'Sometimes, do X' (e.g., where X refers to acting to promote the end), which is a form that makes a clear contrast to the form of perfect duties ('Never Y,' 'Always Z'). The derivative act principles of the form 'Sometimes do X,' however, cannot express the full range of more specific requirements, permissions, and recommendations that we must understand as we think about when, how, and how often to act to promote a given moral end. The universal mid-level principles do not specify these matters, but neither do they imply that any minimal contribution will do. These substantive principles in *The Metaphysics of Morals*, after all, are not the whole of morality. They stand in Kant's moral theory, as it were, between the top level (formulas of the Categorical Imperative) and the bottom level (judgments about particular cases). Such principles, including beneficence, express what are supposed to be requirements on every human being, regardless of time, place, and culture. It should be no surprise that they,

---

conclusion about what is *good* because the predicate 'good' is not explicitly contained in the premise. This is true, of course, but surely Kant's ideas of the unconditional value of humanity and the moral worth of being moved by moral considerations imply that the beneficent acts in question are *good* to do.

[109] Ibid. 61. [110] Ibid. 42.
[111] See the fourth point in the second main section.

by themselves, do not completely specify how we are to act in particular circumstances. Moral deliberation is not simply a matter of determining their entailments for various situations. It is a mistake to suppose that Kant's moral theory, even in *The Metaphysics of Morals*, demands straight-line, top-down application: that is, to think that the Categorical Imperative serves only to generate the mid-level universal principles (such as beneficence), and then all further moral requirements must be deduced from these. We should expect that the mid-level principles of *The Metaphysics of Morals* (that is, whatever substantive moral requirements beyond the Categorical Imperative can be stated as unqualifiedly binding on all human beings) would be less determinative, more 'minimal,' than everything that judgment, guided by the Categorical Imperative, would prescribe for particular situations. These principles are supposed to be abstract expressions of universal moral requirements, not the only moral requirements or the only source of all further moral requirements.

The crucial point here is that, although Kant's general principle of beneficence entails act-duties expressible in the form 'Sometimes, to some extent, do acts that promote the happiness of others,' formulas of this sort cannot by themselves fully capture the more basic duty to adopt the maxim and, all the more, they cannot express the full range of moral considerations that are relevant to particular choices regarding the happiness of others. Consequently, although Kant allows that particular acts of beneficence are sometimes acts that we may permissibly forego, if we please, we must not shut off our moral concern for the happiness of others because we have merely satisfied the 'Sometimes, to some extent, do X' derivative principles. All things considered, sometimes promoting the happiness of others is wrong; sometimes it is obligatory; sometimes it is good but not required; sometimes it is good and even more than required. All this needs to be judged not only from the intermediate principles of imperfect duty that Kant discusses in *The Metaphysics of Morals* but also from the fundamental moral concerns expressed in the formulas of the Categorical Imperative.

8

Personal Values and Setting Oneself Ends

Kant's treatment of various kinds of *moral* evaluation is rich and often disputed. By comparison, his comments on *personal* values are quite limited and relatively ignored.[1] Nevertheless, Kant's idea of personal values is important to his moral theory, in several ways. Most obviously, as all theories acknowledge, moral deliberation must take into consideration what individuals value apart from morality, and an important function of moral principles is to guide judgments about when, how, and within what limits these personal values are to be taken into account. An understanding of what personal values are is presupposed in such judgments. Less obviously, how we understand Kant's idea of personal values can seriously affect our understanding of Kant's grounds for thinking that we are committed to the priority of moral values. In particular, if the idea of personal value is interpreted as commentators often suggest, this seems to lend support to the strong thesis that anyone who has values at all is thereby implicitly committed to objective moral values. Finally, Kant's conception of personal values is significant because, unlike most accounts, it treats the ends that make up an individual's conception of happiness as freely chosen rather than determined by natural sentiment. Although this idea has appealing aspects, it raises troublesome questions.

Several questions, then, should be considered. First, and most generally, what are personal values, in Kant's view, and how do they differ from other sorts of value? Second, does Kant understand personal values in a way that underwrites the strong thesis that anyone who has values at all is thereby committed to objective moral values? Third, is it psychologically realistic or morally appropriate to suppose that we acquire our personal values by deliberately 'setting ends' for ourselves through 'acts of freedom'?

A few preliminary remarks on terminology may be helpful. What I

---

[1] Thanks are due to Andrews Reath and Hilary Bok for their good comments on an earlier version of this essay, presented at the meetings of the Pacific Division of the American Philosophical Association in April 1996. More recently, Adrienne Martin has been particularly helpful.

call *personal values* are things that we, as individuals, care for insofar as these concerns are not driven by prior regard for morality. These values need not be selfish or even concerns for our own well-being. What we care about, apart from morality, is not just our own good. Also our values are not identical with what we desire. In contrast to momentary impulses and unwanted desires, valuing implies a more stable attitude, continually reaffirmed, with some reflective awareness of options. However, to say that something is a *personal value* for someone, as I use this term, is not necessarily to say that it *is* valuable in certain objective, 'agent-neutral' senses. For example, it does not imply that its value is a property that exists independently of the potential reactions of rational and sympathetic observers. Also, whether we have reason to promote another individual's personal values is meant to remain for now an open question, not something settled by definition.

It is tempting to borrow a term from the consequentialist tradition, labeling the values in question *nonmoral values*. There are, however, several reasons to prefer the term *personal values*. First, Kantians hold that what individuals value apart from moral considerations becomes morally important so long as it satisfies the constraints of basic moral principles. So there will be a considerable overlap between these personal values and what we might call 'moral values,' even when there is a conceptual distinction.[2] Calling the personal values 'nonmoral,' then, might be misleading. Second, although in consequentialist theories 'nonmoral values' are determined independently of moral judgments, they are themselves the determinants of moral judgments. That is, what is morally right is simply a function of what can be assessed as valuable independently of moral considerations. Because Kantians reject this last point often associated with consequentialists' use of the term 'nonmoral values,' they may do well to use other terms instead. Third, the term 'nonmoral value' is a broad term that could encompass values regarded independent of all relations to human, or other, evaluators. For example, some say that certain natural phenomena have 'intrinsic value' in no way based on how potential evaluators would respond. Since Kant rejects this possibility, it is better to describe the values in question more specifically as personal values.

My comments are divided as follows. I begin, in the following section, with a sketch of some of Kant's main ideas about moral evaluation, the

---

[2] For example, security from harm is a personal value for a person insofar as the person cares for this above and beyond any self-regarding (or other) moral concern; but Kant argues that it is also a 'moral value' in the sense that it is among the things that 'everyone morally ought to count as an end.'

value of happiness and private ends, and relations among these, largely summarizing what I take to be fairly uncontroversial as interpretation.

Next I raise a question about the interpretation of Kant's position. What value judgments, in Kant's view, do we implicitly make when we set for ourselves personal ends and adopt maxims about how to achieve them? Kant is clear that the value we attribute to our personal ends is 'conditional' and 'relative' in some important sense, but there are different ways of interpreting this. Differences in interpretation here can make a significant difference to how we understand Kant's ethics, especially to how we read Kant's arguments for the Formula of Humanity as an End-in-Itself. Evidence on this issue is not unambiguous, but I suggest that Kant conceives of personal values in a thinner, more subjective way than is often supposed. In significant respects Kant is closer to Hobbes than to Aristotle about personal values.[3] Moreover, there are reasons for preferring to develop Kantian ethics along these lines, even though doing so undercuts what might seem an easy way of arguing that anyone with values at all is committed to objective moral values.

Finally, I address the objection that Kant's account of personal values is too voluntaristic because it exaggerates the extent to which we 'choose' our personal values as opposed to 'finding' them. Kant says that we set ourselves ends by an act of free will, but, if this is understood as a descriptive claim about how we acquire our personal values, it seems quite unrealistic. If, however, we treat the claim as primarily normative, arguably it makes an important point that is not inconsistent with our experience of how personal values are actually acquired.

I. OVERVIEW OF KANT ON MORAL VALUES AND PERSONAL ENDS

For the sake of contrast, consider some of the different kinds of moral evaluation (and values) that Kant distinguishes. To follow the order of the *Groundwork*, first *wills* are evaluated as *good* or *bad* of their kind (i.e., as wills).[4] Good wills are predisposed and committed to following practical reason, the source of moral imperatives for us (as imperfect

---

[3] As will become clear, the main respect in which I suggest Kant is Hobbesian about personal values is not Hobbes's view that they are predominantly self-regarding but his denial that our judgments of what is good from our perspective as individuals imply a claim about what is objectively good. [4] Gg, 7–8 [4: 393–4].

human beings). Kant makes a further evaluative point about the moral and rational priority of maintaining our good will over other (conditionally) good things. That is, a good will, and it alone, is *good without qualification* or, in other words, choiceworthy in any context.[5] Human actions are classified as in accord with, or contrary to, duties of various types, reflecting familiar distinctions between the *obligatory*, the *forbidden*, and the merely *permissible*.[6] There are further distinctions between what is required by *enforceable rights* and what is not, and between what is required in every case and what is *meritorious* (or 'more in the way of duty' than the law requires).[7] Further, some acts are of positive *moral worth*, some (presumably) are of negative moral worth, and some have no moral worth, positive or negative.[8] The relative moral standing of *persons* as *morally better* or worse than others, is also something that in principle could be evaluated, but this is not simply a function of the 'moral worth' of their actions.[9] Having a good will qualifies anyone as a basically good person, and having a bad will means that one is a bad person; but, beyond this, people differ in how *virtuous* they are.[10] This depends on their degree of developed moral strength to face obstacles to duty. More virtuous persons are (morally) more deserving or *worthy of happiness* than less virtuous persons, even though we cannot be sure which are which.[11] Persons are also valued in a noncomparative sense, for all moral agents, good and bad, are attributed a *dignity*, which is 'above price,' an unconditional, incomparable worth, without equivalents.[12]

Further, there are *morally required ends*.[13] Morally permissible personal ends, for example, are not merely valuable to the agents who pursue them, but everyone has some presumptive moral reason to promote or make way for the permissible personal ends of others. We have duties to adopt the happiness of others and our own perfection as ends, though these are 'imperfect' duties that do not determine

---

[5] The interpretation of the special value of good will in the practical sense of 'choice-worthy in all contexts' is explained and defended in the essay 'Is a Good Will Overrated?' reprinted as Ch. 2 this volume.   [6] Gg, 46 [4: 439], MM, 15 [6: 222].
[7] MM, 19–22 [6: 218–22, 227–8].   [8] Gg, 10–13 [6: 397–400].
[9] As Allen Wood emphasizes, Kant discourages comparative evaluations of persons as morally better or worse (superior or inferior in 'inner worth'). We should compare ourselves not with others but with the standard of the moral law. See Allen Wood, *Kant's Ethical Thought* (Cambridge: Cambridge University Press, 1999), 133–9 and MM, 187 [6: 435–6]. Also Kant repeatedly says that we cannot know for sure whether we, or others, have a good will. For example, Gg, 19 [4: 406–7].
[10] MM, 146 [6: 380], 148 [6: 384], 156–7 [6: 394–5].
[11] Gg, 7 [4: 393], MM, 223–5 [6: 480–2].   [12] Gg, 42 [4: 434].
[13] Gg, 39 [4: 430], MM, 150–2 [6: 385–7].

specifically what is to be done to promote the ends.[14] The 'perfection' we must seek includes development of ourselves both as natural beings and as moral beings.[15] Also in addition to a good will and virtue, a developed sensibility (with sympathetic feelings) is a moral value at least in the limited sense that it ought to be cultivated as an aid in fulfilling our duties.[16]

In contrast to these moral evaluations, as individuals we also value various things, not for moral reasons, but because they serve our interests or simply because we take pleasure in them or are directly inclined toward them and we see no sufficient reason to avoid them. These are our 'personal' or 'private' ends and the means that promote them. As we say, they are valuable *to us* as individuals. In Kant's terms, these and the necessary means to fulfill them can only have *price* (as opposed to *dignity*).[17] This is a relative, conditional, and comparable sort of value that things have when they 'can be replaced by something else as [their] equivalent.'[18] It includes both *market price* (e.g., based on universal needs and inclinations) and *fancy price* (e.g., based on individual tastes independent of needs).[19] We also assess things from various other perspectives, for example, aesthetically, as good-of-a-kind, and as good for plants and animals. In ethics, however, what Kant primarily contrasts with moral values are rationally contingent ends and related means, which in Kant's view are things that individuals value when morality is not at issue or serves only as a constraint limiting their range of choices.

Kant implies that, insofar as we are rational, we are guided by *counsels of prudence*, which prescribe the means to happiness.[20] Happiness is variously pictured as a state of well-being and lasting contentment or

---

[14] MM, 153 [6: 390]. Interpretation of the latitude allowed in imperfect duties is controversial. This is discussed at length in 'Meeting Needs and Doing Favors', Ch. 7 in this volume.

[15] MM, 176–93 [6: 421–44].   [16] MM, 204–5 [6: 456–7].

[17] When Kant introduces the term 'price,' he seems to have in mind *things*, such as food and shelter (necessary means) and valuable mementos (cherished objects) rather than personal *ends* (such as to be famous and wealthy). He says, however, that everything in the kingdom of ends has either dignity or price and also that the kingdom includes the 'private' ends of the members (though we 'abstract' from their content). Since only the members, not their private ends, have dignity, we can infer that the sort of value that the private ends have is *price*; G, 41–2 [4: 433–5].

[18] Gg, 42 [4: 434].

[19] Gg, 42 [4: 434–5]. Market price here, we may note, is a specialized notion that is not equivalent to our common idea of 'market value,' for regardless of whether it serves any *universal* needs or inclinations, a thing will have market value in our ordinary sense so long as it is 'fancied' by even one person sufficiently for that person to give something in exchange for it.   [20] Gg, 27 [416], C2, 32–4 [5: 35–7].

Personal Values and Setting Oneself Ends 249

as the satisfaction of our (desire-based) personal ends, i.e., all of these ends or (more plausibly) some semi-coherent subset of compatible ends.[21] Kant frequently says that we have only a vague, somewhat indeterminate idea of what would constitute our being happy and very imperfect knowledge about what is likely to promote it.[22]

Now let us consider in more detail Kant's views about how we value personal ends, within the constraints of morality. To have such an end is not the same as to desire to realize it. As Hobbes emphasized, we find ourselves with many conflicting desires and no possibility of satisfying them all. Rational agents can, and to some extent do, reflect on their options, the circumstances, their initial desires, the likely outcomes of various choices, the source and stability of various preferences, etc., and thereby develop critically goals, plans, and policies that may differ significantly from those they were at first most inclined to. From the perspective of rational deliberation, we must treat this process as a matter of 'setting ends' for ourselves, which we regard as an 'act of freedom,' not completely determined by antecedent empirical causes.[23] Our task in practical deliberation, then, is not the purely intellectual task of finding goals and plans to maximize our utility, understood as a function of prima facie weights fixed by natural facts about our preferences, the probability of various outcomes, etc. Rather, typically, with a vague picture of our wants and possibilities, we must choose our ends, in the end plumping for this or that set, relying on only loose prudential guidelines that rarely (if ever) dictate just one determinate choice.

No one can force anyone to adopt personal ends;[24] and we can always 'abandon' such ends if their pursuit proves immoral or too costly.[25] The

---

[21] See 'Happiness and Human Flourishing', Ch. 6 in this volume.
[22] For example, Gg, 28–9 [4: 417–19], CPrR, 23 [5: 25], 33 [5: 36], MM, 9 [6: 215–16].
[23] MM, 146–7 [6: 381], 149 [6: 384–5], 154 [6: 392]. [24] MM, 146 [6: 381].
[25] Gg, 30 [4: 420]. Kant says that happiness is an end that we all have 'by natural necessity' and so unavoidably, but Kant implies that any particular 'principle of the will' based on this end remains a contingent imperative, a mere 'counsel of prudence' and 'we can always be released from the precept if we give up the purpose' (Gg, 30 [4: 420]). The point, I take it, is that although we cannot altogether give up having happiness as an end, it is a rather indeterminate end the content of which varies from person to person and can change for any given person. So all of the specific 'counsels' directing us to the means to happiness are so flexible and indeterminate that we could, if necessary, avoid what they advise by altering or giving up some particular end that we had previously included in our idea of our happiness. If, for example, a categorical imperative forbids us to take the necessary means to a particular end the achievement of which we had previously counted as part of being happy, then we can avoid the 'counsel' to take it by giving up that particular end as a constitutive part of our conception of happiness. This interpretation makes Kant's view to some extent similar to the Stoic idea that persons of good will can and must, so far as possible, shape their conceptions of happiness to avoid

'freedom' to set ends, no doubt, does not mean that we could choose to pursue a goal toward which we have (in deliberation) neither desire nor moral predisposition, but only that, for practical purposes, these dispositions are not to be seen as fixing the outcome of deliberation independently of the agent's endorsement. These personal ends are rationally contingent; that is, one is not rationally constrained to adopt this or that end. Naturally these ends often vary from person to person, though the ends of different persons at times may be similar (e.g., many aim to be rich) or converging (e.g., many seek to preserve the tropical forests). Rational agents are presumed to act on maxims, and maxims, when fully specified, contain reference to an end as well as to a projected course of action to be taken for the sake of the end. All of this description belongs to a network of ideas we employ when we take up a practical perspective, i.e., reflect on what we have reason to do; but, Kant maintained (controversially) that, despite the legitimacy of practical talk of 'acts of freedom,' all phenomenal events can and must be regarded from an empirical perspective as necessitated by natural causal laws.[26]

Many aspects of Kant's position on the relation of personal ends to morality are clear enough and can be briefly summarized. Some ends are morally permissible to adopt, and others not, as determined by the Categorical Imperative. For example, to pursue fame is in itself permissible; to seek the spread of war as an end is not. Some means to a permissible end are immoral; and if all available means are immoral, we can and must abandon our end. The same object, for example, our health or the welfare of our children, can be both a desired personal end and a morally necessary end. Treating humanity in persons as an end in itself consists, at least in part, in valuing them as sources of (permissible) personal ends. So, at least to some degree, we ought to make the ends of others our own.[27] As noted earlier, this is an imperfect, ethical duty to promote the happiness of others, giving weight to their permissible ends in our own decision making.[28]

---

irreconcilable conflict with higher priorities of will. Kant seemed well aware of the difficulty of altering human *desires*, but he did regard the desire-based *ends* that make up our conception of happiness as ends that we freely set for ourselves.

[26] C1, 464–79 [A 532–57, B 560–86], CPrR, 75–89 [5: 89–106].

[27] Gg, 39 [4: 430], MM, 156 [6: 393]. The extent of the requirement is controversial. See 'Meeting Needs and Doing Favors', Ch. 7 in this volume.

[28] As I interpret Kant, the point is not that each permissible end of every person is assigned some (presumably small) weight in a manner analogous to how others' pleasures are treated under Bentham's hedonistic calculus or even W. D. Ross's principle of beneficence. Ross's procedure, given absence of a general prima facie duty to promote

Also, the moral requirement to respect others requires us not to mock or look down on other human beings because we find their ends trivial, foolish, or distasteful by our standards.[29] The universal principle of justice (*Recht*), the fundamental postulate of practical reason for law, affirms the 'external' liberty of all persons to pursue their own personal ends so far as this is compatible with a system of universal laws respectful of the equal basic liberty right of others.[30] These rights may be coercively defended, and in fact the primary authority of government stems from its obligation to protect this right.

II. WHAT VALUE COMMITMENTS ARE INHERENT IN ADOPTING ENDS?

The preceding summary of Kant's views about moral values and personal ends does not yet address an important interpretative problem. When we set ourselves ends and adopt maxims to achieve them, do we necessarily regard the achievement of the ends as good, and, if so, in what sense? Kant's answer is clear if we are asking about rationally 'legislating' to ourselves the 'ends which are duties,' our own perfection, and the happiness of others. In this special case, willing (or 'legislating') ends (as duties) implies accepting that the end has objective moral value. This is because the ideas that the end has objective moral value and that it is a necessary object of rational willing (as duty) are essentially the same. But, we may still wonder, what value commitments, if any, do we make when we adopt rationally contingent personal ends and maxims to act in pursuit of them? Must we regard these as valuable, and, if so, in what sense? Moral philosophers over time have disagreed significantly on this question, and, contrary to what several distinguished commentators suggest, it is not obvious what Kant's position is.[31]

one's own pleasure, results in actual duties to promote others' small pleasures, even at great sacrifice of one's own pleasure, if all else is equal. (Ross, however, suggests at one point that perhaps our own pleasures should count if we see them under the rubric of 'a person's pleasure' rather than 'my pleasures.') For Kant the point is that we should sincerely adopt the maxim to promote the happiness of others (somehow, to some indeterminate extent) in our decision making. We should count their satisfaction of permissible ends as 'a good thing,' just as we count our own as 'a good thing,' which gives us some reason, but not a compelling reason, to do what would promote the end. In both the *Groundwork* and *The Metaphysics of Morals* Kant also argues, for some cases, a stricter duty of mutual aid, i.e., to help others in dire need when we can without comparable costs. See 'Meeting Needs and Doing Favors', Ch. 7 in this volume.

[29] MM, 209–13 [6: 462–8].   [30] MM, 39–1 [6: 237], 24–6 [6: 230–3].
[31] Christine Korsgaard attributes to Kant a strong version of the idea that to set an

Background: Traditional vs. Hobbes's Ideas of Value

Our problem, then, is to determine what sorts of value judgment, in Kant's view, are implicit in the adoption of personal ends. The background, somewhat oversimplified, includes several points, which may be summarized as follows. A common view in ancient and medieval philosophy was that rational agents desire and will things only under the aspect of goodness.[32] This was not merely a claim about fully rational agents who were desiring and willing in the most completely rational way. The idea was that in choosing, or reflectively endorsing, an end, any minimally rational agent must be *taking it to be good*. When we adopt bad ends, then, this reflects an error in evaluative judgment or a distorted focus of attention. Even imperfectly rational human agents were assumed to be aiming, in some sense, to do what they judged or assumed best for them to do in the situation, what, all considered, they had best reason to do.[33] The standard here was thought to be objective,

---

end is to take it to be objectively good, and she uses this in a regressive argument for the absolute worth of humanity. See 'Kant's Formula of Humanity' in her *Creating the Kingdom of Ends* (Cambridge: Cambridge University Press, 1996), especially 115–17. See also her 'Kant and Aristotle on the Source of Value,' in the same volume, p. 241, and her introduction to Kant's *Groundwork of the Metaphysics of Morals* (Cambridge: Cambridge University Press, 1997), pp. xxi–xxiii. Allen Wood follows Korsgaard's basic strategy of argument but makes modifications. See his *Kant's Ethical Thought*, 111–32, especially 124–32.

In *The Practice of Moral Judgment* (Cambridge, MA: Harvard University Press, 1993) Barbara Herman seems to hold that in adopting maxims we always believe that it would be objectively good to act on them, but (as Adrienne Martin convinced me) the evidence is inconclusive. Herman says that maxims express agents' 'action and intention understood to be good and chosen because good' (p. 217), and she often implies that agents believe their reasons and choices are good, justified, and choice-worthy (pp. 221–3). Sometimes, however, the claim is qualified, for example, saying only that an agent believes her ends good 'in some sense' and 'so far as she is rational' (p. 214).

In 'The Concept of the Highest Good in Kant's Moral Theory', *Philosophy and Phenomenological Research*, 52 (1992), 747–80, Stephen Engstrom seems more clearly committed to the view that adopting an end, such as happiness, reflects the objective goodness of the end. He says, for example, 'in taking something as the object of one's will (that is, in adopting it as an end), one claims it to be good' (p. 760), and he explains further that if something is a good end then all rational agents have reason to make it their end (pp. 755, 760, 764). Neither Herman nor Engstrom, as far as I know, uses these claims in the sort of arguments that Korsgaard and Wood offer against those skeptical about the rationality of moral constraints.

[32] The 'traditional' view that I sketch here no doubt has subtle variations, but it surely includes Aristotle and Aquinas and many of their contemporary followers, notably including Elizabeth Anscombe: see her *Intention* (Ithaca: Cornell University Press, 1963), 76. Here, however, I deliberately pass over historical details and simply stipulate the features I want to contrast with Hobbes's view, for my aim in this section is simply to introduce my interpretative questions about Kant.

[33] The assumption need not be that at each moment we actually intend to do the very

even when hard to discern, a standard any rational person in principle could apply to agents in their particular situations, to determine whether their choice of ends was (or was not) in accord with reason.[34] On this view, even prior to questions about moral right and wrong, certain ends are (objectively) good for an agent to adopt and pursue, not just good *to* the agent, good *from the agent's perspective*, or valued *by* the agent. Moreover, rational agents, as such, are conceived as wanting and choosing what is good because it is good, and so their wanting or choosing does not constitute goodness. Their desires do not set the standard but, rather, their desires are to be indulged, extinguished, or reshaped according to whether or not they fit with an objective conception of what is good for human beings. Although the value of some ends may vary with individual personality and circumstances, it was commonly thought that there are also some objectively good personal ends that all agents should adopt regardless of variations in individual circumstances. Finally, our judgment that an end is good for another person to adopt and pursue was commonly assumed to imply that we have at least prima facie reason not to interfere with that person's attaining the end.[35]

best we can, but something looser, for example, that the *telos* of rational (human) agents is to 'seek' (or tend, in favorable conditions) to fulfill their potential for more and more rational self-governance, even if they often fall short.

[34] The terms 'objective' and 'subjective' have been used in many ways, and so may not be helpful here except as abbreviating what is expressed in other words. Unfortunately, the same seems to be true of the popular terms 'agent-neutral' and 'agent-relative,' introduced by Derik Parfit in *Reasons and Persons* (Oxford: Clarendon Press, 1984), 143. In an early work Thomas Nagel treats 'objective' values as those which give everyone reasons to do or refrain from various acts. For example, to say it is objectively valuable that I enjoy the taste of coffee now would imply that others have reason to help me to have coffee now. 'Subjective' values, by contrast, are merely good for a person: Thomas Nagel, *The Possibility of Altruism* (Oxford: Clarendon Press, 1970). Later, as Christine Korsgaard notes, Nagel treats 'objective' values as what is really valuable as opposed to what seems valuable. See Thomas Nagel, *The View from Nowhere* (Oxford: Oxford University Press, 1986), ch. 8, pp. 138–63, and Korsgaard, *Creating the Kingdom of Ends*, ch. 10, pp. 275–310, especially n. 5, pp. 302–3. What is really valuable, according to Nagel, is determined from an impersonal 'view from nowhere.' More modest ideas of objectivity might include 'true,' 'warranted by good evidence,' or 'capable of truth or falsity and subject to confirmation and mistake (in principle).' Here the 'traditional' view I sketch takes values to be objective in these modest senses, which can apply to what is good *for* an individual, but, beyond this, it takes objective values to give some prima facie reason to everyone at least not to interfere with their realization in others. Objective values, then, may be good for an individual but they are not *merely* so; it is also a good thing, from an impartial or interpersonal point of view, that individuals obtain what is objectively valuable.

[35] This is a further feature of the position that I want to contrast with the Hobbesian one, but some who accept that choices commit us to objective values in some sense may not accept this claim on others as an implication of their idea of objective value. Where Aristotle stands on this is perhaps not obvious, though he evidently thought that the

An extreme version of the view sketched here might add that, together with moral ends, such values always provide agents with sufficient reasons to act one way rather than another. Thus, in principle, there would never be any need for arbitrary choice because reason (moral and nonmoral) would dictate precisely what must be done in each circumstance.

Notoriously Hobbes and many subsequent philosophers take a radically different view of how we evaluate ends. On this view, nothing is good in itself.[36] Goodness is not a Platonic form, an objective property fixed by human nature, or any kind of nonnatural property (divine or otherwise). Judgments that something is good are always, at least implicitly, relativized to a person. Just as nothing can be 'relevant in itself,' but must be relevant to this or that concern, nothing can be 'important in itself' but only important to this or that person or group, or for this or that purpose. Similarly, on the Hobbesian view, when we call things 'good' we at least implicitly relativize the claim to persons. Typically, and always in a state of nature, the implicit reference is to the speaker; for 'good' is just what we call the things we desire, and 'bad' the things to which we are averse, especially when we are well-informed of their consequences for us. It is only a small step to recognize what others are saying when they call things 'good' (to them), and we can easily understand what they are saying as true or at least apt (i.e., revealing what they desire) without our caring, or having any reason to care, about their getting what they call 'good.'[37]

Hobbes accepts, then, a shadow version of the traditional doctrine

flourishing of fellow citizens is supposed to be something that everyone in a *polis* has reason to promote.

[36] Thomas Hobbes, *Leviathan*, ed. C. B. Macpherson (Baltimore: Penguin Books, 1951), part I, 120.

[37] One way of developing the Hobbesian idea that we call 'good' the objects of our reflective ('rational') desires is to add that, while each person calls 'good' (implicitly 'to me') that which he or she reflectively desires, we also naturally learn to communicate better when we can speak of what is 'good to P,' when P is some other agent, using what we take to be P's reflective desires as the standard. Thus, 'This good to P,' for any P, might be said to mean 'This serves P's reflective desires.' This does not leave us, as Hobbes's famous passage might suggest, with a simple noncognitivist impasse in conflict cases, where we each use 'good' only to express what we ourselves (reflectively) desire and we have no way of acknowledging that the other person is making a true and warranted, but relativized, value claim. This move to relativized cognitive evaluations does not, of course, remove the root causes of conflict, but it provides the vocabulary for each to recognize the truth of what the other is saying. I shall assume, then, that for the Hobbesian 'This is good to P' means something more like 'This serves P's reflective desires' rather than '*I* (the speaker) commend this for P' or 'Cheers for P's having this.'

that in choosing an end we take it to be good, but he removes the doctrine's substance and reverses its order of priority. Because the standard of what is good to a person is provided by that person's own, often variable desires, it is not an objective, independent standard from which those desires can be evaluated. There are some ends, Hobbes thought, that all human beings desire, for example, self-preservation. This, however, implies only that each of us has an agent-relative reason to preserve our own lives, not that we have any reason to preserve the lives of others (unless doing so would promote our own survival).

This simple picture is complicated for Hobbes by the fact that people in civil society are supposed to have authorized a secular Sovereign to settle potentially dangerous value disputes.[38] They agree, in effect, to a convention that what is 'good' in such cases is relative to the Sovereign's will, not theirs. That use of 'good' is Hobbes's analogue to a moral use of the term because, by Hobbes's third law of nature, we are bound by justice to obey the Sovereign.[39] Apart from declarations of the Sovereign, we distinguish what is only apparently good to (or for) a person from what is really good to (or for) the person, according to whether the person's desire for the object stems from false beliefs or a realistic understanding of the situation.[40] In this way, reason, relying on experience, helps to correct false beliefs, and so enables one to form more 'rational' desires and so more correct or apt evaluations. This idea of what is good without reference to the Sovereign, though subject to error and correction, is still constructed from ideas about what we desire, or would desire, in various circumstances. In a more complex way, Hobbes's idea of what is good relative to the Sovereign is also determined by our desires, for he argues that we agree to rely on a Sovereign to settle disputes about goodness in order to improve our chances of satisfying our most urgent desires (e.g., for peace). Thus, in Hobbes's view, we continue to call things *good* because of their relation to our desires rather than desiring things because they are good.

This Hobbesian view, then, pays lip service to the old traditional adage that we always desire things under the aspect of the good, but it gives the saying a radical new twist. To desire is not to make a judgment about what is valuable in some sense independent of (informed) desire; it is simply to have an impulse (itch, craving, yearning) or (more steady) inclination (disposition, interest, cherishing). Reasoning may alter our desires for ends by informing us more about them, and it serves

---

[38] Hobbes, *Leviathan*, 120, 226–8, 232–4. [39] Ibid. 201–8. [40] Ibid. 129.

to transfer desire to means to which otherwise we might be indifferent; but reason itself is not a desire or disposition to act, nor does it prescribe any ends or means independently of our desires.[41]

Kant and Hobbes are often contrasted with regard to moral judgments, but my focus here is still on personal values. The question is whether Kant's views on the main points sketched above more closely resemble the Hobbesian or the traditional model. To avoid misunderstanding, however, we should note certain differences between Kant and Hobbes that, though important, do not settle the question.

One notable way in which Kant's view differs from Hobbes's concerns the role of reason in nonmoral cases. Arguably Hobbes, like Hume after him, treats reason as basically an 'inert' cognitive power, implying no substantive dispositions to act one way or the other. Kant holds that there is at least one rational principle of nonmoral practical reasoning, the Hypothetical Imperative, which says in effect 'if you will an end, take the necessary means in your power or give up your end.'[42] This, as I understand it, prescribes how we ought to will in nonmoral cases. It is not simply an empirical proposition about the most effective means to satisfy our desires. It is an imperative of reason, expressing what is analytic of completely rational willing. The rational disposition it expresses, however, is a disjunctive one, not prescribing a particular end but only demanding adjustment of one's means and ends to achieve rational coherence among them. It makes no specific recommendation until it is supplemented with information about a person's ends and the available means. Although noteworthy, this apparent difference between Hobbes and Kant on the nature of instrumental reason does not answer our question about what value judgments, if any, are implicit in adopting ends and maxims. According to Kant, to will (at least provisionally)

---

[41] The interpretation of Hobbes here is controversial. Some hold that Hobbes's view of reason is closer to the traditional natural law view. Alternatively, one might conjecture that he held something like the Hypothetical Imperative (or 'take the most efficient means to what, with adequate information, you most desire') to be his principle/disposition of reason which, when combined with his psychology of predominant death aversion, would yield more or less his 'laws of nature.'

[42] For fuller explanation of this interpretation, see 'The Hypothetical Imperative' and 'Kant's Theory of Practical Reason' in *Dignity and Practical Reason*, 17–32, 124–31. What is analytic of willing an end, on this account, is willing to take necessary means when available or to abandon the end. When the necessary means are immediate and fully known to be necessary, there may be nothing that counts as irrationally willing the end but simultaneously failing to will the means. This is because in such cases if we refuse to take the means, this seems adequate to show that we have in effect abandoned the end. In cases in which the necessary means extend over time and are not always the immediate object of attention, we can irrationally fail to do what a hypothetical imperative prescribes by not either taking up the necessary means or giving up the end.

to take the necessary means to ends we have adopted is an imperative of practical reason. This, however, does not imply that the end or the means have any objective value, beyond our wanting them and regarding them as good *to* us personally.[43]

Similarly, although there are significant differences between Hobbes and Kant about what we naturally desire as an end, these also do not provide an answer to our question about the commitments implicit in adopting ends and maxims. Despite some appearances to the contrary, Kant does not think that our natural desires are quite as thoroughly self-directed as Hobbes supposes.[44] This leaves the question open, however, whether we necessarily take our ends or their necessary means to be objectively good as opposed to being merely wanted or 'good to us.'

A complication, which may cloud the issue, is that Kant held that morality prescribes, as either perfect or imperfect duty, many things that Hobbes and many people today would count as entirely optional. For example, purely self-regarding considerations are often regarded as nonmoral, 'merely prudential' matters. The line between moral and nonmoral for Kant, however, is drawn by the distinction between hypothetical and categorical rational requirements, not the line between 'other-regarding' and 'self-regarding' considerations. Since, according to Kant, it is categorically against reason to destroy one's health in pursuit of pleasure, to kill oneself to ease one's anguish, or to neglect one's

---

[43] Kant's concentration on absolute goodness (for example, in C2, 50–7 [5: 58–66]) may suggest that Kant has no concept of agent-relative value; but he acknowledges that we call the means to what we find agreeable 'good' in a qualified sense. For example, in C2, 54 [5: 62] he writes of actions 'good with reference to our inclination and hence only mediately (relatively to an end, as a means to it)' and later at C2, 55 [5: 64] he implies a contrast between this and the concept of good determined by moral law which, he says, 'deserves this name absolutely.' The concepts of well-being (*das Wohl*) and the useful seem to approximate some of our terms for agent-relative goodness. See also Gg, 25 [4: 414] where Kant presents hypothetical imperatives as representing acts as 'good as a means' and 'necessary in accordance with the principle of a will which is *good in some way*' (my italics). And under a hypothetical imperative that is a rule of skill 'whether the end is rational or good is not at all the question' (Gg, 26 [4: 415]).

[44] The nature and extent of Hobbes's psychological egoism is a matter of controversy, but Gregory Kavka makes a convincing case that it is qualified though extensive. See his *Hobbesian Moral and Political Theory* (Princeton: Princeton University Press, 1986), ch. 2, especially 42–51. There is also no general agreement about whether Kant thought that, apart from morally motivated acts, human motives are thoroughly hedonistic and egoistic. Kant often gives this impression by placing other-regarding desires along with self-centered ones under the concepts 'self-love' and 'happiness,' but arguably Kant uses these terms in a broad sense that is misleading. See Andrews Reath, 'Hedonism, Heteronomy, and Kant's Principle of Happiness', *Pacific Philosophical Quarterly*, 70 (1989), 42–72.

mental capacities from laziness, he concludes that there are self-regarding duties or 'duties to oneself.'[45] Thus, for Kant, one's life, health, and mental development must count as goods in a moral sense as well as whatever nonmoral sense he acknowledges. Moreover, although the various rationally optional ends that individuals adopt for themselves, e.g., learning to play the violin, are commonly regarded as morally optional for both the agent (who may abandon the ends) and for others (who may judge that they have no moral reason to aid in the projects), these ends take on a moral dimension for Kant because we all have an imperfect duty to make it our maxim to promote the permissible ends of others. Except for immoral ends, then, most of the ends that people actually adopt for other than moral reasons turn out, in Kant's ethics, to be ends that it is morally good (an imperfect duty) for others to help (or allow) one to achieve. Our question about personal ends, then, is not whether there are ends that are totally without any moral significance, but about whether in adopting an end on nonmoral grounds we thereby commit ourselves to its having objective value, in a robust sense.

Candidates for Value Judgments without Commitment to Objective and Moral Values

In an important section of the *Critique of Practical Reason* Kant argues that the moral law is not based on a prior conception of goodness independent of rational willing.[46] 'Good' and 'evil' in an unqualified 'absolute' sense apply only to acts, and to be good in this sense is to be the necessary object of a pure rational will. In developing this theme Kant acknowledges various sorts of qualified value judgments that are not based on moral considerations and do not obviously imply further judgments about what is objectively or morally valuable. Perhaps adopting ends and maxims presupposes only these weak, qualified value judgments. If so, we could not argue on conceptual grounds that anyone rational enough to act (by adopting ends and maxims) is implicitly committed to robust objective values that ground moral imperatives. Let us review these weak value judgments that might be thought implicit in adopting ends and maxims. Given Kant's thesis that judgments of 'good' and 'bad' involve practical reason, they must be based on dispositions we have as rational agents, not merely sentiments or natural facts.

[45] MM, 176–97 [421–47].   [46] C2, 50–8 [5: 57–67].

(A) Empirical Facts and Purely Theoretical Judgments

We find that some experiences are pleasant and others painful. This for Kant is not, strictly speaking, evaluation of the experiences as good or bad, for such judgments, he says, always require reason.[47] If, based on past experience, we predict that an experience of some kind will again be pleasant, we use theoretical reason in a modest way; but such judgments, e.g., 'I will probably find that pleasant,' are not themselves assessments of experiences as 'good.' They affirm factual propositions, relevant to evaluations, but they are not themselves reason-giving. Similarly, theoretical reason is presupposed when we judge empirically that certain means are effective, and even necessary, to getting what we desire, such as pleasure and avoidance of pain. These judgments, too, express beliefs about factual propositions rather than evaluations.

(B) Judging Means as Good or Bad

If we make it our end to satisfy certain desires, then the empirical facts about the effectiveness of means can warrant a qualified evaluative judgment.[48] The underlying rational principle is the Hypothetical Imperative, a requirement to take the necessary means to our ends or abandon the ends.[49] On this basis, given certain facts, we can assess acts as *good as a means* to our desired ends, provided we understand that we can abandon particular ends without irrationality and sometimes there may be rationally compelling (moral) reasons to do so. These judgments make use of *practical* reason, employed instrumentally, and so they meet at least a minimum condition for judgments of 'good' and 'bad.' They are, however, only about what is 'good' in a very qualified sense, not implying all-things-considered choice-worthiness.[50]

(C) Prudential Judgments

We also make empirical assessments about what will contribute to our weal or woe, welfare or faring poorly, happiness or unhappiness. These

---

[47] C2, 51 [5: 58].   [48] C2, 51 [5: 58–9], Gg, 25 [4: 414].
[49] The Hypothetical Imperative is the principle behind particular hypothetical imperatives, which Kant says assert that something is good, or ought to be done, because it serves as a means to some end, e.g., happiness. As imperatives, they are 'commands of reason,' not simply descriptive statements about what is needed as a means to happiness (Gg, 24–6 [4: 413–15], C2, 18 [5: 20], MM, 14–15 [6: 221–2]). Also see n. 42.
[50] C2, 34 [5: 62].

judgments involve theoretical reason in several ways, for example, assessing the effectiveness of means, noting what ends are compatible, and exploring options. On this basis, as a matter of practical reason, we can determine that acts are good as a means to our happiness as individuals.[51] These are value judgments, not merely empirical judgments that the acts are likely to promote our happiness. The underlying assumptions are that being happy is an end that everyone has and that the Hypothetical Imperative gives us reason, conditionally, to take the necessary means to our ends. On this basis we judge that the acts are good *for* us.

As noted earlier, however, the concept of happiness is too indeterminate to ground many precise, inflexible prescriptions. We can often abandon some ends, when their pursuit proves costly, and replace them with others, choosing among 'packages' of ends (or conceptions of happiness for us) without needing to judge one set as superior to others. As a result, although both natural desires and rational judgment are involved in these evaluations, there is also room for choice beyond what reason can dictate. This, I suggest later, may be part of the practical import of the idea that we 'set ends' by 'an act of freedom.'

We can judge acts as more or less valuable contributors to our happiness apart from our moral judgments about them. Admittedly, Kant says that a good will, as the condition of 'worthiness to be happy,' is also the condition of all other 'good' things, and this might suggest that even prudential evaluations depend on moral ones.[52] The point of Kant's remark, however, is evidently that, in the final judgment of reason, once all things are considered, any qualified 'good' that is incompatible with maintaining one's good will in a given situation is not worthy of choice in the context. If so, the remark is not a denial that we judge things 'good' from more limited perspectives, even from a perspective focused entirely on what will make us happy. An immoral act, in Kant's view, is never choice-worthy all things considered, but may nonetheless be prudentially good for the agent—worth choosing if nothing but the agent's happiness were relevant. Kant himself sometimes proposes to use 'the good' (*das Gute*), in contrast with well-being (*das Wohl*), in an unqualified sense referring to moral goodness, but he acknowledges that relativized judgments about well-being were traditionally characterized in terms of 'good' (*bonum*) in Latin.[53]

---

[51] C2, 53–4 [5: 61–2], Gg, 26–7 [5: 415–16].
[52] Gg, 7 [4: 393], 10 [4: 396].   [53] C2, 51–4 [5: 61–2].

(D) Morally Constrained Judgments of Instrumental and Prudential Value

In addition to the weak value judgments that Kant explicitly discusses, he implicitly acknowledges value judgments that presuppose moral standards but are not grounded in moral judgment. For example, for some acts, we may not count them as good because they are morally prescribed, but we regard them as good only when they are not morally prohibited. We might judge such an act good as means to the satisfaction of our personal ends insofar as we are conscientious individuals willing to pursue happiness only within the constraints of moral law. Such judgments would be relativized to individuals but constrained by morality. As such, they would not entail that the act is a good thing impersonally, intrinsically, morally, or 'from the point of view of the universe.'[54] Such judgments would give the agent, even the most conscientious agent, personal reasons to act to achieve the ends in question, but whether other people have moral reason to help would remain an open question.

Which, if any, of these relative value judgments do we express or presuppose when we adopt ends and maxims? When we set ourselves a personal end, we thereby also provisionally commit ourselves to regarding the necessary means as instrumental goods relative to our goal. This is a value judgment of type (B). Insofar as happiness is conceived as achieving all of our desire-based ends, then in adopting a personal end we also affirm it as part of our conception of happiness for us. On this basis we judge the means to the end as prudentially good for us. This is a type (C) value judgment. When we adopt a particular maxim in pursuit of a personal end, we are again affirming the end and committing ourselves to the instrumental and prudential value to us of the means specified in the maxim. This involves value judgments of both types (B) and (C). However, because many people who adopt ends and maxims do not aim to be happy only by morally permissible means, the mere adoption of ends and maxims does not imply commitment to live only by morally constrained judgments of instrumental and prudential value (type (D) judgments).

None of these commitments in adopting ends and maxims attributes any impersonal, nonrelative, or moral goodness to our personal ends as individuals. Absent further argument, achieving such ends is still just

---

[54] The term 'from the point of view of the universe' derives from Henry Sidgwick, *Methods of Ethics*, 7th edn. (Chicago: University of Chicago Press, 1962), 420.

good to the agent.[55] Moreover, what makes these various ends and means relative goods to (or for) individuals is not that they fit well with an objective conception of human flourishing. It is rather that individuals endorse them, in at least minimally rational and informed reflection, because they desire (and will) to succeed in their personal projects and to be happy. Although practical reason is presupposed, in these weak, relative evaluations we regard things as good because we desire and will them, not the reverse.

Why Suppose that Adopting Ends Commits Us to More Objective Values?

So far we have found only qualified, relative value judgments implicit in adopting ends and maxims. Without a thorough review of many potentially controversial passages, we could not assure ourselves that Kant accepted only these implications. Several considerations, however, tell against attributing to Kant the strong thesis that adopting ends and maxims carries commitment to objective values that could ground moral claims. All the more, the considerations suggest that contemporary developments of Kantian moral theory would do well to abandon that strong thesis.

A possible source of the idea that all Kantian value judgments are proto-moral is misreading of certain passages in the *Critique of Practical Reason*'s section entitled 'The Concept of an Object of Pure Practical Reason'.[56] Here Kant plainly acknowledges that we do assess things according to the pleasure or pain we anticipate from them. More generally, we evaluate them under the concepts of well-being (*das Wohl*) and woe (*das Übel*), which are special senses of the ambiguous Latin terms 'good' (*boni*) and 'bad' (*mali*). Reason is obviously involved in such judgments, but reason is said to have a higher moral function, displayed in the further judgments of what is good and evil from a fully rational, moral point of view (*das Gute* and *das Böse*). Turning to the

---

[55] By 'good to agents' I do not mean simply 'good in the opinion of the agents' but something more like 'good from the perspective of the agents insofar as they are concerned with furthering their own rationally and morally contingent ends.' These contingent ends need not be their own pleasure, wealth, security, and the like. Pleasure in the anticipation of fulfilling an end plays a role in Kant's empirical explanation of nonmoral motivation, but this does not mean that all nonmoral acts are done for the sake of our own pleasure. Sometimes I substitute the alternative phrase 'good for us,' but this unfortunately can also be construed in different ways. In one sense (physical well-being), to incur physical injuries in defense of a helpless person is not 'good for us,' but it may be good for us in another, broader sense (fulfillment of our highest-priority ends).

[56] C2, 50–8 [5: 57–67].

Latin formula *Nihil appetimus, nisi sub ratione boni; nihil aversamur, nisi sub ratione mali*,[57] Kant notes that it is ambiguous, in fact true under one interpretation and very doubtful under another. What is true and certain, he says, is 'We will (*wollen*) nothing, under the direction of reason, except insofar as we hold it to be good (*gut*) or evil (*böse*).'[58] 'Good' and 'evil' in this context clearly refer to moral goodness and badness, but otherwise interpretation may not be obvious.

What, for example, is the meaning of 'under the direction of reason'? We might suppose, implausibly, that every choice in which practical reason plays any role at all is to be counted as 'under the direction of reason.' If so, then the passage might be construed simply as saying that whenever we act, using at least instrumental reason, we make a definite moral judgment on the act. That is, either we hold the act to be good or we hold it to be evil. This is hardly a compelling interpretation as it implies, contrary to good sense, that we never act purposively with the idea that what we do is merely permissible, i.e., not morally bad or good. Even if we expanded the interpretation to include the merely permissible, it is far from obvious that whenever we are guided by instrumental reason we pass moral judgment on our acts (as good, evil, or permissible). In any case, the interpretation in question would give no support to the controversial strong thesis that adopting ends and maxims implies commitment to the objective moral goodness of our ends and the acts based on our maxims, for it leaves it open that we may adopt ends and maxims that we believe are evil.

In the context, Kant's phrase 'under the direction of reason' probably refers to the definite prescriptions of pure practical reason, not the qualified 'rules' and 'counsels' of instrumental reason. Pure practical reason is what determines moral good and evil, which is the sort of goodness and badness with which Kant is concerned in the passage. Also, hypothetical imperatives do not give decisive directions but always leave us the option of abandoning our ends and suspending a particular way of pursuing happiness, and so they do not give us unequivocal 'direction.' What the 'true and certain' version of the Latin formula most likely means, then, is that insofar as our will is determined by pure practical reason it is only directed towards the morally good (*das Gute*) and against moral evil (*das Böse*). The 'object' of pure practical reason is, in essence, fulfilling moral requirements from duty. Kant does not think that this is the object of all actual choices in which reason plays some

---

[57] 'We desire nothing except under the form of the good; nothing is avoided except under the form of the bad' (C2, 51–2 [5: 59–60]). [58] C2, 52 [5: 60].

role. He does not deny that practical reason, employed instrumentally, plays a guiding role in pursuit of immoral projects as well as morally optional ones; and he does not affirm the Socratic view that wrongdoing is always a result of ignorance of what is good.

The dangerous and doubtful reading of the Latin formula that Kant rejects is the psychological theory that we *always* desire and will under the idea of our welfare or woe (*Wohl* and *Weh*). He does not deny that we sometimes desire and will under these value concepts alone. Indeed, it seems a persistent theme in Kant's writings that all too often we do exactly that, i.e., pick our particular ends and means with our focus exclusively on our welfare rather than what duty requires.

In *Critique of Judgment* Kant again makes comments that, if taken out of context, might encourage the view that whatever we will in any sense we thereby take to be objectively good. For example, he says: 'Good is what, by means of reason, we like through its mere concept.'[59] Later he adds: 'the good is the object of the will (a power of desire that is determined by reason).'[60] Kant's aim in the context is to distinguish the pleasure in beauty, the 'useful', the 'agreeable', and absolute (moral) goodness. We judge things good through our concepts of them, which is different from appreciation of beauty. Our 'liking for the good' is always 'connected' with an 'interest' in it, but here, as elsewhere, 'interest' is a broad term that includes *both* having an *inclination-based* interest in something and taking a *moral* interest in something.[61] Kant notes that, although in common speech things that are merely 'agreeable' are often called 'good,' the concepts are distinct. Judging something good requires the use of reason. Kant's example is food that is tasty (agreeable) but unhealthy (not good).[62] Health is always 'agreeable,' but 'good' only when directed to a purpose. Everyone thinks that happiness ('the greatest sum ... of what is agreeable in life') is a 'true good,' Kant says; but he argues here (as elsewhere) that it is 'far from being an unconditional good.'[63]

This section, then, seems to agree with what Kant has said previously. Although only the moral good is 'good absolutely and in every respect,' we judge at least the means to what is agreeable to be good in a qualified sense. The instrumental use of reason guides our judgment of what is good as means; the full use of reason 'determines' the moral good. It

---

[59] C3, 48 [5: 207].
[60] C3, 51 [5: 209]. Thanks are due to Robert Johnson for insightful comments on this section from which these quotations are drawn.
[61] Ibid. and Gg, 54–8 [448–53], 25n [414].   [62] C3, 50 [5: 208].
[63] Ibid. and Gg, 7 [4: 393], C2, 92–3 [5: 110–11].

seems unlikely, then, that in saying 'the good is the object of the will
... determined by reason,' Kant meant to imply that every act of willing
is directed to the absolute (moral) good. If we were to use reason fully,
taking everything relevant into account, we would not will to do what
we know is immoral; but sometimes, relying on reason in a more partial
way, we do will ends and means that we are aware could not pass moral
scrutiny.[64] Adopting ends and maxims, then, at most implies a commitment to their qualified goodness, relative to what (with partial rational
reflection) we want.

In 'Theory and Practice' Kant again points out the ambiguity of
'good,' which can refer to either the absolutely good or the merely relatively good. Maxims in pursuit of the latter may be evil in themselves.
To prefer one thing over another on the basis of a natural end, such as
happiness, is to regard it better, in degree, relative to our end. Kant
quotes Christian Garve's argument that our preferences reflect what we
perceive as good, which are the states which make up happiness. Kant
replies that this plays on the ambiguity of the word 'good.' Although
we may and should prefer conformity to duty to the immoral pursuit
of any end, our preferences may reflect only what we regard good relative to our natural and chosen ends. Kant adds: 'But to give preference
to one state rather than another as a determinant of the will is merely
an act of freedom (*res merae facultatis*, as the jurists say) which takes
no account of whether the particular determinant is good or evil
in itself, and thus is neutral in both respects.'[65] Evidently, then, to give
preference to something expresses a choice, which is based on what

[64] Kant's distinction between *Wille* and *Willkür* may be relevant here. *Wille* is pure
practical reason and is translated as 'will' by Gregor; *Willkür* is a power of choice and
is translated 'choice' by Gregor. Kant does not always explicitly distinguish these two
aspects of our 'will' (in a broader sense), but contexts of discussion often make it clear
which is appropriate. In the passage in question Kant uses *Wille*: 'das Gute ist das Object
des Willens' (C3, 51 [5: 209]). If Kant sticks to his distinction here, the quote should
mean 'the morally good is the object of pure practical reason.' This was Kant's main
message in the section of the *Critique of Practical Reason* reviewed above. This thesis
allows, however, that we can 'will'—in the other sense—acts and maxims without judging
them to be objectively and morally good. In that sense (choice) we can, and do, 'will'
what we know to be wrong. If Kant is using 'will' more loosely here, then 'das Gute'
must be read more loosely too. Then the message would be that *both* qualified goods
and moral good are determined by the use of reason *in some way*. This, again, would
not imply that in willing (choosing) ends and means we are thereby committed to their
objective or moral goodness.

[65] 'On the Common Saying: "This May Be True in Theory, but It Does Not Apply
in Practice"', in Hans Reiss (ed.), *Kant: Political Writings* (Cambridge: Cambridge
University Press, 1991), 66–7 [8: 283]. Also in *Immanuel Kant: Practical Philosophy*,
ed. and tr. Mary Gregor, 284–5. Nisbet translates *res merae facultatis* as 'a mere thing
of opportunity.'

we regard good in some sense (at least relative to what we want); but preferences and choices are not necessarily for what is morally or objectively good.

Charity directs us, when interpreting a theory, to prefer readings that make it more plausible unless textual considerations to the contrary are compelling. All the more, this policy makes good sense if our aim is to develop a contemporary version of the theory in question.[66] These considerations, as well as strictly textual ones, tell against the strong thesis that adopting ends and maxims implies commitment to objective moral values. Kant was aware that human nature has a dark side, and psychology and recent history fully confirm this. It would be naïve to deny that people often willingly and deliberately choose what they realize could not be justified to others as morally good or even permissible. In fact sometimes they even seem resolutely to pursue what they acknowledge to be imprudent and immoral. To be sure, as Hobbes said, they see what they voluntarily choose as good in some respect; but this does not mean that they see it as good and worthy of choice, all things considered. Guilt, shame, and self-contempt all too commonly express the judgment that the life we are leading is not good, not reasonably to be commended to others, and yet these attitudes can coexist with a stubborn 'will' not to change. When philosophers declare grandly that in choosing for ourselves we are affirming to the whole world that our way of acting is a good way, then, unless they are expressing a trivial logical point, they are attributing to ordinary choice far more commitment than the choosers intend.[67] The widely held view that we acknowledge only 'agent-relative' values is an exaggeration, but it at least recognizes that some value judgments are not, even implicitly, commitments to the impartial goodness of what we value.

Further, if adopting ends and maxims, by itself, implied a commitment to the objective moral goodness of the ends and corresponding

---

[66] For a subtle contemporary discussion of our topic independent of Kant, see David Velleman's 'The Guise of the Good', ch. 5 of his *The Possibility of Practical Reason* (Oxford: Oxford University Press, 2000), 99–122. Velleman concludes: 'Since reasons do not recommend an action by presenting it as a good thing to do, actions performed for reasons need not be performed under the guise of the good.' See also Michael Stocker, 'Desiring the Bad: An Essay in Moral Psychology', *Journal of Philosophy*, 76 (1979), 738–53.

[67] The trivial logical point is that value claims are universalizable in at least the sense that if I judge something to be good (to me) then I imply that anything exactly or relevantly like it would be good (to anyone exactly or relevantly like me) in exactly the same or relevantly similar circumstances. This is trivial because no substantive prescriptions follow until criteria of relevance are supplied.

acts, then this would provide an implausibly easy way to argue that it is irrational not to be moral. To any moral skeptics or professed amoralists we could simply point out that even their most vicious, self-serving acts express commitment to standards of impartial reason, which turn out to condemn what they do. Further argument would be needed to identify and apply the standards, but if the first step were conceded the would-be skeptics would have already taken the hook. All that remains would be to reel them in to a particular conception of the impartial moral standards. Some commentators may welcome this result, but the argument rests on a very thin reed at the first step.

History looks dimly on efforts to demonstrate that anyone rational enough to deliberate from self-interested principles is necessarily committed to moral standards. Kant may appear at times committed to the belief that this is so, but in the end he had to acknowledge that it is an indemonstrable 'fact of reason' for those with reason of the kind we have.[68] Even if, as it may appear, chapter III of the *Groundwork* was an attempt to pull the moral rabbit out of the nonmoral hat, the effort was abandoned in the second *Critique*. In *Religion* Kant clearly acknowledges the predisposition to use instrumental practical reason ('humanity') as conceptually distinct from our predisposition to govern ourselves by moral reason ('personality'), and, although he holds that we have both, he does not suggest that having the one necessitates having the other.[69] Moreover, in chapter II of the *Groundwork*, where some apparently see Kant as arguing from relative values to the absolute value of humanity, Kant insists repeatedly that the arguments of that chapter are still compatible with there being no genuine Categorical Imperative or duties.[70] That is, the arguments are all hypothetical: if there are moral duties, as 'common rational cognition of morality' assumes, then analysis shows there must be a Categorical Imperative; and if so, it must prescribe conformity to universal law and only this. Given all this and the fact that, as rational persons, we each conceive of ourselves (morally) as ends, not mere means for others, then the same basic principle can be expressed as 'humanity in persons is an end in itself.' The conclusion is, and must be, conditional: if there are moral duties, then the Humanity Formula expresses the values at their core. Acknowledging the dignity of humanity is implicit in our moral

---

[68] C2, 28–9 [5: 31–2], 37–8 [5: 42–3].
[69] *Religion within the Boundaries of Mere Reason*, tr. and ed. Allen Wood and George di Giovanni (Cambridge: Cambridge University Press, 1998), 50–2 [6: 26–8].
[70] Gg, 37–8 [4: 428–9], 39–40 [4: 434], 50–1 [4: 444–5].

III. IS KANT'S ACCOUNT OF PERSONAL VALUES TOO VOLUNTARISTIC?

Here is the apparent problem. Kant says that we set for ourselves even our desire-based ends through acts of freedom, but in fact, it seems, the occasions we might describe as deliberately adopting ends are relatively rare.[72] Typically, the ends we adopt are fairly determinate goals that we set ourselves because of other, deeper values that we almost never question. That we pick up many of our personal values from early socialization and continuing cultural influences seems undeniable. Moreover, often we simply 'find' some kinds of experiences immediately delightful and others repulsive. In such cases it seems implausible to insist that a psychological explanation of our pursuing the one and avoiding the other must postulate a deliberate 'act' of end setting. It is natural to suspect that Kant has over-intellectualized the processes by which we come to acquire our personal values. Sometimes it takes persistent self-observation and reflection to become aware of what we most deeply care about independently of morality; but then, though the process of reflection is intellectual, it seems more accurately described as a process of 'discovering' rather than 'choosing' our values.

Three preliminary comments may help to clarify the problem I mean to raise here by distinguishing it from others with which it might be confused.

First, the problem I want to address concerns a specific conflict between Kant's idea of setting ends and our common experience of how we actually come to acquire our values and goals. The issue is not the general problem of free will. To be sure, Kant held that we must attribute 'freedom,' in several senses, to the will of all rational beings.[73]

---

[71] Christine Korsgaard and (later) Allen Wood interpret Kant's argument for the Formula of Humanity as an End in itself in a way that is at odds with my position here. Their arguments, I think, are unsuccessful at least partly because they rely on what (in my view) is the implausible first step. Their reconstructions of Kant's arguments, however, deserve a detailed examination, which I intend to attempt later. See Wood, *Kant's Ethical Thought*, 124–32, and Korsgaard's 'Kant's Formula of Humanity', in *Creating the Kingdom of Ends*, 194–7.

[72] See MM, 146–7 [6: 381], 149 [6: 384–5], 154 [6: 392].

[73] For example, Gg, 52–4 [4: 446–8], 26–7 [5: 29–30], 79 [5: 93–4], MM, 13–15 [6: 213–14].

As rational beings, he argues, we necessarily 'act under the Idea of freedom.'[74] That is, we take ourselves to be able to act as efficient causes without ourselves being determined by 'alien causes,' and so we must regard ourselves also as having a positive freedom or autonomy of the will. No doubt at least part of what Kant meant by saying that adopting ends is 'an act of freedom' alludes to these perennially controversial doctrines, but the issue on which I want to focus is narrower, and (I hope) more manageable, than these. Kant treats setting ourselves ends as a matter of choice. If this is so, his doctrine of free will implies these choices are 'free' in his special senses. But is adopting ends always a matter of choice? Do we, as Kant suggests, choose our personal ends rather than simply finding ourselves valuing and pursuing what is usual or expected? Setting aside its metaphysical implications, saying that we 'set' ourselves ends as an 'act' of freedom still suggests, implausibly, that even our most basic ends are always adopted in an explicit process of deliberate choice.

Second, it is important to distinguish this specific concern from general dissatisfaction with 'existentialist' notions of free choice as arbitrary, utterly detached from both reasons and prior motives. Kant never implies that setting personal ends is a radical existential choice, if this means not made for reasons or influenced by our desires. To the contrary, according to Kant, our desires and aversions, likings and dislikings, provide the motivating background for adopting personal ends. We are not mindlessly driven to our goals by such factors, but they are central to our reasons for endorsing one end rather than another. Our reasons, though not typically compelling in the sense of 'leaving no reasonable options,' can be reconstructed along familiar lines, noting that we desire the end, indicating what there is about it that we find attractive, and explaining how it fits with our other ends and resources. To say that we set ourselves an end implies at least that we assumed that we had options and that it was, in some important sense, 'up to us' to affirm or reject them. How to explain this sense is a perennial philosophical puzzle, but at least it should be clear that, on any reasonable account, being 'up to us' does not imply that the choice was made in the absence of deliberative reasons and natural predispositions.[75]

---

[74] Gg, 53 [4: 448].

[75] My remarks here are meant to be neutral between compatibilist and incompatibilist accounts of free choice. Neither needs to affirm the extreme 'existentialist' idea that free choice is totally independent of natural causes and not based on reasons. My aim will not be to offer a metaphysical account or linguistic analysis of free choice but rather to suggest that certain practical, normative points may be behind what looks like a metaphysical claim.

Third, to say that we set our ends freely does not imply that there are no limits to what we can adopt as our end. Knowing that I cannot fly simply by flapping my arms, I cannot make it my end to do so. So too, despite what Kant himself may have thought, Kantians should admit that people with severe addictions cannot by themselves alter certain behavior patterns and, knowing this, they cannot even make it an end for themselves to do so. The issue at hand, however, is not *what* ends we can adopt but about *how* we come to have the ends we do.

The relevant charge of excessive voluntarism, then, is just that Kant writes as if we acquire our personal values and ends by an explicit act of choice whereas experience suggests that a more gradual and passive process is at work. The best response, I think, is for Kantians to admit the point as a description of our experience but then look for the practical, heuristic value (as well as the danger) of treating end-setting as a matter of deliberate choice. For this purpose we should recall the broad context of Kant's ideas about setting ourselves ends. The context is moral theory, in particular relations between personal ends and morally necessary ends.[76] Kant does not offer us a full psychology or phenomenology of nonmoral evaluation. His practical concern was to say how, morally, we ought to treat others' personal projects and values and, further, to say how in rational deliberation we should view our own projects and values. I begin with the second concern.

Rational deliberation about our own projects and values. When we deliberate about important goals, we normally come to the process with values that we have picked up, without much thought, through various natural and social influences. The personal ends we adopt are often expressions of these acquired values or shaped by them. To deliberate more rationally, however, we can follow the regulative principle to look for new possibilities, to examine our evaluative assumptions, and to question whether, in the light of fuller reflection, we want to reaffirm or abandon those value commitments that we recognize (even 'discover') in the patterns of our past thoughts and behavior. To subject our personal ends and related values to this sort of review, I suggest, is to treat our ends *as if* adopted by acts of freedom. That is, though, strictly

---

[76] In *The Metaphysics of Morals* Kant is concerned with two different kinds of end-setting. First, through our rational wills with autonomy (positive freedom) we prescribe to ourselves 'the ends that are duties'—our own perfection and the happiness of others. Second, we adopt personal ends with a negatively free will (the ability to pursue these or not independently of 'alien causes'). These two types of end-setting are connected in the claim that it is rationally necessary to make it an end for ourselves to further the permissible personal ends of others.

Personal Values and Setting Oneself Ends

speaking, we grant that our initial acquisition of values and goals often cannot be traced to an explicit deliberate choice, we can see them as 'up to us' in the sense that they are subject to review and possible change in our further rational reflections. From an explanatory historical point of view, many values that shape our plans are not deliberately chosen; but, from a deliberative agent's perspective, they fall within a realm of free choice in that we may deliberately alter them if there are good reasons to do so (or no compelling reasons not to). In taking a deliberative stance toward our values and the ends that express them, we presuppose that we can alter them if there is sufficient reason to.[77] The idea that they are 'up to us,' however, is not merely that in fact we have the *ability* to alter them, but that we ourselves, when reflecting rationally, have the normative *authority* to decide whether to endorse or abandon those personal values and ends that (we assume) are within our control. When we reflect morally, Kant thought, we will acknowledge important moral constraints; but these are supposed to be rationally self-legislated. Beyond these moral constraints nothing but our own properly reflective choices determine what are legitimate ends and priorities in our life plans. Neither nature nor the commands of other persons, for example, provide a definitive blueprint that can determine what a rational person must choose in this area.

This idea admittedly goes against the grain of many popular conceptions of rational choice. It implies that in deliberation about our own personal ends, our choice is underdetermined by reason. That is, at least within limits, we can think of these choices as 'up to us' in the sense that we may adopt this end, or that, or another, or reject them all, without being irrational.[78] Even with all available information about what I have

---

[77] This is a conceptual point about deliberation, not a metaphysical or empirical claim about our powers of control. We can deliberate about what personal values and ends to endorse only if we assume that our deliberations will determine, or at least help to shape, those values and ends. We might, of course, find sufficient empirical evidence that certain drives, habits, and cravings are goal-directed but utterly unresponsive to rational reflection. Then we might appropriately deliberate about external means to control them (for example, drugs or aversive conditioning), or their undesirable consequences, but not about whether to retain or abandon them as personal ends. Whether we are sad, or glad, to have these reason-insensitive dispositions, we would need to deal with them as given facts, potentially relevant to some practical deliberations, but unlike the ends, values, policies, and plans that we view as subject to authoritative review and possible change in rational reflection.

[78] Given human nature and our individual inclinations, of course, it is predictable that we will in fact always make certain choices (for example, the cessation of excruciating physical pain that serves no purpose) so long as we are sane and cognitively rational. For a cognitively rational and aware person not to make it an end to stop the pain in this context would be bizarre, contrary to human nature, and incredible, but arguably

enjoyed, my current inclinations, my opportunities, etc., my rational reflection may not yield a particular prescription. This might be due to the fact that available knowledge is still imperfect, but it is far from obvious that even with perfect information we could always determine a particular choice as rationally mandated. Some might conjecture that in such cases reason determines that the weight of reasons is precisely the same for each of many alternatives; but it is doubtful that there is a plausible measure for the weight of reasons here and, even if so, it seems unlikely that such 'ties' would be a common outcome. Instead, we can think of practical reason as in principle determining certain choices, but not all. If so, the best rational deliberation about our personal ends may leave many choices 'up to us' in the sense that they are rationally optional.

This view of reason, at least regarding morally permissible personal ends, fits with Kant's idea that the Hypothetical Imperative, his primary principle of nonmoral reason, always leaves us options if we are willing to adjust our personal ends. The idea is that, if one wills an end and certain means are necessary and available, it is rationally necessary to take those means—or abandon the end. That we can rationally abandon particular personal ends, on this reading, is not merely a psychological or metaphysical claim but rather a point about the kind of reasons favoring the ends, i.e., they are not rationally *compelling*. They are considerations that understandably appeal to us and incline us to include the related goals into our life plans, but not factors from which an argument can be constructed that we must, on pain of irrationality, adopt a certain personal end. We 'explain' our adopting of a personal end by citing the 'reason,' and this presents our decision as an intelligible choice, not merely a random, unmotivated 'picking.' This sort of explanation, however, is very different from claiming that the considerations for adopting the end show, under some necessary principle of rational choice, that there was no rational alternative. On my reading of the Kantian view, for example, even apart from morality, there is no rational requirement to maximize the satisfaction of our given current desires, our expected preferences over time, or anything of the sort.

on Kant's view (and Hume's) it is not strictly contrary to practical reason. In Kant's view, as I understand it, practical reason prescribes only moral imperatives and means to ends that can be abandoned or suspended; and in Hume's view, strictly speaking, we do not have *practical* reason that prescribes ends. I discuss these matters further in 'Pains and Projects: Justifying to Oneself', Ch. 12, pp. 173–88, in *Autonomy and Self-Respect*.

Personal Values and Setting Oneself Ends

Moral Treatment of Others' Personal Ends and Values. Let us turn now to Kant's second, perhaps primary, concern in the contexts of saying that adoption of an end is an act of freedom: the concern to explain how, morally, we ought to regard the personal projects and values of others. Here the idea that we should treat others as if they freely set their own personal ends, even if exaggerated, expresses a valuable moral caution against certain kinds of meddlesomeness. For example, to be charitable to others with due respect, we should not (without special reason) try to second-guess what is really going to make them happy and so deny their requests in favor of something else. In personal relations, as in politics, there is a strong (but not indefeasible) presumption that we should leave room for people to plan and live their own lives, as they choose, within the constraints of moral principle and law. Further, when trying to get someone to adopt a permissible but morally optional project or goal, we should not proceed to do so by manipulative techniques that play on their ignorance or irrationality but rather treat the change as one that is (normatively) 'up to that person to decide' or 'his or her free choice.' That is, we should see the change as ours to influence only by respectfully offering (legitimate) reasons, information, and offers for them to weigh reflectively, free from outside deliberate pressures to 'make them' change.

As before, the practical point is not that we should pretend, contrary to fact, that personal ends were initially acquired through explicit, voluntary acts of choice. The point, rather, would be to treat all of others' legitimate personal ends and values, however they were acquired, as within a sphere of choice 'up to them' to affirm, revise, or abandon in rational reflection in which they are the primary authoritative decision makers. Since, in Kant's view, rational reflection reveals moral constraints on what they can set as an end and what we can do to aid them, ultimately it is others' morally *permissible* personal ends that we need to treat as 'up to them' in the relevant sense. The practical import of the idea that others' permissible ends are up to them is that in our attempts to be beneficent we should normally let them decide how they conceive of happiness for them. As long as their ends are permissible, properly beneficent persons do not impose their ideals of well-being on their beneficiaries.[79] Also, when we pursue our own personal ends, we

---

[79] Apparent exceptions would include cases where people formed their conceptions of happiness in ignorance or under manipulative social influences. In these cases, however, what is primarily called for is not 'imposing' our ideals against their wills but rather counteracting the manipulative forces and ignorance. Also, arguably, moral considerations implicit in the idea of humanity as an end in itself will support placing a priority

must take into account ways in which our pursuits may adversely affect others' attaining happiness as they conceive it. Legal commercial practices are morally suspect, for example, if they subtly undermine aspects of a group's culture that are integral to its members' conception of happiness and are not morally objectionable.

The heuristic value of acting *as if* ends are freely adopted, of course, has its limits. If this meant always turning a blind eye to empirical facts about how we actually come to have the ends we do, it would have unfortunate consequences. If some social conditions encourage us to take up constructive and rewarding goals and projects and others do not, it is obviously worthwhile to learn and make use of this information as we develop and reform our social institutions. If in fact many young people initially take up morally objectionable values in a mindless way and have never been encouraged to reflect on them, this should be relevant both to their responsibility and to how we should treat them. Respecting these cautions, however, is compatible with recognizing the proposed (limited) heuristic of treating personal ends as if freely adopted.

on meeting beneficiaries' basic human needs over merely promoting whatever they count as belonging to their happiness. Further, as Kant notes at MM, 151 [6: 388]: 'It is for them to decide what they count as belonging to their happiness; but it is up to me to refuse them many things they think will make them happy, but that I do not, as long as they have no right to demand them from me as what is theirs.' The general duty to promote the happiness of others is an imperfect duty, typically (not always) leaving many options about whom to help and how.

PART III

Moral Worth: Self-Assessment and Desert

9

Four Conceptions of Conscience

Controversies about the nature, reliability, and importance of conscience have a long history. Diverse opinions reflect not only differences in theological beliefs and political context but also deep divisions in moral theory. Some scholars hold that relying on conscience is a sure path to morally correct, or at least blameless, conduct and that the imperative to follow one's conscience is unconditional, taking precedence over all other authorities. Making moral decisions conscientiously and sticking by them are widely thought to be essential ingredients of integrity, and some would add that they also affirm one's autonomy and individuality.

This sanguine view of individual conscience has not been shared by all, however. Many traditional moralists place more confidence in church and state authority than in private conscience, arguing that those authorities have better access to moral truth or that, practically, giving precedence to individual conscience is a recipe for anarchy. Observing that those people who rely on conscience often approve of radically different practices, including some that may seem outrageous, many reflective people understandably come to doubt that conscience is each individual's unerring access to moral truth. Recalling how often cruel and destructive conduct has been excused in the name of conscience, they naturally question as well even the more modest doctrine that following one's conscience guarantees a *blameless* life.

These controversies provide the background for my discussion, although I shall not address them directly. My more modest aim is to highlight, as a preliminary aid to understanding the larger issues, some of the similarities and differences among four important conceptions of conscience. In particular, I want to call attention to the various ways in which these conceptions interpret the origin, function, and reliability of conscience. How one conceives conscience makes a significant difference regarding one's attitude toward one's own conscience and the (alleged) conscientious judgments of others. So, in contrasting the four conceptions of conscience, I also call attention to the implications of each conception regarding whether and (if so) why one should respect conscience in oneself and in others. More specifically, for each conception, I address the following question: If one conceives conscience in this way, and confidently so, then to what extent and why should one (1) treat the apparent promptings of one's own conscience as one's authoritative guide and (2) respectfully tolerate the conduct of others when they are apparently guided by conscience?[1]

Here I differentiate between various particular 'conceptions' of conscience and a general 'concept' of conscience in a way analogous to John Rawls's distinction between the general concept of justice and various particular conceptions of justice.[2] That is, the several *conceptions* of conscience are specific interpretations, or more detailed understandings, of a general *concept*, or core idea, of conscience. The core idea that they have in common is, roughly, the idea of a capacity, commonly attributed to most human beings, to sense or immediately discern that what he or she has done, is doing, or is about to do (or not do) is wrong, bad, and worthy of disapproval.[3] Moreover, the general concept, I assume, includes the idea that a person's conscience, whatever else it may be, is something that apparently influences (but rarely, if ever, completely controls) that person's conduct. It also is something that, when disregarded, tends to result in mental discomfort and lowered self-esteem.

This general idea leaves open further questions about how conscience is acquired and developed, how it operates, what it purports to 'say,'

---

[1] What do the various conceptions imply, for example, about whether we should endorse and protect other people's reliance on conscience? Which conceptions, if any, imply that the voices of conscience in others are relevant data for our own moral decision making? Do they imply that we must tolerate the conscientious acts of others even when we are convinced that their judgments are mistaken and harmful and, if so, within what limits?

[2] See John Rawls, *A Theory of Justice* (Cambridge, Mass.: Harvard University Press, 1999), 5 ff. The concept of justice, according to Rawls, is specified by the role that different particular conceptions are supposed to have in common. It is, roughly, the idea of publicly affirmed principles that assign basic rights and duties and determine a proper distribution of benefits and burdens in a cooperative scheme. By contrast, the particular 'conceptions of justice' characterized by justice as fairness, utilitarianism, and perfectionism are different ways of specifying what the principles are that should play the general social role of a concept of justice.

[3] Roughly, to say that conscience is a capacity to 'sense or immediately discern' is to say that it is a way of arriving at the relevant moral beliefs about our acts by means of feeling, instinct, or personal judgment. Becoming convinced by conscience that our conduct is immoral is supposed to be distinct from reaching that conclusion by explicitly appealing to external authorities or by engaging in discussion with others, although perhaps most people would grant that public opinion and authoritative pronouncements tend to influence the development of consciences and so may indirectly affect what conscience 'says' on particular occasions.

how trustworthy it is as a moral guide, whether it is universal or found only in certain cultures, what purposes it serves individuals and society, and even whether saying 'her conscience tells her to' is a purely descriptive statement or one that also expresses the speaker's attitudes or moral beliefs. These particular conceptions of conscience are the various ways in which questions such as these are addressed in moral theories, in systems of theology, and also in less articulated, popular ways of thinking that extend (and sometimes distort) religious and scientific ideas prevalent in a culture.

Although it will become evident where my sympathies lie, it is not my aim to argue that one or another of these conceptions is correct or even—all things considered—superior to the others. I do not pretend to be neutral regarding the merits of the various conceptions under discussion, but my primary purpose here is merely to sketch the different conceptions, note significant variations, and draw out some of their practical implications.

Besides this, I have another aim that leads me to make some more explicitly evaluative remarks. The context is my ongoing project to develop a moral theory in the Kantian tradition that is as plausible as possible. This gives me a reason to examine and call attention to the merits and weaknesses of various conceptions of conscience from this perspective. The point is to consider how a reasonable, modified Kantian ethics should interpret conscience and why it should reject other interpretations.[4] Although Kant's own account of conscience is one of the four conceptions to be considered, it is not necessarily the best conception, even for my purposes, simply because Kant proposed it. The reason is that developing a plausible 'Kantian' moral theory requires selectively endorsing some of Kant's claims and rejecting others, according to one's best judgment as to what is both sustainable and most fundamental to the theory. Since a full exposition and defense of such a theory is obviously impossible here, my evaluative remarks should be understood for now as tentative and hypothetical, suggesting reasons that if one adopts certain basic features of a Kantian ethics, it is preferable to interpret conscience in a certain way and not in others.

The four conceptions of conscience, briefly described, are the following: first, a popular religious view that bases a strong confidence in an instinctual conscience on theological beliefs about its origin and

---

[4] I describe features of a Kantian ethical theory that I regard as most plausible—as distinct from aspects of Kant's own view that I regard as untenable—in my previous essays, some of which are collected in *Dignity and Practical Reason*. Others include chs. 1, 2, and 5 in my *Respect, Pluralism, and Justice*, and Chs. 3 and 9 of this volume.

purpose; second, a deflationary cultural relativism that regards conscience as nothing but an unreflective response to the socially instilled values of one's culture, no matter what these happen to be; third, Joseph Butler's idea of conscience as reason, making moral judgments by reflecting 'in a cool hour' on what conduct is morally appropriate, given human nature and the facts of one's situation; and fourth, Kant's narrower, metaphorical conception of conscience as 'an inner judge' that condemns (or acquits) one for inadequate (or adequate) effort to live according to one's best possible, though fallible, judgments about what (objectively) one ought to do.[5]

My comments on the relations of the first three conceptions are too diverse to summarize briefly, but my main suggestions regarding the Kantian perspective are the following: First, Kant's conception of conscience makes room for some central ideas in each of the other conceptions while avoiding aspects of them that, at least from the basic Kantian perspective, are problematic. Furthermore, Kant's own account of conscience does fit coherently with the basic features of his moral theory, even though it might seem at first that 'conscience' should have no place in rationalistic moral theories such as Kant's.

In the Kantian view, we must treat basic moral beliefs as known, or to be determined, through *reason*.[6] When we deliberately try to apply general principles to particular kinds of problems, we use *judgment*, and whether we act on our moral beliefs depends on the strength and goodness of our *wills*. *Conscience*, however, is not the same as reason, judgment, or will. In fact, Kant assigns conscience a limited role in his moral theory. It is not a moral expert with an intuition of moral truth or a moral legislator that makes moral laws or a moral arbitrator that settles perplexing cases. Rather, the role of conscience is restricted to that of an 'inner judge' who scrutinizes our conduct and then imposes sentence on us as guilty or else acquits us of either of two charges: (1) that we

---

[5] 'Adequate effort' here is meant to cover 'due care' in forming judgments about what one ought to do as well as firmness of will in following these judgments. It is intended to cover both of Kant's somewhat different accounts of conscience, which I describe later. The first account is in MM, 26–7 [6: 234–5], 156 [6: 399], and 188–9 [6: 438–40]. The second is in R, 178–9 [6: 185–6].

[6] It is important to note that from the Kantian point of view, reason is not regarded as a faculty of intuition by which we can 'see' certain moral norms as 'self-evident.' However, to say something is determined by reason also does not mean that it is provable in any formal way. Practical reason is not simply instrumental, determining efficient means to our ends. Rather, it is supposed to be a shared capacity of moral agents to think from a common point of view that respects and takes into account the interests of all.

contravened our own (reason-based) judgment about what is morally right or (2) that we failed to exercise due care and diligence in forming the particular moral opinions on which we acted. Presupposing rather than providing our basic understanding of morality, conscience brings into focus a sometimes painful awareness, not that our action is 'objectively' wrong but that we are not even making a proper effort to guide ourselves by our own deepest moral beliefs.

For general moral guidance, especially in perplexing cases, Kant agrees with Butler that we should not rely on instinct but on reason in deliberate reflection. Kant granted that conscience (narrowly construed) should be considered authoritative within its limited sphere, but he also believed a further point that others (such as Butler) might describe as 'respecting the authority of conscience' because they work with a broader conception of conscience. That is, Kant's moral theory holds that each of us must, in the end, treat our own (final) moral judgments as authoritative, even though they are fallible. When others disagree, we must listen to them and take into account their reasons; and when civil authorities demand conformity, we must give due regard to the moral reasons for obeying such authorities. Having taken all this into account, however, each of us must carefully make and rigorously follow our own best moral judgment.[7] To do so, in Kant's view, enables us to live with a clear conscience, but it does not guarantee that our acts are objectively right (since our moral judgment may be misguided).

I. INSTINCTIVE ACCESS TO MORAL TRUTH

Let us begin with a popular religious conception—conscience as God-given instinctual access to moral truth. There are many variations, but for contrast, I shall describe an extreme version. Here are the main themes.

1. Each human being is born with a latent conscience, which (barring certain tragic interferences) emerges into its full working capacity in youth or young adulthood. It is a capacity to identify, among one's own acts, motives, intentions, and aims, those that are morally wrong and

---

[7] It is significant that despite Kant's rigorous condemnation of participating in revolutionary activities, he granted that one must refuse to obey state orders to do what one judges wrong in itself. See MM, 98 [6: 322] and 136 [6: 371]; also Hans Reiss, 'Postscript', in Hans Reiss (ed.), *Kant: Political Writings* (Cambridge: Cambridge University Press, 1991), 267–8; and R, 153n [6: 154].

those that are permissible (i.e., not wrong). Conscience, however, does not identify acts and motives as morally admirable and praiseworthy. At best, conscience is 'clear' or 'clean,' not self-congratulating.

2. That certain acts, such as murder and adultery, are morally wrong is a matter of objective fact, independent of our consciences. That is, what makes such acts wrong is not just that they are, or would be, disapproved of by the agent's conscience or even the consciences of everyone. However, once our conscience has persuaded us that to perform a certain act would be wrong, there arises the possibility of doing a second wrong, namely, violating our conscience. Since this is intentionally doing what we believe to be morally wrong, it is generally regarded as wrong, independently of whether our initial moral belief is correct.[8]

3. In acknowledging the wrongness of an act, our conscience gives us a sense that we cannot comfortably view that act as something that was, is, or will be optional, to be pursued or not according to our interests. It imposes painful feelings of self-disapproval when it recognizes the wrongs of our past or ongoing activities, and it threatens the same when we entertain future plans that it would condemn.

4. Conscience originates as God's gift to human beings, a special access to moral truth that can work independently of church authority and rational reflection.[9] Its authority, moreover, stems from the fact that its content is part of God's own knowledge and/or will. That is, it stems from the part that God chose to make accessible to us, for our guidance, in this special way.[10]

---

[8] The possibility of this second wrong, in regard to our moral beliefs, is the source of a number of traditional puzzles and controversies about conscience. For example, if we 'conscientiously' believe an act to be a duty when it is 'objectively wrong,' then it seems, paradoxically, that we must inevitably do wrong, no matter what we do: either we (unknowingly) do what is objectively wrong or else (intentionally) do what we believe is wrong, which is a wrong of another kind. Philosophers have responded to this puzzle in various ways, depending on whether they grant that conscience can 'err,' whether they believe that there are 'objective wrongs' defined independently of the agent's intention, and whether they judge the source of moral error to be culpable or inculpable in origin. See Alan Donagan, 'Conscience', in Lawrence and Charlotte Becker (eds.), *Encyclopedia of Ethics*, 2nd edn. (New York: Garland Press, 1992), i. 297–9.

[9] Note that the 'natural law' tradition in Western religious ethics, unlike the popular conception, emphasizes individuals' reason as their mode of access to moral truth. This makes the view more similar to Kant's, which is why, for starker contrast, I selected the 'popular' view.

[10] According to some, conformity or nonconformity to God's commands is what constitutes objective right and wrong. According to others, objective features of the acts are what make them wrong. But either way, all who accept the popular religious conception agree that God in fact forbids and disapproves of wrong acts while commanding and approving conformity to duty. All agree that it is generally wrong to act contrary to conscience, but this is not because it is thought that the objective wrongness of acts in general

5. Appealing to conscience is not the same as using rational, reflective judgment to resolve moral questions. Conscience may be partly shaped and informed by such judgments, as well as by public debates, religious education, and the like, but it is pictured as operating not so much like an intellectual moral adviser as like an instinct-governed, internal 'voice' or sign that 'tells' us what we must or must not do, warns us when tempted, and prods us to reform when guilty.[11]

6. Once we have correctly identified and heard its 'voice,' conscience is a reliable source of knowledge of our own moral responsibilities in particular contexts. The story is that God gave each of us a conscience as a guide for our own conduct, not for judging or goading others. Each of us is commanded to follow our conscience and is directly accountable to God for having done so or not. Judging that an act is wrong for us means that it is wrong for everyone unless there is a relevant difference between the cases, but others' cases may differ in so many ways that we have no practical license to make extensive generalizations from what we 'learn' from our own conscience.

A more modest thesis might say that following our conscience is a reliable guide to living a blameless life and not necessarily a guarantee that we will do what is morally correct in every instance. The popular conception I have in mind, however, holds the stronger thesis that the voice of our conscience coincides with what is objectively right or wrong for us to do, that is, what it is correct, on the basis of the known facts, to judge as right or wrong.

Even this strong thesis, however, inevitably leaves a loophole for error. Whether or not we believe that conscience itself is infallible, we must still acknowledge that we can make mistakes about whether what we

consists simply of their being against the agent's conscience. Rather, acts against conscience are typically wrong because, given that conscience is our God-given means of access to the truth about what is objectively right and wrong, the acts that conscience warns us against are truly wrong (independently of that warning).

When I say that the wrongness of acts against conscience is not in general constituted by their being against conscience, the qualification is important. In those special cases in which, owing to error of conscience, the acts (described independently of the agents' beliefs and conscience) are not in fact wrong (even though the agents think they are), the agents still would be doing something wrong (namely, 'intentionally doing what they believe wrong') by acting against conscience. In this special case, the wrongness does consist entirely of the acts being violations of conscience.

[11] Typically our conscience is pictured not as judging the moral quality of particular acts from first principles but, rather, as identifying a limited class of (our own) wrong acts by means of the characteristic painful feelings aroused in contemplating them. This is a feature of several conceptions of conscience that fits well the metaphor of conscience as a warning, nagging, and reprimanding Jiminy Cricket or a tiny angel that follows us through tempting times. Butler's view is a partial exception.

take to be dictates of conscience are authentic. Wishful thinking, fear, childhood prejudices, and indoctrination in false ideologies can imitate or distort the voice of conscience, especially if we have dulled that voice by frequently disregarding it. So in effect, the doctrine that conscience is very reliable, even infallible, with regard to objective right and wrong is subject to practical qualifications. As with some marvelous technologies thought to be virtually 100 percent reliable if used properly by flawless operators under ideal conditions, errors of application occur but are blamed on the user, not the equipment.

What are the implications of this popular conception of conscience with regard to how we should treat it? First, what should our attitude be toward our own conscience? Since by hypothesis, conscience provides reliable access to both moral truth and subjective rightness, we would have good (moral) reason to avoid 'dulling' our conscience, to 'listen' carefully for its signals, and in general to be cautiously guided by what apparently it tells us to do. Several factors, however, can combine to recommend caution even to the firm believer in the popular conception. For example, although conscience is supposed to be a reliable signal of moral truth, it is not necessarily the only, or the most direct, means of determining what we ought to do. When secular and religious authorities, together with the professed conscientious judgments of others, all stand opposed to what we initially took to be the voice of conscience, then these facts should raise doubts. Even assuming that genuine pronouncements of conscience are infallible, we may not be infallible in distinguishing these from our wishes or fears or the echoes of past mentors. In effect, we may need to check our supposed instinctual access to moral truth by reviewing more directly the relevant evidence and arguments, for example, concerning intended benefits and harms, promises fulfilled or broken, and the responsibilities of our social role. To confirm that our instinctive response is a reflection of 'true conscience' rather than a morally irrelevant feeling, we would need to consult other sources, for example, to see whether the response coincides with reflective moral judgment, based on a careful review of pertinent facts in consultation with others.

Without such a check, there is no way to be confident that the instinct on which we are about to rely is 'conscience' rather than some baser instinct. By analogy, suppose that we believe we have an intuitive sense that somehow regularly signals dishonesty in job applicants when this 'sense' is properly identified and used under ideal conditions. Although the suspicions we formed by consulting this intuitive sense might serve as useful warning signs, they would not be a substitute for investigating the candidates' records and seeking direct evidence of dishonest conduct. Only an examination of the relevant facts could ascertain whether what we suppose is an accurate intuitive signal really is so.

Second, how should we regard the consciences of others? Here, again, it is clear that the popular conception, if true, would give us some reason to encourage others to develop and listen to their consciences and to tolerate their conscientious acts within limits. However, we should be cautious in trusting the appearance of conscience, for others are presumably just as subject as we are to self-deception in identifying conscience, and besides, they may intentionally deceive us about what they really believe. Again, when opinions differ, a check seems needed, for how can we reasonably believe another's claim that what he or she is following is really an instinctual 'sense' of moral right and wrong, rather than an instinct of another kind, unless the person can give plausible moral reasons for thinking that what 'the voice' recommends is right?

From a Kantian perspective, the popular religious conception is untenable for several reasons. First, it draws conclusions about ethics from theology, whereas Kant insisted that whatever reasonable beliefs we can have about God must be based on prior moral knowledge, not the reverse. Second, the popular view of conscience as instinctual access to God's mind or will omits (what the Kantian takes to be) the prior and indispensable roles of reason and judgment in determining what we ought to do. For Kantians, what is morally required is ultimately a matter of what free and reasonable people, with a proper respect for one another, would agree to accept as a constraint on the pursuit of self-interest and other goals. That is not the sort of thing that we could claim to know directly 'by instinct.' Once we have a basic grasp of the reasons for moral principles and acknowledge their authority because of this, our respect for the principles may be signaled by unbidden 'pangs' and 'proddings' that feel like instinctual responses. But from the Kantian perspective, what should make us count these as signs of conscience is the plausibility of seeing the feelings as due to the agent's internal acceptance of what he or she judges to be reasonable moral principles.

Third, the popular religious conception regards the voice of conscience—when it has been identified as authentic—to be a completely reliable, even infallible, reflection of moral truth, but Kantian ethics (rightly, I think) rejects the idea that there is any way we can infallibly judge the morality of particular acts. Although Kant himself had confidence that reason could provide certainty regarding basic principles and many substantive duties, the basic Kantian view of moral deliberation and judgment, as I understand it, leaves more room for uncertainty and error than Kant allowed regarding specific moral questions. The reason is that in the Kantian view, moral deliberation and judgment are processes by which we try to identify choices that we could justify to all other reasonable persons, and the processes require subtle application of fundamental moral principles to empirical circumstances that are often uncertain and only partially understood.[12]

II. MERE INTERNALIZED SOCIAL NORMS

Those who cannot accept theological accounts of the origin and function of conscience often adopt an extreme cultural relativist conception, perhaps because they assume this to be the only secular alternative.[13] The term *relativism* is, of course, used loosely to refer to many different ideas, but what I mean by 'an extreme cultural relativist conception' of conscience (or ECR, for short) sees the promptings of conscience as nothing but feelings (1) that reflect our internalization of whatever choice-guiding, cultural norms we have internalized and (2) that serve to promote social cohesion by disposing individuals to conform to group standards. This conception replaces the theological story about the origin and function of conscience with a contemporary sociological hypothesis, but more radically, it goes beyond this empirical hypothesis by claiming that conscience reflects 'nothing but' whatever cultural choice-guiding norms we have internalized. That is, ECR is actually a combination of (1) a widely accepted causal explanation of the genesis and social function of the feelings ascribed to 'conscience' and (2) the controversial philosophical thesis that what is called *conscience* is not, even in the best case, a mode of access to moral truth, knowledge, or objectively justifiable moral beliefs.

What I call *conceptions* of conscience are complexes of beliefs

---

[12] Kant, as we shall see, does at one point claim conscience to be infallible, but there is a catch. It is not an infallible guide to objective moral truth, but only an (allegedly) infallible judgment that we violated our own principles or failed to exercise due care and diligence in moral judgment.

[13] Types of relativism are usefully distinguished in Richard Brandt, *Ethical Theory* (Englewood Cliffs, NJ: Prentice-Hall, 1959), ch. 11, pp. 271–94; William Frankena, *Ethics*, 2nd edn. (Englewood Cliffs, NJ: Prentice-Hall, 1973), ch. 6, esp. 109–10; and James Rachels, *The Elements of Moral Philosophy* (New York: Random House, 1986), 12–24. See also John Ladd (ed.), *Relativism* (Belmont, CA: Wadsworth, 1973); and David Wong, *Moral Relativity* (Berkeley and Los Angeles: University of California Press, 1984).

about how feelings of conscience come about, what purpose they serve, and how reliable they are as a guide to moral truth or well-justified moral belief. Accordingly, what I call ECR is not merely a view of the origin of conscience but also a view of its social function and reliability as a moral guide. Regarding origin, ECR explains the 'conscientious' person's feelings of constraint as due to a learning process by which he inwardly accepts local cultural norms as his standard of self-approval. Regarding function, ECR sees the development of conscience as a way by which social groups secure a measure of conformity to their standards without relying entirely on external rewards and punishments. Regarding reliability, ECR holds that although conscience reliably reflects the local norms that we have taken up from our environment, there is no objective standard by which we can ever determine that some cultural norms, but not others, are morally 'true' or 'justified.'

To avoid misunderstanding, I must stress that this second conception of conscience, the ECR, is not merely the scientist's refusal, as a matter of methodology, to include moral judgments and metaethical doctrines as a part of scientific theory. That attitude, in fact, is one that advocates of other conceptions of conscience may well applaud. Also, ECR is much more than an empirical hypothesis about the origin and social function of feelings attributed to conscience. If it were just that, it would be compatible with a variety of theories about moral justification and truth, including contemporary Kantian theories that disassociate themselves from certain aspects of Kant's metaphysics.[14]

Moral theory is not science, of course, but any moral theory that is worthy of contemporary support should, in my opinion, at least be compatible with empirical explanations regarded as well established in the current scientific community. What especially distinguishes ECR from the other three conceptions reviewed here is its deflationary stance regarding the nature and justifiability of moral beliefs, which is a

---

[14] It is not obvious whether Kant himself could have consistently accepted the particular empirical account that I attribute to ECR, although it is clear that he rejected its 'nothing but' thesis. Kant was deeply committed to the idea that all 'phenomena,' including those associated with human thought and action, are in principle subject to empirical causal explanations when viewed as natural occurrences from a scientific point of view. He also insisted that the same, or corresponding, phenomena related to human action can be 'thought' under practical 'ideas' of free will, rational justification, and so forth when one considers them from an irreducibly different perspective needed to make sense of morality. Many, if not most, contemporary Kantian moral theorists, I think, accept the validity of both the empirical and the practical perspectives but want to reconcile them without Kant's 'transcendental idealism.'

position reached only by a giant step beyond empirical explanation into an area of perennial philosophical controversy.

Returning now to the main task of describing the ECR and its implications, I should note that like my first (theological) conception, the ECR also treats conscience as something experienced as an instinctual feeling rather than as a deliberate judgment about how basic moral principles apply to particular circumstances.[15] Briefly, the picture is something like the following: The origin of conscience is largely early socialization, resulting in cultural norms being so deeply internalized that we respond to them for the most part without thinking about them. The 'voice' of conscience is a felt discomfort, analogous to 'cognitive dissonance,' generated by a conflict between our (perhaps unarticulated) awareness of what we are doing and a cultural norm that we have internalized.[16] The discomfort is a signal not that an objectively true moral principle has been violated or threatened but merely that we are about to step across some line that early influences have deeply etched on our personality. As cultures differ, then, we expect variations in what consciences disapprove. And even when we find uniformities, we regard them merely as signs that different cultures have some common social needs and processes, not that we have discovered universal moral truths.[17]

What are the implications of ECR regarding the attitude we should take toward our own conscience? If ECR is true, virtually everyone will spontaneously feel that certain acts are 'bad' and 'worthy of disapproval,' but how should an informed and reflective person who accepts ECR regard these feelings and respond to them? Clearly, these feelings should be seen for just what they are (according to ECR), namely, a fairly reliable sign that some past, present, or anticipated action of our own violates some cultural norm that we have internalized. The result is that we can expect to experience further internal discomfort and to incur the disapproval of others if we continue acting as before (or as planned). These expectations give a prudent person a self-interested

---

[15] It shows itself in a 'sense,' often painful, that something that one has done, is doing, or is about to do is wrong and blameworthy; it has motivational force; and people are inclined, at least initially, to treat their own consciences as authoritative, a reliable sign of something deeper and more important than mere customs or personal preferences.

[16] See Gilbert Ryle, 'Conscience', *Analysis*, 7 (1940), 31–9. This is reprinted with other discussions of conscience in John Donnelly and Leonard Lyons (eds.), *Conscience* (New York: Alba House, 1973), 25–34.

[17] Virtually all complex societies consist of various subcultures, which may instill somewhat different norms in their participants. This accounts for variations and conflicts of conscience, but it does not alter the fundamental story.

reason to 'heed conscience.' And if a person's culture's norms serve socially useful purposes, that person would have some altruistic reason to obey the promptings of 'conscience.' On the other side, however, those who accept ECR also have reason to try to 'see through,' dispel, or discount the feeling that to violate conscience would be 'wrong,' 'immoral,' or 'unreasonable' by any objective, culturally independent standard. Moreover, when the rewards of acting against conscience outweigh the unpleasantness of residual guilt feelings and predictable social disapproval, then the smart thing to do, believing ECR, would presumably be to stifle conscience or, if need be, simply tolerate the discomfort it causes in order to gain the greater rewards.

If we accept ECR, how are we to view the consciences of others? Since a person with a conscience is liable to suffer inwardly when contravening it and this normally serves as a deterrent, we have a self-interested reason to be pleased when others' consciences discourage behavior that we dislike. Moreover, insofar as we are concerned for the others, we should be glad when their consciences prompt social conformity that is useful to them, but otherwise we should merely pity them for their unnecessary inhibitions and needless suffering.[18]

Kantians obviously reject some features of ECR, but not necessarily all. It is important not to mislocate the major disagreement. Despite what some might suppose, it is arguable that the ECR's empirical hypothesis about the development of conscience, or some similar empirical account, should pose no special problem for the Kantian perspective.[19] The main deep point of disagreement concerns ECR's denial of objective standards of moral reasoning and judgment. This denial is often mistakenly thought to be a logical consequence of the empirical hypothesis, but as the philosophical literature on relativism repeatedly points out, the empirical observations that cultural standards differ and that people tend to internalize their local standards do not, by themselves, prove anything about objectivity in morals or any other field.

---

[18] If obedience to conscience is essential to our sense of integrity and self-respect, then, other things being equal, we should no doubt want to encourage them to act conscientiously. But according to ECR, conscience is not something to be especially treasured, protected, and tolerated, at least not for the reasons suggested by the popular conception—that conscience is God-given, that it signals moral truth and motivates moral conduct, and that even if mistaken, those who try to follow it are obeying a divine/moral imperative (to follow their conscience to the best of their ability).

[19] Contemporary Kantians who reject certain aspects of Kant's metaphysics should expect that the development of conscience can be explained empirically, and in my opinion, there is no need to deny that conscience requires certain cultural contexts in which to develop.

Objectivity, whether in normative or descriptive matters, is not constituted simply by de facto agreement. By the same token, objectivity is not necessarily undermined by de facto disagreement.[20] The issues are more complicated than that and obviously cannot be resolved here, one way or the other. The point of mentioning the issue now is just to stress that although there remains an unresolved disagreement between ECR and the Kantian perspective, the main point at issue is a long-standing, many-sided controversy about moral objectivity (truth, justification, etc.). It is not a debate about whether the feelings attributed to conscience are empirically explicable and tend to reflect social influences that vary from culture to culture.

There is another, more minor difference between ECR and the other conceptions of conscience, including Kant's. This has to do with terminology. ECR, as presented here, treats 'conscience' as a broad descriptive term, covering felt responses to any action-guiding standard internalized in a culture. Having such a broad, evaluatively neutral term to refer to similar phenomena in different cultures is probably useful, for example, as a term of art in comparative anthropological studies. However, I suspect that the term *conscience* is commonly used more narrowly than this. At least the cultural norms attributed to conscience are usually assumed to be 'moral' norms, in a broad sense of 'moral' that contrasts with the norms attributed only to a society's laws, customs, religious rites, or code of etiquette or to specific club rules, gang taboos, prudential maxims, and the like.[21] This point could be accommodated in a more sophisticated cultural relativist (SCR) conception of conscience simply by stipulating that 'conscience' refers to our felt responses to the moral (as opposed to merely legal, customary, etc.) norms that we have internalized from our culture. To call norms 'moral' in this (weak) sense does not imply that the norms are 'true,'

---

[20] It should be noted, to avoid misunderstanding, that the Kantian perspective that I sketch is concerned not with actual, or *de facto*, agreement in the moral opinions of people across the world and history but, rather, with the regulative ideal of what free, reasonable, and mutually respectful people (defined in a certain way) would agree to if they were 'legislating' moral principles (under certain ideal conditions). This theory is subject to many objections, but not that it reduces objectivity to actual contingent agreement in people's moral opinions.

[21] For example, see the distinctions drawn by H. L. A. Hart, *Concept of Law* (Oxford: Clarendon Press, 1961), 163–80; and Kurt Baier, *The Moral Point of View* (Ithaca, NY: Cornell University Press, 1958). To say that the concepts of a group's 'custom,' 'law,' and so on differ from the concept of the group's 'moral' beliefs is not, of course, to deny either that the same prohibitions may belong to several categories or that the borders between categories are often fuzzy.

'correct,' or 'objectively justifiable,' and so a kind of neutrality would be maintained, even though the cases attributed to 'conscience' would be somewhat limited.

I conjecture, however, that even this broad, neutral sense of 'conscience' (SCR) differs in another respect from the narrower, more normative senses of conscience found in ordinary discourse and the other conceptions. If so, this is not in itself an objection to SCR, but to avoid confusion, the difference should be noted. What I suspect is that apart from social science, the term *conscience* is typically used in a partially laudatory sense or tone, implying or expressing the speaker's limited endorsement of the source, if not the content, of the beliefs he or she attributes to conscience. My speculation here can be put in either cognitivist or expressivist terms. That is, when we attribute a person's reluctance to act in a certain way to that person's 'conscience,' then typically either (1) we express an (endorsing) belief about the source of that person's reluctance—that is, that it is generally a reliable sign of what is objectively wrong for that person to do—or (2) we express an (endorsing) attitude toward the source—that is, approval of treating it as a guide generally to be followed. If so, the partial approval (commonly) expressed when we speak of a person's 'conscience' would explain why it sounds a bit odd (or not intended literally) when someone, outside anthropology class, says that Himmler's conscience told him to keep gassing Jews despite his momentary sympathy for them. If, as I suspect, Himmler's norms were fundamentally vicious, self-serving, and subversive of morality, then any bad feelings he may have had when thinking about violating them do not deserve to be called *pangs of conscience* in the usual (partially laudatory) sense.

Similarly, I suspect that Mark Twain had his tongue in his cheek when he attributed to 'conscience' Huck Finn's 'guilty' feelings about helping the slave, Jim, to escape. If it seems odd to say that Huck's conscience made him feel guilty for helping Jim, this may be because we suppose Huck was moved by a genuine (but not articulated) moral reason for helping him. By contrast, we suppose that Huck's reluctance to help Jim reflected no comparable moral commitment, only his having been socialized in an evil system.[22] Given the ways the word *conscience* commonly

---

[22] It is important to distinguish Huck Finn from others who may have had sophisticated, though gravely misguided, moral defenses of the slave system. Huck is described as going through the motions of considering 'reasons' and feeling (painfully) that the reasons would show that he 'should' in some sense not help Jim escape, but I still see it as more plausible to suppose that young Huck internalized his culture's attitudes without

expresses approval, the description of Huck seems paradoxical; it is as if we are told that the 'good' source of moral feelings in Huck is condemning him for doing what his (genuinely good) sense of humanity impels him to do. The oddity reflects the fact that we take the feelings we attribute to conscience as more worthy of attention than the feelings we would describe as merely responses to social upbringing. As perhaps the author intended, the paradox reminds us that far from being a sure sign of wrongdoing, the discomfort experienced in violating cultural norms may be nothing but an unfortunate side effect of doing what is really only decent and humane.

The endorsing function of the word *conscience* should not be exaggerated, however, for in many cases we acknowledge that others' 'consciences' prompt them to do what they think is morally right but what we consider extremely wrong. For example, I might say this of the Inquisitors who ordered heretics burned at the stake if their reasons and motives were convincingly 'moral' ones (e.g., saving the heretics from eternal torture) but applied in conjunction with false empirical and theological beliefs (e.g., burning them was necessary to that end). Alan Donagan believed that utilitarianism was deeply misguided, but he did not deny that people could sincerely follow consciences shaped ('corrupted') by utilitarian standards. Generally, given the common core concept of conscience, those who accept any of our four particular conceptions of conscience should be able to understand much of what others are saying when they speak of conscience.

Still, those who accept a particular normative conception of conscience tend to hold back the usual endorsing connotations of the term, or to cancel them partially, when describing others whom they suspect are making grave moral mistakes. That is, when we suppose that others are sincerely following their moral beliefs but doing what (we believe) is grossly immoral, we are inclined to say 'it was false (corrupt, not genuine) conscience that told him to do that.' Alternatively, we may say, 'You might describe them as conscientious in a sense, but those crimes couldn't have been prompted by conscience as I understand it.'[23]

much thought and that his more humane, moral sense was awakening through his friendship with Jim. Huck had to lie and cross the wishes of his elders to help Jim, but his history did not reveal him as someone with a deep commitment to moral ideals of truth-telling and obedience to adult rules.

For a different view of the 'consciences' of both Huck Finn and Heinrich Himmler, see Jonathan Bennett's challenging essay, 'The Conscience of Huckleberry Finn', *Philosophy*, 49 (1974), 123–34.

[23] These remarks about how those who have a particular normative conception of 'conscience' may speak of those who do not share their conception are in response to

III. REASON REFLECTING IN A COOL HOUR

In his *Fifteen Sermons* (1651) Joseph Butler articulated a conception of conscience as reflective moral judgment. Although as an Anglican bishop, Butler had theological beliefs that he thought supported his conception of conscience, in the *Sermons* he explicitly set himself the task of developing ethics from an empirical understanding of human nature.[24] Human nature, he argued, consists of several faculties, which have an organizing 'constitution' that determines their proper functions and relations.[25] The main aspects of human nature are particular passions, self-love, benevolence, and conscience. *Particular passions* are desires and aversions, loves and hates, for particular objects or events.[26] *Self-love* is a more sophisticated, higher-order desire for the satisfaction of a set of other desires, conceived as our 'happiness.' *Benevolence*, too, involves the desire to satisfy other desires, for it is the disposition to care about the happiness of others.[27]

---

the worry expressed by my commentators that, by my initial account, Kantians would have to say that only Kantians can have consciences. To say this would be a mistake. Clearly, using the broad core concept, we can be quite inclusive in attributing conscience, and those who hold one conception (e.g., Kantian) can acknowledge that anyone who lacks a conscience as Kantians conceive it may still have 'a conscience' as conceived in some other way. As long as we specify what we mean to attribute, we can understand one another, and there is no profit for moral theorists to haggle over who has exclusive title to the honorific term.

[24] From this perspective, he argued that observation of human conduct, properly described in plain English, was in conflict with the cynical views of human motivation expressed by Thomas Hobbes and Bernard Mandeville. Self-love is not, and indeed conceptually could not be, the only concern that moves us. Benevolence, conscience, and particular passions influence and sometimes override self-love. Other British moralists, Butler thought, underestimated the moral significance of self-love and too readily concluded that moral concern is simply concern for the general welfare. See Joseph Butler, *Five Sermons*, ed. Stephen L. Darwall (Indianapolis: Hackett Publishing Co., 1983).

[25] Butler did not pretend to describe human nature in evaluatively neutral terms. More like Plato than Hume, he freely speaks of the purposes for which faculties are 'designed,' always with the assumption that we thrive better as individuals and as a community when each faculty serves its function in a way judged by reason to be appropriate to the whole.

[26] Some are intrinsic, such as to solve a puzzle, to taste a cookie, or to help an injured bird, and some derivative, such as desires for tools, money, or medicine. Particular passions may be good or bad, inner-directed or outer-directed.

[27] These basic dispositions exist in different people to different degrees, Butler thought. How to express them suitably may, to some extent, differ according to this and other contextual features. Although all our basic dispositions are good, unless properly supervised they may pull us in different directions and result in immoral and destructive behavior.

The supervisory faculty, Butler says, is *conscience*.[28] He refers here to our capacity to deliberate reasonably before acting and taking proper account of our nature, circumstances, options, estimated consequences, and certain (supposedly obvious) deontological constraints. Such deliberation requires a time of 'calm,' 'cool' reflection, and the result—our deliberative judgment—is neither purely intellectual nor purely sentimental but, rather, 'a sentiment of the understanding' and 'a perception of the heart.'[29] Conscience has a limited motivational power, but its authority is unchallenged.[30] The reason is that its verdicts are conceived as, all things considered, deliberative judgments of our own reason, a faculty whose natural role is to supervise our conduct and direct us to a life that gives appropriate expression to all our basic natural dispositions. Based on this assumption, Butler argued that the recommendations of conscience, reasonable self-love, and reasonable benevolence coincide, even though they are conceptually distinct.[31]

In sum, Butler holds the following: (1) Conscience is in fact God-given but is recognizable as authoritative without its theological backing. (2) The voice of conscience is not a mysterious signal passively received ('heard') but, rather, is the verdict of our own active, reason-guided

---

[28] This is also described as 'the principle of reflection,' 'the moral faculty,' and 'reason.'

[29] Butler, *Five Sermons*, 69.

[30] That is, human nature is so constituted that anyone with a conscience is disposed to follow it, although sometimes we let other motives overpower it, and human beings with conscience take its judgments to reflect what they ought to do, all things considered, even when its demands are to give up some immediately pressing concern.

[31] More important to my present purposes, in arguing for this conclusion, Butler treats conscience as neither a power of pure 'rational intuition' nor the ability to deduce particular moral conclusions from abstract necessary 'principles of reason.' Admittedly, Butler does suggest that we have an unexplained (intuition-like?) grasp of deontological principles against deception, injustice, and unprovoked violence (*Five Sermons*, 70). But unlike those who identify moral judgment with rational intuition regarding particular cases, Butler seems to think that for the most part with conscience, we make reasoned judgments from a basic moral standard derived from natural teleology. The standard, admittedly vague but not empty, is that we should always do what is appropriate to the constitution of our human nature. That is, we must do what is 'fitting' for human beings, whose (empirically discerned) basic faculties have natural purposes and are related to one another in a structure that, if properly respected, leads to individual happiness and social harmony. Rationalistic natural law theorists agree with Butler that in moral judgment, reason applies general standards, but Butler's position also differs from theirs. For unlike classic natural lawyers, Butler is skeptical about the project of articulating necessary rational first principles of morals so that individuals need only apply them, more or less deductively, to their particular circumstances. When he keeps his theology to the side, Butler offers his basic moral standard as empirical, and he is under no illusion that it can be applied merely by subsuming particular cases under fully determinative general principles. Although Butler articulated this conception of conscience more thoroughly than anyone else I know of, certain main features of his idea, I think, are still widely shared.

judgment, accompanied by corresponding feeling. (3) Conscience does not simply deduce its conclusions from given determinate principles but, rather, is guided by the vague standard of whether our acts are 'fitting' or 'appropriate' to the situation, given our human nature as rational, desiring, self-loving, and yet also benevolent persons. (4) Conscience often motivates us and ought never to be contravened, but at times particular passions, self-love, and even love of others overpower it. (5) Because even small variations in the capacities and specific situations of individuals can matter, what conscience rightly tells one person may differ from what it rightly tells another who seems similarly situated. (6) Each person's conscience is a highly reliable, if not perfect, guide to what is morally required of him or her.[32] (7) Finally, conscience's approval or disapproval is not what makes acts objectively right or wrong, but it provides the agent with an (internally acknowledged) reason, as well as a motive, to do what he or she thinks right, and this is an important part of his or her sense of moral obligation.[33]

If we were to accept this Butlerian conception, what should our attitude be toward our own conscience? Obviously, we would have good reason to cultivate, inform, and guide our conduct by conscience, for conscience would be accepted as a reliable access to moral requirements, a reflection of our own best, reasonable judgment, and a liability to self-loathing if we flouted it. It represents our own reflective conviction about what is 'fitting' to do in the light of a realistic view of our situation and our nature as human beings.

The preceding two conceptions, seeing conscience as an instinctual or conditioned response, left their advocates room for doubts that called for independent, reasoned moral reflection. But in Butler's account, the voice of conscience is already the conclusion of our best, reasoned reflection. If other individuals or state or church authorities disagree with our

---

[32] Butler typically writes as if conscience is perfectly reliable, although he warns that his methodology is to describe the predominant tendencies of human nature, suggesting that allowing a few exceptions would not be incompatible with his main claims (*Five Sermons*, 32). He allows that we can corrupt our nature and then perhaps might live with vice without 'real self-dislike' (p. 18). We might take this to mean that conscience can lose its power to motivate, rather than its ability to distinguish right and wrong correctly. Whether conscience is a 'reliable guide' may also depend on how determined we are to consult it, for Butler often stresses our liability to self-deception, a tendency to 'avert the eyes of the mind' from what we could see if we were willing to look. What is clear is that Butler thought that at least for all practical purposes, we can and should treat our conscience, if consulted honestly and diligently, as a reliable guide to moral requirements.

[33] See Stephen Darwall, *The British Moralists and the Internal 'Ought'* (Cambridge: Cambridge University Press, 1995), 244–83, esp. 282–3.

initial judgment, then this is new information that may call for new reflection; but it remains information to be conscientiously reflected on, not a verdict that any person of conscience can blindly accept. From the point of view of a deliberating conscientious agent, the knowledge that others disagree with our initial moral judgments then becomes part of the description of the next problem we face, and the question is what we should do now. Others' disagreement may be a sign that our initial judgment was based on a self-deceptive picture of the facts or that we were too hasty or emotionally distracted in our initial deliberation. In either case, however, the check is a new use of conscience, not a decision to accept the authority of someone else's judgment over our own.

Perhaps certain public officials do have legitimate authority, in a sense, over an area of our conduct. In Butler's view, however, for us to have grounds to acknowledge their authority, we would have to conclude, in our own conscientious reflection, that given the particular situation (including their social role and their particular pronouncements), it is right for us to do what they command. Far from being a limitation on the moral authority of our conscience, this amounts to treating individual conscience as the ultimate source of the right of public authorities to expect obedience.

What, then, does Butler's account prescribe as a proper attitude toward the consciences of others? Insofar as we want others to conduct themselves morally, we should, other things being equal, favor whatever promotes the cultivation, protection, and employment of informed conscience by others. Although Butler does not discuss political matters, the point does have obvious political implications. He concedes, however, that anyone who claims to make a conscientious judgment may be self-deceived, and obviously others may try to deceive us by claiming to follow their consciences when they know this is not so. Therefore, we can find ourselves in situations in which our best conscientious judgment is that we must hinder, even by force, what another claims to be a conscientious act.[34] Each case of this sort must be judged in its own context.[35]

---

[34] In theory it could even be that one person's conscience tells her to thwart another's opportunity to follow his conscience, even though the second person *correctly* judged his instructions of conscience. Since what we ought to do, all things considered, can depend, among other things, on our social role and past commitments, there is no guarantee that two people, each acting correctly by conscience, will not oppose each other, even after each adequately understands the position of the other. In Butler's view, contrary to what some philosophers have maintained, 'A has a duty to X' does not entail for all others 'it is wrong to prevent A from X-ing.'

[35] Again, as suggested earlier, the fact that the conscientious judgments of other sincere and honest people sharply differ from our own should be grounds for self-doubt and

Four Conceptions of Conscience

From the Kantian perspective, a good feature of Butler's conception of conscience, compared with the previous ones, is that Butler's account promises to preserve the good name of conscience even among those who reject its theological supports.[36] It does so, however, primarily by identifying conscience with a natural capacity to determine our moral responsibilities in a reason-governed, reflective manner and to guide our conduct by these judgments. Conceiving of conscience in this way broadens its secular appeal, but it abandons some of the connotations that Kant and others accept as associated with conscience and as expressed in the familiar metaphors used to describe it.

What I have in mind is the notion that conscience is, in some ways, more like an immediate, instinctive response than the product of a long, careful, process of rational deliberation.[37] We are 'struck' by pangs of conscience; we 'find' ourselves suffering from a guilty conscience; and even when we are reluctant to engage in a moral assessment of our acts, it 'speaks,' 'demands,' 'warns,' 'prods,' 'forbids,' 'rebels,' and at times 'is revolted.' Explicit reflection and judgment seem neither necessary nor sufficient for us to experience the promptings of conscience. Often, it seems, we simply feel its inner demands or reprimands. In stressing this familiar aspect of conscience, Kant's conception, the popular religious conception, and the cultural relativist conception all seem more in line with common thinking than Butler's is.[38]

---

reconsideration. Such conflicts call for review of the relevant facts, for self-scrutiny to identify bias, for effort to counteract self-deception and wishful thinking; but in the end, after due reflection, we must rely on our own best judgment. Others may continue to disagree and may punish us for our conscientious act, but acting conscientiously, and only this, in Butler's view, is acting 'according to our nature' and in a way that warrants self-approval.

[36] I am not arguing here that a theory that 'preserves the good name of conscience' independently of theology is necessarily better than one that does not, for I have not attempted to refute ECR, SCR, or the alleged theological underpinnings of the religious conception. Some may accept the various implications I have noted and yet hold that the claims of conscience should be deflated or, alternatively, that they should be retained in a religious context; and I have not argued otherwise.

[37] I am reminded of a story once related by Gilbert Ryle. A professor of mathematics was laying out a proof and, moving from one step to another, remarked, 'It's obvious that this follows.' A student put his hand up and asked, 'Excuse me, sir, but is it obvious?' The professor then set about to check his move and in the process covered two more boards with an elaborate proof and then at the end remarked. 'Yes, see, it is obvious.' In some ways, 'my conscience tells me' is like 'it is obvious'; it makes a claim to justifiability but is not itself the product of a process of deliberate justification. (If the story is funny, it is because although the professor established the truth of the proposition that he had said was obvious, his elaborate proof could not show that 'it is obvious.' Similarly, by means of moral argument, one can back up a claim regarding the voice of conscience, but the argument does not show that 'conscience said so.')

[38] Reflecting the ordinary sense of our moral terms, I take it, is a prima facie, but by no means decisive, consideration for including a particular conception (e.g., of

From a contemporary (modified) Kantian perspective, there are other problems with Butler's account. For example, it rests on the foundational assumption that as a matter of natural teleology, our particular passions, self-love, benevolence, and reason are structured in a normative hierarchy that assigns to each a place and a function.[39] Again, like Plato and Aristotle, Butler is more inspiring than convincing in his teleological argument that human nature is so constituted that reasonable self-love never recommends injustice. Few would dispute Butler's ideas that moral judgment, at its best, requires the use of reason in wide-ranging, honest reflection 'in a cool hour' and that it should take into account human nature, our individual capacities, and the facts of our situation. But to distinguish moral from other forms of deliberation and perhaps to reach any definite conclusions at all, we need a fuller account of what we are deliberating about, what we are looking for, and what criteria or constraints in such deliberation make its outcome morally binding.

IV. A JUDGE IN AN INNER COURT

Let us turn now to Kant's idea of conscience as judicial self-appraisal.[40] Butler identified *conscience* as the faculty by which we make moral judg-

---

conscience) in our moral theory. An entirely revisionary moral theory is unlikely even to get a hearing, but there are many possible considerations for not automatically adopting current (or even persistent) 'common sense.' For example, it may presuppose what is contrary to (not just beyond) our best scientific knowledge.

[39] Readers will recall that Kant, too, often appeals to (dubious) teleological claims in applying his fundamental principles, but the basic argument for the Categorical Imperative does not rest on these assumptions. It would be contrary to his idea of autonomy to suppose that at the basic level, one might argue for morality from natural teleology.

[40] I assume some basic points, including the following: The principal elements of human nature relevant to moral judgment are *sensuous inclinations*, *reason*, and *will*. The first category includes all ordinary desires and aversions, second-order (e.g., the desire for happiness) as well as first-order ('particular passions'), self-regarding (self-love) as well as other-regarding (benevolence), cultivated desires for pleasures of the mind as well as instinctual cravings for pleasures of the body. Such inclinations are passive, given facts, not the sort of thing we can control at will, and so in themselves are neither good nor bad. Their value neutrality, I think, is Kant's dominant view, despite some unfortunate passages, reminiscent of Plato, about how rational beings wish to be rid of them. Viewed from a practical standpoint, they are presumed to incline but not determine our behavior. *Will*, in one sense, is a power of choice, enabling us to deliberate and 'freely' choose which inclinations, if any, to incorporate into our maxims. *Will* in another sense is the same as *practical reason*. This includes our capacity and disposition, to follow hypothetical imperatives in taking means to our ends, and to recognize and follow cate-

ments, but what Kant calls *conscience* is something distinct that can come into play only after one has made, or accepted, a moral judgment.[41] Moral judgments are simply applications of basic moral requirements (the 'moral law') to more specific circumstances. These basic requirements, articulated in the forms of the Categorical Imperative, are supposed to be part of the rational knowledge of all ordinary moral agents, even though nonphilosophers may not be able to articulate them in their pure abstract form.[42]

gorical imperatives in morally significant situations. Practical reason is a broad term that sometimes includes the functions of conscience, namely, passing judgment on ourselves for acting against our judgment as to what is right (or without sufficient effort to determine what was right) or 'acquitting' ourselves from self-accusations of such guilt.

Kant treats practical reason not merely as a source of abstract truths but as a set of dispositions to govern ourselves in accord with certain norms of decision making. To have practical reason is to be predisposed to deliberate and choose our courses of action in accord with the rational norms expressed in the Categorical Imperative (various forms) and the Hypothetical Imperative (the general principle behind reasoning to particular hypothetical imperatives, namely, 'If one wills an end and finds certain means to that end necessary and available, then one ought to take [will] those means or abandon the end.'). I discuss this general principle in *Dignity and Practical Reason*, chs. 1 and 7.

This is not a stipulative definition of 'practical reason' for Kant, nor does he think it is 'analytic' that practically rational wills accept the forms of the Categorical Imperative. Nonetheless he thinks the point can be argued, at least that it can be shown to be a presupposition of our belief that we have moral duties that we are committed to the Categorical Imperative (in all its forms) and to viewing this as a 'command of reason.' These basic 'rational' dispositions are unavoidable, demanding, and sometimes painful to live by. They are not seen as something unfortunate, alien, or to be resisted but, rather, as basic self-defining norms and so, as it were, imposed on ourselves by ourselves (our 'better self' perhaps). Although not an empirically attributed desire or set of inclinations, practical reason (like these) is a constant and potentially effective element of human motivation. It is attributed to moral agents a priori because analysis (supposedly) reveals it to be a necessary precondition of having duties and obligations, and even of making moral judgments. Moral feelings, such as respect for moral law, are analyzed as the consequences of recognition of how this basic moral/rational disposition can conflict with our inclinations. We can, of course, question Kant's claim that the norms expressed in the Categorical Imperative are necessary principles of reason, but the fact that we are committed to them as authoritative is the essential background assumption that enables us to think of conscience and conscientious judgment as having motivating force.

[41] 'Judgment' is ambiguous in many of the passages on conscience. In one sense it refers simply to drawing more specific conclusions from general moral principles, that is, 'applying' them as when we conclude that 'one mustn't spit in another's face' from 'one ought to respect every person.' In *Lectures on Ethics*, tr. Louis Infield (New York: Harper & Row, 1963), 129, Kant refers to this as 'the logical sense,' as opposed to the 'judicial sense.' The latter is the sort of judgment made by a legal judge who 'condemns or acquits,' sentences, and 'gives legal effect to his judgment.' See also R, 178–9 [6: 185–6].

[42] Intermediate-level principles, articulated in Kant's *The Metaphysics of Morals*, are supposed to be derivable from the basic requirements, together with some general empirical facts about the human condition. The rational capacity to apply the Categorical Imperative and intermediate principles to specific cases, which is judgment (in one sense),

According to Kant, ordinary people normally judge quite well whether their acts are right or wrong, and they do so without much conscious, explicit reflection. However, if subject to strong temptations and confused by philosophical sophistries, they are apt to try to make self-serving exceptions to rules that they generally acknowledge as universal.[43] The result is that although every moral agent is presumed to have an adequate grasp of the fundamentals of the moral point of view, errors of judgment are possible. Obviously, errors of fact, culpable or not, can lead us to a judgment that we would not make if we had a correct, realistic view of our circumstance. But this is not the only source of mistake. Inattention, wishful thinking, and self-deceptive special pleading all can result in misapplications of moral principles that, in the abstract, we know well enough. Presumably, too, we might come to have unjustifiable moral opinions without making any direct judgments of our own, for example, by simply accepting the prevailing standards in our culture or placing complete reliance on the moral judgment of some other person.[44]

These errors of moral judgment, however, do not amount to an erring conscience. In fact, conscience has yet to enter the picture. What, then, is conscience? There are puzzling features about Kant's remarks on conscience, and there seem to be some changes among Kant's several works, but we can summarize the main points as follows:[45]

is not some mysterious special access to moral truth but simply an ability to interpret the principles, perceive relevant features of one's particular circumstances, and arrive at a specific directive by subsuming the case at hand under the principles.

See G, 71–2 [4: 404]. Kant here treats 'judgment' in moral matters as analogous to judgment regarding science and ordinary matters of fact, that is, as the capacity to apply general principles and concepts to more specific circumstances. In writing about conscience as the inner 'judge,' however, the sense is different, the model being a legal judge passing sentence on an accused or acquitting him or her.   [43] Ibid.

[44] We can distinguish, then, these possible sources of mistaken moral beliefs: (a) one makes no moral judgments for oneself but blindly takes on the mistakes of one's adviser or one's culture; (b) one judges badly, or misjudges, what follows from the basic moral law because one is inattentive, careless, and/or self-serving in the process of judgment (implicit or explicit); and (c) one misperceives, or fails to consider as relevant, facts about one's situation that are in fact morally important. Like most moral philosophers in his tradition, Kant did not acknowledge radical ignorance or misunderstanding of the basic moral law as a further source of mistaken moral belief. The errors here are presumably failures to exercise due care in self-scrutiny. Consider, for example, MM, 191 [6: 441]. His theory can allow (even if Kant himself did not) that there might be adult, functioning members of our species who do not know or understand what Kant calls the moral law, but then their norms, if any, would be amoral and their applications of them not erroneous moral judgments but, rather, judgments of some other kind.

[45] Notably there are shifts from Kant's *Lectures on Ethics*, to *The Metaphysics of Morals*, to *Religion within the Boundaries of Mere Reason*. See MM, 160–1 [6: 400–1], 188–91 [6: 438–40], and R, 178–9 [6: 185–6]. There are places where Kant seems to

1. All moral agents have consciences. The belief that this is so is not based simply, or mainly, on observation. Rather, that someone has a conscience is a presupposition of his or her being a moral agent. Moral agency also presupposes practical reason, but practical reason is a broader concept. It includes our capacity and disposition to acknowledge the moral law and to apply the moral law through 'judgment.' But neither of these is identical with conscience.

2. Conscience is mostly described in metaphorical terms, but the metaphors can be unpacked. Conscience is 'an inner judge' that issues verdicts of acquittal or condemnation. Like a trial judge, who is not legislating or merely informing others about the law, conscience 'imputes,' 'reproaches,' and passes 'sentence.' If it judges us to be guilty, we are made to suffer, and at times the result can be torment. The verdict of acquittal brings relief but not happiness. Although the inner 'forum' of conscience is not a real court, we must think of ourselves as playing several roles: that of accuser, defender, and finally a judge who yields a verdict and passes sentence. The metaphor requires that we think of ourselves from different perspectives, but it is important that it also be the same person who accuses and who stands accused. We can also think of conscience as demanding accountability to God, but this is a 'subjective' construal rather than an essential feature of conscience.[46]

3. Although the metaphors suggest that the moral agent is active in the operations of conscience, Kant also describes conscience as like an 'instinct,' as something that we 'find' in ourselves, something that we 'hear' even when we try to run away, and something that 'speaks involuntarily and inevitably.'[47] The point, I think, is to distinguish conscience—as the often painful self-accusation, guilty verdict, and consequent suffering—from the general activities of moral deliberation, reasoning, and judgment. Conscience presupposes and makes use of these activities and thus is not (as in the popular conception) a mere felt clue or symptom that we have done wrong or are about to.

Like a well-grounded judicial verdict and sentence, the 'voice' of conscience imposes a painful awareness of two distinguishable things: (1) that what we have done (or intend to do) is at odds with what, even in

---

use 'conscience' broadly, like Butler, for our capacity to determine whether our acts are right or wrong by applying the basic moral law to them. See, for example, G, 79 [4: 411–12] and 89–90 [4: 422–3].

[46] Carrying the metaphor to an extreme, Kant writes, 'Only the descent into the hell of self-knowledge can prepare the way for godliness' (MM, 191 [6: 441] and 188–9 [6: 438]).

[47] See Kant, *Lectures* (tr. Infield), 129; MM, 65–6 [6: 282–3] and 26–7 [6: 234].

our own judgment, is wrong in the circumstances and (2) that the act is fully imputable to ourselves as a free agent.[48]

In effect, conscience presupposes and uses the results of our general reasoning and judgment in answer to the question 'What sorts of acts, in what circumstances, are morally permissible, and what sorts are morally forbidden?' When we 'compare' or 'hold up' our past (or projected) acts (as we perceive these) to these answers (our general judgments about what is permissible and what is forbidden) and also realize that those acts are (or will be) imputable to ourselves as their 'free cause' (without excuse), then conscience imposes (or threatens) 'sentence,' that is, makes us (as the guilty party) feel bad and yet (as the sentencing judge) feel that the pain is warranted. Here we see that conscience, although working more like an instinct than a capacity for reasoned moral judgment, is not a mere instinct because it depends crucially on that basic capacity.

In *Religion within the Boundaries of Mere Reason*, when discussing 'the guide of conscience in matters of religious faith,' Kant introduces what seems to be a slight variation on this main theme. He first states a strict 'postulate of conscience' about prospective acts, namely, 'concerning the act I propose to perform I must not only judge and form an opinion, but I must be sure that it is not wrong.' This is a special, but quite broad, duty of due care; that is, we must undertake and diligently carry out a moral appraisal of our projected acts (presumably unless we are already sure, from previous appraisal, that the acts are permissible). Metaphorically speaking, 'judgment$_1$' (one sense of 'judgment') is what is responsible for appraising the act diligently, and 'conscience' then 'passes judgment$_2$' (a second sense of 'judgment') on judgment$_1$ as to whether it has fulfilled that responsibility. Paradoxically, then, conscience is 'judgment passing judgment upon itself.'[49] Thus the particular offense of which conscience accuses us is the failure to undertake seriously and carry out diligently a moral appraisal of our acts, a violation of the special duty of due care in making sure that one 'venture nothing where there is danger that it might be wrong.'[50]

---

[48] Also C2, 81–3 [5: 97–9]. See also Kant on imputation, MM, 16 [6: 223] and 19 [6: 227]. In German law, apparently, the two phases of determining whether an agent's act is a legal offense ('objective' guilt) and determining whether the act is 'imputable' to the agent (culpability) are more separate than in our legal system. See Joachim Hruschka, 'Imputation', *Brigham Young University Law Review* (1986), 669–710. A series of articles on imputation, particularly in Kant and in German law, appeared in *Jahrbuch für Recht und Ethik*, 2 (1994), ed. B. Sharon Byrd, Joachim Hruschka, and Jan C. Joerden (Berlin: Duncker & Humblot, 1994).

[49] R, 179 [6: 186].

[50] R, 178–9 [6: 185]. A puzzling passage in *The Metaphysics of Morals* also suggests that what conscience judges is simply 'whether I have submitted [my act] to my practi-

Four Conceptions of Conscience 303

The Metaphysics of Morals also includes something like this duty of due care, a duty to try to 'know (scrutinize, fathom) yourself.' This 'First Command of All Duties to oneself,' Kant says, requires impartiality in appraising ourselves 'in comparison with the law' and sincerity in acknowledging our 'inner worth or lack thereof.'[51]

In the light of this, we can perhaps put the two accounts of conscience together as follows: Conscience is an involuntary response to the recognition that what we have done, are doing, or are about to do is contrary to the moral judgments that we have made (by applying moral law to different types of circumstances). Prominent among the many moral judgments that persons of conscience will have made is that they have the special, second-order duty to submit their acts to the 'inner court' of conscience, scrutinizing them diligently, impartially, and sincerely. Once they submit their acts to appraisal, conscience gives its verdict and 'passes sentence' automatically, for this is just a metaphor for the painful awareness of wrongdoing that such sincere appraisal causes in a person with the basic dispositions of 'practical reason.' Combining Kant's two accounts, we can say that conscience can acquit or condemn with regard to accusations of both violations of first-order duties (e.g., truth telling) and failures to fulfill the second-order duty of due care in scrutinizing and appraising our acts diligently (by 'holding them up' to our judgment of the first-order duties). In both cases, conscience presupposes but is not the same as 'moral judgment' in the sense of 'drawing from the moral law a more determinate specification of our duties.'[52]

cal reason (here in its role as judge) for such a judgment' (MM, 160–1 [6: 400–1]). My best effort to untangle what Kant means there is that the relevance of 'whether I have submitted' is not literally that this is what conscience judges but that it is a background fact that one knows unmistakably and that is part of the suggested argument that conscience cannot err.

Roughly, that argument might be reconstructed as follows: If on the one hand, we did scrutinize our act by our moral standards, we would have known this easily by introspection, and if so, conscience would have 'involuntarily' reached its verdict and (if appropriate) imposed its sentence. Mistakes here are apparently assumed to be impossible because what we compare is all 'internal': our conception of our act and our moral judgment regarding its rightness or wrongness. But if we did not submit our act to our moral standards, we did not make any prior moral judgment on the particular act, and so our conscience (which presupposes such judgments) never operated and so cannot have yielded a false verdict. Mistakes due to bad memory of our past acts and/or deliberations, misjudgments of objective duty, self-deceived conceptions of our acts, and the like are not counted as errors of conscience but as failures antecedent to its operation.

[51] MM, 191 [6: 441].
[52] Presumably it is rare that we have a clean conscience with respect to due care but a guilty conscience with respect to first-order duties, for that would mean that despite the most diligent effort to ensure that our projected acts are not wrong, we nevertheless acted in a way that was wrong even in our own judgment. In other words, we weakly or perversely ignored the conclusion of our diligent search. Assuming this to be rare, we

4. Our judgment about whether certain acts are 'really' right or wrong can be mistaken, and so presumably our consciences may at times be working from mistaken premises regarding this. However, Kant claims that in a sense, conscience itself does not err.[53] Why he thinks this is not entirely clear, but perhaps the basic thought is that conscience is not liable to common 'external' sources of error that may infect ordinary moral judgment. For example, mistakes about the facts of our situation can lead us to make mistakes about what is objectively permissible, but they cannot cause us to err in regard to whether our act as we conceived it was contrary to our judgment about what is right. Mistaking a lost hiker for a moving target on a firing range can lead to the erroneous judgment that shooting at what we see is permissible, but this same misidentification does not mean that the act as intended (e.g., shooting at the target here) was contrary to our moral judgment about it (e.g., that shooting at the target here is permissible). Errors of conscience, if there were any, would have to be a matter of failing, even after we raised the question, to recognize either the fact that what we intentionally did was (or was not) against our best moral judgment or the fact that we had (or had not) exercised due care to determine whether our act was right. Perhaps, despite Kant, errors are possible even in these 'subjective' judgments, but the important point remains that in Kant's sense, even an unerring conscience is in no way a guarantee that what we believe is right is really so.

The implications of the Kantian conception regarding our attitude toward our own conscience should now be clear. Conscience is no substitute for moral reasoning and judgment but in fact presupposes these. A clear conscience is no guarantee that we acted in an objectively right way, and so it is no ground for self-righteous pride or presumption that our moral judgment is superior to that of those who conscientiously disagree. However, insofar as the warnings and pangs of conscience actually reflect our diligent efforts to hold our acts up to our best moral

can suppose that satisfying conscience in the *Religion* sense (due care) typically leads us to satisfy it in the prior sense of *The Metaphysics of Morals* (imputation and judicial judgment of first-order duty violations).

[53] Kant's remarks on this are puzzling. One crucial passage denying 'erring conscience' is MM, 161 [6: 401]. But in the much earlier *Lectures on Ethics*, 132–3, Kant acknowledges 'errors of conscience,' based on errors of fact or errors of law, some culpable, some not. Conscience can be 'natural' or 'instructed' (and apparently at times 'misinstructed'); the natural conscience takes precedence in cases that conflict. Again, however, Kant reaffirms that there can be no nonculpable errors about the basic moral law, that one can mistake something else (e.g., prudence) for conscience but cannot 'deceive' or 'escape' it.

judgments, conscience may be a reliable subjective sign of whether we are doing well relative to our moral beliefs. Conformity to conscience is necessary and sufficient for morally blameless conduct, in Kant's view, even though it cannot ensure correctness.[54] Thus as Kant says, conscience ought to be 'cultivated' and 'sharpened' as well as heeded. Our impartial moral judgments (about what anyone in various situations should do) will not affect our conduct unless they are applied to our own case and the acts in question are imaginatively 'imputed' to ourselves, which is a function of conscience. Again, past misdeeds often call for restorative acts in the present (apology, compensation, etc.), but it is conscience that makes us feel the force of our wrongdoing and thus presumably aids in the recognition of these duties.

How, then, should we view the consciences of others? Many of the same points apply, but there are some asymmetries. Although in moral debate, my appeal to conscience weighs no more than anyone else's, in the end I must heed my own conscience, not that of others. This is not to deny that the conscientious disagreement of others gives us grounds for questioning, listening to their reasons, consulting more widely, and rethinking our initial moral judgment. Also, knowing that others conscientiously disagree may itself be a reason for altering our judgment about what, all things considered, we should do, even if we are fully convinced that these others are mistaken. Here the fact of disagreement serves as new relevant information rather than grounds to suspect our earlier process of judgment. The same would apply if our initial moral judgment turned out to be contrary to legal authority. But in all these cases, our final responsibility is to heed our own consciences, which are based on our diligent effort to judge, all things considered, what is right.

Another asymmetry follows from Kant's view that the basic ends of a virtuous person are his own perfection and the happiness of others. Practical concern for others' happiness, not worries about their souls, should motivate us to avoid tempting others into activities that would cause them to suffer agonies of conscience. But concern for making ourselves morally more perfect, not concern for our own happiness, is what should move us to keep our own consciences clean.[55]

So far I have avoided discussing the content of Kant's moral law, but given more time, I would argue that Kant's idea of the moral law itself gives deep and compelling reasons for taking seriously the moral judgments of others, especially those who use their 'consciences' in sincere

---

[54] 'But if someone is aware that he has acted in accordance with his conscience, then as far as guilt or innocence is concerned nothing more can be required of him' (MM, 161 [6: 401]).   [55] See MM, 151–2 [6: 388].

and diligent self-appraisal. The main idea here is that Kant's basic moral point of view, expressed by the combination of forms of the Categorical Imperative, holds that moral standards are found by analyzing (rational) human willing. They are not perceived in Plato's heaven of Forms or derived from God's will or identifiable with any empirical facts (e.g., about human sympathies). Rather, they are constituted by what reasonable, autonomous persons ideally would 'legislate' for themselves, subject to certain constraints (conceptually) built into the idea of moral reflection. A crucial constraint is that all legislation must respect the value of humanity as an end in itself. This places a priority on our concerns as rational beings, forbids our thinking of human beings as exchangeable commodities, and, especially, puts forward an ideal that policies should be morally justifiable to all.

Kant, I think, had too much confidence that all who take up the moral perspective would reach agreement on moral principles. But in the face of disagreement about matters of vital moral importance, it is clear that his theory implies that the best each of us can do is, first, to make our own moral judgments about what we can sincerely recommend as reasonable to others who will take up the moral legislative point of view and, then, after duly consulting with others and giving due weight to their concerns, to act according to these judgments faithfully but with humility. Universal agreement would be a regulative ideal, perhaps constituting 'correctness' about what is 'objectively' right, but in practice this would only be an aim and a hope.

Given even this brief sketch, it should now be clear that consulting with others and taking into account their reasons for the moral judgments must be an important part of the Kantian process of moral deliberation. This speaks in favor of treating the moral judgments of others respectfully and also of creating the social conditions in which sincere and diligent efforts to make and apply moral judgments are encouraged. It does not support an absolute ban on coercing someone against his or her conscience, but it does urge respect for conscientious resistance even when we believe it is mistaken.

It was no accident, apparently, that Kant developed his special conception of conscience rather than simply incorporating one of the previous conceptions into his moral theory. To review, Kant's special conception fits his basic moral theory in several respects better than other conceptions would.

First, the Kantian conception, unlike the popular religious conception, is not based on theology, and so it is compatible with Kant's doctrine that ethics must precede religion. Moreover, the Kantian conscience reflects Kant's idea that only the use of reason can determine what is moral, for it denies the (popular) view that conscience is a mysterious, instinct-like access to truth about what is morally forbidden.

Second, as opposed to the relativistic conceptions, ECR and SCR, Kant's conception does not deny, but in fact presupposes, the possibility of objective moral judgments, which is a central tenet of Kant's moral theory. Also, ECR and SCR treat *conscience* as a descriptive, or evaluatively neutral, term, but Kantian moral theory would encourage the common practice of speaking of conscience in a partially laudatory way. The reason is that in the Kantian conception, pangs of conscience, unlike most pains, stem from a morally respect-worthy source, a deeply rooted disposition of moral agents to hold up their own conduct to the same moral judgments that they make for others in comparable situations.

Third, as opposed to Butler, Kant clearly avoids making natural teleology foundational for ethics and so avoids making what Kant regarded the mistake of founding morals on 'heteronomy.' Arguably, too, Kant has a more plausible and determinate idea of the standards that should guide reasonable moral reflection. Butler sees conscience as making rational, reflective judgments, but he gives very little hint of the premises from which we are to reason. In addition, Kant's conception of conscience is closer to common sense and ordinary language than Butler's, in that Kant treats conscience not as our general capacity to reflect morally regarding our acts but, rather, as a special disposition to 'find' ourselves involuntarily warning, accusing, and judging ourselves when we compare our acts (as we conceived them) with our moral judgments about the sorts of acts that are right and wrong.

Finally, the special Kantian conception of conscience promises to highlight and give a deep sense to the idea that a person who consistently follows her conscience is a person of integrity. Integrity has been viewed in different ways, of course, but in any sense, I suggest, persons who follow their conscience as understood in the previous conceptions may nonetheless lack a kind of integrity. For example, a person who followed the popular religious conception of conscience would, given his premises, be wise and prudent to do so because conscience is a sign of divinely sanctioned standards, but this seems no guarantee of genuine integrity. The latter presupposes not simply reliable, responsible public behavior but also self-governance by principles that one knowingly affirms for good reasons. One who regularly follows the mysterious 'inner voice' of popular conscience may do so from fear and with little understanding.

Similarly, those who follow conscience in the ECR or SCR sense would reveal a steady disposition to be governed by cultural norms internalized early in life, and this might lead to many of the patterns of public behavior and the freedom from inner conflict that we associate with persons of integrity. But unless they are to some degree critically reflective and selective regarding the local norms they endorse as adults, something important would be missing. They may rest content with cultural norms that encourage deception and manipulation of a sort incompatible with integrity, as commonly understood. And even if their internalized principles happen to be morally decent, they continue to hold them as blind conformists, with too little appreciation of the principles' grounds to qualify them for the virtue of integrity.

Finally, Butler's account of conscience relies so heavily on the alleged facts of natural teleology that even though Butler claims that a person following conscience is a 'a law to himself,' one might argue that his or her ultimate guide is the given 'constitution of human nature,' whose normativity seems to be accepted as a given natural fact, independently of the person's reflective, reasonable endorsement of it. Although this is sufficient for some sorts of integrity, arguably there is a deeper notion of integrity attributable to persons faithful to the Kantian conscience. The latter not only strive to make good moral judgments and govern themselves by their best moral judgments, but they also are supposed to follow a moral law that is itself a reflection of their own autonomous, rational will, not an acceptance of standards found 'in nature.' These notions obviously need interpretation and are subject to doubt, but they are suggestive. Insofar as 'integrity' has to do with being a principled, self-governed person, Kant's account of the conscientious person tries to carry this a step further than even Butler does.

A last caveat may help forestall misunderstanding. Although I have compared different conceptions of conscience partly to show the merits from a broadly Kantian perspective of the special conception that Kant adopted, I do not mean to deny or minimize the many problems with Kant's ethics that are not addressed here. Kant's conception of conscience is a part of his larger moral theory and so is not immune to familiar doubts about, for example, the adequacy of his formulas of the moral law, their alleged status as universal rational principles, and their apparent neglect of animals. Moreover, there are special doubts that one may raise about Kant's account of conscience. For example, even if Kant's metaphors of the accuser, defender, and judge reflect the phenomenology of moral experience for many of us, we may question whether the images stem from excessive preoccupation with legal models that are not essential to, or best for, understanding morality.

In our age we can hardly help but doubt Kant's faith in the universality of conscience. His best defense might be that analysis of 'common rational knowledge of morality' reveals possession of conscience (as Kant conceives it) as a precondition of full moral agency, that is, of being subject to duties conceived as categorical imperatives. But this analytic claim, too, may be doubted. Finally, Kant's ethics is most plausible when seen as a less comprehensive account of morality than he thought. Despite Kant's later work on virtue, his main focus from the beginning is on duty, or what one morally must do, and its presuppositions of freedom, respect for humanity, and the like. However, there are moral values and ideals not readily expressible in this framework, and so it seems there must be more to ethics than Kant acknowledged. Whether these values and ideals are incompatible with the basic Kantian theory has yet, in my opinion, to be worked out.

10

Wrongdoing, Desert, and Punishment

Contemporary Kantians emphasize positive aspects of Kant's moral theory that are appealing, even inspiring, to conscientious persons.[1] For example, Rawls stresses the idea that in acting justly we realize our nature as rational autonomous persons. He says that Kant's ethics should not be regarded as primarily an ethics of duty, but rather an ethics of self-esteem.[2] Others too highlight Kant's idea that we are most fully self-regulating and free when we willingly act from respect for the moral law without ulterior motives. Moral agents, it seems, do not need to be pushed, threatened, and manipulated to do what is right: they need only see the right clearly and exercise the power of will that we must presume they have. Moreover, our main moral duties as individuals with regard to others are to respect them, to honor their rights, and to promote their happiness, not to force them to be good or to make them suffer when they do wrong.[3]

With these upbeat messages ringing in their ears, readers may be surprised when they turn to what Kant says about punishment and conscience. Here a darker, less attractive picture of moral agents seems to be at work. Law, for example, is not to rely on citizens' respect for the legal system. Explicit sanctions for nonconformity, appealing to non-

---

My thoughts on the issues considered here owe much to Herbert Morris. Indeed, I owe more, philosophically and personally, to Morris than I can adequately convey. As a colleague and mentor during my early years at UCLA, he was an inspiring teacher and an invaluable friend. His subtlety, depth, patience, and gentle guidance have been a model for me as well as many others. In a time when philosophical debate was too often verbal warfare, he showed by example how richly different genuine philosophical investigation could be.

[1] My own project for some time has been to see how far Kant's basic moral theory, properly understood and modified as necessary, can be made plausible as at least a candidate for serious consideration in contemporary philosophical discussions. This requires, I think, sympathetic reconstruction and extension of certain core Kantian ideas but also critically abandoning some of Kant's ideas on particular issues that prove to be untenable and unwarranted by Kant's more basic theory.

[2] John Rawls, *A Theory of Justice* (Cambridge, MA: Harvard University Press, 1999), 225.

[3] MM, 147–56 [6: 383–94] and MM, 198–218 [6: 448–74].

moral motives, must be included in the laws.[4] Kant even suggests at one point that the law should be designed so that a race of devils could live in peace under it.[5] The rules of punishment are tough and inflexible: all the guilty must be punished, made to suffer the equivalent of the losses they inflicted, and there should be no pardon for public crimes.[6] Conscience, too, is far from a gentle whisper of moral encouragement.[7] It places us on trial for (perceived) moral failings, accuses us, passes sentence, and makes us suffer.

These two sides to Kant's theory are not strictly inconsistent, but the apparent tension between them invites us to reflect on how each should be understood and how they are related. This is the background context for my discussion here, but I will focus only on certain aspects of the larger issue. My main concern is with relations between *wrongdoing* and *suffering because of one's wrongdoing*. Utilitarians typically deny any necessary connection between these. That is, whether wrongdoers *will* suffer for their misdeeds is a contingent, empirical matter, depending largely on how others respond; and whether we *ought* to make wrongdoers suffer is also a contingent matter, depending on the consequences of doing so. Many have suspected that the utilitarian answer misses a deeper connection. For example, although retributivists grant that, theology aside, it is a contingent question whether wrongdoers *are actually likely to suffer* for their misdeeds, they see it as a moral necessity, independently of the consequences, that wrongdoers *ought to be made to suffer* in proportion to their offenses. What I call *deep retributivism* holds this as a fundamental principle, in need of no further justification. Kant is commonly taken to be a deep retributivist, but in fact there are compelling reasons to interpret his retributivism, at least in his most mature and systematic work, as contingent, limited, and justified (if at all) by principles of another kind. Kant does assume a necessary connection between wrongdoing and suffering at the core of his moral theory. The crucial thesis, however, concerns our liability to suffer in the recognition of our own misdeeds, not our right or duty to make others suffer for theirs. Kant's position, I think, has considerable merit, especially by comparison with the familiar alternatives; but my primary aim here is simply to present it as an intelligible and not implausible reconstruction of Kant's views.

---

[4] MM, 20-2 [6: 218-21].   [5] See PP, 112-23.
[6] See, for example, MM, 104-10 [6: 331-7].
[7] MM, 160-1 [6: 400-1] and MM, 188-9 [6: 438-40]; C2, 82-3 [5: 98-9]; R, 92-3 [6: 76-7], R, 145-6 [6: 144-6], and R, 178-80 [6: 185-7]; LE (tr. Heath), 88-9 [27: 297-8] and 130-5 [27: 351-7].

My plan is this. First, I make some distinctions to clarify the issues to be addressed and the thesis about Kant's theory that I want to defend. Second, I highlight features of Kant's conception of wrongdoing that imply that wrongdoers are necessarily liable to suffer because of their wrongdoing (*the intrinsic **liability** thesis*). Third, I argue that in saying that only the virtuous are worthy of happiness Kant did not endorse the deep retributive idea that we ought to make the vicious suffer because they inherently deserve it (*the intrinsic **desert** thesis*). Fourth, I suggest that, despite appearances, this thesis is not implied by Kant's official theory of punishment either. Despite Kant's undeniably strict 'retributive' policies for determining the degree and kind of punishment, his mature theory of justice implies that the principle that *wrongdoers ought to suffer* can have only a contingent, limited, and derivative role as a practical principle.[8] This interpretation, I argue, is compatible with several famous passages where Kant seems to take a stronger retributive position. Finally, I conclude with a few brief conjectures about the implications of Kant's basic ideas as presented here for further development of a Kantian theory of punishment.

I. UTILITARIAN, DEEP RETRIBUTIVE, AND KANTIAN POSITIONS

If we ask, generally, about the relations between wrongdoing and suffering, the first issue that may come to mind, especially in discussions of Kant, is whether right and wrong are exclusively determined by the consequences of what we do. For example, are acts wrong simply because they cause suffering to others?[9] This is *not* what is at issue here.

---

[8] This has been argued by several scholars in recent years. See B. Sharon Byrd, 'Kant's Theory of Punishment: Deterrence in its Threat, Retribution in its Execution', *Law and Philosophy*, 8(2) (1989), 151–200; Donald E. Scheid, 'Kant's Retributivism', *Ethics*, 93 (1983), 262–82; Sarah Holtman, 'Toward Social Reform: Kant's Penal Theory Reinterpreted', *Utilitas*, 9 (1997), 3–21; and ch. 7 of *Respect, Pluralism, and Justice*. For other interpretations see Jeffrie Murphy, 'Kant's Theory of Criminal Punishment', in Jeffrie Murphy (ed.), *Retribution, Justice and Therapy: Essays in the Philosophy of Law* (Dordrecht, Holland: D. Reidel, 1979), 82–92, and 'Does Kant have a Theory of Punishment?' *Columbia Law Review*, 87(3) (1987), 509–32, and Samuel Fleischacker, 'Kant's Theory of Punishment', in Howard L. Williams (ed.), *Essays on Kant's Political Philosophy* (Chicago: University of Chicago Press, 1992), 191–212.

[9] Here I use the term 'suffering' broadly as a stand-in for a variety of terms that mark subtle distinctions that are important in some other contexts (e.g., 'pain,' 'discomfort,' 'misery,' 'trouble,' 'harm,' 'deprivation,' etc.). The connotation of *undergoing unwelcome experiences* passively is perhaps typically apt in discussions of punishment, but, as Morris points out, *experiencing* pain is not always *suffering* pain, for example, if (as in

Rather, my discussion concerns two other questions, namely: (A) *Are wrongdoers in fact liable to suffer because they have done wrong and, if so, why?* and (B) *Should wrongdoers suffer because of their wrongdoing and, if so, why?* Concerning each question, it is important to consider, for any proposed answer: *Is the claim meant to be necessary or contingent?* Regarding affirmative answers to the second question, we should ask: *Is the principle that wrongdoers ought to suffer meant to be basic or derivative?*

Utilitarians have ready answers to all of these questions.[10] To the first, they are apt to say that wrongdoers are often, but not always, *likely* to suffer as a result of their wrong acts. Whether they will suffer or not is a contingent matter, depending on many natural and social facts, especially about how others respond to what they have done. Wrong acts are those which fail to maximize utility or at least a subset of such acts that are generally so harmful that the utility principle justifies compelling people to avoid them. Although utilitarianism offers reasons for training people so that they will feel bad when they do wrong, it does not hold that recognizing one's act as wrong *necessarily* makes one liable to feel the pain of guilt for doing it.[11] Similarly, although utilitarianism gives us reason to harness and make use of natural feelings of anger at those who harm us, it does not maintain that recognizing that others have done wrong to us *necessarily* means that we are prone to oppose, censure, or break relations with them. Whether a person's acts are wrong depends on the utility of their results; but whether recognition of wrongdoing engages anyone's feelings and attitudes depends on many factors, including prominently how they have been socialized. The utilitarian's position here is directly opposed to Kant's, as I shall explain in Section II.

Utilitarians and retributivists are supposed to divide on the second

---

masochism) one is not disposed to avoid the pain. For this reason, though I shall often continue to use the term 'suffering' in a broad sense, those who welcome the painful experience of guilt feelings as an inseparable aspect of a process of reform and restoration of relations may not, strictly speaking, be *suffering* the pangs of guilt: Herbert Morris, 'Guilt and Suffering', *Philosophy East & West*, 21(4) (1971), 89–110.

[10] Utilitarianism now comes in many varieties, but my remarks here, I believe, apply to most familiar versions.

[11] When I say that someone aware of doing wrong is 'liable to suffer' I mean more than the trivial point that if various, perhaps accidental, circumstances occur something may cause the person to suffer. The point is, rather, that the person is in a condition that makes the ensuing suffering what is an expected, normal realization of a disposition inherent in the recognition. Thus the utilitarian's answer to the first question, strictly speaking, is 'no, there is no such *liability* in wrongdoing, or even in recognition of one's wrongdoing, there is only a contingent "likelihood" given favorable social conditions.'

question, i.e., whether (and why) wrongdoers ought to suffer for what they have done. Assuming the question is a practical, action-guiding one, the *utilitarian* says that whether we ought to bring it about that wrongdoers suffer for their wrongdoing depends on contingent facts about what will maximize utility. *Retributivists*, in general, reply that it is morally necessary that wrongdoers be made to suffer.[12] Those I call *deep retributivists* hold this as a *fundamental* moral principle, which can serve to justify retributive policies of punishment. Others, though often called retributivists, are better regarded as advocates of *mixed theories* in which retributive policies are justified by principles of a different kind.[13] Kant is often taken to be a deep retributivist. Although there is strong evidence against this interpretation, many passages seem to favor it and so the textual evidence, overall, appears quite inconsistent. Some further distinctions, however, help to reconcile most of the apparently contradictory passages.

One important distinction is between *derivative retributive policies* (rules, or principles) that operate within, or even partially constitute, a social practice, such as criminal punishment, and *basic retributive principles* that might be used to justify such practices.[14] When the distinction is ignored, what Kant says forcefully in support of the former is easily taken as an endorsement of the latter, thereby confusing vehement advocacy of a principle with its depth within the structure of the theory.

A further distinction is also needed. What I call *the intrinsic desert*

---

[12] A modest version would say merely that there is some reason, apart from the consequences, for us to bring it about that wrongdoers suffer. This seems to be W. D. Ross's view, for the prima facie duty of justice, as he presents it, is a duty to promote the proportionality of virtue and happiness (W. D. Ross, *The Right and the Good* (Oxford: Clarendon Press, 1930), ch. 2).

[13] By 'retributive policies' I mean such principles as that only the guilty ought to be punished, that all the guilty ought to be punished, that the severity of the punishment should be proportionate to the crime, and that the punishment should 'fit' the crime in kind, as in 'an eye for an eye' and 'he who kills must die.' An obvious example of a mixed theory would be one that held several of these policies quite firmly but tried to justify doing so by appeal to utilitarian concerns, e.g., their value for deterrence, satisfaction of victims, etc. I shall argue that Kant, with regard to judicial punishment, holds a mixed theory, though he is far from a utilitarian in his account of what justifies legal practices and policies.

[14] The distinction between the rules of a practice and what justifies having the practice was made prominent in John Rawls's 'Two Concepts of Rules', *Philosophical Review*, 64 (1955), 3–32. H. L. A. Hart famously employed the distinction in his essays on punishment, e.g., *Punishment and Responsibility* (Oxford: Oxford University Press, 1968). The distinction is also important in essays on Kant's theory of punishment, e.g., in the articles of Byrd and Scheid previously cited, and in Herbert Morris's classic essay, 'Persons and Punishment', *Monist*, 52(2) (1968), 475–501.

thesis is the general idea that it is morally necessary, not just for contingent reasons, that wrongdoers ought to suffer. In other words, the thesis is that, in some sense, it is good in itself that wrongdoers suffer for what they have done. We must distinguish, however, two versions, a practical or action-guiding version and a merely faith-guiding or wish-expressing version. The *practical version* asserts that it is a good thing, apart from the consequences, that we, human beings, make wrongdoers suffer for their wrongs. In other words, the fact that someone has done wrong, by itself, is at least a prima facie reason for us to make the offender suffer. The more anemic, *nonpractical version* asserts that it is *fitting*, or *reasonably to be wished*, that wrongdoers will suffer for their wrongdoing, but it does not understand this as giving *us* any reasons to act.[15] It is meant to guide, not our actions, but faith about what God will do.[16] It is akin to the thought that it is fitting, and so to be hoped, that such a Being will ultimately ensure that *if virtuous we will be happy*; but it goes further, contending that *if vicious we should be unhappy*. That is, it is *fitting* and so there is *presumptive reason* for God to cause human beings to suffer because of their morally bad deeds regardless of any further reasons.

Given these distinctions, Kant's position, I suggest, is best understood as follows. Sometimes, undeniably, he expresses belief at least in the faith-guiding version of the intrinsic desert thesis.[17] That is, he accepts

---

[15] As Gerald Postema has pointed out to me, there are significant distinctions that a fuller discussion would need to take into account. For example, advocates of the non-practical version might have different grounds for rejecting the reason-giving implications that the terms 'good in itself,' 'fitting,' and 'reasonably to be wished' ordinarily have for us. Most obviously, it might be thought that, owing to human imperfection, we lack the knowledge and power required for us to have the authority, or standing, to judge and punish wrongdoers proportionate to their inner moral qualities. Alternatively, it might be held that *assessments of what we have reason to do* are fundamentally distinct from, and partially independent of *evaluations of states of affairs as (intrinsically) good, or fitting*, in the sense that they are (in themselves) *reasonably to be wished for*. Thus, apart from our limitations of knowledge and power, Kant might have embraced the proportionate suffering of wrongdoers, as he did the success of the French Revolution, as an outcome that good people can reasonably hope for without his thereby implying that these are causes to which he, and others, have reason to contribute. This is an implausible view, I think, because of its initial assumption that suffering proportionate to wrongdoing is in itself 'to be wished' and not because 'to be wished' implies 'reasons to seek.' There are complex issues here, however, that I cannot pursue now.

[16] A person's faith, hopes, and wishes about what God ('fittingly') will do may, of course, have an *indirect* influence on the person's conduct. The crucial point is that the belief that 'God has reasons to make the wicked suffer' does not license us to 'help' in the project.

[17] See, for example, LE (tr. Heath), 79 [27: 287], and 309 [27: 553]; C2, 34–5 [5: 37–8], 53 [5: 61], 84 [5: 1099–100], and 103–10 [5: 124–32]; R, 86 [6: 69], 89–90 [6: 73–4], 123–4 [6: 116–17], and 131 [6: 126].

the *general* proposition that *wrongdoers ought to suffer* at least as a principle to guide speculation about what God will do. He definitely does not hold the practical version of the intrinsic desert thesis as a *general* proposition covering all kinds of wrongdoing, including even neglect of imperfect duties.[18] Regarding *criminal punishment* Kant's position admittedly is more controversial. Even here I argue that, despite appearances to the contrary, in his more mature, systematic work Kant does not rely on the intrinsic desert thesis as a basic action-guiding principle. The right and the duty of the state to punish criminals is justified as a part of a system of credible (and so enforced) threats needed to uphold justice by deterring potential lawbreakers. This is directly contrary to the usual impression of Kant's position, despite the good work of Sharon Byrd and others; and so further review of the relevant evidence is called for.

II. THE INTERNAL CONNECTION BETWEEN DOING WRONG AND SUFFERING FOR IT

Unlike typical utilitarians and other externalists, Kant held that to recognize that one has done something morally wrong is necessarily to be liable to painful self-reproach and alienation from others. To see why this is so, let us first review some basic elements of Kant's conception of wrongdoing and then draw out their implications.

(A) Some Elements of a Kantian Conception of Moral Wrongdoing

To describe a conception of moral wrongdoing, as I understand this, is not to give a strict definition or analysis of the concept, but only to articulate some important points about how the term is understood, background assumptions about its proper application, and implications about the relations among those who judge that wrong has been done. In addition, characterizing how we conceive wrongdoing is not the same as laying out all the substantive principles by which we judge what is

---

[18] Throughout my discussion I mean 'wrongdoing' in an ordinary sense, broad enough to include many morally objectionable acts that are not crimes. In his philosophy of law (the *Rechtslehre*) Kant uses terms translated as 'right' (*recht*) and 'wrong' (*unrecht*) in a narrower sense, implying legal enforceability. Thus, in this narrower sense, we would not call an act wrong (*unrecht*) unless convinced that it is of a kind that persons can be justifiably coerced to avoid. This, however, leaves open the question what makes acts *wrong in the sense that implies justifiability of coercion*, for example, whether this depends on contingent facts as it does under utilitarianism.

wrong. Kantian standards for moral decision making are supposed to be expressed in the several formulas of the Categorical Imperative, but here my main interest is not in the criteria by which we judge acts to be wrong but in what we take to follow from such judgments.

I begin with some general points about freedom, maxims, and reasons. A basic feature of Kant's conception is that in order to do something morally wrong one must be a person who satisfies at least minimum conditions of rationality and freedom.[19] Some capacity for memory, foresight, reflection, and self-control is necessary. When a wrong act is imputed to a person, the person is presumed to be the 'free cause' of the act. Leaving aside Kant's troublesome references to 'noumenal' causation, we can assume that he wants at least to exclude many standard cases of permanent and temporary incompetence. To be a free cause is to 'will' an act, and this requires a capacity to reflect on one's options and to adopt and act on personal policies or principles. Moral agents see themselves as having alternatives, and they choose to act as they do for reasons, good or bad. Kant supposes that, for practical purposes, we can think of them as acting on 'maxims' or subjective principles that express what they saw themselves as doing and their rationale for doing it. In attributing a rationale to a person we implicitly invoke general principles of rational choice, for example, that a rational person takes the necessary means to ends that he or she wills (or else abandons those ends).

A significant feature of this Kantian conception is that an imputable action is taken to be more than a causal product of nonrational desires and aversions, seen as given vector forces that pulled or pushed the person to behave as he or she did. We experience feelings and impulses as inclining us to one choice or another, but if we take the act to be imputable we presuppose that these inclinations were not so irresistably compelling that the agent could not have chosen to act otherwise (if there were strong reasons to). Even when we act 'from' inclinations, then we are seen as acting on maxims, i.e., choosing (when one might do otherwise) to adopt and follow the policy of doing what satisfies such inclinations in the sort of context at hand. Greedy acts, then, are not to be understood as behaviors causally necessitated by a strong inner force, but rather as reflections of an agent's at least temporary commitment to a policy of satisfying his urges even at others' expense. All this, it should be noted, is a way of conceiving agents for practical

[19] MM, 11–22 [6: 211–21]. For a fuller explanation, see 'Kant's Theory of Practical Reason', in my *Dignity and Practical Reason*, 123–46.

purposes (e.g., of law and morality). It is supposed to be compatible with understanding human behavior quite differently for other purposes, e.g., for purposes of empirical psychology human behavior can be seen as a part of a system of natural causes.[20]

So far, the background assumptions might apply to reflective agents generally, without special reference to their moral capacities. I turn now to sketch three special ideas about morality.

(1) *Moral duties are, in a sense, self-imposed.* Kant analyzes what he takes to be the ordinary idea of moral duty in a series of steps, the upshot of which is that moral duties, if there are any, are based on unconditional principles to which we are necessarily committed as rational persons with autonomy of the will. When thinking clearly and free from self-deception, we cannot but regard them as authoritative, rational, overriding, and in need of no further justification. They are supposed to be principles constitutive of our practical reason; they do not represent commands of any external authority, but rather the constraints of our own reason. To put it metaphorically, my true (rational) legislative will, as an author of moral law, commands that I, as 'subject', obey its laws; and so, when I do so, I am only obeying myself, or my 'better' self, as it were. One may doubt whether this model of moral agency fits all human beings; sociopaths, for example, may be an exception. The point, for present purposes, is just that, wherever Kant's model of moral agency is applicable, persons are presumed to be deeply disposed to do what they recognize to be their moral duty, regarding it as an overriding rational and self-endorsed requirement rather than simply one among many inclinations. One need not buy into Kant's whole worldview to acknowledge something like this: although often weak, easily distracted, and neglectful of their acknowledged responsibilities, virtually all competent moral agents, when faced with a clear, undoubted case of moral duty, judge and feel it to be overridingly required, independently of potential rewards and punishments, and they would regard themselves less true to themselves if they failed to respect it.

(2) *Every rational person has dignity as a legislator of moral law.* This is a core idea in Kant's later formulations of the Categorical Imperative.[21] Here I take it to be a minimal basic content of moral law; that is, not a moral decision procedure, but an idea that, at least in some rudimentary form, is implicit in moral thinking. Humanity, or rational nature in all persons, is taken to have a special status: it has dignity, an

[20] G, 117–31 [4: 450–63].   [21] G, 95–105 [4: 428–37].

unconditional and incomparable worth, above all price, and without equivalent. The interpretation of these familiar phrases is controversial, but a good clue is Kant's subsequent assertion that what gives humanity this special status is 'the idea of the will of every rational agent as a will giving universal law.'[22] All rational agents are pictured as together lawmakers and subjects in an ideal analogue of a political community, the kingdom of ends, where they legislate not from private interest or commitment to prior authorities but with an impartial regard for the humanity of each co-legislator.[23] We respect this ideal in various ways, but primarily by respecting moral laws, which are seen as constructed by the common practical reason of all moral agents. We honor the ideal by caring for the lives and permissible ends of our fellow legislator/citizens, by consulting and listening to them in moral discussion as persons whose voices count as much as ours in determining what is right, and by appreciating their willingness to reciprocate our efforts to make our shared moral constraints the framework of our mutual relations.

This last point supplements the previous one in an important way. That is, it makes clear that, in addition to regarding moral duties as *self-imposed*, in a sense, we must also see them as what we, *together with all others* (qua rational and autonomous), will for all. (Moral duties are, so to speak, legislated *by* the People as well as *for* the People.) Again, one may endorse the main points here without necessarily accepting everything implied by Kant's special terminology. The core points, for example, might be summarized this way: moral principles are meant to be what reasonable, mutually respecting, appropriately impartial human beings can endorse as a common basis for their reciprocal, moral relations, and we give proper respect to the dignity of fellow human beings by trying our best to conform to what, in our best judgment, those principles are.

(3) *We each are responsible for fulfilling our moral duties, with respect for their rational grounds, and the morality of others is, generally, not our business.* Our basic *ethical* duties are directed toward two ends: 'our own moral perfection and the happiness of others.'[24] To pursue one's own happiness, normally, is not a moral duty. This is not because one should view one's own happiness as less important than others', but because we are already well inclined to pursue our own happiness and also, I think, because a general duty of beneficence to oneself, parallel

---

[22] G, 98–100 [4: 431–2].
[23] G, 100–5 [4: 433–7]. For interpretative comments, see *Dignity and Practical Reason*, 58–66, 226–50.   [24] MM, 150–6 [6: 386–94].

to the duty to others, turns out to be incoherent.[25] The moral perfection of others, however, is generally *their* responsibility, not ours. To be sure, one should not throw temptations in the path of the morally weak, and we have responsibilities for moral education of the young.[26] However, to see to it that others do what they should (ethically) do is not generally among the 'ends that are duties' for us.[27] This is partly because, strictly, to fulfill ethical duties a person must have a good will and be guided by his/her own good will, and, in Kant's view, that is something in the end up to the agent. We might bribe, plead, threaten, and manipulate others to induce *moral-like behavior*, e.g., giving to charity, but without a good will the behavior does not fulfill the ethical duty of beneficence. Officials of the law can rightly use coercion to prevent violations of juridical duties, but whether a person fulfills the indirect ethical duty to conform to juridical duties depends on whether his/her motive is respect for the *moral* law. The main point I want to emphasize here, however, is that, in Kantian ethics, moral agents are, in a sense, *trusted* to govern themselves by moral principles. The law, ideally, imposes sanctions only when their use of their freedom hinders the legitimate freedom of others under universal laws, and even here we are subject to penalties only for 'external acts,' not bad (even wicked) attitudes. Kant does not in general endorse the use of informal social pressures to back up the law and motivate moral behavior beyond the law. Each person's conscience is expected to warn, prod, and motivate reform, but the role for our neighbors' participation in this process is quite limited. The explanation is partly Kant's keen awareness that we are largely ignorant of others' true motives, but even more his thought that we should, in general, respect each person as able, disposed, and potentially willing to meet his or her own responsibilities without external prods.

(B) Implications of Acknowledged Moral Wrongdoing: Self-Blame and Others' Disapproval

Suppose, then, that we realize that we have failed in our moral duties, for example, violating a 'perfect' duty of respect to others or ignoring

---

[25] I argue for this in 'Happiness and Human Flourishing', Ch. 6 in this volume.

[26] MM, 221 ff. [6: 477 ff.]; also Immanuel Kant, *Education* (Ann Arbor: The University of Michigan Press, 1960), 83–121.

[27] Kant suggests that the duty to promote the happiness of others leads to an indirect duty to be concerned with their moral well-being insofar as their doing wrong will lead them to suffer pangs of conscience. Beneficence also should lead us to want to prevent others from wrongfully interfering with the happiness of others, but the basic end here is the (permissible) happiness of those who would be harmed, not the moral goodness of those who would wrongfully harm them (MM, 156 [6: 393–4]).

an imperfect duty to pursue the happiness of others as an end.[28] Given our first point, to recognize that we have done a moral wrong in one of these ways is to be aware that we have acted contrary to our own rationally endorsed commitments, which we cannot help but regard as overridingly authoritative. Thus, we judge that, for insufficient reasons and when we could have done otherwise, we violated an unconditional self-command. What one must experience, then, is more than a mere *conflict of desires* or *regret* at an imprudent decision. The acknowledged violation of moral duty turns oneself against oneself in the way Kant's metaphor of conscience suggests; the sentence is the inevitably painful realization that one has offended against oneself. One did not act in a self-respecting way, and so one's self-esteem is lowered.

Notice that the suffering to which one is liable from violating one's moral principles is not a sanction only contingently connected with the agent's judgment of wrongdoing, e.g., a deliberate 'kicking oneself' to motivate reform. The tendency to suffer, though perhaps blocked in some cases, is inevitable. Moreover, it is presumably not merely a 'necessary evil' that one should wish to be rid of; for the price of losing it, on Kant's view, would be to lose one's effective sense of moral obligation, one's humanity, the ground of one's human dignity.

Drawing from our second point, we can say much the same thing for the discomfort we experience when we recognize that we have damaged our moral relations with others. Insofar as they recognize our serious wrongdoing, they see that we have violated or ignored moral principles to which they, too, are deeply committed, as overridingly authoritative. They, and we, when thinking clearly, see moral principles as constructed by reasonable, mutually respecting persons to provide a moral framework for our interactions that has benefits for all and burdens no one unfairly. Others have willingly constrained themselves by respect for these principles, which they see as structuring a form of life that is fair and mutually beneficial only to the extent that others are willing to reciprocate and do their part. What attitude, then, can we expect from others when they fully recognize our serious wrongdoing? They will not merely deplore unwelcome consequences of our misdeeds, but they will regard us as having struck a blow at something they value, ignored a common bond, failed to respect them as persons worthy of equal consideration. In short, we can expect others to be offended. This applies not only to those whom in particular we have mistreated, but also

---

[28] Our failure could be with respect to satisfying an 'indirectly ethical' duty to obey the law, but, if so, we are concerned with it here as a moral offense, not merely as a legal one.

anyone who takes seriously moral principles as the fair and reasonable framework for our interactions. Even if others do not express their negative attitude, one who acknowledges her wrongdoing must know that she deserves it; and this must be painful, given the basic respect that, in Kant's view, moral agents have for each other. As acknowledged wrongdoers, we grant that others would be correct to judge that we have done wrong, and this amounts to a concession that we deserve the negative attitudes that are inseparably part of that judgment. It does not follow that we deserve more than this, for example, explicit condemnation and deliberate efforts by others to make us suffer. All that is undeniably apt are the reactive attitudes inseparably bound up with recognition of the offense.

Finally, drawing from our third point (regarding individual responsibility), we can add that, given the Kantian model, as acknowledged wrongdoers we will be regarded, by others and ourselves, as having betrayed a trust. The ethical system, and so everyone as an 'author' of it, counts on individuals, outside the domain of law, to cultivate their own moral attitudes and to fulfill their ethical responsibilities without threats and prodding from others. The person who violates or ignores ethical duties breaks this bond of trust, showing herself to be unworthy of it to some degree. Again, this makes the acknowledged wrongdoer open to a justified negative attitude of others—a sense of betrayed trust—to which a moral agent, in Kant's view, cannot be indifferent. Since as wrongdoers, despite our misdeeds, we are (by hypothesis) still deeply committed to the ethical standards that we offend against, we cannot help but regard our wrongdoing as a betrayal of our own commitments as to how one should act. Painful inner turmoil, disappointment in ourselves, seem the inevitable result in normal cases, even if it does not express itself in quite the legalistic forum that Kant pictures 'conscience' to be. Once again, we should note that the discomfort the wrongdoer suffers is an inherent liability in being one moral agent among others, as Kant conceives this. There is no ground here for supposing that this suffering, or even more, should be deliberately imposed to 'get even' with the offender or badger him into better behavior in the future.

To summarize, though wrongdoing may be a special offense against an individual, it is also an affront to each person. Others too regard the moral law as authoritative, identify with its commands, and so cannot help but have a negative attitude in general to those who violate them. They will see offenders as willfully disregarding the principles that, in their best impartial moments, they all endorse as fair and reasonable, their basis for mutual peace and equal opportunity to pursue happiness. So, moral wrongdoing brings not only self-blame but also the disapproval of others who are aware of it. The offense is not merely to oneself and the individuals immediately harmed, but to humanity. As Herbert Morris might say, our moral relations with all other moral agents have been to some degree ruptured and moral agents, who value these, will have reason to make amends.[29]

These points may become clearer by contrast with a utilitarian perspective.[30]

First, utilitarianism typically endorses an externalist conception of right and wrong, and Kant, by contrast, is an internalist. That is, for the utilitarian, unlike Kant, what is right is (in principle) determined by an objective fact (that an option maximizes utility) independent of the agent's intentions and motives. Thus, typically utilitarianism implies that one can have, and judge that one has, a duty without being motivated to do it or to feel remorse for failing to do it.

Second, the utilitarian, then, must attach a motive to moral requirements, supplying moral agents with incentives that have no necessary connection with the requirements. Thus, for example, they will want to instill internal sanctions through training as well as relying on social pressure, rewards and punishments, to induce people to maximize utility.

Third, because utilitarian moral requirements are not essentially self-imposed but are socially instilled, reflection on the *origin* of one's utilitarian 'sense of duty' may not lead one to reaffirm it. Thus, a utilitarian commitment to morality may fail the test of reflective endorsement. This should not be surprising, for people whose stable sentiments always prioritize the general happiness seem quite rare.

Fourth, for the typical utilitarian moral requirements are not, in the same way as for Kant, *offenses against all conscientious people*. In general, of course, *devoted* utilitarians will be *sorry* whenever utility is not maximized; and utilitarian rules of justice (according to Mill) assign rights to individuals, and so each *injustice* does wrong to *some* individual. Utilitarian wrongdoing, however, is not inherently a failure to

---

[29] See, for example, Herbert Morris, 'Guilt and Suffering' and 'A Paternalistic Theory of Punishment', *American Philosophical Quarterly*, 18(4) (1981), 263–71, reprinted in Jeffrie G. Murphy (ed.), *Punishment and Rehabilitation*, 3rd edn. (Belmont, CA: Wadsworth Publishing Co., 1995), 154–68.

[30] The following points are not intended as criticisms of utilitarianism, for the resources of subtle variations of utilitarianism are plentiful and the points in question are themselves open to reasonable controversy.

respect humanity in each person by violating the principles authored by each.

Finally, wrongdoing for utilitarians is not the sort of betrayal of trust that it is for Kant. In fact, utilitarians have every reason not to leave moral motivation to the individual. Social pressure is a necessary and legitimate utilitarian means to get people to make utility-maximizing decisions. Those who violate the utility principle have ignored such pressures; this is different from betraying a trust that others place in us by counting on us to fulfill our own responsibilities without moralizing pressure.

III. DESERT AND WORTHINESS

In Kant's view, then, we are liable to suffer for our wrongdoing regardless of whether others make a special effort to make this happen. In a sense, an offender's pain is fitting, to be expected, and not misguided (i.e., it stems from an accurate self-assessment). This is not yet to say, however, that wrongdoers *deserve* to suffer in any practical sense that entitles others to contribute to their suffering. The question now is whether Kant is committed to this stronger claim, in particular to what I call the *practical* version of the *intrinsic desert thesis*. Kant undeniably thinks that criminals *deserve*, in some sense, to be punished and that anyone who lacks a good will is, to some degree, *unworthy to be happy*. What is less clear is what we are to make of these claims. My suggestion is that they do not amount to an endorsement of the intrinsic desert thesis as an action-guiding (practical) principle.

The question, 'Do wrongdoers *deserve* to suffer?' can be confusing. Consider several notions of desert.

(1) First, it should be noted that, trivially, the *judgment* that someone has done wrong is *deserved* only if the person has in fact done wrong, for this is just to say that the *judgment* is correct and not misplaced. According to the intrinsic liability thesis, persons who recognize that they have done wrong and that this is known by others are for that very reason liable to suffer in some ways (self-blame and damaged relations). Suffering from self-blame is to be expected, and it is not altogether to be deplored because it is beneficial if it leads to reform and restored relations. In a sense, one might say, it is a 'fitting' or 'appropriate' response to wrongdoing because it is a sign that the offender recognizes the wrong and retains some basic moral commitments. As fitting or appropriate it is 'deserved' in this trivial sense. However, to say that

the offender 'deserves to suffer' goes beyond this, in any of several ways.

(2) For example, laws of the state that define legal offenses, Kant held, necessarily impose sanctions for noncompliance, and so we can say that, *relative to such laws*, the law-breaker (legally) *deserves* the sanctions defined by law. This, *by itself*, says nothing about whether the person, morally speaking, deserves suffering and condemnation rather than merely imposition of penalties or 'disincentives.' The concept of crime implies liability to penalties under a system of law,[31] but what, if anything, the legal offender morally deserves depends on many other factors, including prominently whether the laws are just and fairly administered. Judgments about what a person deserves, in the minimal sense used here, presuppose and are derived from the *de facto* system of laws. Without strong further premises, they do not warrant the claim that offenders *morally deserve* to suffer or even that it is morally justified to impose the legal penalties.

(3) In a just and fairly administered legal system that justifiably imposes penalties for offenses, we might say that, under those just laws, offenders *morally deserve* the penalties they receive. Unlike the previous (minimal) idea, this is a notion of moral desert but the judgment of what is deserved still presupposes and derives from prior judgments about the legal system (in this case about what its laws *justifiably* impose on offenders). It is not an independent, freestanding assessment of the deed or character of the agent that could *ground* the claim that the system justifiably imposes the sanctions. Furthermore, it does *not follow* from the fact that an agent has done wrong morally that the wrongdoer morally deserves a penalty in this third sense. Even if moral wrongdoing is necessary for morally deserving the penalty, it is hardly sufficient because the latter requires, further, that the law is justified in placing the deed in question under the system of criminal sanctions.[32]

(4) Moralists often talk as though a person could be morally deserving, or undeserving, in a sense that floats free from systems of law and systems of informal social sanctions. This is what I call *intrinsic moral desert*. It might be thought, for example, that necessarily acts of certain kinds have as an intrinsic property that it is *fit, appropriate, or 'called for' that the perpetrator suffer for it*. Thus, one might suppose that it takes no moral argument but merely conceptual analysis or moral intuition to 'see' that immoral, 'grossly wrong,' or 'wicked' acts make the

---

[31] MM, 130 [6: 362], C2, 34–5 [5: 37–8].
[32] For Kant's distinction between legal offenses and merely 'ethical' failings, see MM, 23–5 [6: 229–31], 31–2 [6: 239], 145–8 [6: 380–3].

agent intrinsically deserving of painful sanctions. I find this a conceptually dubious and morally repugnant idea, but my concern here is merely to show that Kant did not endorse it as a practical, or act-guiding, principle for us.

The main sources of the thought that Kant held that wrongdoers intrinsically deserve to suffer seem to be these: (a) his remarks, sprinkled throughout his works, that a good will is the condition of the *worthiness to be happy* and (b) his tough-sounding remarks about punishment in *The Metaphysics of Morals*. In the remainder of this section, I review typical examples of (a); and in the next section, I turn to (b).

Despite what some passages may suggest, the thesis in question is not grounded in Kant's idea that only moral goodness makes us 'worthy to be happy.' Consider, for example, the famous passage at the beginning of Kant's *Groundwork* in which Kant says 'an impartial rational spectator can take no delight in seeing the uninterrupted prosperity of a being graced with no feature of a pure and good will.'[33] Kant adds, 'a good will seems to constitute the indispensable condition even of worthiness to be happy.'[34] The implication here, and elsewhere, is that a wrongdoer who lacks a good will and virtue is not 'worthy' to be happy, but this does not imply that we are warranted, as individuals or state officials, to inflict suffering on wrongdoers or to deprive them of happiness in any way other than preventing them from attaining it by immoral means. Kant poses a thought experiment about an extreme, atypical case: a scoundrel living with '*uninterrupted* prosperity' despite having '*no* feature of a pure and good will.' Even regarding this extreme case the passage implies only that such scoundrels are not *worthy* of their happy condition, not that anyone is authorized to prevent or interrupt it (as opposed to preventing their seeking it by immoral means). The point, arguably, is addressed to us as persons deliberating about the priorities among the good things in life that we might possess, develop, and pursue—for example, understanding, wit, courage, perseverance, power, riches, honor, health, and happiness. The practical lesson is that we should regard maintaining our good will, and only this, as our highest priority, worth valuing and holding on to in all possible conditions.[35] Happiness, like other conditional goods, is not worth pursuing at the cost of one's good will.

Another relevant passage is Kant's sketch of a moral catechism at the

---

[33] G, 61 [4: 393]. [34] Ibid.
[35] This interpretation is developed at more length in Ch. 2 of this volume.

end of *The Metaphysics of Morals*.[36] Here the imaginary 'teacher' elicits from the 'pupil' that, even regarding others, we should try to adjust our conduct according to judgments as to who is worthy of happiness.[37] The passage, however, does not imply a general warrant to interfere with the happiness of persons who are 'unworthy' of it. Its point is elementary and limited: one should not contribute to the vices of others. The teacher illustrates: one should not wish to give soft cushions to the idle, abundant wine to the drunkard, a charming air to a swindler, or strong fists to a violent man.

In his second *Critique* Kant contends that we ought to strive to promote the highest good, hence we must believe that its realization is possible, and so we must postulate the existence of God (whose power and insight would be necessary to bring about the highest good).[38] The highest good of a person is virtue and happiness together, and 'the highest good of a possible world' is 'happiness distributed in exact proportion to morality (as the worth of a person and his worthiness to be happy).'[39] It would be inconsistent with the will of a perfectly rational being, Kant declares, to allow preventable unhappiness in beings who need happiness and are worthy of it.[40] It is important to note the limits to Kant's claims here. The context is a qualified defense of faith in a God that admittedly cannot be known or comprehended. Kant's suggestion here that we ought to strive to promote the highest good is, arguably, not the introduction of a new duty beyond the system of duties sketched in Kant's other ethical works.[41] That is, our responsibility in striving for the highest good is conscientiously to fulfill our various independently specified duties, as determined by the Categorical Imperative. These are primarily to avoid violating others' rights, to respect them as human beings, to promote their happiness, and to show proper gratitude. These duties are not owed only to the virtuous.[42] Of course, we are to promote only the 'permissible' ends of others, but this does not mean only the ends of those whom we judge morally worthy. In fact,

---

[36] MM, 223–5 [6: 480–2].   [37] MM, 224 [6: 481].
[38] C2, 103–10 [V: 123–32].   [39] C2, 93 [V: 110–11].   [40] Ibid.
[41] See Stephen Engstrom, 'The Concept of the Highest Good in Kant's Moral Theory', *Philosophy and Phenomenological Research*, 52 (1992), 747–80, and Andrews Reath, 'Two Conceptions of the Highest Good in Kant', *Journal of the History of Philosophy*, 26 (1988), 593–619.
[42] That is, the *basic* general principles of duty are not so restricted. (For text citations, see *Dignity and Practical Reason*, 176–95.) This point, of course, is compatible with the common-sense idea that, in particular contexts, one's estimate of the goodness or evil of others' deeds and motives will make some difference to how one judges, from basic principles, that one should treat them.

according to Kant's moral psychology we are so ignorant of the moral worth of others that we could not fairly undertake to make others happy, and unhappy, in proportion to their worthiness. That it is fitting for God to take up this task is a faith-guiding idea that Kant sometimes seems to endorse, but it is not what grounds or determines our responsibilities.

IV. MORAL WORTH AND PUNISHMENT

In Kant's ethical writings, the main suggestions of the intrinsic desert thesis come from his idea of worthiness to be happy. The thesis is also commonly assumed to be embedded in Kant's harsh-sounding remarks about punishment. Do they imply the *deeply* retributive idea that wrongdoing is in itself a reason to make offenders suffer?

In several respects, Kant's position on punishment places him prominently among those commonly regarded as retributivists. He held, for example, not only that (1) only those guilty of legal offenses should be punished but also (2) that all the guilty should be punished regardless of whether punishing the offender in the particular case has any deterrence or reform value. Moreover, he held a version of the idea (3) that the severity of the punishment ought to be proportional to the gravity of the offense. This was (4) the traditional *lex talionis*, i.e., offenders should receive back in degree and (with exceptions) in kind what they inflicted upon others. In addition, as we shall see shortly, the tone of Kant's remarks about punishment expresses a moral condemnation at odds with the consequentialist idea that penal law is merely a 'price system' to discourage undesirable behaviors.

Despite all this, Kant's mature theory of legal punishment is arguably not deeply retributivist.[43] His retributive policies (i.e., 1–4) are not based on the intrinsic desert thesis; nor do they stand as fundamental moral requirements. Rather, they are best understood as derivative features of a practice that requires independent justification. Sharon Byrd, and other scholars, have argued forcefully that the structure of Kant's

---

[43] I limit my discussion here to Kant's main discussion of punishment in *The Metaphysics of Morals*. Kant comments occasionally on punishment elsewhere. See, for example, C2, 34–5 [5: 37–8], 53 [5: 61] and LE (tr. Heath), 80 [27: 286], 307–12 [27: 551–8], 284–5 [27: 552], and 181 [27: 418]. These texts are not without ambiguity, but the *Lectures* clearly assign a deterrence role to state punishment. Both, however, contain suggestions of the intrinsic desert thesis as at least appropriate for a Being of infinite wisdom and power.

theory of law calls for a reconstruction of Kant's theory of punishment as a mixed theory, combining retributive policies (about who and how much to punish) with deterrence considerations playing a role in a complex justification of the practice that employs such policies. Here I will only briefly review the main considerations that make this persuasive, and then turn to several passages which seem to conflict with this interpretative hypothesis.

Kant presents his most thorough and systematic statement on punishment in *The Metaphysics of Morals*. Here Kant makes clear that judicial punishment must be for (intentional) 'external acts' as they can be assessed in a public court of law.[44] The law cannot assess the 'inner' moral worth of offenders because that would require knowing more about the agent's motives and 'will' than we can determine with confidence. The justifying purpose of a practice of punishment, then, cannot be to make wrongdoers suffer according to their intrinsic moral deserts. Kant's justification, in fact, lies elsewhere. The general authority for state coercive powers, on which the right to punish is based, is the authority to 'hinder hindrances to freedom.'[45] The universal principle of justice (*Recht*) determines that each person in a state has a right to a sphere of freedom under universal laws compatible with the freedom of others. State officials have the duty to specify this freedom and to protect it through coercion that hinders those who would interfere with ('hinder') it. The main method that Kant discusses for protecting the specified freedom of the individual is to threaten each person with legal sanctions for violating the law.[46] Such threats are supposed to provide disincentives to all who are inclined to infringe the rightful freedom of others. Assuming sufficient threats and efficient enforcement, rational citizens, even if self-interested, will normally be deterred. The point of this practice, then, is to protect freedom rights or, more broadly, to maintain a condition in which just relations among persons are possible. Threats would be empty and useless unless generally carried out, and so it is not an option to adopt a practice of making threats to deter potential crime but not follow through with punishment whenever the threat fails. Selective execution of threats, for example, excusing offenders whenever punishment would not have deterrence value *in the particular case*, might undermine the deterrence value of threats; but a more serious objection, from Kant's point of view, is that selective enforcement is prima facie unfair and comparatively unjust.

[44] MM, 20–2 [6: 218–21].
[45] MM, 24–5 [6: 230–1]; see also Byrd, 'Kant's Theory of Punishment'.
[46] MM, 4–9 [6: 331–7].

On this understanding, then, deterrence plays a role in the general justification of the practice of punishment, but this is compatible with retributive policies governing judges, juries, and even legislators operating within the framework of the practice. Officials impose punishment on a particular offender, it should be noted, because the law and the retributive policies of the justified practice demand it—or briefly, 'because he is guilty of the crime.' Their aim as enforcers of the law should not be to deter him from future crimes, still less to deter *others* by making an example of him. That, arguably, would be to use him merely as a means. Punishment is imposed as the carrying out of the state's prior legitimate threat *to him*, a legal response required by a justified practice designed to secure the legitimate freedom of all (including him). The practice, if just, allowed him fair opportunity to avoid the penalty, and it is (if Kant is right) a practice that the offender's own practical reason would endorse if reflective about the justification of social institutions apart from special self-favoring attitudes that discount the interests of others. Assuming (with Kant) that disproportionate and degrading punishments are prohibited in the practice, the criminal cannot plausibly argue that punishing him is using him as a mere means to the good of others.[47]

The Metaphysics of Morals contains several often quoted passages which might seem to tell against this line of interpretation and even favor reading Kant as committed to the intrinsic desert thesis. On balance, however, I find even these troublesome passages fail to establish the intrinsic desert thesis. However unappealing, the passages can be understood in a way compatible with the sort of 'mixed theory' interpretation I have (partially) sketched above. Assuming this, the mixed theory interpretation seems clearly more credible because it builds on Kant's basic justification of state coercion without denying Kant's commitment to certain extreme retributive policies. We cannot consider all aspects of this matter, but let us review four famous passages.

(1) Kant writes:

[Judicial punishment] can never be inflicted merely as a means to promote some other good for the criminal himself or for civil society. It must always be inflicted upon him only *because he has committed a crime*.... He must previously have been found *punishable* before any thought can be given to drawing from his punishment something of use for him or his fellow citizens. The law of punishment is a categorical imperative, and woe to him who crawls through the windings of eudaemonism in order to discover something that releases the

---

[47] MM, 106 [6: 333], 130 [6: 362–3], 209–10 [6: 462–4].

criminal from punishment or even reduces its amount by the advantage it promises, in accordance with the pharisaical saying, 'It is better for *one* man to die than for an entire people to perish.'[48]

These remarks, I take it, characterize the rules of the practice of punishment, i.e., the guidelines for officials operating within the framework of a system of criminal law. The point is that officials should impose the legal penalties as prescribed by law in each case, without deviating for pragmatic reasons, for example, reducing a sentence for offenders who volunteer for medical experiments. The accused must be found 'punishable' or guilty and responsible under the law, independently of any consideration of whether imposing sanctions in the particular case will reform them or deter others from similar crimes. (Some previous translations misleadingly translated 'strafbar' as 'deserving of punishment' rather than 'punishable,' thereby encouraging the thought that intrinsic moral desert might be the justification for inflicting suffering.) Although not everyone will agree with Kant's prescriptions here, it should be clear that as policies for officials charged with enforcement of law they leave open the question how the practice of punishment, with such policies, is to be justified. There is no denial here that the fact that the practice tends to deter potential lawbreakers is a significant part of the grounds for maintaining it.

(2) The passage above is followed by another favorite of those who view Kant as the arch-retributivist.

Whatever undeserved evil you inflict upon another within the people, that you inflict upon yourself. If you insult him, you insult yourself; if you steal from him, you steal from yourself; if you strike him, you strike yourself; if you kill him, you kill yourself. But only the law of retribution (ius talionis)—it being understood, of course, that this is applied by a court (not by your private judgment)—can specify definitely the quality and the quantity of punishment; all other principles are fluctuating and unsuited for a sentence of pure and strict justice because extraneous considerations are mixed into them.[49]

Here again, I take it, Kant prescribes a rule for the practice of punishment, not a basic moral principle. The rule is to be applied by a court as the 'principle and measure' of 'what kind and what amount of punishment' public justice requires.[50] The only ground for it offered here is that alternative principles are 'fluctuating' and include 'extraneous considerations,' not that it gives back to criminals what they intrinsically deserve. Rather than justifying the rule for determining the degree and

---

[48] MM, 105 [6: 331]. [49] MM, 105 [6: 332]. [50] Ibid.

kind of punishment, the statement that 'whatever undeserved evil you inflict on others ... you inflict on yourself' simply explains its content. It is not in fact a basic moral principle of Kant's that we ought to inflict on wrongdoers whatever undeserved evil they inflict on others. This is at best a limited principle, applicable only within a practice of criminal law, and standing in need of independent justification. As Kant realizes, we cannot permissibly 'do back' to the worst criminals all the heinous things they have done to their victims; and outside the criminal law, we have no warrant to make people suffer in kind for their moral offenses. The special appeal of the retributive principle, I suspect, is that doing to offenders just what they did to their victims makes vivid the fact that an offender is in no position to complain about the penalty. But, of course, the fact that the offenders cannot complain (consistently with their enacted maxims) does not *by itself* warrant our responding to them in kind, letting their illegal maxims determine the proper legal response. The policy of 'giving back in kind and degree,' as Kant seems to realize, is not a self-justifying basic moral principle but at best a doubly limited working guide, restricted to criminal law and bounded by moral constraints.

(3) Among the sternest passages that Kant's critics are fond of citing is the following.

> Even if a civil society were to be dissolved by the consent of all its members (e.g., if a people inhabiting an island decided to separate and disperse throughout the world) the last murderer remaining in prison would first have to be executed, so that each has done to him what his deeds deserve and blood guilt does not cling to the people for not having insisted upon this punishment; for otherwise the people can be regarded as collaborators in this public violation of justice.[51]

Even if one finds Kant's conclusion here repugnant, it should be noted that it does not endorse punishment because of, or even according to, intrinsic desert. The conclusion can be understood as simply a rigorous application of Kant's extreme retributive *policy* that *all* of the guilty ought to be punished, following *lex talionis* so far as permissible. It reaffirms the idea that those responsible for enforcing the law must apply the legally prescribed sanctions without concern for whether punishment has any deterrent value in the particular case. We may object to these doctrines in the extreme form that Kant presents them, but Kant's illustration of them in the dramatic case of the last day of a civil society

[51] MM, 106 [6: 333].

does not alter the structure of his theory. The need to 'hinder hindrances to freedom' plays a role in justifying the legal practice that authorizes punishment of all the guilty by (qualified) *lex talionis*, but in particular cases the practice requires the strict enforcement of the rules with no further end in view. We may well doubt that Kant's general justification of the practice really supports his inflexible stand that all the guilty must be punished, even in the extraordinary case where the civil order is about to be abandoned. This doubt, however, can be understood as directed to Kant's *application* of his general justification strategy, rather than an *ad hoc* appeal to the intrinsic desert thesis. Even in the extraordinary case, I think, considerations of *comparative justice* make understandable, even if not defensible, Kant's thought that the long-standing (supposedly) just policy of executing murderers should not be abandoned for the few remaining convicts.

When Kant says that the murderous deeds 'deserve' the death penalty, this is also compatible with the hypothesis that what is at issue is not the murderer's inner moral deserts. What his 'deeds deserve,' in the relevant sense, may be determined by just law, and, if so, it cannot be the ground for thinking that the death penalty is just. 'Blood guilt' is a term that conjures up unsavory attitudes, but in the context, Kant's point seems clearly to be a rather common-sense one. That is, those who release an offender whom they ought to punish also do wrong; to some extent they share the offender's guilt, as if they were accomplices (after the fact). There are strong and controversial assumptions at work here, but not clearly the doctrine that offenders should be punished because of their intrinsic moral deserts.

(4) Finally, let us look at a passage where Kant seems to speak more directly of the relation between a punishment and the offender's inner moral quality.

This fitting of punishment to the crime, which can occur only by a judge imposing the death sentence in accordance with the strict law of retribution, is shown by the fact that only by this is a sentence of death pronounced on every criminal in proportion to his *inner wickedness* (even when the crime is not murder but another crime against the state that can be paid for only by death).— Suppose that some . . . who took part in the recent Scottish rebellion believed that by their uprising they were only performing a duty they owed to the House of Stuart, while others on the contrary were out for their private interests; and suppose that the judgment pronounced by the highest court had been that each is free to make the choice between death and convict labor. I say that in this case the man of honor would choose death, and the scoundrel convict labor. This comes along with the nature of the human mind; for the man of honor is acquainted with something that he values even more highly than life, namely *honor*, while the scoundrel considers it better to live in shame than not to live at all. . . . Since the man of honor is undeniably less deserving of punishment than the other, both would be punished quite proportionately if all alike were sentenced to death; the man of honor would be punished mildly in terms of his sensibilities and the scoundrel severely in terms of his. On the other hand, if both were sentenced to convict labor the man of honor would be punished too severely and the other too mildly for his vile action. And so here, too, when sentence is pronounced on a number of criminals united in a plot, the best equalizer before public justice is *death*.[52]

Here Kant seems to imply that punishment ought to be imposed proportionately to the inner wickedness of the offender. This would be at odds with the interpretation that, I have argued, fits best Kant's main claims and arguments about punishment. Most crucially, it would be incompatible with the idea that juridical punishment is concerned only with intentional 'external' acts, known to be contrary to law, rather than with the overall moral quality of the will or character of the agent. Also, it conflicts significantly with Kant's characterization of 'the law of retribution' as calling for proportionality between severity of punishment and gravity of the crime as *measured by the victim's loss*, not by the criminal's degree of moral wickedness.

How can we understand this anomaly? The context is a general discussion of the idea that punishments ought somehow to be fitting and 'equal' to the crime even in cases where literal application of 'like for like' is inappropriate. Kant cites one case where the idea of equality is best served by making the punishments different for a rich man and a poor man; for a small fine for the rich is a milder punishment than it is for the poor. Here, assuming 'the same crime' (culpable insult), the penalty that is superficially 'the same' (a small fine) would constitute more severe punishment for one type of offender than another; and so Kant advocates different penalties that are more nearly equivalent in severity. The example of the Scottish rebels, it seems, allows that what is superficially 'the same crime' may encompass significantly different cases, just as in the first case what is superficially 'the same penalty' covered relevantly different cases. Regarding the rebels, the superficially same penalty (death) is said to be appropriate for what seem to be significantly different criminal acts (rebellion from misguided political loyalty vs. self-serving rebellion).

This raises an apparent objection to Kant's often repeated contention

[52] MM, 106–7 [6: 333–4].

that all rebels should be executed because, Kant says, the honorable rebels are undeniably 'less punishable.'[53] His (rather unconvincing) solution is to suggest that what is superficially 'the same' punishment (death) in this special case would nevertheless preserve appropriate proportionality of crime and punishment. This is because (supposedly) death is a more severe penalty for the dishonorable rebels than for the honorable ones because the former value life with dishonor more than the latter do. The point, on this reading, is to defend *lex talionis* as a general policy, if qualified and applied with sensitivity to relevant distinctions, against apparent counterexamples. Subjective factors, he grants, are sometimes relevant in assessing the severity of punishment (e.g., the rich man's indifference to a small fine).[54] The distinction between motives of agents (e.g., honor vs. malice) is usually *morally* relevant and so, one might think, they should be taken into account in the system of criminal justice.[55] But, in the present case and with few exceptions, Kant held that the courts should not deviate from the standard penalty according to its assessment of the criminals' motives. He argues, in effect, that in the case of the Scottish rebels, the literal application of 'same punishment' (death) for 'same crime' (rebellion) should not be thought morally offensive because, even though that rule disregards motives, the *result* is a morally appropriate proportionality of crime and punishment after all. The example is not an instance of the courts measuring the inner moral desert of the two groups of rebels and meting out punishment accordingly. To the contrary, a policy of judicial disregard for morally relevant differences is defended at least in the case under discussion. Kant apparently accepts that intuitively those with more dishonorable motives should be punished more severely, but he does not imply that courts should vary punishments according to their assessment of the motives of

---

[53] Note that Mary Gregor translates 'strafbar' here as 'deserving,' which misleadingly favors the idea that punishment is for inner desert. (A page earlier, MM, 106 [6: 332], she had rendered 'strafbar' as 'punishable,' thereby avoiding the misleading connotation in others' translations.) In the same paragraph about the Scottish rebels, she renders 'inneren Bösartigkeit' as 'inner wickedness,' which is clearly a deep moral quality of will, whereas the term naturally and more consistently can be rendered as 'inner maliciousness,' which could be a trait of character imputed on empirical evidence. Although Kant held that we cannot know for certain what a person's maxims are and especially whether a person has a good will or not, it would be a mistake, I think, to suppose that *everything* he refers to as 'inner' in a person is inaccessible and so cannot be attributed on the basis of empirical evidence.

[54] MM, 19–20 [6: 228], 106 [6: 332–3].

[55] Kant describes two cases in which he apparently regarded the motive of 'honor' as a mitigating factor, at least in our imperfect world: the woman who kills her illegitimate baby and the soldier who kills another in a duel (MM, 108–9 [6: 335–7]).

the offenders or that legislators should include motives in their definitions of crimes. This, like Kant's other ideas about punishment, is open to serious challenge, of course. My point here is simply to show how far Kant was from the doctrine of punishment for intrinsic deserts.

IV. CONJECTURES FOR A MORE PLAUSIBLE KANTIAN THEORY OF PUNISHMENT

Suppose we take seriously Kant's ideas about how the idea of wrongdoing is, and is not, connected with the idea of the offender's suffering. What difference would this make? Here are a few brief suggestions.

(A) The apparent tension between the harsh retributive tone of Kant's discussion of punishment and his basic ideas about what could justify the practice may be partially resolved. On the suggested reading, for example, acknowledging the role of deterrence in Kant's justification of the practice is compatible with granting that Kant also consistently, though perhaps mistakenly, endorsed strict retributive policies as guidelines governing punishment in particular cases. Like rule-utilitarians, Kantians would distinguish two levels of discussion of punishment: the right and duty to have such a practice at all, and the rules and policies that should govern its application. But the Kantian perspective on the first issue is not, like utilitarianism, exclusively focused on consequences, and so certain objections to two-level approaches to punishment would not apply.

(B) Suppose we assume that, for better or worse, punishment has an expressive function, conveying the moral disapproval of the community to lawbreakers who are thought (with rare exceptions) to have a moral duty to obey the law. Then this expressive or communicative function of punishment would provide the Kantian presumptive reasons for punishing all and only lawbreakers, proportionate to the gravity of their offenses (so far as this is publicly ascertainable).[56] Any reasonable theory will have to balance countervailing factors; but if judicial sentences are in part powerful *statements* to the accused and the community, they should be honest and they are subject to the fairness constraints of comparative justice. Imposing penalties is not just a useful conditioning tactic. To punish disproportionately, without a clear and overriding reason, gives a dishonest, untruthful message. To express disapproval of some and not others for merely pragmatic reasons is generally unfair and dishonest.

[56] This is a main theme of ch. 7 of my *Respect, Pluralism, and Justice*. See n. 8.

(C) The effects of recognition of wrongdoing cited earlier tend not to support but rather tell against *lex talionis*. There are two points to consider. First, 'in kind' punishments are often *more* than is needed to provide incentives to keep lawbreaking to an acceptable level because, with some exceptions, citizens in fact care about avoiding wrongdoing and incurring the consequent disapproval of fellow citizens. If Kant's idea about the moral consciousness of ordinary moral agents is even approximately correct, the justice system does not need to provide disincentives sufficient to make it work even for a 'race of devils.' Second, punishing merely 'in kind' or equivalent to the victim's loss would often be *too little* to serve the general need to hinder hindrances to freedom. This is especially clear when we take into account obvious imperfections in any system of law enforcement—the fact that we can detect and punish only a fraction of actual crimes. Everyone may be disposed to some degree to avoid wrongdoing, but obviously conscience is all too easily overridden. More severe punishments than the victim's loss often seem necessary to provide effective disincentives. Assuming, as I have, that *lex talionis* is not a basic principle but (at best) derivative, appropriate increases in punishment could be fair if justifiable to all from the appropriate Kantian legislative perspective.[57]

(D) As Herbert Morris and others have emphasized, punishment *at its best* can *speak* to the offender, setting in motion natural moral steps toward reform and restoration of relations with others.[58] This is just what Kant's intrinsic liability thesis would lead us to hope for. The appropriate message, however, must be an honest expression of a moral judgment with which the offender can identify. It should appeal to the criminal's conscience, and yet it cannot imply more knowledge of his heart and soul than courts can presume to judge. This last point is a serious constraint. The main point of punishment, on my reading of the Kantian view, is not to moralize. We must acknowledge that punishment is an institution that in fact conveys the moral disapproval of the community, whether this is a good thing or not; and, given this fact, we should try to arrange the institution so that its message is fair and no stronger than the state has the knowledge and moral authority to make.

---

[57] The Kantian moral legislative perspective is the moral point of view that is relevant to deliberations and debates about what more specific moral principles should govern various aspects of life. Attempts to interpret and reconstruct a Kantian account of this vary considerably. My partial attempts to characterize it are in *Dignity and Practical Reason*, ch. 2, pp. 58–66, ch. 10, pp. 196–225, and ch. 11, pp. 226–50, and several essays in *Respect, Pluralism, and Justice*.

[58] For example, Morris, 'A Paternalistic Theory of Punishment' and Joel Feinberg, 'The Expressive Function of Punishment', *Monist*, 49 (3) (1965), 397–423, reprinted in his *Doing and Deserving* (Princeton: Princeton University Press, 1970), 95–118.

Treating offenders as worthless scum, utterly incapable of reform, is obviously contrary to Kantian principles. The official judgment should focus on the alleged offense as appropriately judged by law—guilty or not—not gratuitous assessments of the offenders' moral worth, compared to others. In addition, the moral message is likely to be lost if the punishment is vindictive, merely pragmatic, or based on an inappropriate medical model.

(E) Given Kant's conception of what is involved in acknowledging that we have done wrong, it seems that, contrary to what Kant actually suggests, a kind of 'fear of punishment' could be a morally worthy motive.[59] That is, insofar as this is really a reluctance to face the correctly disapproving judgment of our fellow citizens, it may (indirectly) reflect our respect for them as rational moral agents who are, with us, equal sources of moral obligation whose judgments cannot be reasonably ignored.

(F) Finally, punishment can, and should, avoid treating the individual offender as a mere means to social benefit, although deterrence plays a significant role in the justification of the practice of punishment. Two points should be noted. First, you are not treating someone *merely* as a means in Kant's sense if you are at the same time treating the person as an end in itself. Arguably, then, we are respecting persons as ends if we never treat them by policies that we could not justify to them, assuming that they and we consider the matter from an appropriately impartial, mutually respectful point of view. In principle, a system partly justified by deterrence could be justified to the person who is punished under it. Suppose, for example, that each citizen has a fair share of liberty defined in accord with Kant's universal principle of justice; but suppose that coercion by credible threat of punishment is necessary to support this system; suppose, further, that each has fair opportunity to avoid the penalty (by avoiding the crime); suppose that the justification makes no appeal to utilitarian calculations of the value of one individual's life or liberty against that of others; suppose, finally, that to the extent possible this system is actually accepted and enforced as an ongoing institution in a republican democracy. Given such conditions as these, the criminals seem to have no grounds to complain that they are being treated as mere means. They could have avoided the penalty by accepting a share of liberty comparable to that of others; they must acknowledge that coercive threats are needed to make the system work

---

[59] I develop this theme in 'Punishment, Conscience, and Moral Worth', Ch. 11 in this volume.

and that, in general, the threats must be carried out for the system to be credible. They can only try to complain that the system did not give them an *unfair* advantage over others, and that is not a valid complaint.

Consider, however, the further objection that the offender is still being treated as a mere means because, after all, the threat did not work on him and the carrying out of the threat then is just to preserve the credibility of the system. Is that not treating him, after the crime, as a mere means to uphold the social good of having legal threats be credible? The reply, I think, requires us to keep focused on the executive officials' perspective on the particular case. The judge, jury, and other law enforcement officers are not supposed to carry out the law's threat because they judge this a necessary means to reinforce the credibility of the penal system but because it is their assigned duty in the system of justice. The focus of their attention should not be on how to deter others by 'setting an example.' Their job is to carry out a just law, with its sanctions, as legally prescribed by the system; and one can give a general (though not an absolute) moral justification for their doing so. The law's threat of punishment is to each citizen, but once offenders have ignored it what is relevant is the relation between the law and the individual offenders. They disregarded the legitimate threat addressed to them, and the law has, in general, a morally justifiable right to carry out what it threatened *to them*. By hypothesis, they have no complaint against the system, and the effect of the punishment on others is not now the issue. The court imposes the punishment on individuals because that is the law, not because it is a means to frighten others. At least in this best case scenario, the courts thereby respect the humanity of offenders as an end, though this provides the offenders no escape from the legitimate sanction that, by their free choice, they willfully incurred. The problem that criminals are treated disrespectfully, as mere means to social ends, is undeniably real, but its source is not the broadly Kantian theoretical approach to punishment outlined here but rather the discrepancy between our actual practices and the ideal of justice that Kant attempted to articulate.[60]

---

[60] I am grateful for the support of the Social Philosophy and Policy Center at Bowling Green University while completing this essay. Participants in discussions at Bowling Green and Santa Clara Universities offered helpful comments, and I want especially to thank Bernard Boxill, Sarah Holtman, Jeffrie Murphy, and Gerald Postema for their help and encouragement on this and other projects.

11

Punishment, Conscience, and Moral Worth

In the *Metaphysics of Morals* Kant offers us pieces of a theory of *punishment*, a metaphorical description of *conscience*, and an elaboration of his earlier account of the *moral worth* of actions. My questions concern relations among these.[1] How is conscience analogous to punishment in Kant's theory, and how is it different? What is the role of *fear* of punishment and *pangs* of conscience? Are these morally acceptable motives? Can an autonomy-based moral theory approve of institutions that rely on fear of judicial punishment or of individuals who need to be moved by the painful prodding of conscience? Can there be any moral worth in such motives?

I begin with a sketch of Kant's views about punishment and conscience. Since my main concern is with how punishment and conscience *motivate* us, my plan is simply to highlight some features of Kant's views that are relevant to my questions about motivation. In these background sections I draw from previous discussions of Kant's conceptions of punishment and conscience that treat them separately and in more detail.[2] Some points may be controversial, but my aim for now is simply to summarize my understanding of Kant's conceptions in order to facilitate the later discussion.

The background for what I say about punishment is an ongoing debate about the interpretation of Kant's provocative remarks about punishment, reinvigorated by new challenges to the formerly accepted view of Kant as a prime example of a retributivist.[3] To preview briefly,

---

[1] I am grateful to the participants at the Spindel Conference at the University of Memphis, October, 1997, and especially to Nelson Potter, for helpful comments and discussion.

[2] These discussions include ch. 7 of my *Respect, Pluralism, and Justice*, Ch. 8 of this volume, and chs. 9 and 10 of *Dignity and Practical Reason*.

[3] See, for example: B. Sharon Byrd, 'Kant's Theory of Punishment: Deterrence in its Threat, Retribution in its Execution', *Law and Philosophy*, 8 (1980), 151–220; Donald E. Scheid, 'Kant's Retributivism', *Ethics*, 93 (1983), 262–82; Jeffrie Murphy, *Kant: The Philosophy of Right* (London: Macmillan, 1970), 109–49, and 'Kant's Theory of Criminal Punishment' in his *Retribution, Justice and Therapy: Essays in the Philosophy*

what I suggest is the following: Although Kant does endorse standards of punishment commonly associated with retributivism, his rationale for endorsing those standards is far from the familiar retributivist thought that evildoers inherently deserve to suffer. To the contrary, the retributive elements in Kant's theory are more firmly rooted in considerations of comparative justice and honesty in public expressions of moral judgment. On the other side, although Kant does hold that any legal system must use the fear of punishment to deter citizens from crime, punishment for Kant is far more than a deterrence system of social control—we do not punish 'simply to deter crime.'

The background for my later discussion of motives is this. Endless debates have raged over the interpretation and value of Kant's views about the 'nonmoral' motives of sympathy and compassion, but surprisingly little attention has been given to the place and value of the other motives on which I want to focus: fear of punishment and the prompting of conscience. These incentives, like sympathy and reasonable self-love, have often been thought respectable, even worthy, motives for doing what is right; but they are not unproblematic from the perspectives of Kantian moral theory and reflective common sense. How are we to understand these motives? Can acting from such motives be morally worthy? Are they morally indifferent motives, perhaps necessary at times but of no credit to those who act on them? Or, worse, are they morally objectionable, unworthy of us as free and rational persons?

These are large questions, and my aim is only to raise the issues, offer some suggestions, and invite discussion. Although my initial questions are about Kant's moral theory, as expressed especially in the *Metaphysics of Morals*, my long-range interest extends beyond this. I want to consider whether, as I suspect, there are both important insights and serious flaws in Kant's ethical writings on these topics and, if so, what a reasonable Kant*ian* ethics, suitably revised and supplemented, might say on the issues in question.[4] Ultimately, of course, as philosophers we want to assess this whole Kantian approach, compared to the best alternatives—but that is not the issue at present.

---

of Law (Dordrecht, Holland: D. Reidel, 1979), 82–92; and Sarah Holtman, 'Toward Social Reform: Kant's Penal Theory Reinterpreted', *Utilitas*, 9 (1997), 3–21.

[4] In this paper I am concerned more with interpreting and extending Kant's ethics than with criticizing it, but I hope it is clear that I do not mean to endorse all of the views of Kant's that I summarize and try to understand sympathetically.

I. KANT'S THEORY OF PUNISHMENT: SOME MAIN POINTS

Several ideas about Kant's theory of punishment will be especially relevant when we turn to punishment as a motive.

(1) We have a moral duty to obey the law. There is an important exception, for we must not obey any order to commit acts that are in 'conflict with inner morality.'[5] That case aside, juridical duties are also indirect ethical duties.[6] That is, apart from the exception just mentioned, conformity to the law is a strict moral duty; and making it our principle to do so from duty is a requirement of virtue—even though legal authorities cannot demand this.

(2) This qualified duty to conform to legal requirements is not a freestanding moral axiom but is derived from more fundamental moral premises together with assumptions about the human condition. The more basic ideas are the *Categorical Imperative*, the innate rights to freedom and equality, the universal principle of justice, and its corollary authorizing coercion to 'hinder hindrances to freedom.'[7] From these starting points Kant attempts to derive the duty to establish and maintain a Sovereign legal authority with the right to make laws and to punish lawbreakers.

(3) Although not subject to legal constraint, the Sovereign authority in any legal system can be gravely wrong in its legislation. Errors of fact and judgment are common even when legislators are conscientiously trying to be guided by the moral law. And, of course, legislators are not always conscientious. Nonetheless, the errors and corruption of lawmakers are not in themselves a justification or excuse for disobeying the law.[8] Except when the law orders us to do something 'intrinsically immoral,' legal offenses are *ipso facto* moral offenses.[9]

(4) Lawmakers and judges should determine the manner, extent, and scope of punishment by rules commonly associated with 'retributivism.' That is, (a) all and only those who break the law are to be punished,

---

[5] See MM, 98 [6: 322], 136–8 [6: 371–2], and R, 153n [6: 154n]. See also Hans Reiss's 'Postscript', in *Kant: Political Writings*, ed. Hans Reiss (Cambridge: Cambridge University Press, 1991), 267–8.

[6] MM, 21–2 [6: 220–1].

[7] MM, 17–18 [6: 225–6], 23–4 [6: 229–32], and 29–30 [6: 236–8].

[8] MM, 95–8 [6: 318–23].

[9] This is not to say that the ideas of 'legal offense' and 'moral offense' are the same, but merely that (apart from the exceptions noted) when one commits a legal offense this is also a moral offense (against the moral requirement to obey the law).

(b) the severity of punishment should be proportionate to the gravity of the crime, and (c) the manner of punishment should be 'like for like' ('an eye for an eye') except when physically or morally impossible. Also, (d) punishment presupposes that the agent had the freedom necessary to conform to the law, and (e) punishments degrading to humanity are prohibited.[10] The law should be concerned only with intentional 'external acts' that violate enforceable public requirements.[11] Whether our motives are morally worthy is not the business of the courts. Moral unworthiness is not equivalent or proportionate to legal culpability, even though (with the exception noted) every criminal act is presumably based on a maxim that is morally unworthy to some degree.[12]

(5) Punishment is a practice through which officials and the public express moral disapproval of criminal acts. In this respect punishment differs significantly from many other sorts of disincentives that serve to promote social order. It is not simply a useful public device to control behavior. It expresses public condemnation of 'external' (but intentional) acts contrary to laws that should be obeyed. This expressive aspect of punishment, I think, is an inseparable part of the traditional and common understanding of what it is to *punish* someone, as opposed to merely venting anger, using negative conditioning, or frightening others into conformity. Also, if we suppose (as I do) that Kant took the expressive aspect of punishment for granted, then this helps to narrow the gap between Kant's basic moral premises and his particular rules regarding who should be punished, how much, and in what manner.[13] That is, once we see punishment as, in part, a *statement* of public disapproval, then we can invoke Kant's standards of honesty and fairness to see why, for example, punishments cannot be varied simply for pragmatic reasons and convicted criminals cannot be pardoned whenever it would be useful.[14]

---

[10] MM, 102–9 [6: 328–37]. [11] MM, 23–4 [6: 230].

[12] Kant implies that the degree cannot be determined with any assurance and that it is not the business of the courts to assess.

[13] These are points discussed in ch. 7 of my *Respect, Pluralism, and Justice*. I do not claim that Kant explicitly notes the expressive function of punishment, but only that it would be a natural assumption and helps to make sense of his position. Even more, I do not claim that Kant held an expressive *theory* of punishment of the sort that Joel Feinberg describes in his justly famous paper, 'The Expressive Function of Punishment', *Monist*, 49(3) (1965), 399–423, reprinted in his *Doing and Deserving* (Princeton: Princeton University Press, 1971), 95–118. The expression of official and public disapproval is a constitutive feature of what we commonly understand as *punishment*, but it is a feature that may make the practice of punishment more problematic rather than a feature that explains why the practice is justified.

[14] For example, it is dishonest to express a severe moral judgment on one person and

To forestall misunderstanding, I should add that my suggestion is not that expressing public disapproval is the justifying aim of punishment. Rather, the expressive function is simply a feature of the practice that itself needs to be justified. We should not deprive people of liberty and make them suffer *in order to* express our moral disapproval, but the fact that punishment is a practice through which disapproval is expressed must be taken seriously when we think about how to impose punishment fairly and honestly and also when we consider whether the practice is justifiable at all.

(6) The ultimate justification for having the practice of punishment is not retribution or deterrence, as these are commonly understood. The *lex talionis* is a policy of returning to wrongdoers an equivalent to losses they inflicted on another, but Kant justifies it as 'the only unwavering standard,' not because wickedness inherently warrants the infliction of suffering.[15] Despite some suggestions to the contrary, Kant's premiss is not that it is intrinsically good for criminals to be unhappy in proportion to their moral unworthiness; and he certainly did not think that it is the business of the state to try to bring about such proportionality.

For a long time Kant's theory of punishment was almost universally regarded as the paradigm of retributivism, but recent scholars have rightly called attention to the fact that the need to deter crime plays a crucial role in Kant's justification of the right and duty of the state to punish lawbreakers. But this recognition of the need for deterrence seems at odds with the many passages in the *Metaphysics of Morals* that initially led so many to label Kant's theory *retributivist*. Various commentaries have suggested ways in which deterrence and retribution might be mixed in Kant's theory of punishment. A common first step is to distinguish the rules governing the practice (or institution) of

---

a mild judgment on another if the only difference has to do with external factors, unrelated to their offenses. And it is not fair to profess public disapproval of some offenders on a certain basis but then refuse to make the same judgment on others. These considerations do not fully justify Kant's inflexible policy of proportionate punishment for all of the guilty, but they provide a strong presumption for proportionality.

[15] MM, 105–6 [6: 332]. In a passage referring to the 'inner wickedness' of murderers at MM, 106–7 [6: 333–4] Kant seems to take a different view, but I argue that even this uncharacteristic passage does not imply that it is the business of the state to mete out punishment in accord with inner wickedness. The passage seems to be an *ad hoc* response to a possible worry that, by not assessing the comparative inner moral worth of murderers, strict application of *lex talionis* would make idealistic revolutionaries suffer just as much as vicious ones. Kant argues that, at least in the case of Scottish rebels of 1745–6, execution would have been worse for the vicious revolutionaries. See *Dignity and Practical Reason*, 186.

punishment from the justification of having such practice. Given this distinction, it has been suggested that *deterrence* is the justifying aim of having the institution and *retributive policies* are constitutive features of the institution, features that either promote the justifying end or serve as side constraints.[16] Another proposal is that the *threat of punishment* is justified by the aim of deterring crime, but the *execution of punishment* is justified independently by considerations of justice and the requirement to treat persons as ends in themselves.[17]

These proposals are improvements on earlier one-sided interpretations, but I suspect that they do not yet fully capture the retributive side of Kant's thought. In any case, the suggestion that for Kant the aim of punishment is deterrence seems misleadingly oversimple. Clearly, Kant did not want the operative aim of *judges* (and other enforcement officials) in administering the law to be to deter future crime, either by 'making an example' of convicted criminals or by making them realize the price they will pay for further wrongdoing. This point is rightly acknowledged by commentators who distinguish the working policies of the practice from its 'justifying aim.' Also, Kant makes plain that legislators, in deciding what sanctions to assign to various legal offenses, should be guided by *lex talionis* and a prohibition of degrading punishments, not by a pragmatic policy of assigning whatever will most efficiently deter crime. But, even if these constraints on judges and legislators are considered part of the practice rather than its justification, it would still be misleading to say that for Kant the aim of the practice is to deter crime. That aim has an important role, but it is only part of a much more complex story.

The background of the story includes everyone's innate natural rights to freedom and equality, which in turn must be rooted in the basic moral law expressed in various forms of the *Categorical Imperative*.[18] A crucial premiss is the universal principle of justice (*Recht*), which says (roughly) that it is unjust to hinder the external liberty of another if that hindrance could not take place under a system of laws in which everyone is entitled to liberty equally. In a state of nature, acts against this principle would be violations of 'right' in a slightly attenuated, but still important, sense: they are acts that 'ought to be prohibited by law' and they

---

[16] Scheid, 'Kant's Retributivism', 262–5.
[17] Byrd, 'Kant's Theory of Punishment', 157, 184–98.
[18] This is well presented by Byrd, even though she occasionally writes of deterrence as the justifying aim of threats of punishment—a description, I think, that does not do justice to the fuller understanding of Kant's position that, in most respects, her article shows.

may be coercively opposed even in a state of nature. The often cited corollary of the principle of justice is supposed to express its implicit meaning more fully: violations of the principle can be coercively opposed as 'hindrance to hindrances to (legitimate) freedom.'[19] This points us toward a justification of punishment, but there are obviously more steps needed. For example, we have as yet no specification of how much, in what ways, and by whom coercion may be exercised. Kant fills in some gaps by asserting a moral duty to establish and obey a Sovereign not subject to legal constraints.[20] This, he argues rather unconvincingly, is conceptually necessary for the possibility of justice. Then Kant moves rather quickly to a description of the authoritative powers of the Sovereign and the moral principles which *should* constrain legislation and enforcement even though no one has the right to force the hand of the Sovereign.

Gaps remain, but enough pieces of the story are in place to make clear that it is better to avoid simple descriptions like 'in Kant's theory the justifying aim of punishment is deterrence.' Of course, that waves a hand toward Kant's view, but the trouble is that it points indiscriminately to a whole variety of unKantian deterrence theories at the same time. We could as easily say that punishment is to make justice possible, to protect the legitimate liberties of citizens, or respect the Sovereign's moral and legal right to use coercion to maintain justice. Admittedly, any one of these descriptions would also oversimplify; brief slogans almost invariably do. Punishment for Kant would lose its rationale if threats of punishment never, or rarely, deterred offenders, but 'deterring crime' is not a self-sufficient moral goal and principles specifying whom to punish, how much, and in what ways are far from being settled by seeing what means most efficiently achieve this end—or even the end of 'minimizing violations of justice.'

II. CONSCIENCE: THE INNER JUDGE

Apart from a few brief references, Kant does not make much of the idea of *conscience* in the *Groundwork* or the second *Critique*. In the *Metaphysics of Morals* and later in *Religion* he explains, in metaphorical terms, how he views conscience.[21] His conception of conscience, I

---

[19] MM, 24 [6: 231].   [20] MM, 89 ff. [6: 311 ff.].
[21] G, 89–90 [4: 422], G, 72 [4: 404], C2, 82–3 [5: 98], MM, 27 [6: 235], MM, 160–1 [6: 400–1], MM, 188–9 [6: 438–42], and R, 178–9 [6: 185–6].

think, is distinctive in some respects, and perhaps initially surprising; but in the end it can be seen to fit well with his basic moral theory.

In some popular views, conscience replaces reason as a way of determining what is right. It is viewed as a God-given instinctual sense that tells us whether what we are doing, have done, or are proposing to do is wrong. On this view, although conscience itself may be infallible, its voice (like that of the ancient oracles) can be misunderstood, misheard, or distorted through self-deception, distracting influences, etc. A different conception of conscience was well described in the sermons of Bishop Butler.[22] Butler used 'conscience' as the name of a faculty of reason, able to discern 'in a calm hour' what is fitting for human beings to do in their particular situations. Reason, in Butler's view, relies on a natural teleology of human faculties. We have self-love, benevolence, and particular passions; and conscience is just reflective reason, determining what it is fitting for a person with such natural dispositions to do. In more recent times, cultural relativists treat conscience as nothing but the psychological manifestations of having internalized the social norms of our culture. Kant's view is interestingly different from all of these.

For Kant, *reason* determines the basic principles of right conduct, *judgment* is needed to apply them, and strength of *will* must be developed to follow our best judgments unfailingly. *Conscience*, in Kant's view, does not serve any of these functions. It does not tell us generally what is right: that is the job of reason. Conscience does not tell us what the principles of right imply for more specific situations: that is the job of judgment. And conscience is not the ready power to do what we judge right despite temptations: that is virtue, or strength of will to do right. Our reason can be obscured by self-deception, but conscience seems to speak unavoidably even when we do not want to consult it. Our moral judgments can err, but (Kant says) conscience cannot. Our strength of will can be deficient, but conscience makes us suffer even so. How are we to understand all this?

Kant discusses conscience in metaphorical terms. A person with a conscience has a sort of internal judicial system. It is as if we were called into court to account for our conduct. We accuse ourselves, try to defend ourselves, and then the inner judge of conscience reaches a verdict—guilty or not guilty—and passes sentence. Not a legislator who makes

---

[22] Joseph Butler, *Five Sermons*, ed. Stephen Darwall (Indianapolis: Hackett Publishing Co., 1983).

the laws and not a legal expert who simply informs us of their implications, conscience is the inner judge that either acquits us or condemns us to suffer for our failures. The relevant charge in this court, significantly, is not violation of what is objectively, and correctly, judged to be a moral requirement. Rather, the relevant charges, in effect, are of two kinds: (1) that we have failed *to act in accord with our own general moral judgments*, e.g., the judgments we make about right and wrong when not specifically focused on our own situation, and (2) that we have failed in our *duty of due care* by not being sufficiently serious and careful in determining in particular what our duties are.[23]

When we judge what is right in general we are supposed to be guided by the moral law; but making such judgments is not the job of conscience. Rather, conscience holds up our *acts-as-we-perceive-them* for comparison with the *general-moral-judgments-that-we-accept* (e.g., regarding others) in order to see whether we have acted well by our own lights. And conscience also has the second task: to pass judgment on whether we have been careful and diligent in our initial moral judgments about what generally human beings may do in various situations. In this second capacity, Kant remarks, paradoxically, that conscience is 'judgment passing judgment upon itself.'[24]

Conscience, so conceived, cannot err, Kant says.[25] His view is understandable, even if exaggerated. The idea is that, although we can make mistakes in our particular judgments about what morality objectively requires in various situations, we are not liable to the same sorts of mistakes when we compare 'inner' thoughts—i.e., what we *intend* to be doing in the situation as we perceive it and what we *think* that human beings may do in such a situation. Errors of fact, for example, can lead to misjudgments about whether our actual acts were permissible, but those errors do not prevent us from seeing (when it is so) that our acts-as-we-perceive-them are at odds with our moral judgments-as-we-accept-them. No doubt, contrary to Kant, we can make errors even in comparing these 'inner' thoughts. If so, Kant's denial that there can be an 'erring conscience' is an exaggeration, not strictly true. But a significant contrast remains between judgments of conscience and judgments of objective duty, as Kant conceives these. That is, the latter are vulnerable to many sources of error that the former are not. Misunderstanding the material facts about the situation that we are in, for example, commonly leads to mistakes about what it is objectively right

---

[23] Here I put together ideas from Kant's *Metaphysics of Morals* and his *Religion within the Boundaries of Mere Reason*. The duty of due care is from R, 178–80 [6: 185–7].

[24] R, 179 [6: 186].   [25] MM, 160–1 [6: 401].

to do in that context, but that sort of error does not affect the judgment of conscience.[26]

Conscience, then, is like judicial punishment in several ways. Both condemn or acquit us by judging fallible conceptions of our acts by normative standards that may not be objectively justifiable. *At best* both the laws of the judicial system and the moral judgments at work in conscience are made with respect and proper understanding of the moral law: the public legislator's in the first case and the individual moral agent's in the second. But public lawmakers in determining the judicial standards can be foolish and corrupt, and, despite Kant's greater faith in them, individual agents are obviously not immune to ignorance and vice when they apply their basic understanding of the moral law to specific situations. Kant thought that, though imperfect, both the laws of the state and the demands of conscience must be followed. Kant admits these may conflict when the laws of the state require a person to do something in conflict with 'inner morality', but in all other cases an informed conscience is supposed to demand conformity to public laws, no matter how bad the laws are. Thus, apart from a (rarely mentioned) exception, the imperatives to follow law and conscience are both strict.

There are differences, of course. The range of public law is narrower than that of conscience, for it is restricted to external acts that may be coerced. Conformity to conscience is supposed to be sufficient for a *morally blameless* life; but conformity to public law, obviously, is not. But even here there is a parallel: conformity to public law is supposed to be sufficient for a *legally blameless* life, i.e., for immunity from judicial punishment and condemnation.

Let us focus now on how punishment and conscience function as motives. Both have a dark side, and a brighter side; or, better, each of them, I suggest, can be interpreted as an unworthy motive or as a worthy motive. Conscience is usually regarded as an admirable motive, but it may not be. Fear of punishment is usually regarded as an unworthy motive, but it need not be.

---

[26] 'Objectively right' here raises questions. Unlike many consequentialists, Kant is not primarily concerned with what is 'right' independently of the knowledge and understanding of the agent. The universal law formulas, for example, test agents' subjective principles (maxims) and so the results always depend, in a way, on how they conceive the situation they are in. But Kant also has, I think, a notion of objective right as what reason would prescribe *given a correct assessment of the facts, a clear understanding of the basic moral law, and no distorting influences on judgment*. Kant apparently thought that the well-intentioned Scottish rebels mentioned at MM, 106–7 [6: 333–4] did what was objectively wrong in this sense even though they mistakenly judged what they did to be morally justified (and so, as some say, they were 'subjectively right').

III. A PROBLEM: FEAR OF PUNISHMENT AS AN APPARENTLY UNWORTHY MOTIVE

Kant's ethics is famous for its insistence that moral agents have autonomy of the will. They recognize moral requirements, then, as what they must do, irrespective of anticipated rewards and punishments. Only acts from duty have moral worth; and, even if acting from other motives is quite natural and unobjectionable in many situations, when the duty is clear, evident, and salient, to conform to duty from motives that are utterly unrelated to a will to do right seems at least morally suspect. It falls short of a Kantian ideal, and perhaps it displays insufficient attention to the (imperfect) duty to strive for moral perfection. Even common opinion, for example, would think it 'unworthy' of a human being (and not just failure to achieve a special moral praiseworthiness) to rescue a drowning rich man with mind and heart focused on potential reward money—even if one would have managed to do it 'from duty' had the man been poor. Does Kant's theory of punishment, as sometimes thought, represent a retreat from these bold moral ideas? Is it, perhaps, a sign of Kant's willingness to compromise with hard realities of human nature?

Why might we suspect this? One line of thought might run as follows: Despite Kant's eloquence in favor of fulfillment of duty from respect for moral law, when he turns to the problem of how to establish and maintain a just social order under laws, he advocates a legal system that does not require a moral motivation and would suffice even to keep order among fiends. The law, he says, is to be concerned only with 'external' acts and so disregards the moral worth of the agent's motives, enforcing the same strict requirements whether the offender's motives were high-minded or base. Now this might seem to reflect a weakening of Kant's professed faith in the capacity of every moral agent to do his/her duty from respect for the moral law alone. Why, we might wonder, should we utterly disregard this capacity when concerned with matters of law and justice, resting our trust entirely in citizen's fear of punishment rather than their will to do what is right?

This worry rests partly on misunderstanding. Kant never denies that moral agents *can* be just from respect for the moral law. In fact, since all juridical duties are 'indirectly ethical duties,' Kant implies that we have an (imperfect) ethical duty to conform to them from respect for the moral law that grounds them. And that we ought implies that we can, at least often and increasingly so, if we strive for moral perfection. We must presume, then, that we can be law-abiding citizens because we acknowledge our duty, under justice, to follow the law. Perhaps most people do, at least under good social conditions. Kant's claim that a legal system should be designed to be effective, even among egoists with no moral sense, does not imply that most citizens will follow it with that attitude or that they would resort to crime without such tough-minded law enforcement. Coercion (e.g., through punishment) is needed, Kant thought, to make a just social order possible, but this only implies that we cannot do without coercion at least as a 'fall back' motivation provided to the weak and corrupt. It does not imply that each and every citizen needs to be moved by fear of punishment, nor even that the weak and corrupt always need this.

There is, however, another possible source of the suspicion of Kant's reliance on threats of punishment. This is the thought that by advocating a system thoroughly reliant on nonmoral incentives, such as the fear of punishment, Kant endorses a motivation that is, from a Kantian point of view, unworthy of morally mature human beings, a rather ugly motive needed only by the weak and corrupt. To be fair, the critic will not say that Kant *recommends* the motive of fear of punishment, but does he not rest content with it as a crucial pillar of human society, as a motivational attitude that, though unworthy in itself, is acceptable to exploit and use for good ends? Even if threats are necessary for extreme cases, one might think, a social system that by design relies exclusively on threats expresses contempt for our better natures.

This worry is more interesting than the last and it is not entirely rooted in misunderstanding of Kant's views. However, I suggest that, with suitable supplement, Kant's main points about the morality of punishment allow for a more appealing way of thinking about the problem. The practice of punishment, even as Kant interprets it, can and should tap into finer motives than mere amoral fear of legally inflicted pain and deprivation. To be sure, the practice does serve to provide protection to the liberties of law-abiding citizens by means of threatening unwanted consequences to would-be offenders who refuse to be moved in any other way; but, despite the impression that Kant may at times give, that is far from the entire picture about how the practice of punishment draws upon our motivational resources. In order to lay background for this suggestion, I turn next to an analogous motive: the prompting and pangs of conscience.

IV. AN ANALOGOUS PROBLEM: CONSCIENCE AS AN APPARENTLY UNWORTHY MOTIVE

A bad conscience 'hurts,' and, as we have seen, Kant treats this pain as analogous to the suffering imposed on lawbreakers by the system of criminal justice. If fear of punishment is an unworthy motive for doing what duty requires, then it would seem that it is equally unworthy to do one's duty from fear of a bad conscience. And if the system of criminal justice systematically relies on threats that exploit our unworthy fear of punishment, and so expresses contempt for our better natures, the same would seem to he true of conscience. It prods, pricks, nags, and even torments moral offenders, pressuring them (it seems) to change their ways. It helps to prevent us from sliding into immoral practices, it seems, because we are aware that our conscience, that inner judge, will exact a heavy price if we do. It does not simply inform us of what is right but warns us, threatens us, and reminds us of the sanctions it will impose for disobedience.

Obviously, we need a distinction here. There are different ways that we can respond to conscience. In the worst case, of course, a person may be moved solely by a desire to avoid the discomforts of a bad conscience. We sometimes say, for example, 'I couldn't sleep if I did *that*,' suggesting that all that holds us back from doing something awful is a desire to avoid insomnia. Actually, this is often said with false modesty: it is not 'cool' to display one's moral commitments. If it is really the pangs of *conscience* (in Kant's sense) that the agent fears, then the agent must believe that the act expected to bring on the pain is wrong and contrary to his or her own moral judgment. On Kantian and other internalist moral theories, no one could be indifferent to violating his or her own moral judgments. So, on these theories, it is not even possible to care only about the pain incurred when one transgresses conscience; moral agents necessarily have some regard for doing what they believe right. Nonetheless, it is possible to be exclusively focused on the discomforts that violating conscience will bring, and thus also possible to be moved on particular occasions just by a desire to avoid those discomforts. The ugliness of this worst case motivation is highlighted when we realize that, if that is all that deters the agent, then he or she might violate conscience and then take a pill to block the discomfort if that were possible. If all that keeps me from betraying a friend is that it would cause me to lose sleep, then I must be quite ready to do it if I have an adequate supply of (nonaddictive) sleeping pills.

The worst case just described may not be the only possibility, but the alternative is not yet clear. Given that we often speak with respect of deeds motivated by conscience, it would be very odd to suppose that these were simply a matter of someone's choosing to avoid pain. If conscience were viewed simply as a faculty that 'informs' us what we ought to do, then we might praise these 'conscientious' acts as nothing more than acts guided by our moral beliefs or, in other words, instances of 'acting from duty.' But that idea is not available to Kant, for, as mentioned, he held that we determine what we ought to do through reason and judgment, not conscience. Kantian conscience speaks, after self-accusation and self-defense, as a judge who enforces the law, passes sentence, and so makes us suffer for our misdeeds. Or, in advance, it threatens, or warns, of the sentence and consequent suffering that we can expect if we do not scrupulously try to avoid wrongdoing. So, it seems, being motivated by conscience (as Kant conceives it) must be like being motivated by fear of punishment in that anticipation of *pain inflicted for wrongdoing* plays a significant role.

It is not obvious, then, that it is morally worthy to be motivated by conscience. Whether it is so depends on how, more specifically, we understand that motive in particular cases.

V. ANTICIPATION OF GRIEF AND CONCERN TO DO MORALLY WORTHY ACTS

Let us consider some other cases in which an apparently simple motive can be understood in different ways.

Anticipation of Grief

Suppose, to explain our giving life-preserving aid or advice, we said, 'We would grieve terribly if you died.' We might be expressing the attitude that we want to prevent the untimely death of the other person in order to satisfy our desire to avoid pain for ourselves. But that is not the only possibility. In many cases the remark would be more plausibly understood as an expression of love, a deep attachment manifested in our disposition to experience pain when those we love suffer or meet an untimely death. The experience of grief, so understood, is painful, but what 'hurts' is the recognition of their loss and our inability to continue a cherished relationship with them. If we hope that others will grieve for us when we die, at least for a short while, this is not because we want them to suffer but because we hope that they will remember us with love and respect and we know that, at least for most human beings, such memories are inevitably painful for a while after the death of a loved one.

Sometimes we cannot, in fact, have the good we want in a situation without some necessary pain, but we can readily imagine what it would be like to do so and wish that this were possible. For example, at present doctors may sometimes need to manipulate injured limbs and then to rely on the patient's reports of pain in order to identify the injured parts; but we can imagine and wish that they could get the information otherwise. Again, we may in fact be unable to work our hardest to accomplish challenging projects without suffering anxiety in the process and being liable to painful disappointment if we fail, but we can imagine this and wish it were possible. With grief it seems different: it is hard to imagine loving someone deeply and yet experiencing no pain when first facing and remembering the good we have both lost. Even if we can imagine that drugs or Stoic training could enable us to love, face the loss, and yet feel no pain, it is far from obvious that transforming ourselves in these ways would be worth what we would lose in doing so.

How, then, might the thought that we would grieve for someone lead to our doing something? As the idea 'crosses our mind,' as we say, we are imaginatively entertaining 'how it would be' if the loved one died, and this typically is an unpleasant, even painful, thought. But why? It is not quite like imagining ourselves having a headache, which is unpleasant to anticipate simply because we dislike being in pain. We shudder, and recoil, at the thought of the untimely death of loved ones because we value them, not just because we hate to be in pain. The thought moves us (for example, to act protectively) not like a painful itch that drives us to scratch, but like a jarring 'wake up call' that focuses our attention on something we value for its own sake.

Concern to Do Morally Worthy Acts

Some Kantians may look with suspicion at an analogy between the motives of love and conscience, and so let us also look at another complex motive—one that seems to have a Kantian moral dimension. Acting from duty is supposed to be morally worthy; acts from other motives, apart from this, are supposed to lack moral worth. But suppose that someone is strongly *motivated to do acts that are morally worthy*?

Is this a morally worthy motive, the sort of motive that makes acts deserving of moral esteem?

It all depends on how, more specifically, we understand the motive. There are several possibilities, some morally admirable, some ugly. What would be morally admirable? This, for Kant, is acting out of respect for the moral law, nothing less. But, given Kant's theory, the description 'acts that have moral worth' picks out just those acts that fulfill duty and are motivated by respect for moral law. So, on one possible reading, 'a concern to do acts that have moral worth' can be a stand in (for Kantians) for *doing one's duty from duty,* even though strictly 'having moral worth' is not the same idea as 'fulfilling duty from duty.' Consider an analogy.[27] Suppose papers deserve As only if they are academically excellent by the usual standards of clarity, cogency, understanding of issues, originality, etc. Genuinely good students will be primarily concerned with academic excellence rather than getting A grades *per se*. But, assuming fair and proper grading, they will take for granted that A papers are academically excellent. They may even express this concern when they say that they are working for As, i.e., trying to do all A work. Referring to the desired papers as 'A papers' serves (approximately) to *pick out* the intended set of papers, but not by describing the essential features for which they are valued. Similarly, a good person whom we may describe as 'trying to act in a morally worthy way' may be ultimately concerned, not so much with deserving moral esteem, but with doing what is right because it is right.

But there is also a less sympathetic way to understand the concern to do acts of moral worth. Assuming for now that 'morally worthy acts' are 'acts deserving of moral esteem,' the agents' focus of attention could be exclusively on their own moral records and how others should view them.[28] There are much worse motives, no doubt. At least the concern

---

[27] Here is an alternative analogy. When sorting apples, I'm asked why. I say, 'I want to select all the really bright red ones.' The inquirer might wonder, a bit perversely, why I am so 'hung up' on color. But suppose I am assuming that the bright red ones are tastier, more nourishing, etc., and my main concern, after all, was to select the tastier, more nourishing apples. When I explained why I was sorting the apples as I was, I referred to a visible identifying mark rather than the object of my ultimate concern, as we often do, unless some one explicitly presses us to explain our more basic or ground-level motivation. By analogy, to say 'I want to do acts of moral worth' (or, more naturally, 'I want to act in a morally worthy way') may express a basic respect for the moral law even though that is not mentioned explicitly.

[28] A promising alternative idea of moral worth, developed by Robert Johnson in a manuscript not yet published, understands 'morally worthy acts' from the deliberative stance as those morally worthy of choice, i.e., those whose maxim is such that

in question is to *deserve* esteem for one's deeds, not merely to *receive* it. But, still, the motive may not reflect a morally worthy respect for moral law. Admittedly, what we might call 'wanting to deserve their esteem' can be a complex motive that *includes* respect for the standard that must be met to deserve esteem; but we can imagine the less admirable case in which we have no direct respect for the standards themselves but only want to be in a position where others *should* be prepared to praise, approve, and esteem us. The more common case, no doubt, is wanting that others *actually* praise, esteem, and approve of what we do, but we may entertain (and even 'act out') *fantasies of deserved but unrecognized esteem* for doing morally heroic deeds. Here it would be, in a sense, our having 'moral worth,' rather than following the moral law, that we valued. And, if we understand the motive in this way, there is no moral worth in acting from concern for moral worth.

The bottom line, again, is that simply described motives often need a fuller explanation before we can think clearly about how to assess them. Having seen how this is so with regard to anticipation of grief and concern to do what is morally worthy, let us return to consider *conscience* as a motive.

VI. MOTIVATION BY CONSCIENCE: WORTHY AND UNWORTHY VERSIONS

It is clear that being motivated directly and exclusively by aversion to the discomfort, insomnia, and even torments that conscience may cause us is not a morally admirable motive for doing what we know is the right thing to do. But conscience, as Kant sees it, does not move us to do our duty simply by holding up an inspiring ideal that draws us joyfully to realize our nature as rational autonomous persons. It warns, threatens, accuses, and generally disturbs our peace of mind. Since mere aversion to pain is not a morally worthy motive, especially when our duty is definite, how can anticipation of a tormented conscience play a motivational role in the life of a good person? Is it merely a regrettable but necessary 'backup' motive, not in itself an expression of our higher

(compared with other maxims for the situation) it is worthy of choice by a good will, when choosing as such. This makes the idea that 'only acts from duty have moral worth' not so much a lesson about how to allocate praise and esteem, as often thought, but more a lesson about the reasons that should be primary for us when we know, and are deliberately considering, that we have a duty in a situation.

nature but merely a natural device that serves a purpose when better motives fail?

The analogies with grief and concern to do morally worthy acts suggest a way of approaching these questions. Although we can be concerned in an unworthy way about the pain that a bad conscience brings, sometimes what seems to be merely 'wanting to avoid the pain' may in fact be a deeper, and better, motive. The pain may be a natural human reflection of our recognition that we have failed to show full respect for the moral standards that we recognize as authoritative. A bad conscience hurts because, sometimes in spite of ourselves, we care about whether we make our moral judgments with due care and live by them. Conscience often warns, prods, and jars us to reform, but not by a simple stimulus–response reflex mechanism. Nor does it move us merely by prompting us to act under a freely chosen maxim of pain avoidance. Rather, the hurting conscience—the painful awareness that the inner judge has passed sentence—alerts us and makes us more vividly aware of our respect for the moral law and its requirements, as far as we can judge, on the particular occasion. Its phenomenology, no doubt, has a basis in natural human psychology, but it is morally significant because it expresses our recognition and acceptance of the authority of moral reasons. Pangs of conscience, we might say, are a particular form of the dark side of 'respect for moral law' that Kant describes in the *Critique of Practical Reason*: they are instances of the general fact that our recognition of the legitimate claims of others strikes down our self-conceit. They turn our mind, painfully, not to the discomfort of violating our moral standards, but to those standards themselves. Our respect for the moral law shows itself, in a natural human way, by the fact that we cannot hold our acts up to the law and see that we fall far short without experiencing the glaring difference with discomfort. The metaphors regarding conscience may be overworked, but the central point remains: being motivated by conscience may be (and one hopes often is) fundamentally a matter of being motivated by respect for morality, and so ultimately by respect for the legitimate claims of others and our own better nature.

Our analogies also suggest that even what we describe in suspect ways may actually be instances of acting from respect for the moral law. This is because, as before, our description may simply pick out the intended acts by an identifying feature that is not the essential object of our concern. For example, given Kant's assumptions, 'avoiding what would cause me the discomforts of a bad conscience' identifies the same set of acts as 'avoiding what would be a failure to live by my best moral judgments.' If our governing intention is to avoid the acts described in the second way, then we are moved by respect for the moral law. Even if we pick out the set of acts we mean to avoid by the first description, our basic motive may still be respect for the moral law—though we did not explicitly mention the essential feature that makes these acts morally worthy. So, in several ways, what we think of as 'being moved by conscience' may be more, and better, than 'being moved by aversion to pain.'

VII. FEAR OF PUNISHMENT AS A MOTIVE: WORTHY AND UNWORTHY VERSIONS

Socrates, as described in Plato's *Crito*, looks down on the fear of punishment as an unworthy motive, but paradoxically he later seems to include as a reason for not escaping prison his belief that then he would be *rightly* condemned and punished as one who would destroy the laws. Perhaps he disapproved of the *fear* of punishment because he saw it as a raw, unexamined emotion whereas, by contrast, his aversion to being subject to *justified* punishment and condemnation was a motive that he could rationally approve on due reflection. Kant's view, I suspect, was similar, or ought to have been.

Recall our background assumptions. Certain special cases aside, the judicial punishment should be carried out without interference—even in an imperfectly just system.[29] Lawbreakers are presumed to be not only in violation of a legal requirement but also in violation of their indirectly ethical duty to conform to all moral requirements from duty. Even if the law unjustly forbids what would not be wrong to do apart from the legal prohibition, the act that violates the prohibition is presumed to be wrong because it disobeys legitimate state authority. The presumption, then, is that those convicted of crimes have intentionally and freely done acts of a kind for which they can be rightly condemned and punished. They have also shown a failure to act on respect for the moral law when they needed to. So, although the law is not (in Kant's view) in the business of full moral assessment of the character, motives, and moral worth of citizens, we can suppose, at least for practical purposes, that criminals in normal cases have acted wrongly and from less than

---

[29] The special cases, as mentioned earlier, are where the law demands of the citizen that he or she commit an act 'immoral in itself.' Such acts for Kant no doubt included rape, sodomy, murder, etc.

worthy moral motives.[30] Moreover, punishments express public condemnation, and, if justly imposed, they convey their message honestly and equally for citizens who commit the same crime.

What about the motive of fear of punishment, then? We have seen how it can be understood as something unworthy, second best, or at least short of the Kantian ideal. But how could it be something better?

Suppose, first, that we understand 'fear,' not as a raw terror in anticipation of future pain or loss, but more broadly as a strong aversion to an outcome that is felt *and judged* to be a bad thing. Fear of this sort could be, in part, an attitude stemming from values endorsed in rational reflection. Like Kantian 'respect,' it could be essentially a motivating recognition of authority that is also experienced as a feeling. Those who speak approvingly of 'fear of God,' I suspect, sometimes have something like this in mind.

Whether we call the motive 'fear' or not, the sort of aversion to punishment that has the best claim to moral significance is not a knee-jerk reaction, but a commitment to a policy (or maxim) to avoid incurring the *justified* moral disapproval of fellow citizens expressed in judicial punishment (when properly applied). Even if a crime is not immoral apart from its being authoritatively prohibited, Kant's presumption is that we would be wrong (barring certain exceptional cases) to violate the legal prohibition. So, whether or not the laws are good, avoiding the justified disapproval of others expressed through punishment can be a principled policy rather than a mechanical response to impulse. We can understand it as a maxim freely adopted by a moral agent.

Moreover, the maxim need not fall under a more basic maxim of self-love. That is, our reason for affirming it is not necessarily that it serves as a means to a personal nonmoral end—such as avoiding embarrassment and financial loss. The essential and sufficient ground may be a commitment to doing what is right with respect to the laws of the land. Although discomfort at the thought of being justly punished may be the first sign that we are in danger of violating our moral commitment, the analogy with pangs of conscience suggests that what the discomfort reveals need not be an aversion to pain but rather an unwillingness to betray our moral standards. We may 'pick out' what we want to avoid by the description 'avoiding (justified) punishment,' but the essential feature of our concern may be something deeper, namely, avoidance of

[30] There is a gap, I think, between Kant's idealized assumptions (especially regarding criminals' freedom and moral knowledge) and the realities of our world, but I am setting aside for now doubts about Kant's background assumptions.

wrongdoing. If so, the ultimate ground is respect for the moral law, which is, for Kantians at least, a morally worthy motive.

Some may object that all efforts to defend a morally significant 'fear of punishment' are trivial, for the following reason. The motive under consideration, it might seem, is simply a hybrid, a combination of disparate elements—a moral concern to avoid wrongdoing *per se* plus a nonmoral aversion to incurring the negative responses of others. We all know that Kant holds that the first is morally worthy, the second is not, and whether an act is morally worthy depends on which motive is actually operative in the case. So, after all, the suggestion that there might be morally worthy fear of punishment is nothing but a new spin on old doctrines.

A new spin may, in fact, help to correct old misunderstandings, but what I am suggesting is more than this. A principled (and felt) aversion to incurring the justified disapproval of our fellow citizens for our intentional acts is not simply a conjunction of a concern to do right and a desire to maintain a good reputation. In the best case, the pain we want to avoid is inseparable from the recognition that we have done wrong. Moreover, for us as human beings, the inseparability is deep. Even if it would be godlike to care only to do right without any regard for the approval of others, this is not an option for us—nor should we wish it to be. In fact, a proper regard for the opinion of others is an expression of respect for them as fellow legislators of moral law. It also respects their capacity, as moral equals, to judge in particular cases what is right and what is wrong. To suppose that our respect for moral law is utterly independent of any concern for what others think, so that we have only pragmatic and self-interested grounds to avoid their reasonable moral disapproval, is a kind of moral arrogance incompatible with recognition of the humanity of each person as an end in itself. Respect for moral law is, in an important way, like respect for law (i.e., legal authority) in a just democratic community. Respect for law in a just democracy is ultimately respect for our fellow citizens, and respect for moral law in Kant's basic theory, as I understand it, is ultimately respect for humanity in each person. If so, what we call 'fear of punishment' can, at its best, be a specific form of respect for moral law and so a worthy motive. Insofar as its source is autonomous recognition of 'the moral law within,' it is—like response to conscience at its best—a form of *self-respect* as well.

Why does all this matter?[31] Presumably, as moral philosophers, we

---

[31] I am grateful to Andrews Reath for having encouraged me to address this question, for readers may well have doubts about it.

are trying to achieve a better understanding of our moral concepts, and recognizing the strengths and weaknesses of classic moral theories, such as Kant's, may well be useful for this purpose. But, more specifically, how we view punishment as a motive is a significant part of how we understand our moral relations with others. Moralists often seem to believe that only they, and perhaps a few others, obey the law from admirable motives whereas the vast majority who obey the law do so only because they want to avoid the pain and deprivations that the law threatens. This belief encourages a self-righteous attitude that is deeply contemptuous of others: because 'they' lack moral motivation, 'we' must determine what is right and keep 'them' in line by threats. I doubt that the underlying belief can be sustained empirically, and I suspect that it stems from a confusion. It is observed, no doubt correctly, that the prospect of punishment is a significant aspect of the motivation of most law-abiding citizens, but it is not noticed that the thought of punishment can motivate in quite different ways. What we call 'fear of punishment' is in fact complex and ambiguous. Understood in one way, it is a morally unworthy motive but probably not the sole or primary explanation of why most citizens are law abiding. Understood in another way, fear of punishment is probably a motivating factor for most citizens but not a motive that altogether lacks moral worth. If my conjecture here is correct, we who conscientiously obey the law do not stand to most fellow citizens as the high-minded to the contemptible. Rather, we all relate to each other as imperfect moral agents who, despite lapses, generally show their respect for each other by maintaining a reasonable moral aversion to incurring the justified disapproval of their peers, as would be expressed in just punishment. Although Kant does not say all this, it is compatible, I believe, with the main features of his moral and political theory.

12

Moral Dilemmas, Gaps, and Residues

No one, I suspect, accepts everything that Kant said about moral matters, but many remain hopeful that Kant's ideas, suitably modified and supplemented, might be developed into an ethical theory that meets most familiar objections and remains worthy of serious consideration. The project of developing such a Kantian theory, however, faces formidable obstacles. Prominent among these are problems concerning conflicts of duty. Alan Donagan has addressed at length the most familiar problem of this sort: the charge that Kantian principles generate unresolvable moral dilemmas.[1] Although correct and important in its main thesis, I think that Donagan's defense of a Kantian position concedes too much in one way and too little in another. Moreover, the objection to which Donagan responds is not the only problem Kantians must face regarding moral conflicts.

For example, even if Kantian moral theory does not absolutely command incompatible courses of action, it is hard to deny that the theory has *gaps*. If so, it may leave us to face tragic moral conflicts without guidance and without reason to expect that there is, even in theory, a best option. What is worse, Kantian theory seems to give conscientious moral agents the wrong message *after* they had to make such choices. If they had 'good wills,' why should they have any personal regret or special concern for those they have harmed? We commonly expect people to feel bad when they knowingly cause harm to others, even if there was nothing morally better they could have done. But does this make sense from a Kantian perspective? How, in fact, can a Kantian say that they 'should feel' anything at all?

I want to thank Gene Mason, Henry West, Martin Gunderson, Andrews Reath, David Cummiskey, Geoffrey Sayre-McCord, Terrance McConnell, Walter Sinnott-Armstrong, and David Weber for their comments. I am also grateful for helpful discussions at the Minneapolis and Duluth campuses of the University of Minnesota, and the University of California, Riverside.

[1] Alan Donagan, *The Theory of Morality* (Chicago: University of Chicago Press, 1977), 'Consistency in Rationalist Moral Systems', *Journal of Philosophy*, 81 (1984), 291–309, and 'Moral Dilemmas, Genuine and Spurious: A Comparative Anatomy', *Ethics*, 104 (1993), 7–21.

In what follows, I explain these problems more fully and sketch some lines of response that I think are reasonable and compatible with Kantian ethical theory, broadly construed. My discussion will be divided as follows. (I) I mention a variety of reasons why philosophers have been interested in cases of moral conflict, distinguish some different issues raised by such cases, and identify the questions that will be my main concern. (II) I summarize some common features of theories that, for purposes of discussion, I shall count as 'Kantian.' (III) I review critically Alan Donagan's response to the objection that Kantian theory generates unresolvable moral dilemmas. (IV) I grant that Kant's moral theory has gaps, but suggest that such indeterminacy may be better than the alternatives. (V) I describe what I take to be common and reasonable views about how conscientious persons should feel *after* they have acted in cases of tragic moral conflicts. (VI) I respond to the suspicion that Kantian moral theory is deeply incompatible with these common expectations. I conclude that Kantians should agree that those forced to make hard choices in practical moral dilemmas have grounds for agent-regret and special concern for those they have harmed, even if they acted with good will. In a sense, this is just how they should feel.

I. QUESTIONS ABOUT PRACTICAL MORAL DILEMMAS

Conscientious people at times find themselves in situations I shall call *practical* moral dilemmas. That is, they confront situations in which important, and apparently decisive, moral considerations seem to demand incompatible courses of action, condemning all their options, and they see no reasonable way to resolve the conflict. In the most dramatic cases they know that they will cause grave harm whatever they do. Through no fault of their own, principles and values that they assumed could never be compromised pull at them from opposite directions, threatening to tear apart that unity of soul long supposed to be the only indestructible reward of virtue.

There are some moral conflicts that we cannot resolve simply because we lack relevant information. Often we must act under uncertainty, sometimes almost in darkness, with regard to facts that, if known, would leave us in no doubt about what we should do. But in the conflict situations on which I want to focus here, the moral tension that the conscientious person experiences is not due to missing information. The problem is that, even given the facts as we see them, the moral values and principles to which we are committed seem to draw us strongly to opposing conclusions without offering any non-arbitrary way to choose between them. What we need is not more facts, it seems, but a better way to think about the facts we have.

Literary and religious classics offer a rich array of stories to illustrate the problem. Antigone, for instance, felt that she must either dishonor her brother or disobey the king, and Abraham thought (before being told otherwise) that he must sacrifice his son or disobey God.[2] Films and novels suggest further dramatic examples: in the film *High Noon*, the sheriff's bride must abandon either her pacifist convictions or her husband and his just cause; in the film and novel *Sophie's Choice*, Sophie must lose both her children or accept the fiendish Nazi demand that she select which child is to die; and in John Fowles's novel *The Magus*, a mayor can save eighty villagers from Nazi atrocity only by personally beating to death two guerillas whom he regards morally innocent. Philosophers, of course, have invented a further range of now-familiar stories having to do with runaway trolleys, fat men stuck in caves, and so on. Ordinary life offers more mundane but still significant cases of moral conflict that are encountered as having no reasonable, or even acceptable, resolutions.

Philosophers have had a special fascination with such cases, for various reasons. *Teachers of ethics* like to use dramatic cases of moral conflict to capture the attention of lethargic students, perhaps unintentionally luring them into philosophy with the false hope that what is practically difficult becomes easy after one has studied a bit of moral theory. Those doing serious work in *applied ethics* are often called upon to give moral advice on real and urgent cases of moral conflict, and so, understandably, they want to discuss past and hypothetical cases in an effort to stimulate the thinking of professionals who must soon face such decisions.

For *moral theorists*, the examples of apparent moral dilemmas offer a challenge, testing the resources of their theories as well as their skills as casuists. As advocates of particular theories, they typically want to defend and confirm their theories by showing how the theories can resolve apparent moral dilemmas. As critics, they often hope to expose the limitations of other theories by demonstrating that the theories remain silent on cases that clearly call for a moral response; and, more ambitiously, they may try to prove a theory incoherent by arguing that

---

[2] The cases I mention have often been cited to illustrate the moral conflicts of the sort I describe, but it is not important for my purposes that the reader sees these particular examples as practical moral dilemmas.

the theory yields contradictory prescriptions in hard cases. Some conclude from the prevalence of practical moral dilemmas that what we call 'morality' is a fragmented cluster of incommensurable ideals and principles that in ordinary circumstances serve well enough, but in crisis situations lead to nothing but ambivalence and tragedy. Others see apparent moral dilemmas as colorful entries into some intriguing metatheoretical questions, such as whether admitting the existence of genuine moral dilemmas is compatible with moral realism and a satisfactory deontic logic.

Questions about practical moral dilemmas, of course, are not merely of interest to professional philosophers. On the contrary, they are prompted by concerns that any conscientious person might have when facing such moral conflicts.

The first concern naturally is the immediately practical one, (1) *How can I find a way to resolve the dilemma?* That is, a conscientious person will want to continue to ask whether there are new options, previously overlooked facts, and alternative perspectives on the conflict that favor one course of action over the other, thus revealing the dilemma to be merely apparent.

If this effort fails repeatedly, despite one's best efforts, the tension and frustration of the search may well prompt the more abstract question, (2) *Can it really be, as it seems, that I will be morally wrong whichever option I take?* Could this be so, one might well wonder, even after all things are considered, including the extraordinary circumstances of the case and the fact that one has searched so hard to find something morally permissible to do?

An affirmative answer may seem too paradoxical to accept. But even so, if efforts to resolve the dilemma continue to fail, the conscientious agent might still wonder, (3) *Can it really be, as it seems, that morality pulls me so strongly in opposite directions and yet lacks the resources to determine which way, all things considered, I should go?* Is it possible that there simply is no resolution, that no further facts or reflection can help me, and so I must make an arbitrary choice? The question here is not whether morality prescribes too much but whether it prescribes too little. That is, the concern is not whether morality makes demands that we cannot meet but whether it is silent when we want advice.

Now suppose that, though still unable to find a morally satisfactory resolution to the conflict, the conscientious agent decides that to delay action longer would be even worse than embracing other options, and so simply seizes one horn of the dilemma, causing, as expected, grave harm.[3] Imagine that even afterward, despite more reflection and consultation with others, the agent finds no reason to change his initial assessment of the conflict. Now further questions arise, questions about 'moral residues.' Most obviously, there is a new practical question to face about how to *act* in the aftermath of the dilemma. That is, (4) *What should I do now? For example, must I make reparation, compensate, or apologize to those I have harmed or to their survivors? Do I have a special obligation to comfort or ameliorate the plight of the injured?*

No matter how they decide these questions concerning residual obligations, conscientious agents who have seriously harmed others by the stand they have taken in a practical dilemma may feel regret and experience painful guilt, or guilt-like, feelings. Then they may well wonder whether these painful feelings are morally important responses or merely insignificant side effects that they would do well, if possible, to ignore or be rid of. More generally, they may ask, (5) *Now that I have taken a stand in an unresolved practical moral dilemma, what should my attitudes and feelings be about myself and those I have harmed?*

This last question is not about what one should *do*, either in confronting a practical moral dilemma or afterward; rather, it is about how one should *be* after having made a hard choice in a situation of serious moral conflict. It concerns the *attitude* one should take, how one should *feel*, and how one should *regard* oneself and those one has harmed when, despite one's best efforts, one has had simply to seize one horn of an unresolved practical moral dilemma. This question may be prior to the preceding question about what one should do, and it would remain significant even if there was nothing compensatory or ameliorative one could do, for example, because the injured parties died without survivors.

For present purposes I set aside the controversial topic of how Kantian principles and procedures can determine what we ought to *do* in various situations. That is, I address questions (2), (3), and (5), but not (1) and (4). In sum, the issues are: Can one, within a broadly Kantian perspective, acknowledge that there are genuine moral dilemmas, tragic gaps in moral theory, and morally significant residues of feeling and attitude?

---

[3] Although there are serious moral conflicts of other kinds, to simplify I will assume that in 'practical dilemmas' to be discussed here the agents know that they will cause serious harm to someone, no matter what they do.

II. SOME FEATURES OF KANTIAN MORAL THEORY

Since our project is to investigate how Kantian moral theory can respond to questions about practical moral dilemmas, we need at least a preliminary account of what is to count as 'Kantian' for purposes of our discussion. Theories that are called Kantian vary widely, and there is room for reasonable disagreement about which of Kant's beliefs a theory must preserve in order to use the label without disrespect. Here I merely stipulate some main features of 'Kantian theory' as I intend to understand it in my subsequent discussion.

1. Kantian ethics is primarily *addressed to concerns we have as rational moral agents*, as we deliberate conscientiously about what we ought to do. Morality must make sense from this first-person, deliberative point of view. Standards of how we evaluate, praise, and blame others are secondary, derivative, and of less practical importance. It is not the task of moral philosophy to give third-person perspective, empirical explanations of moral phenomena (e.g., how we talk, behave, and feel). Although presumably such explanations are possible, moral principles and the conception of the agent that they presuppose are not reducible to these.

2. Moral 'oughts' purport to express categorical imperatives or judgments based upon these.[4] At least this is so in paradigm cases of moral 'oughts' that strictly prescribe or prohibit specified actions. These *express rational requirements on choice* that are not grounded in either the need to take necessary means to one's particular contingent ends or one's general desire for happiness. If I have a strict ('perfect') duty not to do something, then no matter what the competing reason, I must not do it; for me to choose otherwise would be wrong and contrary to reason.

3. Categorical imperatives and the moral judgments derived from them express rational prescriptions *in a vocabulary of constraint* ('must,' 'bound,' 'obligatory,' 'duty,' 'Do it!') that reflects how recognizing a rational moral requirement is experienced by those ('imperfect wills') who know that they can satisfy the requirement but also know that they can and might violate the requirement and choose instead to pursue some conflicting desire-based end. To acknowledge that one is morally bound to do something goes beyond thinking that it would be

---

[4] See G, 82–4 [4: 417–17], ch. 1 of *Dignity and Practical Reason*, and Ch. 1 of this volume.

'a good thing to do *if possible.*' Rather, it expresses a sense that this is the course of action, *among those open to the agent*, that is rationally and morally demanded.

Acknowledging a moral duty is also more than believing that one is under an actual command of some person or group. Moral duties are 'commands *of reason*,' that is, 'oughts' based on considerations generally recognizable as reasonable, whether actually commanded by someone or not. Individual and group authorities can, and at times do, issue commands that are so demanding that their subjects cannot obey them in all circumstances, and they may have reasons for refusing to accept 'I could not comply' as an excuse.[5] But Kantian 'commands of reason' are essentially directives for deliberating agents that tell them *how to choose among options* presumed to be available to them in their situation. Kant opposed the facile use of 'I can't' as a bad-faith excuse; for example, presuming without adequate grounds that one is inwardly too weak or frail to do what (Kant believed) duty requires. But his concept of duty implies that what is manifestly physically impossible for a person to do cannot be that person's duty, all things considered, to do or even to 'will' to do.[6]

4. Moral 'oughts' express a deep, self-identifying, and inescapable disposition of moral agents, who have reason and autonomy of will, to acknowledge certain considerations as overridingly authoritative and so internally binding.[7] Therefore, if I am a moral agent, I cannot be indifferent to what I judge I morally ought to do in the way I might be indifferent to what I believe conforms to prevailing social norms or maximizes general utility. For fully developed moral agents, then, the first and virtually inevitable penalty for moral failure is self-condemnation: one identifies oneself, in a sense, as moral lawmaker and judge as well as lawbreaker, and so it is painful to acknowledge '*I* should have, *I* could have, and yet *I* chose not to.'

5. It is a fundamental moral principle that humanity in each person is to be regarded as an end in itself. We are to attribute dignity, an

---

[5] The possibility of moral dilemmas in command moralities is noted by Donagan in his 'Moral Dilemmas, Genuine and Spurious: A Comparative Anatomy'.

[6] In some cases, Kant thought, the rational case for doing or achieving something if it were an option is so compelling that we should assume on faith that it is an option, even though empirical evidence suggests otherwise. For example, unlike more typical cases, regarding 'perpetual peace' and the 'highest good,' we are apparently to determine our duty first without being constrained by prior empirical assessments of what is possible for us and our likelihood of success. Even here, though, duty is seen as the rational choice among options presumed to be open.

[7] G, 108–16 [4: 440–8], and ch. 5 of my *Dignity and Practical Reason*, 76–96.

unconditional and incomparable worth, to all human beings, insofar as they are presumed to have the capacity for rational and moral living.[8] In part we acknowledge this dignity by trying to restrict our personal policies to those we judge, in reasonable and appropriately impartial reflection, to be policies that would be rationally acceptable for anyone to adopt for relevantly similar circumstances. We can think of the policies and acts that would be acceptable for everyone, in the relevant sense, as just those policies and acts that would conform to the 'universal laws' that moral legislators would accept if trying to work out a reasonable system of moral principles under certain ideal conditions ('the kingdom/realm of ends').[9]

6. These general principles are supposed to establish a strong presumption against willful deception and manipulation. For example, trying to motivate people to avoid practical dilemmas by cultivating in them a false sense of guilt would not be an option for Kantians.

7. When thinking from a practical moral perspective rather than an empirical scientific perspective, we conceive typical human actions as done intentionally—for reasons—by agents presumed capable of choosing to act differently. We understand or explain an action from this point of view by attributing to the agent a rationale. A rationale is not a *causal* explanation, as this is usually understood, but a reconstruction of the beliefs, intentions, aims, policies, and deepest commitments that (we suppose) made up the agent's *normative* reasons for ('freely') choosing to do what he or she did. Thus, we think of actions as typically done intentionally on the basis of agents' judgments as to what they had good reason to do, given their perceived options, aims, commitments, and implicit norms of rational choice. A person's judgment can be unreflective, clouded, and perhaps suspended under pressures of various kinds, but, at least in serious moral cases, we still typically attribute to the agent the final capacity and responsibility to use and follow judgment. ('He *let* his feelings overpower him,' we say.) Conscientious agents, when acting to do what duty requires, are conceived as acting on their *judgment* that the particular act was (overridingly) good to do, based on a *rationale* that includes both their deep disposition (*Wille*) as rational moral agents to acknowledge the moral law as authoritative and their commitment to a personal policy (maxim) of conforming to it.[10]

---

[8] G, 95–8 [4: 427–30] and 102–3 [4: 435–6].
[9] For a fuller account of my interpretation of these points, see chs. 2, 3, 10, and 11 in *Dignity and Practical Reason*, and ch. 2 of *Respect, Pluralism, and Justice*.
[10] Kant's view contrasts with Hume's in that 'reason' does 'move us,' but this is not

8. In human beings practical judgments and feelings are not usually separable.[11] Our moral judgments have an impact on our sensibility. For example, we *feel* respect for the moral law because we acknowledge its validity, we *feel* respect for people because we judge their acts to exemplify the moral law, and we *feel* moral contentment or remorse because we judge ourselves to be innocent or guilty. Normally, when we make a moral judgment we experience a corresponding affective response, and this is so familiar, expected, and deeply human that, barring special explanation, we are very reluctant to believe a person who claims to make a moral judgment but altogether lacks the usual corresponding affect. For example, we would naturally doubt the sincerity (or self-awareness) of someone who said, 'It is wrong to humiliate women, I know, but I love to do it and I have no bad feelings about doing it.' Feelings of constraint or revulsion are not the ultimate *grounds* of the judgment that it is wrong for one to treat others with disrespect, but, given normal human sensibility, such feelings are among the expected signs that one genuinely recognizes that such treatment violates the basic norms of morality and reason to which one is committed.

III. ARE GENUINE MORAL DILEMMAS POSSIBLE?

What makes this question particularly challenging for Kantians is that Kant held that ethics is based on reason and that a rational moral system

to deny Hume's point that judgments and beliefs motivate only when combined with an underlying disposition to act that is part of the character of the person. Kantian 'reason' is not merely the cognitive capacity for discerning 'relations of ideas' and 'matters of (empirical) fact' that Hume stipulated. To attribute reason to a ('free') agent is, in part, to attribute a deep disposition (*Wille*) to acknowledge as authoritative (and so to follow) certain very abstract, higher order norms, which (Kant argues) are the Hypothetical and Categorical Imperatives. This disposition, presupposed in moral agents as an invariable background fact, is part of human nature, but an aspect characterized as 'rational' rather than 'sensuous.' Moral judgments move us because they subsume particular cases under these basic norms (toward which we are all presumed to be motivationally disposed). It may be doubted that 'reason' in this strong sense, should be attributed to everyone, but the idea is not as mysterious as contemporary Humeans like to suppose.

[11] Kant conjectured that there could be purely rational ('holy') wills who lacked sensibility (and thus moral feelings) and yet could still discern by reason the same basic propositions about what is good to do that we imperfect human beings experience as categorical imperatives. He also thought that the core of our capacity for moral judgment is logically independent of our disposition to have certain feelings. He held, for example, that we can discern the most general principles that reason prescribes without relying on our feelings as either data or 'sensors.' Kant's critics are no doubt right to suspect that moral feelings, judgments, and behavioral dispositions are connected in more complex ways than Kant realized, but my discussion does not presuppose Kant's most extreme views about the separability of rational judgment and feeling.

cannot admit genuine conflicts of duty, and yet despite this Kant presents principles in his *Groundwork* and *The Metaphysics of Morals* that, when applied to hard cases, seem to yield conflicting prescriptions. I begin with a few remarks about this second point.

The first natural question upon confronting a practical dilemma is, 'How can I find a way to resolve the (apparent) dilemma?' The Kantian answer to this, although long and complex in detail, is easy to summarize: Review the facts of the case, explore your options, and be guided by the ideas expressed in the various versions of the Categorical Imperative. Alternatively, if you are convinced (as I am not) that Kant's system of principles in *The Metaphysics of Morals* is derivable from his fundamental principles, then the answer is: Use that system, with casuistry and good judgment, to work out what to do in your conflict situation. Unfortunately, it has seemed to many that these procedures not only leave some apparent dilemmas unresolved but also that they themselves *generate* dilemmas.

The Metaphysics of Morals, for example, includes many unqualified principles that apparently can conflict: they include not only prohibitions of adultery, murder, and slavery but also 'perfect' duties against lying, rebellion against lawful government, and any form of disrespect for others. Also, at least one form of the Categorical Imperative (if thickly interpreted)[12] seems more liable to generate practical dilemmas than to solve them. This is the Formula of Humanity, which attributes an unconditional and incomparable value to each person. The problem is that sometimes it seems that one cannot fully respect the value of humanity in one person without violating it in another.

Alan Donagan has argued ingeniously against the facile assumption that Kant's principles *actually* generate unresolvable conflicts in *real* cases. The stories offered as posing dilemmas, he argued, often turn out to overlook distinctions between 'doing' and 'letting,' between the consequences of one's acts and the consequences of others' responses to one's acts, and so on.[13] To the same end, I suggested in an earlier paper one way a Kantian could try to resolve moral conflicts that stem from the Formula of Humanity.[14] The basic idea is to take the Formula of Humanity as prescribing a basic moral attitude, not a decision procedure to be applied case by case. If it is understood as expressing a value

---

[12] By 'thick' interpretations I have in mind quite substantive, action-guiding readings like that of Donagan in *The Theory of Morality* and mine in ch. 2 of *Dignity and Practical Reason*. I discuss the distinction between 'thick' and 'thin' interpretations in ch. 5 of my *Respect, Pluralism, and Justice*.
[13] Donagan, *The Theory of Morality*, 50–1, 112–42.
[14] See ch. 10 of *Dignity and Practical Reason*.

that can be incorporated into procedures for moral reflection on how *general principles* of conduct should be specified, what exceptions they should allow, and so on, then at this higher level of deliberation we may find reasons for adjudicating apparent (first-order) moral conflicts one way or another.

Unfortunately, neither Donagan's procedures for resolving apparent moral dilemmas nor mine guarantee success in all cases. What one must do, in either case, is to examine each apparent dilemma, with the background facts and arguments that seem to generate it, as it arises. Donagan had remarkable confidence that, with an exception to be considered later in this essay, such *ad hoc* investigations could resolve all the apparent dilemmas generated by Kant's Formula of Humanity and the system of moral precepts derivable from it. Here I think Donagan conceded too little to Kant's critics; for, despite all Donagan says, it seems to me that extraordinary circumstances can put one in a situation, through no fault of one's own, in which one has to break a promise or tell a lie even though doing so would be forbidden by the rigorous precepts accepted by Kant and Donagan.[15] But I shall not press the point here, as it is incidental to my main project.

Instead, let us consider what follows if Kant's actual principles and precepts sometimes unequivocally prescribe incompatible courses of action.[16] Must Kantians then concede that genuine moral dilemmas are possible? The answer, as Donagan has made clear, is, No, because there are other theoretical options.

To see this, consider the following propositions that Kant himself held: (a) to have a moral duty is to be under a practical command of reason; (b) reason cannot issue incompatible practical commands, and so (c) there can be no genuine conflict of duties; (d) the moral principles presented in Kant's works are correct, as stated, without need for further qualification; and (e) these principles, judiciously applied, will not in fact impose incompatible demands on anyone.

If, as suggested above, we suppose that Kant's principles sometimes lead to incompatible demands, we reject (e). Contemporary Kantians can still hold on to Kant's central tenets (a)–(c) if they are willing to deny (d). In other words, Kantians can still deny the possibility of

---

[15] Kant's intermediate moral precepts are in *The Metaphysics of Morals*. Donagan's comparable system of (first order) moral precepts, which is somewhat less rigoristic than Kant's, is in Donagan's *The Theory of Morality*, ch. 3. Donagan comments on Kant's system in 'The Structure of Kant's Metaphysics of Morals', *Topoi*, 4 (1985), 61–72.

[16] Note that even Donagan concedes this, since he thinks that Kant's principles allow genuine moral dilemmas that are created through the agent's prior wrongdoing.

genuine moral dilemmas if they are willing to modify the particular principles in Kant's moral system that generate the apparent dilemma. Many contemporary Kantians would grant that Kant's particular precepts, for example, those about lying and disobedience to civil authorities, need to be modified to allow more exceptions, regardless of whether the precepts generate dilemmas.[17] Even Donagan, who believed that Kant's principles do not need much modification to avoid troublesome dilemmas, conceded that the principles *would* have to be revised *if* they generated incompatible prescriptions to *innocent* persons.

Given that apparent conflicts resulting from Kant's principles leave them a choice, Kantian theorists, in my opinion, will preserve more of the central and distinctive features of Kant's ethics by rethinking the arguments leading to apparent dilemmas and, if necessary, revising Kant's system of principles than by taking the alternative course, which would be to abandon the rationalist conception of duty that refuses to tolerate moral dilemmas. That is, assuming (e) above is false, it is better to abandon (d) than (a)–(c).

A revision of Kant's system of principles to avoid dilemmas, we should note, need not be undertaken in a piecemeal fashion. Rather than trying to modify each particular principle separately, a Kantian revisionist might insure the whole system of principles against dilemmas by a qualification: if the principles, as so far stated, unequivocally prescribe incompatible courses of action, then take that judgment as only provisional and count both courses, or at least one, as permissible in the special circumstances.[18]

To summarize: Is it *possible*, then, that I can be in a situation in which I will be *wrong no matter what I do?* The answer Kantians should give, in my view, is No. The reason lies in the Kantian conception of moral judgments discussed in Section II, (1)–(3). The primary function of moral judgments (expressed by 'ought,' 'duty,' and 'wrong') is to express rational demands on our *wills* as deliberating agents, telling us which among our (perceived) options to choose to take. If all options seem to be morally condemned and yet we cannot avoid taking one or another of them, then we must rethink the issue, for we cannot coherently judge, from this Kantian point of view, that every choice we could make would

---

[17] MM, 182–4 [6: 429–31] and 95–8 [6: 318–23].
[18] If the particular principles in irreconcilable conflict each strictly follow from the basic principle (the Categorical Imperative), under some interpretation, then the qualification amounts to a concession that the basic principle itself (as so interpreted) is not absolutely binding but must be understood as leaving a permissible option in dilemma-like cases.

be strictly wrong, such that doing it in that actual situation would be contrary to duty, all things considered. If rethinking yields no practical resolution, we can conjecture that Kant's system permits a resolution that we have been as yet unable to see, or we can admit that Kant's principles need to be amended. In either case, however, we must concede that, despite appearances, at least one available option must be permissible.

My remarks here obviously draw from Donagan's admirable discussions of moral dilemmas, but there is an important difference between his position and the Kantian position I have just described. Donagan argued that rationalist ethical theories must reject the possibility of genuine moral dilemmas *except when the agent got into a dilemma situation through his own fault*.[19] Suppose, for example, I promised a person to do something and then wrongly promised someone else that I would do what I knew was incompatible with my fulfilling the first promise. On Donagan's view, rationalist ethics can concede that at this point *I will do wrong no matter what I do*. He held, however, that even if all my options are contrary to duty, one option may still be morally *worse* than another and, if so, I should *do the lesser evil*.[20] The lesser evil, as well as the greater, remains condemned by inflexible moral principles, and so I cannot avoid doing wrong; but I can and should try to control the damage and minimize the offense.

Donagan found in Thomas Aquinas's work a precedent for his idea that rationalist ethics can tolerate moral dilemmas *when (but only when) the agent is already at fault*, but he had at least two further motives for making this exception to his general denial of moral dilemmas.

First, Donagan wanted to defend a system of quite rigorous moral precepts modeled on (but not identical with) Kant's system in *The Metaphysics of Morals*. Donagan thought that he could show, with subtle casuistry and attention to detail, that most cases alleged to be dilemmas resulting from his own precepts turn out to be spurious. Cases in which guilty agents themselves generated the problem, however, he acknowledged to be more intractable. To argue that moral dilemmas do not arise even in these cases, he would have had to admit many more exceptions into his system of moral precepts than he thought tolerable.

Second, if we allow no exceptions to our denial of moral dilemmas, then the following objection arises. Suppose I make a promise and then

---

[19] See Donagan, *The Theory of Morality*, 143–9.
[20] See Donagan, *The Theory of Morality*, and 'Consistency in Rationalist Moral Systems'.

wrongfully make a second promise knowing that I cannot keep both. If I keep the first and not the second, supposing this to be morally best in the circumstances, then neither 'I could not keep both' nor 'I was wrong to have made the second promise' is an adequate defense when the second promisee complains, 'But, nonetheless, you did wrong in breaking your promise to me.' By conceding that there can be moral dilemmas resulting from the agent's misconduct, Donagan could grant the objector's judgment, 'Having wrongly made the second promise, you would have then done wrong, no matter what you had done.'[21]

Whatever his motives, by conceding that there can be genuine unresolvable conflicts of duty Donagan abandoned a feature of Kant's ethics that seems to me quite central. What is lost is the idea that moral principles and precepts can guide the decision making of every deliberative agent, the guilty as well as the innocent, to choices they can make without further wrongdoing. So conceived, morality acknowledges that human beings are imperfect and often guilty, but it calls upon each at every new moment of moral deliberation to decide conscientiously and to act rightly from that point on. No matter how guilty in the past, each person is respected as now able to do and be responsible for doing only what duty permits and always what duty requires, all things considered, in her or his situation.[22] To say that every option is wrong—strictly contrary to duty—in fact makes no sense if *duty* is understood in the Kantian way described earlier. It would be like saying that practical reason, after due reflection, unequivocally directs you now to refuse to take any of your available options, including doing nothing. A perverse secular authority might 'demand' this and then pretend to justify punishment by citing your noncompliance with his orders; but no one should confuse his orders with the voice of practical reason.[23]

---

[21] See Donagan, *The Theory of Morality*, 284–5.

[22] Note that Donagan's ideal system of precepts will require those in a self-generated dilemma to take whichever option is a violation of a duty of lesser gravity, even though it blocks the conclusion that the option is a permissible act. Some might think that this is guidance enough, but, as I suggest below, there is something positive and attractive about a Kantian system that respects each person as able at each time to act rightly for the right reasons, not merely to conscientiously choose a less offensive way to continue to do wrong.

[23] This is not to deny that the perverse commander might have good reasons from his perspective for giving the orders he knows you cannot fulfill. The point is that for Kant, and for a long tradition before and after, 'reason' refers to what is conceived as a common faculty that guides us to conclusions (in logic, in science, and in morals) that are not so agent-relative. It is conceived as a faculty that demands consistency among the beliefs and norms that it endorses, that has a purpose of guiding its possessors to think and act well, and that does not in the end frustrate its own purposes. Normally we must presume its verdicts are just what we ourselves conclude in our own best reflections, but

Let us reconsider the motives mentioned above that inclined Donagan to grant that there can be moral dilemmas if the agent is at fault. One was the desire to maintain, without further modification, a quite inflexible system of moral precepts. Donagan saw that to deny moral dilemmas without qualification, a Kantian would have to modify his system of moral precepts, as needed, to ensure that, whatever the situation, agents have at least one permissible option. For Donagan and others fully confident of his system of strict precepts, this consideration makes sense; but its appeal is quite limited. For example, to those who share my sense that modifications in the Donagan/Kant systems of precepts are needed *even apart from worries about dilemmas*, a wish to avoid modifying the precepts is not a very compelling reason for tolerating moral dilemmas.

Consider, then, the second motive that inclined Donagan to grant that there are moral dilemmas created by the agents' misconduct: Donagan's belief that this concession is necessary to make moral sense of the second promisee's complaint in the two-promise story. It is arguable, however, that our moral intuitions about this case can be accommodated by less drastic measures. Assuming that in this case the second promise was wrongly made and breaking it would have been morally worse (or no better) than breaking the first, we do not need to say that the promisor was morally *wrong*, or *ought not*, to have broken the second promise. We can say, instead, that the agent is to blame *for making* the second promise and that in breaking the promise he *incurred further obligations* to the second promisee. He incurs these further obligations not because he was *wrong* to break the second promise, but because in doing so he disappointed legitimate expectations that he knowingly and wrongfully raised. Now he must apologize and try to make up for the damage he caused, for, although his breaking of the second promise was the right thing to do, it was foreseeable as the (morally) necessary extension of his earlier moral offense: the making of the second promise. By denying that the promisor was in a genuine moral dilemma, then, we do not provide him with a blanket excuse from liability to blame and

conceptually these are not identical. If, in considering theoretical paradoxes or apparent moral dilemmas, our reflections stop with 'Believe and don't believe' or 'Do and don't do,' we have to admit we have not yet found what (if anything) reason directs, for these are not really choice-guiding directives. Kant, of course, famously insisted that 'reason' in its speculative use disposes us to seek more and more unconditional explanations and so drives us toward 'antinomies.' But Kant does not leave us with the antinomies as the final verdict of reason; instead he uses these apparent conflicts of reason as grounds for accepting the noumenal/phenomenal distinction that supposedly dissipates the conflicts.

compensation. The complaining second promisee was right to suggest that breaking a promise is a *kind* of act that is *normally* wrong, but not to suggest that the agent's choice to break that promise, in the actual situation, was wrong, all things considered. When morally *required* to do what is called 'the lesser of two evils,' we must be *permitted* to do it and thus doing it, from the best motives, is not really an 'evil.' If we created the problem, however, we are to blame for that, and consequently we are obligated to compensate for the damage we do in response to the problem.

Now one might argue on Donagan's behalf that there may be less substantive difference than at first it seems between his view and the Kantian position as I have presented it. The differences, and apparent incompatibility, may be partly due to matters of terminology. For example, when Donagan says that in a moral dilemma (of the sort he allows) the agent cannot avoid doing something *impermissible, wrong*, and *contrary to duty*, he may be using these words in a special way. Perhaps what he *means* is just that given his situation, the agent cannot avoid doing something contrary to a set of rules that morality and reason prescribe to all *in an initial position of innocence* as rules that *at that initial point* they should resolve to follow, and can follow, without exception. Perhaps, too, 'impermissible' and 'wrong' for Donagan imply the undisputed point that the agent may be liable to compensate for damages and subject to blame (at least for prior choices leading to the moral necessity to do 'wrong'). If he were to interpret the relevant terms in this special way, Donagan *could* say, without incoherence, that in some situations morality and reason demand that a person do something 'wrong' and 'impermissible,' namely the 'lesser evil.'[24] Then, so construed, his contention that there can be fault-generated moral dilemmas would not be in conflict with the *substantive* Kantian point that, whatever the situation, there is something a conscientious person can then choose to do without being blameworthy *for that choice*. Donagan's point in saying that there can be fault-generated moral dilemmas, then, would be simply to say that if we act badly, we may incur blame and further liability by putting ourselves into situations in which everything we can then do is incompatible with what *innocent* people can and should do. So understood, the contention

---

[24] Note that 'lesser evil' will have to be defined with a special spin, too, to avoid the implication that the agent is somewhat evil in choosing it. It will be, perhaps, the option that does less harm (an 'evil') to others or the option that, were the agent not in the dilemma, would be a less grave offense than the other option. Some cases are discussed in ch. 6 of *Respect, Pluralism, and Justice*.

would no longer be one that a Kantian, as characterized here, need deny; but I suspect it also falls short of what most people understand when they say that there are genuine moral dilemmas.

But even if it turns out that there is no deep substantive *incompatibility* between our Kantian view and Donagan's position, as construed above, nonetheless the way each uses 'duty,' 'wrong,' and so on seems to reflect a significant difference in focus and attitude. What I have in mind is that the Kantian use of these terms, and its corresponding refusal to admit moral dilemmas of any kind, seem especially suited to express an attitude of respect for persons, conceived of as Kantian moral agents.

Here, somewhat simplified, is the familiar Kantian picture. Moral agents are in general conceived of as knowing the moral law and acknowledging its authority, as capable of following it for the right reasons, and as responsible for bringing themselves to do so. Although we know that the effects of our choices are not entirely up to us, we must never suppose that external natural forces or other human beings could prevent us from having a good will, the sole source of moral worth. No matter what crimes and moral offenses they have committed, moral agents should be viewed as capable of radical reform at any time. All human beings have a dignity grounded in these capacities, and by realizing them they can become worthy of the highest moral esteem. We carry responsibilities incurred by past commitments and offenses, and we are responsible for having the right intentions regarding the future; but these are only aspects of our primary responsibility, which is to make our present choices at each moment as directed by morally informed reason.

Now my thought is that the Kantian position on dilemmas respects and highlights this conception of a person in a fitting way insofar as it allows that, no matter how grave their past crimes and moral offenses, a person *can choose* at any time to be fully conscientious and *to do no further wrong*. Neither nature, nor other persons, *nor one's own past failures*, on this view, can rob one of the opportunity, and responsibility, to 'go and sin [i.e., violate duty] no more.'

For example, suppose, as an unlikely but possible occurrence, that a gang member has a fundamental change of heart while taking part in a kidnapping and robbery. Though now eager to do what is right, he may be so deeply entangled in the web of crime that the only way for him now to save innocent lives is to carry on for a while, even receiving stolen goods, driving the getaway car, and helping to hold the hostage until he can reveal his intentions without further endangering innocent people. He has no moral choice, I am supposing, but to do further *illegal* things that also violate moral precepts that, in all *normal* conditions, everyone should abide by. Undeniably, he can be justly punished, and he may owe compensation. He will also have a credibility problem, for he has no way to convince others that he had a moral conversion in the midst of the sequence of crimes. Nevertheless, assuming he really acted for moral reasons from the moment of his change of heart, the Kantian position respects his ability to reform by refusing to count his post-reform conscientious acts as, all things considered, *morally wrong* in the context.

Now, as I granted, one *can* understand 'wrong' (as Donagan may have) in a sense that allows one to coherently describe the case quite differently, but the Kantian refusal to use 'wrong' in that way and thus its categorical denial of moral dilemmas serve to call attention to the conception of a person as primarily responsible to govern himself as reason directs at each moment, regardless of past errors. By saying that after his change of heart the kidnapper, acting in good conscience, did not violate moral duty or do anything 'evil' (not even a 'lesser' one), we highlight the Kantian ideas that morality never demands more than one can do, that one is always able and responsible to will conscientiously, and that, if one acts with a good will, one has thereby a moral worth undiminished by other features of the act and situation, however regrettable these may be.[25]

IV. ARE THERE GAPS IN KANTIAN THEORY?

A theory has gaps if it provides no way, even in principle, to determine what one should, or even may, do in some cases. That is, even given all pertinent facts about a case, a theory with gaps lacks the resources to determine for all acts whether they are obligatory, forbidden, or neither. The idea is not just that the theory's decision procedures are somewhat abstract and complex, and that therefore reasonable people might occasionally apply them differently. This would be true of virtually any action-guiding theory. When a theory has gaps, it simply has no procedures for deciding some issues. An example of a theory with (many)

---

[25] I fully understand and share, but set aside here, doubts about whether this conception of persons as moral agents actually fits every sane adult human being. Kant had a faith regarding this that was not uncommon for his time, but those of us who doubt it need to reflect seriously on how a more realistic assessment would require limitations in the application of Kantian theories.

gaps is Ross's intuitionism, which asserts there are several basic prima facie duties and no theory-governed way to judge what to do when these prima facie duties conflict. An example of a theory that (in principle) has no gaps is hedonistic act utilitarianism, which holds that acts are *permissible* if they produce at least as much balance of pleasure over pain as any alternative, *obligatory* if they produce a greater balance than any alternative, and *wrong* otherwise.

Some theoretical gaps may be practically unimportant, whereas others may prove to be deeply troubling. If a consequentialist theory grants that some personal goods are incommensurable, it will have gaps; but these may not in fact make the theory significantly harder to apply than standard consequentialist theories. Gaps make an important practical difference, however, when they stem from a claim that very basic moral values are incommensurable and yet also virtually absolute. Consider, for example, the idea that each human life has a sacred, incalculable, and incomparable value. This is not a minor incommensurability. It urges us most strongly, and without any explicit qualification, to try to preserve every human life, and yet it forbids us to adjudicate conflicts by comparing and weighing the worth of some lives against the worth of others, or more lives against fewer. A theory that said this, and no more, would repeatedly expose us to tragic conflicts: cases in which, although the outcomes are vitally important, basic incommensurable values pull relentlessly toward incompatible choices and our moral guidelines fail to determine what we should (or even may) do.

Does Kant's ethical theory have gaps? If we concentrate on Kant's famous universal law formula of the Categorical Imperative, scholars may disagree, but there are many reasons at least to suspect gaps. Kant himself seemed at times to think that he had offered a procedure for testing maxims by which an agent could determine, for all cases, whether proposed acts would be morally forbidden, required, or (merely) permissible. But the procedure requires selecting a maxim for each act and determining what one 'can will' as universal law, and these requirements, especially the first, introduce considerable indeterminacy into the procedure. Critics have often charged that applying the universal law procedure results in conflicts of duty; and even if, following Kant, we stipulate that this can only be a conflict in the 'grounds' of obligation, it is not clear that Kant's universal law procedure can always determine which ground should override in these *apparent* conflicts of duty.[26] Some say that the procedure is only a negative test, condemning

[26] MM, 16–17 [6: 224].

some maxims as wrong without certifying every maxim that passes as not wrong; and if so, again, we have gaps. Kant's defenders have addressed some of these problems with remarkable ingenuity in recent years, but few, if any, are bold enough to defend Kant's universal law formula as successfully offering a determinate ('gapless') moral decision procedure.

Consider Kant's formula that humanity in each person is always to be treated as an end in itself. On some interpretations the formula is 'thin' or completely 'formal,' yielding no practical conclusions independently of other considerations. So viewed, the formula neither introduces nor closes 'gaps' in Kant's theory. On a more common substantive reading, however, the humanity formula declares that persons, or each person's 'rational nature', has an unconditional and incomparable worth. Unlike 'price,' this value 'admits of no equivalent.' Although not the same as 'human life,' 'rational nature' is supposed to be a basic and incommensurable value, just as 'life' was for the 'sanctity of life' advocates mentioned earlier. What is required by valuing *humanity* as an end is more complex and indefinite than what is required by regarding human *life* as sacred, and it is not so evident with Kant's formula as it is with the sanctity of life theory that we will be driven to acknowledge many unresolvable, tragic conflicts.[27] Nevertheless, it seems hard to deny that, when interpreted substantively, Kant's idea of the incomparable value of humanity in each person could sometimes draw us powerfully toward opposing courses of action, without telling us definitively 'Do this,' 'Do that,' or even 'You may do either.'

Sophie's choice and my earlier example from John Fowles's *The Magus* seem to illustrate the point, and one can also think of examples in which the conflicts involve degradation, deprivation, and deceit rather than loss of life. Any particular example may be questioned, but the general point that the humanity formula (on a substantive reading) is liable to generate more conflicts than it can resolve seems more obvious than any particular example can demonstrate. Acknowledging that *each* person (or something 'in' each person) has a (substantive) value naturally leads to prima facie conflicts, just as virtually any recognition of multiple values does. But then counting these potentially conflicting values as *unconditional*, *incomparable*, and *without equivalent* prevents us from resolving conflicts by the familiar methods of weighing, balancing, and trading off one value against another. Kantians can propose other procedures for deciding what to do in these cases, but the

---

[27] See chs. 2 and 10 of *Dignity and Practical Reason*.

proposals go beyond the humanity formula itself. So, in sum, although the extent of the problem remains open, it seems only reasonable to grant for now that Kant's ethical theory has 'gaps,' even gaps that can leave us without help regarding some tragic choice problems. The same will hold for any Kantian revisionist theory if it has not shown how it plugs the gaps.

Is it a serious objection to a theory that it has gaps of this sort? Several considerations suggest that even the best moral theories may need to admit gaps. Moreover, we may even have reasons to welcome them.

First, it is not necessarily a theoretical virtue of an ethical theory that it eliminates gaps. Life itself is complex and often tragic. Ethical theories represent the efforts of various limited human beings to highlight important recurrent values; to articulate, organize, and inevitably simplify the results of many generations of moral experience and moral thinking. The theories are constructed by individuals with different hopes, purposes, and theoretical ideals. Thus they are bound to be imperfect and limited in what they can do for us. Theories that satisfy ideals of neatness, completeness, and elegance may serve some purposes less well than theories that unabashedly highlight the moral conflicts we experience. Theories that offer precise unequivocal decision procedures help to satisfy philosophical yearning for neatness and closure, but the cost is often ignoring or distorting the deeply felt value conflicts that originally led us to moral theorizing. Having gaps, then, is not unqualifiedly a defect in a theory. Gaps may reflect important features of our moral experience that closure would distort.

Second, insofar as our interest in theories is practical, it makes a significant difference how frequent and important the cases are in which its gaps expose us to tragic conflicts. Fortunately, we are not forced every day to face choices like those of Antigone, Abraham, Sophie, Bernard Williams's 'Jim,' those trapped by the fat man in the cave, and so forth. If our best theory abandons us only in these extreme cases, then perhaps we can live with this. In any case, merely closing gaps in theory does not necessarily help us settle our perplexities in practice. For example, theological and consequentialist theories can avoid gaps in theory by stipulating what counts as 'duty,' 'wrong,' and 'permitted' in terms of God's rational commands or sums of intrinsic value; but this is no practical advantage if we have no effective ways to discern God's rational will or to identify and calculate with intrinsic values.

Third, the incommensurable values that open gaps in Kantian theory may help to explain why we should strive to avoid tragic moral conflicts. The background thought is this: Whatever their position on dilemmas and gaps, everyone should agree that we ought *generally* to avoid getting ourselves into tragic situations in which we have no further choice but to cause severe harm and to contravene the normal constraints of decent conduct. The point needs to be qualified, for at times the only way to avoid tragic choices is to refuse positions of power, to disengage from political struggles, and to retreat into a less challenging private world in which tragic conflicts are avoided by isolating oneself from the major world problems. Some means of escaping tragic conflicts, then, are cowardly and not to be encouraged, but the general point stands: we should want to *use all honorable means* to avoid creating or falling into tragic dilemma-like situations.

What moral motives do we have to avoid these situations? What will deter us from simply welcoming dilemma-like conflicts as an opportunity to enjoy with impunity the exercise of powers that one is normally forbidden to use? Some have thought that seeing tragic conflict situations as *genuine moral dilemmas* gives us the moral motivation we need to prevent such situations from arising. Because we want not to do wrong, we would be motivated not to fall into real moral dilemmas; for these are seen as situations in which we cannot avoid doing wrong, no matter what we choose. Ruth Marcus suggests that this is an advantage of holding that there are genuine moral dilemmas.[28]

But tolerating moral dilemmas is not necessary to provide a strong motivation to avoid tragic situations of moral conflict.[29] The Kantian position also provides a strong motivation, and yet it denies the possibility of genuine moral dilemmas. By attributing an unconditional and incomparable worth to rational nature in each person, Kant's humanity formula affirms that we have powerful moral reasons to not destroy, damage, dishonor, or discount any person, which is what we would be forced to do if we allowed ourselves to fall into tragic conflict situations.[30] Obviously, we have a strong reason in advance to do everything

---

[28] See Ruth Barcan Marcus, 'Moral Dilemmas and Consistency', *Journal of Philosophy*, 77 (1980), 121–36; reprinted in Christopher Gowans (ed.), *Moral Dilemmas* (New York: Oxford University Press, 1987), especially pp. 188, 197–9.

[29] Terrance McConnell has been helpful on this point, as well as others.

[30] Here I am conceding that the strong moral prescriptions implicit in the humanity formula, such as to preserve lives and avoid deception, are defeasible, but not that the humanity formula itself is a defeasible or prima facie principle. It affirms absolutely that one must always treat humanity in each person as an end, but the idea of valuing humanity as an end is complex, many-sided, and indefinite enough to permit some flexibility of application. It encompasses many strong moral presumptive considerations that in crisis situations cannot all be satisfied. Note, too, that I rely here on a 'thick' interpretation of the humanity formula, as opposed to a 'thin' or formal reading that Kant also suggests.

that we permissibly can to avoid later being forced to do what we have powerful moral reason not to do.

In sum: Although the incalculable worth of humanity in each person opens a gap in Kantian theory, leading us to admit that there may be some unresolvable tragic moral conflicts, the same idea directs us in the strongest terms to abhor what we would need to do in such conflict situations and so to use all permissible means to prevent those situations from arising.

Fourth, it is not always a good idea to try to settle potential conflicts before one faces them. There may be psychological and moral costs, and no practical need, to have them settled in advance. This seems obviously so in many mundane cases, but my conjecture now is that even in developing general normative theories it may be better to leave some questions open.

The conjecture is suggested by an analogy. Think of individuals who are utterly devoted to their children, their partners, their vocations, and their personal standards of how people should treat each other. If they guide themselves by their commitment to these highest values in a realistic and flexible way, in favorable conditions they are likely never to face a situation in which they must *sacrifice* any of the values for another. Of course, they will need to compromise, adjust their schedules, and live with the fact that they wish they could do more than they can. But they do not need to rank their values. They do not have to ask in advance what their priorities would be if, through horrible misfortune, they could not continue to live a life that expresses their full respect for all of these values. Treating their several values, for all practical purposes, as supreme and yet incommensurable serves to frame a way of life for them, and so they reasonably confess that if forced to make a radical choice they 'would not know what to do.'[31] Living in the faith that they can reconcile the things that they most cherish enables them to live with a virtually unqualified, self-defining commitment to each value. This, we can imagine, energizes their pursuits and motivates them to anticipate and forestall crises in which the values could not be reconciled. Also, importantly, it enables them to enjoy special relationships that are built upon the similar and reciprocal commitments of others.

---

[31] We may disapprove of this refusal to rank values if the conflict is of a particular kind, say, between one's family and one's vocation (e.g., Gauguin) or between one's vocation and one's integrity; so my point is more intuitive if we focus on conflicts in which the choice is between the various persons one loves.

If actually forced to make the hard choice to sacrifice one of their highest values, they might in fact cope and eventually restructure a new life, as people often do when their normative world collapses. Then again, they might not; but even in this worst case, they would not necessarily have been better off to have ranked their values in advance. Doing so would probably not have prevented the loss or made them immune to the pain, and it would have robbed them of the benefits of unqualified, wholehearted commitment. To try to make a *serious* decision in advance as to which basic values they *would* sacrifice *if* faced with various imagined crises seems not only unnecessary but also potentially self-destructive. Like Sophie, but without any evident need to do so, they would make a self-fracturing choice, in effect forcing themselves to put a price on commitments that in their hearts they regard as priceless.

Parallel considerations are worth considering when we reflect about whether moral theories should provide determinate answers for all possible contingencies. Moral theories are constructed for different purposes, but let us consider their practical function. Insofar as they are meant to be normative, or action-guiding, for *that* purpose, it is undeniably a merit that they offer guidance for the significant moral decisions we actually face, the more the better, if *other things are equal*. To provide answers to purely hypothetical questions about imaginary cases or extremely rare cases is not crucial for practical purposes, although *how* a theory answers such questions, if it does, can confirm or shake our confidence in its acceptability. There is, then, a presumption for determinacy in normative theories, but this is only a limited presumption. To give no guidance, for example, is better than giving clearly unacceptable guidance. The question now is whether the analogy with incommensurate personal values suggests a further way the presumption might be rebutted.

Suppose that, as Kant thought, we hold some of our basic *moral* values as incommensurable and virtually absolute. Imagine further that although the effort to reconcile tensions and prima facie conflicts among these values sometimes requires us to adjust, balance, and reinterpret these values, we rarely, if ever, face situations in which we must make the radical choice to abandon, sacrifice, or permanently subordinate any of the values for others. Refusing to rank these values, let us suppose, helps to motivate us to anticipate and circumvent situations in which we would be forced to make such radical choices. As with personal values, imagine that our unreserved commitment to these moral values energizes us to realize them more fully and provides the foundation for special relationships with those who have similar and reciprocal commitments.

Given this situation, a moral theorist who insisted that we must treat our basic values as commensurable and subject to ranking would be in some ways like someone who thinks that we should prioritize all of our personal values in anticipation of the horrible choices that extreme circumstances could force upon us. In *both* cases, closure comes with costs: we would have to put a price on what previously we held, for all practical purposes, as priceless. Moreover, relative to the Kantian view, the shift to commensurability *in moral theory* seems to involve an *extra* cost, for if we are not to view others as having an incomparable worth we cannot claim any such value for ourselves. Thus, adopting a price model for all evaluations would require not merely a change in one's self-conception but also a lowering of one's self-esteem.[32]

V. RESIDUAL FEELINGS AND ATTITUDES COMMONLY EXPECTED

Our final issue concerns whether the Kantian position about residual feelings and attitudes is compatible with what we ordinarily expect. What are these expectations? For present purposes and tentatively, I suggest the following.

1. *Nonmoral responses.* Some responses we might expect are worth mentioning only to separate them from the morally significant responses that are my main concern. We would commonly anticipate, for example, that those who made hard choices in practical moral dilemmas might have various personal concerns, the absence of which might be unusual but would not mark one as morally defective. These might include *fear* that those whom one injured might retaliate, *anger* at whomever or whatever caused one to be in the dilemma, *regret* that one's social image has been tarnished, *desire for reassurance* from friends, distasteful *memories*, and *worries* that similar problems will disturb one's peace of mind again.

2. *Judgment of 'not guilty' for the choice.* By hypothesis, the agents

---

[32] This is a theme of 'Social Snobbery and Human Dignity', in *Autonomy and Self-Respect*, 155–72, esp. p. 171. My point is not that theorists should pretend, for pragmatic reasons, that basic values cannot be ranked despite strong non-pragmatic argument that they can, but rather that, lacking such argument, we need not necessarily deplore the gaps opened by leaving certain basic values unranked.

did not create the problem by previous wrongdoing, they deliberated conscientiously, they honestly concluded that they had no better option, and they have not changed their minds in retrospect. I imagine that most people, understanding all this, would not expect the agents to judge themselves to be morally *guilty* or blameworthy *for what they chose to do*. For the agents to judge that, in the fullest sense, they were *guilty* and so blameworthy, they must, I assume, believe that they did wrong, all things considered and without excuse. Admittedly, in advance and in retrospect, our agents saw the option they chose as *apparently* wrong, that is, *as far as they could discern*, condemned by moral considerations no less (or more) than an alternative they had. But this is not to say that they concluded, then or later, that what they did, or their choosing it in the situation, was actually wrong, all things considered. We may expect that, if duly modest, they will admit that they *might* have chosen to do otherwise if they had *known* more, had more *time* to think, or had a more developed *capacity* for moral judgment. Thus, they might admit that what they did could have been 'wrong' in a sense that abstracts from the agents' knowledge, opportunities, and capacities; but moral guilt and blameworthiness are commonly understood to be determined by how well one conducted oneself given one's available knowledge, opportunities, and capacities, not by whether one did wrong in the sense that abstracts from these factors.[33] *Even* when using the latter sense, modest agents only have reason to say, 'I *might* have done what was wrong,' not 'I *did* what was wrong.'

It seems unreasonable, then, for our agents to judge themselves to be guilty, and so we can suppose other people who understand the agents' situation would not expect them to judge themselves to be guilty. Of course, we often blame people who *claim* to have acted in a practical dilemma, but this is usually because we do not believe them. That is, we suspect that, contrary to what they say, they did not try hard enough to find a better option or did not honestly believe their options were morally equivalent. In saying that we would not 'expect' them to judge themselves as guilty for what they have done, I mean that we would not suppose that they *should* judge themselves as guilty and we would not look down on them for regarding themselves as not guilty. We might, of course, *predict and anticipate* (i.e., 'expect' in another sense) that

---

[33] One can, of course, be culpable for acts and omissions that result in one's ignorance, limited opportunities, and stunted capacities, but this general point is not relevant here because we are assuming that our agents are in the practical dilemmas through no fault of their own and so their limited knowledge, opportunities, and capacities are not the result of their wrongdoing or vice.

some would *regard* themselves as guilty, even while admitting they could have done no better; for we know that at times people make irrational, even inconsistent, judgments, especially concerning innocence and guilt.

3. *Guilt for other things and quasi-guilt feelings.* Although not expecting agents to regard themselves as guilty *for what they chose to do* in a practical dilemma, we should not be surprised if they had some other genuine and appropriate feelings of guilt. They may realize, for example, that even though they were not to blame for *what* they did, the *manner* in which they acted was callous, clumsy, or weak. They may suspect themselves of *mixed motives*, even of having enjoyed causing grave harm to innocent persons. The episode may cause them to reflect on their character, calling to mind past neglects and misdeeds; or it may reveal how arrogant and self-righteous they have been in posturing as too 'pure' ever to do the sort of thing that they have just done. But whether it is appropriate for a person to feel guilty about these further matters will depend on the special features of the particular case.

Besides all this, our agents may experience *displaced* guilt, *natural* guilt, or *associated* guilt. That is, in thinking of what they did in the practical dilemma, they may *feel* bad, even quite awful, about themselves in a way they say 'feels like guilt,' but the feeling is explained by something other than their judgment that they were at fault in their decision. *Displaced guilt feelings* are genuine but misdirected, perhaps unconsciously, to something other than that for which the person is really guilty. *Natural guilt feelings*, if there are any, would be emotional discomforts and dispositions, not stemming from self-regarding *moral judgments* and not rooted in social learning, to turn against oneself after behaving in certain ways. A tendency to feel bad and act self-destructively after knowingly killing a parent or companion might be thought to be an example. *Associated guilt feelings* are similar in that they do not reflect the agent's actual moral judgments, but are feelings we have because our emotional responses do not discriminate finely enough between morally distinct but otherwise similar behaviors. For example, although one may not actually *judge* oneself morally guilty after killing a loved one (purely) by accident, the horror may be so intense that one cannot help but feel as if one is to blame.[34]

Although we should not be surprised if, after facing practical moral dilemmas, our agents experience guilt-like feelings (displaced, natural,

---

[34] So-called 'residual guilt feelings' are perhaps a special case of associated guilt feelings. One feels residual guilt for behavior that one was earlier socialized to accept as wrong but no longer thinks wrong. Here our feelings fail to take note, as it were, of a change in intellectual judgment about the same behavior.

and associated guilt), I doubt that we would 'expect' such feelings, that is, think that this is how the agents *should* feel. Strong feelings of *displaced* and *associated guilt* in conscientious people who are not at fault are typically seen as regrettable psychological problems, invoking sympathy rather than blame; and *natural guilt*, if it exists, must be acknowledged as a universal and inevitable tendency, for good or ill, rather than a reaction that moral agents 'should' have and can be disparaged for lacking. The tendency to feel these kinds of quasi-guilt to some degree may be socially useful, but when felt by those who have conscientiously faced practical moral dilemmas, they seem to be an *undeserved* or misplaced burden of suffering. If we found someone who was free from these tendencies but who felt guilty when and only when *appropriately judging* himself to *be* guilty, then probably most of us would count that person *fortunate and healthy* rather than lacking in something that a good person must have.

4. *Moral responses expected of everyone.* We expect that morally good people who are aware of the dilemma and its aftermath will have various moral feelings and attitudes toward those who have suffered, toward the community, and toward the agent in the practical dilemma, considered simply as persons involved in a situation of this kind. For example, we expect everyone to regret the fact that someone had to face the agonizing choice and that some innocent persons suffered. Everyone, we suppose, should hope that such choices can be avoided in the future. We might expect, too, that anyone would want the victims and the community not to misunderstand what has occurred, for example, to realize that, although it may appear otherwise, the agent was conscientious and could find no better option. The event may have ruptured normal moral relations, provoked powerful desires for vengeance, and contributed to a general climate of suspicion and moral skepticism. If so, we suppose that a good person, knowing all this, would deplore the outcome and want to change it. We anticipate and allow that the *intensity* of responses will vary with persons' relations to the problem; for example, depending on whether they were players, immediate witnesses, or simply people who read about the problem in the papers. But to respond to some degree in the ways I have suggested seems normally expected of people independently of their role in the dilemma situation or their special relations to the individuals in question.

5. *Personal, or individual-relative, moral responses.* The agent in a practical moral dilemma is not just anyone. There are special responses that we expect of the person who faced the choice and caused the harm. We expect such agents to have deep personal regrets about what they

have done to the *particular individuals* they have harmed. The appropriate attitude is *not just* regret that *someone* was harmed, especially not merely that someone was harmed *by someone*. The agents need to acknowledge that their actions, although justifiable in the extraordinary circumstances, put them in a special relation to the actual victims in the situation. This is *not* to say that they should feel *more regret* for harming that individual than they *would have had* if they had injured a different person in a comparable situation, but they should deplore the fact that they injured *that very person*, not just that they injured someone (or someone like him).[35]

Agents often feel, and are expected to feel, a special deep sadness, if not horror, that they themselves have done what they have done, even though they were unable to find anything morally more acceptable to do. We may call this *agent-regret*, but must remember that it does not imply that the agent wishes she had done something different, *given the options*. It is not simply wanting to avoid the *appearance* of having done wrong, nor need it be a part of self-righteous obsession with the purity of one's moral record compared to that of others. The regretting agents need not be so presumptuous as to think that from an *impartial moral point of view* it would have been better if someone else had to make the tragic decision, but *personally* they cannot be indifferent to the fact that they themselves, rather than someone else, were the agents. As in serious cases of causing harm accidentally or in the course of duty, agents often feel their lives somehow *marred*, *tainted*, *made worse* than they would have been.[36]

What is puzzling is not so much that people react to tragic choices this way, but that they are expected to. That is, we seem to think that, in some sense, people *should* have the attitudes and feelings that typically they do. Recall the tragic choices posed by *The Magus* or *Sophie's Choice*, and Truman's decision to use atomic bombs to end the Second World War. Or, if you doubt that these were really practical dilemmas, then construct your own best example. Then imagine that, having knowingly caused many deaths as they 'plumped' for one horn of the dilemma, the agents said sincerely, not masking deeper feelings:[37] 'There

---

[35] Perhaps one should feel more regret for harming, say, one's brother than a stranger, but the concern should be particularized in either case. The regret that one killed this stranger may be of the same degree as the regret that one would have had for killing that stranger, but in neither case should it be merely regret that 'I killed someone.'

[36] I say more about this in 'Moral Purity and the Lesser Evil', in *Autonomy and Self-Respect*.

[37] I borrow the label 'plumping' for these choices from Simon Blackburn.

was nothing better to do, as far as I could tell. It's a pity that someone had to do this (or something as bad) and people died. But I am content, even proud, that I wanted to avoid doing anything wrong, and I did. My life is no worse for doing what I did, I have no more reason to feel concern for the people I killed than you do, and, other things being equal, I would happily take up the job of making the hard choice again if someone had to do it.' Something seems missing here: attitudes and feeling we suppose any decent person would have.

VI. A KANTIAN PERSPECTIVE ON RESIDUES OF ATTITUDE AND FEELING

What should Kantians say about the attitudes and feelings one should have after facing a practical moral dilemma?

1. *Should a conscientious person who takes a stand in an unresolved practical dilemma feel guilty?* Here Kantian theory coincides with reflective ordinary opinion (as described above). That is, both agree that the agents should not feel guilty in the robust sense that implies a *judgment* that they are in fact guilty. Since there are no *genuine* moral dilemmas, at least one of the agents' options must have been permissible. For example, Sophie must have been morally permitted either to save her daughter, to save her son, or to refuse to select between them. Since practical dilemmas are only apparent dilemmas, it is still conceivable that more fully informed or subtle moral judges could see that *only* one of her options is 'permitted,' the rest being 'wrong' in a sense that abstracts from the agent's perspective. But the agents facing practical dilemmas must choose within the limits of their perspectives or, as Kant would have it, on a 'maxim' that reflects how they see the problem. Now, taking this into account, *what they do*, described as is now morally relevant, is *to 'plump' for one option with a good will but with a nonculpable inability to discern that one option is morally preferable to another*. Described in this way, what they do is not *wrong* in the primary sense that takes into account the agent's perspective (knowledge, intention, and motive).[38] Therefore, there is no warrant for the

---

[38] This allows, however, that what they did, described independently of their inability to discern a morally better option, was (unbeknownst to them) in fact 'wrong' in a sense (e.g., a rights violation) that detaches from knowledge, motives, and circumstances. Practical dilemmas, on the Kantian view, are only apparent dilemmas; and what follows from the denial of genuine dilemmas is that at least one option must be permitted (in the 'detached' sense), not that both are. What makes the conscientious agent in a

judgment 'I *am* guilty for doing it' that is normally implicit in the self-description 'I *feel* guilty for doing it.'[39] 'Displaced,' 'natural,' and 'associated' guilt feelings may be experienced, but one can have these feelings without thinking that what one did was wrong, all things considered.

The first conclusion, then, is that Kantians should agree with ordinary opinion that agents *should not, strictly speaking, feel guilty* when they act conscientiously in practical moral dilemmas.[40] The argument, in sum, is that *feeling bad* about what one has done does not amount to *feeling guilty* in the fullest sense unless it reflects the *judgment* that one *is guilty*, and Kantians should not judge that conscientious agents who act in practical dilemmas are in fact guilty. The argument for this negative conclusion does not presuppose the dubious general thesis that because feelings cannot be called up and extinguished at will, it is *always* inappropriate to make 'should' and 'ought' judgments about feelings. This general thesis is clearly incompatible with common opinion. Unfortunately, the general thesis is strongly suggested by many of Kant's remarks, which is why we must now turn to the following question.

2. *How does it make sense to say that a person 'should feel' one way or another?* Common opinion holds that certain special regrets and concerns for the injured should be felt by anyone who has made the hard choice in a practical moral dilemma. But in Kantian theory this cannot be understood in a straightforward way.

Why not? The Kantian primary moral 'ought' or 'should' is a command of reason, addressed to the will of imperfect moral agents, who can follow it but might fail. Addressed to the deliberative agent, it says, 'Choose this from among your options, whether you feel like it or not.' But substitute 'to feel regret' for 'this' here and the result seems to be nonsense. We cannot simply choose how to feel at the moment,

---

practical dilemma guilt free is not that his act was not wrong in the detached sense, but that he did his best and so was not wrong to choose it, given his understanding and motive.

[39] 'But if someone is aware that he has acted in accordance with his conscience, then as far as guilt or innocence is concerned nothing more can be required of him' (MM, 161 [6: 401]). What is needed to accord with conscience, Kant says, does not require actually satisfying the 'objective judgment as to whether something is a duty or not,' in which one 'can indeed be mistaken at times,' but only satisfying 'my subjective judgment as to whether I have submitted it to my practical reason . . . for such a judgment,' which (Kant says) is a matter about which one cannot be mistaken (MM, 161 [6: 401]).

[40] 'Acting conscientiously' in a practical dilemma, of course, must be understood not as 'acting as conscience dictates' but as 'acting without contravening conscience after conscientiously reflecting on what to do.'

whereas obligation and duty are the moral 'necessity of a free action under a categorical imperative of reason.'[41] Thus Kant says, 'There can be no duty to have a moral feeling or to acquire it.' It is a self-contradiction, for example, to suppose that we have a duty to have feelings of love, respect, or even 'hatred of vice.'[42]

The point here does not depend on a 'two worlds' picture of feeling as caused and human behavior as uncaused. Kant does assume that, from a practical point of view, we must view our actions as freely chosen in a way that our feelings are not. The point, however, is not that feelings fall under empirical causal laws whereas human behavior does not; for, on Kant's view, everything that occurs is in principle subject to causal explanation when viewed empirically. Kant relies on his idea that we can and must view the same phenomena from two different perspectives, empirical and practical, depending on our purposes, even though neither perspective is reducible to the other and they seem incompatible. Assuming this, Kant granted that from the empirical point of view both feelings and behavior are subject to causal explanation; but he thought, as most of us do, that from the practical point of view we consider what we do, or at least *will* to do, as immediately 'up to us,' whereas how we feel is not. For example, a doctor can simply choose whether or not to clean her patient's festering wound, but not whether or not to enjoy the task. From my deliberative standpoint, my feelings are like other things over which I lack direct practical control, for example, your choices and attitudes, and my headaches, heart rate, and dreams.[43] Hence, Kant thought, moral imperatives can only

---

[41] See MM, 15 [6: 222–3]. 'Duty' is 'the action to which a person is bound,' the 'matter' of 'obligation.'

[42] MM, 161–2 [6: 402–3].

[43] Qualifications are needed here. I may find that I feel sad every time I play a certain piece of music while looking at old photos of a deceased friend, and so I could try to make myself feel sad by this means, predicting success as well or better than many things I decide/choose/will to do, for instance, finish a paper by the deadline. I might even say, 'Tonight I choose to be sad,' and then set about to make myself sad by the music and pictures. But this possibility of choosing our feelings seems of little help when we return to our problem of making sense of the common expectation that I feel guilt, remorse, sympathy for the injured, and so on. If I had to use devices analogous to the music and pictures to work up the expected feelings (on the appropriate occasions), I would not be meeting those expectations but rather still showing myself morally defective (by the standards of common opinion). So the fact that I cannot do this with regular success is only part of the story.

Ordinarily, I think, we want the appropriate moral feelings in agents who have done wrong and caused harm, and so on, not as an end in itself but as expressions of the agent's genuine moral commitments. Compare: We want our friends to grieve our death not because we value for its own sake their suffering on our account but because absence of grief, given human nature, would be a rather sure sign that they lacked the sort of

command actions, not feelings, and so 'should feel' never expresses a direct requirement of duty.

One might imagine that Kant's view can be reconciled with common opinion by emphasizing our capacity to develop our sensibilities and so *indirectly* influence the feelings we have at later times. But this strategy does not seem promising. Granted, we can sometimes and to some extent control our feelings by circuitous means—for example, by distracting ourselves when we are angry and putting ourselves into environments in which friendly feelings typically grow. In fact Kant in *The Metaphysics of Morals* says that it is a conditional and indirect duty to cultivate affections as a means of promoting active benevolence.[44] But when common opinion *expects* agents to feel regret and says that they *should* feel it, the main point, surely, is not that they should now do things to cause sentiments of regret to well up in them, for example, visit the morgue or the family of their victims.[45] Nor is the point that they should take steps to develop a disposition to regret on later occasions, for example, through psychotherapy or association with more sensitive people. They should feel regret *now*.

Given that they cannot interpret 'should feel' as a moral command, the best strategy for Kantians is to construe the 'should' here as one of normative expectation. Consider, for example, the parent who tells a child just returning from the store, 'You should have a dollar in change!' or a doctor who tells her patient, 'You should have a higher red cell count.' Both express disappointment at finding something less than expected or normal. This may not in itself be a problem, but as a symptom of deeper trouble it causes concern. Absence of expected *feelings* may be symptomatic of problems too. Suppose, for example, after a husband or wife happily departs to Hawaii for what he or she professes to be the funeral of an old friend and then a week of 'nothing but tedious work,' the spouse left behind remarks suspiciously, 'He [or she] should have felt sad.' The point is not that the departing spouse should have tried to work up some sad feelings or to cultivate a disposition to sadness on such occasions in the future. Rather, if there was nothing amiss with the spouse's aims, attitudes, commitments, and value judg-

attitude, commitment, preferences, and dispositions that we hoped and expected them to have.

[44] MM, 204–6 [6: 456–8].

[45] Even Kant says that we have a duty not to avoid places of suffering where sympathetic feelings are likely to be aroused, but what common opinion expects is not just these indirect future-oriented measures but appropriate feelings at the time they are called for (MM, 204–6 [6: 456–8]).

ments, he or she *would* almost certainly have felt sad; and so the absence of sadness was a bad sign.

Similarly, the thought that those who harm others in practical dilemmas, or even accidentally, should feel regret or sorrow may be interpreted as the idea that such feelings are normally to be expected in moral agents who have the aims, attitudes, commitments, and value judgments that they should have. Absence of the expected feelings would not be morally bad in itself but merely symptomatic of moral defects in the agent. The expectations would rest upon the Kantian point that in human beings, as a matter of fact, our moral judgments and commitments are *typically* accompanied by corresponding feelings. Normally, we might add, we find these virtually inseparable: that is, we experience and express our judgments and commitments in an emotional way. We are to blame, if at all, not for the absence of affective responses *per se*, but for culpable defects of judgment and will of which lack of affect is a typical symptom. These defects, on the Kantian view, are seen as directly 'up to us,' unlike the affective aspect of our feelings. Thus it is our responsibility to alter our defective will and judgment immediately, not later. If we do, we can expect that, as a rule, corresponding changes in how we feel will eventually follow.

Kantians, then, can understand claims about how we 'should feel' as expressing the 'should' of expectation rather than of obligation. What makes such claims *morally* significant is that the defects signaled by the absence of the expected affective responses are *moral* defects. Let us think of *attitudes* broadly as including the aims, policies, value judgments, and commitments that express the agent's 'will' and so are, in the appropriate sense, within the control of the agent. Then we can say that feelings are morally significant at least insofar as they are expressions of morally relevant attitudes. Thus the more basic question underlying 'How should we feel?' is 'What attitudes should we adopt?' We can understand our remaining problems then as concerned directly with attitudes, and only indirectly with feelings.

3. *Why should the agents, or even bystanders, care about the outcomes of practical dilemmas?* Why, for example, should I think that it is a bad thing that someone was injured or killed by someone? After all, by hypothesis, the agents in our practical dilemmas maintained a good will, which is supposed to be the only unconditional good and the condition of all values. Also, by hypothesis, agents did what was right, given the situation as they perceived it, and they were not acting from culpable ignorance. So the Kantian reason for deploring the resulting injury or death cannot be a general opposition to immorality. Further, Kantian

theory denies that there are 'intrinsic values,' natural or nonnatural, that exist prior to and independent of the will of rational agents. So Kantians cannot say that the pain, or even death, that was caused by the agent is *in itself* a bad thing in the way utilitarians might understand this. How, then, is it bad?

Here it may help to distinguish what I shall call the extreme hard-line Kantian position from a moderate one.[46] The extreme hard-line Kantian insists that only immoral choices (or 'willings') are to be considered objectively bad, strictly speaking; everything else is considered bad only in a derivative sense or relative to individual tastes and preferences. On this view, although as individuals we tend to find such things sad and distasteful, the pains, injury, and death of others *must* be regarded as 'bad things' *only* in the sense that they are 'things we would normally be wrong to choose to bring about.'[47] When these misfortunes occur naturally, result from accidents, or are caused in the performance of duty, the hard-line Kantian (with the Stoics) tries to maintain the attitude, 'What is that to me?' for he sees such things as not in themselves bad and sees no reason to indulge his own empathetic suffering when it can do nothing for the victims.[48] On the hard-line view, morally good persons as such need only be concerned with their own acts and motives. Some of their duties, to be sure, direct them to aim to promote certain effects and to try not to cause others; for example, they must try to aid the needy and avoid killing innocent people. Perhaps, too, as Kant said, they should cultivate some sympathy to counterbalance the selfish and malicious inclinations that commonly tempt people from the path of duty. But apart from such concerns, which are derivative from a commitment to do one's duty, the hard-line Kantian says that morally good persons may have an attitude of indifference to the pains, injuries, and deaths of human beings when these result from natural causes, the unpreventable behavior of others, or their own dutiful acts.

This hard-line Kantian position seems so clearly opposed to common opinion that Kantians who hope for some reconciliation with common

---

[46] The moderate position, in my opinion, is a plausible and more sympathetic reconstruction of Kant's views; but the hard line at least echoes some of Kant's remarks. Both are compatible with the basic Kantian position sketched earlier.

[47] Note that this is not exactly the idea of prima facie wrong made familiar by W. D. Ross. There may be absolutely nothing against doing something 'normally wrong' in an atypical case; but there is always something against doing what is 'prima facie wrong' in Ross's sense.

[48] Kant expresses admiration for the Stoic wise man's refusal to suffer for the fate of a friend he could not rescue, but nonetheless urges the cultivation of compassionate natural feelings. See MM, 205 [6: 457].

opinion have good reason to find, or develop, a more humane position on these matters. The roots of this more moderate view are in Kant's idea that humanity in each person is an end in itself. Like other formulations of the Categorical Imperative, Kant's humanity formula expressly addresses how we should act, but in explaining the grounds for this act-guiding principle Kant expresses the broader requirement to conceive of humanity in each person as an end in itself.[49] The required conception is really an *evaluative attitude*, for it means regarding each (rational) human being as 'something whose existence is in itself of absolute value,' as having 'dignity,' as above all 'price.' The basic disposition to acknowledge this evaluative stance as morally and rationally appropriate is not something we choose, but is supposed to be inherent in all moral agents.[50] What we are required to do, can do, but might fail to do, is to affirm and adopt this attitude as our own overriding commitment. To do so, I suggest, is to let the idea of human dignity guide not only our actions and policies but also our judgments about what is good and bad among the things not under our control.

Suppose, for example, some people have just suffered horrible deaths from some natural or accidental disaster. Upon learning of it, those with the right moral attitude will no doubt do what they can to aid secondary victims and to minimize the risk of recurrences. But they will also regard it a very bad thing that the people suffered and died needlessly; and this is a judgment that is more than a morally optional 'wish' or personal preference. The right attitude leads one immediately to see and deplore the tragic fate of the victims and not merely to focus on one's own future-oriented tasks. Even if the tragedy was utterly beyond human control, the moral attitude is reflected in the 'will' that it not be so, were this possible.[51]

---

[49] G, 96 [4: 429].

[50] This is important if we are to make sense of the claim that people 'ought' to commit themselves fully to the attitude in question. If sociopaths totally lacked the basic disposition to acknowledge other persons as ends, then one could not say, in a Kantian sense, that they ought to so regard and treat them. Moral 'oughts' are meant to express the sense of being bound because of principles that agents themselves are deeply disposed, as moral agents, to acknowledge as rationally authoritative and so see as (in a sense) expressive of themselves. A too-seldom noted consequence is that if one thinks that Kant's faith that virtually all sane adult human beings have such dispositions is unwarranted, then one should also see Kant's ground for attributing moral duties, rights, and dignity to *all* human beings as undermined.

[51] The hard-line Kantian supposes that we can will only our own actions, but the moderate view allows that, in a broader sense, one can have a 'will' toward other possible states of affairs. Here one's 'will' expresses what one is prepared to hope and cheer for, to plead and pray for, to welcome openly, or to dread and bemoan, to protest and cry out against, to resist becoming 'resigned' to, whether these can affect outcomes or not.

Returning to the issue at hand, the moderate, but not the hard-line, Kantian can agree with common opinion that we should have concern for those who suffer as a result of how someone acts in a practical dilemma. In deploring these misfortunes as well as other tragedies and outrages that are not our fault, we are expressing the basic moral attitude that counts each human being as having a special value. We may at the same time, of course, express *personal* grief and sympathy for the victims, but this goes beyond the attitude that can be morally expected of everyone. What is required of all is at least the judgment that it was a bad thing, even apart from further consequences, that human beings were injured and killed. This is not to say that the injuries and deaths had a property of 'intrinsic badness' that is independent of our wills. On the contrary, in saying that these were bad things to happen, we *express* our will, broadly construed: 'Would that such things not occur!'

4. *Why should Kantians care particularly about the individual victims?* Assuming now that Kantians can explain why we should regret that *someone* was injured or killed, how can they explain why we should have a *particular* concern for the *very individuals* who were harmed?[52] After all, the formula of humanity tells us to treat persons with dignity because of something quite general: their rational nature. Is it not enough, then, that I regret that *a person*, considered abstractly as a rational being, was injured? Why need I care, beyond that, about *the individual victim*—Harry, Tanya, or whoever?

The answer requires a closer look at what it means to value a person, or a person's humanity, as an end. Humanity, for Kant, is in part a rational 'capacity to set ends, any ends whatsoever.' Apart from the 'obligatory ends' that all rational agents are supposed to share, each person freely adopts certain personal ends as his or her own. We are naturally inclined to pursue various goals, but our inclinations do not finally determine what our ends are. We each shape our own vague conception of happiness as we select our particular goals and policies. Unless our ends are immoral, by endorsing personal ends we are, in a sense, creating (person-relative) values. That is, we confer a new status on some-

---

Note that to be so 'prepared' is not merely to 'wish' or 'feel' passively, without judgment or choice. Kant seems to endorse the less narrowly restricted idea of 'will' in MM, 13–14 [6: 213–14].

[52] Note: I do not assume that common sense says that one must care more for that person than one would care for another person who was injured, as might be the case if the person was one's mother, but only that a personalized, individual-directed caring is in order.

thing that may have previously been of no value to anyone: now it gives *us* reasons to value various means, and it gives *others* moral reason not to hinder arbitrarily our achievement of those particular ends. To value humanity in persons, then, is not simply to favor rational decision making abstractly or to promote ends that *every* rational agent *must* endorse. It requires *valuing* persons *as the authors of their own personal ends*, which means that these ends must have weight with us simply because they are permissible ends that the individuals have endorsed.[53]

Having reason, inclinations, will, and freedom are supposed to be the shared general features of all moral agents, but individuals are in large part identified as 'the very individuals they are' by the different sets of ends (or 'projects,' as some say) that they choose to endorse. So, we must conclude, the formula of humanity itself implies that we must acknowledge and give appropriate weight to the individuating, special ends of each person.

Since we obviously cannot, and need not, give attention to the individuating features of every person on earth, this moral imperative must be understood as applicable relative to context. In practice, we must pay special regard to the particular, self-defining ends of those with whom we most closely interact, the people related to us in ways that make our individual attention most relevant. For example, it is important for me to be alert and responsive to the special projects and aspirations of my family and students who come to me for advice; but it is surely not required that I probe into personal matters as I check out a library book, pay for my groceries, or greet a passing stranger. Even in these routine exchanges, however, there are subtle but important ways of acknowledging the other person as an individual. A pleasant comment, a sincere 'Thank you,' or even just a friendly demeanor can signal recognition of a person as an individual, suggesting a readiness to deal on a more personal level if circumstances should call for this.

These considerations establish a presumption that the agents in practical dilemmas, and perhaps even close witnesses, have moral reason to concern themselves with the victims as individuals and not simply as abstractly conceived moral agents. What needs to be done to express this varies with the case; but the minimal attitude of 'regretting that *someone* was harmed,' which may be an appropriate response to a news report of injuries in a foreign war, seems obviously insufficient for the

---

[53] See G, 95–6 [4: 427–9] and Christine Korsgaard, 'Kant's Formula of Humanity', *Kant-Studien*, 77 (1986), 183–202.

agents in the tragic practical dilemmas we have been considering. By knowingly doing what causes someone serious harm contrary to all normal moral expectations, the agents put themselves in a non-routine relationship to their victims, a relationship in which the personal concerns of the individuals harmed become highly relevant.

5. *Why should the agents in practical dilemmas have any special personal regrets?* Why should the *agents* regard the forced choice as a tragedy for themselves as well as for those they harmed? Why should they think of their lives as marred or made worse by what they have done? Why regret being the agent rather than merely a bystander? After all, the agents are not guilty; and they have no reason to think that it would have been morally better to have done something different. The idea of a 'moral stain,' that is, a metaphysical property that can attach to a person (like social stigma) no matter how good the person's will, has no place in Kantian ethics. Moreover, from a general moral point of view, it is not worse that the particular agents, rather than others, caused the harm. Our conscientious agents who act in practical dilemmas are, by hypothesis, spotless within the limits of their knowledge and abilities. They may even have had a good will throughout their lives. What more does it take to have an unmarred, regret-free moral life?

To see why agent-regret is to be expected we need to take a broader view of our lives as moral agents situated in a dangerous world. On the Kantian view, we must be committed to the unconditional value of every human being, but we know that everyone is highly vulnerable. If we are to honor the commitment, we must make it a permanent life project to do all that is physically and morally possible to avoid causing serious harm to people. Although a good person typically accepts this project without much explicit thought, it requires steady vigilance in daily activities (such as driving) and extraordinary efforts in crisis situations (such as responding to crime, medical emergencies, and threats of war). Realizing that we cannot altogether avoid causing harm to others, we need to think hard about which harms are justified in various contexts; and we need to try to avoid situations that would force us to cause harm in the line of duty. For similar reasons, the moral project requires us to try hard to avoid falling into practical dilemmas, for these, again, leave a conscientious person no alternative to causing serious harm.

This background provides a natural explanation of why morally conscientious persons feel their lives made worse by what they must do in practical dilemmas. When forced to cause serious harm to others in a practical dilemma, they have to that extent failed in a fundamental life project. By hypothesis, the failure is not their fault, but it is bound to bring disappointment, frustration, and regret. Agents who did not regard their personal lives as made worse by causing serious harm in a practical dilemma would give strong evidence of not having been deeply committed to the moral project. The attitude of personal regret, although not in itself morally required, is morally significant insofar as it is a natural expression of conscientious agents' deep and self-identifying commitment to preserve and respect humanity in each person. The regret is (normatively) expected because lacking it is a symptom that one does not take one's basic moral responsibility seriously. If we understand that agents were conscientious in facing their practical dilemmas and guiltless in falling into them, we should not lower our moral esteem for them; but we should be able to see how, from the agents' perspective, their lives fall short of what they deeply hoped for.

An analogy may be helpful here, although analogies are also liable to mislead. The view of most players and avid fans of a sports team is that it is not enough for players to have the attitude, 'I will do my best but I don't care about the outcome of the game.' They want players to make winning an end, something they care about beyond their own performance or any rewards. This attitude motivates players to play harder, but the attitude is valued, apart from this, as an expression of a shared commitment that binds them together. But if players strive to win with all their hearts and yet fail, then, even though it is no fault of their own, they will almost inevitably experience disappointment, regret, and unhappiness about that brief part of their lives. The liability to regret is inseparable from whole-hearted commitment, in sports and in the attempt to live morally. But there is a crucial disanalogy. In both cases, absence of regret signals weakness of commitment; but only in the latter case is it cause for *moral concern*. Commitment to the goals of a sports team is optional; but, at least on the Kantian view, we 'ought' to be wholeheartedly committed to moral ends. This is because the moral commitment, unlike the other, is supposed to be the full expression of our nature and common bond as reasonable and autonomous human beings. It is necessary, so to speak, to be true to ourselves and to others.

One final note. Consequentialists have their own answers to the questions raised here, and I have not argued that the Kantian position is superior. Indeed, for the most part, the challenge has been just to find Kantian answers that are more plausible than the completely untenable answers it might seem at first that Kant was committed to. However, one comparative point is worth mentioning: the Kantian position presented here does *not* appeal to the idea that it is *useful* to foster feelings of agent-regret *as a means* to make people more reluctant to cause harm and violate useful norms *on other occasions*. All the more, Kantians could not endorse a policy of encouraging people to feel guilty when they are not really guilty, even if this would be useful. Perhaps some utilitarians also reject these strategies in the end, but for Kantians the systematic manipulation and deception required would be immediately repugnant.

BIBLIOGRAPHY

ALLISON, HENRY E., *Kant's Theory of Freedom* (Cambridge: Cambridge University Press, 1990).
ANNAS, JULIA, *The Morality of Happiness* (New York: Oxford University Press, 1993).
ANSCOMBE, G. E. M., *Intention* (Ithaca: Cornell University Press, 1963).
—— 'Modern Moral Philosophy', *Philosophy*, 33(124) (1958), 1–19.
ARISTOTLE, *Nicomachean Ethics*, in Richard McKeon (ed.), *The Basic Works of Aristotle* (New York: Random House, 1941), 935–1112.
—— *Nicomachean Ethics*, tr. Terence Irwin (Indianapolis: Hackett Publishing Co., 1985).
BAIER, KURT, *The Moral Point of View* (Ithaca, NY: Cornell University Press, 1958).
BARON, MARCIA, 'Imperfect Duties and Supererogatory Acts', *Jahrbuch für Strafrecht und Ethik/Annual Review of Law and Ethics*, 6 (1998), 57–71.
—— *Kantian Ethics (Almost) without Apology* (Ithaca: Cornell University Press, 1995).
—— 'Kantian Ethics and Supererogation', *Journal of Philosophy*, 84 (1987), 237–62.
BARRY, BRIAN, *Theories of Justice* (Berkeley: University of California Press, 1989).
BAXLEY, ANNE MARGARET, 'Kant's Theory of Virtue; The Importance of Autocracy', PhD Dissertation, University of California, San Diego, 2000.
BENNETT, JONATHAN, 'The Conscience of Huckleberry Finn', *Philosophy*, 49 (1974), 123–34.
BENTHAM, JEREMY, *A Fragment on Government and An Introduction to the Principles of Morals and Legislation*, ed. Wilfred Harrison (Oxford: Blackwell, 1960).
BITTNER, RUDIGER, *What Reason Demands*, tr. Theodore Talbot (New York: Cambridge University Press, 1989).
BLACKBURN, SIMON, *Spreading the Word* (Oxford: Oxford University Press, 1984).
BONESANA, CESARE, Marchese di Beccaria, *On Crimes and Punishments* (New York: Bobbs Merrill, 1963)
BRANDT, RICHARD B., 'The Concept of Rational Action', *Social Theory and Practice*, 9 (1983), 143–64.
—— *Ethical Theory* (Englewood Cliffs, NJ: Prentice-Hall, 1959).
—— *A Theory of the Good and the Right* (Oxford: Clarendon Press, 1979).

BRANDT, RICHARD B.,'Toward a Credible Form of Utilitarianism', in Hector-Neri Castaneda and George Nakhnikian (eds.), *Morality and the Language of Conduct* (Detroit: Wayne State University Press, 1965).

BRINK, DAVID O., *Moral Realism and the Foundations of Ethics* (Cambridge: Cambridge University Press, 1989).

BROAD, C. D., *Five Types of Ethical Theory* (London: Routledge & Kegan Paul, 1930).

BUTLER, JOSEPH, *Five Sermons*, ed. Stephen Darwall (Indianapolis: Hackett Publishing Co., 1983).

BYRD, B. SHARON, 'Kant's Theory of Punishment: Deterrence in its Threat, Retribution in its Execution', *Law and Philosophy*, 8(2) (1980), 151–200.

CHISHOLM, RODERICK, 'Supererogation and Offense: A Conceptual Scheme for Ethics', *Ratio*, 5 (1963), 1–14.

COOPER, JOHN, *Reason and Human Good in Aristotle* (Cambridge: Harvard University Press, 1975).

CRISP, ROGER and SLOTE, MICHAEL, *Virtue Ethics* (Oxford: Oxford University Press, 1997).

CUMMISKEY, DAVID, *Kantian Consequentialism* (New York: Oxford University Press, 1996).

DARWALL, STEPHEN, *The British Moralists and the Internal 'Ought'* (Cambridge: Cambridge University Press, 1995).

——*Impartial Reason* (Ithaca: Cornell University Press, 1983).

DENNETT, DANIEL, *Elbow Room* (Cambridge, MA: MIT Press, 1984).

DONAGAN, ALAN, 'Conscience', in Lawrence and Charlotte Becker (eds.), *Encyclopedia of Ethics*, 2nd edn. (New York: Garland Press, 1992), i. 297–9.

——'Consistency in Rationalist Moral Systems', *Journal of Philosophy*, 81 (1984), 291–309.

——'Is There a Credible Form of Utilitarianism?', in Michael Bayles (ed.), *Contemporary Utilitarianism* (New York: Doubleday Anchor Books, 1968), 187–202.

——'Moral Dilemmas, Genuine and Spurious: A Comparative Anatomy', *Ethics*, 104 (1993), 7–21.

——'The Structure of Kant's Metaphysics of Morals', *Topoi*, 4 (1985), 61–72.

——*The Theory of Morality* (Chicago: University of Chicago Press, 1977).

DONNELLY, JOHN and LYONS, LEONARD (eds.), *Conscience* (New York: Alba House, 1973).

EISENBERG, PAUL, 'Basic Ethical Categories in Kant's *Tugendlehre*', *American Philosophical Quarterly*, 3 (1966), 255–69.

ENGSTROM, STEPHEN, 'The Concept of the Highest Good in Kant's Moral Theory', *Philosophy and Phenomenological Research*, 52 (1992), 747–80.

FALK, DAVID, 'Guiding and Goading', *Mind*, 62 (1953), 145–71; reprinted in Falk, *Ought, Reasons, and Morality* (Ithaca: Cornell University Press, 1986), 42–66.

FEINBERG, JOEL, 'The Expressive Function of Punishment', *Monist*, 49(3) (1965), 397–423; reprinted in Feinberg, *Doing and Deserving* (Princeton: Princeton University Press, 1970), 95–118.
—— 'Psychological Egoism', in Feinberg, *Reason and Responsibility*, 7th edn. (Encino, CA: Dickenson Publishing Co., 1978), 489–500.
—— 'Supererogation and Rules', *Ethics*, 71 (1961), 276–88.
FIRTH, RODERICK, 'Ethics and the Ideal Observer', *Philosophy and Phenomenological Research*, 12 (1952), 317–45.
FLEISCHACKER, SAMUEL, 'Kant's Theory of Punishment', in Howard L. Williams (ed.), *Essays on Kant's Political Philosophy* (Chicago: University of Chicago Press, 1992), 191–212.
FRANKENA, WILLIAM K., *Ethics*, 2nd edn. (Englewood Cliffs, NJ: Prentice-Hall, 1973).
—— 'The Naturalistic Fallacy', *Mind*, 48 (1939), 464–77.
FREUD, SIGMUND, *Civilization and Its Discontents*, tr. Joan Riviere (London: Hogarth Press, 1930).
GIBBARD, ALLAN, 'A Noncognitivist Analysis of Rationality in Action', *Social Theory and Practice*, 9 (1983), 199–221.
—— *Wise Choices, Apt Feelings* (Cambridge, MA: Harvard University Press, 1990).
GOWANS, CHRISTOPHER W. (ed.), *Moral Dilemmas* (New York: Oxford University Press, 1987).
GREGOR, MARY, *Laws of Freedom* (Oxford: Blackwell, 1963).
GUYER, PAUL, 'Kantian Foundations for Liberalism', *Jahrbuch für Strafrecht und Ethik/Annual Review of Law and Ethics*, 5 (1997), 121–40; reprinted in Guyer (ed.), *Kant on Freedom, Law, and Happiness* (Cambridge: Cambridge University Press, 2000).
—— (ed.), *Kant's Groundwork of the Metaphysics of Morals: Critical Essays* (Lanham, MD: Rowman and Littlefield, 1998).
HALE, SUSAN (JAKE), 'Against Supererogation', *American Philosophical Quarterly*, 28 (1991), 273–84.
HAMPTON, JEAN, *Hobbes and the Social Contract Tradition* (Cambridge: Cambridge University Press, 1986).
HARE, R. M., *Freedom and Reason* (Oxford: Oxford University Press, 1963).
—— *The Language of Morals* (Oxford: Clarendon Press, 1952).
—— *Moral Thinking* (Oxford: Clarendon Press, 1981).
HART, H. L. A., *Concept of Law* (Oxford: Clarendon Press, 1961).
—— *Punishment and Responsibility* (Oxford: Oxford University Press, 1968).
HERMAN, BARBARA, 'Mutual Aid and Respect for Persons', *Ethics*, 94 (1984), 577–602.
—— *The Practice of Moral Judgment* (Cambridge: Harvard University Press, 1993).
HEYD, DAVID, *Supererogation: Its Status in Ethical Theory* (Cambridge: Cambridge University Press, 1982).

HILL, THOMAS E., Jr., *Autonomy and Self-Respect* (Cambridge: Cambridge University Press, 1991).
—— *Dignity and Practical Reason in Kant's Moral Theory* (Ithaca: Cornell University Press, 1992).
—— *Respect, Pluralism, and Justice: Kantian Perspectives* (Oxford: Oxford University Press, 2000).
HOBBES, THOMAS, *Leviathan*, ed. C. B. Macpherson (Baltimore: Penguin Books, 1951).
HOLTMAN, SARAH, 'Kant, Justice, and the Augmentation of Ideal Theory', PhD Dissertation, The University of North Carolina at Chapel Hill, Chapel Hill, 1996.
—— 'Kantian Justice and Poverty Relief', *Kant-Studien* (forthcoming).
—— 'Toward Social Reform: Kant's Penal Theory Reinterpreted', *Utilitas*, 9 (1997), 3–21.
HRUSCHKA, JOACHIM, 'Imputation', *Brigham Young University Law Review* (1986), 669–710.
HUME, DAVID, *Enquiries Concerning Human Understanding and Concerning the Principles of Morals*, 3rd edn., ed. L. A. Selby-Bigge and P. H. Nidditch (Oxford: Clarendon Press, 1978).
—— *Moral and Political Philosophy*, ed. Henry D. Aiken (New York: Hafner, 1948).
—— *A Treatise on Human Nature*, ed. L. A. Selby-Bigge (Oxford: Clarendon Press, 1995).
HURKA, THOMAS, *Perfectionism* (New York: Oxford University Press, 1994).
JAMES, WILLIAM, *The Will to Believe and Other Essays* (New York: Dover, 1956).
KANT, IMMANUEL, *Anthropology from a Pragmatic Point of View*, tr. Mary Gregor (The Hague: Martinus Nijhoff, 1974).
—— 'An Answer to the Question: What is Enlightenment?', tr. H. B. Nisbet, in *Kant: Political Writings*, ed. Hans Reiss (Cambridge: Cambridge University Press, 1970), 54–60.
—— *Critique of Judgment*, tr. Werner S. Pluhar (Indianapolis: Hackett Publishing Co., 1987).
—— *Critique of Practical Reason*, tr. Mary Gregor (Cambridge: Cambridge University Press, 1997).
—— *Critique of Pure Reason*, tr. Norman Kemp Smith (New York: St. Martin's Press, 1965).
—— *Education*, tr. Annette Churton (Ann Arbor: The University of Michigan Press, 1960).
—— *Groundwork of the Metaphysics of Morals*, tr. H. J. Paton (New York: Harper and Row, 1964).
—— *Groundwork of the Metaphysics of Morals*, tr. Mary Gregor (Cambridge: Cambridge University Press, 1998).
—— *Lectures on Ethics*, tr. Louis Infield (New York: Harper and Row, 1963).

—— *Lectures on Ethics*, tr. Peter Heath and J. B. Schneewind (Cambridge: Cambridge University Press, 1997).
—— *The Metaphysics of Morals*, tr. Mary Gregor (Cambridge: Cambridge University Press, 1996).
—— 'On a Supposed Right to Lie because of Philanthropic Concerns', in Immanuel Kant, *Grounding of the Metaphysics of Morals*, tr. James Ellington, 3rd edn. (Indianapolis: Hackett Publishing Co., 1993), 63–7.
—— 'On the Common Saying: "This May Be True in Theory, but It Does Not Apply in Practice"', tr. H. B. Nesbit, in *Kant: Political Writings*, ed. Hans Reiss (Cambridge: Cambridge University Press, 1970), 61–92.
—— *Perpetual Peace*, tr. H. B. Nesbit, in *Kant: Political Writings*, ed. Hans Reiss (Cambridge: Cambridge University Press, 1970), 93–130.
—— *Practical Philosophy*, tr. and ed. Mary Gregor (Cambridge: Cambridge University Press, 1996). A comprehensive anthology of Kant's ethical writings.
—— *Religion within the Boundaries of Mere Reason*, tr. and ed. Allen Wood and George di Giovanni (Cambridge: Cambridge University Press, 1998).
KAVKA, GREGORY S., *Hobbesian Moral and Political Theory* (Princeton: Princeton University Press, 1986).
KENNY, ANTHONY, *Aristotle on the Perfect Life* (Oxford: Oxford University Press, 1992).
KORSGAARD, CHRISTINE M., *Creating the Kingdom of Ends* (Cambridge: Cambridge University Press, 1996).
—— 'Kant's Analysis of Obligation: The Argument of Foundations I', *Monist*, 73 (1989), 311–40; reprinted in *Creating the Kingdom of Ends*, 43–105.
—— 'Kant's Formula of Humanity', *Kant-Studien*, 77 (1986), 183–202; reprinted in *Creating the Kingdom of Ends*, 106–32.
—— 'Kant's Formula of Universal Law', *Pacific Philosophical Quarterly*, 66 (1985), 24–47; reprinted in *Creating the Kingdom of Ends*, 77–105.
—— *The Sources of Normativity* (New York: Cambridge University Press, 1996).
—— 'Two Distinctions in Goodness', *The Philosophical Review*, 92(2) (1983), 169–95; reprinted in *Creating the Kingdom of Ends*, 249–74.
KRAUT, RICHARD, *Aristotle and the Human Good* (Princeton: Princeton University Press, 1989).
LADD, JOHN (ed.), *Relativism* (Belmont, CA: Wadworth, 1973).
LEWIS, C. I., *An Analysis of Knowledge and Valuation* (La Salle, IL: Open Court, 1947).
LOEB, DON, 'Full Information Theories of the Good', *Social Theory and Practice*, 21 (1995), 1–30.
LONG, A. A. and SEDLEY, D. N., *The Hellenistic Philosophers* (Cambridge: Cambridge University Press, 1987).
LYONS, DAVID, *Forms and Limits of Utilitarianism* (Oxford: Clarendon Press, 1965).

MANNISON, D. S., MCROBBIE, M. A., and ROUTLEY, R. (eds.), *Environmental Philosophy* (Canberra: Australian National University Research School of Social Sciences, 1980).

MARCUS, RUTH BARCAN, 'Moral Dilemmas and Consistency', *Journal of Philosophy*, 77 (1980), 121–36; reprinted in Christopher Gowans (ed.), *Moral Dilemmas* (New York: Oxford University Press, 1987).

MCGOLDRICK, PATRICIA, 'Saints and Heroes: A Plea for the Supererogatory', *Philosophy*, 59 (1984), 523–8.

MELLEMA, GREGORY, *Beyond the Call of Duty: Supererogation, Obligation, and Offense* (Albany: State University of New York Press, 1991).

MILL, JOHN STUART, *On Liberty*, ed. Elizabeth Rapaport (Indianapolis: Hackett Publishing Co., 1978).

MONTAGUE, PHILIP, *Utilitarianism* (Indianapolis: Hackett Publishing Co., 1979).

—— 'Acts, Agents, and Supererogation', *American Philosophical Quarterly*, 26 (1989), 100–11.

MOORE, G. E., *Ethics* (1912; Oxford: Oxford University Press, 1965).

—— *Principia Ethica* (1903; Cambridge: Cambridge University Press, 1959).

MORRIS, HERBERT, 'Guilt and Suffering', *Philosophy East & West*, 21(4) (1971), 89–110.

—— 'A Paternalistic Theory of Punishment', *American Philosophical Quarterly*, 18(4) (1981), 263–71.

—— 'Persons and Punishment', *Monist*, 52(2) (1968), 475–501.

MURPHY, JEFFRIE, 'Does Kant have a Theory of Punishment?', *Columbia Law Review*, 87(3) (1987), 509–32.

—— *Kant: The Philosophy of Right* (London: Macmillan, 1970).

—— 'Kant's Theory of Criminal Punishment', in *Proceedings of the Third International Kant Congress*, ed. Lewis White Beck (Dordrecht: D. Reidel, 1972), 434–41; reprinted in Murphy (ed.), *Retribution, Justice and Therapy: Essays in the Philosophy of Law* (Dordrecht: Reidel, 1979), 82–92.

—— (ed.), *Punishment and Rehabilitation*, 3rd edn. (Belmont, CA: Wadsworth, 1995).

NAGEL, THOMAS, *The Possibility of Altruism* (Oxford: Clarendon Press, 1970).

—— *The View From Nowhere* (Oxford: Oxford University Press, 1986).

NELL [O'NEILL], ONORA, *Acting on Principle: An Essay on Kantian Ethics* (New York: Columbia University Press, 1975).

NIETZSCHE, FRIEDRICH, *Beyond Good and Evil: Prelude to a Philosophy of the Future*, tr. Marion Faber (Oxford: Oxford University Press, 1998).

—— *On the Genealogy of Morality: A Polemic*, tr. Maudemarie Clark and Alan Swensen (Indianapolis: Hackett Publishing Co., 1998).

OLSON, ROBERT G., *The Morality of Self-Interest* (New York and Chicago: Harcourt, Brace, and World, Inc., 1965).

O'NEILL, ONORA, *Constructions of Reason* (Cambridge: Cambridge University Press, 1989).

——'Constructivism in Kant and Rawls', in Samuel Freeman (ed.), *The Cambridge Companion to Rawls* (Cambridge: Cambridge University Press, 2002).
——*Towards Justice and Virtue: A Constructive Account of Practical Reasoning* (New York: Cambridge University Press, 1996).
PARFIT, DEREK, *Reasons and Persons* (Oxford: Clarendon Press, 1984).
PATON, H. J., *The Categorical Imperative: A Study in Kant's Moral Philosophy* (London: Hutchison, 1947, and Philadelphia: University of Pennsylvania Press, 1971).
PERRY, RALPH BARTON, *General Theory of Value: Its Meaning and Basic Principles Construed in Terms of Interest* (New York: Longmans, Green, 1926).
——*Realms of Value* (Cambridge, MA: Harvard University Press, 1954).
PLATO, *Euthyphro*, tr. Lane Cooper, in Hamilton, Edith and Cairns, Huntington (eds.), *Plato: The Collected Dialogues* (Princeton: Princeton University Press, 1989), 169–85.
POGGE, THOMAS, 'The Categorical Imperative,' in Paul Guyer (ed.), *Kant's Groundwork of the Metaphysics of Morals: Critical Essays* (Lanham, MD: Rowman and Littlefield, 1998), 189–213.
——'Is Kant's *Rechtslehre* Comprehensive?', *Southern Journal of Philosophy*, 36, supplement (1997), 161–87.
POTTER, NELSON T. and TIMMONS, MARK (eds.), *Morality and Universality: Essays on Ethical Universalizability* (Dordrecht: Reidel, 1985).
PYBUS, ELIZABETH M., 'A Plea for the Supererogatory: A Reply', *Philosophy*, 61 (1986), 526–31.
RACHELS, JAMES, *The Elements of Moral Philosophy* (New York: Random House, 1986).
RAND, AYN, *The Virtue of Selfishness* (New York: New American Library, 1964).
RAWLS, JOHN, *Collected Papers* (Cambridge, MA: Harvard University Press, 1999).
——*Political Liberalism* (New York: Columbia University Press, 1993).
——*A Theory of Justice* (Cambridge, MA: Harvard University Press, 1999).
——'Two Concepts of Rules', *Philosophical Review*, 64 (1955), 3–32.
REATH, ANDREWS, 'Two Conceptions of the Highest Good in Kant', *Journal of the History of Philosophy*, 26 (1988), 593–619.
——'Hedonism, Heteronomy, and Kant's Principle of Happiness', *Pacific Philosophical Quarterly*, 70 (1989), 42–72.
REISS, HANS (ed.), *Kant: Political Writings*, tr. H. N. Nisbet (Cambridge: Cambridge University Press, 1991).
ROSATI, CONNIE S., 'Persons, Perspectives, and Full Information Accounts of the Good', *Ethics*, 105(2) (1995), 296–325.
ROSEN, ALLEN D., *Kant's Theory of Justice* (Ithaca: Cornell University Press, 1991).
ROSS, W. D., *Kant's Ethical Theory* (Oxford: Clarendon Press, 1954).

Ross, W. D., *The Right and the Good* (Oxford: Clarendon Press, 1930).
Rousseau, Jean-Jacques, *The First and Second Discourses together with Replies to Critics*, ed. and tr. Victor Gourevitch (New York: Harper and Row, 1986).
Ryle, Gilbert, 'Conscience', *Analysis*, 7 (1940), 31–9.
Scanlon, T. M., *What We Owe To Each Other* (Cambridge, MA: Harvard University Press, 1998).
Scheid, Donald E., 'Kant's Retributivism', *Ethics*, 93 (1983), 262–82.
Schneewind, J. B., *Moral Philosophy from Montaigne to Kant*, ii (Oxford: Oxford University Press, 1990).
Selby-Bigge, L. A. (ed.), *British Moralists* (Indianapolis: Bobbs-Merrill, 1964).
Sher, George (ed.), *Moral Philosophy* (San Diego, New York, and Chicago: Harcourt Brace Jovanovich, 1987).
Sherman, Nancy, *The Fabric of Character* (Oxford: Oxford University Press, 1989).
Sidgwick, Henry, *The Methods of Ethics*, 7th edn. (Chicago: University of Chicago Press, 1962).
Singer, M. G., *Generalization in Ethics* (New York: Alfred A. Knopf, 1961).
Singer, Peter, 'Famine, Affluence, and Morality', *Philosophy and Public Affairs*, 1 (1972), 229–43.
—— *Practical Ethics*, 2nd edn. (Cambridge: Cambridge University Press, 1993).
Slote, Michael, *Beyond Optimizing: A Study of Rational Choice* (Cambridge, MA: Harvard University Press, 1989).
—— *From Morality to Virtue* (New York: Oxford University Press, 1992).
Smart, J. J. C. and Williams, Bernard, *Utilitarianism: For and Against* (Cambridge: Cambridge University Press, 1973).
Statman, 'Who Needs Imperfect Duties?', *American Philosophical Quarterly*, 33(2) (1996), 211–24.
Stocker, Michael, 'Desiring the Bad: An Essay in Moral Psychology', *Journal of Philosophy*, 76 (1979), 738–53.
—— 'The Schizophrenia of Modern Moral Theories', *Journal of Philosophy*, 73 (1976), 453–66.
Thomas, Lawrence, *Living Morally: A Psychology of Moral Character* (Philadelphia: Temple University Press, 1989).
Tiberius, Valerie, 'Deliberation about the Good: Justifying What We Value', PhD Dissertation, The University of North Carolina at Chapel Hill, Chapel Hill, 1997.
Trianosky, Gregory, 'Supererogation, Wrongdoing, and Vice: The Autonomy of an Ethics of Virtue', *Journal of Philosophy*, 83 (1986), 26–40.
Urmson, J. O., 'On the Interpretation of the Philosophy of J. S. Mill', *Philosophical Quarterly*, 3 (1953), 33–9.
—— 'Saints and Heroes,' in A. I. Melden (ed.), *Essays in Moral Philosophy* (Seattle: University of Washington Press, 1958), 198–216; reprinted in Joel Feinberg (ed.), *Moral Concepts* (London: Oxford University Press, 1969), 60–73.

VELLEMAN, DAVID, *The Possibility of Practical Reason* (Oxford: Oxford University Press, 2000).
WILLIAMS, BERNARD, *Ethics and the Limits of Philosophy* (Cambridge, MA: Harvard University Press, 1985).
——*Moral Luck: Philosophical Papers, 1973–1980* (New York: Cambridge University Press, 1981).
WOLF, SUSAN, 'Above and Below the Line of Duty', *Philosophical Topics*, 14 (1986), 131–48.
——'Moral Saints', *Journal of Philosophy*, 79 (1982), 419–39.
WONG, DAVID, *Moral Relativity* (Berkeley and Los Angeles: University of California Press, 1984).
WOOD, ALLEN, *Kant's Ethical Thought* (Cambridge: Cambridge University Press, 1999).

INDEX

a priori method 13–22
Abraham 364
altruism 99n., 100, 105–6, 108–15, 118–24
analytic mode of argument 15–16, 21
animals, nonhuman 155n. 55, 308
Antigone 364
Aquinas 374
Aristotle 26, 43, 164, 167, 171
authority (authoritative) 27, 163, 278, 321–2, 329
autonomy 31–36, 40, 318–19

Baron, Marcia 209n. 25, 211n. 27, 213n. 32, 217n. 42, 234–43
Baxley, Anne Margaret 56n. 34
Beccaria, Cesare 80
Bentham, Jeremy 113
Brandt, Richard 154
Butler, Joseph 141, 293–8, 347
beneficence, duty of 102–4, 112–15, 118–24, 187–91, 193, 201–3, 206–18, 222–35, 242–3
blame 54–6; blameworthiness 387; self-blame 321–3

common sense 59, 127–39, 159–60, 341
conscience 340–1, 346–9; concept of 278–9; popular religious conception 281–6, 306–7; cultural relativist conception 286–92, 307; Butler's conception 293–8, 307–8; Kantian conception 48, 280–1, 298–309, 346–9; conscience as a motive 340–1, 352–3, 356–8
conscientiousness 100n. 3, 101–3, 103n.
consent (or agreement); actual 57–70, 77, 84–6, 94; possible 67–95; hypothetical 67–95
consequentialism 126, 146–8, 150n. 41, 162–3, 230–4

constructivism 61–4, 91–3
Cummisky, David 207n. 20, 213n. 32, 211n. 27, 217n. 42, 218–34, 242–3

desert 315, 324–6; intrinsic desert thesis 314–16, 324–6; intrinsic liability thesis 312–13, 324, 337–8
deliberative rationality, models of; common sense 128–39; self-interest 139–43; coherence-and-efficiency 143–6; consequentialist 146–51; Kantian 151–63
Donagan, 232, 353, 371–79
duty 26, 234–6; to oneself 190–1, 206–11, 257–8; juridical vs. nonjuridical 113, 342; perfect vs. imperfect 103, 113, 181n. 42, 203–11, 214n. 34; wide vs. narrow 220–4, 223n. 55

egoism 93–4, 99n., 100–6, 139n., 141–2
empirical method 15–16
ends; ends that are duties 206, 247–8; personal 125–6, 244–74; see also Formula of Humanity as an End-in-itself
esteem 217–18

feelings (sentiments, emotions); altruistic, benevolent or sympathtic 100, 105–6, 108–13, 119, 225–6; see also moral feelings
flourishing, human 164–8, 191–200
Formulas of the Categorical Imperative; as system 155–7, 174n. 24; related to mid-level principles 242–3; Formula of Universal Law 42, 68–73, 120–4, 155–7, 177, 233, 380–1; Formula of Humanity as an End-in-itself 69–73, 177, 371–2, 381–3, 397–9; Formula of

Formulas of the Categorical (*cont.*):
  Autonomy 31; Kingdom of Ends
  Formula 73–6
Fowles, John (*The Magus*) 364
freedom 34–6, 178–80, 197–9;
  external vs. internal 178n. 32; *see
  also* autonomy
Freud, Sigmund 184n. 21

good, *see* value
good will 37–60
government, purpose of 178–81
grief 353–4
guilt, feeling guilty 387–9, 391–2

happiness 108, 164–75, 181–200
heteronomy 31–4; *see also* autonomy
High Noon (film) 364
Himmler, Heinrich 49, 291, 291n.
Hobbes, Thomas 77, 100, 104, 156, 254–8
Holtman, Sarah 179
Huck Finn 291–2, 291n.
Hume, David 17, 18, 39, 100, 104n. 7, 141, 144n. 28
Hutcheson, Francis 15, 17

impartiality 149–51, 161–3
imperatives 24; categorical 22–32, hypothetical 24, 32, 46n. 20; the Hypothetical Imperative 152–3, 272, 259; *see also* Formulas of the Cateogrical Imperative
integrity 307–9
intelligible world 20, 36

James, William 111
Johnson, Robert 355n. 28
judgment 298–305, 299n. 41
justice 79–80, 102, 176–81, 202, 212, 316, 345–6, 329

Kagan, Shelly 232
Kavka, Gregory 99
Korsgaard, Christine M. 233, 268

legislation 75–6; *see also* legislative perspective
Locke, John 77
lying 20, 176, 209

Marcus, Ruth Barcan 383
maxims 74–5, 203–7
Mill, John Stuart 234
Moore, G. E. 50–2, 87, 170–1
moral, dilemmas 363–6, 370–9, 387–402; moral gaps 379–86; moral feelings 29, 386–402
moral worth 247, 355n. 28; of actions 30n., 31, 215n. 37, 215–18; of agent 54–6, 326–8; as a motive 354–56
Murphy, Jeffrie 232

naturalism 18–20, 87–8, 155n. 52
Nietzsche, Friedrich 183

O'Neill, Onora 93n.
original contract 77–84, 90–91
other-regarding interests 134–6

Perry, Ralph Barton 154
perspectives, empirical vs. practical 19, 20, 36, 317–18; deliberative 89, 100n. 3, 106–12, 115–18, 270–2; legislative 157–9, 337n. 57
Plato 92n., 358
praise (praiseworthiness), 54–6, 201
prima facie duties, *see* Ross, David
principles, subjective vs. objective 24; 'counting principles' of rational choice 72n. 19
promises 68–70, 209, 374–6
prudence 17, 190, 190n. 56, 199, 194–5, 259–60
punishment 301–16, 328–39, 340–6, 349; justification 313–16, 328–336; policies 312–16, 314n. 13, 328, 330–6; as a motive 338–9, 340–1, 350–1, 358–61

Rand, Ayn 183
Rawls, John 74, 88, 144
reason, legislative 94; practical vs. theoretical 35–6, 196n. 61
regret 389–91, 400–2
relativism, extreme cultural 286–90; sophisticated cultural 290–2
respect 29; for moral law 41, 319–20, 360
retributivism 314; retributive policies 328, 330–6; retributive justifications

of punishment, *see* intrinsic desert thesis; deeply retributive theories 311, 314, 328; *see also* punishment
rights 99, 162
Ross, David 113–14, 175, 250n. 28, 380
Rousseau, Jean-Jacques 77–8, 80

self-interest 100, 104, 125n., 125–6, 130–4, 139–43
self-love 108, 120–24
Singer, Peter 134n. 13
Slote, Michael 137, 182–3, 183n. 43
sociopath 34
Socrates 358
Sophie's Choice (novel and film) 364
supererogation 215–18, 156n. 39, 236–43

Thomas, Lawrence 106n.
Tiberius, Valerie 184n. 49
Twain, Mark 291–2

utilitarianism 106, 126, 146–7, 173–4; act vs. rule 173n., 313, 323–4; *see also* consequentialism

value 43, 185; agent-relative vs. agent-neutral 170n. 14, 253n. 34; dignity 157, 233, 248, 248n. 17, 318; highest good or summum bonum 182, 327–8; instrumental 259–62; intrinsic 50–2, 146–51, 170–1; judgments of value 252–68; moral 244–8; nonmoral 168, objective vs. subjective 253n. 34; personal, *see* ends, personal; prudential 259–62, qualified 264–8; unqualified goodness 43–4, 50–60, 170
valuing 184, 184n. 50
virtue 55–6, 168n. 4, 199–200
virtue ethics 164–71, 182–3

weakness of will 116–24, 117n.
Wolf, Susan 217
Wood, Allen 268
wrongdoing 316–24

Printed in the United States
131460LV00002B/14/P